LSAT

LAW SCHOOL ADMISSION TEST

LSAT

LAW SCHOOL ADMISSION TEST

Complete Preparation for the *NEW* Test

Gino Crocetti
National Program Director
Sexton Educational Programs
and
B. M. Clarke, J.D.

ARCO PUBLISHING, INC.
New York

First Edition, Third Printing, 1983

Published by Arco Publishing, Inc.
215 Park Avenue South, New York, N.Y. 10003

Library of Congress Cataloging in Publication Data

Crocetti, Gino.
Law school admission test.

1. Law schools—United States—Entrance examinations.
I. Clarke, B.M. II. Title.
KF285.Z9C76 340'.07'1173 82-1825
ISBN 0-668-05427-1 AACR2

Printed in the United States of America

TO
PATRICIA A. PORTER, J.D.
WHO HAD THE FIRST WORD

CONTENTS

THE NEW LSAT FORMAT

SIX SECTIONS—35 MINUTES EACH + 30-MINUTE WRITING SAMPLE

FOUR SECTIONS PLUS TWO EXPERIMENTAL (NOT COUNTED TOWARD YOUR SCORE)

TOTAL NUMBER OF QUESTIONS (COUNTED TOWARD YOUR SCORE) = 114–115 IN FOUR SECTIONS

SECTION	TIME	NO. OF QUESTIONS
LOGICAL REASONING	35	26
ANALYTICAL REASONING	35	24–25
READING COMPREHENSION	35	28
ISSUES AND FACTS	35	35–38
EXPERIMENTAL SECTIONS—	35	??
REPEATS OF 2 OF ABOVE SECTIONS	35	??
WRITING SAMPLE	30	—
	4 hours	113–117 counting questions

You will not generally be able to tell the experimental sections from the other sections.

Some variation in the number of questions in the Analytical Reasoning and Issues and Facts section is possible.

The other sections might possibly vary a question or two in length from test to test, but it is unlikely.

See also page 8, "All About the LSAT," for more details.

LSAT

LAW SCHOOL ADMISSION TEST

Part I

About the New LSAT and General Test-taking Information

READ THIS FIRST—HOW TO USE THIS BOOK

WHY INSTRUCTIONS FOR A BOOK?

The book that you hold in your hand is different from other preparation books in several ways that will help you get a better LSAT score.

First, there is much more instructional material in this book than in other preparation books. The Instructional Overviews for each type of question are substantial reviews of what the question type is all about and how to master it. They are not filled out with just more drill work. They really teach you something.

Second, the answer explanations are not only longer than usual, but they discuss all the answer choices—including the reasons that the wrong choices were attractive. There are no one sentence explanations. There are, after all, four wrong answers to cope with for every right answer.

Third, this book offers a complete program of preparation including both general test-taking hints and specific hints for each type of question in the Instructional Overviews and in the answer explanations, many of which are longer than the questions they explain.

Fourth, there is a separate Attack Strategy for each question type, including detailed timing recommendations on sections and question types where students have had trouble in the past.

Fifth, the treatment of the new Writing Sample section not only reviews some of the basic rules of good writing, but gives you a fail-safe method of making sure that you will have something to write about.

Sixth, the problems in the four practice tests (there are actually six practice sections for each of the LSAT question types) are just like the test. There will be no surprises.

Seventh, there is nothing in the book that is not going to be on the test. There are no "extras" that only fill up the book without helping your score. Everything you need is here, while anything you don't is not.

For all these reasons we want to tell you how to get the full value of this book towards getting the best possible LSAT score.

THE IMPORTANCE OF THE LSAT SCORE

You know the LSAT score is important. It is used both as a cutoff and as one of two major criteria in evaluating your application. Consult the *Prelaw Handbook* published by the Association of American Law Schools. Law school by law school, the charts showing the LSAT scores and grade point averages of all their applicants and which ones were admitted are more eloquent than we could ever be. These matters and the new scoring and question structure of the LSAT are discussed more fully in the next chapter, "All About the New LSAT."

WHY AND HOW PREPARATION IS EFFECTIVE

The LSAT is intended by its makers to test mental and academic skills that they regard as taking a long time to develop. These skills are usually referred to as "the ability to read, understand, and reason" but are somewhat narrower than that designation might imply. There are three separate ways that preparation can raise your score.

1. UNDERSTANDING THE TEST: Preparation will help you to know what each section of the test is about. Good preparation will also analyze each subtype of question and explain what it is asking. Also included in this area of benefit are such technical matters as knowing whether to guess (yes on the LSAT), how the timing works, etc.

2. IMPROVING YOUR TEST-TAKING SKILLS: Good test-taking skills improve the efficiency of your other academic and mental skills. There are many different test-taking skills. One of the most difficult to master is knowing just which other skills should be used for different question types. That skill is fully explained in this book. Other test-taking skills include the order in which parts of the section should be read and the emphasis to be given to each, how to tell the answer choices apart, key words to beware of, what you DON'T have to worry about, and how to avoid various simple errors.

3. IMPROVING YOUR "ABILITY TO READ, UNDERSTAND, AND REASON": Or at least the mental and academic skills that go by that name on the LSAT. Reading, reasoning, and problem-solving are skills that you use every day, and which like all skills can be improved. One of the most effective ways of improving any skill, and the one used in this book, is clear identification of errors and the appropriate times to use various subparts of these skills.

Perhaps an analogy to a "physical" skill will help (no skill is purely physical; there is always a major mental element). A tennis player may have a dozen excellent shots, but still play poorly because he does not know when to use them to best advantage or he lacks one shot that he needs.

You may be in a similar position. You have spent years learning a large number of mental and academic skills, but if you don't know which ones to use on which parts of the test you won't do as well as you should. Similarly, you can probably benefit from brushing up, or perhaps learning in the first place, some of the skills needed for the LSAT.

We won't pretend that a five-year-old could pick up this book and then get a perfect score on the LSAT. But you are not five years old and you don't need a perfect score, just a better one. A better score is just what you will get if you master the skills presented in this book.

WHAT YOU NEED TO DO

How then shall you use this book? We will give you guidance in three areas: How to evaluate your needs and resources, how to set up a workable study plan, and how to study this sort of material effectively. Naturally there is some overlap between these three areas.

The first and most important thing that you need to do is take this book seriously. If you are just going to read a page here and there, casually do some problems without regard to timing, and never read the explanations—well, in that case, you are not going to benefit nearly as much as you could. It takes work and commitment—YOUR work and YOUR commitment.

Now, having been stirred to action, here is what you do.

Evaluating your Needs and Resources

The most valuable resource you have in this work is your time. You may have a great deal of time or you may have only a little. You need to set priorities so that you can get the most return for the time invested.

Actually, your needs are not too complicated to evaluate. You should assume that you need to study closely each of the Instructional Overviews, unless you are previously both familiar AND successful with the kinds of questions it treats. If you think you don't need to study one or two of the Instructional Overviews, do the appropriate sections in the first practice test as a check. Unless you get over 85% right, study the Overview. By the way, as a first exercise in logical reasoning, note that the use of 85% as a criterion in this context does not mean you should expect to get 85% of every section right on the test. As is explained in the next chapter, the LSAT scoring doesn't require that criterion. Even if you can get 85% right without help, you could still probably benefit from further study.

In addition to the overviews, every student should read the next two chapters on the nature of the LSAT and general test-taking strategies. You should also read the first part of the chapter on anxiety just to check yourself out, and read all of it if you find that you have even a small overanxiety problem.

That leaves the practice tests. You must take at least one test as a full-dress rehearsal. That is the highest priority after the instructional material. It is good to do all of the practice tests, but if time does not permit, you can do extra sections of the question types that give you difficulty. The Writing Sample, while not unimportant, is not as important as the other sections, as explained in the next chapter and the Writing Sample Instructional Overview.

As you study and do the practice tests, you will develop a list of your problem areas, which will direct your further studying. The development of this list is described later, in the section on effective studying.

Now consider your time. Do not overestimate how much time you have. If you think you have four hours every day, say instead that you have two hours five days a week. If you actually have the extra time, you can always do more studying, but if you plan on more than you actually do, you will feel bad and your priorities may become distorted. Be conservative.

Even if it is just 45 minutes a day, that is fine. Just make sure that it is actually 45 minutes and not 20 minutes of telephone calls and only 25 minutes of study. Regular study in small amounts is much better than occasional larger periods. The practice tests that you take as complete tests should be done in one sitting.

Take a piece of paper right now and write down all the time you want to dedicate to studying for the LSAT between now and the test date. If you don't know the test date, consult the official LSAT bulletin.

Setting Up a Workable Study Plan

Once you know how much time you have, you are halfway to having a plan that will work. Each week, you should plan exactly on which topics or tests you will work. You cannot plan the entire process at the beginning because you won't know how long things take until you have done some of them. Allow TWICE as much time as your best estimate of the time it really takes. If you actually do finish quicker, you'll feel good and there is no harm done. You will find your margin used up very quickly.

Never plan two things for the same time. For the best results, your study time must be totally dedicated to study. If you can do some extra review of your notes while commuting, so much the better, but make that extra time, not prime time.

In sum then, the keys to setting up a workable plan are dedicated time, conservative estimation, and advance planning in writing. Aside from helping you to remember when you are to study for the LSAT, putting the plan in writing will remind you to reschedule the hours which will inevitably be superseded by some "emergency" or special event.

Effective Studying for the LSAT

In addition to the organizing ideas just mentioned, there are several studying hints that are particularly helpful with this type of material.

1. ALWAYS HAVE A POSITIVE ATTITUDE. Start every session with the thought of how much better off you will be because you will know even more after studying than you did before.

2. STUDY IN SHORT SEGMENTS, with rest breaks in between. Most people should study in 20-minute segments with a five-minute review at the end for a total of 25 minutes of studying. Then completely relax yourself and think of nothing at all for two minutes or so. If you rush right into another topic, even another LSAT topic, your memory of the first topic will not be as good. No one should go more than 40 minutes without stopping, reviewing, and resting. It just isn't efficient. You will learn better in short periods.

3. TAKE MEANINGFUL NOTES. Take notes in a separate notebook and not in the margins of this book. Don't rely only on highlighting. Write complete notes that will mean something to you at a later time.

4. PREVIEW, READ, WRITE, AND REMEMBER. Rapidly preview the chapter you are studying. Then read it carefully, taking good notes. Finally, after you are finished, close the book and try to recall all the major ideas of the chapter. If you have any difficulties, check yourself against your notes. If they are unclear or incomplete, check the book. The very act of trying to remember will engrave the material in your memory far better than merely rereading it once or even twice.

5. DO EACH EXERCISE OR PRACTICE TEST BY THE "TRAC" METHOD. The initials TRAC stand for Time, Rework, Analyze, and Check for clues:

Time:	First do the exercise or test in the time limit. However, mark the questions carefully to indicate the answer choices you have eliminated and the choices and questions about which you felt unsure.
Rework:	Before you check your answers, rework all of the questions about which you were unsure and indicate to yourself whether you came up with the same answer or a different one.
Analyze:	Now check the answer key and try to analyze any remaining errors for yourself, armed with the knowledge of the right answer. Do a full analysis.

Check for clues: Now read the answer explanations for all of the questions which gave you trouble the first time through the material—not just the ones of which you are still unsure. Look for the clues in the problem and the answer choices which you missed the first time through. Try to see how you might have worked your way to them, or seen them more easily.

This entire process will usually take from two to four times as long as the time limit for the section.

NOTE: The key to improvement in reviewing the exercises is NOT merely understanding the explanation of why the right answer was correct, but, just as important, you must try to see exactly what clues in the problem lead you to the right explanation and the right answer. After all, on the day of the test that is what you will have to do—find the answers, not just understand someone else's explanation of them.

Remember that practice is very important in making sure that you have not only understood but also mastered the skills you learn from this book. To be helpful, your new skills must be familiar friends, not just acquaintances.

6. LEARN ATTACK STRATEGIES AND TIMINGS. These are the basic summaries of the application of the material in the Instructional Overviews. Consciously use them whenever you are doing problems, even if you think the problem is easy.

7. VIVID IMAGES ARE EASY TO REMEMBER. Whenever you want to remember something from this book or elsewhere, you will find a vivid image easier to remember. For instance, if you want to remember the TRAC method, you might think of yourself "tracking" across a giant book, and savagely cutting away the wrong answers leaving only correct answers and uncertain questions. Then a new round of conquest without the clock shining overhead as a sun and fewer problems still can withstand your glorious assault. . . . You get the idea. The stranger the image, the easier it is to remember. Don't worry if it is a little weird—you don't have to tell anyone about it, just use it to help remember something.

8. REST. This has been mentioned, but is worth repeating. Rest for at least two to five minutes at the end of each study session. Don't think of anything, or just imagine yourself at your favorite secluded spot, alone, gazing at the sky.

GOOD LUCK AND GOOD STUDYING!

ALL ABOUT THE NEW LSAT

PURPOSE OF THE LSAT

The LSAT is a standardized test intended to assist law schools in making admissions decisions by giving a standard assessment of mental skills considered to be important to the study of law. The LSAT scores are designed to be a measure of the "ability to read, understand, and reason" according to the Law School Admissions Council, the consortium of law schools which owns and controls the LSAT.

The purpose of a standard measure is to permit the law school admissions decisions to be based, at least in part, on an "objective" comparison of all the candidates—no matter what their college or background. There has been some controversy about the degree to which the laudable goal of "objectivity and total evenhandedness" has been met. There is no similar disagreement about the importance that the law schools place on the LSAT scores in making their admissions decisions.

At base, the purpose of the LSAT is to be part of the criteria for law school admissions, and your purpose in taking it is to do as well as you can so you will have the best possible chance of getting into the law school of your choice.

FORMAT OF THE NEW LSAT

Starting with the June 1982 administration of the LSAT, the question types, the timing, and the scoring system have all been radically changed. We will discuss the old LSAT only when such discussion can help you prepare for the new LSAT.

The format of the new LSAT is simpler than the old. All six of the sections will be 35 minutes long and there are only four types of questions—reading comprehension, logical reasoning, analytical reasoning, and issues and facts. (A brief description of each question type follows. For more details see the specific chapters devoted to each.) There is also a writing sample which is discussed in detail later in this chapter and in the Writing Sample Instructional Overview. Another simplification is the scoring system, which now runs from a low score of 10 to a high score of 50. The old 200 to 800 range has been abolished for the LSAT. Your score is still based solely on the number of questions you answer correctly, with no deduction for incorrect answers.

Here is a very brief description of each question type.

READING COMPREHENSION questions are based on a reading passage and ask you to demonstrate your understanding of the passage by answering questions about the structure, meaning, and implications of the passage. This type of question was on the LSAT many years ago in a somewhat different form. Similar questions appear on several other standardized exams, such as the SAT, GMAT, and GRE.

LOGICAL REASONING questions are based on very short arguments. You are asked to demonstrate your understanding of the arguments by choosing answers that describe the argument, weaken or strengthen it, identify its premises, or state its conclusions or implications. This is the only question type on the new LSAT which also appeared on the old LSAT.

ANALYTICAL REASONING questions are based on a set of information which you must organize in order to answer the questions. Diagrams of various sorts are helpful. This is also referred to as "logical games" and is not dissimilar to games found in various magazines. A similar version of this question type appears on the GRE.

In ISSUES AND FACTS questions, a fact situation, a dispute, and a pair of "legal"-sounding rules are presented. The questions ask you to classify various issues according to a preset answer schema as being unimportant to the dispute, deducible from the facts, needing further rules or facts to resolve the issue, and requiring a choice between the two rules. See the Instructional Overview for a fuller description.

As with previous LSAT's, not every section of the test administered to you will actually be used to compute your LSAT score. Your score will be based on the sum of your answers to four of the six sections—one section of each of the four question types just presented. Your work on the other two sections is only your contribution to the research and development of future LSAT's. One of the major purposes of the change to equal-length sections was to make it impossible for students to know which sections will count toward their LSAT score and which ones won't. Unfortunately, that purpose has been quite well-served and you will not be able to tell which sections are to be counted in your case and which are not.

Furthermore, LSAT's will now present "operational" and "non-operational" sections (as they are called) in any order whatever and in different orders for different students. Thus, your test booklet may be ordered like this:

1. reading, 2. logic, 3. issues, 4. logic, 5. analytic, 6. analytic.

Another student's test booklet may be like this:

1. logic, 2. issues, 3. reading, 4. issues, 5. analytic, 6. reading.

And the two booklets might have none of the same sections in the same places—even though the same four sections that count will appear somewhere on every version of the test booklet used at a particular administration.

The bottom line is that you must do all the sections.

The four operational sections of the new LSAT will have a total of 110 to 120 questions that count towards your score. While some format variation will occur, a typical test would be:

Reading Comprehension	28 questions, 4 passages
Logical Reasoning	26 questions
Analytical Reasoning	24–25 questions, 4–5 problem sets
Issues and Facts	35–38 questions, 6–7 problem sets

The format and timing of each question type is discussed in much greater detail in the Instructional Overview for that question type.

SCORING OF THE NEW LSAT

There are several issues related to scoring which are worth discussing briefly. First, how your score is derived from the answers you give to the questions. Second, how that score is expressed on the 10-to-50 scoring scale. Third, how the new scoring scale will be used with the old scale by the law schools.

There is no penalty for wrong answers. This means that when the testing service puts your answer sheet into the computer, the only thing that the computer considers is the number of questions you answered correctly. The number of right answers in the operational sections is then entered into a formula which gives the score on the 10-to-50 scale. The formulas for different forms of the test will differ somewhat to reflect the somewhat different degrees of difficulty of the various versions of the test. Each question answered correctly will probably be worth slightly less than half a point, so getting 80 out of 116 questions right might, for this hypothetical formula, give a score slightly below 35. We won't go into all the fine details of the scoring systems any further, since your job on the test is to get as many right as possible, whatever the scoring formula.

The new scoring range of from 10 to 50 permits only 41 different scores. The previous range of 200 to 800 permitted 601 different scores to be reported. The Law School Admissions Council felt that there was too much spurious precision in the old scoring range, and thus too much temptation for admissions officers to use differences smaller than the standard error of approximately 30 points in making admissions decisions.

THE NEW LSAT SCORES ARE NOT INTENDED TO BE COMPARABLE WITH THE OLD LSAT SCORES IN OTHER THAN A GENERAL WAY. There is no conversion formula; percentiles will be used where comparisons are needed. During a transition period of one or two years, law schools are supposed to accept either type of score, 200–800 or 10–50. There will doubtless be difficulties for the admissions officers, but since you will be taking the new test, you do not have anything to worry about.

USE OF THE WRITING SAMPLE BY THE LAW SCHOOLS

Usually at the beginning of the test, you will be asked to do a writing sample based on a vacuous question that will be given to you. The sole purpose of this writing sample is to give the law schools an idea of your spontaneous writing abilities, done in a situation where it is definitely your work alone. The writing sample is not looked at by the testing service, but only photocopied and sent directly to all the law schools who are receiving your LSAT scores.

As will be discussed in the Writing Sample Overview, a rough survey of law school admissions officers indicates that the writing sample will usually be used as a "tie-breaker" or secondary credential of much less importance than the LSAT score. However, a very poor writing sample could seriously undermine an otherwise strong application at many schools. While a very strong writing sample will not equally redeem an otherwise weak application, it may be the deciding factor where your application is approximately as strong as someone else's.

REGISTRATION FOR THE LSAT AND LSDAS

You can obtain registration materials for both the LSAT and the Law School Data Assembly Service (LSDAS) required by most law schools in the same package either from your college's prelaw advisor or dean, or by writing to:

Law School Admission Services
Box 2000
Newtown, PA 18940

You should register well in advance of the test and should get your materials as soon as possible. The registration booklet also contains a full-length sample test which you should do as part of your preparation. While this test lacks answer explanations, it is very useful in the later stages of your preparation.

SPECIAL ADMINISTRATIONS OF THE LSAT

Special arrangements can be made for the physically and visually handicapped, for persons whose religious beliefs forbid taking the test on a Saturday, and for some other persons with special needs. The key to making satisfactory arrangements is time. If you want to make any special arrangements for taking the LSAT, communicate immediately with the Law School Admissions Services at the address just given.

GENERAL TEST-TAKING STRATEGIES

In the last chapter, "All About the New LSAT," we discussed the intellectual skills needed to do well in each specific section (see also our chapter on "How to Recognize and Reduce Test Anxiety" for further hints). Later we will provide attack strategies aimed at each section. At this point, we need to take up the more general problem of working within the limits of a standardized test such as the LSAT. The LSAT is to a very large extent a game—a game with its own rules—and the winners and the losers are selected within that framework. This artificiality produces some surprising anomalies. For example, it is conceivable, though extremely unlikely, that a person could score a perfect LSAT just by guessing, and it is also conceivable that a person could turn in a very low score because he picked not the best but the second-best answer on every problem. The test, you see, has this very large blind spot: The machine reads only correct answers—those little black marks on the answer sheet. No one receives any credit for the "thinking" which went into solving the problem. Unless the mark is there in the appropriate spot, the machine will assume the student simply could not answer the question (no partial credit is given for an "almost" answer).

Four Points to Remember

Since you are aware of the limitations of the LSAT, you can turn those limitations to your own advantage. We make the following four suggestions regarding taking the LSAT: (1) preview sections, (2) be attentive to the time, (3) guess when necessary, and (4) watch carefully how you enter your answers on the answer sheet. Let us develop each one of these in a little more detail.

Previewing sections. When the proctor announces that it is time to begin work on a section (remember, each section is separately timed and you will not be allowed to work ahead in other sections, nor will you be allowed to return to a section once time has been called on that section), take a few seconds to preview the material. This procedure is beneficial in two ways. First, it has a calming effect. Instead of beginning work in a frantic manner, you can take a deep breath and remind yourself of the strategy which you have learned for approaching that particular section. Your eye may fall onto a question stem which looks familiar and this will trigger associations. In other words, you will be in a better state of mind to begin work in a systematic fashion. A second benefit of previewing is that you guard against the unexpected. In this book we have followed faithfully the layout which ETS (Educational Testing Service) has officially announced for the LSAT. ETS is under no legal or moral compunction, however, to abide by every detail of this information. To be sure, ETS is not likely to spring a whole new test or new question type on students (that is inconceivable), but it is not out of the realm of possibility that they could make some last minute adjustments in the test format. For example, it is conceivable that ETS would add two logical reasoning questions to a section, bringing the total number of questions to twenty-eight. Similarly, the Analytical Reasoning section may have only twenty-four questions in four problem sets. If you make it a practice to preview the section before you begin work, you cannot be caught out by any such adjustments in the test.

Timing. A second very important point, which should be always on your mind, is the critical nature of timing. Remember the computer which grades your paper has no mechanism for judging the depth of your thought. It gives the same credit for a lucky guess as it gives for a well-thought-out answer, and it gives the same credit for a tentative "I'm not sure about this" answer as it gives for a firm "This has to be it" answer. So your entire effort must be aimed at maximizing the *total number of correct answers*—without regard to incorrect answers and without regard to the amount of thought which went into finding the answer.

To make this clear, let us compare the performance of two hypothetical students. One student is a very meticulous thinker. He attacks the Logical Reasoning section in a very careful manner, checking his work. At the end of the thirty-five minutes, he has answered only eighteen questions, but he has gotten fifteen of those correct—missing only three. Another student works more quickly—not that he is careless; it is just that he knows the importance of the time limit—he attempts to answer all twenty-six of the questions. Some of them he sees immediately, so he does not bother to recheck his work. Others he can see would take a long time to solve, so he makes his best guess. On still others, he was able to limit his choice to two of the five possibilities, answering when he knew it would be a bad investment of his time to keep working toward a certainty which he knew might never materialize. Our second student answered twenty-six questions, but he missed eight questions, giving him a total of eighteen questions answered correctly. Now, at first glance it might seem that our careful student is the better student, and under different circumstances (in the real world) that may be so. But on the LSAT, our second student is the better performer—by a total of three questions, eighteen correct as compared with only fifteen correct. This demonstrates the importance of careful attention to the time limit. To guide you in learning how quickly you must work, keep the following points in mind:

1. Do not spend too much time on any one problem. Remember, each question on the test is worth the same; the difficult questions are not extra-credit questions. It just does not pay to spend extra time answering a hard question when there may be some easy questions left for you to answer.

2. Do not look for certainty. There will be many times when you have eliminated all but two answers. At that point you will probably want to work some more on the problem, thinking to yourself "If I give this another minute or so, I will definitely figure it out." *This is a mistake.* If you use that minute in answering another problem (taking your chances with a fifty-fifty guess on the first one), you will be better off in the long run than if you try answering only one problem with certainty.

3. Do not try to be "super" accurate. While it is true that the LSAT places a premium on careful reading and attention to detail, you must still work quickly. Rest assured that there are no cheap tricks, such as words written in invisible ink, that you have to find. Try for comprehension, but learn to do it quickly.

4. Finally, there is obviously some trade-off between accuracy and speed, and the optimal point will vary from individual to individual. The best thing to do in preparing for this test is to work to find that point for yourself—remembering that it is the number of correct answers, not the accuracy rate, which determines the LSAT score.

Guessing. The third point of general strategy is: when in doubt, GUESS—and this rule applies equally to problems you did not have time to do. The scoring mechanism of the LSAT differs from other standardized tests you may have taken in that it does not penalize you for an incorrect answer. Obviously, since there is no penalty for a guess, and since there is a chance that you will happen across the correct answer, you should always enter an answer for every question.

Answer sheets. Finally, it goes without saying that you must be attentive to the mechanics of the testing process; specifically, you must be careful in your management of your answer sheet. As obvious as this is, some students will make a coding error in completing the answer sheet, e.g., putting the answer intended for question twenty-four in the slot for the answer to question twenty-five. Interestingly enough, this kind of mistake seems to be randomly distributed across the scoring range; that is, the very best students seem just as likely to make this kind of error as their colleagues who did not score as well. In order to avoid making this error we suggest:

1. Keep a separate record of answers in the test booklet (yes, you may write in the test booklet). You get no credit for marks made in the test booklet (only for those answers coded on the answer sheet), but circling the answer you believe to be correct and placing a question mark by those you intend to come back to will provide you with a separate record of your choices. Should you then discover that you have made an error in coding answers, you can retrieve the information more easily.
2. Code answers in blocks. Rather than coding answers one-by-one (which requires needless paper shuffling), work a group of problems, say four or five, without coding answers (keeping your independent record in the test booklet). Then, when you find a convenient breaking point, e.g., turning a page, take that opportunity to record those answers. Coding in blocks will minimize the danger of a coding error, and it will also save time. Obviously, it is important to watch the time. Make absolutely certain that the proctor does not call time before you have had the opportunity to record answers. It may be a good idea, as time draws to a close, to record answers one by one. In any event, you should practice this technique at home before attempting to use it on the actual LSAT.

A final note. It is not enough to merely understand the Instructional Overviews and answer explanations. Your success on the LSAT depends on mastering the ideas presented in the book, through practice, so that they are second-nature to you and will be truly available to you during the test.

HOW TO RECOGNIZE AND REDUCE TEST ANXIETY

HOW TO USE THIS CHAPTER

This chapter will help you to recognize, minimize, and control test anxiety while you prepare for and take the LSAT.

Many students are tense and anxious about the LSAT. Indeed, you need a certain amount of adrenalin flowing in order to do your best on the exam. However, too much tension can be a serious problem for some students. Overanxious students are often unable to think clearly, read quickly and precisely, or remember accurately during the exam. Needless to say, their scores suffer.

This chapter provides a step-by-step program for discovering and addressing these problems. Even if you do not have a severe overanxiety problem, you will probably benefit from following the guidelines contained in this chapter. We will first discuss the nature and sources of anxiety. Then we will analyze the elements of anxiety and give you some hints on how to reduce these problems during your preparation for the test. This is followed by some specific hints on how to recognize and control tension during the test itself.

WHAT IS ANXIETY AND WHERE DOES IT COME FROM?

One definition of anxiety calls it a state of "uncertainty, agitation or dread, and brooding fear." This pretty well describes the feelings of all too many test-takers. Anxious students may find themselves sweating, trembling, or gripped with muscle tension, racing hearts, and pounding pulses.

One critical fact about anxiety that most students don't know or ignore is that it is not solely a phenomenon of the testing room. The seeds of anxiety are sown long before the test and some of the best weeding-out of anxiety can also be done before the test—as part of your preparation for the LSAT.

CONTROLLING ANXIETY BEFORE THE TEST

Let's take each part of the definition of anxiety and see how you can control and minimize it.

UNCERTAINTY: Standardized tests such as the LSAT ask the test-taker to be definite and precise. While speed is not the major problem on the LSAT, most of the problems have to be done fairly quickly.

The best way to combat uncertainly on the LSAT is to focus your study time on issue recognition, which is actually one of the major skills required of a lawyer and asked for by the test. Many students study problem explanations simply to see if they can follow along with the explanation. Certainly that is required, but it is just as important to look for the clues in the question or the passage which tell you that a certain approach or issue is important in this particular problem. This book tries to help you to do that in the discussions of the basic problem types and in the answer explanations. For Analytical Reasoning problems, for instance, you will learn how to tell map problems from names and occupations problems, and in knowing what the problem type is you will know how it should be approached.

But there is another, deeper level of uncertainty with which you must cope. When you first read a problem there will ALWAYS be a moment of ignorance when you don't know what to do. Sometimes the moment is very short, and other times noticeably long. Many anxious students feel this moment of ignorance and become convinced that they can never do the problem. If they take too long to talk themselves out of this defeatist attitude, they lose valuable time.

Let's do an experiment. What is 2 + 2?

"Four," you said to yourself so rapidly it seemed instantaneous.

What is 19 + 19?

For most people this takes a little longer than 2 + 2. However, you have little doubt that you can do the addition so you get right to work and in a few seconds you have the answer. The fact that there was a moment of ignorance when you were asked to add 19 + 19 was absolutely no indication that you could not do it. All it meant was that you had to work it out rather than pull it directly from memory like 2 + 2.

LSAT problems are more complicated than 19 + 19, but the same principle applies—JUST BECAUSE THE ANSWER OR APPROACH DOESN'T COME IMMEDIATELY TO MIND HAS PRACTICALLY NOTHING TO DO WITH WHETHER YOU CAN GET THE ANSWER OR NOT.

The antidote to uncertainty has three parts:

1. Carefully studying the instructions and different types of problems so that you can recognize what they require for solution. This should take the form of outlined notes and memorized attack strategies and problem recognition clues.

2. Becoming tolerant of your moment of ignorance.

3. Learning that perfection is not the goal. The LSAT scoring system was explained earlier in this book. It is expected that everyone will miss some questions and a very respectable score may well be the result of a situation where you are certain of fewer than half the questions. If you do not remember this clearly, reread that section of the chapter describing the LSAT.

AGITATION: This is essentially the physical part of the anxiety syndrome—the muscle tension, trembling hands, sweaty palms or brows, pounding pulse, and shortness of breath. Few students experience all of these symptoms, but the significance of these physical symptoms is that they will let you know that you are overanxious and that it is time to do something about it.

Agitation is rarely severe, even on the day of the test. The most common part of the agitation syndrome is muscle tension, usually in the neck, shoulders, arms, or lower back. Such tensions can tire you out and distract you from the task at hand—scoring your best on the test.

In your study sessions prior to the LSAT the best way to reduce tensions is to always be totally relaxed before and during your study sessions. The simplest and most direct way to relax is to follow these steps:

1. Sit in a comfortable chair (your study chair should be comfortable) in a reasonably undisturbed location.

2. Close your eyes, roll your head and shoulders, and take a deep breath—letting it out slowly.

3. Starting with your toes, tense each muscle in your body slowly and then relax it—along with its tension—in a slow rhythm.

4. Once you have relaxed your body just float there for a minute or two breathing slowly but deeply.

It is also a good idea to do a relaxation exercise at the end of your study session. If you have had successful experiences with other methods of relaxation, you can certainly use them either in addition to or in place of the ones described here. However, a method which is not focused on relaxation so much as some other object such as on a mantra, a center, etc., is not as likely to be helpful in this particular context.

Using this technique regularly will help you to apply the following anxiety-reducing technique for your use during the test.

DREAD AND BROODING FEAR: While this is much more extreme than most students will ever feel, fear of the test is usually the result of a lack of confidence, from whatever source. If you have previously had bad experiences with tests, you should remind yourself each time you study for this test that you are better prepared this time.

Another trick that some students play on themselves is to always focus on their difficulties with a problem and their errors. Although it is true that studying your errors can help you to correct them, it is also true that you should always keep in mind the things you are doing right. Many times you can be making life tough for yourself by using the wrong standard to measure your performance. Perfection is not, as was previously mentioned, the proper reference point.

As the song says, "accentuate the positive."

CONTROLLING ANXIETY DURING THE TEST

Your main job during the test is to answer questions. Sometimes, you may be a little overanxious. If you are, it can be helpful to recognize the signs of overanxiety and take action to relieve the anxiety during the test so that it doesn't become a problem. There are three signs of overanxiety during the test and three ways of relieving it.

Recognizing Overanxiety

1. As previously noted, the most common sign of anxiety is muscle tension. While you can expect to be a little stiff from sitting in a chair for several hours, you will notice excess tension if it is present.

2. If you find yourself reading and rereading sentences or questions without really grasping what you have read, this is the result of overanxiety and not your inability to read the material on the test.

3. Assuming that you have not been so foolish as to have been up late partying the night before the test, any sleepiness that you might feel is the result of anxiety and not fatigue.

Reducing Overanxiety

If you find that you might be becoming a little overanxious you can do the following things:

1. Remember that you are well-prepared. You know a lot about all the types of problems and you CAN work on them.

2. Reduce the tension by moving your muscles. Stretch, rotate, shake your arms. Be sure to get up and move during the break in the test. Don't worry how it looks, just do it.

3. Do a relaxation exercise. You shouldn't take the time during the test to do a full-dress exercise, but you can do a shorter version which can be very effective during the test.

—Take a deep breath and hold it for just one second.

—Close your eyes, blank your mind, and let out the breath while you relax your upper body (without falling off your chair).

The whole thing should take only four or five seconds. Don't take any longer. If you keep it short, you can do it as often as you need to, even after every question if you need to. You should practice this exercise before the day of the test.

AN OUNCE OF PREVENTION

When you are at the test you may be near someone who is very nervous. Don't talk about the test. Similarly, you should not talk about the test during the break. Use the break to stretch, drink, go to the bathroom, and relax. If you want to **calmly** review your guidelines for a section which has not yet appeared, that is fine. Just don't give anyone else an opportunity to make themselves feel good by telling you what they think you have done wrong.

Part II

Review of LSAT Question Types

LOGICAL REASONING INSTRUCTIONAL OVERVIEW

PRELIMINARIES

A Logical Reasoning section on the LSAT will contain 26 questions and have a time limit of 35 minutes. A candidate may have a test form which includes more than one LOGICAL REASONING section, in which case only one of the two Logical Reasoning sections will be scored. The other will contain trial questions being tested for validity so they can be used on future exams. Once again, we stress that since test-takers have absolutely no way of determining which questions, if any, on their test formats are trial questions, they must treat each and every question as though it were vital to their test scores. The Logical Reasoning section or sections can appear as any of the exam's six sections.

Now, the very title of this section—*Logic*al Reasoning—causes some students to worry, for it suggests to them that they will be tested on the formal rules of logic. They imagine that they will encounter problems using Latin terms and mathematical symbols and notations. Fortunately, this is not the case. Doing well in this section does not depend upon having had any official instruction in logic, such as a college course in symbolic logic, and the official LSAT bulletin stresses this point:

> It should be emphasized that the questions do not presuppose knowledge of the terminology of formal logic. You would not be asked, for example, to evaluate an argument by describing it as *argumentum ad hominem* but would be expected to recognize the unreasonableness of an attack on a person when an attack on an idea is more appropriate.

Instead, the section is actually a test of two skills—reading ability and reasoning power—both of which are essential to the practice of law. Of course, it cannot be denied that a student who has had formal training in logic, for example the standard introduction to logic offered by most college philosophy departments, may find occasion to put that training to use in this section, but many brilliant thinkers have never received so much as a single hour of instruction in the rules of thinking.

The value of a course in logic is not so much that it teaches a student anything new—after all, we all *do think* even if we do not *know how* it is that we think. Rather, the value of a logic course is that it brings some order or structure to what we do quite naturally. Perhaps an analogy drawn from athletics might make the point clear. Some people are natural sprinters and can run very fast. Nonetheless, a good coach can show even the most gifted runners how they can improve their performances. The same is true of thinking. Some people are naturally brilliant thinkers, others are not; but whatever the level of natural ability, everyone could definitely benefit from "coaching" in this area. In this Instructional Overview, we will try to offer some hints on how to sharpen up your analytical abilities. It must be emphasized, however, that the material we present is not new. This is not like a course in organic chemistry where a student can get a good grade simply by memorizing all the formulas. Instead, we are just trying to make you *aware* of what you have always done—to put you in touch with your thought processes.

As you read this material, then, you should try to make it your own by fitting it into your own thought patterns. For example, we may use a newspaper ad to illustrate the danger of not attending to detail.

> Seventy-three percent of the doctors surveyed said they would, if asked by a patient, recommend Lite Cigarettes with their low tar and nicotine for patients who smoke.

Does the ad claim that many *doctors* are encouraging people to smoke Lite Cigarettes? Not exactly, for the claim made by the ad is carefully qualified in several respects. First, the ad speaks of a certain *percentage* of doctors without saying how many doctors were questioned. Second, the doctors who did respond did not say they *do* recommend Lite Cigarettes; the ad says specifically they *would* recommend Lite Cigarettes *if* a patient asked them about cigarette smoking. And third, the final phrase of the ad also makes a very important qualification: The doctors would make such a recommendation for those patients who *do* smoke already. We can see from this very simple illustration that there is a great difference between the general impression created by this advertisement and what the advertisement really says. And this is one skill you need to develop: careful reading with attention to detail.

It should be obvious, then, that it does absolutely no good to memorize the instruction: Read carefully! Instead, as you study these materials, make cross-connections to similar material which you have encountered, for example, another advertisement. Also, you should practice being alert. Someone who is really aware of the importance of careful reading is always attending to detail. This is not to suggest that good thinkers are paranoid about people trying to trick or deceive them, and the *LSAT Bulletin* is explicit on this point as well. The problems do not involve cute tricks. But careful thinkers are always paying attention. Learning to be a careful thinker involves practice. We would never imagine that an athlete could learn to run faster or jump higher by just listening to a lecture on muscle structure. We know very well that the athlete has to take that information and incorporate it into his training regimen. Fortunately, the practice field for logical thinking is everyday life. Think carefully about everything you hear or read.

Our approach here will not concentrate on classifying actual LSAT Logical Reasoning problems. The kinds of questions that ETS prepares for this section are too numerous for simple classification. Instead, we will try to give a highly condensed course in basic logic, pointing out the most common argument forms and fallacies that appear on the LSAT. Then, in our answer explanations to the practice tests that follow, we will study the question stems ETS uses in the Logical Reasoning section to test whether a candidate can recognize these forms and fallacies. If you feel you would benefit from further reading in logic and have the time to pursue these studies, we recommend the standard college textbook on elementary logic: *Introduction to Logic,* Irving M. Copi (Macmillan Publishing Co.: NY, 5th ed., 1978), particularly chapters one through seven.

STRUCTURE OF AN ARGUMENT

An *argument* is a group of statements or assertions, one of which, the *conclusion,* is supposed to follow from the others, the *premises.* Some arguments are very short and simple:

Premise: No fish are mammals.
Conclusion: No mammals are fish.

Others are extremely lengthy and complex, taking up entire volumes. Some arguments are good, some are bad. Scientists use arguments to justify a conclusion regarding the cause of some natural phenomenon; politicians use arguments to reach conclusions about the desirability of government policies. But even given this wide variety of structures and uses, arguments fall into one of two general categories, depending on the kind of *inference* which is required to get *from the premises to the conclusion.* An inference which depends solely on the meanings of the terms used in the argument is called a *deductive* argument. All other arguments are termed *inductive.* So all arguments have three parts—premise(s), inference, conclusion; and the difference between deduction and induction is the kind of inference. Let us take a look at some examples.

A *deductive* argument is one in which the inference is guaranteed by the meanings of the terms:

Premises: All bats are mammals.
All mammals are warm-blooded.
Conclusion: Therefore, all bats are warm-blooded.

We know that this argument has to be correct just by looking at it. No research is necessary to show us that the conclusion *follows automatically* from the premises. This argument is what the logicians call a *valid argument,* by which they mean that the conclusion does follow from the premises; or more precisely, *if* the premises are true, then the conclusion must also be true. We must be careful to distinguish "truth" from "validity." Logic is an "arm-chair" science. The logician is concerned with the *connection* between the assertions. He is concerned only incidentally, if at all, with the ultimate truth of those assertions.

We might think of logic, then, as analogous in function to a computer. The computer generates outputs on the basis of inputs; if the input is correct (and the computer is functioning properly), then the output will also be correct. But if the input is wrong, then the output will be correct only as a matter of luck. So, too, the logical thinker takes the input which is given to him and he processes it; he says, in effect, "I myself know nothing about bats personally; but if the information you have given me is correct, then the conclusion is also correct." In deductive logic, we speak of arguments as being logical or illogical, or, using the more technical terms, we speak of them as being "valid" or "invalid." We never refer to an *argument* as being "true" or "false." The statements used in making the argument may be true or false, but the deductive argument itself—the inference from premises to conclusion—can only be valid or invalid, logical or illogical, good or bad, but never true or false.

An *inductive* argument also moves from premises to a conclusion, but it uses a different kind of inference: a probable inference. For example:

Premise: My car will not start; and the fuel gauge reads "empty."
Conclusion: Therefore, the car is probably out of gas.

Notice that here, unlike our deductive argument, the conclusion does not follow with certainty; it is not guaranteed. The conclusion does seem to be likely or probable, but there are some gaps in the argument. It is possible, for example, that the fuel gauge is broken, or that there is fuel in the tank and the car will not start because something else is wrong. Since we have used the terms "valid" and "invalid" to apply to deductive arguments, we will not want to use them to apply to inductive arguments. Instead, we will speak of inductive inferences as being "strong" or "weak," and we realize that no conclusion which follows inductively is guaranteed. Some inductive conclusions are very strong:

Premise: This is an ordinary coin I am tossing.
Conclusion: Therefore, it will not come to rest on its edge.

It is of course possible that the coin will land on its edge—but very, very unlikely. Some inductive conclusions are very weak:

Premise: This year the July Fourth picnic was rained out.
Conclusion: Therefore, every year the July Fourth picnic is rained out.

But regardless of the relative strength of the argument, both of these examples have the same inductive form. The conclusions do not follow from the premises as a matter of logic.

FINDING THE CONCLUSION

Locating the conclusion of an argument and defining its exact scope is the first step in evaluating the strength of any argument. You cannot begin to look for fallacies or other weaknesses in a line of reasoning or even find the line of reasoning until you have clearly identified the point the author wishes to prove. Any attempt to skip over this important step can only result in misunderstanding and confusion. We have all had the experience of discussing a point for some length of time only to say finally, "Oh, now I see what you were saying, and I agree with you." Of course, sometimes such misunderstandings are the fault of the speaker, who perhaps did not clearly state his position in the first place. This is particularly true in less formal discourse, such as conversation, where we have not carefully prepared our remarks before the discussion begins; but it can also occur in writing, though in the case of writing the proponent of a claim generally has the opportunity to consider his words carefully, and is therefore, one would hope, less likely to misstate his point. Often, however, the misunderstanding cannot be charged to the speaker or writer and the blame must be placed on the listener or the reader.

Careful thinkers will obviously want to know precisely what is being claimed in an argument they are examining. They know it is a waste of their mental energy to attack a point which has not been advanced by their opponents but is only the product of their own failure to pay careful attention. In order to help you become more sensitive to the importance of finding the exact point of an argument, we will discuss conclusions in two steps: (1) locating the main point of an argument, and (2) defining exactly the main point of any argument.

Locating the Main Point

Sometimes the main point of an argument is fairly easy to find—it is the last statement in the paragraph:

> Since this watch was manufactured in Switzerland, and all Swiss watches are reliable, this watch must be reliable.

Here the conclusion or the point of the line of reasoning is that part which is underlined. The argument also contains two premises: "This watch was manufactured in Switzerland" and "all Swiss watches are reliable." The same argument could be made, however, with the statements presented in a different order:

> This watch must be reliable since it was manufactured in Switzerland and all Swiss watches are reliable.
>
> or
>
> This watch must be reliable since all Swiss watches are reliable and it was manufactured in Switzerland.
>
> or
>
> Since this watch was manufactured in Switzerland, it must be reliable because all Swiss watches are reliable.

So we cannot always count on the conclusion of the argument being the last sentence of the paragraph even though sometimes it is.

Instead, it is always necessary to ask "what is the main point of this argument?" Or perhaps "what is the author trying to prove here?" If the conclusion is not the last statement in a passage, it may be *signaled* by indicator words. We often use transitional words or phrases such as *therefore, hence, thus, so, it follows that, as a result,* and *consequently* to announce to the reader or listener that we are making an inference, that is, that we are moving from our premise(s) to our conclusion. For example:

> Ms. Slote has a Masters in Education, and she has twenty years of teaching experience, therefore (hence, thus, etc.) she is a good teacher.

Here the conclusion is "she is a good teacher," and the premises are "Ms. Slote has a Masters in Education" and "she has twenty years of teaching experience."

In some arguments the premises rather than the conclusion are signalled. Words which signal premises include *since, because, for,* and others which normally connect a dependent clause to an an independent one. For example:

> Since Rex has been with the company twenty years and does such a good job, he will probably receive a promotion.
>
> or
>
> Rex will probably receive a promotion because he has been with the company twenty years and he does such a good job.
>
> or

> If Rex has been with the company twenty years and has done a good job, he will probably receive a promotion.

In each of the three examples just presented, the conclusion is "Rex will probably receive a promotion" and the premise is that "he has been with the company twenty years and does a good job."

Not all arguments, however, are broken down by the numbers, so to speak. Sometimes inattention on the part of the author or speaker, or sometimes matters of style, result in an argument which does not include a prominent signal of any sort. In such a case, the readers or listeners must use their judgments to answer the question "what is the author or speaker trying to prove?" For example:

> We must reduce the amount of money we spend on space exploration. Right now, the Soviet Union is launching a massive military buildup, and we need the additional money to purchase military equipment to match the anticipated increase in Soviet strength.

In this argument there are no key words to announce the conclusion, nor is the conclusion the last sentence or statement made in the passage. Instead, the reader must ask, "What is the author trying to prove?" Is the author trying to *prove* that the Soviet Union is beginning a military buildup? No, because that statement is used as a premise in the larger argument, so it cannot be the conclusion. Is the main point that we must match the Soviet buildup? Again the answer is "no," because that, too, is an intermediate step on the way to some other conclusion. Is the author trying to prove that we must cut back on the budget for space exploration? The answer is "yes," that is the author's point. The other two statements are premises which lead the author to conclude that a cutback in space exploration is necessary.

Sometimes an argument may contain arguments within the main argument. Thus, the argument about the need for military expenditures might have included this sub-argument:

> The Soviets are now stockpiling titanium, a metal which is used in building airplanes. And each time the Soviet Union has stockpiled titanium it has launched a massive military buildup. So, right now, the Soviet Union is launching a massive military buildup.

Notice that now one of the premises of an earlier argument is the conclusion of a sub-argument. The conclusion of the sub-argument is "the Soviet Union . . . buildup," which has two explicit premises: "The Soviets are now stockpiling titanium" and "a stockpiling of titanium means a military buildup." So in trying to find the main point of an argument one must also be alert to the possibility that an intermediate conclusion may also function as a premise in the main argument.

Defining the Main Point

Once the main point of the argument has been isolated it is necessary to take the second step of exactly defining that point. In particular, one must be attentive to any qualifying remarks made by the author. In this regard it will be helpful to ask three questions: (1) How great a claim (or limited a claim) is the author making? (2) Precisely what is the author talking about? And (3) What is the author's intention in making the claim?

The first of these questions reminds us that authors will frequently qualify their claims by using words such as *some, all, none, never, always, everywhere,* and *sometimes*. Thus, there is a big difference in the claims:

> All mammals live on land.
> Most mammals live on land.

The first is false, the second is true. Compare also:

> The United States and Russia have always been enemies.
> For the past thirty years, the United States and Russia have been enemies.

Again, the first statement is false and the second is true. Finally, compare:

> It is raining and the temperature is predicted to drop below 32°F, therefore it will surely snow.
> It is raining and the temperature is predicted to drop below 32°F, therefore it will probably snow.

The first is a much less cautious claim than the second, and if it failed to snow the first claim would have been proved false, though not the second. The second statement claims only that it is probable that snow will follow, not that it definitely will. So someone could make the second claim and defend it when the snow failed to materialize by saying, "Well, I allowed for that in my original statement."

The second group of elements to pay attention to are the descriptive words used in a passage. Here we cannot even hope to provide a list, so the best we can do is present some examples.

> In nations which have a bicameral legislature, the speed with which legislation is passed is largely a function of the strength of executive leadership.

Notice here that the author makes a claim about "nations," so (at least without further information to license such an extension) it would be wrong to apply the author's reasoning to *states* (such as New York) which also have bicameral legislatures. Further, we would not want to conclude that the author believes that bicameral legislatures pass different laws from those passed by unicameral legislatures. The author mentions only the "speed" with which the laws are passed—not their content. Let us take another example:

> All of the passenger automobiles manufactured by Detroit auto makers since 1975 have been equipped with seat belts.

We would not want to conclude from this statement that all *trucks* have also been equipped with seat belts since the author makes a claim only about "passenger automobiles", nor would we want to conclude that *imported cars* have seat belts for the author mentions Detroit-made cars only. Finally, here is yet another example in which the descriptive terms in the claim are intended to restrict the claim:

> No other major department store offers you a low price and a seventy-five-day warranty on parts and labor on this special edition of the XL-30 color television.

The tone of the ad is designed to create a very large impression on the hearer, but the precise claim made is fairly limited. First, the ad's claim is specifically restricted to a comparison of *department* stores, and *major* department stores at that. It is possible that some non-major department store offers a similar warranty and price; also it may be that another type of retail store, say an electronics store, makes a similar offer. Second, other stores, department or otherwise, may offer a better deal on the product, say a low price with a three-month warranty, and still the claim would stand—so long as no one else offered exactly a "seventy-five-day" warranty. Finally, the ad is restricted to a "special edition" of the television, so depending on what that means, the ad may be even more restrictive in its claim.

The final point in understanding the conclusion is to be careful to distinguish between claims of fact and proposals of change. Do not assume that if an author claims to have found a problem, he also knows how to solve it. An author can make a claim about the cause of some event without believing that the event can be prevented or even that it ought to be prevented. For example, from the argument:

> Since the fifth ward vote is crucial to Gordon's campaign, if Gordon fails to win over the ward leaders he will be defeated in the election.

you cannot conclude that the author believes Gordon should or should not be elected. The author gives only a factual analysis without endorsing or condemning either possible outcome. Also, from the argument:

> Each year the rotation of Earth slows a few tenths of a second. In several million years, it will have stopped altogether, and life as we know it will no longer be able to survive on Earth.

you cannot conclude that the author wants to find a solution for the slowing of Earth's rotation. For all we know, the author thinks that the process is inevitable, or even desirable.

To summarize this discussion of conclusions, remember you must find the conclusion the author is aiming at by uncovering the structure of the argument. (Did the author try to prove this, and if so, did he use this as a premise of a further argument?) Then pay careful attention to the precise claim made by the conclusion.

FINDING THE PREMISES

In our discussion of conclusions, we implicitly treated the problem of finding the premises of an argument, for in separating the conclusion from the remainder of the paragraph, we also isolated those premises explicitly used by the author in constructing his chain of reasoning. In this section, we do not need to redo that analysis, but it will be useful if we describe three important kinds of assumptions an author might make—value judgments, factual assumptions, and definitional assumptions. Then we will discuss the significance of assumptions.

One very important kind of assumption is the *value judgment.* For example, if we argue that the city government should spend money to hire a crossing guard to protect school children walking to school, we have implicitly assumed that the lives of school children are important and, further, that protecting these lives is a proper function of city government. Another kind of assumption is the *factual assumption.* For example, "The ball struck the window and the glass shattered." So the person who threw the ball broke the window. Here the explanation uses the factual assumption that it was the ball that broke the glass—and not some super ray fired by a Martian at the same time. Finally, a third group of assumptions, *definitional assumptions,* are those called into play when we use vague terms. For example, the person who threw the ball is to blame for the broken window, because a person is responsible for his misdeeds. Here the conclusion rests upon the assumption that throwing the ball is, by definition (at least under the circumstances) a misdeed.

With this in mind, we can turn to a discussion of the importance of assumptions in evaluating an argument. In our discussion of conclusions, we noticed that the conclusion of one argument may function as a premise of yet a further argument. With a little imagination, we could construct an argument in which there might be twenty, thirty, or even more intermediate links in the chain of reasoning joining the initial premise and the final conclusion. Of course, in practice our arguments are hardly ever so complicated. Usually, we require only three or four steps. For example, we may reason:

> Since there is snow on the ground, it must have snowed last night. If it snowed last night, then the temperature must have dropped below 32°F. The temperature drops below 32°F only in the winter. So, since there is snow on the ground, it must be winter here.

We can easily imagine also extending this string of situational assumptions in either direction. Instead of starting with "there is snow on the ground," we might have backed up one further step and reasoned, "If there is a snowman on the front lawn, it must be because there is snow on the ground"; and from the presence of the snowman on the front lawn we could have reached the conclusion that it is winter here. Or we might extend the argument to yet another conclusion. Using the additional premise "If it is winter here, it is summer in Australia," we could reason from "there is a snowman on the front lawn" to "it is summer in Australia."

In practice, however, we do not extend our arguments indefinitely in either direction. We stop at the conclusion we had hoped to prove, and we begin from what seems to us to be a convenient and secure starting point: "If there is snow on the ground, then it must have snowed last night." Now it is obvious that the strength of an argument depends in a very important way upon the legitimacy of its assumptions; in fact, defeating an assumption is the most effective way of attacking any argument. Let us consider examples of arguments using our three types of assumptions.

A very simple factual assumption is the following:

Premises:	If there is gasoline in the tank, my car will start.
	I checked and there is gasoline in the tank.
Conclusion:	Therefore, my car will start.

A very effective attack on this argument can be aimed at the first premise. One would want to object that the situational premise "if gas, then car starts" is unacceptable because it ignores the fact that there are other reasons the car may fail to start, e.g., the battery is dead, the distributor cap is wet, the engine was stolen. Now the conclusion "my car will start" no longer has any support. Of course it is possible that the car will start, but whether it does or not will not be determinable from the specific argument we have just defeated.

An example of a value judgment is the following:

Premises: The government should help people who might hurt themselves.
Cigarette smoking is harmful to people.
Conclusion: Therefore, the government ought to prevent people from smoking.

One way of attacking this argument is to attack the value judgment that the government ought to protect people from themselves. That might be done by talking about freedom or individual rights, and it will not be possible to clearly *defeat* the assumption of value. In our first argument, the assumption was a question of fact—causal laws in the physical universe—and could be resolved by empirical evidence. In arguments resting on value judgments, it may never be possible to get final agreement. But for purposes of evaluating the strength of an argument, one way of *pursuing the issue,* which is to say, one way of objecting to the argument, is to reject the value judgment upon which it rests.

Finally, a definitional assumption is similar to a valuational one:

Premises: An inexperienced person will not make an effective Supreme Court Justice.
A person with only ten years of legal practice is inexperienced.
Conclusion: Therefore, a person with only ten years of legal practice will not make an effective Supreme Court Justice.

This argument is a valid deductive argument, but that does not mean it is unassailable as it applies to the real world. One way of attacking the argument is to question its second premise by insisting that ten years is long enough to make a person experienced. Of course, that might be disputed, but at least that is a possible line of attack on the argument. After all, if it could be *proved* that ten years of practice makes one experienced, then the conclusion of the argument must be considered to have been defeated.

Hidden Premises

In each of our three examples, the attack on the argument was fairly easy to find. To be sure, there were others available to us; but at the very least we knew one way of attacking the argument would be to question the assumptions on which it rested. Unfortunately, the attack is not always this easy to find because many times arguments are built upon hidden or concealed assumptions, and this is not necessarily because the proponent of the argument is intentionally hiding something which he knows will weaken his argument. Since an argument could be extended backward indefinitely (But why do you believe that? So why do you think that? What is your reason for that?), the starting point of an argument is always a bit arbitrary. Even someone who is giving what he thinks to be a correct and honest argument will make some assumptions which he does not explicitly acknowledge.

Argument: The ground is damp, so it must have rained last night.
Hidden premise: Rain is the only thing which causes the ground to become damp.
Argument: Homosexuality is a sin; therefore, there should be laws against such practices.
Hidden premise: The government ought to enforce morality.
Argument: John is the perfect husband; he never cheats on his wife.
Hidden premise: Any husband who does not cheat on his wife is a perfect husband.

So, in evaluating an argument, it is always important to be aware of the possibility of hidden assumptions which might be open to attack. This is particularly true if one finds an argument which on the surface appears to be logically correct, but reaches a conclusion which seems factually impossible, or one which seems valuationally or judgmentally absurd. In such a situation, it is a good idea to look for a hidden assumption which makes the argument work. Of course, even though the conclusion seems strange, it might just be correct, in which case careful thinkers admit that their initial reactions to the argument were wrong, and they change their minds. Similarly, a reasonable appearing conclusion can be based on inadequate or wrong argumentation.

With regard to premises, then, we have learned that every argument rests upon them. An explanation of events usually rests upon factual premises, and a proposal for action rests upon value judgments. And both kinds of arguments will make definitional assumptions. It should also be kept in mind that since a complex argument is made of sub-arguments, a final factual conclusion may ultimately have a value judgment somewhere in the argument supporting it, and by the same token a final value judgment may have a factual premise somewhere in the argument supporting it. Many times the assumptions of an argument will not be explicitly mentioned by the author; they may be hidden. But whether an assumption is explicit or just implicit, it is of critical importance to the argument, and for this reason attacks on premises can be very powerful.

EVALUATING INFERENCES (INDUCTIVE)

In the preceding two sections, we described the importance of finding the conclusion and the premises of an argument. We now turn our attention to techniques for evaluating the inference which is supposed to link the conclusion to the premises. Our discussion of inductive inferences is a checklist of the most important kinds of fallacies which appear on the LSAT. You should not, however, allow yourself to think that you can memorize the list and apply it mechanically to Logical Reasoning problems. The classification we present is somewhat artificial, and discretion is required in using it. We will discuss seven fallacies: The *ad hominem* attack, circular reasoning, appeals to irrelevant considerations, false cause, hasty generalization, ambiguity, and false analogy.

Ad hominem Attack

This is any argument which is directed against the source of the claim rather than the claim itself. Since there are times when such attacks are useful, as when the credibility of the speaker is at issue, we must be careful to distinguish the illegitimate *ad hominem* attack from the legitimate attack on a person's credibility. An illegitimate *ad hominem* argument is one which ignores the merits of the issue in favor of an attempt to discredit the source of the argument where the credibility of the speaker is not at issue. For example:

> We should not accept Professor Smith's analysis of the causes of traffic accidents because we know that she has been unfaithful to her husband.

Setting aside such outlandish speculations as the possibility that Professor Smith has killed her husband in a fake accident (and remember that the *LSAT Bulletin* specifically warns against such speculation), we can see that there is no connection between Smith's analysis of accidents and her infidelity to her husband. So this is an illegitimate attack. A student who wants to see further examples of such attacks need only read the daily newspaper with particular attention to any political campaign or other political struggle. On the other hand, there are attacks on the credibility of speakers which are legitimate. We are all suspicious of the claims made by sales persons, and rightly so! More generally, it is legitimate to take account of any possible self-interest in making a statement. For example:

> General: The Army needs more and bigger tanks. Even though they are expensive, they are vital to the nation's security.
> Politician: And if I am elected governor, I will cut taxes and put an end to crime.

In these cases, it is not wrong to point out that the speaker's vision may be clouded by his own interest in the outcome of the matter.

Circular Reasoning

A second fallacy commonly used on the LSAT is that of circular reasoning. Any argument which includes the conclusion it hopes to prove as one of its premises is fallacious because it is circular. For example:

> Beethoven was the greatest composer of all time, because he wrote the greatest music of any composer, and he who composes the greatest music must be the greatest composer.

The conclusion of this argument is that Beethoven was the greatest composer of all time, but one of the premises of the argument is that he composed the greatest music, and the other premise states that that is the measure of greatness. The argument is fallacious, for there is really no argument for the conclusion at all, just a restatement of the conclusion.

Appeals to Irrelevant Considerations

A third type of fallacy which you might encounter in a Logical Reasoning section on the LSAT is any appeal to irrelevant considerations. For example, an argument which appeals to the popularity of a position to prove the position is fallacious. For example:

> Frederick must be the best choice for chairman because most people believe that he is the best person for the job.

That many people hold an opinion obviously does not guarantee its correctness—after all, many people once thought airplanes couldn't fly. Another appeal to an irrelevant consideration might be an illegitimate appeal to authority. For example:

> The theory of evolution is only so much hogwash, and this is clearly proved by the fact that Professor Edwards, who got an M.A. in French Literature from Yale University, says so.

In this case, the authority is not an authority on the topic for which authority is needed. Now, there may be legitimate appeals to authority. For example:

> Inflation erodes the standard of living of those persons who are retired and have fixed incomes such as savings or pensions; and Professor Jones, an economist who did a study on the harms of inflation, concluded that over 75% of retired people live on fixed incomes.

In this case, the appeal to authority is legitimate. We often must defer to the expertise of others, but we must be careful to select our sources of authority so that we find ones which are unbiased and truly expert.

False Cause

A fourth type of fallacy, and one of which the LSAT is fond, is the fallacy of the false cause. An argument which commits this error attributes a causal relationship between two events where none exists—or at least the relationship is misidentified. For example:

> Every time the doorbell rings I find there is someone at the door. Therefore, it must be the case that the doorbell calls these people to my door.

Obviously, the causal link suggested here is backwards. It is the presence of the person at the door which then leads to the ringing of the bell, not vice versa. A more serious example of the fallacy of the false cause is:

> There were more air traffic fatalities in 1979 than there were in 1969; therefore, the airways are more dangerous today than they were ten years ago.

The difficulty with this argument is that it attributes the increase to a lack of safety when, in fact, it is probably attributable to an increase in air travel generally.

Hasty Generalization

A fifth fallacy is that of hasty generalization. In our discussion about the structure of an argument, where we distinguished inductive from deductive arguments, we remarked that the best one can hope for in an inductive argument is that it will *probably* be true. We pointed out that some arguments are very strong, while some are weak. A common weakness in an inductive argument is the hasty generalization; that is, basing a large conclusion on too little data. For example:

> All four times I have visited Chicago it has rained; therefore, Chicago probably gets very little sunshine.

The rather obvious difficulty with the argument is that it moves from a small sample—four visits—to a very broad conclusion, Chicago gets little sunshine. Of course, generalizing on the basis of a sample or limited experience can be legitimate:

> All five of the buses manufactured by Gutmann which we inspected have defective wheel mounts; therefore, some other buses manufactured by Gutmann probably have similar defects.

Admittedly this argument is not airtight. Perhaps the other uninspected buses do not have the same defect, but this second argument is much stronger than the first.

Ambiguity

A sixth fallacy which the LSAT has used in the past is that of ambiguity. Anytime there is a shifting in the meaning of terms used in an argument, the argument has committed a fallacy of ambiguity. For example:

> Man is only one million years old. John is a man. Therefore, John is only one million years old.

The error of the argument is that it uses the word *man* as two different meanings. In the first occurrence *man* is used as a group; in the second occurrence *man* designates a particular individual. Another, less playful, example:

> Sin occurs only when man fails to follow the will of God. But since God is all powerful, what He wills must actually be. Therefore, it is impossible to deviate from the will of God, so there can be no sin in the world.

The equivocation here is in the word *will*. The first time it is used, the author intends that the will of God is God's wish and implies that it *is* possible to fail to comply with those wishes. In the second instance, the author uses the word *will* in a way which implies that such deviation is *not* possible. The argument reaches the conclusion that there is no sin in the world only by playing on these two senses of "will of God."

False Analogy

A seventh, and final, fallacy which might appear on the LSAT is that of false analogy. We do sometimes present legitimate arguments from analogy. For example:

> The government should pay more to its diplomats who work in countries with unstable governments. The work is more dangerous there than in stable countries. This is very similar to paying soldiers combat premiums if they are stationed in a war zone.

The argument here relies on an analogy between diplomats in a potentially dangerous country and soldiers in combat areas. Of course, the analogy is not perfect—no analogy can be more than an analogy. But some analogies are clearly so imperfect that they have no persuasive force. For example:

> People should have to be licensed before they are allowed to have children. After all, we require people who operate automobiles to be licensed.

In this case, the two situations—driving and having children—are so dissimilar that we would probably want to say they are not analogous at all—having children has nothing to do with driving.

While the ingenuity of the test-makers can result in Logical Reasoning problems that do not precisely fit these fallacies of induction, there will be very few problems on the test which have any other sort of inductive reasoning errors. The practice tests in this book contain many illustrations of each kind of problem with full explanations. There are also problems which show how these different errors can be combined in one problem.

EVALUATING INFERENCES (DEDUCTIVE)

In the last section, we discussed some common inductive fallacies; in this section, we turn our attention to deductive reasoning. You will recall from the first section that a deductive inference differs from an inductive inference in that the deductive inference—if it is valid—is guaranteed by the meanings of the terms used in the argument. The argument form we most often associate with the study of logic is the syllogism, a term which will be familiar to anyone who has studied basic logic:

> All trees are plants.
> All redwoods are trees.
> Therefore, all redwoods are plants.

Ancient and medieval thinkers devoted a great deal of study to the various forms of syllogisms and other logical structures, and their treatments are full of technicalities—technicalities which we can safely ignore. All that one requires for the LSAT is a working knowledge of the forms without all the jargon. Thus, although we have employed some technical terms in these materials, this was strictly for purposes of organization, and you need not commit these to memory. Our discussion will treat four groups of deductive arguments: direct inferences, syllogisms, implications, and relational sequences.

Direct Inferences

By a direct inference, we mean a conclusion which follows from a single premise. For example, from the statement "no birds are mammals" we can conclude "no mammals are birds," since there is no individual which is a member of both the group bird and the group mammal. From "no birds are mammals" we could also reach the conclusion that "all birds are not mammals," but this is really nothing more than a grammatical restructuring of the original form, whereas the statement "no mammals are birds" is actually an inference (it is a totally new claim).

Setting aside possible variations in grammatical structure ("no B are M" = "all B are not M," "some B are M" = "some B are not non-M," etc.), we may organize such assertions into four groups, depending on whether they make a claim about "some" on the one hand or, on the other hand, either "all" or "no" members of groups and whether they are "affirmative" or "negative." In order to save space and also to show that our techniques are generally applicable—that is, not dependent on any particular content—we will find it convenient to use capital letters as substitutes for terms. Thus, "all birds are mammals" becomes "all B are M," which could also stand for "all bats are myopic," but nothing is lost in the translation since we are concerned with the formal relations and not the actual substantive or content relations between sentences. Using capital letters, we set up the following scheme so that we have sentences which make affirmative claims about all of a group, negative claims about all of a group, affirmative claims about part of a group, and negative claims about part of a group.

	Affirmative	Negative
General	All A are B.	No A are B.
Specific	Some A are B.	Some A are not B.

Before we proceed any further, there is one very important point regarding use of the word *some* which we must make. The LSAT follows the logician in using the word *some* to mean only "at least one." So a statement of the sort "some A are B" means *only* that there is at least one A which is also a B. The statement does *not* imply, as well, that there are some A's which are not B's. Similarly, the statement "some A are not B" means that there is at least one A which is not a B; it does *not* imply that there are also some A's which are B's. Notice that this is at variance with our ordinary conversational usage of the word *some.* In conversation a person who states "Some of the students have not turned in their term papers" probably wants us to understand that some students have turned in their papers, but this additional implication depends upon the context in which the statement is made. Strictly speaking, as a matter of logic, the statement "some students have not turned in their term papers" means just that—"some students have not turned in their term papers"—and does not further mean that some students have turned in their term papers. It is conceivable that no student has turned in a term paper; still, the statement "some students have not turned in their term papers" would be accurate. Even though it only partially describes the situation—*some* as opposed to *all*—it does give an accurate description of that part it describes.

Perhaps a little thought experiment will clarify the point. Imagine that you are standing in front of an opaque container with marbles in it, and you are asked to pick marbles blindly from the container. You pick a marble which happens to be red. At that point, we ask you to describe the color or colors of the marbles in the container. You can say, "Some of the marbles are red" (setting aside the difficulty that the red marble is no longer in the container, for we are talking about the marble population without regard to such technicalities). This statement is obviously true since you hold the proof in your hand. Now, if you draw the remaining marbles from the container, one of two situations will develop. Either all of the remaining marbles will prove to be red, in which case you can say, "All of the marbles are red," or not all of the remaining marbles will prove to be red in which case you can say, "Some of the marbles are not red." But since our first statement, "Some of the marbles are red," was proven to be true by the fact that you held a red marble in your hand, and since a true statement does not become false with the passing of time (again, setting aside such difficulties as demonstrative pronouns, such as "this is a live cat"—ten years later it is dead—and time-dependent statements, such as "Nixon is *now* President"), the statement "some marbles are red" remains true even if it should turn out that "all marbles are red." What this shows is that the statement "some marbles are red" is not logically inconsistent with—does not contradict—the statement "all marbles are red." Similarly, "all M are R" not only does not contradict "some M are R," but the latter statement must actually follow from the former. A moment's reflection will also show that a similar relationship exists between the statements of the negative form, "some M are not R" and "no M are R." The only possible exception would be a Logical Reasoning question which consists of a discussion between two persons in the form of a transcript. If the tone is *very* conversational, one of the speakers *might* mean *some* in its everyday sense.

To return to our four kinds of statements:

Using Venn or Circle Diagrams. It is also fairly apparent that there are interrelationships among all the statement forms. For example, if "all A are B" is true, then both "no A are B" and "some A are not B" must be false. One way of exhibiting these relationships is through the use of Venn or circle diagrams. (These are also used in Analytical Reasoning problems.) We will use a circle to mark off a "logical area." So a circle which we label "A" separates the field of the page into two spaces, A and not-A. The interior of the circle is the space where all A's are located, and anything located outside the circle is not an A (it is a non-A):

Diagram 1:

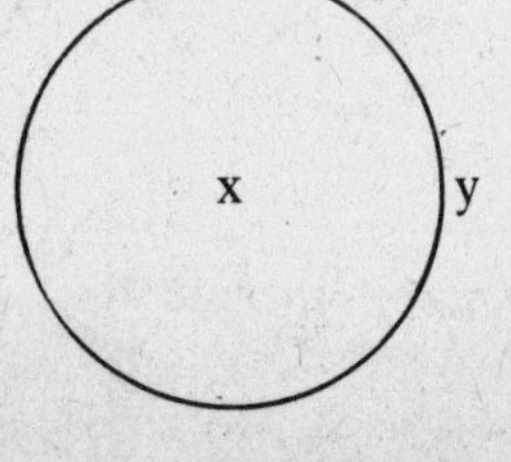

In Diagram 1, *x* is an A, but *y* is not an A, which is to say *y* is a non-A. Now if we draw two overlapping circles, we can represent not only two groups, A and B, but also the intersection of those groups:

Diagram 2:

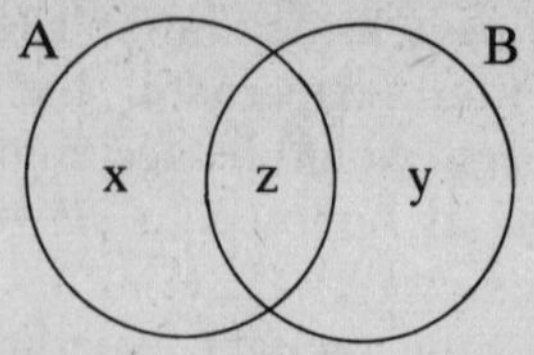

In Diagram 2 *x* is an A, which is not, however, a B; *y* is a B, which is not, however, an A; and *z* is something which is both A and B.

If it is true that "all A are B," then it is not possible for something to be an "A but not also a B," so we blot out that portion of our circle diagrams which contains the area "A" but not also "B":

Diagram 3:

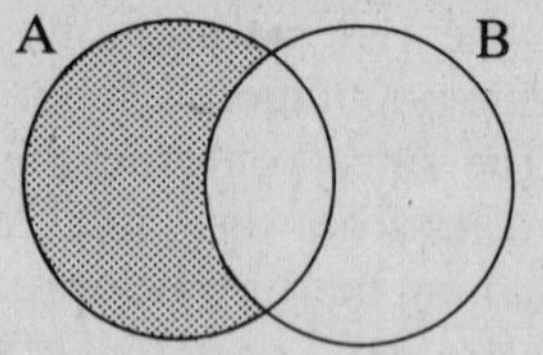

Now if it is true that "all A are B," then:
"no A are B" is false. (All the A are B.)
"some A are B" is true. (All the A are within the B circle.)
"some A are not B" is false. (That area is eliminated.)
If it is false that "all A are B," that might be because "no A are B":

Diagram 4:

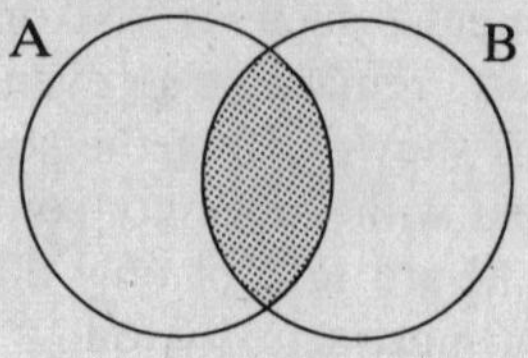

However, it might also be because "some, though not all, A are not B":

Diagram 5:

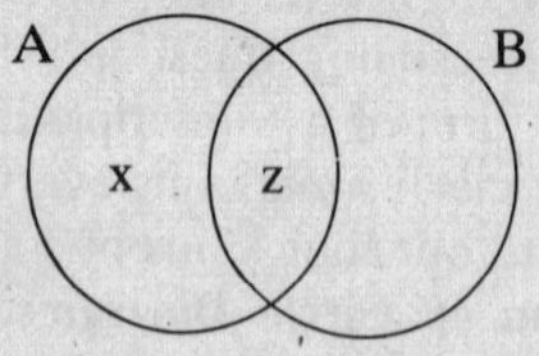

Both situations are consistent with "all A are B" being a false statement. So, if it is false that "all A are B," then:
"no A are B" might be true or false. (We cannot choose between Diagram 4 and Diagram 5.)
"some A are B" might be true or false. (We have no basis for choice.)
"some A are not B" is true. (This is the case with both Diagram 4 and Diagram 5.)
If it is true that "no A are B," then there is no overlap between the two:

Diagram 6:

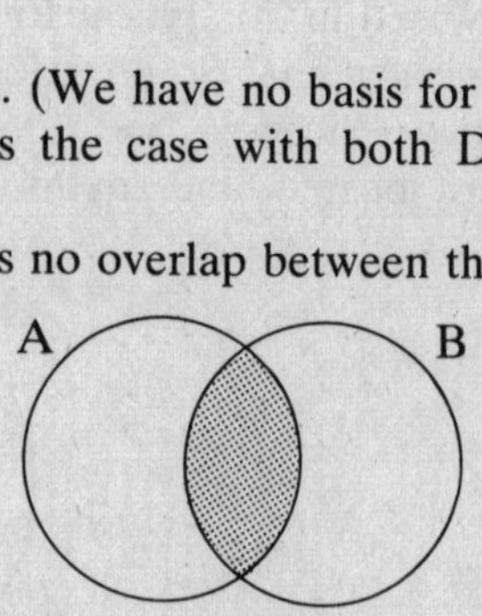

So, "all A are B" is false. (There is no overlap.)
"some A are B" is false. (There is no overlap.)
"some A are not B" is true. (That part is left open.)

But if "no A are B" is false, that might be because "all A are B":

Diagram 7:

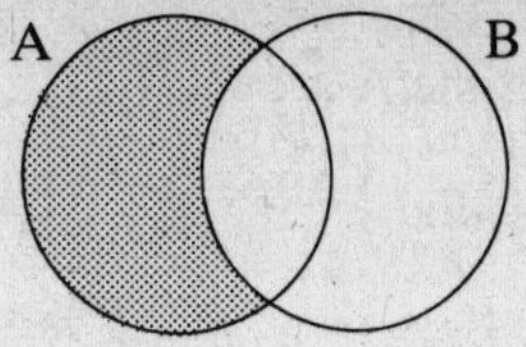

But it might equally well be because "some, though not all, A are B":

Diagram 8:

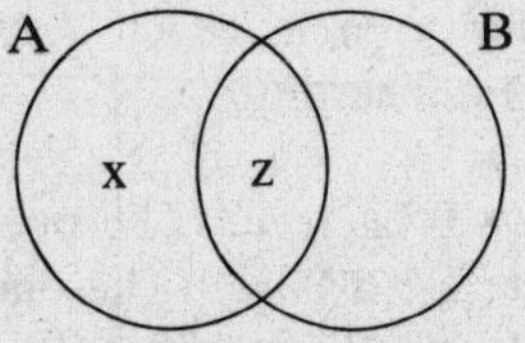

Therefore, "all A are B" might be true or false. (There is no basis for choice.)
"some A are B" is true. (See diagrams 7 and 8.)
"some A are not B" might be true or false. (There is no basis for choice between diagrams.)

If it is true that "some A are B,"

Diagram 9:

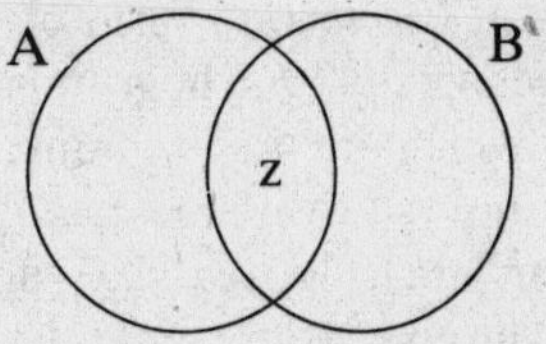

then, "all A are B" might be true or false. (See discussion of *some*.)
"no A are B" is false. (See Diagram 9.)
"some A are not B" might be true or false. (See also discussion of *some*.)

If it is false that "some A are B," this can only be because there is no overlap between the two circles:

Diagram 10:

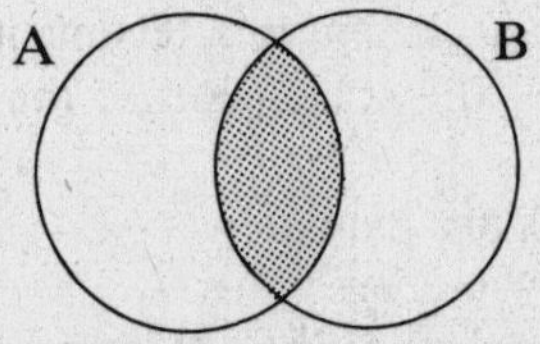

Therefore, "all A are B" is false. (There is no overlap at all.)
"no A are B" is true. (As shown by Diagram 10.)
"some A are not B" is true. (That area is left open.)

If it is true that "some A are not B":

Diagram 11:

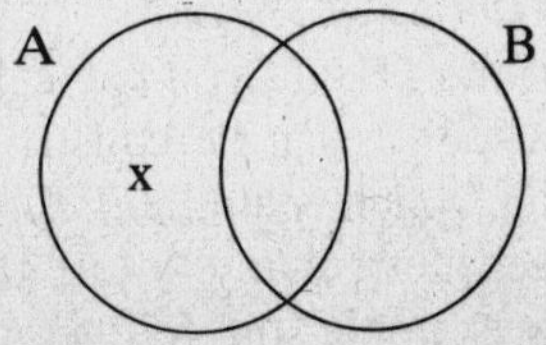

then, "all A are B" is false. (Shown by the *x* in Diagram 11.)
"no A are B" might be true or false. (The *x* does not close off the overlap of A and B, but then again we do not know that there are individuals with the characteristic A and B.)
"some A are B" might be true or false. (See the reasoning just given for "no A are B.")

If it is false, that "some A are not B":

Diagram 12:

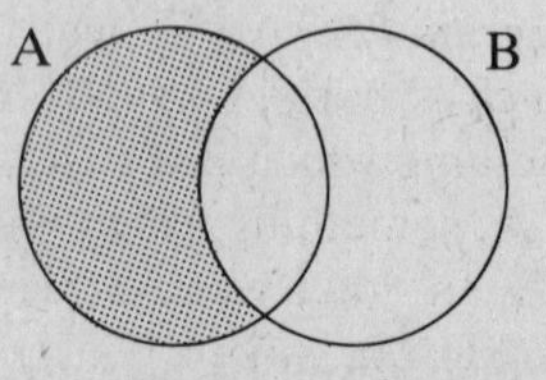

then the area of the A circle which does not overlap the B circle is empty, as shown by diagram 12. Therefore:

"all A are B" is true. (The one is contained in the other.)
"no A are B" is false. (The one is contained in the other.)
"some A are B" is true. (In fact, all are, but see our discussion of "some.")

A word of caution: Do not memorize all the relationships just presented. The circle diagrams will provide an aid for thought and practice, and they will also prove useful in our study of the second form of deductive inference: the syllogism.

Syllogisms. Technically, a syllogism is supposed to be constructed from three statements, two of which are assumptions, and the third the conclusion. However, since the LSAT is not a test of technical knowledge of logical forms, it may use the term "syllogism" in a looser way, applying that term to an argument with four, or perhaps even five, statements. For example:

All trees are plants.
All redwoods are trees.
This tree is a redwood.
Therefore, this tree is a plant.

If we analyzed this argument in a technical way, we would say it includes not one, but two syllogisms—the conclusion of the first forming a premise of the second:

All trees are plants.
All redwoods are trees.
Therefore, all redwoods are plants.

All redwoods are plants.
This tree is a redwood.
Therefore, this tree is a plant.

But for purposes of the LSAT, you can call the first argument a syllogism as well.

Of course, a syllogism can be constructed using negative statements as well. Now, depending on which statement forms are used and how the terms are arranged, we can construct many different syllogisms. Not all of these, however, would be valid. For example, the following syllogism is valid.

All A are B.
No B are C.
Therefore, no A are C.

We can show its validity by using a variation on our circle diagrams. Now we have three terms rather than two terms. Remember that two terms or groups might be related in three ways: An A which is not a B, a B which is not an A, and something which is both A and B. When we add our third term, C, we have to allow for something which is a C, but not an A or B; something which is a C and B, but not an A; something which is a C and A, but not a B; and something which is C, B, and A. In other words, there are seven possible combinations.

1. an A, but not a B or C
2. a B, but not an A or C
3. an A and B, but not a C
4. a C, but not an A or B
5. an A and C, but not a B
6. a B and C, but not an A
7. an A, B and C

These seven possibilities can be shown on a three-circle diagram:

Diagram 13:

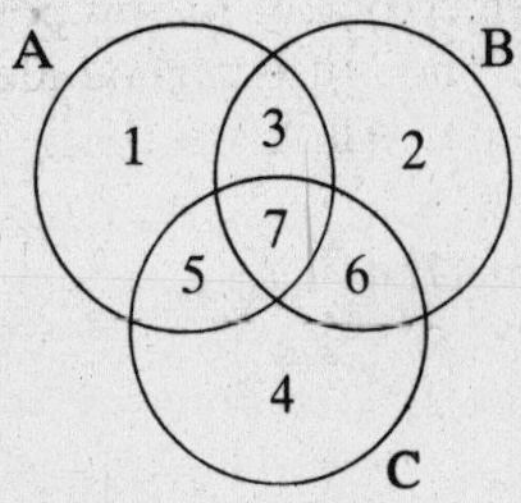

Using our three-circle diagrams, we can show the validity of the syllogism constructed at the beginning of this paragraph. Since our first premise states that "all A are B" we can eliminate the areas of the diagram which are within the A circle but not within the B circle. This corresponds to areas 1 and 5 in Diagram 13.

Diagram 14:

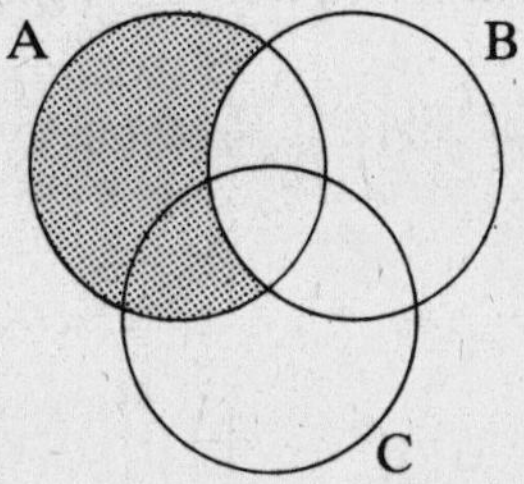

Our second premise states that "no B are C," so we must eliminate those areas, corresponding to 6 and 7 on Diagram 13, which allow that something might be a B and a C. (Notice that something which is an A, B, and C—area 7—is automatically something which is a B and a C.)

Diagram 15:

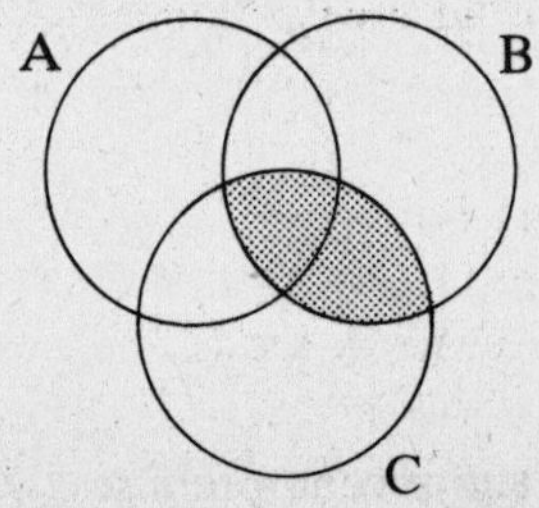

Now if we enter both premises one and two on the same diagram, we have:

Diagram 16:

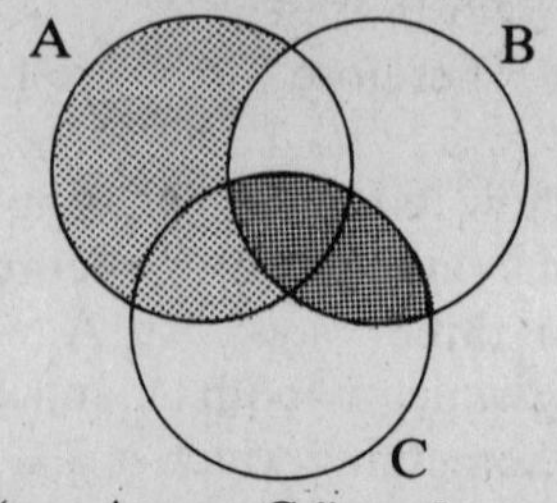

The conclusion of our syllogism asserts that "no A are C," and our diagram confirms this. The only area of A left open is within the B circle; all A but non-B areas have been erased.

Another example of a valid syllogism is:

All A are B.
Some C are A.
Therefore, some C are B.

In a syllogism in which one of the propositions uses "some" and the other proposition uses "all" or "no," it is a good idea to enter the "all" or "no" information first. So we enter first, "all A are B":

Diagram 17:

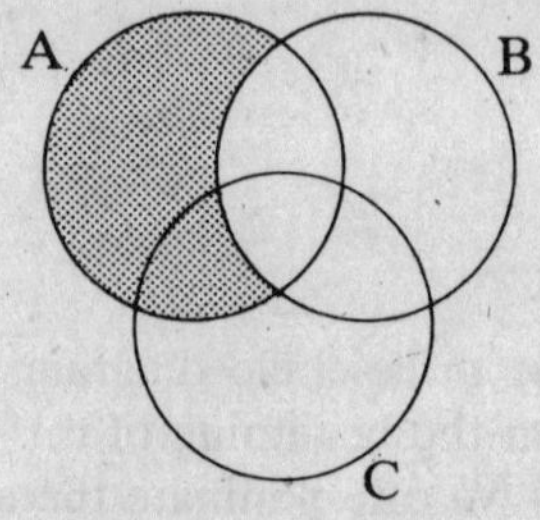

Then we enter "some C are A" by putting an *x* in the area of C and A. Since there is only one such area left, the *x* must be placed so:

Diagram 18:

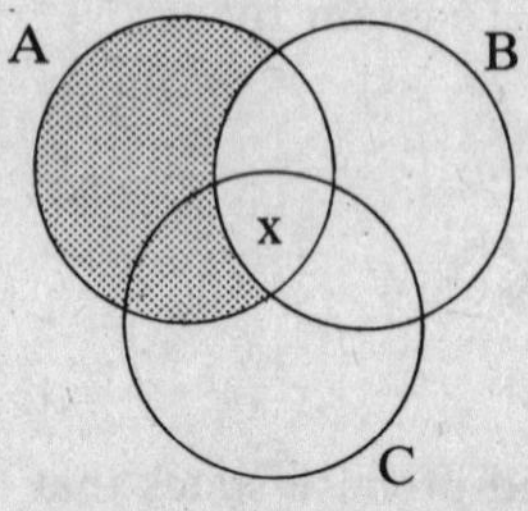

Now the diagram shows the validity of our syllogism: there is at least one C which is also a B.

An example of an *invalid* deductive argument is the syllogism which has the form:

No A are B.
No B are C.
Therefore, no A are C.

We enter the first and second premises:

Diagram 19:

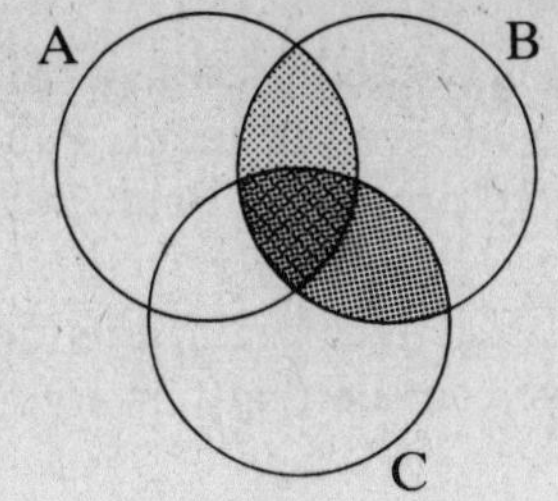

But then we observe that the overlap of A and C is still open, so our conclusion that "no A are C" is not warranted, that is, it does not definitely follow from our premises. So, too, the following argument is invalid.

Some A are B.
Some B are not C.
Therefore, some A are not C.

Since there is no premise which begins with "all" or "no," we are forced to start with a premise which begins with "some." We take premise number one first. "Some A are B," but we have no way of determining whether or not the A's which are B's are also C's. So we will leave open those possibilities:

Diagram 20:

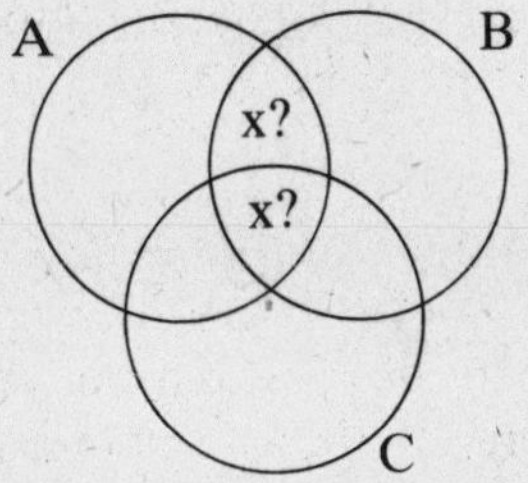

Now we add the information "some B are not C," again keeping open the possibility that that something might be a B and an A or a B but not an A:

Diagram 21:

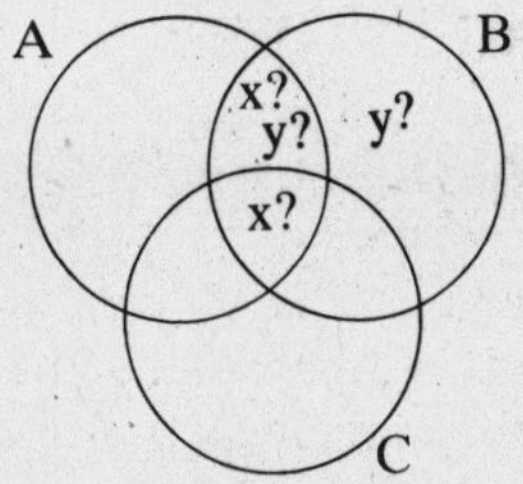

Diagram 21 shows that the conclusion, "some A are not C," does not follow from our premises because we do not definitely know the locations of our *x*'s or *y*'s, as indicated by the question marks.

Implications

Thus far, we have treated deductive inferences which involved relationships among terms. Now we treat a group of deductive arguments, which we will call implications, that are based on the connections of *sentences* as opposed to *terms*. An example of an implication argument is:

> If John is elected president, Mary is elected vice-president, and if Mary is elected vice-president, Paul is elected secretary. Therefore, if John is elected president, Paul is elected secretary.

If we employ our capital letters again, this time using each letter to stand for a clause (or sentence), we can see that our argument has the form:

> If J, then M.
> If M, then P.
> Therefore, if J, then P.

Notice that our entire argument is phrased in the conditional. Our conclusion does not state that "Paul is elected secretary." It states rather that "*if* J, then P," and that entire conditional statement is the conclusion of our argument.

Another common form of implication is illustrated by the argument:

> If John is elected President, Mary is elected vice-president. John is elected President. Therefore, Mary is elected vice-president.

The form of the argument is:

> If J, then M.
> J.
> Therefore, M.

Notice that this argument differs from our conditional argument, for our second premise definitely asserts "John is elected president." Now, since the validity of an argument is dependent only upon its form, it is clear that any argument which has this form is valid. This form of argument must not, however, be confused with the superficially similar but invalid form:

> If A, then B.
> B.
> Therefore, A.

The first premise asserts only that A is followed by B; it does not assert that an occurrence of situation B is necessarily preceded by an occurrence of situation A. For example, the following argument is not valid.

> If an object is made of clay, it will not burn. This object will not burn. Therefore, this object is made of clay.

There are many objects which will not burn and which are not made of clay—those made of steel for example. So *any* argument which has this form is invalid.

Another common form of implication which is valid is illustrated by the argument:

> If John is elected president, then Mary is elected vice-president. Mary is not elected vice-president. Therefore, John is not elected president.

It has the form:

> If J, then M.
> Not M.
> Therefore, not J.

Since the first premise states that an occurrence of situation J will be followed by an occurrence of situation M, and since the second premise tells us that situation M did not occur, we can logically conclude that situation J did not occur, for if J had occurred so, too, M would have occurred. A similar but invalid argument form is illustrated by the argument:

> If John is elected president, then Mary is elected vice-president. John is not elected president. Therefore, Mary is not elected vice-president.

That this argument is invalid is demonstrated by the consideration that the first premise states only that an occurrence of J is followed by an occurrence of M. The premises do not establish that M can occur *only* if J also occurs. The first premise says "if J, then M," not "M only if J." So any argument of the form "If A, then B. Not A. Therefore, not B." is *invalid.*

Not all valid implicational forms have been shown; our illustrations are intended to illustrate the technique of substituting capital letters for sentences. This allows us to isolate the general *form* of an argument, which makes analyzing or comparing that form easier.

Relational Sequences

There is a final group of deductive arguments which we call relational sequences. A simple example is provided by the argument:

> A is greater than B.
> B is greater than C.
> Therefore, A is greater than C.

Since these arguments are susceptible to treatment by using pictorial devices, we have treated them in the section on Analytical Reasoning, where such devices are introduced. For the present, remember that you *may* find Analytical Reasoning-type problems also included in Logical Reasoning, but of course you can use Analytical Reasoning techniques to solve them. If these sorts of problems appear in the Logical Reasoning sections, they will usually be in paragraph form and will have only one question associated with them. Accordingly, they are simpler diagrams than those on the Analytical Reasoning section.

LOGICAL REASONING TEST STRATEGY

As we indicated earlier, the difficulty with the Logical Reasoning section of the LSAT is that there is such a variety of question stems that it is difficult to provide a mechanical procedure for approaching such problems. The following tips, however, may help make our somewhat abstract discussion of logic easier to apply to actual LSAT-type problems. In any event, you should keep in mind that the materials presented thus far are merely an overview. There is much more detailed discussion of specific problems in the practice tests contained in this book.

Preview question stem. The first point of attack in the Logical Reasoning section is to read the question stem (the part to which the question mark is attached) before reading the paragraph or sample argument. The reason for this suggestion is easily explained. There are many different questions which one might ask about an argument: "How can it be strengthened?"; "How can it be weakened?"; "What are its assumptions?"; "How is the argument developed?"; and so on. If you read an argument without focusing your attention on some aspect of it, all of these aspects of argumentation (and even more) are likely to come to mind. Unfortunately, this is distracting. The most efficient way to handle the Logical Reasoning questions is to read the stem of the question first. Let that guide you in what to look for as you read.

Find the conclusion. This is always helpful, even when it is merely a descriptive statement. Keep in mind the importance of finding the exact conclusion for structuring the argument and assessing its strengths or weaknesses.

Attack the answer choices. The differences between the answer choices often help you isolate the issues in the problem. Attack the answer choices by:

1. always reading all the answer choices
2. eliminating obviously incorrect choices
3. contrasting remaining choices to isolate the relevant issues

Remember that you are only trying to choose the best answer. The best is often not perfect and the less than best—and thus incorrect—answers often have some merit.

For special Logical Reasoning questions. Many of the Logical Reasoning questions are straightforward questions about how to attack and defend arguments. Some questions, however, are ETS inventions and involve special twists of thinking. To assist you in answering some of these, keep in mind the following points:

- For a question that asks, "Which of the following arguments is most similar?," remember that you are not supposed to correct the argument. You are supposed to find an answer choice with a similar structure—even if the original argument contains a fallacy. Also, be careful to notice exactly what is to be paralleled—all of an argument, one speaker, or whatever.
- For a question that asks, "Which of the following statements is the most reliable?," look carefully at the qualifications of the author in relation to the topic on which he is writing, and also look for elements of self-interest in the statement.
- For a question involving deductive reasoning, try using a Venn (circle) diagram, a relational line, or some other pictorial device.

- For a question that requires you to complete a paragraph, keep in mind that you must complete the structure of the argument as a whole as well as the particular sentence. This means that an answer choice which repeats something already said is not correct. The correct answer must be the *completion* of the thought.
- When the question stem asks for the identification of assumptions, it is seeking implicit or unstated premises which—like all premises—are necessary to the argument.
- When the question stem asks for weakening ideas, it is usually a matter of attacking implicit assumptions which justify the application of the evidence to the conclusion(s).
- When the question stem asks for strengthening ideas, the correct answer might be merely an explicit statement of a previously implicit premise.
- When the question stem asks what the second person in an exchange has interpreted the first person to mean, two things are important: (1) The second person has *mis*interpreted the first person and, thus, (2) the correct answer must relate to the second person's comments, not to those of the first.
- *Cave Distractum:* Watch out for *superficial* similarities of subject matter between answer choices and argument. Wrong answers often mention irrelevant details.

READING COMPREHENSION INSTRUCTIONAL OVERVIEW

INTRODUCTION

"Reading comprehension?" you snort. "I know how to read." And you do. But somehow you still make errors on reading comprehension problems.

While reading is a skill that you have practiced nearly all your life, it is one that you—like almost everyone else—could probably improve greatly. We don't mean just speed, or even primarily speed, but COMPREHENSION—getting the meaning, the whole meaning, and nothing but the meaning. Having made that global statement, let us focus on the much narrower and simpler task of improving your score on the Reading Comprehension section of the LSAT.

We will approach this task by first describing the Reading Comprehension section in some detail; second, by identifying different kinds of reading tasks and approaches that you will need on the section; third, by analyzing the types of questions you will be asked and the answer choices among which you will be choosing; and, fourth, by developing an attack strategy for this section.

STRUCTURE AND TIMING OF THE READING COMPREHENSION SECTION

On the LSAT you will typically see Reading Comprehension (hereafter RC) sections which give you 35 minutes to do 28 problems. The problems will usually be based on four passages with seven questions on each passage, though some variations are possible. The passages will usually be writings that are, or could be, from textbooks, journal articles, academic essays, and the like. While they will not often be intrinsically interesting to you personally, they are fairly well written with definite structure and considerable implicit meaning. Later we will discuss this further. The topics presented will range widely and will usually include passages from the humanities and social sciences, with some fairly technical-sounding passages from such fields as economics, psychology, and occasionally even physical sciences. The topics are not really important since in principle you can always answer all of the questions even if you have no knowledge of the field other than what the passage tells you.

You will often, correctly, be told: THE RC SECTION IS NOT A TEST OF KNOWLEDGE, BUT ONLY OF READING SKILLS. While this is basically true, it is also true that you are expected to use two general areas of knowledge—language and common sense. The linguistic knowledge required is not knowledge of esoteric vocabulary, but the ability to read closely and know the precise relationships expressed by common words. Common sense knowledge is merely what any reasonably alert college graduate could be expected to know. For example:

Cows are the source of beef, cows are deliberately raised by humans for food and not simply harvested like fish, China is a country, theology has to do with God, etc.

Many students are very worried that their reading speed is inadequate for the test. They often base this feeling on the experience of having wanted more time than was available for the reading sections of this or other tests. READING SPEED IS NOT THE KEY TO THE LSAT. You will only have to read about 115 words per minute, perhaps less, for the whole section, including passages, questions, and answer choices. This is well within the capacities of virtually any college graduate. Of course there is one other little matter—you have to think about the questions and answer them.

The passages will range from 400 to 700 words in length, but since there are about as many words in the questions and answers as in the passages, the different passage lengths don't really make too much difference to your timing plans. You should budget your time as follows:

TIME ALLOCATION FOR READING COMPREHENSION SECTION WITH 4 PASSAGES, 7 QUESTIONS EACH.

TASK	**TIME**	
PREVIEW OF SECTION	1 minute maximum	
PASSAGE #1		
Preview Question Stems	½ minute	
Read Passage	3–4 minutes	
Answer Questions	4–5 minutes	
Total for Passage		8½ minutes
PASSAGE #2 (same as #1)		8½ minutes
PASSAGE #3 (same as #1)		8½ minutes
PASSAGE #4 (same as #1)		8½ minutes
	TOTAL SECTION	35 minutes

The most important thing for you to remember about this timing recommendation is that it is not rigid. It is certain that you will not follow it exactly for most passages, so don't worry. The second most important thing is that you spend more time answering the questions than reading the passage. While this will not always be possible with a longer or more obscure passage, it is what you should strive to do. The questions and answers between them will have nearly as many words to read as the passage, words that are not all connected together. In addition, you will have to think about the answer choices to the questions since many are rather close, as we will discuss later. While it is true that you have to think about the passage while you read it, there is still more work to be done with the questions than with the passage. Furthermore, your natural impulse is to feel that if you could memorize the passage all your troubles would be over and the questions would answer themselves. Nothing could be further from the truth. Practically none of the RC questions will merely ask you to parrot back what was in the passage. At the least, you will need to use different words and often you will need to work from underlying structures and implicit ideas, again as we will discuss later. All of this means that your goal is to read the passage carefully but briskly once, thinking all the while, and then to work the problems briskly but carefully.

Two previews are mentioned in the timing schema. The preview of the section is simply checking the timing and the total number of questions, and leafing quickly through the section to see how many passages there are and that they are essentially as described in the book. If there are some variations, you will adjust your timings accordingly. The total time available for each question, on the average, is 75 seconds, which is broken down approximately as 5 seconds for previewing the question stem, 30–35 seconds per question for reading the passage (which still takes however long it takes), and 35–40 seconds per question for reading and answering it.

The previewing of the question stem that we recommend is a very quick reading of just the part of the question which asks the question, not the answer choices or roman numeral propositions, if any. There are three purposes to this preview. First, it can alert you to most of the questions that concern details or have references to specific parts of the passage ("line 20" or "first paragraph," etc.); this foreknowledge can save you time and improve accuracy, though it only applies to a few questions. Second, it can give you some idea of the topic and approach of the passage so that you can more easily follow it; this can be particularly helpful when the passage has a broad range, or a beginning that is quite different from its body. Third, by giving you some clues and structure for your reading of the passage, this preview can combat both fatigue and boredom. As interested as you are in your score, you may find the passages less than thrilling. If you can persuade yourself that it is a detective game—which it is, of sorts—you might keep up your interest and do better.

Most students find previewing the questions very helpful and reassuring. Try this technique on the practice tests in this book. If you personally find that you are not comfortable with it and you can do well without the preview of the questions, drop it. Everyone should preview the section, and the quicker the better.

DIFFERENT KINDS OF READING AND HOW TO DO THEM

Four aspects of reading will concern us here.

1. literal versus implicit meaning
2. precision versus imprecision
3. active versus passive reading
4. "test reading" versus "real-world" reading

These are not entirely separate ideas, nor will you find them strange. You have been reading successfully for many years and all we will try to do in this section is help you to improve by making you conscious of and emphasizing the reading skills most used on the LSAT.

We will use the following short passage as the basis of our discussions of both the different kinds of reading and the different kinds of questions on the LSAT. Whenever a question is asked about the passage, try to answer it before you read the explanation.

One dependable characteristic of the cattle cycle is the biologic time lag in the production process.

Heifers are not bred for their first calf until they are 14 to 18 months old. Then the gestation period is 9 months. The calf, in turn, won't reach mature slaughter weight for another 17 to 19 months, depending on the individual calf's rate of gain and the feeding program.

Consequently, it takes up to 4 years from the time a cattle producer's heifer is born until her offspring reaches slaughter weight. If this offspring is retained to expand the herd rather than sent to slaughter, it could be about 5½ years from the time the first calf is retained in the herd until an offspring reaches slaughter.

Because of the time lag, beef production continues to increase well beyond the time price signals change. This happened in the 1974–76 period. Beef production kept increasing despite the large financial losses to cattle producers.

Literal Versus Implicit Meaning

Literal meaning is the meaning of the passage that is explicitly stated. For instance:

1. What is the period of gestation in cattle?

The answer is found by looking up the period in the second paragraph of the passage (or by memory) and noting that it is 9 months.

2. What happened to beef production and prices during 1974–76?

In the last paragraph it is stated that the production kept increasing despite lower prices and large losses.

Although it is hard to do anything with a passage if you do not even see its literal meaning, most of the questions and most of the information in a passage—even one as simple and descriptive as this one—is carried in the implicit meanings. There are many kinds of implicit meanings, but they are all essentially the same idea. The connections between the different parts of the passage and the fact that the specific literal ideas are presented in particular orders and with particular emphases and relationships conveys additional meaning. There is, of course, no absolute dividing line between explicit and implicit. Some ideas can be understood in several ways.

3. What is a heifer?

A young female of the cattle species. This could be known by prior knowledge (not much of that on the LSAT, though) or you could see that it is implied from the statement in the passage that heifers are the cattle which give birth, hence female by our common knowledge of mammalian reproduction, and are young since it is the earliest they can be bred. The latter is a little less sure than the former.

4. What is the cattle cycle referred to in the first sentence?

Here we begin to get into what the answer is not. The cattle cycle is not the generations of cattle or the process of getting one cow from another. That would be the biologic cycle perhaps. We know this because if something (the biologic cycle) is a characteristic of something else (the cattle cycle), then the characteristic is not likely to be the whole thing.

What, then, is the cattle cycle? The last paragraph tells us that there is a price movement as well, and that the price movement and the biologic movement have been out of synchrony. This leads to the idea that the cattle cycle is some sort of cycle involving the prices, the production or number of cattle, and the biologic cycle of cattle. Since it is referred to as a cycle, it presumably goes up and down. Therefore, we might see a further question of this sort.

5. What probably happened to beef prices and cattle supplies after 1976?

Since the cycle had been on a down price and up cattle supplies part of the cycle through 1976, one would expect a reduction in herd size and an increase in prices after 1976. This would be followed by a natural desire for the cattle producers to increase their herds to take advantage of the higher prices (deduced from the cyclic nature of things, reinforced by common sense applied to basic business). This would gradually lead to a general increase in cattle supplies and an eventual decrease in prices, thus completing the cycle.

6. How long does a cattle cycle probably take?

This is not a question that can be answered with great confidence. One would actually have to work with the answer choices to some extent as will be described in the section on questions. However, we CAN imply from the passage that the cycle must involve at least 6 years or more since it will take at least that long for the herds to have increased through two generations. An answer choice of less than 5 years would be too short to allow really major changes in cattle supplies and one longer than 15 years (maybe 10) would not be good since it would not recognize the building up of oversupply. The upper limit is much less certain than the lower.

We will leave this topic now, though it will be carried forward further in the discussion of the kinds of questions which you will be asked, and the proper approaches to them. Many examples of this sort of reading are explained in the answer explanations for the practice test RC sections.

Precision in Reading

Many of the implications which you will be called upon to see in the passages on the test will be strong or weak or even possible because of the precise wording of the passage. It is very important, however, to remember that precision is not the same as subtlety. An example of precision is the difference between *can* and *will* in these two sentences:

> Inflation can be controlled.
> Inflation will be controlled.

These sentences have very different meanings. The first states that it is possible to control inflation, while the second states that not only can it be controlled, but also that this happy outcome will occur. The difference is not subtle in any way, even though it turns on a single word.

In the passage about cattle, the first sentence used the word *cycle,* and we were able to learn a lot from the fact that the cattle situation was a cycle. If the sentence had only referred to a "problem" or an "industry" we would have known much less about what was happening.

There are too many possible sentences for us to hope to classify them all for you, nor is that needed. There is one fundamental idea which you need to apply: EVERYTHING COUNTS.

In order to fully understand this injunction, that everything counts, let us remember just what the test-writers are interested in and with what sorts of passages you will be dealing. The test-writers want to see how well you can get the fullest understanding—comprehension—from a passage. To permit a good test of that skill, they will usually give you passages that—unlike much writing—are highly structured and fairly well written. We must immediately point out that interest, vitality, and style are not within the scope of the writing we are now describing, though some passages have those qualities. What we are referring to is the fact that the authors of the passages have thought about the structure of their sentences and paragraphs and about their choice of words rather carefully. We may assume that whatever words or structures are in the passages are intended to convey every bit of meaning that can reasonably be wrung from them.

Thus, if the word *cycle* is used, you must conclude that it was precisely a cycle that was meant and not merely an event, period, or circumstance.

Many words are particularly important in terms of understanding the strength or scope of a statement, such as: *some, all, every,* etc. The significance of these words is fully discussed in Instructional Overviews for both Logical Reasoning and Analytical Reasoning problems.

How, you may be wondering, can the reader possibly catch all of this precision in less than 39 readings of the passage? The answer to this reasonable question is contained in the third aspect of reading we will treat in this section.

Active Versus Passive Reading

Every piece of reading is done differently. If you are reading a book in bed at night in order to relax and go to sleep, you will probably read more slowly and without as much attention to detail than if you were studying the same book in order to write a major analytic paper on it. But no matter how fast or with how much concentration you are reading, you are always thinking about what you are reading as you are reading it.

When you are watching television or looking up at the clouds after a summer picnic, you may be doing practically nothing but passively receiving visual stimuli.

When you read, however, your understanding depends on how much thinking you are doing while you are reading. Indeed, even pure memorization of a passage will be improved if you have done some good thinking about it while you were reading.

Active reading, then, is reading accompanied by sustained, intense thought about the passage being read: not a conscious counterpoint to the passage, but just feeling the gears whirring underneath, where most thought occurs.

As we have mentioned, it is the structure and implicit meanings of the passage that will be the major subjects of the questions on the test. Therefore, you will want to be constantly trying to "dig the bones" of the passage. Here are some of the questions you should be considering as you read:

—How is this idea connected to previous ones in the passage?
—What is likely to follow (from) this idea?
—What is the author's purpose in making this particular statement at this particular place in the passage?
—What does this prove, exemplify, demonstrate, etc.?
—Is this a continuation of some previous idea or the introduction of a new line of thought?

Connections, connections—that is always your concern. Always working while you are reading is your method of finding them in the time available. You do this all the time; all that you need to do on the LSAT is do this a little bit more.

"Test Reading" versus "Real-world" Reading

When you are reading an article in the real world you are trying to link what the article is telling you to everything else that you know. This is the most powerful sort of reading that you can do. In practice, of course, you don't quite manage to make a complete cross-referencing to everything you know about every topic, but you probably pretty well cross-reference to a lot of what you know about the specific topic of the passage and related topics.

On the test you don't do the same thing. The LSAT is not a test of your previous knowledge of the topic of the passage, nor of any particular previous knowledge at all except language and reading skills. All the test is concerned with is the INTERNAL linkages within the passage. This makes your job much easier. "All" you have to do is correlate all of the parts of the passage with each other and understand whatever can be implied from that. While there are hard and easy questions, you will find after a while that the difficulty of the questions is largely a matter of the range of answer choices and not so much a matter of the passage's difficulty. Focusing on the internal linkages within the passage actually reduces the work a great deal.

ANSWERING THE DIFFERENT TYPES OF RC QUESTIONS

We will analyze RC questions in two ways: formal structure and linkage to the passage. In the latter we will analyze the different types of question stems and what they are asking of you. Then we will discuss the fundamental rules for answering RC questions prior to developing an attack strategy in the next section.

Formal Structure

The directions ask you to select the best answer choice out of the five available. This means just what it says. The correct answer choice will be better than any of the others. It may be all but perfect and surrounded by other good choices, or it may be fairly poor and surrounded by totally unacceptable choices. While all of the correct answer choices have merit, there are wrong answer choices which also have merit and some correct ones whose main claim is the poverty of their competition. For this reason you always read all of the answer choices.

The question stem for the RC question, as for most verbal questions, sets up a criterion by which to judge the answer choices. Any answer choice may relate to the criterion in three basic ways: definitely meets the criterion, definitely fails the criterion, or it is not known how it relates to the criterion. Therefore, when the question asks which answer choice is, for example, true, the incorrect answer choices may be either false or indeterminate. In addition, two or more of the answer choices may have some measure of truth and you have to choose the one which is most strongly deducible.

When the question states that all of the answers are, for example, agreeable to the author EXCEPT . . . , then the incorrect answers are agreeable, though the agreeableness of some may be more strongly supported than that of others, and the correct answer choice may be either known to be disagreeable or something whose agreeableness is not determinable.

For Roman Numeral format questions, you can make good progress even if you only know one or two of the propositions. Use the ones you know to eliminate answer choices. This also applies to Analytical Reasoning.

The strength and scope of the questions and the answer choices is very important, and as noted in the Precision Reading section, this issue is discussed in other Instructional Overviews in even more detail.

Linkage to the Passage

Each and every question that you face on the test has the unstated introductory clause "In light of what the passage says or implies. . . . " Some questions actually say "according to the passage," or "according to the author," etc. But you will always have that in your mind whether it is stated or not.

While it is possible to consider every question to be asking for you to make some sort of inference, we shall first sort out some other slightly more restricted sorts of questions before addressing the general topic of inference questions as the residual category of questions. We will discuss the following kinds of questions:

—Specific details (0–3)
—Purpose (2–4)
—Tone (2–4)
—Identity of author or other person (0–2)
—Use of evidence (2–4)
—Main idea, including title (5–9)
—Logical reasoning or method of argument (0–2)
—Inference, implication, author agree, trend, or stated or implied (6–15)

The numbers in parentheses following each question type are a very approximate indication of the typical range of frequency for that question type in a 28-question RC section. The types are not utterly distinct, and some variants, combinations, or just plain oddball questions are perfectly possible, but there won't be many.

Specific Details Questions. There may be a few questions which essentially ask you to report something which is specifically stated in the passage. These would be questions such as questions 1, 2, or 3, previously discussed. If you see this sort of question, be very careful in checking the answer choices for qualifiers and limiters that may be the difference between one choice and another. Also, more than one quality or descriptor may go with a particular idea and the correct answer choice may be somewhat more comprehensive than the incorrect ones.

Purpose of the Passage or Author. If the passage is just a description of something, then the purpose will be to describe whatever the passage describes. The purpose can also be explanatory of some aspect of the passage which is implicit. In the illustrative passage abut the cattle cycle, for example, you might have the following:

7. What is the author's purpose in writing the passage?
   (A) To describe the problems of ranchers
   (B) To justify the cattle cycle
   (C) To explain how the cattle cycle can lead to apparently irrational actions by cattle producers

(A) has the merit of saying that some problem is being explained, which is true of the passage. It is not, however, especially the problem of ranchers, but of cattle producers. This is a matter of precision reading.

(B) has the merit of referring to the cattle cycle, which is certainly a major part of the passage. However, *justify* means to show why something is good, usually in spite of appearances to the contrary. The cycle just is, and the author isn't in favor of it.

(C) is the best answer since it amounts to saying that the purpose of the passage is to justify the cattle producers' actions as being not irrational in the least because of the lag time. *Justify* might be too strong anyway, so the use of *explain* in (C) is better.

Thus, a purpose must match the passage as precisely and completely as possible. Generally, it will reflect the bulk of the passage similar to the way a main idea problem does as discussed on the next page.

The only exception would be a passage which makes a specific proposal for some change. In that case, the purpose of the passage was to make the proposal.

Tone of the Passage. As for any other question, the answer chosen must have a basis—preferably a strong one—in the passage. This passage might be described as factual, objective, explanatory, and so on. It would be too strong to call it apologetic or alarmed or worried. Some tone questions have single-word answer choices; others have longer choices. The longer the choices, the more accurately they can reflect the texture of the passage—factual but concerned.

Identity of Author or other Person. Usually this is a matter of time and job description. Typically the inferences are a bit on the thin side, and frequently fall far short of perfection. In the illustrative passage, the perfect description might be "an agricultural economist writing in the late 1970's." The time could not be before 1977, and the job must be something to do with economics or agriculture. An answer choice such as "Congressional aide" is tempting, but there is nothing "Congressional" about the passage. There is no basis.

Use of Evidence. This question type asks you to identify the role of some piece of evidence or sub-argument in the overall scheme of things. Occasionally, the role of a piece of evidence in the development of a sub-argument or a quoted argument may be sought. The basic type would be of this sort:

8. What does the author demonstrate by referring to "large financial losses" in the last paragraph?
   (A) foolishness of cattle producers

(B) financial weakness of cattle producers
(C) poor prospects of small cattle producers
(D) inevitability of the biologic time lag
(E) futility of trying to plan anything in cattle production

As discussed for #7, the author does not feel that the cattle producers are especially foolish, but is explaining the difficulties they face, hence (A) is inadequate. (B) has a superficial appeal since large losses surely cannot strengthen the financial strength of the cattle producers, but that is not related to the flow of the actual passage, which is concerned with explaining the interactions of the cattle and biologic cycles. (C) fails on precision reading grounds since nothing is said in the passage about small producers as such. The prospects of all cattle producers are tainted by the seeming unavoidability of the cattle cycle, but "small" is unfounded.

(D) is the best answer because of the author's purpose in mentioning the losses (and low prices) is to show just how inevitable the biologic lag is. Even when they lose money, they still have to increase the production of beef (slaughter) since they started growing the animals years previously. This highlights the need ALWAYS to consider your answer in light of the actual passage.

(E) is appealing because it captures the feeling of inevitability just referred to in (D). However, the word *anything* is far too strong since the passage is only describing a part of the cattle production process.

Main Idea Including Title. In the previous two problems we had different statements of the main idea of the passage. It is important in the longer passages that you will see on the test that you make certain that the main idea answer choice that you choose covers as much of the passage as possible. No significant part should be left out if it can be avoided. Typically, several of the answer choices in this type of problem are quite good and you have to examine the differences between the various answer choices closely in order to choose the correct one. Any outright error would eliminate an answer choice, but scope and fit are usually the final issues you must consider. Always be aware of how well the answer choices reflect the range of ideas, generality, causality, or other connecting ideas and strength of the passage.

A title question is treated the same way except that the potential titles are usually shorter than the answer choices in a main idea question, which means that the fit to the passage will be somewhat rougher.

Logical Reasoning or Method of Argument. You will occasionally have a question that is essentially a Logical Reasoning question. Treat it the same way you would if it appeared on the Logical Reasoning section. Method-of-argument and premises questions would be the most likely.

Inference, Implication, etc. This large class of questions is unified not so much by the varied question stems as by the method of attack. Questions 4, 5, and 6 are all examples of this question type. Let us take one more example:

9. All of the following may be inferred from the passage EXCEPT
   (A) Weight is a more important determinant of a calf's readiness for slaughter than age.
   (B) Successful cattle producers usually have either considerable ready capital or substantial lines of credit.
   (C) The cattle cycle is a dependable phenomenon and will continue indefinitely.

(D) It would be an improvement over current practice if market prices coordinated with beef supplies.
(E) The 1974–76 period was not an unusual one for cattle producers.

(A) can be inferred from the second paragraph. This is practically stated since the only reference to "slaughterability" is in terms of weight. (B) is much more implicit and derives from some of the same considerations as (E). The passage makes it clear that the cattle cycle is a cycle—a repetitive event. The biologic lag is dependable and it was the biologic lag which led to the mismatch between prices and supplies, and thus the losses. Therefore, cyclical losses (presumably offset by gains at other times) are typical of cattle producing, hence (E). If cyclical losses are typical, then any successful cattle producer must have some way of surviving these losses, hence (B).

(C) and (D) are both candidates for not being inferable, but by definition of the problem, one will turn out to be inferable and the other won't. (C) has two ideas in it about the cattle cycle. One is that the cycle AS A WHOLE is dependable and the other is that it will continue indefinitely. The first is only very weakly supported. The fact that it is a cycle is all that we needed for (E) and (B). (C) adds the modifier *dependable*. The only thing which is known to be dependable is the biologic lag (cycle) which, while important to the cattle cycle, is not necessarily the whole thing. Furthermore, we must see what the author means by *dependable* in the passage. When he refers to the biologic lag, he means that it is both necessary and of fairly well-defined duration. While the cattle cycle appears to be occurring, neither its necessity nor the regularity of its timing are known to be.

(D), on the other hand, has a somewhat weaker claim, which is thus easier to infer. (D) holds that the current situation, where the market prices and beef supplies are not in synchrony, is not as good as one where they would be in synchrony. This is supported by the last paragraph's reference to price signaling change in beef production (thus, one should follow the other), and to a lesser extent, by the author's basically sympathetic view of the cattle producers' problems.

On a test, many of these ideas will not come to you neatly sorted out in reference to each answer choice, but will derive from a close examination of each choice and its differences from the other answer choices.

ATTACK STRATEGY FOR READING COMPREHENSION

The final section of the Instructional Overview will review a number of tips, tricks, and traps for RC questions. Here we will summarize our discussion in the form of an attack strategy for this type of question.

1. **Preview section (1 minute).** Check layout, time, number of questions and passages.

2. **Do each passage separately.** Do not jump back and forth between passages.

FOR EACH PASSAGE

3. **Preview the question stems only (½ minute).** Become alert to specific references and idea of passage.

4. **Read passage actively, briskly, precisely (3–4 minutes).** See linkages, structural clues, and flow. Checkmark specific references known from preview.

FOR EACH QUESTION (4–5 MINUTES FOR 7 QUESTIONS):

5. **Read question and all answer choices.** Read precisely and actively. Watch for key words. Identify question type.

6. **Choose answer choice by elimination and contrast.** Focus on differences between answers to eliminate. Resolve close calls by strength of inference and closeness to main idea of passage.

7. **Refer back to passage only when necessary or for specific-detail questions.**

8. **Do not get hung up on one question or one passage.**

Tips, Tricks, and Traps

This section is a listing of hints that may help to improve your speed or accuracy on RC passages.

1. Topic sentences. Most paragraphs will have a topic sentence giving the idea of the paragraph. This sentence is usually the first or last sentence.

2. Structural clues in passage. The following items are all clues to the structure of a paragraph or passage and should be noted by you as you read. In each case ask yourself how this structural clue advances the ideas of the passage.

—Comparison (finding similarities, what is basis)
—Contrast (finding differences, what is basis)
—Causes (exactly what causes what, and how)
—Sequences (order and basis of order)
—Processes (steps and underlying idea, what next)
—Metaphors or images (how do they work, what in the image represents what in the world, what does it prove, where does it lead)
—Quotations and examples (what does it prove, why is it at this point in the passage)
—Numbers and dates (don't memorize, do they connect to anything else, do they limit the other ideas)
—Generality and specificity (is this a universal situation, limited, limited to what, how)
—Modifiers (why is it this kind of thing, what is the significance of the modifier, what else also is this way)
—Where is the evidence/conclusion (if one is given look for the other, either can be first)
—Definitions (do you understand it and how it works in the development of the passage's ideas)
—Buzzwords, jargon, technical terms (what you need to know about them is in the passage, but the definition might be implicit—note if it isn't defined)

3. Flow of the argument. It is usually important to notice when the argument is definitely continuing in the same vein or when it is making a change. The change may only be within a sentence or it may be a basic change in the flow of the entire passage. Many words and phrases indicate these ideas, but here are a few examples:

—Flow continuers: *and, also, in addition to, moreover, thus, since, because, then,* etc:
—Flow changers: *instead, on the other hand, unless, despite, although, but,* etc.

4. Key words. The following words are the kinds of words which are likely to be important in interpreting questions, answers, and passages. This list is only exemplary, not exhaustive: *always, never, ever, possible, definite, impossible, exactly, precisely, necessar(y)(ily), primar(y)(ily), most, least, unless, without, entire, all, no, part(ial)(ly),* etc.

5. Reading speed and speed reading. It is better to read faster with the same or increased comprehension. It is true that many persons do not read as fast as they could, even maintaining the same comprehension. Many people report increased comprehension as well as speed with a speed reading course. Leaving aside the question of the comprehension tests having been given by the speed reading schools, this is reasonable since the essence of speed reading is better concentration and mental and physical discipline. Both of those should increase speed and also comprehension.

However, the key limit on the LSAT is comprehension, not speed. Just as the increased concentration resulting from speed study often yields increased comprehension, the increased concentration resulting from comprehension study almost always results in increased speed. If you have only a few weeks to study for the LSAT, you should concentrate on improving your comprehension through practicing precise and active reading. If you make sure that you don't let yourself slack off on the speed, you will probably find that your speed has increased along with your comprehension.

One thing that can slow down your speed, regardless of the level of your comprehension, is vocalizing or subvocalizing as you read. Vocalizing is the practice of making slight motions with your lips, tongue, or jaw as you read. This limits you to approximately the speed at which you could read aloud, which is much slower than you can read without vocalizing. Biting a pencil while you read will both reveal vocalizing (the pencil will wiggle) and can discourage it (bite down on the pencil).

Subvocalizing is the practice of "sounding" each word to yourself in your mind as you read. This is fairly common and also slows down your reading without any compensating advantages. This is more difficult to detect and eliminate and you should not look for complete change in this area in a short time. Try to mentally hum a nonsense syllable tune like "ta-ra-ra-BOOM-dee-ay" while you are reading. You will find that with a little practice you can read and mentally hum at the same time. Then stop the humming and try to keep the words flowing in the same way (but faster). Another technique uses reading material printed in narrow columns like a newspaper cut out so only one column is visible. Read it very rapidly several times in succession. You should eventually be able to go faster than the subvocalization. Once you have felt what reading is like without the subvocalization, you can both notice and desist more easily. Another, more abstract approach is to concentrate on the leap/link to the next word or words. This tends to break the one-word-at-a-time element of subvocalization and is good reading strategy anyway.

6. Eyes. Physically we can all read a thousand words a minute unless there is something wrong with our eyes. Mentally, that is usually not so practical. The point is that if you feel eyestrain or have a lot of trouble physically reading, you should go to an ophthalmologist or optometrist and have your eyes checked. It probably is the tension of studying, but if you do need glasses or some other treatment, get it at once.

7. Practice makes better, but only if it is practice of the right things. For everything that you read from now to the test, especially the practice tests in this book, analyze them carefully and check any errors you might make to see which clue(s) you missed—so you won't miss them next time.

ANALYTICAL REASONING INSTRUCTIONAL OVERVIEW

FUNDAMENTAL CONCEPTS OF ANALYTICAL REASONING PROBLEMS

Analytical Reasoning questions (hereafter AR questions) will be asked in a section which will present 24 or 25 questions to be answered in 35 minutes. These questions will be presented in four to six sets of questions per section.

AR questions are fundamentally matters of organizing a system of conditions, or being able to see and use the structure of some set of information. In other words, it is the linkages within the information that are the focus of the questions. The set of information will consist of a series of statements which may be a simple listing—numbered—accompanied by a further explanatory paragraph or presented in paragraph form, or a combination of these formats. The information set will be accompanied by from three to six, or even seven, problems—though four to six questions per set is the most likely situation.

We will now discuss the kinds of information which are included in an AR problem set and the kinds of questions that are asked about that information. Then we will discuss methods of attack which apply to all AR questions, preliminary to discussing the detailed approaches to the major kinds of AR questions. It is very important that you be familiar with the basic ideas which apply to all AR questions before you study the special techniques for specific kinds of AR problems.

Nature of the Information Set

In addition to the preceding remarks, it is useful to analyze a little more closely just what is occurring with AR information sets, so that you can more confidently, accurately, and quickly attack these problems. There are three kinds of information that can be given to you in an information set: outline, linkages, and specifics. ALL ARE IMPORTANT to answering the questions.

The **outline** is that portion of the information which tells you generally what sort of situation it is. For example:

> Three sailors are assigned to three different ships.
> The chief of a tribe is selecting hunters and trackers for a hunting expedition.
> Twelve people are seated in a restaurant at four tables.

This outline information is usually presented first, and it is the first step in understanding the problem. If three sailors are on three different ships, then each goes to one ship and our task is clearly to figure out who goes where, or some such. If people are seated in a restaurant, then only one person sits in a given seat and they would generally be expected to face the table so you can tell left from right by considering them all facing the table. The hunting expedition will require some hunters and some trackers, and they are probably going to be different people.

The point is that the situations will usually be everyday in their outlines and the common sense nature of the situation can give you useful—indeed necessary—information about the problems. Do not feel that the purpose of the problem is to trick you, for that is absolutely not true. Some outlines and situations have more realism than others, and a few may be totally abstract.

The **linkages,** conditions, or relationships are the connections between the various parts of the problem. These usually contain the bulk of the information given in the information set, and they will often be the major items with which you will work. You must, however, not divorce them from the outline. Sometimes, to be sure, the outline is not critical, but even when not necessary, most test-takers find it helpful in keeping track of things. Most of the substance of the diagrams that you will draw will be derived from the linkages given in the problem.

A linkage and the outline can sometimes overlap a bit. In the hunting party, the requirement that there be at least two hunters on the trip can be viewed as either a linkage or as part of the outline. It doesn't really matter, so long as you don't forget about it. THERE WILL BE VERY LITTLE INFORMATION GIVEN WHICH IS NOT USED FOR ANY OF THE PROBLEMS. *(Little,* but not necessarily *none.*)

A more typical linkage would be: If tracker X goes, hunter Y cannot go. Sometimes the reason for the linkage will be explained and sometimes it won't. If it is, then the same reasoning may be used implicitly in a problem or for setting up a further linkage.

> Tracker X can't go with Hunter Y, because two members of the same family may not be risked on a single trip.

If this linkage was followed with the detail that P and Q were in the same family, then you would know that P and Q couldn't both go on the trip either.

Linkages can be of different sorts and they can also be of different strengths. We are not referring here to the variations in the specific situations you will see on the exam, but rather LOGICAL variations, since this section does rely on basic logical relationships, usually not even as advanced as those found in the harder of the Logical Reasoning problems. The variations of linkages are of several types:

COMMON TYPES OF VARIATION IN LINKAGES
Exclusion/Inclusion
All the time/Part of the time
Can/Will
Some/All
Likes, prefers, desires/Must, cannot, etc.
Relative in position or reference/Absolute in position or reference

Naturally, these elements are usually combined in a given linkage.

> Mary must sit two seats to the left of George.

This is absolute in connecting George to Mary, but relative in the placement of Mary in that her position is stated as relative to George rather than at any particular seat—as George moves, so does Mary. The direction from George to Mary is definitely left (as opposed to simply two seats in either direction).

The key to linkages is that they are very precise as to what they say and what they do not say. More will be said of this later.

Specifics are NOT unimportant. They are items which are not connections between one item and another but absolute statements, such as: Jim is on the third boat; or M is a hunter. They are not dissimilar to an absolute linkage involving only one characteristic of one item.

Completeness of the Information

In most AR problem sets, the information given will not be totally complete, though this can vary from problem set to problem set. Sometimes the information will be virtually complete; once you have delved its final depths, only a few of the possible interrelationships are not specified in full. Often the information will not be very complete at all, with only a small number of possible relationships being specified and the left rest to the manipulation of the questions. All you have to do is be willing to cope with whatever level of completeness the particular problem happens to have.

What AR Questions Do

Having erected some sort of system of linkages in the information set, there are several different kinds of questions which the test can ask you. Each has its own charms. The major types of questions are: analysis, new specifics, new conditions, partial information, and changed or deleted conditions or linkages. Some questions combine these basic forms, and there are always a few seemingly oddball questions, which can be combinations of the major types, perhaps with information from the outline being required.

The most common AR questions are the analysis, new specifics, and new conditions questions—with the first two probably being the more numerous. (Remember that the distinction between a condition and a specific is somewhat arbitrary.)

Analysis questions are ones which explore the given information. The more complete the information that is given, the greater the number of analysis questions which are likely to be asked, which is only common sense. Why set up a whole structure if they are not going to ask you about it? Having figured out the seating arrangement mandated by a problem set, for example, an analysis problem will simply ask who sits next to Aunt Jane or who sits three chairs from Harry, etc. A variant of the analysis problem is one which either asks how many possibilities there are, or asks you to identify possible or impossible combinations, arrangements, orders, etc.

New specifics questions are usually the most common when the information set is not very complete. In these problems a new specific is given, such as "X will go on the hunting trip." You are then asked to analyze who else can or cannot go, or how many possibilities are left for tracker, etc.

New conditions questions introduce a new condition and then ask for an analysis of the situation. Usually the new condition is no more complex than the ones already present in the problem.

Each of the three question types just described absolutely require that, in principle, you consider all of the information given in the information set. The two to be described next use only part of the information given in the information set.

Partial information questions will usually occur when the information set has numbered statements that the question can clearly refer to. This type of question will ask what could be known from only some of the original information statements. For example, it might ask what would follow from statements I, III, and V. It is efficient to do this sort of question first since the final structure of linkages that you construct from all of the information may not be helpful. The final structure might, for instance, exclude a possibility which is still available when only part of the information is used.

Changed or deleted conditions or linkages questions do just what their names imply: They ask you to analyze the situation that would result if one of the conditions was changed or deleted. A deleted conditions or linkages question can be handled by putting together all of the other information first, answering this question, and then adding in the linkage in order to address the rest of the questions. Often the changed or deleted conditions question can just as easily be done in its listed order. When a linkage is modified, it is usually easiest to start with the completed structure and modify it as indicated by the question—though occasionally a fresh start is easier, time permitting.

GENERAL APPROACHES TO ANSWERING AR PROBLEMS

The overall approach is to separate the tasks of arranging the information and answering the questions. In cases where the information is complete, or nearly so, the arrangement of the information will naturally take much longer than when relatively little original information is given. We will first discuss overall timing for AR questions. Then we will discuss the fundamental rules of arranging information for AR questions. In the next section we will discuss the identification and treatment of specific types of information by creating diagrams suitable to that particular information.

Timing

Timing is an important issue on all sections of the test, but many students find that they need to watch their time most closely when doing AR questions. If there are 25 questions in 35 minutes, which is typical, you have 84 seconds per question. That is not too helpful a piece of information, however, without some interpretation. It does, however, give the measure of the time available for each problem set. This total time for each set needs to be further divided. You have two tasks to accomplish within the time allotted for each set of problems: arrangement of the information into usable form, and answering the questions. While no hard and fast rules can be laid down, since the problems vary in several ways, a general idea of how your time should be divided can be gleaned from a VERY brief preview of the question stems, that is to say, the part of the question which asks the question—not the answer choices, and not any roman numeral statements which may be running around in the question (technically they are part of the answer choices).

The purpose of the preview is very limited. Like the preview in Logical Reasoning and Reading Comprehension, the purpose is to get information to plan the assault on the problem. Unlike those sections, no specific information about the actual problem is sought. All that the preview can usefully give you is two things: (1) an idea about how to divide your time between arranging and answering, and (2) advanced knowledge of partial information, and deleted or changed conditions questions which may best be answered out of order as previously discussed. THAT IS IT! Don't try to memorize the questions. Anything like that is generally a waste of time.

THE PREVIEW SHOULD TAKE NO MORE THAN 5 SECONDS PER QUESTION! If you don't have the discipline to skim them that fast, only preview two of them in 10 seconds and if you don't have the discipline to do that, don't preview at all. You can't possibly do the problems until you have the information organized, so anything but a skim is a complete waste.

The findings of the preview can be evaluated as follows. If all of the questions, or all but one, are "if" questions, then it is likely that the information is not very complete and most of your time will be spent with the questions. If few or none of the questions are "if" questions, then probably most of your time should be spent on arranging the information. The main reason for even bothering to find out how your time should be spent is to avoid anxiety in complete information problems when ½ to ⅔ of your time might be spent on organizing the information.

If you find partial information, or deleted or changed conditions questions, then you may do those questions first, especially the partial information ones.

SHORT AND LONG TIME ALLOTMENTS FOR AR PROBLEM SETS*
(in minutes)

NUMBER OF	COMPLETE INFORMATION		PARTIAL INFORMATION		TOTAL
QUESTIONS	ARRANGING	ANSWERING	ARRANGING	ANSWERING	TIME
3	2½	1½	1	3	4
4**	3½	2	1½	4	5½
5**	4½	2½	2	5	7
6**	5	3½	2½	6	8½
7	5½	4½	3	7	10

*Based on 24 total questions, which is probable.
**These are the most probable lengths.

Lest this chart seem too overwhelming, remember that it is only a guide and its main purpose is to impress upon you that the division of time between arranging and answering information is very variable indeed. The only fairly ironclad timing is the total time for a problem set.

Fundamental Rules for Arranging AR Information

Arranging the information in the AR question set is at least as important as the answering of the questions, since the latter depends on the former. In addition, all of the rules and understandings which are necessary for proper arrangement of the information are equally necessary for manipulating the information for all of the questions, except perhaps the pure analysis question.

The instructions for this section indicate that "it may be helpful to draw a diagram." While it is true that some students do not need to draw diagrams for some of the AR problem sets, these are few and far between, and they usually will be mentally making some sort of diagram or organizing structure. That is fine if you are both very good at these sorts of problems and very experienced at them. But everyone, whether they make diagrams or not, should abide by the following fundamental rules for arranging the information. You probably already follow them instinctively, but a review will ensure that you do so consistently and completely.

There are five rules. Three of the rules are general, and apply in similar ways to some of the other sections of the test. Two of the rules primarily apply to AR. You can remember them as PLICC (pronounced "plick").

—Precise reading is always necessary, but there are no tricks.
—Logical rules should always be followed as shown in the Logical Reasoning Instructional Overview.
—Independence criterion applies totally. Carry nothing from one question to the next.
—Chain your information together, one item at a time.
—Cherish your ignorance. Knowing what you don't know is at least as important as knowing what you do know.

Let us examine each of these principles by itself.

PRECISE READING does not mean paranoia. As mentioned in the other instructional overviews, precise reading means paying attention to what each sentence actually says. The LSAT warns you to be particularly alert to words that describe or limit relationships or linkages. Words particularly important in AR information sets are: *only, exactly, never, always, must be/can be/cannot be, some, all, no, entire, each, every, except, but, unless, none, if, more/less, before/after, possible/impossible, different/same, taller/shorter, lighter/heavier, least/most,* any superlative (*-est*), *maximum* (*at most*), *minimum* (*at least*).

There are many others and you should be particularly alert for words which derive their meaning from the specific situation—the outline—because they are ones which you may easily miss because of their unique character.

The proper approach to all the reading on the AR section is one of bland but analytical acceptance. You are not disputing what is said at all, you are merely analyzing it for just precisely what it does say so that you can file it away properly and draw the proper conclusions from it.

The LOGIC on the AR section is all essentially deductive logic. There is virtually no inductive work to be done at all. Some of the questions might possibly seem to require some sort of generalization, but only do this if it is clearly required by the question. The only complication is that most of the time you will not have everything tied down completely, but will need to consider different contingencies or possibilities constantly.

The INDEPENDENCE CRITERION applies to this section as to all sections. It is absolutely critical that you never carry anything forward from one question to the next. To be sure, the test-makers usually try to avoid having questions which change the basic conditions in different ways right next to each other, but there are many ways that you might carry things forward. The most common is by making alterations to your basic diagram for a particular problem, and then forgetting that the alteration is based on information that applies only to one problem and using it in another problem. The solution to this is to either not make marks on your main diagram at all, or be prepared to redraw all or part of it for a couple of questions. This need not be as onerous as it sounds, since the redrawing is usually only required in situations where the original information was not too complete anyway.

Another facet of the independence criterion is that you only look for the items, people, and things which are actually stated in the problem. If they ask how many people could possibly be on the porch, you only consider the persons mentioned in the problem and not your cousin Sue and your Uncle Mike. Keep within the problem's parameters. Also be careful not to make any unnecessary, and thus unwarranted, assumptions about the connections being discussed in the passage: *Taller* does not necessarily mean *heavier;* a husband is not necessarily older than his wife; a woman is not necessarily smaller or lighter or weaker than a man; staying at a party longer does not necessarily mean that one drank more. In other words, be careful NOT to make ordinary inductions about the situation which are not required by the problem itself.

CHAIN your information together. This is *critical* in both the arrangement of the information into a diagram, and the interpretation of the diagram for the solution of problems. More mistakes are probably made on the AR section through improper chaining than any other single cause.

The process of chaining has three parts: breakdown, linking and review. The first step is **breaking down** the information to be arranged into individual items of information. Frequently, the original information set will contain sentences which have several items of information in them. You cannot enter all of these items at once, but must separate them and enter them one at a time into the diagram which you will be constructing. For example:

Mary will not sit at the same table as Bob or Jane.

This sentence contains two items of information: (1) Mary is not at the same table as Bob, and (2) Mary is not at the same table as Jane. These should be entered separately and these should be reviewed separately because each one may have separate implications that need to be followed through separately.

Linking means that you cannot enter an item into the diagram unless you have something to hook it on to. Here is a simple example:

I. A is larger than B.
II. C is larger than D.
III. B is larger than C.

If we make a diagram in which we say that left is smaller and right is bigger, then we can enter these items as follows:

	←SMALLER——LARGER→	
Enter I.	B	A

If you now try to enter II at once, there is no way to link it to the information you have about B and A, since II concerns neither, and there is no information in the diagram yet about either C or D. Try entering II yourself and see that wherever you enter it into the diagram it isn't very helpful. All you can do is to indicate that there is no real connection between I and II, and you have essentially two separate diagrams. While there are some problems which do end up with something of that sort, you do not want to do it unless you have to, because you might be missing some deductions you need in order to answer problems. For example, if we make two lines on our diagram:

```
         ←SMALLER——LARGER→
I.            B          A
II.              ←D——C→
```

Even this is open to misinterpretation since we might accidentally suppose that $B = D$ or $A = C$ or that $C > B$.

You should hold off entering II until you have some sort of linkage.

```
                           ←SMALLER——LARGER→
Enter III instead                C     B     A
Now II can be entered      D     C     B     A
```

Which gives the final relationship for these three items of information. Note that there are many deductions which can be made from the diagram listed: $D < B$, $D < A$, $C < A$. One of the virtues of a diagram of this sort is that when it can be made—and it is not always appropriate—it saves you having to write down all the deductions without running any risk of not seeing them if you need them for the solution of a problem.

There are some sorts of diagrams, as we shall see, where the outline of the problem can be used to set up a structure that immediately guarantees that all information can be usefully entered, or where there is so little information that all that can be diagrammed is a few linkages. In these cases you still have to be very careful to separate each item of information from others and to enter it only as it can be linked, but the linkage requirement is much less onerous and would not usually require holding off on entering any items.

Review is the process of evaluating the possible deductions that can be made between the item of information which is under review and every other single item of information already entered and every other possible combination of the items already entered. This doubtless sounds like a terrific amount of work and it sometimes is, but if you use a little common sense you will only be doing the work necessary for the problems. The key here, as in all test problems, is to look for connections. In this case it is connections between the item of information you are reviewing and the other items already entered into your diagram or structure. If your item says Bob is the son of Mary, you can look for the following connectors:

Mary, or other relatives of Mary, who will also be relatives of Bob.
Bob not being the husband or sibling of Mary, etc.
Anything to do with being male.
Anything to do with being younger than someone else since Bob must be younger than Mary.
Anything to do with being a son in general.

Examples of previously coded items that could relate to the preceding item using these ideas are:

Mary is married to Andy; thus, Andy is Bob's (step)father.
Mary is younger than Jim; thus, Jim is older than Bob.
The pilot is a female; thus, Bob is not the pilot.
John is an only child; thus, John is not Bob's brother, and not the son of Mary.

The point of all this is that it is the easiest thing in the world to overlook a deduction in the heat of the test. You can guard against making that serious error by developing the ironbound habit of always reviewing carefully each item as you use it. It will save you many errors and much wasted effort in the AR section.

CHERISHING YOUR IGNORANCE is primarily a matter of not tricking yourself into thinking you know more than you do. There is a natural pressure to get the last drop of deduction out of the information, but many questions turn as much on clearly knowing the limits of your knowledge in the situation as on having made all possible deductions. In fact, the two often work together, with some answer choices being wrong for one reason and some for the other.

The review of logic which is contained in the "Logical Reasoning Instructional Overview" has many valuable pointers on logic and you should be as careful to do good reasoning in the AR section as you are in the Logical Reasoning section. However, let us review some particularly pertinent points of logic here as well, to warn you of some of the errors that might make you accidentally fail to cherish your ignorance.

1. *SOME* only means "at least one," and there is no implication whatever that because "some elephants are gray" there are some (any) elephants which are not gray. All elephants might be gray. From "some X are Y" you cannot conclude that "some X are not Y." If you are told that "not all Q are S," then you can conclude that "some Q are not S."

2. ALL A ARE B does not tell you anything about the B which are not A. There may be B which are not A, or maybe not; it is just a possibility.

3. ONLY D ARE E equals ALL E ARE D and the same strictures apply.

4. MARY CANNOT WORK WITH GEORGE is the same as "if Mary, then not George," which is the same as "if George, then not Mary." Error can creep in when there are several statements of this sort:

Mary cannot work with George.
George cannot work with Tom.

You have to be a little careful with this situation. While it is true that if George is included, both Mary and Tom cannot be included, there is no other linkage between Mary and Tom. Mary CAN work with Tom, but is not required to be with him as far as these two statements alone are concerned.

5. TRANSFORMATIONS often occur in AR problems. When a couple marries, they may become the caste/tribe/etc. of the husband or the wife, or they may be arbitrarily assigned some designation. Thus, "a woman of caste M becomes caste P upon marriage" means that the woman may be referred to as either "a pre-marriage caste N woman" or "a married caste P woman." This kind of multiple referencing can also occur in any problem where more than one characteristic is assigned to an individual person or thing. If the biggest dog lives in the third house with Jim, then they might ask you about the location of Jim's dog or the size of Jim's dog or the location or owner of the biggest dog, etc.

6. NECESSARY VERSUS SUFFICIENT. Just because all elephants must be gray doesn't mean that everything that is gray is an elephant. Classifications

into groups are typically done on the basis of more than one characteristic. This is easy to spot in real life since we know perfectly well that there are other gray things, even other gray animals such as squirrels and donkeys. When the situation is abstract or unrealistic we don't have that reality check and have to ask logically and consciously if the condition of being a Z is sufficient to make something automatically a W or if it is an open question, or if it is even impossible.

7. COUNTING POSSIBILITIES. You will sometimes be asked to count the number of possible different arrangements of some situation. There are two thorns of which to beware. First, you must determine whether it is just bunches of things that are at issue or whether order matters in some way. For example, if you are making up the hunting party referred to earlier in the chapter, it does not seem to matter whether the trackers are Bob and Jane, or Jane and Bob, so that is just one possibility. On the other hand, if the question is discussing the slate of officers for an election, it is quite different if Jane is president and Bob vice-president, or the other way around. That would be two possibilities. There can also be an issue of physical rotation, as discussed later when seating-type diagrams are discussed.

DRAWING THE RIGHT DIAGRAM FOR EACH AR PROBLEM

Almost every problem will require a diagram (for most students) as previously discussed. We strongly recommend that you practice drawing diagrams of all sorts so that you will always be prepared for any problem you might see on the test. If you get to the actual test and you can easily keep it all in your head, fine! Do it! But most people need to keep at least a few notes, and a diagram is usually the most efficient way to keep the notes.

We will now be discussing several different types of diagrams and ways of deciding which one is best for a particular problem. Although it is helpful to start with the best diagram, the choice of diagramming method is not something that you should spend a very long time over. If you are paying the proper attention to the information in the problem set, you will generally find yourself being guided to the right diagramming technique because it will be the one that fits. Thus, it is important to have some familiarity with several different techniques. In addition to the material presented in the Instructional Overview, you should definitely review the explanations for all of the AR sections in the practice tests and closely follow the construction of the diagrams there.

Using the Outline

The outline of the problem is the statement of the general situation as discussed in the early part of this Instructional Overview. The outline is the first piece of evidence to be used in deciding which type of diagram will be most efficient for a particular set of AR problems. The second piece of evidence is the nature of the linkages which are given in the problem. A third important piece of evidence is sometimes provided by the form of the questions in the AR problem set. First, we shall discuss these three types of evidence and explain how to interpret them; then we will detail the different types of diagrams.

The outline is usually the most important piece of evidence leading you to the correct form of diagram. In every case, the purpose of the diagram is to arrange the information in the AR problem set in the most natural and useful way. It is only common sense that the proper arrangement depends on the nature of the information being arranged.

If the situation is a seating arrangement, then a diagram of the table is indicated, though other things may also be needed. If the situation is colors and sizes and fuels of six trucks, then you know that you will need to make a table or two to correlate all the information. If the situation is one in which a process is described whereby persons change status or location according to given rules, then you need to make a chart which will allow you to make the required transformations quickly and accurately, forwards and backwards. The outline is also usually the key to identifying the special types of diagram situations described below.

The linkages are helpful in diagnosing the problem because they may be the point in the presentation at which the various possibilities are raised. You know there are six trucks, but you don't know that their fuel is an issue until a linkage raises it. There are sometimes problem sets where the major issues are limited, but the linkages deal with additional issues. For example, if the issue is which sailor goes with which boat, there might be a linkage telling you that one of the boats is bigger than another, or one of the sailors is blond. As such, these are not major arranging issues, but subsidiary ones that help to limit possibilities.

The questions are often helpful in deciding about the arrangement of the information. As previously noted, if there are many "if" questions, it is likely that there is not too much information being given, and that it will not completely describe the situation. This means that most of the information will be linkages, and a few parameters such as in the hunting party situation described briefly at the beginning of this Instructional Overview. In such cases the diagram is usually limited to a pure linkage format as described in the following paragraphs. If the questions ask about an issue—Which sailor had the red hair?—then you know that you are going to have to know something about red hair, or at least hair color in general. A large number of analysis questions usually indicates that a table or physical analog diagram is likely to be helpful, though this is not always the case.

Specific Diagramming Techniques

We shall discuss three major categories—Physical Analog, Pure Linkage, Tables—and the combination of the last two types. Pure linkage and table diagrams apply, in principle, to virtually all problems. The physical analog diagrams apply to some special cases that may appear and which are most efficiently handled with these special techniques. Let us deal with the special situations first.

Physical analog. All this means is that the diagram you will make is a picture of the situation in some direct way. One simple example would be a problem set where the issue (or one of the issues) was the relative weight of a group of individuals. What you do is establish some direction as representing heavier and the opposite direction as representing lighter. This could be up and down or left and right or even diagonally if that seems good at the time (though we don't recommend that). For example:

←LIGHTER———HEAVIER→.

Sometimes there may be more than one such parameter in a problem, such as louder/quieter and faster/slower, or whatever it may be. These are simple problems provided that you remember the fundamental rules for diagramming (PLICC).

Sometimes there is a residuum of uncertainty in the problem. This can occur in two ways. First consider the propositions:

←LIGHTER——HEAVIER→.

I. A is heavier than B. B A

II. A is heavier than C. C A

The problem is how to indicate that you do NOT know the relationship between B and C, though A is the heaviest. Use arrows to indicate ranges of possibilities:

←LIGHTER——HEAVIER→.
B A
←C→

This accurately notes that B might be greater than, less than, or equal to C. If we add to this another proposition, that "C is heavier than D," we end up with two somewhat separate lines, which still can be used to answer questions.

←LIGHTER——HEAVIER→.

III. C is heavier than D. B A
←D——C→

Another example of a physical analog diagram is when there is a situation that is a map; that is, there are directions north, east, west, and south just like a map, and the issue is to draw the map so that questions can be answered. Again, close adherence to the fundamental rules of diagramming is essential—indeed it is always essential, and the failure to repeat this warning for every problem type is simply to save you reading the same thing ten times, but do remember it.

With a map situation, you will either be making a map of streets, avenues, lanes, etc., or ones of towns, blocks, areas, etc. In either case, you should always assume that the map is a rectilinear grid or checkerboard unless something in the problem says otherwise. Always interpret any direction given as precisely that direction. North means "directly north." Precise directions should always be used in making the diagram. In answering the questions always use precise directions, unless there is no possible answer that way—in which case you can use "northwards" instead of "north." This is very rare. Do not assume that you know how long any streets are unless you are told. Also, be careful to observe the same sort of care with double references that you have to do with heavier/lighter diagrams as was discussed in the preceding paragraphs.

A third kind of physical analog is the Venn diagram (circles to represent categories or groups), which is explained in detail in the "Logical Reasoning Instructional Overview." The Venn should be used when the situation is primarily one of interacting or overlapping groups with only some individuals in the problem. Typical propositions for such questions are "no X are Y," "only M can be Y," etc. Remember that Venns cannot be used with more than three groups at once. The relationships among four groups cannot be adequately represented by four circles on a flat piece of paper. If there is this sort of question on your test and it seems to have four groups, just make the Venn for the three most discussed groups and then fit in the fourth one verbally as you need it.

A fourth common type of physical analog diagram is the seating diagram. This actually applies to any situation where a physical arrangement is at issue: beds, lines, shelves, seats, cars, garages, etc. Typically, a seating problem will have a combined diagram with several linkages being used as well as the seating diagram. In fact, it is common for you to have to construct a different seating chart for each question based on the requirements of the linkages and the question.

A problem often encountered with seating diagrams is when more than one arrangement is possible. For example:

I. F, G, H, and J are sitting at a four-sided table, one on each side.
II. F is opposite G and H is opposite J.

There are two basic arrangements:

	F			F	
H		J	J		H
	G			G	

Also, F could be sitting in any one of the four seats, as far as we know at this time, so there could be $2 \times 4 = 8$ arrangements. Thus, it matters whether you are simply asked who is opposite/next to whom, or who is in the seat closest to the window, etc.

Pure linkage. These diagrams are used when all, or virtually all, of the information is in the form of linkages. This situation is usually accompanied by questions primarily of the added detail or condition type. Therefore, what you need is a diagram that will quickly and accurately let you travel through the linkages, both forwards and backwards, in order to ascertain the results of the added details or conditions.

The "classic" pure linkage problem would be one such as the hunting party situation we have mentioned at several points in this overview. Let us lay this out as if it were a full problem.

The chief of the Inagway tribe is selecting a hunting party, which will consist of two hunters and two trackers.

G, H, J, and K are hunters and M, N, and P are trackers.

G and P cannot go on the trip together because they are from the same family, and P does not get along with M so the chief cannot send both P and M together.

1. If P goes on the trip, who else must go?

2. If G goes on the trip, who else cannot go?

We see that we have to be concerned in this instance with the linkages among a group of seven individuals who are subdivided into two groups—hunters and trackers. While it would be all right to just have the seven listed as a single group, it makes sense to have them sorted out as much as possible. We know that the hunter/tracker designation will matter since there are limits placed on the situation based on that division—two of each. (Of course, if there were no sub-groups, then you would treat the whole group together.)

As we analyze the outline we see that we should have the two groups just mentioned—hunter and trackers. We also see that the only other information is in the form of linkages—who cannot go with whom—and a condition that there must be two of each in the party. The "if" questions—added details or conditions—confirm that linkage is the major issue.

There are several methods that can be used to chart the linkages we have been given. The two simplest are *labelled arrows* and *pseudo-algebra.* Don't let the names put you off—we had to call them something—and it doesn't matter what you call the diagram so long as you get the questions right.

Most people prefer the labelled arrows method, so let us describe that first. After you have the outline in mind—here the idea that there are two groups to interrelate—you just draw arrows from individual to individual to indicate their linkages. Here are several sample arrows with labels:

X←NEVER WITH→Y X←ALWAYS WITH→Y

X←ONLY WITH→Y X←BEFORE/TWO DAYS/AFTER→Y

X←WITH ONLY ONE OF { →Y OR →Z }

Note that while most arrows will point both ways, it is possible for a condition or linkage to be stated so that the arrow only works one way. If a condition states that X could only go if Y could go too, that is only one way. Y might go even if X did not. In the hunting party case we would draw the following diagram:

HUNTERS	TRACKERS
Choose two	Choose two
G←NOT WITH ———→	P←NOT WITH→M
H	N
J	
K	

This diagram makes it easy to answer the questions.

1. If P goes, then neither M nor G can go. This means that since two trackers are required, N must go. However, on the hunter side, we have three candidates for two seats, and cannot say who MUST go.
2. If G goes, then only P is excluded; M and N must go, but that isn't what the question asked.

Two additional points about labelled arrows. You may easily find that the arrows are not straight as an arrow. That is just fine. All you are interested in is what the linkage is as shown by the arrow. The direction means nothing here since you have not assigned it any meaning (unlike some of the physical analog diagrams). As a corollary of that point you may find that your arrows sometimes cross. That is OK, too. If direction means nothing, then the fact that the arrows cross means nothing, since crossing is a function of direction.

Pseudo-algebra is just a fancy way of saying that you can borrow some algebraic notation, such as "=," "not=," etc., and use it for your own purposes and with your own meanings. If you are not comfortable with math, you should definitely use the labelled arrow method. Pseudo-algebra is not really quite as good since we are using signs which have other meanings, and that multiplicity of meaning can sometimes confuse us.

In the hunting party example, we would do the following:

HUNTERS	TRACKERS
G NOT=	P NOT= M
H	N
J	
K	

You can see the similarities between this method and the other. The question answering is the same.

One difficulty with the pseudo-algebra is when two items must go together (in whatever way things go together in that problem set). You indicate this by "X=Y" and you have to be careful to remember that that symbolism does NOT mean that X and Y are the same thing.

If you have your own methods and they work, fine. They are probably essentially the same idea as these, but just using your own symbols.

Tables. Tables (and scorecards) are particularly helpful when your task is to sort out some situation where, in principle, there is only one actual arrangement but you may not have been given enough information to complete the sorting out. For example:

I. There are three sailors, F, G, and H, who are a bosun, gunner, and cook on ships 101, 201, and 301, not necessarily in that order.

II. G and H are in a different navy than F, but in the same navy as each other.

III. Yesterday the bosun was transferred from ship 101, where he was serving with the gunner, to ship 201.

1. Who serves on ship 301?
2. The rank of which sailor(s) is (are) not definitely known?

The information seems fairly complete and the two questions are both analysis questions. Thus, we expect to be able to develop a fairly complete picture of the situation, though question 2 indicates that there might still be uncertainties—even when all the available information is arranged. Since it is a "sorting out" type of situation, a table or scorecard is likely to be helpful. We will have a table that will have three columns and four rows for the three locations or individuals, and the four types of information we know about each individual—name, rank, boat, and navy.

The reason that we have referred to a scorecard will become clear as we use the table. The purpose of a scorecard is to enable you to figure out who the players are. Similarly, the purpose of the table or scorecard here is to enable you to figure out who the "players" are.

NAME			
RANK			
BOAT			
NAVY			

You can also just draw a table with vertical and horizontal boxes, or even just keep the columns separate. If you are not very neat, it is probably best to draw lines in both directions.

Two key ideas from the outline of the situation are that each of the sailors is different in every way (except two in the same navy) and that the possibilities listed are the only ones with which you need to be concerned. It is this very restricted view that makes these problems possible and reasonable, so keep it in mind. One sailor is on each boat and if you know where two of them are, you also know where the third one is.

Let us enter item II first. Even though you might think that it would be a little easier to enter III first, it is never so much easier that you should spend any time trying to figure out the order to enter items of information. Get right to work. Enter them in the order given. As previously discussed, the existence of partial information problems, or changed or deleted conditions problems, or inability to enter the item, are the only exception to the rule of entering the information in the order presented.

There are actually two items of information in proposition II separated by *but,* but they are so straightforward that we can safely enter them simultaneously—after considering them separately.

NAME	F	G	H
RANK			
BOAT			
NAVY	different	same as H	same as G

There are no further implications to be drawn at this point.

Now let us enter the next statement, which also has several items of information in it. The sentence's main clause states the bosun was transferred from 101 to 201. This tells us the following: (1) the bosun is now on 201, and (2) ships 101 and 201 are in the same navy.

Deduction 2 deserves some study since it is a good example of the interactions that can occur between the outline or general situation and further items. In statement II we learned that two of the sailors were in the same navy, and the third was in a different navy. Now while it is perfectly true that servicemen from different nations do serve on each other's ships and boats for various reasons, the usual situation is that the crew of a naval vessel are all members of the naval service of that country, as opposed to that of another country. This justifies deduction 2.

There is another deduction to be made from this part of the statement: (3) G and H are on 101 and 201, though we don't know which sailor is on which ship. This is inferable from the connecting link of navy membership: G and H, like 101 and 201, are in the same navy, while the third boat and sailor are in another navy. We can also deduce: (4) the bosun is either G or H, since he is on ship 201. While (1) would almost inevitably be the first deduction to come to mind, (2), (3), and (4) could be reached in various orders and expressed with various wordings.

The second part of proposition III tells us that the gunner is on 101. While it is "true" in the real world that he might have been transferred since yesterday, the real world is not the only (or even the main) guide. The problem says nothing of the gunner's being transferred; therefore, he was not transferred. Let us enter what we know so far into the diagram:

NAME	F	G		H
RANK		gunner	or	bosun
BOAT		101	or	201
NAVY	different	same as H		same as G

There is still much to be deduced from this situation by the review of the interactions of all of the now-known items. Since we know that the three different sailors all had different boats and different ranks, the process of elimination lets us reach two more deductions: (5) F is the cook, and (6) F is on 301. Entering this we get the final diagram:

NAME	F	G		H
RANK	cook	gunner	or	bosun
BOAT	301	101	or	201
NAVY	different	same as H		same as G

We are now in a position to answer any questions that might be asked about this situation. To answer the particular questions previously raised:

1. F serves on ship 301.
2. The ranks of G and H are not definitely known.

If you have a problem set which does not concern the piecing together of the real identity and characteristics of some set of individual persons or things, then you might find yourself using a straight table method in which you would list all of the different kinds of information which you expect to have to arrange (and add to this table as you need to), and then carefully enter each item and check it against every other entry that you have made. The straight table method is the most generally applicable method, and can in principle be used for every kind of problem, but it is not nearly as efficient as the other methods—for the problems to which the other methods apply.

In the case of the sailors, for example, you would have made the following headings for your set of tables:

RANK (1 EACH TYPE)			NAME (INDIVIDUALS)			BOAT (1 EACH TYPE)		
BOSUN	COOK	GUNNER	F	G	H	101	201	301

You would probably not make a separate table for navy, though you could. The method of execution is simply to enter each and every item and deduction in the tables. The tedious BUT ABSOLUTELY NECESSARY part is that you have to enter many connections in two places. When you find out that F is on boat 301, you have to enter "on 301" under F and "F" under 301. This double connection is noted in the scorecard form of table by the fact that F and 301 are in the same column. If you don't put everything in, you almost might as well not bother. You also have to be very disciplined in making sure that you follow these rules of entry, derived from the fundamental rules of diagramming:

1. Consider only one piece of information at a time.
2. Cross-check that piece with every other entry already in the table, looking for deductions or for connections to yet other entries.
3. Whenever a deduction is found, it must be entered at once, and then BOTH the deduction and the original piece of information must be checked against every piece of information starting from the beginning again. It is tedious but it works. Do it!

Combinations. Combining the table or scorecard method with the linkage method is common. Sometimes it is merely a matter of it being more convenient to record as a linkage some slightly out-of-the-way piece of information, such as navy status in the preceding example. Other times there is fairly complete information about one aspect of the situation and only linkage information about another. Do not hesitate to record something as a linkage, even if you end up putting it into a table later when there is some further deduction or other information on the same point.

SUMMARY REVIEW OF ATTACK STRATEGY FOR AR PROBLEM SETS

For the entire AR section, you should preview the number of questions and total time printed at the top of the first page of the section. You should also spend five or ten seconds seeing how many problem sets there are, and approximately how many questions there are for each.

FOR EACH PROBLEM SET you should follow this attack strategy. Remember, however, that this one listing is only a summary of the ideas of the previous pages, and you cannot substitute reading this outline for reading the entire overview.

1. Quickly preview the question stems only. (Five seconds each.) Note the partial information questions.
2. Skim the information set quickly to get an idea of the outline of the situation. (Fifteen seconds.)
3. Evaluate the outline of the situation. (Ten seconds.)
4. Quickly decide on the basic diagram method you will use. Note, for your peace of mind, the completeness of the information and the likely proportions of arranging and answering times.

   Physical analog—greater/lesser
   —mapping
   —Venn diagrams (circles)
   —seating

   Linkages—few analysis questions, incomplete information
   Scorecard—tables with definite outcome
   Tables—most general method

5. Enter the information using PLICC. Enter in order given except—enter first the propositions used for partial information questions.
   Precise reading
   Logical rules
   Independence criterion
   Chain information
   Cherish ignorance
6. Answer the questions, remembering the different types.
   —Analysis
   —Partial information
   —Deleted or changed conditions or linkages
   —New conditions
   —New specifics
7. Watch time closely. Don't spend too much on one problem and don't run overtime for the problem set.

FINAL NOTE

You are most likely to see questions on the LSAT AR sections which describe an incomplete situation in which in the conditions are mainly for the questions beginning with the word "if." With these sets, most of the work is in the answering of the question. Occasionally, the conditions are such that an original diagram is unfruitful. This happens when there is a physical situation, such as seven offices next to each other in one corridor, and seven workers, placed one to an office, but the given conditions only regard relationships among the workers, with no information on how any worker fits into any particular office. If they tell you that G is to the right of H, you can put down a diagram stating that G is not in the left-most office, but if they tell you that G is two offices away from H and J two away from K, you cannot fill in the diagram until you get to the questions which will give you further information. Such problems are equally difficult compared to other problems as long as you do not worry that a beginning diagram is not feasible. In general, when you have gone as far as you can with a piece of information, try to answer the question or, failing that, specify the area that is preventing an answer.

Note that the major difference between complete and incomplete situations lies in whether the information is contained in the question stems (incomplete) or in the original conditions (complete). The moves in complete and incomplete questions sets are the same. Your work on the practice tests will be most valuable to you if, when given a particular situation, you try to master the logical moves being made and understand the reasons for these moves.

ISSUES AND FACTS INSTRUCTIONAL OVERVIEW

INTRODUCTION

Many students believe that the Issues and Facts section is the one section of the LSAT which is a real test of aptitude for legal studies, while the other sections are just filler. This is a SERIOUS ERROR! Every section on the the exam is designed to test two skills—reasoning and reading—and the Issues and Facts section is no exception to this rule. It is no more, but no less, a test of those skills than the other three sections (Logical Reasoning, Reading Comprehension, and Analytical Reasoning). Although the section uses rules couched in legal-sounding language, these principles are only hypothetical. And even if it should turn out that the rules used on the Issues and Facts section are accurate restatements of some law, this coincidence between the LSAT and the real world will be purely fortuitous. So students who have had no prior legal training need not worry that they will be at any disadvantage; in fact, our experience is that students who have some knowledge of the law often create for themselves needless difficulties which the student who has no such knowledge never has to face. The Instructional Overview of this section, therefore, will emphasize reading and reasoning. After previewing the section's structure, it will issue three warning notes, then look at the structure of legal decision making, analyze the instructions, and finally provide an attack strategy.

SECTION STRUCTURE

Keeping in mind, as always, the possibility of some minor variations in test format, you should expect to find an Issues and Facts section on your LSAT containing 35–38 questions to be answered in 35 minutes. If there is more than one such section on a given test, the likelihood is that only one will actually be a "live" section, while any others are just "experimental." We repeat, however, that since you cannot know which is the "live" section, you must treat all questions as though they were going to be scored.

The Issues and Facts section consists of six or seven problem sets, each problem set containing four to seven questions. A problem set consists of three elements: the facts, the rules, the dispute and the questions. The facts will present a case history, that is, a series of events which led to a legal case or dispute. The description of the facts will be 100 to 200 words long. Following the facts and the dispute, there will be two rules, each rule some 20 to 50 words in length. Following the rules and facts, there will be four, five, or six questions which raise different aspects of the case. After reading the questions, you are supposed to classify the aspect of the case raised by the question according to the following scheme:

(A) a relevant question the answer to which requires a choice between two rules

(B) a relevant question the answer to which does not require a choice between the two rules, but does require further facts or rules
(C) a relevant question that can be readily answered from the facts or rules or both
(D) an irrelevant question the answer to which does not affect, or only tangentially affects, the outcome of the dispute

THREE WARNING NOTES

This section is deceptively easy for two reasons. First, for those who have some familiarity with legal principles, it is all too easy to imagine that one has already mastered the knowledge required for the section—but as we have already noted, this section is not a test of previously acquired knowledge. Second, for people who do not appreciate the precision with which lawyers must work, this section contains other pitfalls. Therefore, before we get to a discussion of the specifics of this section, we issue the following warnings.

Warning note 1. Do not use any previous knowledge of the law. Again we emphasize that the laws used on the LSAT are hypothetical only. Most people who have learned something about the law of the jurisdiction in which they reside *incorrectly* imagine that this is *the* law. In fact, no jurisdiction has all of the same laws as any other jurisdiction. The laws of Alaska will differ in many ways from those of Texas. The important point to be learned here is that there is no "the" law, so the test-writers could use a principle which is actually a law somewhere, though not in the particular jurisdiction you know. Now, if this advice is sound (as it is) for people who have worked with the law (as police officers or secretaries), then it applies with even greater force for people who have only read about the law in books. So, forget anything you may have learned about the law—answer the questions only on the basis of the rules you are given. This applies also to procedural questions: DO NOT WORRY ABOUT HOW TO PROVE IT! While it is true that in the real world lawyers sometimes have difficulty with witnesses and evidence, on the LSAT, if it is mentioned in the facts, take it as proven. The only time you would worry about a question of evidence is when a rule specifically makes it an issue. In short, don't try to be Perry Mason on the LSAT.

Warning note 2. Read carefully. Although the rules which are used on the LSAT are only imaginary, you will nonetheless have to treat them as though they were actual rules of law. It cannot be overemphasized that each and every word in a rule of law is important. Take the following example:

> A party to a contract who breaches his contract is liable for only those damages he could have foreseen would result from a breach at the time he entered into the contract.

There are several important phrases in this rule. First, the party is liable only "for those damages he could have foreseen." In other words, if you promise to deliver a package for a fee, and you forget to do it, you will be liable for reasonable damages, but you will not be liable for something you could not have foreseen would happen. To take an example, if someone offered you five dollars to deliver a package, and they said, "this is important," you would not be liable for one million dollars if it turned out the package contained a critical document for a million-dollar deal. On the other hand, suppose someone gave you a library book and said, "I will give you five dollars to deliver this book, and if you fail I will owe the library twenty dollars." If you lose the book, then you are liable, because you knew the amount of the possible loss when you took on the job. There is a second critical phrase in the rule: "at the time he entered into the contract." In other words, you might know at the time you decide not to complete a bargain that some dire result will occur, yet you might still not be liable for it—if you were not aware of the dire result at the time you entered the contract. For example, suppose you were asked to deliver a library book, and you are aware that your failure to do so might result in a loss of twenty dollars, so you agree. Later, you learn that a million-dollar deal depends upon your prompt delivery of that book. What if you then fail to deliver—even though you knew a lot of money was riding on you? Well, according to the rule, you would not be liable for the million dollars. The rule states that you must be aware, *at the time you entered into the contract,* of the extent of the harm which might result if you failed to complete the bargain. Now, this may surprise some people—cut against the grain, as it were—and if so, this serves also to reinforce our first warning about holding opinions concerning the law. In any event, the point here is that you must carefully read each rule you encounter.

Warning note 3. Do not strain at gnats. Many people imagine that lawyers are trained to distort words, but this is simply not so. But someone who holds this opinion will misread a rule such as "If a person injures another person by his carelessness, he must compensate the injured person." Now it must be allowed that the "he" in this sentence is not without ambiguity. It might be insisted that the "he" refers to the injured person. On that reading, the injured person is supposed to compensate himself for another's carelessness. Need we say, however, that such a reading is just plain silly? Nevetheless, some students will try to be clever in just this way—to say, "Yes, but there is another possible reading." Now there is nothing wrong with this in principle—it is just that it will not get you a good score on the LSAT. So the rule is, think carefully, but if you find yourself coming up with absurd interpretations, forget them.

THE STRUCTURE OF LEGAL DECISIONS

Legal decisions are extraordinarily intricate matters. Generally speaking, a judge must decide a number of preliminary issues or questions—some of them quite complicated—before he is in a position to give a final decision in the case. Since this section is supposed to be a test of your ability to think in this way, it would be well if we explained a bit about the difference between *ultimate* and *penultimate* issues or questions. By the ultimate issue, we mean the final outcome of the case; by the penultimate issue, we mean any question which the judge might have to settle as a way of reaching the ultimate outcome of the case. Let us take a contract dispute as an example.

> Suppose that Jones is suing Smith for damages for Smith's failure to finish a contract with Jones. Jones asserts that Smith promised to repair Jones's shoes by Wednesday. Jones asserts also that Smith did not do the work by Wednesday, and as a result Jones could not go to the ball and marry the princess. So Jones did not live happily ever after.

Let us first take a simple rule of law which states, "A party who breaches his contract is liable for the damages which the non-breaching party to the contract suffers as a result of the breach." Now, what must be shown if Jones is going to win?

One thing which comes immediately to mind is that Jones must show that there was a contract in the first place. Obviously, if there was no contract, Jones has no case (at least not on the grounds of contract). Secondly, Jones must show that there has been a *breach* of the contract, and that, too, is obvious. Surely, Smith does not have to pay if he actually did the work he promised. Finally, it must be shown that Jones suffered some injury as a result of the breach of contract. After all, the rule says the injured party is to be compensated for the *loss* he suffers, but if he suffers no loss, then no compensation is due. Notice that each of these three elements is essential to the final outcome of the case, but that each element is also, in a manner of speaking, only a part of that decision. Perhaps a second example will reinforce the point. Let us take the rule, "A person who intentionally attacks and kills another person is guilty of murder, unless the killing was justified as a matter of self-defense." Now, here, to prove that murder has occurred, there are also several elements. Was there a killing? Was the killing intentional? Was it a matter of self-defense?

All of this is fairly obvious. The ultimate decision is based upon penultimate considerations; that is, there are some preliminary questions to answer before the final decision can be made. At this point, let us introduce another consideration. A rule may not be self-contained. For example, what is self-defense? Well, some cases are clear-cut. A person who without warning attacks another person for his money is not acting in self-defense. A person who is fighting for his life against an assailant or who has been attacked without provocation is clearly acting in self-defense. In the middle, however, are many possible cases which are not easily resolved. Suppose that Smith heard that Jones intended to kill him. Smith is in no immediate danger, and Smith could even have Jones arrested and put in jail. Yet, Smith decides to confront Jones, knowing that Jones will attack him. Smith arms himself with a pistol. He confronts Jones, and when Jones, as Smith expected, attacks him, Smith shoots Jones to death. Is *that* self-defense?

The case suggests difficulties. It is an open question whether Smith can justify his actions by self-defense. On the one hand, Jones had threatened to kill Smith. But on the other hand, Smith went out of his way to find an opportunity to have to defend himself. This suggests that we need some further guidance before we make our decision. That is, we just do not have enough information yet about what is or what is not self-defense to determine whether Smith's actions were self-defense.

Finally, let us consider what happens when two rules of law conflict with one another. In the real world, conflicts in the law result from the development or evolution of legal doctrines. A hundred years ago, judges might have used the rule, "A property owner owns unlimited airspace above his land, and anyone who crosses that airspace without permission is trespassing." The invention of the airplane and the subsequent growth in air travel made this rule obsolete. It has been replaced with rules more favorable to the commercial use of airways, such as, "A property owner owns the airspace above his land only to a height of 300 feet." So in the real world of law, at some point a court had to *make a choice* between these two rules. The court could not have applied both of them because that would have lead to contradictory results. The case was one involving a choice between conflicting rules.

It is also possible, however, that a rule will contain a number of exceptions or qualifications, and these exceptions are like separate rules in themselves which contradict (they are *exceptions*) the general rule. The rule we analyzed earlier regarding murder and self-defense can be rendered as two rules:

1. A person who intentionally kills another person is guilty of murder.
2. A person who intentionally kills another person as a matter of self-defense is not guilty of a crime.

Both rules may fit the facts of the same situation; but only one of them can be chosen to govern any given case, because they give different results. In other words, a court must make a choice between the two rules. Fortunately, the LSAT does not require you to actually make the choice. As we will see shortly, all you have to do is recognize that *a choice* is required. You do not have to worry about how the conflict between the rules came to be, nor figure out how the conflict should be resolved.

In conclusion, the way legal decisions are structured is such that there are preliminary issues and final outcomes. The preliminary issues (was it self-defense, was there a contract, was it careless conduct) may or may not be decidable on the basis of what is already known. Sometimes such issues require additional rules (a more precise definition of self-defense, what is required to make a contract), and occasionally they even require that a court get more facts (how fast over the speed limit was he driving, how close to the house was he standing when he started to burn the leaves). Further, even when all the rules and facts are available, it may be that a choice has to be made as to which rule governs the situation at hand.

THE INSTRUCTIONS

The information from the last section will guide us in trying to figure out what it is that the LSAT has in mind with their instructions for Issues and Facts. Let us keep in mind that the LSAT will present two rules. Oftentimes, though not necessarily always, these will conflict. Further, these rules should contain some concepts such as "self-defense" and "intentional" which it will be necessary to apply to the facts. These observations already suggest what the four answer choices are driving at.

ISSUES AND FACTS DIRECTIONS

Directions: Each of the following sets consists of a fact situation, a dispute and two rules. The rules may conflict, but you are to apply each rule independently. Do not treat a rule as subsidiary or as an exception to the other rule. The rules are followed by questions. You are to select from the following lettered choices (A) through (D) the one that best describes each question in the way it relates to the application of one or both of the rules to the dispute. Blacken the corresponding space on the answer sheet.

(A) a relevant question the answer to which requires a choice between the two rules
(B) a relevant question the answer to which does not require a choice between the two rules, but does require further facts or rules
(C) a relevant question that can be readily answered from the facts or rules or both
(D) an irrelevant question, the answer to which does not affect, or only tangentially affects, the outcome of the dispute

Answer choice (D) is anything which is irrelevant. Every lawsuit involves a lot of information which is just not relevant to the issues to be decided. In a way, for example, the names of the parties are usually not relevant (though they may be). The ages of the parties are not usually relevant (though at other times they are). The sex of the parties is sometimes relevant (and at other times not). Deciding a legal case means separating the essential points from the inessential points for that particular case, and that is what category (D) is for: Identify all of those points which are *not* immediately relevant to the dispute at hand.

Now, we should observe that the remaining three answer choices are all called "relevant" issues of some sort. This indicates that an issue is either totally irrelevant or nearly so, Answer Choice (D), or it bears on the dispute somehow. There will be few, if any, close calls as to whether something is relevant to the resolution of the dispute or not. Most of the difficulty with (D) answer choices will be questions that are clearly something that is involved in the fact situation, or is of concern to the parties on general principles, but is NOT relevant to the resolution of the dispute. For example, the severity of injuries in an automobile accident is obviously very important to the injured parties, but may be of no consequence in assigning blame for the accident since the fact that one driver ran a stop light makes him at fault whether there are great or small injuries, or indeed no injuries at all.

The penultimate questions are the (B)s and the (C)s. These are concepts which "trigger" the application of a rule, that is, determine whether the rule is applicable or not. If there is sufficient guidance in the problem and rules to make a determination one way or the other about such a concept, then a question asking about it must be answered as (C). If, however, there is not enough information, because not enough facts are provided or because some key term is not precisely defined, then the correct answer must be (B). Some examples will help clarify the meaning of these two categories:

Let us take as a rule:

> A person who reasonably believes that he is about to be the victim of a violent crime may defend himself by whatever means he thinks necessary.

And let us take two different fact situations. In the first,

> Jones is walking down a dark street. Smith approaches him, pulls out a knife and says, "I'm going to kill you." Jones, who is a karate expert, kicks Smith in the kneecap, breaking Smith's leg.

Setting aside for a moment with what crime either might be charged, we can ask, "Did Jones reasonably believe himself about to be the victim of a violent crime?" There can be no doubt that the answer to this question is "yes." Since the answer to our question is that we know Jones was reasonable in his belief, the correct LSAT answer is (C). That is, we know definitely that Jones was reasonable in his belief that he was about to be the victim of a violent crime.

Let us take another example using the same rule:

> Smith, a professional athlete, is walking down the street when Johnny, a five-year-old boy, says to Smith, "I am going to beat you up." Smith pushes the child to the ground, breaking the child's arm.

In this case, did Smith *reasonably* believe that the child was about to inflict violence on him? The answer is an obvious "no." But again, since we have sufficient information to resolve the issue, our answer choice on the LSAT must be a (C). We do have sufficient information to resolve the issue. Nothing else is required. Note, then, the following important point:

> A (C) answer may be entered when there is sufficient information to determine that a concept does *not* apply as well as when there is sufficient information to determine that it does apply.

The (B) answer has a slightly different complexion. An aspect of a case may be a (B) because it requires either additional facts or additional rules. Let us take the problem with additional facts first.

Suppose we had a rule which stated:

> A person who attacks another person with the intent to inflict deadly violence is guilty of assault.

And further suppose that we take the facts:

> Ellie learned that her husband Grover had another woman as a lover. Ellie followed Grover to a rendezvous with his lover. When she saw Grover with his lover Linda, she attacked Linda with a stick. Ellie beat Linda repeatedly, saying, "You must be punished."

Now, we can set aside the question whether Linda died or not because the rule does not mention that. The question we must raise is whether Ellie intended to inflict deadly violence on Linda. This is an open question. To be sure, there is reason to believe that she did. But again, there is reason to believe that she did not intend for the violence to be deadly: She used a stick rather than a gun. The point is not to argue for either of these positions. Rather, the point is that without further information, we simply cannot determine whether the intent was there.

A similar situation occurs when we lack sufficient guidance from the law to make a decision. Take the following rule for working purposes:

> A government employee on official business is not personally liable for any accident he causes as a consequence of the demands of that business.

For facts let us take:

> Smith, an employee of the federal government, was driving in a government car to Easton. Her most direct route was Highway 20, and Smith took that route. Smith knew that her boyfriend Jones worked at a service station along her route. Although she did not need gas, she wanted to stop and say hello to him. She decided that a short break would be a good idea as a matter of safety, and further that it could not hurt to have the oil and air checked as well as the windshield cleaned. As Smith pulled into the service station where her boyfriend worked, she carelessly ran over the pet iguana of the service station's owner.

The obvious question which comes to mind is whether Smith is liable for the pet iguana. Here, as in contrast to the problem immediately preceding, there are many facts. Smith had a boyfriend, but on the other hand she could have used a break. Further, the car could be checked. But, then again, why stop there as opposed to some other service station? The point here is that the issue is not settled by what we *know*. We need further guidance in the form of a rule to tell us which of these facts is important and which others can be safely discarded. So again we have an answer choice (B).

With regard to answer choice (B), we make the important note:

> An answer choice (B) is appropriate where there is a concept which is not sufficiently defined to allow its application or where there is not enough factual information to allow the application of an adequately defined concept.

The final question which a case might raise would be a choice between two conflicting rules, answer choice (A). It is very important to understand what the LSAT means by a conflict. In the real world, a general rule with an exception, such as the murder and self-defense rule which we used in the preceding section, would not be regarded as an inconsistent rule. Rather, we would say there is the exception which takes a situation out of the general rule, so that the general rule does not govern that situation. For example, we would say this is a case of self-defense, so the general rule regarding murder does not apply here. And it would seem to us that we have not disregarded a conflicting rule, but that we have applied one large, internally consistent rule: Do X generally, but do Y in the following special cases. IF you see such a rule as a single rule on the LSAT, you should treat it just as we have discussed. BUT if you saw this laid out as TWO separate rules on the LSAT, *you must regard them as conflicting.*

What allows us in the real world to treat the general rule with exceptions as one consistent principle is that we accord priority to one rule or the other, that is, we say this rule is supposed to *override* that rule in this situation. But the directions for this section specifically state: " . . . you must not automatically suppose that one of the two rules takes precedence over the other. You must accept that the rules are of equal importance." If we pay attention to this aspect of the directions, we will treat the exception and the general rule as being of equal importance, so that deciding whether a situation is to be governed by the general rule or the exception requires a choice between two co-equal and independent principles.

To reinforce these points, let us take a look at some examples of pairs of rules which conflict.

> I. Any physical entry upon the surface of land owned by another without the owner's express or implied consent to the entry is a criminal trespass.
>
> II. A police officer or an officer of the court has an absolute privilege to enter upon land belonging to another for the purpose of executing official duties without obtaining the owner's consent.

In a case involving official action by a police officer or an officer of the court, these two rules conflict. If a police officer pursues a criminal suspect onto private property, is he guilty of trespass? According to Rule I the officer may be (if all the other conditions are met, e.g., lack of owner's consent); but according to Rule II the officer cannot be guilty of trespass since he enjoys a privilege. A choice must, therefore, be made between the two rules. If Rule I is chosen, perhaps the officer is guilty of trespass. If Rule II is chosen, the officer is definitely not guilty of trespass. Again, we remind you that you will not have to choose either rule. You have only to point out that a choice is required. Incidentally, suppose the facts stated that Officer Smith, in his squad car, was chasing suspect Jones, who was driving a stolen car. Jones drives across Johnson's front yard and around the house. Smith follows him, hot on the trail. Did Smith obtain the owner's consent to enter the property? The obvious answer is that "no, he did not," so if the LSAT asks the question, "Did Smith obtain the owner's consent?", the correct answer is (C). It can be deduced from the facts that no consent was given. On the other hand, suppose Smith pursued Jones's car into the parking lot of the supermarket on Sunday, when the supermarket is not open. Assume further that there is a sign which says: "No parking on Sunday." However, the owner of the supermarket does not enforce this. In fact, the owner would prefer no one parked there on Sunday, but to avoid generating ill-will he allows neighborhood residents to park there on Sunday. Did the owner give his implicit consent for people to enter his parking lot on Sunday, despite the presence of the sign? This raises an issue which is not easily answered. On the one hand, the owner specifically says, "No parking." On the other hand, the owner does allow parking. This question is an open question. We need more guidance from rules about specific actions and implicit consent. Therefore, such a question should be classified a (B) on the test.

Here is another set of rules:

I. A person who is injured by the carelessness of another may not recover damages for his injuries if he contributed to the accident in any way by his own careless conduct.

II. Even a person who has contributed to an accident by his own carelessness may recover damages suffered as the result of someone else's careless act, provided that that other person had the last clear chance to avoid the accident but failed to take advantage of it.

The kind of case in which these two rules conflict is as follows. Jones was driving his car down the expressway at 65 miles per hour in a 55-mile-per-hour zone. Smith was entering the expressway. Though Smith usually wore glasses and was required to wear them when he drove, he had forgotten to wear them that morning. As a result, he misjudged the speed of Jones's approach. Jones saw Smith enter and could have changed lanes, but Jones blew his horn instead, expecting that Smith would give way. By that point, however, Smith was too far onto the road and had nowhere to go. The two cars collided. Can Smith recover from Jones for any damage caused in the accident? The answer to this question is that one must choose between the two rules. Rule I precludes Smith's recovering, because Smith's own carelessness contributed to the accident. Rule II, however, says that Smith may recover even though he was himself careless, because Jones had the last clear chance to avoid the accident (by changing lanes) but he failed to use it.

Let us take one more example.

I. An oral agreement for the sale of goods valued at less than $500 is enforceable according to its terms.

II. A contract where the subject matter is illegal is not enforceable in a court of law.

Suppose that Smith verbally agrees to sell Jones a quantity of illegal drugs; Jones arrives with the money, but Smith refuses to go through with the deal. Can Jones prevail against Smith in court? To answer this question we would have to choose between the two rules. According to Rule I, the contract will be enforceable provided that it is within the $500 limit, but Rule II provides that the contract is not enforceable since it deals with illegal drugs. What if the contract had been for the sale of some legal item? This question would require further information, since we do not know whether the item is worth more than $500, so the correct answer to this question is (B).

There is one final point regarding the directions upon which we should touch: the independence criterion. This has two aspects. First, a section of Issues and Facts will contain several different problem sets (facts and rules). You must make certain that you answer each question on the basis of the rules provided for *that set.* Do not use information from another problem set. Second, sometimes questions will add information. To illustrate, let us return to our last set of rules regarding contracts. A question in that problem set might be: "Suppose Smith took Jones' money and gave Jones the drugs. Then later Jones changed his mind. Could Jones get his money back from Smith?" This question supplements the facts given in the passage, but these additional facts are available only for answering the one specific question. You are not to carry them through and use them to answer other questions *even* in the same problem set.

AN ATTACK STRATEGY FOR ISSUES AND FACTS

Now that we have discussed the underlying substance of this section and the directions, we are in a position to develop a plan of attack for the section. Point by point the strategy looks like this:

Step 1: Preview the Rules.
Step 2: Read the Facts and the Dispute.
Step 3: Reread the Rules.
Step 4: Answer the Questions.

Let us take each of the steps in turn.

Step 1: Preview the rules. Actually, this is more a suggestion than a hard-and-fast rule. Many students will find that previewing the rules is like previewing the question stems in the other sections of the test. It will guide their reading of the facts, enabling them to concentrate on relevant material while screening out details which are not important at all. For example, if we preview a set of rules which say:

I. A person who breaks into residential premises belonging to another with the intention to steal objects therein, and who does steal objects, is guilty of burglary.

II. A person who commits what would otherwise be a crime is not guilty of that crime if he acted under a threat of serious bodily injury or death.

Having previewed the rules, we know we should be on the alert for certain details: Was there a threat of injury or death? Did someone break into residential premises? Did someone steal objects on the premises?

Make sure that the preview is just that—a preview. You should not *study* the rules before you have read the facts; the idea is just to give yourself a little extra guidance. In any event, you should practice attacking problem sets in both ways (reading and not reading the rules) and adopt whichever approach seems to you to be the more effective.

Step 2: Read the facts and the dispute. In reading the facts and the dispute, keep two things in mind. First, although this is a time-pressure part of the test (35 questions in 35 minutes), you cannot afford to skim anything. You have got to pay very careful attention to detail. Someone who speed-reads may overlook an important adverb such as "carelessly" or "intentionally" which is critical to solving the problems. So read as quickly as possible without sacrificing comprehension. As we have noted elsewhere, only practice will allow you to determine where the trade-off between speed and accuracy is for you as an individual. Second, in organizing in your mind the material you are reading, you may find it helpful to keep in mind a list of important groups of details that are often significant.

PEOPLE: Who are the parties involved in the action and what are their peculiar characteristics? Obviously, you must learn to keep the parties straight, that is, who did what and to whom. Beyond that, you should be attentive to status and relations between parties. Were they strangers? Was he a member of the family? Were they married at the time? Was she a doctor? Was he a guest?

PLACES: Where did the action take place? Was it in a public park or in a private home? Did it occur in a residential building or in a commercial building? Was it on the high seas or in the marina? Did it occur in New York or in California?

TIME ELEMENTS: How long did the injured party wait before he brought his suit? When was the problem discovered? For how long did he agree to work? Was it dark at the time of the accident?

MENTAL CHARACTERISTICS: Did she mean to do it? Was she careless in her actions? Did he hope to profit by his act? Was he aware at the time that he was making a false statement? Did he know the car was stolen?

KEY LEGAL TERMS: Was it reasonable? Was it foreseeable? Was it intentional? Was it accidental? Was it careless?

Of course, this list is not exhaustive and it is not intended to be. Rather, we have included it to suggest some of the important things to look for in your reading of the facts of a problem. The more you practice with this section, the better able you will be to pick out the important details.

3. Read the rules. After having read the facts, you need to return to the rules. Your first look at the rules was merely an overview—to familiarize yourself with their general content. Now, however, you have got to reread them with careful attention to detail. Although there are no hidden tricks in this section (as we have already noted), the section does place a premium on careful reading. Do not let a key word slip past you. Be alert for qualifiers such as *all, every, each, no one, only when, provided, if, and, or, unless, except, cannot, must,* and so on. Beyond that, you have to pay attention to each and every word in the rule. Sometimes a key word such as *subsequent* can change the entire meaning of a rule.

4. Answer the questions. This step seems obvious enough, but you should try to approach the questions in a systematic way. Use the following approach:

Would the *answer* to this question
give me information which would
help me apply either rule? → NO ⟶ (D)
↓
Yes, go to second step.
↓
Does this question raise an issue
which can be resolved on the basis
of information given in the facts
or in the rules? → YES ⟶ (C)
↓
No, go to third step.
↓
Is the answer to this question different
if I use Rule I as opposed to Rule II? → YES ⟶ (A)
↓
No, the answer must be
(B), but to check ask:
↓
Do I lack sufficient information or
guidance to definitely answer this? → YES ⟶ (B)
↓
No, go back to step one
and re-think your answers.

Let us complete our discussion of this section by looking at an example:

FACTS: Herbert, age seventeen, and his brother George, who was three years younger than Herbert, wanted to buy a motorcycle. They did not have enough money for the model they wanted, so they decided to steal what they needed. The two entered a small grocery store owned by Hannah, and George told Hannah, "Hand over all the money; my brother has a gun." Although Herbert did not have a gun, he had put his finger in his pocket so as to give the impression of a gun. Hannah turned over the day's receipts to George, and the two brothers fled. Hannah called the police, and the police drove her around the neighborhood until she spotted Herbert and George.

DISPUTE: The police arrested the brothers and charged them with robbery. They pleaded not guilty.

RULES: I. A person who uses force or violence or the threat of force or violence to take property belonging to another from that person's possession is guilty of robbery.

II. A juvenile, any person under the age of sixteen, cannot be convicted of a crime.

1. Is Herbert guilty of robbery?
2. How much money did George and Herbert take from Hannah?

3. If Herbert had had a gun and shot Hannah, would he be guilty of murder?
4. Is George guilty of robbery?

The first step in answering this question set is to preview the rules. Glancing at the rules suggests that you should read to see if there was force or violence or at least the threat of force or violence. Further, was property taken from someone else? Was there a juvenile involved in the case? Then you read the facts of the case and the answers to the questions we have just raised become clear. Yes, there was a threat of force (even if there was no force). Yes, there was a juvenile involved, George. Also, one of the parties was not a juvenile. And property—money—was taken from Hannah.

Then we proceed to answer to questions.

1. Is Herbert guilty of robbery? The attack approach says, first you ask whether the answer to this question would give information enabling you to apply a rule. The answer is "yes," for it would tell you how to apply Rule I. So you go to step two. Does it raise an issue which can be resolved on information and rules already given? The answer is, again, "yes." You have information for all the critical elements. So you go to the third step. Do you get different answers using different rules? No; applying Rule I, you find Herbert is guilty of robbery since all of the elements are there in the facts. Applying Rule II, you find that it does not apply to Herbert, so there is no conflict, answer (C).

2. How much money did George and Herbert take from Hannah? First step: Will the answer to this question be useful in applying either of the rules? No, since neither of the rules mentions anything about amount. So the answer is (D), on the basis of the first step alone. Now, a different result would follow if the rule for robbery had stipulated some minimum amount needed to make the crime robbery. Then, the answer to this question should be (B), since such a rule would make the amount important, while the facts are silent as to the amount.

3. If Herbert had had a gun and shot Hannah, would he be guilty of murder? Notice here that you are dealing with one of those questions which adds additional information, and keeping in mind the independence criterion, you know you are to use it only in answering this particular question. In applying step one, you must keep in mind that the problem structure has been somewhat altered—you are asking about murder now. So step one, would the additional information help you determine whether Herbert is guilty of murder? Yes, so you can rule out (D). Does it, however, raise a question which can be answered on the basis of information you already have? No, because you do not know what is necessary to prove murder. Does the answer require a choice between the rules? Again, no, since Herbert is not a juvenile, and further the question pertains to murder, not robbery. Finally, do you lack information? Yes, you need to know more facts (did Hannah die), and you need another rule (what constitutes murder). So the correct answer is (B).

4. Is George guilty of robbery? The issue is relevant, for the answer would tell you how the rules are to be applied. So (D) is not correct. Does the question raise an issue which can be resolved on the basis of information given? No, because you get different results using the two different rules. Of course, once you reach the conclusion that there is a conflict between the two rules, you know the answer must be (A), so your third step is just a matter of form.

WRITING SAMPLE INSTRUCTIONAL OVERVIEW

PURPOSE OF THE ESSAY

In addition to the four types of standardized, multiple-choice questions that will appear on the LSAT, the test will also include a writing sample. The writing sample will be a short essay on a selected topic to be written in 30 minutes while in the examining room. The writing sample will not be graded, but a copy of the essay will be forwarded with your score report to each school receiving your LSAT score. The point of requiring a student to write an essay while in the examining room is to give a law school admissions committee a piece of writing definitely done by the student alone. The questions will not cover any topic requiring special knowledge. Paper and pens will be provided at the test center.

The underlying purpose in requiring the essay is to give a law school admissions committee another perspective on a candidate's ability; in this case, to give some idea of how well a student writes. The idea is that this can mitigate to some extent the severity of the artificial, multiple-choice format of the rest of the test. Exactly what role the writing sample is to play in the admissions process is decided by each law school. At a conference of college pre-law advisors, we conducted an informal survey of law school representatives.* Many schools said they would use the sample to help choose between otherwise equally qualified candidates. Very few law schools said they would rely heavily upon the writing sample. Most law schools appear to be adopting a middle-of-the-road approach. The writing sample will not figure heavily in the initial screening-out of applications, but it may be used to make decisions in difficult cases. For example, a student with marginal qualifications for a particular law school might be accepted if he wrote a really good essay, and a student of similar background could be rejected on grounds that his writing sample was just not acceptable. Since no one is assured of a seat at a top law school, applicants to those schools who write a very poor essay will likely suffer.

At this time, we should move quickly to reassure you that this section is *not* so important as the other four sections. It is important to keep in mind that law schools will likely use the LSAT as a screening device (coupled with the Grade Point Average). This means the LSAT is a threshhold requirement that must be met before the writing sample even enters the picture. Moreover, the length of the sample is such that you are not really writing a "term paper." In 30 minutes, *no one* is going to be able to write the definitive essay on the topic he is given—and no one is expected to do so. This writing sample is just a check to see

---

*Northeast Association of Pre-Law Advisors, June 1981, Albany, New York.

that you can write clearly and grammatically. It is not to determine whether you would be a great novelist. And finally, the questions will be drafted so that they are vacuous—answers will in no way depend on content. At the conference we just mentioned, the following topic was suggested as appropriate by Professor Walter Raushenbush of the University of Wisconsin Law School, and then president of the Law School Admissions Council:

> It is better to construct classrooms without windows, since the view provided by the windows tends to distract students.

Since everyone taking the LSAT presumably has classroom experience as a student, everyone will have some thoughts on the subject. The idea from the point of view of the LSAT is to select a topic that neither requires nor rewards special knowledge, so that the only things to be demonstrated are organization and expression (the second is clearly more difficult).

The objective of the exercise, then, is to say something—anything—and say it clearly, concisely, and correctly. We will discuss the Writing Sample section of the test from two points of view: what to say and how to say it.

What to Say

Since the topics for this section are chosen because they are devoid of content, finding something to say about them will be at once easy and difficult. It should be easy because you will not find yourself "stumped" for an answer. There is no correct answer to this section—only good writing. But it is also true that finding something to say on a topic on the spur of the moment is sometimes unnerving. ("What if I can't think of something to say?") So before we try to cook up a recipe for this section, let us issue the following warning notes:

Don't be afraid to take a position, but you do not have to be controversial. On the one hand, you need not be afraid that you will step on the toes of some admissions officer. On the other hand, do not go out of your way to be controversial. Taking the topic just mentioned as an example, you might want to argue that the vision needs a respite from looking so long at one teacher. This will not suggest to the admissions committee that you do not like teachers and that you will not like them. Lawyers are trained to endure and even to flourish in the midst of controversy. Admittedly it is difficult to find a controversial point to make about windows in the classrooms, but we feel that a wrong tack to take with that question would be: "The bourgeois, capitalist pigs try mind control by blocking out the student's view of the real world, thereby making him more pliable to their evil demands." So, do not be afraid to make your point, but don't go out of your way to stir up trouble.

This is not a hidden psychological test. You are not looking at blots. You are demonstrating that you know how to write clearly. You need not be afraid that someone is going to try to read between the lines of your essay. Using our example, one might write: "Windows serve a useful function. Since most classes are two hours long, a distant perspective provides relaxation for the eyes as well as a moment of respite for the mind." No one is going to read this and say, "Here we have a student who can't concentrate." Of course, you don't want to make an obviously bad point: "I like windows in a classroom since I get bored easily, and like to spend my time looking outside." But it should be obvious that there is a great difference between these two points.

Do not try to do too much. After you have practiced a few topics, you will have a pretty good idea of what you can hope to accomplish in the time allotted. The biggest problem for students is not going to be having too little to say, but trying to say too much. Your little essay must be structurally complete. That is, it must have a beginning, a middle, and an end. You do not want to run out of time before you have completed your thought. Far better to write a nicely balanced and self-contained essay on the short side, than a longer piece that stops in the middle of the next to the last paragraph. Make sure you can chew what you bite off.

Do not use any legal terminology. The LSAT is not a test of what you already know about the law, and law school admissions officers are not going to be impressed with your essay just because you flavor it with *henceforth, heretofore mentioned, above cited, and/or, his and/or hers,* or similar terms. Such terms have no place in your essay. Your best bet is to try to write naturally, as though you were speaking to someone sitting across the table (though you should avoid slang expressions you might use in conversation).

With these comments in mind, let us now turn to a system for organizing some thoughts about vacuous topics. The system has three steps: define, organize, and execute. Briefly, we mean you should approach the topic by defining the pressure points in it, then select those points you plan to make and put them in a small outline, and, finally, write the essay. By finding the pressure points in the topic, we mean focusing on the nouns and key modifiers, and isolating some connection between concepts. In treating the topic we have been using, we would begin with a little mental "doodling."

> Classrooms: What purpose do they serve? How can they best accomplish it?
> Windows: What is their function? Do they have more than one function (ventilation and light as well as view)?
> Distract: How seriously do they distract? Do they interfere with classroom function?
> Student: What age is the student?

These musings would suggest many points, but we would select only three (at least two and no more than four). For example:

1. The function of the classroom is to provide a location for teaching and learning. To what extent do windows interfere with that function?
2. Even assuming windows are somewhat distracting, they serve other useful functions. They provide light for study, and ventilation, and maybe they are relaxing.
3. If there is a problem with distraction, the way to handle it is on an individual basis (teacher-student), not by eliminating windows entirely.

Since you cannot realistically expect to write more than 250 to 500 words in the time limit, those three points, plus an introductory paragraph and a brief conclusion, should be just enough material.

You could not hope to anticipate all the vacuous questions which the LSAT will use on your administration. You should be prepared to put a little thought into your answer so that you get something which is a bit original but not trite.

Here are four approaches which will probably be applicable to any topic. If you try to follow any one of them slavishly, your essay will reflect the fact that you did not do any real thinking. But we provide them (a) in the hope that they will jog your thinking, leading you in the direction of some worthwhile comment, and (b) as a fail-safe mechanism (if you're really caught with your outline down, don't just sit there, do something!).

One approach which is always available is the "I disagree for three reasons" approach. No matter what the topic, you should be able to think up three reasons on which to disagree with it:

> I disagree with the statement about classroom windows for three reasons. First, windows are only one possible source of distraction. A student who does not want to pay attention will always find something to occupy his mind. Second, windows provide an additional safety feature for many classrooms, another escape route in the event of an emergency. Third, keeping students enclosed in a small space is demeaning.

This is only a sketch of an introductory paragraph. You would then proceed to develop each point in the paragraphs following. In any event, it seems to us that the "I disagree" approach, while somewhat artificial, is always available to you. If nothing good really comes, think up two or three arguments against the statement. Of course, if you just cannot bring yourself to disagree with the topic, then you may use the "I agree for three reasons" variation on this approach. But you will probably find it easier to disagree with than to support the topic.

If you really cannot find enough to say on either side of the topic, you can take a second but weaker approach: equivocate. That is, you can say, "On the one hand. . . . But on the other. . . . " This avoids the necessity for ever reaching a conclusion. The advantage of equivocation (finding something to say when you really cannot devise a strong comment) also has a disadvantage: The essay may show that quality too strongly. But if you are really in a bind for something to say, you can at least think up a point or two on each side.

A third, stronger approach is to take the topic to task for having oversimplified matters. In a way, you avoid taking issue with the topic, but your comments can have some substance. For example, you might write on the topic we have been using:

> While it may be true that windows are a distraction, the proposal that we eliminate all windows from the classroom is too simplistic. There are times when windows are not only not distracting but highly desireable, for example, during non-instructional hours. There are methods for achieving the effect desired without actually eliminating the windows: Installing venetian blinds or some other window covering, which can be removed; or arranging the seating facilities so students have their backs to the windows.

A fourth and final fail-safe approach, and it is not the strongest, is "quibbling." It is always open to you to take issue with the terms used in the topic. The beauty of this approach is that it requires virtually no thought. All you have to do is isolate the three most important concepts, for example, student, classroom, distraction, and proceed to quibble:

> It is difficult to assess the validity of the claim made by the topic since the key terms are not defined. There are many kinds of classrooms, and classrooms serve many functions. Students are not an homogeneous group; some are mature, others are very young. Finally, there are serious distractions and there are not so serious distractions.

And you can develop a thought or two about each point.

By now, you should be reassured that you will be able to find something to say. Before we begin a discussion of "how to say it," we should mention that your essay should have some organizational scheme which ties it together. You should begin with an introductory paragraph containing a statement of purpose which briefly mentions the three points you will develop:

> In this essay, I plan to present three arguments against the conclusion that classrooms should not have windows. One, the distraction cannot be that serious. Two, there are less drastic means for coping with whatever distraction windows may actually cause. Three, some distraction is valuable.

Then you write three short paragraphs, of four or five sentences each, on each of your points. Finally, you include some kind of conclusion: "These three arguments raise serious questions about the validity of the conclusion. At least it has been shown that the issue is not totally one-sided." The main objective of this scheme is to give the essay a balanced and complete look.

No approach is going to be self-applying, but at least you can rest assured that you will have something to say. Now we can turn to the question of how to say it.

How to Say It

As we have stressed, this section is going to be used by law schools to see whether a student can properly write English. So, as important as finding something to say is the way in which you say it. Obviously, this means composing sentences which are free of grammatical errors. Beyond that, however, you should strive for conciseness and clarity of expression. We understand that it is difficult to take this general instruction and apply it to a specific exercise: "Right, I agree, write clearly. But how do I do that?" Our best advice here is to do some practice. In the practice exams which follow we have provided four sample topics with sample answers. But you can practice on your own by selecting a topic—anything which pops into your mind—and writing a short essay on it. If you feel the need, you can use these two questions for additional practice:

—A speaker is more effective if he uses a lectern or podium because he will then make fewer unnecessary and distracting movements.

—It is better to bring household garbage outside as infrequently as possible because it is more efficient to carry fewer large loads than more smaller loads.

As you write your essay, you should keep in the front of your mind the injunction: "Square the corners." By that we mean, (1) each sentence should express a single, simple thought, and (2) each sentence is composed in your mind *before* you begin to write it down.

Now, it must be allowed that for those people who write for a living, these injunctions are not absolute. Most of this overview is addressed to students who are a bit "rusty" in their writing skills. An athlete who is a bit out of condition would not attempt to run a marathon but would select a more manageable distance. So too here, if your writing skills are not in peak condition, slow down a bit. First, make each sentence express a single thought. Rather than trying to tack on qualifications and exceptions to an already long sentence, break it down:

Wrong:	Although it might be argued that some students will be distracted, but there is no proof of this presented, it is still the case that many students would benefit from the relaxing effect of open scenery, and that could even help them learn.
Better:	There is no proof presented that students are distracted by windows. Even assuming some students are distracted, many other students might find the view relaxing. A relaxed student should be a better learner than one who is tense—and learning is the goal of the classroom.

Second, think through the entire sentence before you begin to write. Many errors in writing are the result of an attempt to change structures in mid-sentence. Verb tenses shift; points of view get mixed up; verbs get left out; pronouns get confused; and many other things happen—if the sentence is not already formed when the writing begins. For example:

Wrong:	Even if a student is somewhat distracted, they may be even better able to concentrate when their attention returns to the teacher.

This sentence contains a grammatical error. The pronoun "they," which begins the main clause of the sentence, is plural. But it refers to "student," which is singular. This type of error usually occurs when writers do not have the complete thought or sentence in mind when they begin to write. They lose track of what they have said and shift from the singular to the plural. The best way for you to avoid such errors is to have a good idea of what the completed sentence will say before you begin to write it down.

In addition to "squaring the corners," we offer the following warnings against common errors of grammar and style. The list is not exhaustive, but it does cover some of the most fundamental mistakes.

Watch for Subject-Verb Agreement. Everyone remembers that a verb must agree with its subject, and by and large we all observe this rule. Where we tend to get into trouble is with sentences with subjects modified by prepositional phrases or other material which comes between the subject and its verb.

Wrong:	This distraction, which occurs in students with more limited attention spans, are easily avoided by arranging desks so that the eyes of a student is directed away from the windows.

Two errors of subject-verb agreement occur here: "distraction . . . are" and "eyes . . . is." In this sentence, a clause including two prepositional phrases comes between the first subject and its verb, and it is therefore likely that one of the two nouns "students" or "spans" was mistaken for the subject when the writer chose a verb. A prepositional phrase ("of a student") comes between the second subject and its verb, and the writer has mistaken "student" for the subject of the verb and written "is."

Be wary of pronouns. Many people misuse pronouns. The two most common mistakes in pronoun reference are incorrect number and incorrect case. Sometimes students use a singular pronoun where a plural pronoun is needed and *vice versa* (incorrect number):

Wrong:	The easiest solution is to have the teacher order each student to keep their eyes directed toward the blackboard.

In this case the choice of the pronoun "their" is incorrect. The pronoun must refer to "student," which is singular; but "their" is plural. Consider the next example:

Wrong:	Under this seating arrangement, all of the people in the classroom, except the class monitor and she, will face the blackboard, not the windows.

In this sentence, the use of the pronoun "she" is incorrect because it is in the wrong case. The pronoun here functions as the object of a proposition ("except"), and it should therefore be in the objective case ("her"). One sure way of avoiding errors in the use of pronouns is to avoid unnecessary pronouns.

Better:	Under this seating arrangement, all of the people in the classroom, except the class monitor and the teacher, will. . . .

Avoid the "notorious" dangling modifier. As a general rule, make sure that your modifiers are close to the words they are intended to modify. Be especially wary of the introductory modifier.

Wrong:	While strolling through Central Park, a severe thunderstorm required my companion and me to take shelter in the band shell.

Given the construction of the sentence, it is made to appear that the severe thunderstorm was strolling through the park. When a modifying idea starts a sentence and is set off with a comma, the modifier must be taken to modify the first noun or noun phrase after the comma. A related error to be avoided is the squinting modifier, which is placed so that it may modify either one of two things, producing ambiguity in the sentence.

Wrong:	Paul told Mary that he would wed her down by the old mill.

Did Paul tell Mary down by the old mill that he would wed her, or did Paul tell Mary that he would wed her and that the wedding would take place down by the old mill?

Avoid the passive voice. As we have mentioned, it is important to write in straightforward declarative sentences. These sentences are easily used, and they express thoughts clearly. But many students imagine that the more stilted the construction, the better the writing:

Wrong:	When the notice was received by me. . . .
Correct:	When I received the notice. . . .
Wrong:	The cake was baked by the chef to please. . . .
Correct:	The chef baked the cake to please. . . .

We do not imply here an absolute prohibition against the passive voice. We only say that a law school admissions committee will be favorably impressed by straightforward and direct composition—even if that writing is a bit dry. But they will not be favorably impressed by needlessly complicated and imprecise sentences.

Avoid slang. Whatever else you do, do not allow slang to slip into your writing.

Wrong:	Let the kids do their own thing. Its too heavy a trip to always have the teacher, the man, laying this guilt business on you. No windows would be a head trip. Some of the kids would wind up at the shrink's. So just lay off, and let them be themselves.

In conversation we often use expressions that are just not acceptable in formal writing. Can you dig that?

What not to say. You are in command of the Writing Sample. Unlike the other sections, in which you are *forced* to choose from among ETS's answers, the writing sample allows you to construct and write your own answer. It will be possible, to a certain extent, to "fake it." We have already discussed "faking" the *content* of the answer. However, if you are not sure about the meaning or spelling of a word, find an alternative. There is absolutely no reason to expose yourself to the possibility of error when you could avoid that danger entirely by using another phrase. So WHEN IN DOUBT, LEAVE IT OUT.

Writing neat. What we have tried to do in this section is reassure you that you will not be caught without anything to say. The questions will be drafted in such a way that you will be able to think of a point or two—and probably more. The important thing is to express yourself clearly in order to impress upon the admissions officers that you can write, a skill every lawyer needs. Finally, although good penmanship is not a prerequisite to being a good lawyer, your writing will be read by some fairly important people. Present yourself in a way of which you can be proud. Some people have naturally beautiful handwriting, others do not. But everyone can make his handwriting legible. It is only courteous to write clearly, so that the people who have to read your essay can do so easily. So write slowly (without sacrificing coverage), and try to use your best handwriting. Print if necessary.

In the practice tests, you will find some sample topics and essays. Do not take these answers as the final word. They are only illustrations of what you might say about a given topic. You will have to bring your own thinking to this section. But, as we have said, you will surely have something to say, and you'll probably have more to say than time enough in which to say it. Practice being concise and clear.

FINAL NOTE

The Writing Sample topics will sometimes ask you to write a position paper and put yourself in the place of a legislature, administrator, or a judge. This defines your status in relation to the problem. The main purpose of the assignment is to help students become involved in the topic. You are not expected to display any special knowledge appropriate to the position into which you are being transported.

Usually, you are given some report regarding each side of the question. The ideas that are presented in the topic should not be avoided simply because they are in the topic statement. You will be expected to address the issue. It is also important to avoid making assertions of a viewpoint. There are always obvious and cogent objections. If you oppose a decision, recognize all sides of the argument and address it directly. The essay is an exercise in clear thinking and written expression. Straightforwardness and clarity are most important.

Part III

Four Full-Length Practice Examinations

ANSWER SHEET—PRACTICE EXAMINATON 1

SECTION I

1 Ⓐ Ⓑ Ⓒ Ⓓ Ⓔ	6 Ⓐ Ⓑ Ⓒ Ⓓ Ⓔ	11 Ⓐ Ⓑ Ⓒ Ⓓ Ⓔ	16 Ⓐ Ⓑ Ⓒ Ⓓ Ⓔ	21 Ⓐ Ⓑ Ⓒ Ⓓ Ⓔ
2 Ⓐ Ⓑ Ⓒ Ⓓ Ⓔ	7 Ⓐ Ⓑ Ⓒ Ⓓ Ⓔ	12 Ⓐ Ⓑ Ⓒ Ⓓ Ⓔ	17 Ⓐ Ⓑ Ⓒ Ⓓ Ⓔ	22 Ⓐ Ⓑ Ⓒ Ⓓ Ⓔ
3 Ⓐ Ⓑ Ⓒ Ⓓ Ⓔ	8 Ⓐ Ⓑ Ⓒ Ⓓ Ⓔ	13 Ⓐ Ⓑ Ⓒ Ⓓ Ⓔ	18 Ⓐ Ⓑ Ⓒ Ⓓ Ⓔ	23 Ⓐ Ⓑ Ⓒ Ⓓ Ⓔ
4 Ⓐ Ⓑ Ⓒ Ⓓ Ⓔ	9 Ⓐ Ⓑ Ⓒ Ⓓ Ⓔ	14 Ⓐ Ⓑ Ⓒ Ⓓ Ⓔ	19 Ⓐ Ⓑ Ⓒ Ⓓ Ⓔ	24 Ⓐ Ⓑ Ⓒ Ⓓ Ⓔ
5 Ⓐ Ⓑ Ⓒ Ⓓ Ⓔ	10 Ⓐ Ⓑ Ⓒ Ⓓ Ⓔ	15 Ⓐ Ⓑ Ⓒ Ⓓ Ⓔ	20 Ⓐ Ⓑ Ⓒ Ⓓ Ⓔ	25 Ⓐ Ⓑ Ⓒ Ⓓ Ⓔ
				26 Ⓐ Ⓑ Ⓒ Ⓓ Ⓔ

SECTION II

1 Ⓐ Ⓑ Ⓒ Ⓓ Ⓔ	8 Ⓐ Ⓑ Ⓒ Ⓓ Ⓔ	15 Ⓐ Ⓑ Ⓒ Ⓓ Ⓔ	22 Ⓐ Ⓑ Ⓒ Ⓓ Ⓔ	29 Ⓐ Ⓑ Ⓒ Ⓓ Ⓔ
2 Ⓐ Ⓑ Ⓒ Ⓓ Ⓔ	9 Ⓐ Ⓑ Ⓒ Ⓓ Ⓔ	16 Ⓐ Ⓑ Ⓒ Ⓓ Ⓔ	23 Ⓐ Ⓑ Ⓒ Ⓓ Ⓔ	30 Ⓐ Ⓑ Ⓒ Ⓓ Ⓔ
3 Ⓐ Ⓑ Ⓒ Ⓓ Ⓔ	10 Ⓐ Ⓑ Ⓒ Ⓓ Ⓔ	17 Ⓐ Ⓑ Ⓒ Ⓓ Ⓔ	24 Ⓐ Ⓑ Ⓒ Ⓓ Ⓔ	31 Ⓐ Ⓑ Ⓒ Ⓓ Ⓔ
4 Ⓐ Ⓑ Ⓒ Ⓓ Ⓔ	11 Ⓐ Ⓑ Ⓒ Ⓓ Ⓔ	18 Ⓐ Ⓑ Ⓒ Ⓓ Ⓔ	25 Ⓐ Ⓑ Ⓒ Ⓓ Ⓔ	32 Ⓐ Ⓑ Ⓒ Ⓓ Ⓔ
5 Ⓐ Ⓑ Ⓒ Ⓓ Ⓔ	12 Ⓐ Ⓑ Ⓒ Ⓓ Ⓔ	19 Ⓐ Ⓑ Ⓒ Ⓓ Ⓔ	26 Ⓐ Ⓑ Ⓒ Ⓓ Ⓔ	33 Ⓐ Ⓑ Ⓒ Ⓓ Ⓔ
6 Ⓐ Ⓑ Ⓒ Ⓓ Ⓔ	13 Ⓐ Ⓑ Ⓒ Ⓓ Ⓔ	20 Ⓐ Ⓑ Ⓒ Ⓓ Ⓔ	27 Ⓐ Ⓑ Ⓒ Ⓓ Ⓔ	34 Ⓐ Ⓑ Ⓒ Ⓓ Ⓔ
7 Ⓐ Ⓑ Ⓒ Ⓓ Ⓔ	14 Ⓐ Ⓑ Ⓒ Ⓓ Ⓔ	21 Ⓐ Ⓑ Ⓒ Ⓓ Ⓔ	28 Ⓐ Ⓑ Ⓒ Ⓓ Ⓔ	35 Ⓐ Ⓑ Ⓒ Ⓓ Ⓔ

SECTION III

1 Ⓐ Ⓑ Ⓒ Ⓓ Ⓔ	6 Ⓐ Ⓑ Ⓒ Ⓓ Ⓔ	11 Ⓐ Ⓑ Ⓒ Ⓓ Ⓔ	16 Ⓐ Ⓑ Ⓒ Ⓓ Ⓔ	21 Ⓐ Ⓑ Ⓒ Ⓓ Ⓔ
2 Ⓐ Ⓑ Ⓒ Ⓓ Ⓔ	7 Ⓐ Ⓑ Ⓒ Ⓓ Ⓔ	12 Ⓐ Ⓑ Ⓒ Ⓓ Ⓔ	17 Ⓐ Ⓑ Ⓒ Ⓓ Ⓔ	22 Ⓐ Ⓑ Ⓒ Ⓓ Ⓔ
3 Ⓐ Ⓑ Ⓒ Ⓓ Ⓔ	8 Ⓐ Ⓑ Ⓒ Ⓓ Ⓔ	13 Ⓐ Ⓑ Ⓒ Ⓓ Ⓔ	18 Ⓐ Ⓑ Ⓒ Ⓓ Ⓔ	23 Ⓐ Ⓑ Ⓒ Ⓓ Ⓔ
4 Ⓐ Ⓑ Ⓒ Ⓓ Ⓔ	9 Ⓐ Ⓑ Ⓒ Ⓓ Ⓔ	14 Ⓐ Ⓑ Ⓒ Ⓓ Ⓔ	19 Ⓐ Ⓑ Ⓒ Ⓓ Ⓔ	24 Ⓐ Ⓑ Ⓒ Ⓓ Ⓔ
5 Ⓐ Ⓑ Ⓒ Ⓓ Ⓔ	10 Ⓐ Ⓑ Ⓒ Ⓓ Ⓔ	15 Ⓐ Ⓑ Ⓒ Ⓓ Ⓔ	20 Ⓐ Ⓑ Ⓒ Ⓓ Ⓔ	25 Ⓐ Ⓑ Ⓒ Ⓓ Ⓔ

SECTION IV

1 Ⓐ Ⓑ Ⓒ Ⓓ Ⓔ	6 Ⓐ Ⓑ Ⓒ Ⓓ Ⓔ	11 Ⓐ Ⓑ Ⓒ Ⓓ Ⓔ	16 Ⓐ Ⓑ Ⓒ Ⓓ Ⓔ	21 Ⓐ Ⓑ Ⓒ Ⓓ Ⓔ	26 Ⓐ Ⓑ Ⓒ Ⓓ Ⓔ
2 Ⓐ Ⓑ Ⓒ Ⓓ Ⓔ	7 Ⓐ Ⓑ Ⓒ Ⓓ Ⓔ	12 Ⓐ Ⓑ Ⓒ Ⓓ Ⓔ	17 Ⓐ Ⓑ Ⓒ Ⓓ Ⓔ	22 Ⓐ Ⓑ Ⓒ Ⓓ Ⓔ	27 Ⓐ Ⓑ Ⓒ Ⓓ Ⓔ
3 Ⓐ Ⓑ Ⓒ Ⓓ Ⓔ	8 Ⓐ Ⓑ Ⓒ Ⓓ Ⓔ	13 Ⓐ Ⓑ Ⓒ Ⓓ Ⓔ	18 Ⓐ Ⓑ Ⓒ Ⓓ Ⓔ	23 Ⓐ Ⓑ Ⓒ Ⓓ Ⓔ	28 Ⓐ Ⓑ Ⓒ Ⓓ Ⓔ
4 Ⓐ Ⓑ Ⓒ Ⓓ Ⓔ	9 Ⓐ Ⓑ Ⓒ Ⓓ Ⓔ	14 Ⓐ Ⓑ Ⓒ Ⓓ Ⓔ	19 Ⓐ Ⓑ Ⓒ Ⓓ Ⓔ	24 Ⓐ Ⓑ Ⓒ Ⓓ Ⓔ	
5 Ⓐ Ⓑ Ⓒ Ⓓ Ⓔ	10 Ⓐ Ⓑ Ⓒ Ⓓ Ⓔ	15 Ⓐ Ⓑ Ⓒ Ⓓ Ⓔ	20 Ⓐ Ⓑ Ⓒ Ⓓ Ⓔ	25 Ⓐ Ⓑ Ⓒ Ⓓ Ⓔ	

SECTION V

1 Ⓐ Ⓑ Ⓒ Ⓓ Ⓔ	6 Ⓐ Ⓑ Ⓒ Ⓓ Ⓔ	11 Ⓐ Ⓑ Ⓒ Ⓓ Ⓔ	16 Ⓐ Ⓑ Ⓒ Ⓓ Ⓔ	21 Ⓐ Ⓑ Ⓒ Ⓓ Ⓔ
2 Ⓐ Ⓑ Ⓒ Ⓓ Ⓔ	7 Ⓐ Ⓑ Ⓒ Ⓓ Ⓔ	12 Ⓐ Ⓑ Ⓒ Ⓓ Ⓔ	17 Ⓐ Ⓑ Ⓒ Ⓓ Ⓔ	22 Ⓐ Ⓑ Ⓒ Ⓓ Ⓔ
3 Ⓐ Ⓑ Ⓒ Ⓓ Ⓔ	8 Ⓐ Ⓑ Ⓒ Ⓓ Ⓔ	13 Ⓐ Ⓑ Ⓒ Ⓓ Ⓔ	18 Ⓐ Ⓑ Ⓒ Ⓓ Ⓔ	23 Ⓐ Ⓑ Ⓒ Ⓓ Ⓔ
4 Ⓐ Ⓑ Ⓒ Ⓓ Ⓔ	9 Ⓐ Ⓑ Ⓒ Ⓓ Ⓔ	14 Ⓐ Ⓑ Ⓒ Ⓓ Ⓔ	19 Ⓐ Ⓑ Ⓒ Ⓓ Ⓔ	24 Ⓐ Ⓑ Ⓒ Ⓓ Ⓔ
5 Ⓐ Ⓑ Ⓒ Ⓓ Ⓔ	10 Ⓐ Ⓑ Ⓒ Ⓓ Ⓔ	15 Ⓐ Ⓑ Ⓒ Ⓓ Ⓔ	20 Ⓐ Ⓑ Ⓒ Ⓓ Ⓔ	25 Ⓐ Ⓑ Ⓒ Ⓓ Ⓔ
				26 Ⓐ Ⓑ Ⓒ Ⓓ Ⓔ

SECTION VI

1 Ⓐ Ⓑ Ⓒ Ⓓ Ⓔ	8 Ⓐ Ⓑ Ⓒ Ⓓ Ⓔ	15 Ⓐ Ⓑ Ⓒ Ⓓ Ⓔ	22 Ⓐ Ⓑ Ⓒ Ⓓ Ⓔ	29 Ⓐ Ⓑ Ⓒ Ⓓ Ⓔ
2 Ⓐ Ⓑ Ⓒ Ⓓ Ⓔ	9 Ⓐ Ⓑ Ⓒ Ⓓ Ⓔ	16 Ⓐ Ⓑ Ⓒ Ⓓ Ⓔ	23 Ⓐ Ⓑ Ⓒ Ⓓ Ⓔ	30 Ⓐ Ⓑ Ⓒ Ⓓ Ⓔ
3 Ⓐ Ⓑ Ⓒ Ⓓ Ⓔ	10 Ⓐ Ⓑ Ⓒ Ⓓ Ⓔ	17 Ⓐ Ⓑ Ⓒ Ⓓ Ⓔ	24 Ⓐ Ⓑ Ⓒ Ⓓ Ⓔ	31 Ⓐ Ⓑ Ⓒ Ⓓ Ⓔ
4 Ⓐ Ⓑ Ⓒ Ⓓ Ⓔ	11 Ⓐ Ⓑ Ⓒ Ⓓ Ⓔ	18 Ⓐ Ⓑ Ⓒ Ⓓ Ⓔ	25 Ⓐ Ⓑ Ⓒ Ⓓ Ⓔ	32 Ⓐ Ⓑ Ⓒ Ⓓ Ⓔ
5 Ⓐ Ⓑ Ⓒ Ⓓ Ⓔ	12 Ⓐ Ⓑ Ⓒ Ⓓ Ⓔ	19 Ⓐ Ⓑ Ⓒ Ⓓ Ⓔ	26 Ⓐ Ⓑ Ⓒ Ⓓ Ⓔ	33 Ⓐ Ⓑ Ⓒ Ⓓ Ⓔ
6 Ⓐ Ⓑ Ⓒ Ⓓ Ⓔ	13 Ⓐ Ⓑ Ⓒ Ⓓ Ⓔ	20 Ⓐ Ⓑ Ⓒ Ⓓ Ⓔ	27 Ⓐ Ⓑ Ⓒ Ⓓ Ⓔ	34 Ⓐ Ⓑ Ⓒ Ⓓ Ⓔ
7 Ⓐ Ⓑ Ⓒ Ⓓ Ⓔ	14 Ⓐ Ⓑ Ⓒ Ⓓ Ⓔ	21 Ⓐ Ⓑ Ⓒ Ⓓ Ⓔ	28 Ⓐ Ⓑ Ⓒ Ⓓ Ⓔ	35 Ⓐ Ⓑ Ⓒ Ⓓ Ⓔ

EXAMINATION FORECAST

Section Number	Type	Minutes	Questions
Section I	Logical Reasoning	35	26
Section II	Issues & Facts	35	35
Section III	Analytical Reasoning	35	25
Section IV	Reading Comprehension	35	28
Section V	Logical Reasoning	35	26
Section VI	Issues & Facts	35	35
	Writing Sample	30	—
Total Time		4 hours	

A 15-minute break should be taken after Section IV.

The Writing Sample will usually be given before the rest of the LSAT and is found at the end of the Practice Test in this book.

PRACTICE EXAMINATION I

SECTION I

Time—35 Minutes
26 Questions

Directions: In this section, the questions ask you to analyze and evaluate the reasoning in short paragraphs or passages. For some questions, all of the answer choices may conceivably be answers to the question asked. You should select the *best* answer to the question, that is, an answer which does not require you to make assumptions which violate commonsense standards by being implausible, redundant, irrelevant or inconsistent. After choosing the best answer, blacken the corresponding space on the answer sheet.

1. There are no lower bus fares from Washington, D.C. to New York City than those of Flash Bus Line.

   Which of the following is logically inconsistent with the above advertising claim?

   I. Long Lines Airways has a Washington, D.C. to New York City fare which is only one-half that charged by Flash.
   II. Rapid Transit Bus Company charges the same fare for a trip from Washington, D.C. to New York City as Flash charges.
   III. Cherokee Bus Corporation has a lower fare from New York City to Boston than that of Flash.

   (A) I only
   (B) II only
   (C) I and II only
   (D) I, II, and III
   (E) None of the statements is inconsistent

Questions 2 and 3

Roberts is accused of a crime, and Edwards is the prosecution's key witness.

I. Roberts can be convicted on the basis of Edwards' testimony against him.
II. Edwards' testimony would show that Edwards himself participated in Roberts' wrongdoing.
III. The crime of which Robert is accused can only be committed by a person acting alone.
IV. If the jury learns that Edwards himself committed some wrong, they will refuse to believe any part of his testimony.

2. If propositions I, II, and III are assumed to be true and IV false, which of the following best describes the outcome of the trial?
   (A) Both Edwards and Roberts will be convicted of the crime of which Roberts is accused.
   (B) Both Edwards and Roberts will be convicted of some crime other than the one with which Roberts is already charged.
   (C) Roberts will be convicted while Edwards will not be convicted.
   (D) Roberts will not be convicted.
   (E) Roberts will testify against Edwards.

3. If all four propositions are taken as a group, it can be pointed out that the scenario they describe is
   (A) a typical situation for a prosecutor
   (B) impossible because the propositions are logically inconsistent
   (C) unfair to Edwards, who may have to incriminate himself
   (D) unfair to Roberts, who may be convicted of the crime

(E) one which Roberts' attorney has created

Questions 4 and 5

There is a curious, though nonetheless obvious, contradiction in the suggestion that one person ought to give up his life to save the life of one other person who is not a more valuable member of the community. It is true that we glorify the sacrifice of the individual who throws herself in front of the attacker's bullets saving the life of her lover at the cost of her own. But here is the____(4)____: Her life is as important as his. Nothing is gained in the transaction; not from the community's viewpoint, for one life was exchanged for another equally as important; not from the heroine's viewpoint, for she is ____(5)____; and not from the rescued lover's perspective, for he would willingly have exchanged places.

4. (A) beauty of human love
   (B) tragedy of life
   (C) inevitability of death
   (D) defining characteristic of human existence
   (E) paradox of self-sacrifice

5. (A) dying
   (B) in love
   (C) dead
   (D) a heroine
   (E) a faithful companion

6. It is a well-documented fact that for all teenaged couples who marry, the marriages of those who do not have children in the first year of their marriage survive more than twice as long as the marriages of those teenaged couples in which the wife does give birth within the first twelve months of marriage. Therefore, many divorces could be avoided if teenagers who marry were encouraged not to have children during the first year.

   The evidence regarding teenage marriages supports the author's conclusion only if
   (A) in those couples to which a child was born within the first twelve months, there is not a significant number in which the wife was pregnant at the time of marriage
   (B) the children born during the first year of marriage to those divorcing couples lived with the teenaged couple
   (C) the child born into such a marriage did not die at birth
   (D) society actually has an interest in determining whether or not people should get divorced if there are not children involved
   (E) encouraging people to stay married when they do not plan to have any children is a good idea

7. CLARENCE: Mary is one of the most important executives at the Trendy Cola Company.

   PETER: How can that be? I know for a fact that Mary drinks only Hobart Cola.

   Peter's statement implies that he believes that
   (A) Hobart Cola is a subsidiary of Trendy Cola
   (B) Mary is an unimportant employee of Hobart Cola
   (C) all cola drinks taste pretty much alike
   (D) an executive uses only that company's products
   (E) Hobart is a better tasting cola than Trendy

8. ERIKA: Participation in intramural competitive sports teaches students the importance of teamwork, for no one wants to let his teammates down.

   NICHOL: That is not correct. The real reason students play hard is that such programs place a premium on winning and no one wants to be a member of a losing team.

   Which of the following comments can most reasonably be made about the exchange between Erika and Nichol?
   (A) If fewer and fewer schools are sponsoring intramural sports programs now than a decade ago, Erika's position is undermined.
   (B) If high schools and universities provide financial assistance for the purchase of sports equipment, Nichol's assertion

about the importance of winning is weakened.

(C) If teamwork is essential to success in intramural competitive sports, Erika's position and Nichol's position are not necessarily incompatible.

(D) Since the argument is one about motivation, it should be possible to resolve the issue by taking a survey of deans at schools which have intramural sports programs.

(E) Since the question raised is about hidden psychological states, it is impossible to answer it.

9. Clark must have known that his sister Janet and not the governess pulled the trigger, but he silently stood by while the jury convicted the governess. Any person of clear conscience would have felt terrible for not having come forward with the information about his sister, and Clark lived with that information until his death thirty years later. Since he was an extremely happy man, however, I conclude that he must have helped Janet commit the crime.

Which of the following assumptions must underlie the author's conclusion of the last sentence?

(A) Loyalty to members of one's family is conducive to contentment.

(B) Servants are not to be treated with the same respect as members of the peerage.

(C) Clark never had a bad conscience over his silence because he was also guilty of the crime.

(D) It is better to be a virtuous man than a happy one.

(E) It is actually better to be content in life than to behave morally towards one's fellow humans.

10. Current motion pictures give children a distorted view of the world. Animated features depict animals as loyal friends, compassionate creatures, and tender souls, while "spaghetti Westerns" portray men and women as deceitful and treacherous, cruel and wanton, hard and uncaring. Thus, children are taught to value animals more highly than other human beings.

Which of the following, if true, would weaken the author's conclusion?

I. Children are not allowed to watch "spaghetti Westerns."

II. The producers of animated features do not want children to regard animals as higher than human beings.

III. Ancient fables, such as *Androcles and the Lion*, tell stories of the cooperation between humans and animals, and they usually end with a moral about human virtue.

(A) I only

(B) II only

(C) I and II only

(D) III only

(E) I, II, and III

11. There is something irrational about our system of laws. The criminal law punishes a person more severely for having successfully committed a crime than it does a person who fails in his attempt to commit the same crime—even though the same evil intention is present in both cases. But under the civil law a person who attempts to defraud his victim but is unsuccessful is not required to pay damages.

Which of the following, if true, would most weaken the author's argument?

(A) Most persons who are imprisoned for crimes will commit another crime if they are ever released from prison.

(B) A person is morally culpable for his evil thoughts as well as for his evil deeds.

(C) There are more criminal laws on the books than there are civil laws on the books.

(D) A criminal trial is considerably more costly to the state than a civil trial.

(E) The goal of the criminal law is to punish the criminal, but the goal of the civil law is to compensate the victim.

12. In his most recent speech, my opponent Governor Smith accused me of having distorted the facts, misrepresenting his own position, suppressing information, and deliberately lying to the people.

Which of the following possible responses by this speaker would be LEAST relevant to his dispute with Governor Smith?

(A) Governor Smith would not have begun to smear me if he did not sense that his own campaign was in serious trouble.
(B) Governor Smith apparently misunderstood my characterization of his position, so I will attempt to state more clearly my understanding of it.
(C) At the time I made those remarks, certain key facts were not available, but new information uncovered by my staff does support the position I took at that time.
(D) I can only wish Governor Smith had specified those points he considered to be lies so that I could have responded to them now.
(E) With regard to the allegedly distorted facts, the source of my information is a Department of Transportation publication entitled "Safe Driving."

13. Politicians are primarily concerned with their own survival; artists are concerned with revealing truth. Of course, the difference in their reactions is readily predictable. For example, while the governmental leaders wrote laws to ensure the triumph of industrialization in Western Europe, artists painted, wrote about, and composed music in response to the horrible conditions created by the Industrial Revolution. Only later did political leaders come to see what the artists had immediately perceived, and then only through a glass darkly. Experience teaches us that ___________.

Which of the following represents the most logical continuation of the passage?

(A) artistic vision perceives in advance of political practice
(B) artists are utopian by nature while governmental leaders are practical
(C) throughout history political leaders have not been very responsive to the needs of their people
(D) the world would be a much better place to live if only artists would become kings
(E) history is the best judge of the progress of civilization

14. A parent must be constant and even-handed in the imposition of burdens and punishments and the distribution of liberties and rewards. In good times, a parent who too quickly bestows rewards creates an expectation of future rewards which he may be unable to fulfill during bad times. In bad times, a parent who waits too long to impose the punishment gives the impression that his response was forced, and the child is likely to interpret this as ___________.

Which of the following represents the most logical continuation of the passage?

(A) a signal from his parent that the parent is no longer interested in the child's welfare
(B) a sign of weakness in the parent
(C) indicating a willingness on the part of the parent to bargain away liberties in exchange for the child's assuming some new responsibilities
(D) an open invitation to retaliate
(E) a symbol of his becoming an adult

15. As dietician for this 300-person school I am concerned about the sudden shortage of beef. It seems that we will have to begin to serve fish as our main source of protein. Even though beef costs more per pound than fish, I expect that the price I pay for protein will rise if I continue to serve the same amount of protein using fish as I did with beef.

The speaker makes which of the following assumptions?

(A) Fish is more expensive per pound than beef.
(B) Students will soon be paying more for their meals.
(C) Cattle ranchers make greater profits than fishermen.
(D) Per measure of protein, fish is more expensive than beef.
(E) Cattle are more costly to raise than fish.

Questions 16 and 17

New Weight Loss Salons invites all of you who are dissatisfied with your present build to join our Exercise for Lunch Bunch. Instead of putting on even more weight by eating lunch, you actually cut down on your daily caloric intake by exercising rather than eating. Every single one of us has the potential to be thin, so take the initiative and begin losing excess pounds today. Don't eat! Exercise! You'll lose weight and be healthier, happier, and more attractive.

16. Which of the following, if true, would weaken the logic of the argument made by the advertisement?
    I. Most people will experience increased desire for food as a result of the exercise and will lose little weight as a result of enrolling in the program.
    II. Nutritionists agree that skipping lunch is not a healthy practice.
    III. In our society, obesity is regarded as unattractive.
    IV. A person who is too thin is probably not in good health.

    (A) I only
    (B) I and II only
    (C) II and III only
    (D) III and IV only
    (E) I, II, and III

17. A person hearing this advertisement countered "I know some people who are not overweight and are still unhappy and unattractive." The author of the advertisement could logically and consistently reply to this objection by pointing out that he never claimed that
    (A) being overweight is always caused by unhappiness
    (B) being overweight is the only cause of unhappiness and unattractiveness
    (C) unhappiness and unattractiveness can cause someone to be overweight
    (D) unhappiness necessarily leads to being overweight
    (E) unhappiness and unattractiveness are always found together

18. Since all swans which I have encountered have been white, it follows that the swans I will see when I visit the Bronx Zoo will also be white.

    Which of the following most closely parallels the reasoning of the preceding argument?
    (A) Some birds are incapable of flight, therefore, swans are probably incapable of flight.
    (B) Every ballet I have attended has failed to interest me; so a theatrical production which fails to interest me must be a ballet.
    (C) Since all cases of severe depression I have encountered were susceptible to treatment by chloropromazine, there must be something in the chloropromazine which adjusts the patient's brain chemistry.
    (D) Because every society has a word for *justice,* the concept of fair play must be inherent in the biological makeup of the human species.
    (E) Since no medicine I have tried for my allergy has ever helped, this new product will probably not work either.

Questions 19–21

The blanks in the following paragraph mark deletions from the text. For each question, select the phrase which most appropriately completes the text.

Libertarians argue that laws making suicide a criminal act are both foolish and an unwarranted intrusion on individual conscience. With regard to the first, they point out that there is no penalty which the law can assess which inflicts greater injury than the crime itself. As for the second, they argue that it is no business of the state to prevent suicide, for whether it is right for a person to inflict fatal injury on himself as opposed to others is a matter between him and his God—one in which the state, by the terms of the Constitution, may not interfere. Such arguments, however, seem to me to be ill-conceived. In the first place, the libertarian makes the mistaken assumption that deterrence is the only goal of the law. I maintain that the laws we have proscribing suicide are ____(19)____.

By making it a crime to take any life—even one's own—we make a public announcement of our shared conviction that each person is unique and valuable. In the second place, while it must be conceded that the doctrine of the separation of church and state is a useful one, it need not be admitted that suicide is a crime___(20)___. And here we need not have recourse to the possibility that a potential suicide might, if given the opportunity, repent of his decision. Suicide inflicts a cost upon us all: the emotional cost on those close to the suicide; an economic cost in the form of the loss of production of a mature and trained member of the society which falls on us all; and a cost to humanity at large for the loss of a member of our human community. The difficulty with the libertarian position is that it is an oversimplification. It assesses the evil of ___(21)___.

19. (A) drafted to make it more difficult to commit suicide
(B) passed by legislators in response to pressures by religious lobbying groups
(C) written in an effort to protect our democratic liberties, not undermine them
(D) important because they educate all to the value of human life
(E) outdated because they belong to a time when church and state were not so clearly divided

20. (A) which does not necessarily lead to more serious crimes
(B) without victim
(C) as well as a sin
(D) which cannot be prevented
(E) without motive

21. (A) crimes only in economic terms
(B) suicide only from the perspective of the person taking his life
(C) laws by weighing them against the evil of the liberty lost by their enforcement
(D) the mingling of church and state without sufficient regard to the constitutional protections
(E) suicide in monetary units without proper regard to the importance of life

22. All high-powered racing engines have stochastic fuel injection. Stochastic fuel injection is not a feature which is normally included in the engines of production-line vehicles. Passenger sedans are production-line vehicles.

Which of the following conclusions can be drawn from these statements?
(A) Passenger sedans do not usually have stochastic fuel injection.
(B) Stochastic fuel injection is found only in high-powered racing cars.
(C) Car manufacturers do not include stochastic fuel injection in passenger cars because they fear accidents.
(D) Purchasers of passenger cars do not normally purchase stochastic fuel injection because it is expensive.
(E) Some passenger sedans are high-powered racing vehicles.

23. During New York City's fiscal crisis of the late 1970's, governmental leaders debated whether to offer federal assistance to New York City. One economist who opposed the suggestion asked, "Are we supposed to help out New York City every time it gets into financial problems?"

The economist's question can be criticized because it
(A) uses ambiguous terms
(B) assumes everyone else agrees New York City should be helped
(C) appeals to emotions rather than using logic
(D) relies upon second-hand reports rather than first-hand accounts
(E) completely ignores the issue at hand

24. Judging by the content and the source of the following statements, which is the most trustworthy?
(A) A journeyman plumber and his apprentice: "We have examined the water main at 34th and Broadway, and it looks like the T-valve rusted shut due to lack of maintenance."
(B) Chairman of the Physics Department: "The principal cause of divorce today is the fact that the family is no longer economically or sociologically viable."
(C) Witness under oath: "I stand by my original statement, Congressman. I took the money only because I planned to trap the gangsters and turn them over to the F. B. I."

(D) Ph.D. student in mathematics: "Using calculus and deviant, non-Euclidian geometries, I can prove that God created Earth and man exactly 53 years ago."
(E) University administrator: "Our university has never discriminated in admitting students, regardless of race, color, or creed, during our entire 175-year history."

Questions 25 and 26

Statistics are a blessing to mankind. They allow us to prove all manner of things which might otherwise be disregarded by sound common sense. For example, in the past two hundred and twenty-five years, the Mississippi River has shortened by nearly two hundred miles. That is very nearly a mile a year. Extrapolating from this data, it is easy to see that during the most recent ice age, the Mississippi was nearly one million miles long and stuck out over the Gulf of Mexico like a radio antenna. And furthermore, one thousand years from now, the river will be less than one mile long, and New Orleans and Tokyo will be joined by several toll bridges; and their joint city council will be worrying about the problems of mass transit.

25. The logic of the above argument is most similar to which of the following?
(A) The average life expectancy of people in the United States has increased from 65 years to 70 years during the past two decades; therefore, our children can expect to live longer than our grandparents.
(B) The federal budget has increased 50% in the last ten years; therefore, given the increase in population and the growing demand for services it will probably increase as much again in the next ten years.
(C) Susan grew from four feet-six inches tall on her twelfth birthday to five feet three inches tall on her sixteenth birthday. At this rate, we can expect her to be six feet nine inches tall on her twenty-fourth birthday.
(D) The number of books published annually increased by 25% from 1975 to 1980, and it will probably increase by the same percentage from 1980 to 1985.
(E) Infant mortality in this country dropped by ⅓ during the decade of the 1970's, primarily as a result of increased awareness of the health hazards of pregnancy; since most people are now aware of these hazards, we cannot expect a similar drop during the 1980's.

26. The author's main purpose is to
(A) encourage people to study statistics
(B) suggest new lines of study
(C) ridicule the use of stastistics
(D) question the evidence of geological studies
(E) compare Tokyo and New Orleans

STOP

IF YOU FINISH BEFORE TIME IS CALLED, CHECK YOUR WORK ON THIS SECTION ONLY. DO NOT WORK ON ANY OTHER SECTION IN THE TEST.

SECTION II

Time—35 Minutes
35 Questions

Directions: Each of the following sets consists of a fact situation, a dispute and two rules. The rules may conflict, but you are to apply each rule independently. Do not treat a rule as subsidiary or as an exception to the other rule. The rules are followed by questions. You are to select from the following lettered choices (A) through (D) the one that best describes each question in the way it relates to the application of one or both of the rules to the dispute. Blacken the corresponding space on the answer sheet.

(A) a relevant question the answer to which requires a choice between the two rules
(B) a relevant question the answer to which does not require a choice between the two rules, but does require further facts or rules
(C) a relevant question that can be readily answered from the facts or rules or both
(D) an irrelevant question, the answer to which does not affect, or only tangentially affects, the outcome of the dispute

Set 1

FACTS: In 1970, Jerome was walking along a public beach in the town of East Harwood and found a tin box containing $10,000 which had been washed up on the shore. Jerome took the box and told no one about it except his aunt, Pauline. In 1972, Jerome told a business associate, Kinch, that he had several thousand dollars to invest and was looking for some business venture. Kinch told Jerome that he knew of something and Jerome gave Kinch the $10,000 he had found. Kinch had planned to invest the money in Sedco, an electronics firm, but Sedco went bankrupt. Instead, Kinch decided to gamble with the money. Kinch planned to return the first $20,000 in winnings to Jerome, keeping anything over that amount for himself. Kinch lost the entire $10,000. He told Jerome about his loss in early 1973. Jerome was angry but told Kinch that he, Jerome, would say nothing about it, provided that Kinch would pay him back at $1,000 a year. Kinch promised he would, and for the first six years Kinch payed Jerome the money. Then, Kinch stopped paying, and he and Jerome argued. Jerome went to the police with his story.

DISPUTE: Kinch contests the charge of embezzlement.

RULES: I. One who has lawfully acquired property owned by another person and who then misappropriates the property for his own use is guilty of embezzlement.

II. A criminal action which is commenced five years after the alleged wrong was committed is barred by the statute of limitations, and is therefore void.

1. Did Kinch misappropriate Jerome's money?

2. Has the statute of limitations run out?

3. Did Jerome lawfully acquire the $10,000 in the first place?

4. When did Jerome learn what Kinch had done with the money?

5. Can Kinch be convicted of embezzlement for his use of the $10,000 Jerome gave him?

6. Can the judge require Kinch to finish repaying Jerome the remainder of the $10,000?

Set 2

FACTS: Ralph owned and operated a pawn shop at which he also bought and sold gold, precious stones, old coins, stamps, and similar items. On several occasions he purchased items from Dorothy which he suspected were stolen, but he never inquired where Dorothy had obtained them. Ralph once told a buyer in response to a question regarding the origin of some article, "I don't know, and I don't want to know." Dorothy was, in fact, working with a gang of thieves, and all of the articles Ralph had purchased from her had been stolen. One day Dorothy brought in several stamps and offered to sell them to Ralph. Ralph recognized the stamps as a part of a collection belonging to Briggs. When he questioned Dorothy as to how she had acquired the stamps, Dorothy said, "My brother gave them to me." Ralph knew Dorothy did not have a brother, but he did not pursue the matter. Ralph paid Dorothy $100 for five stamps. Several days later, an undercover detective came into Ralph's store and hinted that he was interested in purchasing some valuable stamps. Ralph showed the detective the five stamps he had purchased from Dorothy and quoted a price of $1,000. The detective then revealed his identity and informed Ralph that the stamps had been stolen ten days earlier from Briggs' collection.

DISPUTE: Ralph was arrested and charged with the crime of receiving stolen property, but pleaded not guilty at his arraignment.

RULES: I. To constitute the crime of receiving stolen goods, the property must have been stolen and must retain that character when the receiver acquires it, and the receiver must have known for a fact that the property was stolen at the time he took the goods.

II. In order to be found guilty of receiving stolen goods, the receiver need not have had specific knowledge that the goods were stolen, provided that there was constructive knowledge that they were stolen, that is, that the receiver had information sufficient to make a reasonable person suspicious about the origin of the goods.

7. Is Ralph guilty of receiving stolen property?

8. Did Ralph specifically know that the stamps had been stolen?

9. Did Dorothy personally steal the stamps?

10. Did Ralph have constructive knowledge that the stamps were stolen?

11. Were the stamps stolen goods?

12. What was the actual value of the stamps?

Set 3

FACTS: Dawson, an out-of-work musician, approached Martha and John Williams, owners of a home in a suburban neighborhood, and told them that a tree growing next to their house was dead and that it should be removed before it blew down on the house during a storm. Dawson told the Williamses that he would do the job for $250. The Williamses knew the tree should go, but they had delayed having it removed because a tree surgeon had quoted them a price of $750 for the job. Martha expressed some concern about Dawson's ability to handle the job, but Dawson reassured Martha that, despite his inexperience, he thought he could handle the job, and also that he was "insured and bonded." In fact, Dawson was not insured and bonded; and when Martha asked Dawson for the name of his insurance company, Dawson gave them the name of a company he had seen in a magazine. John tried to call the company, but the lines were busy. Although the Williamses still had some misgivings, they agreed to Dawson's terms. Three days later, on Saturday, Dawson came back to the Williams' home and proceeded to cut down the tree. Dawson misjudged the height of the tree and allowed it to fall on the Williams' house, causing extensive damage.

DISPUTE: The Williamses sued Dawson for the damage done to their home. Dawson contested.

RULES: I. If a person knowingly and intentionally deceives another person by making a false representation of fact and that other person relies on the misrepresentation, the first person is liable for damages to the second person.

II. A person may not recover damages for false representation if he could have ascertained the true state of affairs by taking reasonable precautions, and thereby have averted the injury.

13. Did the Williamses fail to take a reasonable precaution which might have protected them from Dawson's misrepresentation?

14. If a house belonging to a neighbor had been damaged when Dawson cut down the tree, could the neighbor have recovered damages from Dawson?

15. How far away from the house was the tree located?

16. Can the Williamses recover from Dawson for the damage done to their house when it was struck by the tree?

17. If Dawson had been "insured and bonded," could the Williamses recover from Dawson for misrepresentation?

18. Assuming that the Williamses had refused to pay Dawson anything for his work, if the Williamses won their suit against Dawson, would Dawson be entitled to deduct the fee for his services from what he must pay the Williamses?

Set 4

FACTS: Julio was driving to work one morning when he saw his neighbor, Rivera, walking toward a bus stop. Julio stopped and offered Rivera a ride. Rivera got into the car and offered to give Julio the bus token she had planned to use in exchange for the ride. Julio laughed and said, "No need. This ride's on me." Julio and Rivera then began an animated conversation. Several minutes later, Julio prepared to enter the expressway which would take Rivera and him to their destinations. As he entered the acceleration lane, he noticed another vehicle approaching in the right lane. Julio said to Rivera "This baby's got all the acceleration I need," and gave the car full power. Julio had misjudged the speed of the oncoming vehicle, and the two cars collided. The impact forced Julio's car across the shoulder of the highway and onto the grass adjoining the roadway, where it finally came to rest against a fence. Rivera suffered a broken arm, and cuts and bruises.

DISPUTE: Rivera sued Julio for her injuries. Julio contested.

RULES: I. A person who negligently operates an automobile is liable for all injuries which result from his negligence.

II. An automobile driver is not liable to a guest passenger who is transported gratuitously except for his gross negligence, the failure to use even slight care.

19. How fast was the other vehicle travelling when it collided with Julio's car?

20. Was Julio guilty of gross negligence in the operation of his vehicle?

21. Is Rivera entitled to recover from Julio for the injuries she sustained in the accident?

22. Was Rivera a gratuitous guest in Julio's car at the time of the accident?

Set 5

FACTS: Livingston, Cane County police officer, was working out of uniform at a part-time job, directing traffic at a raceway in a neighboring county. Livingston saw a car pull into the raceway's parking lot that matched the description of a hit-and-run vehicle for which the police had been searching. As Livingston approached the car for a closer look, his police identification in hand, the driver jumped from the passenger side of the car and fled. Livingston chased the driver, and when he caught him, he said, "You are under arrest for hit-and-run driving." Then, before Livingston had a chance to say another word, the driver of the car, Darby, blurted out, "I didn't mean to do it. I didn't even know I had hit the old lady until I got home." Livingston then informed Darby that he had the right to remain silent and the right to counsel, and took Darby to the police station for booking.

DISPUTE: Darby was charged with the crime of hit-and-run driving. At the trial the prosecutor called Livingston to recount what Darby had said at the time of his arrest. Darby's attorney objected, arguing that Darby had not been advised of his legal rights and that the statement, which the prosecution needed to obtain a conviction, was not admissible as evidence.

RULES: I. A person who has been taken into custody by police authorities may not be interrogated by police until they inform him of his right to remain silent and his right to an attorney, and any statement obtained in an official interrogation in violation of this rule may not be used as evidence against him.

II. An utterance which is voluntarily and spontaneously made by a person under arrest before authorities have an opportunity to advise him of his legal rights is not received in violation of the defendant's rights and may be used as evidence against him.

23. Can Darby be convicted of hit-and-run driving?

24. Is Darby's confession to Livingston admissible as evidence against him in the trial?

25. Was Livingston acting in the capacity of a police authority at the time he arrested Darby?

26. Was anything Darby might have said after Livingston advised him of his rights admissible as evidence against Darby?

Set 6

FACTS: Bert, a world-famous adventurer, announced that he was organizing a dive to search for the *S.S. Harcourt,* a luxury liner lost in deep ocean waters, which was believed to have been carrying several million dollars in gold bullion at the time it sank. Three other attempts to locate the ship had failed, and on the third attempt a diving team of six people was lost in the deep waters. Sweet, an experienced diver with his own boat and equipment, learned of Bert's plan and contacted Bert. Bert and Sweet agreed that they would be partners in the venture. Sweet would provide his equipment and expertise, and Bert would finance the venture, paying personnel and purchasing special equipment which Sweet recommended they use. They agreed to a fifty-fifty split of anything they might recover after expenses. Bert and Sweet both agreed that they would have a better chance of succeeding if they waited until the summer months, so they agreed to wait three months before beginning final preparations. In April, Sweet told Bert he thought they should begin to ready the expedition, but Bert told Sweet in response that he had changed his mind about the idea and was going to drop it. Despite Sweet's insistence that he and Bert had an agreement, Bert remained adamant.

DISPUTE: Later, Sweet sued Bert for $3 million, half of what he had hoped the expedition would recover from the *Harcourt.* Bert objected.

RULES: I. When one party to a contract fails to carry out his part of the bargain, the injured party is entitled to damages which are equal in amount to the net gain he anticipated he would realize had there been no breach.

II. Where the damages resulting from a breach of contract are uncertain and highly speculative, the court will award only nominal damages of $1.00.

27. What would have been the cost of actually conducting the search for the *Harcourt?*

28. What is the measure of damages Sweet is entitled to receive?

29. Was the recovery of gold from the *Harcourt* a speculative matter?

30. Why did Bert decide not to go ahead with the expedition?

Set 7

FACTS: Simpson brought his expensive sports car into Warren's garage for a tune-up. Warren told Simpson the job would take two days and then took Simpson's name and address down on a form and gave Simpson a copy of the form with the notation "Tune-up. Ready Friday. $75." The form also bore the legend "Not responsible for property left after 30 days." Simpson left the garage and was crossing the street to catch a bus when he was run over by a passing truck. Warren did not actually see the accident, but the noise attracted his attention. He immediately deduced what must have happened and telephoned for an ambulance. The ambulance arrived and the medics ministered to the unconscious Simpson. Warren asked one of the medics before they drove off to the hospital how serious Simpson's injuries were. The medic responded that the injuries were very severe and that he doubted Simpson would recover. The following day Warren read a report of the accident in the newspaper which stated that Simpson had been killed. The report was incorrect. Although Simpson was very seriously injured, he did survive. Warren, thinking however that Simpson had died, decided to sell Simpson's car. Two weeks after Simpson's accident, Warren found a buyer and sold the car for $8,000. Simpson spent three months in the hospital. After he was discharged, he returned to Warren's garage only to find that Warren had sold the car and that Warren refused to give Simpson the money. Simpson reported the incident to the police.

DISPUTE: Warren contests the charge of wrongfully taking Simpson's property.

RULES: I. The crime of larceny consists of an unauthorized taking of possession of property belonging to another with knowledge that it belongs to another, and with intent at the time possession is taken to keep or dispose of the property without ever returning it to the owner.

II. The crime of conversion occurs when a person who is properly in possession of property belonging to another turns that property to his own use by disposing of it in a manner inconsistent with the interests of the true owner.

31. Is Warren guilty of the crime of larceny?

32. If Simpson had actually died, would Warren have been guilty of the crime of larceny?

33. If Warren had kept the car for over 30 days and Simpson had not reclaimed it in that time, would Warren have been guilty of misappropriating Simpson's property?

34. If Simpson had actually died in the accident, who would have been entitled to possession of Simpson's car?

35. Is Simpson liable to Warren for the value of the work Warren did on the car?

STOP

IF YOU FINISH BEFORE TIME IS CALLED, CHECK YOUR WORK ON THIS SECTION ONLY. DO NOT WORK ON ANY OTHER SECTION IN THE TEST.

SECTION III

Time—35 Minutes
25 Questions

Directions: Each group of questions is based on a set of propositions or conditions. Drawing a rough picture or diagram may help in answering some of the questions. Choose the best answer for each question and blacken the corresponding space on your answer sheet.

Questions 1–5

I. There are five pieces of lost luggage lined up in a row by themselves for customs inspection; the items weigh variously five, ten, fifteen, twenty, and twenty-five pounds. The items to be identified are a trunk, a box, a crate, a suitcase, and a hatbox; and the nationalities of the owners are American, Belgian, German, Swedish, and Turkish, not necessarily in that order.
II. The fifth item weighs ten pounds.
III. The Swedish traveller's luggage has luggage on both sides of it.
IV. The Turkish traveller owns the item weighing fifteen pounds.
V. The traveller who owns the five-pound second item has lost a box.
VI. The American owns the item in the middle, which weighs 20 pounds.
VII. The German does not own the hatbox, which weighs less than all but one of the other items.
VIII. The item on the left is the heaviest and is a trunk.

1. Which of the following can be derived from statements I, III, and VI?
   (A) The Swede owns the first or second item.
   (B) The Swede owns the first or fourth item.
   (C) The Swede owns the second or fourth item.
   (D) The Swede owns the third or fourth item.
   (E) The Swede owns a ten-pound box.

2. What does the German own?
   (A) a 25-pound trunk
   (B) a 25-pound box
   (C) a 25-pound crate
   (D) a 10-pound hatbox
   (E) a 5-pound hatbox

3. Which of the following statements is false?
   (A) The Turk's missing luggage is heavier than the Belgian's.
   (B) The five-pound item plus the American's item weigh the same as the German's item.
   (C) The Turk's missing luggage weighs more than the Swede's.
   (D) The American's missing luggage weighs more than the German's.
   (E) The crate is not next to the twenty-five-pound item.

4. Which of the following is true?
   (A) The first item is owned by the Swede.
   (B) The ten-pound item is owned by the Belgian.
   (C) The suitcase is owned by the Turk.
   (D) The crate is owned by the American.
   (E) The box is owned by the German.

5. Which of the following additional pieces of information would, if true, allow the determination of the types of luggage which weigh 15 and 20 pounds?

   I. The crate weighs more than the suitcase.
   II. The crate is twice as heavy as the hatbox.
   III. The combined weight of the box and hatbox equals the weight of the suitcase.

   (A) I only
   (B) I and II only
   (C) I and III only
   (D) II and III only
   (E) I, II, and III

Questions 6–10

A construction company is building a pre-fabricated structure which requires specialized crane operators for five different parts of the job. Six operators are available: R, S, T, U, V, and W, and each phase will take one day and will be done by a single operator. Though an operator may do more than one phase of the job, no operator will work two days in a row.

Both R and S can handle any phase of the job.
T can work only on days immediately following days on which S has worked.
U can work only on the days that T can.
V can work only on the third and fifth days of the job.
W can work only on the fourth day of the job.

6. Which of the following are true?
   I. R could do up to three of the phases of the job.
   II. S could do up to three of the phases of the job.
   III. T could do up to two of the phases of the job.

   (A) I only
   (B) II only
   (C) III only
   (D) II and III only
   (E) I, II, and III

7. If S works the first day of the job, which of the following is (are) true?
   I. Only T or U can work the second day.
   II. T, U, or R could work the second day.
   III. R, S, or W could work the third day.

   (A) I only
   (B) II only
   (C) III only
   (D) I and III only
   (E) I, II, and III

8. If R works the first day, which of the following are true?
   I. S must work the second day.
   II. S cannot work the third day.
   III. Only T, U, or V can work on the third day.

   (A) I only
   (B) II only
   (C) I and II only
   (D) I and III only
   (E) I, II, and III

9. If R works on both the first and third days, then which of the following most accurately describes the possibilities on the fourth day?
   (A) Only S is eligible to work.
   (B) Only R, S, T, or W are eligible to work.
   (C) Only S or W are eligible to work.
   (D) Only R, S, or W are eligible to work.
   (E) Only S, T, U, or W are eligible to work.

10. R, S, and V do not work on the third day; therefore,
   (A) R worked on the first day.
   (B) Only S can work on the fourth day.
   (C) Only R can work on the fourth day.
   (D) Only W can work on the fourth day.
   (E) Either T or U worked the second day.

Questions 11–15

The parties to an important labor negotiation are two representatives of management, Morrison and Nelson; two representatives of labor, Richards and Smith; and the Federal Meditator, Jones. They are meeting at a round table with eight seats, and the order of seating has become a significant psychological part of the negotiations.

I. The two representatives of management always sit next to each other.
II. The two representatives of labor always sit with one seat between them.
III. Both sides like to make sure that they are as close to the mediator as the other side is, and no closer to the opposing side than necessary.
IV. The mediator prefers to have at least one seat between himself and any of the other negotiators.

11. If conditions I, II, and IV are met, which of the following is necessarily true?
   (A) Jones sits next to one of the management representatives.
   (B) Morrison sits next to one of the labor representatives.
   (C) One of the labor representatives will sit next to either Morrison or Nelson.

(D) Either Richards or Smith sits next to Jones.
(E) None of the above are necessarily true.

12. If conditions I, II, and III are met, which of the following is NOT a possible seating arrangement of the negotiators, starting with Jones and going clockwise around the table?
(A) Jones, Morrison, Nelson, empty, empty, Richards, empty, Smith
(B) Jones, Nelson, Morrison, empty, empty, Smith, empty, Richards
(C) Jones, Richards, empty, Smith, empty, empty, Nelson, Morrison
(D) Jones, Smith, Richards, empty, empty, empty, Morrison, Nelson
(E) All of the above are possible seating arrangements.

13. The Secretary of Labor joins the negotiations and sits across the table from the mediator. If all of the conditions are still met as much as possible, which of the following is true?

I. A labor representative will sit next to the secretary.
II. A management representative will sit next to the secretary.
III. Both a labor representative and one from management will sit next to the mediator.

(A) I only
(B) II only
(C) I and II only
(D) I and III only
(E) I, II, and III

14. If the two sides meet without the mediator and sit so that Morrison is seated directly opposite Smith, which of the following is possible?
(A) Richards and Nelson will both be seated to Morrison's left and to Smith's right.
(B) Richards will be as close to Morrison as he is to Smith.
(C) Nelson will be separated from Richards by one seat.
(D) Nelson will be separated from Smith by three seats.
(E) Nelson and Richards will be seated directly across from each other.

15. If, under the original conditions, Morrison's aide joins the negotiations and sits next to Morrison, which of the following is not possible?
(A) Richards sits directly opposite Morrison.
(B) Richards sits directly opposite Morrison's aide.
(C) Smith sits directly opposite Nelson.
(D) Smith sits directly opposite Morrison's aide.
(E) Morrison's aide sits next to Jones.

Questions 16–20

The coach of the Malibu University swimming team is planning his strategy for the rest of his team's meet with the State University swim team. Each event is scored on the basis of five points to the winner, three points for second place, and one point for third place. The score is currently tied, but the coach thinks his team can win because they have greater depth than the other team. The State University team has only enough good swimmers to just fill out their two entries for each of the last three events with one strong entry and one weak one. The last events are the individual medley, the medley relay, and the freestyle relay. Each relay team has four members. The coach considers these facts:

State's top individual medley racer is sure to win, but their second entry can only manage a time of four minutes even.

16. What is the minimum number of points that Malibu has to score in the last three races in order to win the meet?
(A) 14
(B) 13
(C) 12
(D) 11
(E) 10

17. If State's swimmers take first and third in the individual medley race, which of the following results for the last two races would still let Malibu win?
(A) first place only in both races

(B) first place in one race and second and third in the other
(C) second and third in both races
(D) first in one race and at least first and third in the other
(E) there is no way for Malibu to win the meet

18. Malibu swimmer George can only swim in one more race. He and Jim are the only Malibu swimmers who can beat four minutes in the individual medley. Under which of the following conditions would it be advantageous for George NOT to swim in the individual medley race?
(A) if adding George will move the medley relay team from fourth to third
(B) if adding George to the freestyle relay team will move it from third to second
(C) if adding George to one medley relay team allows shifting of swimmers so that they finish first and fourth instead of second and third
(D) if adding George to the medley team allows shifting swimmers so that the results are a first and third in one race and a second and third in the other, rather than just two firsts
(E) there are no conditions under which it is advantageous to hold George out of the individual medley race

19. If Malibu places second and third in the individual medley race, at least how many of its entries must score points in order to guarantee that Malibu will win the meet?
(A) 2
(B) 3
(C) 4
(D) 5
(E) cannot be determined from the information given

20. State's top individual medley swimmer is disqualified. If Malibu's two swimmers in that race finish in 3 minutes 57 seconds and 3 minutes 58 seconds respectively, which of the following is false?
(A) If State places first and fourth in the other two races, they will still win the meet.
(B) If Malibu places first and third in one relay, they do not even have to swim in the other in order to win the meet.
(C) If three of Malibu's remaining swimmers score points, Malibu could still lose the meet.
(D) If all four of State's relay teams score points, State could still lose the meet.
(E) Even if only three of State's relay teams score points, State could still win the meet.

Questions 21–25

Lois wants to take four courses this semester. There are only seven courses in which she is interested that do not conflict with her job: Three science courses—biology, chemistry, and physics—and four humanities courses—English, French, music, and writing. To meet college requirements she must take two science courses this semester. There are some scheduling problems, however: English overlaps both chemistry and music, which are sequential; biology is given at the same time as French.

21. If Lois decides she will take English, what will her other three courses be?
(A) biology, physics, and chemistry
(B) biology, physics, and writing
(C) biology, physics, and French
(D) physics, chemistry, and writing
(E) physics, writing, and French

22. If the chemistry course is changed to a time which Lois cannot make, and she decides to take music, which of the following would be her schedule?
(A) biology, physics, English, and music
(B) biology, physics, French, and music
(C) biology, physics, writing, and music
(D) physics, English, French, and music
(E) physics, writing, English, and music

23. If Lois takes four courses this semester, she cannot

I. take French and not take chemistry
II. take music and not take chemistry
III. take English and not take physics

(A) I only
(B) II only
(C) III only

(D) I and II only
(E) I and III only

24. Which of the following must always be true?
    I. Lois must take physics if she takes music.
    II. Lois must take chemistry if she takes French.
    III. Lois must take French if she takes chemistry.

(A) I, II, and III
(B) II and III only
(C) I and II only
(D) III only
(E) II only

25. If the physics course is moved to the same time as English, and Lois takes physics, what further problem(s) does she face?
(A) She won't be able to take two science classes.
(B) She won't be able to take biology.
(C) She won't be able to take writing.
(D) She won't be able to take either biology or French.
(E) She won't be able to take four courses which interest her.

STOP

IF YOU FINISH BEFORE TIME IS CALLED, CHECK YOUR WORK ON THIS SECTION ONLY. DO NOT WORK ON ANY OTHER SECTION IN THE TEST.

SECTION IV

Time—35 Minutes
28 Questions

Directions: Below each of the following passages, you will find questions or incomplete statements about the passage. Each statement or question is followed by five lettered words or expressions. Select the word or expression that most satisfactorily completes each statement, or answers each question in accordance with the meaning of the passage. After you have chosen the best answer, blacken the corresponding space on the answer sheet.

It has always been difficult for the philosopher or scientist to fit time into his view of the universe. Prior to Einsteinian physics, there was no truly adequate formulation of the relationship of time to the other forces in the universe, even though some empirical equations included time quantities. However, even the Einsteinian formulation is not perhaps totally adequate to the job of fitting time into the proper relationship with the other dimensions, as they are called, of space. The primary problem arises in relation to things which might be going faster than the speed of light, or have other strange properties.

Examination of the Lorentz-Fitzgerald formulas yields the interesting speculation that if something did actually exceed the speed of light, it would have its mass expressed as an imaginary number and would seem to be going backwards in time. The barrier to exceeding the speed of light is the calculation that only an infinite mass can move at exactly the speed of light. If this situation could be leaped over in a large quantum jump—which seems highly unlikely for masses that are large in normal circumstances—then the other side may be achievable.

The idea of going backwards in time is derived from the existence of a time vector that is negative, although just what this might mean to our senses in the unlikely circumstance of our experiencing this state cannot be conjectured.

There have been, in fact, some observations of particle chambers which have led some scientists to speculate that a particle called the tachyon may exist with the trans-light properties we have just discussed.

The difficulties of imagining and coping with these potential implications of our mathematical models points out the importance of studying alternative methods of notation for advanced physics. Professor Zuckerkandl, in his book *Sound and Symbol,* hypothesizes that it might be better to express the relationships found in quantum mechanics through the use of a notation derived from musical notations. To oversimplify greatly, he argues that music has always given time a special relationship to other factors or parameters or dimensions. Therefore, it might be a more useful language in which to express the relationships in physics where time again has a special role to play, and cannot be treated as just another dimension.

The point of this, or any other alternative to the current methods of describing basic physical processes, is that time does not appear—either by common experience or sophisticated scientific understanding—to be the same sort of dimension or parameter as physical dimensions, and is deserving of completely special treatment, in a system of notation designed to accomplish that goal.

One approach would be to consider time to be a field effect governed by the application of energy to mass; that is to say, by the interaction of different forms of energy, if you wish to keep in mind the equivalence of mass and energy. The movement of any normal sort of mass is bound to produce a field effect that we call positive time. An imaginary mass would produce a negative time field effect. This is not at variance with Einstein's theories, since the "faster" a given mass moves, the more energy was applied to it and the greater would be the field effect. The time effects predicted by Einstein and confirmed by experience are, it seems, consonant with this concept.

1. The "sound" of Professor Zuckerkandl's book title probably refers to
   (A) the music of the spheres
   (B) music in the abstract

(C) musical notation
(D) the seemingly musical sounds produced by tachyons
(E) quantum mechanics

2. The passage supports the inference that
(A) Einstein's theory of relativity is wrong.
(B) The Lorentz-Fitzgerald formulas contradict Einstein's theories.
(C) Time travel is clearly possible.
(D) Tachyons do not have the same sort of mass as any other particles.
(E) It is impossible to travel at precisely the speed of light.

3. The tone of the passage is
(A) critical but hopeful
(B) hopeful but suspicious
(C) suspicious but speculative
(D) speculative but hopeful
(E) impossible to characterize

4. The central idea of the passage can be best described as being which of the following?
(A) Anomalies in theoretical physics notation permit intriguing hypotheses and indicate the need for refined notation of the time dimension.
(B) New observations require the development of new theories and new methods of describing the new theories.
(C) Einsteinian physics can be much improved on in its treatment of tachyons.
(D) Zuckerkandl's theories of tachyon formation are preferable to Einstein's.
(E) Time requires a more imaginative approach than tachyons.

5. According to the author, it is too soon to
(A) call Beethoven a physicist
(B) adopt proposals such as Zuckerkandl's
(C) plan for time travel
(D) study particle chambers for tachyon traces
(E) attempt to improve current notation

6. It can be inferred that the author sees Zuckerkandl as believing that mathematics is a
(A) necessary evil
(B) language
(C) musical notation
(D) great hindrance to full understanding of physics
(E) difficult field of study

7. In the first sentence, the author refers to "philosopher" as well as to "scientist" because
(A) this is part of a larger work
(B) philosophers study all things
(C) physicists get Doctor of Philosophy degrees
(D) the study of the methods of any field is a philosophical question
(E) the nature of time is a basic question in philosophy as well as physics

An action of apparent social significance among animals is that of migration. But several different factors are at work causing such migrations. These may be concerned with food-getting; with temperature, salinity, pressure, and light changes; with the action of sex hormones; and probably combinations of these and other factors.

The great aggregations of small crustaceans found at the surface of the ocean, swarms of insects about a light, or the masses of plankton in the lakes and oceans are all examples of nonsocial aggregations of organisms brought together because of the presence or absence of certain factors in their environment, such as air currents, water currents, food or the lack of it, oxygen, or carbon dioxide, etc.

Insects make long migrations, most of which seem due to the urge for food. The migrations of the locust, both in this country and elsewhere, are well-known. While fish, such as salmon, return to the same stream where they grew up, such return migrations are rare in insects, the only known instance being in the monarch butterfly. This is apparently due to the fact that it is long-lived and has the power of strong flight. The mass migrations of the Rocky Mountain and the African species of locust seem attributable to the need for food. Locusts live, eat, sun themselves, and migrate in groups. It has been suggested that their social life is in response to the two fundamental instincts—aggregation and imitation.

Migrations of fish have been studied carefully by many investigators. Typically, the migrations are from deep to shallow waters, as in the herring, mackerel, and many other marine fish. Freshwater fish, in general, exhibit this type of migration in the spawning season. Spawning habits of many fish show a change in habitat from salt to fresh water. In the North American and European eels, long migrations take place at the breeding season. All these migrations are obviously not brought about by a quest for food; for the salmon and many other fish feed only sparingly during the spawning season, but are undoubtedly brought about by metabolic changes in the animal initiated by the interaction of sex hormones. If this thesis holds, then here is the beginning of social life.

Bird migrations have long been a matter of study. The reasons for the migration of the golden plover from the Arctic regions to the tip of South America and back in a single year are not fully explainable. Several theories have been advanced, although none have been fully proved. The reproductive "instinct," food scarcity, temperature and light changes, the metabolic changes brought about by the activity of the sex hormones, and the length of the day all have been suggested, and ultimately several may prove to be factors. Aside from other findings, it is interesting to note that bird migrations take place year after year on about the same dates. Recent studies in the biochemistry of metabolism, showing that there is a seasonal cycle in the blood sugar that has a definite relation to activity and food, seem to be among the most promising leads.

In mammals, the seasonal migrations that take place, such as those of the deer, which travel from the high mountains in summer to the valleys in winter, or the migration of the caribou in the northern areas of Canada, are based on the factor of temperature, which regulates the food supply.

Another mystery is the migration of the lemming, a small ratlike animal found in Scandinavia and Canada. The lemming population varies greatly from year to year, and at times when it greatly increases a migration occurs in which hordes of lemmings march across the country, swimming rivers, and even plunging into the ocean if it bars their way. This again cannot be purely social association of animals. The horde is usually made up entirely of males, as the females seldom migrate.

8. The reasons for the migrations of birds may ultimately be determined by scientists working in the field of
   (A) population studies
   (B) biology
   (C) metabolism chemistry
   (D) reproduction
   (E) genetics

9. A characteristic of migration is the return of the migrants to their former home areas. This is, however, not typically true of migrating
   (A) birds
   (B) insects
   (C) mammals
   (D) fish
   (E) crustaceans

10. The reproductive instinct is probably not a factor in the actual migration of the
   (A) salmon
   (B) lemming
   (C) golden plover
   (D) monarch butterfly
   (E) deer

11. The main purpose of the passage is to
   (A) show that social factors may be of lesser importance to understanding animal behavior than first appears
   (B) present a new theory in regard to biological evolution
   (C) teach the reader how to evaluate a natural phenomenon
   (D) describe a phenomenon that has not yet been satisfactorily explained
   (E) show how species behave similarly under the same conditions

12. However mysterious, the migration of the lemmings cannot be considered one of social association since
   (A) usually only males migrate
   (B) migrations occur only with population increases
   (C) it is probably due to the absence of some factor in the environment
   (D) the migrants do not return
   (E) migrations occur when there is a food scarcity

13. If the author of the above passage were called on to explain the apparently social behavior of ants or bees in their hills and hives, we may infer that he would probably
   (A) refuse to speculate in any way

(B) compare the hills and hives to human cities
(C) find their behavior mysterious
(D) first seek to find other than purely social explanations
(E) deny that the apparent social behavior could really be social in nature

14. All of the following are posited as reasons for migration *except*
(A) lack of food
(B) hormonal changes
(C) temperature changes
(D) sexual and reproductive instincts
(E) peer pressure

Foods are overwhelmingly the most advertised group of all consumer products in the United States. Food products lead in expenditures for network and spot television advertisements, discount coupons, trading stamps, contests, and other forms of premium advertising. In other media—newspapers, magazines, newspaper supplements, billboards, and radio—food advertising expenditures rank near the top. Food manufacturers spend more on advertising than any other manufacturing group, and the nation's grocery stores rank first among all retailers.

Throughout the 1970's, highly processed foods have accounted for the bulk of total advertising. Almost all coupons, electronic advertising, national printed media advertising, consumer premiums (other than trading stamps) as well as most push promotion come from processed and packaged food products. In 1978, breakfast cereals, soft drinks, candy and other desserts, oils and salad dressings, coffee, and prepared foods accounted for only an estimated 20 percent of the consumer food dollar. Yet these items accounted for about one-half of all media advertising.

By contrast, highly perishable foods such as unprocessed meats, poultry, fish and eggs, fruits and vegetables, and dairy products accounted for over half of the consumer food-at-home dollar. Yet these products accounted for less than 8 percent of national media advertising in 1978, and virtually no discount coupons. These products tend to be most heavily advertised by the retail sector in local newspapers, where they account for an estimated 40 percent of retail grocery newspaper ads.

When measured against total food-at-home expenditures, total measured food advertising accounts for between 3 to 3.7 cents out of every dollar spent on food in the nation's grocery stores. A little less than one cent of this amount is accounted for by electronic advertising (mostly television) while incentives account for 0.6 cents. The printed media accounts for 0.5 cents and about one-third of one cent is comprised of discount coupon redemptions. The estimate for the cost of push promotion ranges from 0.7 to 1.4 cents. This range is necessary because of the difficulty in separating nonpromotional aspects of direct selling—transportation, technical, and other related services.

Against this gross consumer cost must be weighed the joint products or services provided by advertising. In the case of electronic advertising, the consumer who views commercial television receives entertainment, while readers of magazines and newspapers receive reduced prices on these publications. The consumer pays directly for some premiums, but also receives nonfood merchandise as an incentive to purchase the product. The "benefits" must, therefore, be subtracted from the gross cost to the consumer to assess the net cost of advertising fully.

Also significant are the impacts of advertising on food demand, nutrition, and competition among food manufacturers. The bulk of manufacturers' advertising is concentrated on a small portion of consumer food products. Has advertising changed the consumption of these highly processed products relative to more perishable foods such as meats, produce, and dairy products? Has the nutritional content of U.S. food consumption been influenced by food advertising? Has competition among manufacturers and retailers been enhanced or weakened by advertising? These are important questions and warrant continued research.

15. The author's attitude toward advertising can be characterized as
(A) admiring
(B) condemning
(C) uncertain
(D) ambivalent
(E) inquisitive

16. As used in the passage, the term "push promotion" means
(A) coupon redemption

(B) retail advertising
(C) advertising in trade journals
(D) direct selling
(E) none of the above

17. The author implies that advertising costs
(A) are greater for restaurants than for at-home foods
(B) should be discounted by the benefits of advertising to the consumer
(C) are much higher in the United States than anywhere else in the world
(D) for prepared foods are considerably higher than for natural foods for all media
(E) cause highly processed foods to outsell unprocessed, fresh foods

18. The purpose of the article is to
(A) warn about rising food advertising costs
(B) let experts see how overextended food advertising has become
(C) describe the costs of food advertising and the issues yet to be understood about its effects
(D) congratulate the food industry on its effective advertising
(E) calculate the final balance sheet for food advertising

19. All of the following are stated or implied to be important topics for further research EXCEPT
(A) effects of advertising on food and nutrient consumption patterns
(B) effects of advertising on food manufacturer competitive patterns
(C) effects of advertising on meat consumption patterns
(D) effects of advertising on out-of-home eating patterns
(E) effects of advertising on "junk" food consumption patterns

20. According to the passage, all of the following are definitely false EXCEPT
(A) total food advertisements in newspapers cost more than those on television
(B) less money is spent advertising food than automobiles
(C) more of the food advertising budget is spent on push promotion than television ads
(D) less money is spent on food store advertising than on clothing store ads
(E) food advertising is the leading group in radio advertising

21. If it were discovered that the nutritional content of the U.S. food supply were degraded by the advertising of highly processed foods, and such advertising were totally banned, which of the following would be a possible result of the ban that could be inferred from the passage?
(A) The subscription costs of publications might rise.
(B) The cost of cable television might rise.
(C) The cost of free television might rise.
(D) Fewer consumers would watch certain television shows.
(E) No possible effect can be forecast based on the passage.

Educators are seriously concerned about the high rate of dropouts among the doctor of philosophy candidates and the consequent loss of talent to a nation in need of Ph.D.'s. Some have placed the dropout loss as high as 50 percent. The extent of the loss was, however, largely a matter of expert guessing.

Then a well-rounded study was published. It was based on 22,000 questionnaires sent to former graduate students who were enrolled in 24 universities between 1950 and 1954 and seemed to show many past fears to be groundless.

The dropout rate was found to be 31 percent, and in most cases the dropouts, while not completing the Ph.D. requirements, went on to productive work.

They are not only doing well financially, but, according to the report, are not far below the income levels of those who went on to complete their doctorates.

The study, called "Attrition of Graduate Students at the Ph.D. Level in the Traditional Arts and Sciences," was made at Michigan State University under a $60,000 grant from the United States Office of Education. It was conducted by Dr. Allan Tucker.

Discussing the study, Dr. Tucker said the project was initiated "because of the concerns frequently expressed by graduate faculties and administrators that some of the individuals who dropped out of Ph.D. programs were capable of completing the requirements for the degree.

"Attrition at the Ph.D. level is also thought to be a waste of precious faculty time and a drain on university resources already being used to capacity. Some people expressed the opinion that the shortage of highly trained specialists and college teachers could be reduced by persuading the dropouts to return to graduate school to complete the Ph.D. program."

"The results of our research," Dr. Tucker concluded, "did not support these opinions."

The study found that:

(1) Lack of motivation was the principal reason for dropping out.

(2) Most dropouts went as far in their doctoral programs as was consistent with their levels of ability or their specialties.

(3) Most dropouts are now engaged in work consistent with their education and motivation.

(4) The dropout rate was highest in the humanities (50 percent) and lowest in the natural sciences (29 percent)—and was higher in lower-quality graduate schools.

Nearly 75 percent of the dropouts said there was no academic reason for their decision, but those who mentioned academic reasons cited failure to pass qualifying examinations, uncompleted research and failure to pass language exams.

"Among the single most important personal reasons identified by dropouts for noncompletion of their Ph.D. program," the study found "lack of finances was marked by 19 percent."

As an indication of how well the dropouts were doing, a chart showed that 2 percent of those whose studies were in the humanities were receiving $20,000 and more annually while none of the Ph.D.'s with that background reached this figure. The Ph.D.'s did extremely well in the $7,500 to $15,000 bracket with 78 percent at that level against 50 percent for the dropouts. This may also be an indication of the fact that top salaries in the academic fields, where Ph.D.'s tend to rise to the highest salaries, lag behind other fields.

In the social sciences 5 percent of the Ph.D.'s reached the $20,000-plus figure as against 3 percent of the dropouts, but in the physical sciences they were neck-and-neck with 5 percent each.

Academic institutions employed 90 percent of the humanities Ph.D.'s as against 57 percent of the humanities dropouts. Business and industry employed 47 percent of the physical science Ph.D.'s and 38 percent of the physical science dropouts. Government agencies took 16 percent of the social science Ph.D.'s and 32 percent of the social science dropouts.

As to the possibility of getting dropouts back on campus, the outlook was glum.

"The main conditions which would have to prevail for at least 25 percent of the dropouts who might consider returning to graduate school would be to guarantee that they would retain their present level of income and in some cases their present job."

22. After reading the passage it could be suggested that
    (A) the majority of humanities doctoral students received inadequate academic preparation for graduate studies
    (B) the majority of engineering students are less well-read than humanities students in their respective areas
    (C) undergraduate students are poorly motivated
    (D) doctoral candidates in the natural sciences are better prepared for their studies than those in other fields.
    (E) humanities students generally have less money than other students

23. After reading the article, one would refrain from concluding that
    (A) colleges and universities employ a substantial number of Ph.D. dropouts
    (B) Ph.D.'s are not earning what they deserve in nonacademic positions
    (C) the study was conducted efficiently and is probably valid
    (D) many Ph.D. dropouts do not have what it takes to earn the degree
    (E) optimism reigns in regard to getting Ph.D. dropouts to return to their pursuit of the degree

24. The article states that
    (A) not having sufficient funds to continue accounts for more Ph.D. dropouts than all the other reasons combined
    (B) in fields such as English, philosophy, and the arts, the dropouts are doing

better in the highest salary brackets than the Ph.D.'s

(C) at the $10,000 earning level, there is a higher percentage of dropouts than the percentage of Ph.D.'s

(D) in physics, geology, and chemistry, the Ph.D.'s are twice as numerous in the higher salary brackets than the dropouts

(E) the government agencies employ twice as many dropouts as they do Ph.D.'s

25. It would be fair to infer that Dr. Tucker agrees with the statement that

(A) there are students admitted to doctoral programs who should be content not to finish them

(B) a well-motivated student will never have to drop out of a doctoral program

(C) substantial scholarship aid is available to most dropouts who wish to return to school

(D) dropping out of a doctoral program reflects badly on all concerned

(E) the cooperation of their present employers would be needed for most dropouts to return to their doctoral work

26. Research has shown that

(A) all dropouts are substantially below Ph.D.'s in financial attainment

(B) the incentive factor is a minor one in regard to pursuing Ph.D. studies

(C) the Ph.D. candidate is likely to change his field of specialization if he drops out

(D) about one-third of those who start Ph.D. work do not complete the work to earn the degree

(E) there are comparatively few dropouts in the Ph.D. humanities disciplines

27. Dr. Tucker based his distinction between higher and lower quality graduate schools on

(A) degrees and publications of the faculty

(B) estimates made by deans of graduate schools

(C) later attainments of the students

(D) libraries, facilities, and endowment size

(E) a basis not mentioned in the passage

28. What may we infer was Dr. Tucker's reasoning in stating that the dropouts were not wasting precious faculty time and draining away university resources?

(A) The dropouts were self-selected by lack of motivation.

(B) The rate was highest in the poorer schools.

(C) Most dropouts were using their education in their work.

(D) There wasn't enough money for many of the dropouts to continue.

(E) Some dropouts were earning more than most non-dropouts.

STOP

IF YOU FINISH BEFORE TIME IS CALLED, CHECK YOUR WORK ON THIS SECTION ONLY. DO NOT WORK ON ANY OTHER SECTION IN THE TEST.

SECTION V

Time—35 Minutes
26 Questions

Directions: In this section, the questions ask you to analyze and evaluate the reasoning in short paragraphs or passages. For some questions, all of the answer choices may conceivably be answers to the question asked. You should select the *best* answer to the question, that is, an answer which does not require you to make assumptions which violate commonsense standards by being implausible, redundant, irrelevant or inconsistent. After choosing the best answer, blacken the corresponding space on the answer sheet.

1. Children in the first three grades who attend private schools spend time each day working with a computerized reading program. Public schools have very few such programs. Tests prove, however, that public-school children are much weaker in reading skills when compared to their private-school counterparts. We conclude, therefore, that public-school children can be good readers only if they participate in a computerized reading program.

   The author's initial statements logically support his conclusion only if which of the following is also true?
   (A) All children can learn to be good readers if they are taught by a computerized reading program.
   (B) All children can learn to read at the same rate if they participate in a computerized reading program.
   (C) Better reading skills produce better students.
   (D) Computerized reading programs are the critical factor in the better reading skills of private-school students.
   (E) Public-school children can be taught better math skills.

2. Is your company going to continue to discriminate against women in its hiring and promotion policies?

   The above question might be considered unfair for which of the following reasons?

   I. Its construction seeks a "yes" or "no" answer where both might be inappropriate.
   II. It is internally inconsistent.
   III. It contains a hidden presupposition which the responder might wish to contest.

   (A) I only
   (B) II only
   (C) I and II only
   (D) I and III only
   (E) I, II, and III

Questions 3 and 4

Ms. Evangeline Rose argued that money and time invested in acquiring a professional degree are totally wasted. As evidence supporting her argument, she offered the case of a man who, at considerable expense of money and time, completed his law degree and then married and lived as a house-husband, taking care of their children and working part time at a day care center so his wife could pursue her career.

3. Ms. Rose makes the unsupported assumption that
   (A) an education in the law is useful only in pursuing law-related activities
   (B) what was not acceptable twenty-five years ago may very well be acceptable today
   (C) wealth is more important than learning
   (D) professional success is a function of the quality of one's education
   (E) only the study of law can be considered professional study

4. The logical reasoning of Ms. Rose's argument is closely parallelled by which of the following?
   (A) A juvenile delinquent who insists that his behavior should be attributable to the fact that his parents did not love him.

(B) A senator who votes large sums of money for military equipment, but who votes against programs designed to help the poor.
(C) A conscientious objector who bases his draft resistance on the premise that there can be no moral wars.
(D) When a policeman is found guilty of murdering his wife, an opponent of police brutality who says, "That's what these people mean by law and order."
(E) A high school senior who decides that rather than going to college he will enroll in a vocational training program to learn to be an electrician.

5. Most of us are politically apathetic, notwithstanding the fact that every four years we read superficial news analyses of the issues in the national elections. Without such apathy, the corruption which afflicts many local governments would not be possible anywhere at anytime.

Which of the following is the best description of the point up to which the author is leading?
(A) People who are politically apathetic are ultimately responsible for corruption in local government.
(B) When a person is politically apathetic, he belongs to the majority party.
(C) No one can sustain a high level of political involvement for more than four years.
(D) Local government corruption is universal.
(E) People who are politically apathetic are directly involved in corrupting officials of their local governments.

6. The following sentences are a scrambled paragraph.

I. One way to solve gridlock is to reduce the number of vehicles driving on the city's downtown streets.
II. How can the city speed the flow of traffic on its streets?
III. The easiest way to increase significantly the speed at which traffic moves in the city is to solve the problem of gridlock, those crippling traffic jams at major intersections.
IV. Right now, many cars commute into the city via three toll bridges.
V. If the tolls were raised, fewer people would drive into the city.

Which of the following arrangements of these sentences is most logical?

(A) I, III, IV, V, II
(B) III, IV, V, I, II
(C) IV, V, I, II, III
(D) II, III, I, IV, V
(E) II, IV, V, I, III

7. An independent medical research team recently did a survey at a mountain retreat founded to help heavy smokers quit or cut down on their cigarette smoking. Eighty percent of those persons smoking three packs a day or more were able to cut down to one pack a day after they began to take End-Smoke with its patented desire suppressant. Try End-Smoke to help you cut down significantly on your smoking.

Which of the following could be offered as valid criticism of the above advertisement?

I. Heavy smokers may be physically as well as psychologically addicted to tobacco.
II. A medicine which is effective for very heavy smokers may not be effective for the population of smokers generally.
III. A survey conducted at a mountain retreat to aid smokers may yield different results than one would expect under other circumstances.

(A) I only
(B) II only
(C) III only
(D) II and III only
(E) I, II, and III

8. JOCKEY: Horses are the most noble of all animals. They are both loyal and brave. I knew of a farm horse which died of a broken heart shortly after its owner died.

VETERINARIAN: You're wrong. Dogs can be

> just as loyal and brave. I had a dog who would wait every day on the front steps for me to come home, and if I did not arrive until midnight, he would still be there.

All of the following are true of the claims of the jockey and the veterinarian EXCEPT:

(A) Both claims assume that loyalty and bravery are characteristics which are desirable in animals.
(B) Both claims are, in principle, untestable, so neither can be empirically confirmed or denied.
(C) Both claims assume that human qualities can be attributed to animals.
(D) Both claims are supported by only a single example of animal behavior.
(E) Neither claim is supported by evidence other than the opinions and observations of the speakers.

9. Rousseau assumed that human beings in the state of nature are characterized by a feeling of sympathy toward their fellow humans and other living creatures. In order to explain the existence of social ills, such as the exploitation of man by man, Rousseau maintained that our natural feelings are crushed under the weight of unsympathetic social institutions.

Rousseau's argument described above would be most strengthened if it could be explained how

(A) creatures naturally characterized by feelings of sympathy for all living creatures could create unsympathetic social institutions
(B) we can restructure our social institutions so that they will foster our natural sympathies for one another
(C) modern reformers might lead the way to a life which is not inconsistent with the ideals of the state of nature
(D) non-exploitative conduct could arise in conditions of the state of nature
(E) a return to the state of nature from modern society might be accomplished

10. Every element on the periodic chart is radioactive, though the most stable elements have half-lives which are thousands and thousands of years long. When an atom decays, it splits into two or more smaller atoms. Even considering the fusion taking place inside of stars, there is only a negligible tendency for smaller atoms to transmute into larger ones. Thus, the ratio of lighter to heavier atoms in the universe is increasing at a measurable rate.

Which of the following sentences provides the most logical continuation of this paragraph?

(A) Without radioactive decay of atoms, there could be no solar combustion and no life as we know it.
(B) Therefore, it is imperative that scientists begin developing ways to reverse the trend and restore the proper balance between the lighter and the heavier elements.
(C) Consequently, it is possible to use a shifting ratio of light to heavy atoms to calculate the age of the universe.
(D) Therefore, there are now more light elements in the universe than heavy ones.
(E) As a result, the fusion taking place inside stars has to produce enough atoms of the heavy elements to offset the radioactive decay of large atoms elsewhere in the universe.

Questions 11 and 12

SPEAKER: The great majority of people in the United States have access to the best medical care available anywhere in the world.

OBJECTOR: There are thousands of poor in this country who cannot afford to pay to see a doctor.

11. Which of the following is true of the objector's comment?

(A) It uses emotionally charged words.
(B) It constitutes a hasty generalization on few examples.
(C) It is not necessarily inconsistent with the speaker's remarks.
(D) It cites statistical evidence which tends to confirm the speaker's points.
(E) It overlooks the distinction the speak-

er draws between a cause and its effect.

12. A possible objection to the speaker's comments would be to point to the existence of
    (A) a country which has more medical assistants than the United States
    (B) a nation where medical care is provided free of charge by the government
    (C) a country in which the people are given better medical care than Americans
    (D) government hearings in the United States on the problems poor people have getting medical care
    (E) a country which has a higher hospital bed per person ratio than the United States

13. We must do something about the rising cost of our state prisons. It now costs an average of $132 per day to maintain a prisoner in a double-occupancy cell in a state prison. Yet, in the most expensive cities in the world, one can find rooms in the finest hotels which rent for less than $125 per night.

    The argument above might be criticized in all of the following ways EXCEPT
    (A) it introduces an inappropriate analogy
    (B) it relies on an unwarranted appeal to authority
    (C) it fails to take account of costs which prisons have but hotels do not have
    (D) it misuses numerical data
    (E) it draws a faulty comparison

Questions 14–16

The blanks in the following paragraph indicate deletions from the text. For questions 14 and 15, select the completion that is most appropriate.

I often hear smokers insisting that they have a *right* to smoke whenever and wherever they choose, as though there are no conceivable circumstances in which the law might not legitimately prohibit smoking. This contention is obviously indefensible. Implicit in the development of the concept of a right is the notion that one person's freedom of action is circumscribed by the____(14)____. It requires nothing more than common sense to realize that there are situations in which smoking presents a clear and present danger: in a crowded theater, around flammable materials, during take-off in an airplane. No one would seriously deny that the potential harm of smoking in such circumstances more than outweighs the satisfaction a smoker would derive from smoking. Yet, this balancing is not unique to situations of potential catastrophe. It applies equally as well to situations where the potential injury is small, though in most cases, as for example a person's table manners, the injury of the offended person is so slight we automatically strike the balance in favor of the person acting. But once it is recognized that a balance of freedoms must be struck, it follows that a smoker has a *right* to smoke only when and where ____(15)____.

14. (A) Constitution of our nation
    (B) laws passed by Congress and interpreted by the Supreme Court
    (C) interest of any other person to not be injured or inconvenienced by that action
    (D) rights of other persons not to smoke
    (E) rights of non-smoking persons not to have to be subjected to the noxious fumes of tobacco smoking

15. (A) the government chooses to allow him to smoke
    (B) he finally decides to light up
    (C) his interest in smoking outweighs the interests of other persons in his not smoking
    (D) he can ensure that no other persons will be even slightly inconvenienced by his smoking
    (E) there are signs which explicitly state that smoking is allowed in that area

16. The author's strategy in questioning the claim that smokers have a right to smoke is to
    (A) cite facts which are not generally known
    (B) clarify a key term
    (C) entertain argument on a hypothetical case
    (D) uncover a logical inconsistency
    (E) probe the reliability of an empirical generalization

17. Some judges are members of the bar. No member of the bar is a convicted felon. Therefore, some judges are not convicted felons.

    Which of the following is logically most similar to the argument developed above?

    (A) Anyone who jogs in the heat will be sick. I do not jog in the heat, and will therefore likely never be sick.
    (B) People who want to avoid jury duty will not register to vote. A person may not vote until he is eighteen. Therefore, persons under eighteen are not called for jury duty.
    (C) All businesses file a tax return, but many businesses do not make enough money to pay taxes. Therefore, some businesses do not make a profit.
    (D) All men are excluded from the women's dormitory, but some men are polite. Therefore, some polite men are not allowed in the women's dormitory.
    (E) The Grand Canyon is large. The Grand Canyon is in Arizona. Therefore, Arizona is large.

Questions 18 and 19

A study published by the Department of Education shows that children in the central cities lag far behind students in the suburbs and the rural areas in reading skills. The report blames this differential on the overcrowding in the classrooms of city schools. I maintain, however, that the real reason that city children are poorer readers than non-city children is that they do not get enough fresh air and sunshine.

18. Which of the following best describes the form of the above argument?

    (A) It attacks the credibility of the Department of Education.
    (B) It indicts the methodology of the study of the Department of Education.
    (C) It attempts to show that central city students read as well as non-city students.
    (D) It offers an alternative explanation for the differential.
    (E) It argues from analogy.

19. Which of the following would LEAST strengthen the author's point in the argument above?

    (A) Medical research which shows a correlation between air pollution and learning disabilities.
    (B) A report by educational experts demonstrating there is no relationship between the number of students in a classroom and a student's ability to read.
    (C) A notice released by the Department of Education retracting that part of their report which mentions overcrowding as the reason for the differential.
    (D) The results of a federal program which indicates that city students show significant improvement in reading skills when they spend the summer in the country.
    (E) A proposal by the federal government to fund emergency programs to hire more teachers for central city schools in an attempt to reduce overcrowding in the classrooms.

20. Some judges have allowed hospitals to disconnect life-support equipment of patients who have no prospects for recovery. But I say that is murder. Either we put a stop to this practice now, or we will soon have programs of euthanasia for the old and infirm as well as others who might be considered a burden. Rather than disconnecting life-support equipment, we should let nature take its course.

    Which of the following are valid objections to the above argument?

    I. It is internally inconsistent.
    II. It employs emotionally charged terms.
    III. It presents a false dilemma.

    (A) I only
    (B) II only
    (C) III only
    (D) II and III only
    (E) I, II, and III

21. If Paul comes to the party, Quentin will leave the party. If Quentin leaves the party, either Ralph or Steven will ask Alice to dance. If either Ralph or Steven asks Alice

to dance, and if Quentin left the party, Alice will refuse; but if Quentin did not leave the party, Alice will accept.

Assuming that Paul does come to the party, which of the following can be logically deduced from the information above?

(A) Quentin leaves the party with Alice.
(B) Alice accepts Steven's offer to dance.
(C) Alice refuses an offer to dance from either Steven or Ralph.
(D) Either Ralph or Steven asks Alice to dance.
(E) Had Quentin not left the party, Alice would have accepted an offer to dance.

22. All students have submitted applications for admission. Some of the applications for admission have not been acted upon. Therefore, some more students will be accepted.

The logic of which of the following is most similar to that of the argument above?

(A) Some of the barrels have not yet been loaded on the truck, but all of the apples have been put into barrels. So, some more apples will be loaded onto the truck.
(B) All students who received passing marks were women. X received a passing mark. Therefore, X is a woman.
(C) Some chemicals will react with glass bottles, but not with plastic bottles. Therefore, those chemicals should be kept in plastic bottles and not glass ones.
(D) All advertising must be approved by the Council before it is aired. This television spot for a new cola has not yet been approved by the Council. Therefore, it is not to be aired until the Council makes its decision.
(E) There are six blue marbles and three red marbles in this jar. Therefore, if I blindly pick out seven marbles, there should be two red marbles left to pick.

23. New Evergreen Gum has twice as much flavor for your money as Spring Mint Gum, and we can prove it. You see, a stick of Evergreen Gum is twice as large as a stick of Spring Mint Gum, and the more gum, the more flavor.

Which of the following, if true, would undermine the persuasive appeal of the above advertisement?

I. A package of Spring Mint Gum contains twice as many sticks as a package of Evergreen Gum at the same price.
II. Spring Mint Gum has more concentrated flavor than Evergreen Gum.
III. Although a stick of Evergreen Gum is twice as large in volume as a stick of Spring Mint Gum, it weighs only 50% as much.

(A) I only
(B) II only
(C) I and II only
(D) II and III only
(E) I, II, and III

24. Judging from the tenor of the following statements and the apparent authoritativeness of their sources, which is the most reasonable and trustworthy?

(A) FILM CRITIC: Beethoven is really very much overrated as a composer. His music is not really that good; it's just very well-known.
(B) SPOKESMAN FOR A MANUFACTURER: The jury's verdict against us for $2 million is ridiculous, and we are sure that the appeals court will agree with us.
(C) SENIOR CABINET OFFICER: Our administration plans to cut inefficiency, and we have already begun to discuss plans which we calculate will save the federal government nearly $50 billion a year in waste.
(D) FRENCH WINE EXPERT: The best buy in wines in America today is the California chablis which is comparable to the French chablis and is available at half the cost.
(E) UNION LEADER: We plan to stay out on strike until management meets each and every one of the demands we have submitted.

25. A very famous doctor had testified at an important trial. The opposing attorney knew the doctor was well-qualified and had given an honest opinion, so there was no possibil-

ity of attacking the content of his testimony. The attorney and the doctor, however, knew one another socially, and the attorney asked the following questions:

Q: Doctor, you have been a practicing physician in this city for how long?
A: 30 years.
Q: During that time, you have treated some of our city's most prominent citizens, haven't you?
A: Yes.
Q: Were you, by any chance, ever asked to treat former Judge Owens?
A: Yes, I was his personal physician for many years.
Q: I haven't heard of him in some time. Do you know where he is?
A: He has died.
Q: Oh—that's too bad. Did you ever treat former Ambassador Clinton?
A: Yes, also for many years.
Q: And where is he now?
A: I am afraid he is dead, also.
Q: I am sorry to hear that.

The attorney continued along these lines until he had asked about a dozen very prominent citizens whom he knew the doctor had treated and were dead. He ended his questioning to the appreciative chuckles of the jury.

The passage contains a(n)
(A) lesson in good cross examination
(B) textbook example of how not to cross-examine a witness
(C) valuable instructive tool for younger lawyers
(D) humorous anecdote
(E) illustration of intense courtroom drama

26. PUBLIC ANNOUNCEMENT: When you enroll with Future Careers Business Institute (FCBI), you will have access to our placement counseling service. Last year, 92% of our graduates who asked us to help them find jobs found them. So go FCBI for your future!

Which of the following would be appropriate questions to ask in order to determine the value of the preceding claim?

I. How many of your graduates asked FCBI for assistance?
II. How many people graduated from FCBI last year?
III. Did those people who asked for jobs find ones in the areas for which they were trained?
IV. Was FCBI responsible for finding the jobs or did graduates find them independently?

(A) I and II only
(B) I, II, and III only
(C) I, II and IV only
(D) III and IV only
(E) I, II, III, and IV

STOP

IF YOU FINISH BEFORE TIME IS CALLED, CHECK YOUR WORK ON THIS SECTION ONLY. DO NOT WORK ON ANY OTHER SECTION IN THE TEST.

SECTION VI

Time—35 Minutes
35 Questions

Directions: Each of the following sets consists of a fact situation, a dispute and two rules. The rules may conflict, but you are to apply each rule independently. Do not treat a rule as subsidiary or as an exception to the other rule. The rules are followed by questions. You are to select from the following lettered choices (A) through (D) the one that best describes each question in the way it relates to the application of one or both of the rules to the dispute. Blacken the corresponding space on the answer sheet.

(A) a relevant question the answer to which requires a choice between the two rules
(B) a relevant question the answer to which does not require a choice between the two rules, but does require further facts or rules
(C) a relevant question that can be readily answered from the facts or rules or both
(D) an irrelevant question, the answer to which does not affect, or only tangentially affects, the outcome of the dispute

Set 1

FACTS: Kimberly and her husband Paul lived in a suburban home which Kimberly owned. The lot on which the house was built sloped gradually from east to west. Houston owned the lot which bordered Kimberly's property to the west. In 1960 Houston hired a landscaping firm to redo his lot. The firm graded Houston's land so that the edge of Houston's property at the Houston-Kimberly boundary line was six feet lower than Kimberly's property. The landscapers built a retaining wall of cinder block to keep Kimberly's lot from eroding. Kimberly died in 1970, and her will provided that "Paul is to receive the house in which we lived and the property on which it is located to have for as long as he lives. Upon his death, my sister, Fredrika, is to receive the house with no restrictions." Paul continued to live in the house. In 1975, the retaining wall at the eastern boundary of Houston's property gave way, taking with it a large section of the neighboring property. Although Paul urged Houston to have the wall fixed, Houston insisted that Paul should have to pay for half of the repairs. Paul refused. Finally, the erosion became so bad that the portion of Paul's house closest to the Houston lot began to sink.

DISPUTE: When Fredrika learned of the situation, she sued Houston to compel him to repair the wall and for compensation for the damage done to the house. Houston contested.

RULES: I. Damages for permanent harm to real property can only be recovered by one who at the time of the damage is the owner of the property.

II. Anyone having a present or future possessory interest in real property may bring a suit to prevent damage from occurring to the property.

1. Is Fredrika the owner of the property on which Paul is living?

2. Does Fredrika have a future possessory interest in Kimberly's property?

3. How old was Paul when Fredrika initiated her law suit?

4. If the court orders Houston to pay for repairing the wall, will Paul be required to pay half the cost?

5. Is Fredrika entitled to maintain her suit for compensation for damage done to the house?

6. Is Fredrika entitled to maintain her suit to force Houston to repair the retaining wall?

Set 2

FACTS: Eberly was a wealthy businessperson who invested in, among other things, rare art objects. Some of the objects which Eberly owned he lent to museums, others were placed in storage, and still a few others he displayed in his home. Eberly's favorite painter was the American artist John Singer Sargent. Eberly knew that another collector, Jordon, owned a Sargent portrait of which Eberly was very fond. Jordon died; and when Eberly learned of his death, he contacted the executor of the estate to try to buy the painting. The executor advised Eberly that the painting had been bequeathed to a nephew, Haffner, and suggested that Eberly take the matter up with Haffner. The executor also said that the value of the painting had been appraised at $175,000. Eberly offered Haffner $190,000 for the painting. Haffner agreed but told Eberly that the painting was then on five-year loan to a museum in Berlin, so he would not be able to deliver for another two years. Eberly and Haffner then signed a contract for the delivery of the painting two years thence, payment to be made on delivery. Two years later, when time came to carry out the contract, Haffner had a change of heart and decided to keep the painting. When Eberly showed up with a certified check for $190,000, Haffner refused to go through with the deal.

DISPUTE: Eberly sued Haffner for breach of contract. Haffner contested.

RULES: I. A party who breaches his agreement must pay damages to compensate the injured party, and the measure of those damages is the net value of the transaction to the injured party had the contract been performed.

II. In contracts the subject matter of which is unique so that it is impossible to find a substitute for actual performance of the agreement, the remedy for breach of contract is to force the breaching party to give the promised performance.

7. What was the value of the painting at the time Haffner was to have delivered it?

8. Is Eberly entitled to money compensation from Haffner for Haffner's breach of contract?

9. Was the subject matter of the contract between Eberly and Haffner unique?

10. Is Eberly entitled to receive possession of the painting from Haffner?

11. Did Sargent paint as many pictures during his lifetime as Picasso painted during his lifetime?

Set 3

FACTS: Oliver went into Garvey's Drugstore one afternoon to have a prescription filled. One of Garvey's assistants filled the prescription. As Oliver was leaving, he saw a gold watch lying in the doorway to the drugstore. Part of the watch was resting on the marble threshhold of the store, and part of the watch was lying on the public sidewalk. Oliver picked up the watch and walked back into the store. He asked Garvey's assistant if a customer had reported a lost watch. The assistant said no one had mentioned a lost watch to him. Oliver then gave the assistant the watch, telling him to put it on the shelf in case the owner came looking for it. Oliver added, "But if no one claims it, the watch is mine." After three months, no one had claimed the watch, so Oliver asked Garvey to give it to him. Garvey, however, wanted to keep the watch for himself, so he refused.

DISPUTE: Then Oliver sued Garvey to force Garvey to give the watch to him. Garvey objected.

RULES: I. A finder of lost property is entitled to possess that property against anyone except the true owner.

II. When lost property is found on private premises, the owner of those premises is entitled to keep the property as against anyone except the true owner.

12. Was Garvey the owner of the premises on which the watch was found?

13. If the true owner of the watch turns up, who is entitled to possession of the watch?

14. Was the watch on the drugstore's premises or on the public sidewalk when Oliver found it?

15. What is the value of the watch which Oliver found?

16. If the watch was found by Oliver on property owned by Garvey, is Oliver entitled to recover possession of the watch from Garvey?

17. Who is the true owner of the watch?

Set 4

FACTS: Brenda suspected that her boyfriend George was seeing another woman. One evening, after George left Brenda at her apartment, Brenda followed George. George drove to an apartment complex about fifteen minutes from that where Brenda lived. Brenda, following close behind in her car, watched George enter an apartment on the ground floor. She waited for five minutes and then knocked on the door. A woman, Wanda, answered the knock, and Brenda asked to speak with George. Wanda responded, "There is no George here." In fact, Wanda did not know George had come into the apartment, because George had come to see Ellen, Wanda's roommate. Brenda, however, became very angry, thinking that Wanda was hiding George. She shouted at Wanda to move out of her way or she would break her jaw. Wanda refused to move, and Brenda struck Wanda several times with her fists. Wanda then gave way and Brenda ran into the apartment. She found George and Ellen in the kitchen. When she saw Ellen, she threatened to beat her up. George then moved between Ellen and Brenda to prevent Brenda from reaching Ellen; Brenda ran at Ellen but could not reach her because George blocked the way. George, however, suffered a cut lip as Brenda struggled to get around him. Meanwhile, Wanda had called the police who arrested Brenda.

DISPUTE: Brenda pled not guilty to the charge of assault.

RULES: I. A person who willfully attacks and injures another person, no matter how slightly, is guilty of criminal assault.

II. Any person who intends to commit a crime, and but for circumstances beyond his own control would have succeeded in committing that crime, is guilty of a separate crime of attempt to commit that crime.

18. Did Brenda's attack on Wanda constitute a criminal assault?

19. How serious was George's injury?

20. If Brenda's conduct is otherwise classified as a crime, is she excused from criminal liability because she was justifiably in a rage at the time she committed the act?

21. Did Brenda's attack on Ellen constitute a criminal assault?

22. Did Brenda criminally assault George?

Set 5

FACTS: Sydney was driving with his sister, Charlotte, in his car on a rainy afternoon when the car skidded off the road. The accident occurred in the country far away from any stores, and there was no other traffic in sight. Sydney was not injured, but Charlotte was knocked unconscious and was bleeding profusely from a head wound. Sydney immediately applied direct pressure to the wound to stop the bleeding, but he was only partially successful. He then tried to start the car, but the engine had been damaged in the accident. Sydney then noticed a house near the scene of the accident. He ran over to the house and pounded on the front door, but no one was home. Sydney saw that the door was slightly ajar, so he walked in and found a telephone. Sydney telephoned the police who, in turn, called for an ambulance. As Sydney was leaving the house, the owner Frank returned home. Frank was not sympathetic to Sydney's plight and insisted Sydney should have waited until Frank returned home. The ambulance picked up Charlotte, who had regained consciousness. She was treated for a scalp wound and then released.

DISPUTE: Later, Frank sued Sydney for trespass. Sydney contested.

RULES: I. A person who enters onto property belonging to another without the owner's consent, no matter how minor the intrusion, is liable to the property owner for his trespass.

II. A person who, believing himself confronted with a life or death situation, enters onto the premises of another without having obtained prior permission from the owner is not liable for actions even though he did commit a trespass.

23. Was Sydney actually confronted with a life or death situation when he entered Frank's house?

24. Where was the telephone located in Frank's house?

25. Did Sydney's actions in entering Frank's house constitute a trespass for which he is liable to Frank?

26. Must Sydney compensate Frank for the reasonable value of the telephone service?

27. Did Sydney commit a trespass when he entered Frank's house?

Set 6

FACTS: Benny, owner of Benny's Clothing Store, had been plagued by increasing losses due to shoplifting of merchandise. In an effort to curtail losses, Benny put in a security system using mirrors and electronic surveillance devices. He also hired a security guard to monitor the devices. One day the security guard, Russell, noticed a shopper, Cindy, acting in a suspicious manner. Russell called Benny, and the two of them watched Cindy with cameras. Soon, Cindy picked up several articles of clothing, pushed them into a large bag she was carrying, and began to make her way toward the door. Russell and Benny both left the surveillance room and rushed to the front of the store to stop Cindy. While Cindy was out of the view of Russell and Benny, she became nervous and removed the articles from her bag. She dropped them on a counter and began to move nervously toward the exit. At the exit, Benny stopped Cindy and told her he was holding her on suspicion of shoplifting. Cindy did not try to resist, and Benny escorted her to his surveillance room. After five minutes, Cindy tried to leave, but Russell stood in front of the door and would not let her. Later when the police arrived they searched Cindy's bag, only to learn that she was not carrying any articles from the store in it.

DISPUTE: Later, Cindy sued Benny for false imprisonment. Benny contested the suit.

RULES: I. A person who causes the freedom of movement of another to be restricted, by incarceration or otherwise, without that person's consent has falsely imprisoned that person and must compensate him for any physical discomfort, inconvenience, embarrassment, or physical injury.

II. The owner of property may take reasonable steps to protect his property from theft, including detention of persons who attempt to carry off such property.

28. Did Benny falsely imprison Cindy?

29. What was the value of the articles of clothing which Cindy had put into her bag while Benny and Russell were watching her?

30. Was it reasonable for Benny to detain Cindy on suspicion of shoplifting?

31. Is Benny liable to Cindy for any discomfort, inconvenience, or embarrassment she suffered while Russell kept her in the surveillance room?

Set 7

FACTS: Herman owned a small lake-side cottage for which he paid $10,000. He used the cottage in the summer for weekend fishing trips, and for two weeks each year during his vacation. One winter, Deekins bought the piece of land next to Herman's cottage and converted the house on it into a bar and discotheque. The discotheque stayed open until 4:00 A.M. six nights a week, playing loud music which kept Herman awake. Not only that, but each morning Herman's own property would be littered with cans and bottles thrown there by the patrons of the discotheque. When Herman complained to Deekins, Deekins refused to do anything about the noise, but did offer to clean up Herman's property. Herman was insistent about having the noise turned off by midnight each night, but Deekins refused, explaining that the crowds did not really start to come in until eleven at night. Deekins then told Herman he would buy Herman's property. Herman thought that might be a way to get away from the discotheque. He reasoned he could take the money and buy another cottage farther up the lake. But Deekins offered Herman only $5,000. When Herman insisted on $10,000, Deekins laughed and told Herman no one would pay $10,000 for a cottage next door to a disco.

DISPUTE: Herman then sued Deekins for maintaining a nuisance. Deekins contested.

RULES: I. The owner of property, whose enjoyment of that property is diminished by the activities of a neighboring or nearby property owner, is entitled to compensation equal to the diminution in the value of his property.

II. A property owner may bring an action for nuisance, any activity on a nearby or neighboring property which interferes with his use of his property, to force abatement of the nuisance, that is, to force the other property owner to desist from the activity which constitutes a nuisance.

32. Did Deekins' discotheque constitute a nuisance so far as Herman's property was concerned?

33. Can Herman force Deekins to close his discotheque?

34. Can Herman recover compensation from Deekins because his property is no longer worth what it was before Deekins opened his establishment?

35. If Deekins is able to stop his customers from littering on Herman's property, is the discotheque still a nuisance?

STOP

IF YOU FINISH BEFORE TIME IS CALLED, CHECK YOUR WORK ON THIS SECTION ONLY. DO NOT WORK ON ANY OTHER SECTION IN THE TEST.

WRITING SAMPLE

Time—30 Minutes

Directions: Write an essay about the question listed below. You may support or attack the question, or discuss it in any way that you wish. Be sure to make your points clearly and cogently and to write as neatly as possible. Write your essay within the margins of the pages. Additional paper may be used as scratch paper, but only these pages can be used for the actual essay.

TOPIC: The Congress should adopt a national beverage for the United States.

ANSWER KEY
PRACTICE EXAMINATION I

SECTION I

1. E
2. D
3. B
4. E
5. C
6. A
7. D
8. C
9. C
10. A
11. E
12. A
13. A
14. B
15. D
16. B
17. B
18. E
19. D
20. B
21. B
22. A
23. E
24. A
25. C
26. C

SECTION II

1. C
2. C
3. D
4. D
5. A
6. B
7. A
8. C
9. D
10. C
11. C
12. D
13. C
14. B
15. D
16. A
17. C
18. B
19. D
20. C
21. A
22. C
23. B
24. C
25. B
26. C
27. B
28. A
29. C
30. D
31. C
32. C
33. B
34. B
35. D

SECTION III

1. C
2. A
3. D
4. B
5. E
6. E
7. B
8. C
9. C
10. A
11. C
12. D
13. D
14. B
15. A
16. A
17. D
18. B
19. A
20. A
21. B
22. C
23. E
24. E
25. E

SECTION IV

1. B
2. E
3. D
4. A
5. C
6. B
7. E
8. C
9. B
10. B
11. A
12. A
13. D
14. E
15. E
16. D
17. B
18. C
19. D
20. C
21. A
22. D
23. E
24. B
25. A
26. D
27. E
28. C

SECTION V

1. D	8. B	15. C	22. A
2. D	9. A	16. B	23. E
3. A	10. C	17. D	24. D
4. D	11. C	18. D	25. D
5. A	12. C	19. E	26. E
6. D	13. B	20. E	
7. D	14. C	21. E	

SECTION VI

1. B	8. A	15. D	22. C	29. D
2. C	9. C	16. A	23. D	30. C
3. D	10. A	17. D	24. D	31. A
4. B	11. D	18. C	25. A	32. C
5. B	12. B	19. D	26. B	33. A
6. B	13. C	20. B	27. C	34. A
7. B	14. B	21. C	28. C	35. C

EXPLANATORY ANSWERS

SECTION I

1. **(E)** This question is primarily a matter of careful reading. The phrase "no lower bus fares" must not be read to mean that Flash uniquely has the lowest fare; it means only that no one else has a fare lower than that of Flash. It is conceivable that several companies share the lowest fare. So II is not inconsistent with the claim made in the advertisement. III is not inconsistent since it mentions the New York City to Boston route, and it is the Washington, D.C. to New York City route which is the subject of the ad's claim. Finally, I is not inconsistent since it speaks of an *air* fare and the ad's language carefully restricts the claim to *bus* fares.

2. **(D)** We take the first three propositions together and ignore the fourth since we are to assume it is false. Robert cannot be convicted without Edwards' testimony (I), but that testimony will show that Edwards participated in the crime (II). But if Edwards participated in the crime, Roberts cannot be convicted of it because he is accused of a crime which can be committed only by a person acting alone (III). Either Edwards will testify or Edwards will not testify—that is a tautology (logically true). If Edwards testifies, according to our reasoning, Roberts cannot be convicted. If Edwards does not testify, Roberts cannot be convicted (I). Either way Roberts will not be convicted. (E) cannot be correct since we have no way of knowing, as a matter of logic, whether Edwards will or will not testify. We know only that *if* he does certain consequences will follow and *if* he does not other consequences will follow. (A) can be disregarded since the crime is one which only a solo actor can commit (III). (C) is incorrect because we have proven that, regardless of Edwards' course of action, Roberts cannot be convicted. Finally, (B) is a logical *possibility,* which is not precluded by the given information, but we cannot logically deduce it from the information given.

3. **(B)** Examine carefully the connection between II and IV. Suppose Edwards testifies. His testimony will show he, too, has committed some wrong (II); but when the jury learns this, they will not believe any part of that testimony (IV), which means that they will not believe Edwards committed the wrong—a contradiction. Since II and IV cannot both be true at the same time, the scenario they describe is an impossible one—like saying a circle is a square. The remaining answers are all distractions. There is nothing in the information to suggest that the situation was created by Roberts' attorney, so (E) is incorrect. (C) and (D) are value judgments which cannot be inferred from the information given and so are wrong—even if the situation is *difficult* for them, what reason is there for concluding that it is unfair? In any event, the situation is not even difficult for Roberts, who will be acquitted (see our analysis of the preceding question). (A) is wrong, and remember the LSAT does not presuppose you have any information about the law or its workings.

4. **(E)** In the very first sentence, the author remarks that this is "curious" and a "contradiction," so the only correct answer choice will be one which follows up on this idea as (E) does when it speaks of *paradox*. Nothing which precedes the blank suggests that the author is speaking of "beauty" or "tragedy," so (A) and (B) can be disregarded. As for (C), the passage does speak about death, but not of death's inevitability; rather it dwells on death under certain circumstances which may not be inevitable.

As for (D), while death may characterize human existence, the kind of death mentioned—self-sacrifice—is not indicated to be an inherent part of all human life.

5. **(C)** The author is explaining why the sacrifice is meaningless. From three different perspectives, he shows that it can have no value. The community does not win, because both lives were equally important. The lover who is saved does not profit, and that is shown by the fact that he would be perfectly willing to do the transaction the other way. If he has no preference (or even prefers the alternative outcome, his death), it cannot be said that he benefited from the exchange of lives. Finally, the need to prove that the action has no value to the heroine; he says she does not benefit, because she is not in a position to enjoy or savor, or whatever, her heroism. The reason for that is that she is *dead* (C), not dying (A), for dying would leave open the possibility that her sacrifice would bring her joy in her last minutes, and then the author's contention that the transaction has *no* value would be weakened. (D) is wrong, for it is specifically stated that she is a heroine, so it is an inappropriate *completion* of the sentence. (B) and (E) may both be true, but they do not explain why the action has no value to anyone.

6. **(A)** The main point of the passage is that pregnancy and a child put strain on a young marriage, and so such marriages would have a higher survival rate without the strain of children. It would seem, then, that encouraging such couples not to have children would help them stay married; but that will be possible only if they have not already committed themselves, so to speak, to having a child. If the wife is already pregnant at the time of marriage, the commitment has already been made so the advice is too late. (B) and (C) are wrong for similar reasons. It is not only the continued presence of the child in the marriage which causes the stress, but the very pregnancy and birth. So (B) and (C) do not address themselves to the *birth* of the child, and that is the factor to which the author attributes the dissolution of the marriage. (D) is wide of the mark. Whether society does or does not have such an interest, the author has shown us a causal linkage, that is, a mere fact of the matter. He states: If this, then fewer divorces. He may or may not believe there should be fewer divorces. (E) is wrong for this reason also, and for the further reason that it says "do not *plan*" to have children. The author's concern is with children during the early part of the marriage. He does not suggest that couples should never have children.

7. **(D)** Peter's surprise is over the fact that an important executive of a company would use a competitor's product, hence (D). (B) is wrong because Peter's surprise is not that Mary is unimportant; rather he knows Mary is important, and that is the reason for surprise. (E) is irrelevant to the exchange, for Peter imagines that regardless of taste, Mary ought to consume the product she is responsible in part for producing. The same reasoning can be applied to (C). Finally, (A) is a distraction. It has legal overtones, but it is important to always keep in mind that this section, like all sections of the LSAT, tests reasoning and reading abilities—not knowledge of business or law.

8. **(C)** The dispute here is over the motivation to compete seriously in intramural sports. Erika claims it is a sense of responsibility to one's fellows; Nichol argues it is a desire to win. But the two may actually support one another. In what way could one possibly let his fellows down? If the sport was not competitive, it would seem there would be no opportunity to disappoint them. So the desire to win contributes to the desire to be an effective member of the team. Nothing in the exchange presupposes anything about the structure of such programs beyond the fact that they are competitive, that is, that they have winners and losers. How many such programs exist, how they are funded, and similar questions are irrelevant, so both (A) and (B) are incorrect. (D) is close to being correct, but it calls for a survey of *deans*. The dean is probably not in a position to describe the motivation of the *participants*. Had (D) specified par-

ticipants, it too would have been a correct answer. Of course, only one answer can be correct on the LSAT. Finally, (E) must be wrong for the reason cited in explaining (D); it should be possible to find out about the motivation.

9. **(C)** Clark was unhappy if he had a clear conscience but knew, or Clark was happy if he knew but had an unclear conscience. It is not the case that Clark was unhappy, so he must have been happy. Since he knew, however, his happiness must stem from an unclear conscience. (A), (D), and (E) are incorrect because they make irrelevant value judgments. As was just shown, the author's point can be analyzed as a purely logical one. (B) is just distraction, playing on the connection between "governess" and "servant," which, of course, are not the same thing.

10. **(A)** The author's point depends upon the *assumption* that children see both animated features and "spaghetti Westerns." Obviously, if that assumption is untrue, he cannot claim that his conclusion follows. It may be true that children get a distorted picture of the world from other causes, but the author has not claimed that. He claims only that it comes from their seeing animated features and "spaghetti Westerns." Presumably the two different treatments cause the inversion of values. The intention of the producers in making the films is irrelevant since an action may have an effect not intended by the actor. Hence, II would not touch the author's point. Further, that there are other sources of information which present a proper view of the world does not prove that the problem cited by the author does not produce an inverted view of the world. So III would not weaken his point.

11. **(E)** The point of the passage is that there is a seeming contradiction in our body of laws. Sometimes a person pays for his attempted misdeeds, and other times he does not pay for them. If there could be found a good reason for this difference, then the contradiction could be explained away. This is just what (E) does. It points out that the law treats the situations differently because it has different goals: Sometimes we drive fast because we are in a hurry; other times we drive slowly because we want to enjoy the scenery. (B) would not weaken the argument for it only intensifies the contradiction. (D) makes an attempt to reconcile the seemingly conflicting positions by hinting at a possible goal of one action which is not a goal of the other. But, if anything, it intensifies the contradiction because one might infer that we should not try persons for attempted crimes because criminal trials are expensive, yet we should allow compensation for attempted frauds because civil trials are less expensive. (C) and (A) are just distractions. Whether there are more of one kind of law than another on the books has nothing to do with the seeming contradiction. And whether persons are more likely to commit a second crime after they are released from prison does not speak to the issue of whether an unsuccessful attempt to commit a crime should be a crime in the first place.

12. **(A)** The question stem asks us to focus on the "dispute" between the two opponents. What will be relevant to it will be those items which affect the merits of the issues, or perhaps those which affect the credibility of the parties. (C) and (E) both mention items—facts and their source—which would be relevant to the substantive issues. (B) and (D) are legitimate attempts to clarify the issues and so are relevant. (A) is not relevant to the issues nor is it relevant to the credibility (e.g., where did the facts come from) of the debaters. (A) is the least relevant because it is an *ad hominem* attack of the illegitimate sort.

13. **(A)** The point of the passage is that artists see things as they really are, while politicians see things as they want them to be. (B) is wrong, for if anything, it is the politicians who see things through rose-colored glasses, while the artists see the truth of a stark reality. (C) can be overruled, for the passage implies that political leaders are responsive to the needs of people—it is just that they are a little late. Moreover, the point of the

passage is to draw a contrast between artists and politicians; and even if the conclusion expressed in (C) is arguably correct, it is not as good an answer choice as (A), which *completes* the comparison. (D) has no ground in the passage. Be careful not to move from an analysis of facts—artists saw the problems earlier than the politicians did—to a conclusion of value or policy—therefore we should turn out the politicians. The author may very well believe that as sad as these circumstances are, nothing can be done about them, e.g., things are bad enough with the politicians in charge, but they would be much worse with artists running things. (E) also finds no ground in the passage.

14. **(B)** The argument for even-handedness is that it avoids the danger that actions will be misinterpreted. If a parent is overly generous, a child will think the parent will always be generous, even when generosity is inappropriate. By the same token, if a parent does not draw the line until he is pushed to do so, the child will believe that he *forced* the parent's response. A parent, so goes the argument, should play it safe and leave himself a cushion. (D) makes an attempt to capture this thought but overstates the case. The author implies only that this may show weakness, not that the child will necessarily exploit that weakness and certainly not that the child will exploit it violently. And if the author had intended that thought, he surely would not have used the word "retaliate" which implies a *quid pro quo*. Both (A) and (E) have no basis in the passage, and neither is relevant to the idea of rewards and punishments. (C) does treat the general idea of the passage, but it confuses the idea of weakness with the more specific notion of willingness to bargain.

15. **(D)** The key phrase in this paragraph is "beef costs more per pound than fish." A careful reading would show that (A) is in direct contradiction to the explicit wording of the passage. (B) cannot be inferred since the dietician merely says, "I pay." Perhaps he intends to keep the price of a meal stable by cutting back in other areas. In any event, this is another example of not going beyond a mere factual analysis to generate policy recommendations (see #13) unless the question stem specifically invites such an extension, e.g., which of the following courses of action would the author recommend? (C) makes an unwarranted inference. From the fact that beef is more costly one would not want to conclude that it is more profitable. (E) is wrong for this reason also. (D) is correct because it focuses upon the "per measure of protein" which explains why a fish meal will cost the dietician more than a beef meal, even though fish is less expensive per pound.

16. **(B)** I would undermine the advertisement considerably. Since the point of the ad is that you will lose weight, any unforeseen effects which would make it impossible to lose weight would defeat the purposes of the program. II is less obvious, but it does weaken the ad somewhat. Although the ad does not specifically say you will be healthier for having enrolled in the program, surely the advantages of the program are less significant if you have to pay an additional, hidden cost, i.e., health. III, if anything, supports the advertisement. IV is irrelevant since the ad does not claim you will become too thin.

17. **(B)** This question is like one of those simple conversation questions: "X: All bats are mammals. Y: Not true, whales are mammals too." In this little exchange, Y misunderstands X to have said that "all mammals are bats." In #17, the objection must be based on a misunderstanding. The objector must think that the ad has claimed that the only cause of unhappiness, etc., is being overweight, otherwise he would not have offered his counter-example. (A) is wrong because the ad never takes a stand on the *causes* of overweight conditions—only on a possible cure. This reasoning invalidates (C) and (D) as well. (E) makes a similar error, but about effects, not about causes. The ad does not say everyone who is unhappy is unattractive or vice versa.

18. **(E)** The sample argument is a straightforward generalization: All observed S are P. X

is an S. Therefore, X is P. Only (E) replicates this form. The reasoning in (A) is: "Some S are P. All M are S. (All swans are birds, which is a suppressed assumption.) Therefore, all M are P." That is like saying: "Some children are not well-behaved. All little girls are children. Therefore, all little girls are not well-behaved." (B), too, contains a suppressed premise. Its structure is: "All S are P. All S are M. (All ballets are theatrical productions, which is suppressed.) Therefore, all M are P." That is like saying: "All little girls are children. All little girls are human. Therefore, all humans are little girls." (C) is not a generalization at all. It takes a generalization and attempts to explain it by uncovering a causal linkage. (D) is simply a *non sequitur*. It moves from the universality of the *concept* of justice to the conclusion that justice is a *physical* trait of man.

19. **(D)** The author is attempting to argue that laws against suicide are legitimate. He argues against a simplistic libertarian position which says suicide hurts only the victim. The goal of the law, he argues, is not just to protect the victim from himself. A society passes such a law because it wants to underscore the importance of human life. Reading beyond the blank in the second paragraph makes clear the author's views on the value of human life. (A) flies in the face of the explicit language of the passage. The author does not defend the law as being a deterrent to suicide. (B) might be something the author believes, but it is not something he develops in the passage. He is not concerned here with explaining how the laws came to be on the books; he is concerned only with defending them. If anything, (B) would be more appropriate in the context of an argument against such laws. (C) also is something the author may believe, but his defense of the suicide law is not that it protects liberties—only that it serves a function and does not interfere with constitutional liberties any more than laws that prohibit doing violence to others. (E) is wrong for the same reasons that (B) is wrong. It seems to belong more in the context of an argument against suicide laws.

20. **(B)** With the comments in #19 in mind, it is clear that (B) must be correct. The author wants to make the point that suicide is not a victimless crime; it affects a great many people—even, he claims, some who were never personally acquainted with the suicide. Again, reading the whole passage is helpful. (A) is a joke—obviously suicide does not lead to more serious crimes. That is like saying the death penalty is designed to rehabilitate the criminal. (C) simply focuses on the superficial content of the sentence: One, it's talking about church and state, so (C), which mentions sin, must be correct. (D) is wrong because the author is not concerned to defend the laws as deterrents to suicide, as we discussed in #19. Finally, (E) is irrelevant to the point that the entire community is affected by the death of any one of its members.

21. **(B)** This third question, too, can be answered once the comments of #19 are understood. The key word here is "oversimplification." The libertarian oversimplifies matters by imagining that the only function of the law is to protect a person from himself. This is oversimplified because it overlooks the fact that such laws also serve the functions of (1) underscoring the value of life, and (2) protecting the community as a whole from the loss of any of its members. (A) is incorrect because the libertarian does not make this error but the related one of evaluating the function of the law only from the perspective of the suicide. (C) is wrong, for the author apparently shares with the libertarian the assumption that a law must not illegitimately interfere with individual liberty. His whole defense of the laws against suicide is that they have a legitimate function. (D) is wrong for the same reasons that (C) of #20 is wrong. Finally, (E) is very much like (A).

22. **(A)** (C) and (D) are wrong because they extrapolate without sufficient information. These are very much like answers (C) and (E) in #15. (E) contradicts the last given statement and so cannot be a conclusion of it. That would be like trying to infer "all men are mortal" from the premise that "no

men are mortal." (B) commits an error by moving from "all S are P" to "all P are S." Just because all racing engines have SFI does not mean that all SFI's are in racing engines. Some may be found in tractors and heavy-duty machinery.

23. **(E)** This is a very sticky question, but it is similar to ones which have been on the LSAT. The key here is to keep in mind that you are to pick the BEST answer, and sometimes you will not be very satisfied with any of them. Here (E) is correct by default of the others. (A) has some merit. After all, the economist really isn't very careful in his statement of his claim. He says "here we go again" when there is no evidence that we have ever been there before. But there is no particular term he uses which we could call ambiguous. (B) is wrong because although the economist assumes some people take that position (otherwise, against whom would he be arguing), he does not imply that he alone thinks differently. (C) is like (A), a possible answer, but this interpretation requires additional information. You would have to have said to yourself, "Oh, I see that he is against it. He is probably saying this in an exasperated tone and in the context of a diatribe." If there were such additional information, you would be right, and (C) would be a good answer. But there isn't. (E) does not require this additional speculation and so is truer to the given information. (D) would also require speculation. (E) is not perfect, just BEST, by comparison.

24. **(A)** Again, we remind you that the correct answer will not always be free from objection. In these statement-credibility questions, some objections could be raised against all answers, but do not go overboard. Take the information pretty much at face value. For example, (B) is wrong because the physicist is speaking about matters outside of his expertise. Now, it is conceivable that he has also done studies in economics and sociology and is qualified to make this statement, but that requires us to speculate—to add information. (A) does not require this. We have a journeyman plumber, an expert, speaking in his own field. (C) is unreliable, and we can see the blatant element of self-interest. The same is true with (E). (D) is wrong, to a certain extent, for the same reason that (B) is wrong and also because of the wildly implausible content of the statement.

25. **(C)** The point of the passage is a humorous one. It is clearly silly to try to extend a past trend, which you know to be limited, into the indefinite future. (A) is a reasonable inference because there is no reason to believe the limits have been reached. That is, that people's life expectancies will not continue to grow at modest rates at least until the next generation. Of course, we would not want to say, "Therefore, five hundred years from now, the average life expectancy will be twelve centuries." (B) also is a reasonable extension, particularly since it cites a possible cause for the growth. (D) does not cite a cause but is just a simple extrapolation. (C) is better than (D), because there is nothing on the face of (D) that suggests it reaches an unlikely conclusion, i.e., Susan will be 6 feet 9 inches. (E) is very much like (B) in that it cites causal factors in making a projection, but it reverses the conclusion: It projects the trend will cease, and for that additional reason is not most nearly similar to the question stem.

26. **(C)** As was noted above the author wants to make a humorous point. He does not attack the geological studies, they are merely his foils—they set up the punch line. So (D) is wrong. (E) is wrong for the same reason. The author could as easily have picked Peking or Sydney. (A) and (B) are wrong because they attribute a serious intent to the author rather than a flippant one.

SECTION II

Set 1

OVERVIEW: The possible conflict between these two rules is not difficult to find. A case in which a person misappropriates a property, but the events occurred more than five years earlier, presents us with a choice. According to the first rule, that person has committed a crime. According to the second rule, that person cannot be convicted of the crime.

1. **(C)** It is clear from the facts that Kinch took Jerome's property on the condition that he would invest it. Later he used the property for other purposes—not just Jerome's purposes, but his own as well. He planned to gamble with Jerome's money but he did not intend to give all the winnings (if any had materialized) to Jerome.

2. **(C)** Again we can deduce an affirmative answer to this question. The statute of limitations specifies a five year time limit for such actions. Kinch misappropriated the money before 1974 (it is not clear from the facts whether it was in 1972 or in 1973), and then six years passed (Kinch paid the money for the first six years).

3. **(D)** Whether or not Jerome originally acquired the money lawfully, it is clear that Kinch was not the owner. So Kinch took someone else's property and that is all we need to know to apply either rule.

4. **(D)** The statute of limitations is pegged to the time the crime was committed. It is apparently unimportant when the victim discovered that the crime was committed.

5. **(A)** This is the conflict outlined in the set overview. Kinch's actions do fit the provisions of Rule I, so by that rule alone he ought to be convicted of embezzlement. But Rule II, which specifies a time limit, precludes a conviction.

6. **(B)** Since Kinch's actions occurred more than five years ago, he cannot be convicted of embezzlement. But that does not necessarily mean that Kinch is off the hook altogether. It may be that the judge can require Kinch to finish repaying the money he promised to Jerome. We do not know that, but it certainly seems a reasonable possibility. So the correct answer here must be that we require more information to make our decision.

Set 2

OVERVIEW: The conflict between these two rules will come out if there is a case in which the person who took stolen goods did not specifically know for a fact that the goods were stolen, yet had enough information to lead him to suspect that the goods were stolen. The point of Rule II is apparently to prevent someone saying "I do not want to know where you got this," and proceeding to act with impunity simply because he does not have specific information.

7. **(A)** This is the conflict just described. Ralph did not know for a fact that the goods were stolen. It is consistent with the facts to speculate that the stamps were sold from Briggs' collection and eventually found their way into Dorothy's hands. We are not suggesting this did happen; we only want to point out that Rule I does not apply to Ralph's actions since he did not know for a fact how the stamps reached him. On the other hand, Rule II would hold Ralph guilty of receiving stolen property. It does not require specific knowledge, only that the receiver have reason to believe the property is stolen.

8. **(C)** We know that Ralph did not know the stamps were stolen for a fact or how they were stolen if they were. This is a very important question for the application of Rule I. Without such knowledge, a person cannot be guilty on Rule I.

9. **(D)** This question asks about information which is irrelevant. All that Rule I requires (and it is the more restrictive of the two) is that the receiver know the goods to be stolen. It does not go further to require that the receiver also know *how* or by *whom* the goods were stolen. Ralph might be convicted even under Rule I, provided he knew the stamps were stolen even if he did not know who did the dirty deed or when.

10. **(C)** This question does not require any legal knowledge, for the term "constructive knowledge" is defined in the rule. Did Ralph have information sufficient to make

a reasonable person suspicious? The facts of the case clearly indicate he did, so answer (C). Now, it will not do to strain at gnats—but maybe Ralph did not know. The rule does not require that Ralph really know. The rule requires only that Ralph have had information which would make most people suspicious, and most people would have been made suspicious. And if they chose to ignore the information, that does not mean the information was not sufficient to make a reasonable person suspicious, it means only that someone chose to *ignore* the information.

11. **(C)** At first glance, you might have thought this was a (B). After all, Ralph did not have specific knowledge the stamps were stolen. But the detective informs us that the stamps were stolen. Notice also that this cannot be irrelevant, since one of the most important aspects of the crime of receiving stolen goods is that the goods were, in fact, stolen.

12. **(D)** Rule I, which establishes the elements for the crime, does not specify any amount as necessary. So the answer to this question, even if we had it, would not help us apply the rule.

Set 3

OVERVIEW: The conflict, if any is presented by the facts, will probably materialize around the question of reasonable precaution. Rule I establishes, without qualification, that a person who has been deceived by another's false representation can recover. But Rule II introduces the notion that a person cannot recover even if he was deceived if there was an opportunity for him to protect himself which he failed to use. In this case, the Williamses were suspicious and did make an attempt to delve into Dawson's claim about insurance. But they made only one attempt. They gave up after a busy signal. Most people, given the importance and value of the house, would have tried again, and they would not have let Dawson go to work until they were satisfied that he did really have insurance.

13. **(C)** As we have just argued, the Williamses did fail to take the reasonable precaution of persisting in calling the company to determine whether Dawson was really insured with them. Now, it will not do to argue, "Well, but they did try." The second rule requires that they take "reasonable" precautions, not the easiest or simplest. To make a telephone call is hardly burdensome; and most people would persist until they got an answer on the question. Or they would not have let Dawson try the job.

14. **(B)** Here we have a question which adds new facts, creating essentially a new case. It seems clear that a neighbor could not recover from Dawson on grounds of misrepresentation since Dawson did not represent anything, truly or falsely, to a neighbor. Nonetheless, the neighbor may have some claim against Dawson. But to establish that, we will need another rule.

15. **(D)** Dawson blew it, and the tree dropped onto the house. Exactly how Dawson erred is not relevant to the question of whether Dawson misrepresented a state of affairs.

16. **(A)** This is the conflict. Rule I indicates that the Williamses are entitled to recover, because Dawson made his misrepresentation. But Rule II qualifies that by requiring that the Williamses take reasonable precautions to protect themselves from the misrepresentation. We have shown in #13 that the Williamses did not take such precautions, so Rule II reaches a different result from that of Rule I.

17. **(C)** This question alters the facts of the case. If this alternative scenario had come about, the Williamses would have had no action for *mis*representation, even if the tree had completely destroyed the house. After all, how could they complain about a false representation of fact, if the representation was actually true?

18. **(B)** Even if Dawson ends up compensating the Williamses for the damage he caused to their home, Dawson did get rid of the tree. He can argue that he is entitled to be paid

for that work. Whether or not he is so entitled is an issue which needs further explanation. We just do not have enough guidance to make the decision, and that is the nature of answer (B).

Set 4

OVERVIEW: If the case is one involving a gratuitous or non-paying passenger, we may find a conflict between the two rules. In our case, Julio picked up Rivera and offered to transport her for free. Rivera is a non-paying guest. When she is injured, we find there is a conflict between the two rules. According to Rule I, Rivera is entitled to compensation because Julio was careless (he misjudged the speed). But according to Rule II, Julio is not liable since Rivera was a non-paying guest and Julio did use some care (he looked back).

19. **(D)** How fast Julio was driving might be an issue in determining how careless he was, but the speed of the other vehicle is not important since it was Julio's carelessness which caused the accident.

20. **(C)** Although Julio was careless, he was not grossly careless. Notice that we do not need another rule, because Rule II defines gross negligence for us: "The failure to use even slight care." As we noted in the set overview, Julio did use some care—he looked back and, though he misjudged, he thought he could make it.

21. **(A)** This is the conflict situation outlined in the set passage. Since Julio was careless, ordinarily he would be liable. But Rule II creates an exception to this general rule, and as we learned in the Instructional Overview to this question type, an exception is to be treated as a rule equal to the general rule.

22. **(C)** Since a gratuitous guest is one who does not pay (gratuitous is not a legal term—we just give it its ordinary meaning of non-paying), Rivera must be a gratuitous passenger.

Set 6

OVERVIEW: At first glance the rules seem to offer many possible conflicts, but a closer look shows that the chance of conflict is virtually non-existent. The first rule pertains to interrogations—that is, the asking of questions. The second rule applies to a time when no questions have been asked. It would be difficult to imagine a situation in which the two could conflict since a question-asking scenario cannot coincide with a scenario in which no questions are asked.

23. **(B)** Notice that the facts inform us that the admission made by Darby is essential. Without it, Darby will not be convicted. Notice further, as explained in the set overview, that Rule I does not apply unless there has been an interrogation or question asking. Darby was never questioned. He just blurted out his statement. This means that Rule II applies and the statement is admissible. Now, if we stop at this point, we would erroneously conclude that Darby will be convicted, answer (C). But if we are more careful, we will say to ourselves: we do not know of what the crime hit-and-run driving consists. We would need further information to conclude that Darby will be held guilty. While the admission is a necessary element of the case, it is not in and of itself sufficient to guarantee a conviction.

24. **(C)** Only Rule II applies to Darby's admission. The facts show us that the admission was voluntary (he was not coerced) and that it was spontaneous (Darby blurted it out). He had not yet been advised of his rights, but that is not critical since the utterance was voluntary and spontaneous. So applying Rule II, we get our answer to the issue raised by this question and an answer (C).

25. **(B)** What constitutes acting with authority? There are facts in this situation which cut both ways. On the one hand, Livingston was carrying his I.D., and Livingston was an officer. On the other hand, Livingston was not actually doing police work, and Livingston was out of uniform, and he was not in his own jurisdiction. Which of these consid-

erations is decisive? The appropriate response is that we do not know and require further rules.

26. **(C)** The answer to this question is a straight-line deduction from the first rule. Since Livingston did give Darby his rights (as the last clause of Rule I states), anything after that is admissible.

Set 6

OVERVIEW: The conflict in this case arises over the appropriate remedy. Rule I specifies that the usual remedy for a breach of contract is money compensation equal to the expected gain. But Rule II says that in some cases, where the expected gain is speculative—that is, uncertain—the compensation is only $1. One of the most striking features of the facts we are given is the uncertain nature of the venture to recover the gold. Other expeditions had ended in failure. This suggests that a choice between the rules is required. According to Rule I, the appropriate recovery is the expected gain, but Rule II dictates that only $1 in damages be paid.

27. **(B)** Since the first rule specifies that damages are to be equal to *net* gain, the cost of the expedition becomes important. According to the terms of the contract, Sweet could expect to gain half of the gold recovered *after* expenses were paid. So, far from being irrelevant, the cost of the expedition, had it been held, would have been an important determinant of Sweet's share in the take.

28. **(A)** This is the conflict described in the set overview. On the one hand, the venture was highly speculative, so Rule II seems to say that the damages ought to be only $1. On the other hand, Rule I specifies that Sweet is entitled to the gain he would have realized had the breach of contract not occurred.

29. **(C)** Our arguments, thus far, show that the venture was speculative. We do not need some further rule to define this term for us. The word *speculative* is a straightforward ordinary English word, not a legal term. Speculative means uncertain. Was the recovery of gold a certainty, or was it speculative? Since others had tried and failed to recover the gold from the deep ocean waters, we are entitled to conclude that yet another expedition might fail.

30. **(D)** Why Bert decided not to go ahead is irrelevant. That he did decide to forgo the operation is essential to setting up the lawsuit for the questions. After all, had Bert completed his part of the bargain, we would not have had any questions. But his reasons for not going ahead do not help us in applying the two rules regarding the appropriate damages once Bert has breached his contract.

Set 7

OVERVIEW: There is a very important difference in the kinds of situations governed by our two rules. Larceny requires a *taking* of property from another. In conversion, the property is freely given to the receiver who then *converts* or misuses it. In our case, Simpson gave the property to Warren for a purpose (fixing the car), so Warren cannot be guilty of larceny. He is guilty of conversion, however, because he took property which had been given to him for one purpose and turned it to his own purposes—he sold it and kept the money.

31. **(C)** This question does not require us to choose between the two rules. We can deduce that Warren is not guilty of larceny because he never *took* the car from Simpson's possession.

32. **(C)** Our explanation for #31 applies with equal force here. Simpson's death would have been irrelevant since Warren never took the car in the first place. Therefore, the answer to the question raised here is "no," and since we are able to answer "no," we must assign this issue the category (C).

33. **(B)** Warren knew Simpson had been seriously injured. If Simpson failed to return, Warren might conclude that Simpson was

still in the hospital. On the other hand, Warren did have that disclaimer: "Not responsible." This should indicate that the problem is open. We have a situation where we can say "On the one hand . . . but on the other . . . " In such cases, (B) is the correct answer.

34. **(B)** In #32, we pointed out that Simpson's death would have been irrelevant to the question of whether Warren had committed larceny. Simpson's death would not, however, be irrelevant to the question of who was entitled to the car. After all, if Simpson is gone and has no heirs, maybe the car remains where it is. We do not know this as a matter of law, but we can appreciate that we need further rules before we decide the question.

35. **(D)** This is irrelevant to the question of who is entitled to possession of the car. It is not a (B). While we do not know the answer to the question (is he liable), we do not need the answer in order to determine whether Warren is guilty of larceny or conversion.

SECTION III

Questions 1–5

Arranging the Information

There are four things to know about each piece of luggage: Position, type, weight, and owner. Five pieces times four kinds of information about each piece is a grid of 5 × 4 = 20 boxes.

Question stem 1 should be done first since it uses only part of the information, but since none of the questions asks about contradiction or redundancy, the order in which the particular information statements are done after question 1 is answered will not make any difference. Questions 2, 3, and 4 indicate that pretty much the entire story is known about the luggage, but question 5 indicates that at least two parts of the grid will not be definitely completed.

The grid outline from statement I:

POSITION	1	2	3	4	5
TYPE					
WEIGHT					
OWNER					

Entering item II:

POSITION	1	2	3	4	5
TYPE					
WEIGHT					10 lbs
OWNER					

Entering item III:

POSITION	1	2	3	4	5
TYPE					
WEIGHT					10 lbs
OWNER	not Sw	Sw?	Sw?	Sw?	not Sw

Entering item VI:

POSITION	1	2	3	4	5
TYPE					
WEIGHT			20 lbs		10 lbs
OWNER	not Sw	Sw?	Amer	Sw?	not Sw
	not Amer	not Amer		not Amer	not Amer

At this point Question 1 is answerable, as shown in the following "Answering the Problems" section.

Now we enter the other items of information. IV can only be partially entered since there is only the negative inference to be made that anything not fifteen pounds cannot be the Turk's, which needs to be kept in mind in entering each further piece of information. V can be entered now:

POSITION	1	2	3	4	5
TYPE		box			
WEIGHT		5 lbs	20 lbs		10 lbs
OWNER	not Sw	Sw?	Amer	Sw?	not Sw
	not Amer	not Amer		not Amer	not Amer
		not Turk			not Turk

Now enter VII, since VI has already been entered. VII tells us that the hatbox weights ten pounds (second from lightest), and thus is the fifth item, and it is not owned by the German.

POSITION	1	2	3	4	5
TYPE		box			hatbox
WEIGHT		5 lbs	20 lbs		10 lbs
OWNER	not Sw not Amer	Sw? not Amer not Turk	Amer	Sw? not Amer	not Sw not Amer not Turk not Germ

Notice that we can now do some more with the owner line; since 5 cannot be any of the other four, it must be Belgian.

OWNER	not Sw not Amer not Belg	Sw? not Amer not Belg not Turk	Amer	Sw? not Amer not Belg	Belg

Now we enter VIII. Since this is the last item, we expect to have many interactions and to all but complete the remaining blanks at this point. Here is what it looks like after filling in only the direct information in VIII:

POSITION	1	2	3	4	5
TYPE	trunk	box			hatbox
WEIGHT	25 lbs	5 lbs	20 lbs		10 lbs
OWNER	not Sw not Amer not Belg	Sw? not Amer not Belg	Amer	Sw? not Amer not Belg	Belg

Our further deductions are these:

—Since the Turk has a fifteen-pound item, his cannot be in position 1, which makes position one not American or Swedish or Belgian or Turkish, and thus must be German.

—Since the weights are known for positions 1, 2, 3, and 5, position 4 must be the last possibility: fifteen pounds *and* position 4 must, therefore, also be the Turk's item.

—Since the ownership of item 1 is German, 3 American, 4 Turkish, and 5 Belgian, therefore 2 must be Swedish.

—The crate and the suitcase might be in either position 3 or 4. Note that question 5, which indicated that there was some uncertainty in the final grid, would not directly name the uncertain portions of the grid, but refers to them through the weights, which are certain. This is typical.

Thus, the final grid looks like this:

POSITION	1	2	3	4	5
TYPE	trunk	box	crate suitcase	suitcase crate	hatbox
WEIGHT	25 lbs	5 lbs	20 lbs	15 lbs	10 lbs
OWNER	Germ	Sw	Amer	Turk	Belg

Answering the Problems

1. **(C)** As can be seen from the preceding third diagram, these statements tell us that the Swede owns the second or fourth item since his luggage is surrounded by other luggage and had to be either 2, 3, or 4, and the American is 3. Choices (A) and (B) incorrectly allege position 1 is possible. (D) errs in saying that position 3 is possible when that is the American. (E) refers to the ten-pound box, which is position 5 and not surrounded by other luggage.

2. **(A)** This is answered from the grid. The German owns a 25-pound trunk, not a 25-pound box or crate. VIII by itself rules out answers (B) and (C). V by itself rules out items (B) and (E).

3. **(D)** The American's luggage is 20 pounds and the German's 25, thus, (D) is false and the answer sought. (A) is true since Turk=15 pounds, and Belgian = 10. (B) is true since American = 20, German = 25, and 20 + 5 = 25. (C) is true since Turk = 15 and Swede = 5. (E) is true even though the exact location of the crate is unknown—it is position 3 or 4—while the trunk is position 1, thus, not next to it.

4. **(B)** The 10-pound hatbox is owned by the Belgian. (C) and (D) cannot be known since those items' positions are not certain. (A) and (E) are simply false.

5. **(E)** Each of the statements is sufficient. Anything which will distinguish the crate from the suitcase or tie down either one of them will do the trick. One of them is 20 pounds and owned by the American, the other is 15 pounds and owned by the Turk.

   I. works since it tells us the crate must be the 20- pound item.

II. works since it tells us that the crate is the 20- pound item.
III. works since it tells us that the suitcase is the 15- pound item.

Questions 6–10

Arranging the Information

Since this is a flow or process situation where the interest is on who can go when, the information should be arranged to show that:

No two days in row
R, S anytime
T only after S (but not necessarily after S)
U = T
V = 3 or 5
W = 4

6. **(E)** All three statements could be true.
I and II are possible since both R and S could do the first, third, and fifth days of the job.
III is possible, but only when S does the first and third days of the job, since T must follow S.

7. **(B)** Only II is possible. We wish to chart possibilities for the first three days, but we are especially interested in the ones which permit T and U to work on the second day, since that affects I and II. S on the first day makes T and U possible on the second day:

	FIRST DAY	SECOND DAY	THIRD DAY
	S	T or U	R, S, or V
OR	S	R	S or V

Thus, we see that T, U, or R are possible on the second day, which eliminates I. I could also fail if R worked the first day and S worked the second day. II is OK because it has no "only."
III fails because W can work only on the fourth day.

8. **(C)** Only I and II are true. If R works the first day, only S can work the second day because T and U can only follow S and V and W can only work the third and fourth days, respectively. If S works the second day, he cannot work the third.
III is not true, because R could follow S and do the third day.

9. **(C)** As we saw in problem 8, if R works the first day, S must work the second day, but here R works the third day. U and T cannot follow R, eliminating answer choices (B) and (E). R cannot follow himself, which eliminates (B) (again) and (D). Since W can work the fourth day, (A) fails to cover all of the possibilities and (C) is correct.
Note that it is more accurate to say only so and so can work and have that describe the only persons who can work than it is to include all who can work plus some who can't.

10. **(A)** (B), (C), and (D) focus on the fourth day's possibilities. (B) and (C) fail because they ignore W, who can also work on the fourth day. (D) fails because S could also work the fourth day.
Thus, we must consider the previous days as (A) and (E) ask. If R, S, and V did not work the third day, who did? W couldn't, so it must have been either T or U, who worked the THIRD day, not the second as (E) would have it. Thus, (E) is out and (A) in. If T or U worked the third day, then S must have worked the second day since those two can only follow S. Only R and S can work the first day and since they can't work two days in a row, R must have worked the first day.

Questions 11–15

Arranging the Information

Since all of the questions are "if" or conditional questions, we can except that the original arrangement of information will not give a single, definite answer. Further, since question 11 uses only some of the information, we should start with that, adding the other conditions as we do the other problems.

Conditions I and II set up blocks which can then be moved. The management block is two seats and the labor three, with an empty one in the middle of the labor block. We do not know which of the two members of each side will occupy which of the seats in their block. IV sets up another block of three seats for the meditator with him flanked by two empty seats.

Answering the Problems

11. **(C)** The three conditions used result in three blocks of 3, 3, and 2 seats, which adds up to eight. Thus, we will have a definite arrangement, although left and right could switch:

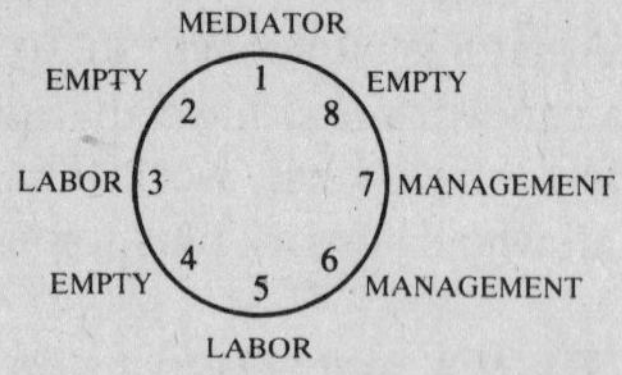

We don't know who particularly is in the seats, only the grouping. (C) correctly notes that one labor person will sit next to one management person, whichever pair it might be.

(A) and (D) fail because IV specifically states that Jones will have empty seats on either side of him.

(B) fails only because we do not know which management representative will occupy the seat next to a labor representative.

(E) fails when (C) succeeds.

12. **(D)** In contrast to problem 11, IV is out and III is in. This means that the mediator will not have empty seats by him, but since III requires that the two parties be equally near the mediator, the nearer member of each side will be seated next to the mediator. Thus, the seating will be:

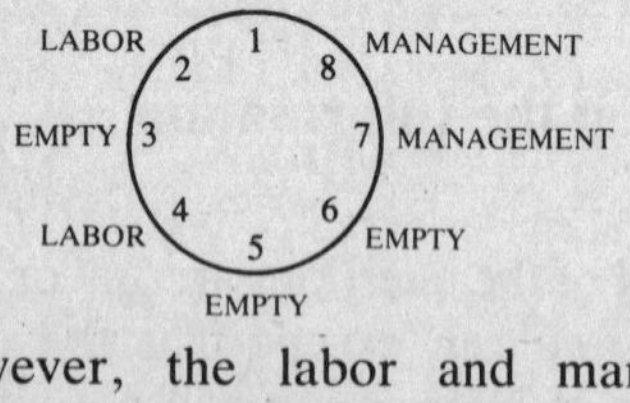

However, the labor and management parties could also switch sides to produce the following arrangement:

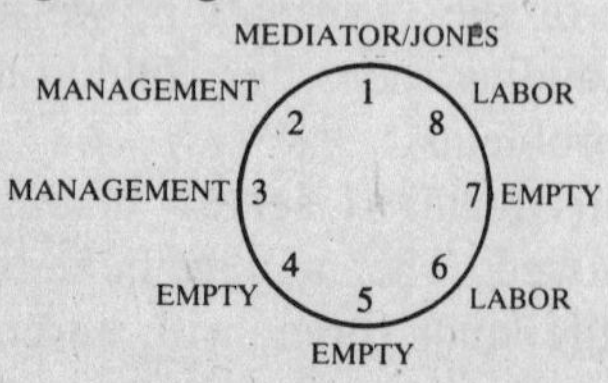

This is significant because the question asks specifically about the clockwise ordering of the negotiators. Since either labor negotiator could occupy either of the labor seats and either of the management negotiators could occupy either of the management seats, there are plenty of possibilities. The correct answer choice will be one which violates one of the basic rules I, II, or III.

(D) is correct because it has the two labor negotiators sitting next to each other in violation of condition II. All of the others satisfy the ideas of having management on one side of the mediator and labor on the other; management together and labor seated with a seat between.

13. **(D)** The Secretary sits opposite the mediator, and ALL the other conditions apply AS MUCH AS POSSIBLE. This means that some might be sacrificed. I and II say "always" while III and IV say "like" and "prefer." I and II take precedence. Here is the diagram with the Secretary opposite the mediator and I and II satisfied:

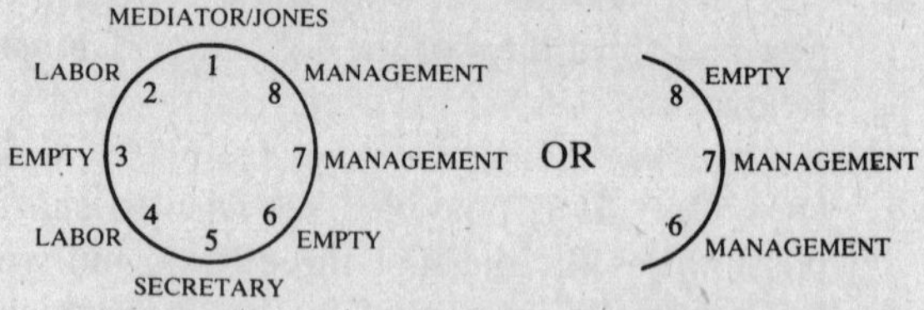

The diagram shows that conditions I and II could be met with the management negotiators either next to the mediator or next to the secretary. Condition III would have the management team sit next to the mediator. Condition IV cannot possibly be met without violating II, and since it is only a preference, it goes by the board. Thus, the final diagram is the preceding main one and the alternative listed on the right is eliminated by condition III.

Statements I and III in the problem are true, but II is false, as the diagram shows.

14. **(B)** Even though the mediator is absent, all of the applicable conditions are still in force, which are just I and II. III and IV do not apply since they refer to the mediator, who is not present. The only part of III that applies is keeping them away from each other. Here is the diagram:

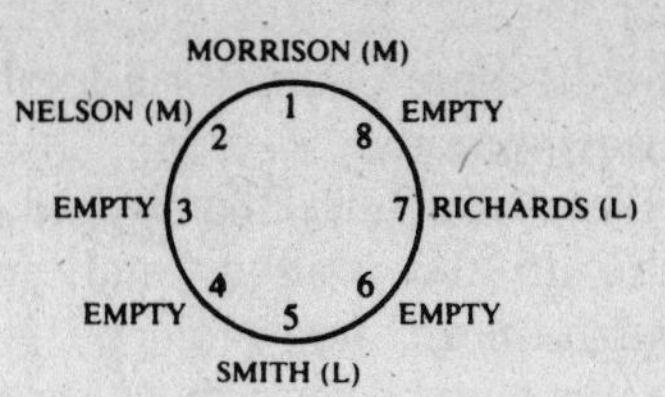

OR

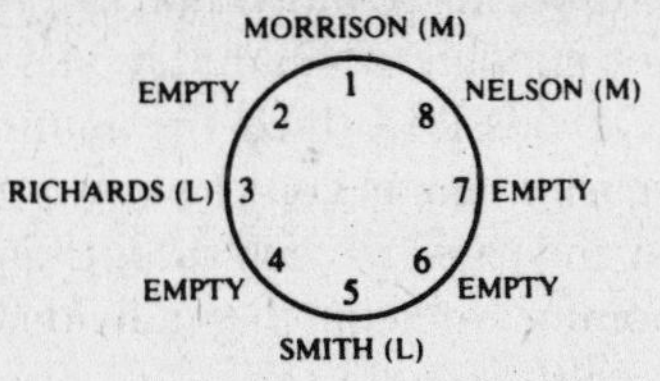

These are the only two possibilities because they want to be as far away from each other as possible so Richard and Nelson would not sit next to each other, eliminating (A). (B) is not only possible, but necessary.

(C) does not fit the diagram. (E) is not possible since these two sit in different relations to the two negotiators who do sit opposite each other. (D) is unlikely in the first place, and amounts to sitting opposite Smith, which is where Morrison is.

15. **(A)** This problem puts us back to the situation with the mediator and all of the conditions operating. Since Morrison and Nelson always sit next to each other, the aide must be on the other side of Morrison, making the management side a block of three seats in a row: Aide, Morrison, Nelson. But the aide and Nelson could flip-flop from one side of Morrison to the other. There are now six people, leaving only two empty chairs. Since one of those empty chairs must be between the two labor negotiators, there cannot be empty chairs on both sides of the mediator; thus, the mediator must be flanked by occupied seats. The middle management seat is Morrison. The diagram:

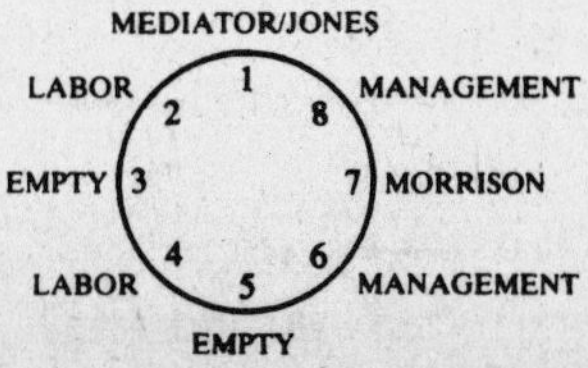

Since the two labor seats can also flip-flop between Smith and Richards, we must be careful.

(A) is not possible because the seat opposite Morrison must be empty. The aide and Nelson are opposite the two labor seats so (B), (C), and (D) are possible. (E) is possible if that is where he happens to be.

Questions 16–20

Arranging the Information

Previewing the questions indicates that the total points and the breakdown of points are the key issues. Nine points are awarded for each race (5 + 3 + 1), times three races yields 27 points at issue. Since the teams are tied now, 14 points in the last three races will win the meet. Since there are two entries from each team in each race, the most that a team could win in a single race is 8 points (5 + 3). For keeping track of the results for each alternative raised by the problems a simple chart might be used:

	Ind Med	Med Relay	Free Relay
FIRST (5)			
SECOND (3)			
THIRD (1)			
TOTAL (9)			

Answering the Questions

16. **(A)** This was answered in the preceding discussion, 14 points will win the meet.

17. **(D)** You don't need to keep track of both teams' points once you know that 14 is the magic number. If State won first and third in the individual medley, then Malibu won second and three points. Therefore, Malibu needs eleven more points to win the meet. (D) provides exactly eleven (5 + 5 + 1). (A) yields only 10 (5 + 5), (B) only 9 (5 + 3 + 1), (C) only 8 (3 + 1 + 3 + 1). The incorrectness of (E) is proved by the validity of (D).

18. **(B)** The individual medley is set up with the idea that State's top swimmer is sure to win, with only second and third being at issue. If George swims, Malibu's two swimmers will earn four points (3 + 1) but if George doesn't then State's second swimmer will get the point for third place and Malibu will get only three points for second place. Thus, the loss to Malibu if George does not swim in the individual medley is one point.

There are two ways of computing the point value of the various coaching moves being contemplated. Both are correct and either one will work, but you have to use one or the other consistently. In this discussion, we are counting only the effect of the coaching move on Malibu's score. One could have said that taking George out of the individual medley will take away one point from Malibu AND give one to State, thus, causing a difference of two points.

In order for it to be advantageous for Malibu for George to swim in another race, the net-increase in the other race will have to be at least two points. If it is only one point there is no advantage.

(A) will add only one point for third (1−0), no advantage.

(B) will add two points (3−1), so IS an advantage.

(C) will add one point (5−(3 + 1)), no advantage.

(D) will add nothing; Malibu scores ten points either way.

(E) is, of course, not true given (B), but would not be an advantage anyway.

19. **(A)** This is a two-step problem. First, you must calculate how many points are needed; second, how many swimmers are needed to win those points. Fourteen is the magic number and Malibu has scored four in the individual medley, leaving ten. Two firsts will do the trick.

20. **(A)** Since the disqualified swimmer cannot score, the situation posited is that Malibu wins first and second in the individual medley, since State's other swimmer cannot beat four minutes even. This means that the score is 8 to 1 in favor of Malibu.

(A) is false because this would only earn State 10 more points for a total of 11 when 14 was needed.

(B) is true since that would add 8 more points to the Malibu total, making 16—enough for victory.

(C) is true because those three swimmers might be two thirds and a second, totalling only 5 points (3 + 1 + 1) which, when added to the 8 won in the individual medley, is only 13—not enough to guarantee victory.

(D) is possible since the minimum that four scoring teams could win is 8 points for second and third in each race. Eight plus the one point earned in the individual medley only totals nine.

(E) is possible since the three might be two firsts and a second, which would be 13 points to add to the one from the individual medley, yielding the magic total of 14.

Questions 21–25

Arranging the Information

In arranging this sort of information where there are sub-groups and the major conditions appear to be the cross connections between their members—as here with the two types of courses—the information may be arranged with an algebraic notation which here would give rise to the equations C NOT = E, B NOT = F, and E NOT = M, with the added notation that there must be two of B, C, or P chosen. To this must be added new deductions as they are made for each problem.

Another way of diagraming this information—which works well for situations of this particular sort, though it is not as general as the algebraic approach—is to list the two groups and connect different items with an annotated line indicating what sort of connection is being made: must go with, cannot go with, etc. Here this would look like this:

SCIENCES (must = 2) — OTHER COURSES

CHEMISTRY ←NOT WITH→ ENGLISH ←NOT WITH→ MUSIC

BIOLOGY ←NOT WITH→ FRENCH

PHYSICS — WRITING

Arrows are helpful in case the relationship is just a one-way situation, though that is not too common.

A further deduction would be that English and French can not go together since either one of them forbids one of the sciences, and if they were both scheduled there would only be one science—which is not permitted.

Answering the Questions

21. **(B)** A step-by-step approach is the key. If Lois takes English, then chemistry and music are out. If chemistry is out, then physics and biology are the two sciences she must take. If biology is scheduled, then French is out. This leaves choice (B). The other answers all include some subject not possible. (A) is not wrong because it has three sciences. That is possible. (A) is wrong because chemistry can't be scheduled with English.

22. **(C)** If chemistry is out, then once again biology and physics are required. Biology precludes French and music displaces English, leaving answer choice (C).

    In any case choices (A) and (E) are impossible because they have both English and music. Choice (B) is out because French cannot be with biology. Choice (D) cannot be scheduled since it has both French and English, which cannot be combined, as previously explained.

23. **(E)** I and III work by the same logic. In each case the taking of one of the non-science courses eliminates one of the science courses from consideration, thus requiring the other two science courses. II is trying to trap you into saying that since neither music nor chemistry can combine with English, they must combine with each other. This is not true. It is possible to have a curriculum of music, physics, biology, and writing.

24. **(E)** I here is trying the same trick as II in problem 23; it does not always have to be true. II must be true since French eliminates biology, and requires the other two sciences. III need not be true since a curriculum of chemistry, biology, writing, and music is but one counter-example.

25. **(E)** With Lois taking the physics, now scheduled at the same time as English, she cannot take English, chemistry, or music because they overlap with the new physics time. Only French or biology may be taken, plus writing. This means that only three courses can be taken (E), though two science courses can still be taken—eliminating (A). (B), (C), and (D) are eliminated by the schedule just discussed.

SECTION IV

1. **(B)** (A) and (D) are simply not related to the passage at all.

   (B), (C), and (E) have some merit. (E) has the merit of being a topic in the book, but it is not clear that sound is a good reference to quantum mechanics. While quantum mechanics is mentioned by the book as a thing to be symbolized, the book also has to discuss the symbolization of music, and that seems to be much more related to sound than quantum mechanics.

   Both (B) and (C) have the merit of referring to the music, but with a title that refers to "sound" AND "symbol," it seems likely that the sound part refers to music and the symbol part to the notational system, rather than the other way around.

2. **(E)** (A) becomes unlikely when the first paragraph calls Einsteinian physics a "truly adequate" system, even though it may not be totally correct. Another key to not choosing this otherwise appealing answer choice is the reference to the Theory of Relativity, which is not specifically mentioned at all, and also the last paragraph's reiteration of the correctness of Einstein.

   (B) is referred to in the passage as a specification of the strangeness of Einsteinian physics, and thus is part of them, rather than contradictory to them. (C) fails because of the several cautionary statements such as the "unlikely" event of our ever experiencing a reversed time flow.

(D) refers to the imaginary mass of tachyons, but the passage says only that the tachyon "may" exist, not that it does.

(E) has the flag word *precisely* which tells you that the answer choice is not referring to going faster than light, but to attaining exactly the speed of light. The need to move an infinite quantity of mass to go exactly the speed of light is referred to as a barrier, and is intuitively unlikely.

3. **(D)** "Speculative" is certainly a fair characterization of the passage. (D) is preferable to (C) because the passage is hopeful that some of these speculative things may come to pass, rather than suspicious of anything. (E) is an unlikely choice for any question of this sort.

4. **(A)** As is usual with this sort of question, there are several good answers among which to choose. (D) is clearly wrong because Zuckerkandl is not stated to have any theories of tachyon formation. (E) similarly fails for lack of reference to the passage. Its only appeal is its obscurity.

(A), (B), and (C) require closer inspection. (C) seems to find that Einsteinian physics cannot treat tachyons, but actually it is predicted by the formulas associated with Einsteinian physics that such strange things as reverse time flow might occur, so (C) is out. The primary difference between (A) and (B) is the question of whether it is the notation and theories on the one hand, or the observations on the other which indicate the need for improved notation. (B), while a good abstract statement of the progress of science, does not cover the waterfront on this passage. The only observations cited in the passage support the theoretical speculations rather than disconfirm the theories. Hence, (A).

5. **(C)** It is certainly not too soon for (D), since that has happened. It seems likely that the time for (A) will never arrive, but it is not discussed in the passage. The author is clearly not satisfied with the current notational system, and thus (E) is definitely in order. While (B) has merit because the author does not endorse Zuckerkandl's ideas, (C) has more merit since (C) is definitely stated to be far from accomplishment, if indeed it is possible at all, as previously discussed for #2 (C).

6. **(B)** In the author's admitted oversimplification of Zuckerkandl, he says that music might be a better language for physics. Better than what? Better than math which is, thus, also seen as a language. (D) fails because of the word *great,* though even without that disqualifier, it would be inferior to (B).

7. **(E)** Without attempting to probe the nature of philosophy, which is certainly not an issue on a test question, (E) best links the topic of the passage to philosophy. (A), (B), and (C) are flack and (D) should not seem very good. Perhaps the nature of any field is a philosophic question, but the methods must usually be just technical matters within the field.

8. **(C)** This can be treated as a detail question with reference to the end of the next to last paragraph. (B) is unlikely since it is far more general than the tone of the passage, which refers to many rather specific ideas within biology. (A) also is unlikely since this is either unrelated or too general. A preview of this question would have made it trivially easy.

9. **(B)** While it is true that an answer may not be correct simply because you happen to know it to be true from common knowledge, an answer that you know from common knowledge to be totally false is only going to be correct if the passage specifically makes the point. In this question, birds (A), mammals (C), and fish (D) are generally known to migrate back and forth. The passage also cites examples of that for these types of animals.

The passage leaves a small ambiguity between migration and aggregation. However, the use of the crustacean example in the second paragraph is by way of explaining non-social forces rather than as an example of strict migration. The third paragraph is the source for saying (B) is correct.

10. **(B)** While the passage is not dispositive of the influence of the reproductive instinct for (C), (D), and (E), (B) is better since only the males migrate, and thus reproduction is not an issue. Do not confuse reproduction with species survival and start speculating that the male lemmings leave because food is scarce and their leaving will ensure the survival of their offspring, or whatever. Such thought is not required on this test.

11. **(A)** The first two sentences of the passage suffice to justify (A). (B) and (E) are well beyond the scope of the passage. (C) and (D) have some merit, but (D) fails because the tenor of the passage is to show that an explanation that has been made is perhaps inadequate. (C) might be an ultimate use of this or any other similar passage, but is not the immediate, identifiable purpose.

12. **(A)** This is a question the answer to which must be taken from the passage. Among human beings there are many aggregations of males which are considered social, but here the author has said otherwise and you must follow his lead.

13. **(D)** The basic idea of the passage, as we saw in #11, is to show that social factors may be less important than they first appear. This supports (D). (E) is too strong, since the author did not totally deny the existence of social actions or significance to all animal behavior. (A) would only be the correct answer to this sort of question if there were specific grounds given in the passage for the refusal to speculate. (B) is seeking social significance, which this author would apparently rather not do. (C) is flack.

14. **(E)** The only difficulty with this problem is that (E) is so totally unrelated to the passage that it seems too easy to be true. All of the others are specifically mentioned as reasons for the migration of some animals. Note that they need not all apply to any single migratory behavior.

15. **(E)** The author is curious about the amount and effects of advertising, hence (E). No value judgments are made in the passage which could support (A), (B), or (D). (E) weakly reflects the author's desire to learn more about advertising.

16. **(D)** This term is not explicitly defined, but at the end of the fourth paragraph the range in costs of "push promotion" is explained by difficulties in separating out the elements of direct selling, hence (D). (A), (B), and (C) are unlikely from the second paragraph, which distinguishes them from "push promotion."

17. **(B)** (B) is stated in the next to last paragraph. (A) fails since restaurants are nowhere mentioned. (C), while true in the real world, is not stated in the passage. (D) has the difficulty that both *prepared* and *natural* are not in the passage and it is not entirely clear that these are identical to *highly processed* and *highly perishable,* respectively. Given the merit of (B), (D) can be eliminated. (E) is simply false, since highly processed foods are stated to account for only 20 percent of the food dollar.

18. **(C)** (C) describes the article perfectly. (A) and (D) fail for want of such value judgments in the passage. (E) is not done in any final way, though some discussion is given of the topic. (B) is not stated, and may even go against the tenor of the passage since a statement that something is large does not imply that it is too large.

19. **(D)** (A), (B), and (C) are explicitly stated at the end of the last paragraph. (E) is implied because of the concern about highly processed versus less-processed foods. (D) is not there since no mention of restaurant versus home eating is made.

20. **(C)** This is a bit of a detail question, but general considerations can help. Food advertising is, overall, #1 in dollar value, which eliminates (A) and (D) since we are looking for an exception to falseness. (E) speaks to radio ads only, and the first paragraph stated that in radio food is near the top.

The other two discuss the breakdown of the food advertising dollar among the different media. The fourth paragraph states that television is less than 1 cent, incentives 0.6

cent, print 0.5 cent, and push promotion 0.7 to 1.4 cents. This shows that (A) is false and (C) is indeterminate, which is to say not definitely false, and thus, the correct answer.

21. **(A)** (A) results from the author's attempt at a balance sheet where he states that food ads subsidize publications. While it is true that free television is also subsidized by food ads, its cost will not rise since it is free. Cable television is not mentioned in the passage as having ads at all, so (B) is out, and the author does not claim that people watch programs for the ads as (D) would have it. (E) fails when (A) succeeds.

22. **(D)** The passage notes that the dropout rate is highest for humanities and lowest for natural sciences. (A) is not supported, however, since academic preparation was not the leading cause of dropping out. (B) is not known since engineering is not singled out, and the depth of reading is not mentioned. (C) refers to undergraduates and does not apply to graduate students. (E) is unknown, though there is some chance that it is true—but only if the money problem is equally divided among all the students, which we do not know.

    (D) is the best answer because *prepared* can refer to the critical motivational factors as well as to academic preparation. Since (D) and (A) are very similar, the fact that (A) refers specifically to academic preparation and (D) does not should alert you to the propriety of interpreting (D) to mean all sorts of preparation.

23. **(E)** The study's results were reported "glumly" in this regard at the end of the passage. (A), (B), and (D) are essentially stated, while the validity and efficiency of the study cannot be evaluated from the article.

24. **(B)** (B) is stated in the discussion of salaries. (A) fails because financial problems affected only 19%, not a majority. The other answers are false.

25. **(A)** Since the study's second conclusion was that most dropouts had gone as far as they could, this can be inferred. (B) is false since motivation was only the major problem, not the only one. (C) fails for the same reasons as #23(E) succeeded. (D) is not true since the study found that the dropouts were using their education and were succeeding in the world. (E) fails because of the word *most.* The condition applies to only a fraction of the 25% referred to as needing to maintain their income levels.

26. **(D)** This is a detail question answered in the third paragraph. The others are all false, except (C) which is not mentioned.

27. **(E)** No basis is given in the passage. Thus, while all of the other answer choices are reasonable ideas, none is supported by the passage.

28. **(C)** The fear that the dropouts were wasting university resources is opposed by the finding cited in (C). The education is being used. None of the others would explain the view that there was not a great waste, though (B) has some slight merit. The money referred to in (D) is not necessarily university money.

SECTION V

1. **(D)** The author's recommendation that public schools should have computerized reading programs depends upon the correctness of his explanation of the present deficiency in reading skills in the public schools. His contrast with private-school students shows that he thinks the deficiency can be attributed to the lack of such a program in the public schools. So one of the author's assumptions, and that is what the question stem is asking about, is that the differential in reading skills is a result of the availability of a computerized program in the private-school system and the lack thereof in the public school system. (E) is, of course, irrelevant to the question of *reading* skills. (C) tries to force the author to assume a greater burden than he has undertaken. He claims that the reading skills of public-school

children could be improved by a computerized reading program. He is not concerned to argue the merits of having good reading skills. (A) and (B) are wrong for the same reason. The author's claim must be interpreted to mean "of children who are able to learn, all would benefit from a computerized reading program." When the author claims that "public-school children can be good readers," he is not implying that all children can learn to be good readers nor that all can learn to read equally well.

2. **(D)** The question contains a hidden assumption: That the person questioned agrees that his company has, in the past, discriminated. So I is applicable, since the speaker may wish to answer neither "yes" nor "no." He may wish to object to the question: "But I do not admit that our company has ever discriminated, so your question is unfair." III is just another way of describing the difficulty we have just outlined. II is not applicable to the question. Since a simple question never actually makes a statement, it would seem impossible for it to contradict itself. A contradiction occurs only between statements or assertions.

3. **(A)** There are two weaknesses in Ms. Rose's argument. One will be treated in the explanation of the following question—she reaches a very general conclusion on the basis of one example. We are concerned for the moment with the second weakness. Even if Rose had been able to cite numerous examples like the case she mentions, her argument would be weak because it overlooks the possibility that an education may be valuable even if it is not used to make a living. Importantly, Rose may be correct in her criticism of the man she mentions—we need make no judgment about that—but the assumption is nonetheless *unsupported* in that she gives no arguments to support it. (B) plays on the superficial detail of the paragraph—the inversion of customary role models. But that is not relevant to the structure of the argument; the form could have been as easily shown using a woman with a law degree who decided to become a sailor or a child who studied ballet but later decided to become a doctor. (D) also is totally beside the point. Rose never commits herself to so specific a conclusion. She simply says professional education is a waste; she never claims success is related to quality of education. (E) is wrong because Rose is making a general claim about professional education—the man with the law degree was used merely to illustrate her point. (C) is perhaps, the second-best answer, but it is still not nearly as good as (A). The author's objection is that the man she mentions did not use his law degree in a law-related field. She never suggests that such a degree should be used to make money. She might not have objected to his behavior if he had used the degree to work in a public interest capacity.

4. **(D)** As we noted at the beginning of our discussion of item 3, there is another weakness in Rose's argument: She takes a single example and from it draws a very general conclusion. (D) exemplifies this weakness. Here, too, we have a person who rests his claim on a single example, and obviously this makes the claim very weak. (E) mentions education, but here education is a detail of the argument. The form of the argument—a foolish generalization—is not restricted to education. (A), (B), and (C) are all wrong because they do not reflect the form of the argument, a generalization on a single example.

5. **(A)** The logical conclusion of the argument is that those who are apathetic are ultimately responsible for the corruption in local governments since that corruption would not have occurred unless they had been apathetic. (B) confuses the reading matter. The author says most of us are apathetic; do not confuse the majority of the *population* with the majority *party*. (C) does not follow from the author's remarks. The four-year period apparently refers to a presidential election period. These mark the peaks of political activity, not the maximum length of political involvement. (D) does not follow from the paragraph. The author says that wherever political corruption in local government occurs, it is the result of apathy. He does not say

that such corruption is universal. (E) overstates the case. While the author claims that apathy is, in the final analysis, what *allows* corruption to occur—and that since we can prevent apathy, we can prevent corruption, so we must be in some sense responsible for it—he does not say that the apathetic are *directly* involved in the wrongdoing.

6. **(D)** Once you realize that II must be the first in the series, the question is relatively easy. II is the opening sentence of the paragraph; it just cannot follow any of the other sentences. As for (E), which also begins with II, while IV and V are coupled in the correct order, I cannot precede III. III should come before I since it not only uses the term *gridlock,* but also gives an explanation of what the term means. Although (A) orders the I-III pair correctly, it puts II as the last sentence; but, as was just pointed out, II makes no sense unless it introduces the paragraph. (B) and (C) must be wrong for all of the reasons just mentioned

7. **(D)** The ad is weak for two reasons. First, although it is addressed to smokers in general, the evidence it cites is restricted to heavy (three-packs-a-day) smokers. Second, the success achieved by the product was restricted to a highly specific and unusual location—the mountain retreat of a clinic with a population trying hard to quit smoking. Thus, II will undermine the appeal of the advertisement because it cites the first of the weaknesses. III also will tell against the ad since it mentions the second of these weaknesses. I, however, is irrelevant to the ad's appeal since the cause of a smoker's addiction plays no role in the claim of this ad to assist smokers in quitting or cutting down.

8. **(B)** Notice that there is much common ground between the jockey and the veterinarian. The question stem asks you to uncover the areas on which they are in agreement, by asking which of the answer choices is NOT a shared assumption. Note that the exception can be an area neither has as well as an area only one has. Examine the dialogue. Both apparently assume that human emotions can be attributed to animals since they talk about them being loyal and brave (C), and both take those characteristics as being noble—that is, admirable (A). Neither speaker offers scientific evidence; each rests content with an anecdote (E) and (D). As for (B), it would seem that some kind of study of animal behavior might resolve the issue. We could find out how horses and dogs would react in emergency circumstances—do they show concern for human beings, or do they watch out for themselves? Importantly, it may be wrong to attribute such emotions to animals, but whatever *behavior* is taken *by the speakers* to be evidence of those emotions can be tested. So their claims—animals *behave* in such a way—are, in principle, testable.

9. **(A)** Although we do not want to argue theology, perhaps a point taken from that discipline will make this question more accessible: "If God is only good, from where does evil come?" Rousseau, at least as far as his argument is characterized here, faces a similar problem. If man is by his very nature sympathetic, what is the source of his non-sympathetic social institutions? (A) poses this critical question. The remaining choices each commit the same fundamental error. Rousseau *describes* a situation. The paragraph never suggests that he proposed a *solution.* Perhaps Rousseau considered the problem of modern society irremediable.

10. **(C)** The last sentence of the paragraph is very important. It tells us that the proportion of light atoms in the universe is increasing (because heavy ones decay into light ones, but the reverse process does not occur) and that this trend can be measured. By extrapolation back into time on the basis of present trends, scientists can find out when it all began. (B) and (E) are incorrect for the same reason. The author describes a physical phenomenon occurring on a grand scale. He never hints that it will be possible for man to reverse it (B). Further, (E) is in direct contradiction with information given in the paragraph: The ratio is not stable because the stars do not produce enough heavy atoms to offset the decay. (D) cannot be inferred from the passage. Although the

ratio of light to heavy atoms is increasing, we should not conclude that the ratio is greater than 1:1. And, in any event, this would not be nearly so logical a conclusion to the passage as (C). Finally, (A) is a distraction. It picks up on a minor detail in the passage and inflates that into a conclusion. Moreover, the passage clearly states that the process which keeps the stars going is fusion, not decay.

11. **(C)** It is important to pay careful attention to the ways in which a speaker qualifies his claims. In this case, the speaker has said only that the *great majority* of people can get medical care—he does not claim that *all* can. Thus, built into the claim is the implicit concession that some people may not have access to medical care. Thus, the objector's response fails to score against the speaker. The speaker could just respond, "Yes, I realize that and that is the reason why I qualified my remarks." (A) is incorrect for the only word in the objector's statement which is the least bit emotional is "poor," and it seems rather free from emotional overtones here. It would have been a different case had the objector claimed, "There are thousands of poor and starving people who have no place to live. . . . " (D) is wrong for two reasons. First, the evidence is really not statistical; it is only numerical. Second, and more important, the evidence, if anything, cuts against the speaker's claim—not that it does any damage given the speaker's qualifications on his claim; but it surely does not strengthen the speaker's claim. Finally, inasmuch as the speaker does not offer a cause-effect explanation, (E) must be wrong.

12. **(C)** There are really two parts to the speaker's claim. First, he maintains that the majority of Americans can get access to the medical care in this country; and, second, that the care they have access to is the best in the world. As for the second, good medical care is a function of many variables: Number and location of facilities, availability of doctors, quality of education, etc. (A) and (E) may both be consistent with the speaker's claim. Even though we have fewer assistants (A) than some other country, we have more doctors and that more than makes up for the fewer assistants. Or, perhaps, we have such good preventive medicine that people do not need to go into the hospital as frequently as the citizens of other nations (E). (B) is wrong for a similar reason. Although it suggests there is a country in which people have greater access to the available care, it does not come to grips with the second element of the speaker's claim: that the care we get is the best. (C), however, does meet both because it cites the existence of a country in which people are *given* (that is the first element) *better* (the second element) care. (D) hardly tells against the speaker's claim since he has implicitly conceded that some people do not have access to the care.

13. **(B)** The chief failing of the argument is that it draws a false analogy. Since prisons are required to feed and maintain as well as house prisoners (not to mention the necessity for security), the analogy to a hotel room is weak at best. (C) focuses on this specific shortcoming. Remember in evaluating the strength of an argument from analogy it is important to look for dissimilarities which might make the analogy inappropriate. Thus, (A) and (E) are also good criticisms of the argument. They voice the general objection of which (C) is the specification. (D) is also a specific objection—the argument compares two numbers which are not at all similar. So the numerical comparison is a false one. (B) is not a way in which the argument can be criticized, for the author never cites any authority.

14. **(C)** Note the word *right* is italicized in the first sentence of the paragraph. The author is saying that this idea of a right can be only understood as the outcome of a balancing of demands. The smoker has an interest in smoking; the non-smoker has an interest in being free from smoke; so the question of which one actually has a *right* to have his *interest* protected depends upon which of those interests is considered to be more important. In some cases the balance is easily struck; in other cases it is difficult; but

in all cases, the weighing, implicitly or explicitly, occurs. (C) captures the essence of this thought. In the case of smoking, the interests of both parties must be taken into account. (A) is a distraction. It is true the passage treats "rights," and it is also true that our Constitution protects our rights; but the connection suggested by (A) is a spurious one. It fails to address itself to the logic of the author's argument. The same objections can be leveled against (B). The wording of (D) makes it wrong. The passage is concerned with the demands of the non-smoker *to be free from* the smoke of others, not with whether he himself chooses to smoke. (E) is premature. At this juncture the author is laying the foundation for his argument. He is speaking about rights in general. He reaches his conclusion with regard to smoking only at the end of the paragraph. (See discussion of the following question.) (E) is wrong also because it mentions the "rights" of non-smoking persons. The whole question the author is addressing is whether the non-smoking person has a *right,* as opposed to an interest or a mere claim.

15. **(C)** Here is where the author makes his general discussion of the balancing of interests to determine rights specifically applicable to the question of smoking. A smoker will have a *right* to smoke when and where his interests outweigh the interests of those who object, and (C) provides a pretty clear statement of this conclusion. (A) overstates the author's case. While it may be true that ultimately it will be some branch of the government which strikes the balance of interests, the phrase "chooses to allow" does not do justice to the author's concept of the balancing. The government is not simply choosing: It is weighing. Of course, since the balance may or may not be struck in favor of the smoker, (B) is incorrect. (E) confuses the problem of enforcement with the process of balancing. The passage leads to the conclusion that the balance must be struck. How that decision is later enforced is a practical matter the author is not concerned to discuss in this passage. Finally, (D), like (A), overstates the case. The smoker has an interest in being allowed to smoke, just as much as the non-smoker has an interest in being free from the smoke. A balance must be struck by giving proper weight to both. The author never suggests that the interests of the smokers can be completely overridden. Thus, for example, a smoker may have a more powerful interest in smoking than a non-smoker has in his being free from smoke, if the non-smoker can—with some small inconvenience—protect himself from the smoke.

16. **(B)** The whole passage is to clear up a misunderstanding about the concept of a *right.* The author explains that the term is misused since most people fail to realize that the right is not absolute, but is qualified by the interests and claims of other persons. While it is true that this is not generally known, (A) is incorrect because the author's *strategy* in argument is to clarify that term, not merely to bring up facts to support a contention which is already well-defined. (C) also fails to describe his strategy. It is true that the author mentions hypothetical cases, but that is a detail, not his principal strategy. As for (D), though the author argues that smokers who claim an unqualified right to smoke are wrong, he does not argue that they have fallen into contradiction. Finally, although the author argues that the general claim of smokers is ill-founded, the general claim he attacks (smokers have a right to smoke) is not an induction based on *empirical* evidence. A person who makes such a claim is not generalizing on observed instances (All swans I have seen are white. . . .), he is making a conceptual claim.

17. **(D)** Let us use our technique of substituting capital letters for categories. The sample argument can be rendered:

Some J are not B. (Some Judges are not Bar members)

No B are F. (No Bar members are Felons)

Therefore, Some J are not F. (Some Judges are not Felons)

This is a perfectly valid (logical) argument. (D) shares its form and validity:

Some M are P. (Some Men are Polite)
No M are D. (No Men are Dorm-allowed)
Therefore, Some P are not D. (Some Polite Men are not Dorm-allowed)

(E) has the invalid argument form:

G is L.
G is A.
Therefore, A is L.

(B) and (C) are both set up using more than three categories; therefore, they cannot possibly have the structure of the sample argument which uses only three categories:

(B)—people, people who want to avoid jury duty, people who do not register to vote, persons under eighteen

(C)—business, entities filing tax returns, business making enough money to pay taxes, business making a profit.

Finally, (A) does not parallel the sample argument since it contains the qualification "likely."

18. **(D)** The author's argument is admittedly not a very persuasive one, but the question stem does not ask us to comment on its relative strength. Rather, we are asked to identify the form of argumentation. Here the author suggests an alternative explanation, albeit a somewhat outlandish one. Thus, (D) is correct. (E) is incorrect because the claim about fresh air and the country is introduced as a causal explanation, not an analogy to the city. (C) is wrong for the author accepts the differential described by the report; he just tries to explain the existence of the differential in another way. By the same token we can reject both (A) and (B) since the author takes the report's conclusion as his starting point. Although he attacks the explanation provided by the *report* which was published by the Department of Education, he does not attack the *credibility* of the *department* itself. Further, though he disagrees with the *conclusion* drawn by the report, he does not attack the way in which the *study* itself was *conducted.* Rather, he disagrees with the interpretation of the data gathered.

19. **(E)** The question stem asks us to find the one item which will not strengthen the author's argument. That is (E). Remember, the author's argument is an attempt (to be sure, a weak one) to develop an alternative causal explanation. (A) would provide some evidence that the author's claim—which at first glance seems a bit far-fetched—actually has some empirical foundation. While (B) does not add any strength to the author's own explanation of the phenomenon being studied, it does strengthen the author's overall position by undermining the explanation given in the report. (C) strengthens the author's position for the same reason that (B) does: it weakens the position he is attacking. (D) strengthens the argument in the same way that (A) does, by providing some empirical support for the otherwise seemingly far-fetched explanation.

20. **(E)** Perhaps the most obvious weakness in the argument is that it oversimplifies matters. It is like the domino theory arguments adduced to support the war in Vietnam: either we fight Communism now or it will take us over. The author argues, in effect: Either we put a stop to this now, or there will be no stopping it. Like the proponents of the domino theory, he ignores the many intermediate positions one might take. III is one way of describing this shortcoming: The dilemma posed by the author is a false one because it overlooks positions between the two extremes. II is also a weakness of the argument: "Cold-blooded murder" is obviously a phrase calculated to excite negative feelings. Finally, the whole argument is also internally inconsistent. The conclusion is that we should allow nature to take its course. How?—by prolonging life with artificial means.

21. **(E)** We can use our technique of substituting capital letters for clauses to keep track of the relationships:

If P, then Q.
If Q, then R or S.
If R or S, then A.
And if not Q, not A.

Notice that we have used "R or S" to symbolize "either Ralph or Steven will ask Alice to dance," but we could have used a single letter, say K, to represent both since nothing turns on the further breakdown of the clause. Also, "A" symbolizes "Alice will refuse," so "not-A" symbolizes the opposite, "Alice will accept." (A) cannot be deduced. The assumptions we are working with are phrased in the conditional: If, then. Although we know "*If* Q, then R or S," we do not know whether Q did or did not come to pass. Similarly, (C) can be rejected, because we do not know whether it is Q or not-Q. (B) would be wrong in any event since we have no way of deducing from "Alice will accept R or S" the conclusion "Alice will accept S." (D) cannot be deduced since we do not know whether Q is the case or not-Q is the case. Finally, (E) is phrased in the conditional, "If not-Q, then not-A." That is equivalent to the second part of our third assumption, so (E) is deducible from the information supplied in the question stem.

22. **(A)** The question stem has the form:

All S are AP. (All Students are APplicants)

Some AP are AC. (Some APplicants are ACcepted)

Some *more* S are AC. (Some more Students are ACcepted)

Notice that (A) preserves very nicely the parallel in the conclusion because it uses the word *more.* Thus, the error made in the stem argument (that some *more* students will be *accepted*) is preserved in (A): *more* apples will be *loaded.* (B) has a valid argument form (All S are W, X is an S, therefore, X is a W) so it is not parallel to the sample argument. (C) is not similar for at least two reasons. First, its conclusion is a recommendation ("should"), not a factual claim. Second, (C) uses one premise, not two premises as the sample argument does. (D) would have been parallel to the sample argument only if the sample had the conclusion "some more applications must be acted upon." Finally, (E) contains an argument which is fallacious, but the fallacy is not similar to that of the question stem.

23. **(E)** The advertisement employs the term "more" in an ambiguous manner. In the context, one might expect the phrase "more flavor" to mean "more highly concentrated flavor," that is, "more flavor per unit weight." What the ad actually says, however, is that the sticks of Evergreen are *larger,* so if they are larger, there must be more *total* flavor. All three propositions, if they are true (as we are asked to assume they are), are good attacks on the ad. First, in I, it is possible to beat the ad at its own game. If flavor is just a matter of chewing enough sticks, then Spring Mint is as good a deal because, flavor unit for flavor unit, it is no more expensive than Evergreen. Second, II would also undermine the ad by focusing on the ambiguity we have just discussed. Finally, III also uncovers another potential ambiguity. If the ad is comparing volume rather than weight, Spring Mint may be a better value. After all, who wants to buy a lot of air?

24. **(D)** Again, we remind ourselves that we are looking for the most reliable statement. Even the most reliable, however, will not necessarily be perfectly reliable. Here (D) is fairly trustworthy. We note that the speaker is an expert and so is qualified to speak about wines. In (A), the speaker is making a judgment about something on which he is not qualified to speak. Also, in (D) there is no hint of self-interest—if anything the speaker is admitting against a possible self-interest that American chablis is a better buy that French chablis. By comparison, (B) and (C), which smack of a self-serving bias, are not so trustworthy. Finally, (E) sounds like a statement made for dramatic effect and so is not to be taken at face value.

25. **(D)** The whole point of the passage is that the attorney really had nothing legitimate to say about the doctor's testimony, so he had a bit of fun with the cross-examination. (E) has to be wrong, for the little story is lighthearted, not serious. Neither (A) nor (C) can be correct because the introduction to the

question-and-answer sequence says specifically that the attorney knew there was nothing to be done by way of cross-examining the doctor. (B) is even farther removed from a correct answer than either (A) or (C), since if one takes the anecdote seriously rather than as it was intended (humorously), he will conclude the cross-examination was effective rather than ineffective.

26. **(E)** This advertisement is simply rife with ambiguity. The wording obviously seeks to create the impression that FCBI found jobs for its many graduates and generally does a lot of good for them. But first, we should ask how many graduates FCBI had—one, two, three, a dozen, or a hundred. If it had only twelve or so, finding them jobs might have been easy; but if many people enroll at FCBI, they may not have the same success. Further, we might want to know how many people graduated compared with how many enrolled. Do people finish the program, or does FCBI just take their money and then force them out of the program? So II is certainly something we need to know in order to assess the validity of the claim. Now, how many of those who graduated came in looking for help in finding a job? Maybe most people had jobs waiting for them (only a few needed help), in which case the job placement assistance of FCBI is not so impressive. Or, perhaps the graduates were so disgusted they did not even seek assistance. So I is relevant. III is also important. Perhaps FCBI found them jobs sweeping streets—not in business. The ad does not say what jobs FCBI helped its people find. Finally, maybe the ad is truthful—FCBI graduates found jobs—but maybe they did it on their own. So IV also is a question worth asking.

SECTION VI

Set 1

OVERVIEW: The rules here present two different remedies for damage to property. According to the first, only the owner is entitled to recover damages for the injury to property. According to the second, anyone having a possessory interest in the property (present or future) can prevent the damage from occurring, as opposed to receiving compensation for the injury to the property. The difficulty presented in our facts is that we do not have enough information to determine who is the *owner* of the property. Is it Paul, who gets it for as long as he lives, or it is Fredrika who cannot get it until Paul dies, or perhaps both of them are owners? It turns out in the final analysis that there is no conflict between the rules. The application of the first rule does not preclude an application of the second, and vice versa.

1. **(B)** As we noted in the set overview, this is an important question in deciding how the rules should be applied, but the answer is one not available to us. To handle this question, we would need some further clarification of the term "owner."

2. **(C)** It is clear from the facts of the case that Fredrika does have some future interest in the property. While we cannot say that she is definitely the owner at this time (see #1), we can conclude that she is in line to possess the property one day. So, regardless of whether Fredrika can claim under Rule I, it appears that she does have the proper status to claim under Rule II.

3. **(D)** Paul's age is irrelevant. Fredrika cannot come into possession of the house until Paul dies. She cannot sneak up on Paul as he gets older, moving a little more furniture in on each birthday, taking over another room every five years.

4. **(B)** While it may be that Paul is not required to pay any part of restoring the wall, this issue is raised by Houston, who insists that Paul should. We obviously do not have a rule to decide this point, so we should call the question a (B).

5. **(B)** This question, as we noted earlier, does not raise a conflict between the two rules; rather, it poses the problem of determining whether Fredrika is the owner, as opposed to Paul. For this we need more information.

6. **(B)** This must be classified as a (B) for the same reason that #5 is a (B).

Set 2

OVERVIEW: The conflict between these two rules will arise when there is a performance promised which is unique, that is, cannot be replaced by a similar performance. The facts of our case provide us with a pretty good example of such a performance, a unique painting. Notice several clues have been sown for you to reap. Sargent is Eberly's favorite artist. Eberly was fond of this particular painting. This tips us off that the painting is unique—it cannot be replaced by a Picasso (who is not Eberly's favorite artist) nor by any other Sargent painting (Eberly is fond of *this one*). Now, this raises the necessity for a choice between the two rules. By the terms of Rule I, Eberly is entitled only to money damages. By Rule II, Eberly is actually entitled to receive the painting.

7. **(B)** One of the critical elements in applying Rule I is determining the value of the lost transaction. The value depends in part on how much the painting was worth at the time that Haffner failed to deliver.

8. **(A)** This is the conflict we outlined earlier. The big question in this case is whether Eberly is entitled to receive money damage from Haffner or whether he is entitled to actually get the painting from Haffner. Deciding which is the appropriate remedy requires a choice between the two rules.

9. **(C)** A critical element in Rule II is the uniqueness of the subject matter of the contract. The term "unique" is defined as something which cannot be replaced. In the set overview we pointed out the reasons for the conclusion that the subject matter of this contract—a particular painting by a favorite artist—could not be replaced.

10. **(A)** This is really the same question as #8. The answer for it can only be had by deciding which of the two rules will govern the case. Only if Rule II is selected over Rule I can an affirmative answer to the question be given, which shows us a conflict between the rules is involved.

11. **(D)** While the number of Sargent paintings in existence might be relevant in determining whether any one painting had the status of being unique, it is surely not the case that a comparison of the sort suggested by this question is useful in determining whether the Sargent painting is unique.

Set 3

OVERVIEW: Rule I lays down a general principle that the finder is entitled to possess property against the whole world save for the true owner. Rule II runs contrary to this and says that if a finder discovers the lost item on private property, it is the owner of the private property and not the finder who is entitled to possession. So by Rule I, the order of ownership runs: (1) True owner, (2) Finder, and (3) Rest of world, but on Rule II the order is: (1) True owner, (2) Owner of premises where found, and (3) Rest of world.

12. **(B)** Clearly an important element of Rule II is the identity of the owner of private property. Notice that the facts, however, do not state whether Garvey owns the premises where the store is located. He could conceivably rent them, in which case the landlord would be the owner of those premises.

13. **(C)** In the set overview, we determined that under both rules the true owner is ranked first in priority. So applying either of the two rules, the true owner would be entitled to possession.

14. **(B)** The facts state that the watch was half on the drugstore premises and half on the sidewalk. So there is an argument for both positions: It was on the sidewalk, it was in the drugstore. A decision here does not require a choice between our rules, since this is applicable only in Rule II. Rule I does not draw a public-private property distinction. But since Rule II does not define the distinction in this case, we need the guidance of some other rule.

15. **(D)** The rules govern the disposition of found property without regard to the value of that property. So this question raises an

issue which is relevant under neither of the two rules.

16. **(A)** This brings out the possible conflict in the set of rules. If it is established that Garvey is the owner of the store premises (see #14), then Rule II states that Garvey is entitled to possession of the watch. But Rule I awards possession of the watch to Oliver, so we find a conflict. A choice must be made between the rules.

17. **(D)** This dispute is between Garvey and Oliver. We know that if the true owner shows up, he is entitled to the watch. But in order to determine whether it is Garvey or Oliver who gets the watch *in the true owner's absence,* we do not need to know who the true owner is.

Set 4

OVERVIEW: The way these rules are set up, no single action could be both assault and *attempted* assault. So if a question asks, "Which of the two crimes was committed," a choice between the rules would be required. As the questions in this problem set are actually presented, this question is never asked and we will not find an (A) answer in the group.

18. **(C)** Brenda's actions show that she did willfully attack and injure Wanda. Since there actually was an assault, we know that Rule II does not govern (see the set overview), so no choice is required here. Rule I definitely applies, and Rule II definitely does not apply, so we enter answer (C).

19. **(D)** This issue is specifically made irrelevant by the wording of Rule I—"no matter how slightly."

20. **(B)** Notice that an additional issue is raised by the "if" clause of this question. We are supposed to assume that Brenda is guilty of something, but then we are asked whether she is relieved of liability because of the circumstances. There is at least an argument that her uncontrollable rage would have some bearing on this question, so we will need some further guidance in the form of a rule to formulate an answer to this question.

21. **(C)** Just as we were able to determine the answer to #18 so, too, we can determine here that Brenda did *not* criminally assault Ellen. She never got to her because George intervened. But even a negative conclusion is still a deduction, so the answer to this question is (C).

22. **(C)** Just as in #21 we were able to answer the question in the negative, here, too, we deduce a conclusion in the negative. Since Brenda was going after Ellen, she did not willfully attack George. But even the conclusion that she did not assault George is sufficient to enter an answer (C).

Set 5

OVERVIEW: The first rule sets up the general principles that anyone who enters onto someone else's premises has trespassed and must pay damages. Now, Rule II does not change the definition of trespass. It, too, says that anyone who, without consent of the owner, enters onto someone's premises is a trespasser. But II differs from I in that II stipulates that no damages are due. Our facts show that Sydney is a trespasser, so both rules agree here. He entered Frank's house without Frank's permission. The conflict between the two rules arises only when we ask if Sydney is required to pay damages for his trespass. Rule I says that he must, no matter how slight his intrusion, while Rule II says that Sydney does not have to pay damages because he clearly believed he was acting in a life or death situation.

23. **(D)** A good, careful reading of Rule II shows that this is a (D), or irrelevant. Rule II does not require that the actor actually be involved in a life or death situation; it requires only that the actor *believe* he is.

24. **(D)** This, too, is made irrelevant by the wording of one of the rules. Rule I says that a trespass occurs without regard to the significance of the intrusion. So even if the telephone were only just inside the door, when Sydney entered he committed a trespass.

25. **(A)** This question raises the conflict we discussed in the set overview. Although both rules agree that Sydney has committed a trespass, they give different results on the issue of damages.

26. **(B)** Notice that the rules speak of compensation for the intrusion. Although the question of damages for the intrusion requires a choice between the two rules, neither rule addresses the issue whether Sydney must pay for something he used. It certainly seems reasonable that he is entitled to use Frank's phone given the circumstances, but it also seems reasonable that he might be required to pay for the call. That, in any event, is a question which requires another rule.

27. **(C)** As we have noted before, both rules are in agreement on this point.

Set 6

OVERVIEW: Rule I sets up the actions for a civil wrong called false imprisonment. Rule II carves out an exception. It states that although an act might be false imprisonment, the owner of property is entitled to take such action provided that it is needed to protect his property. In the facts of our case, there is no question but that Cindy was falsely imprisoned—at least according to the definition provided by Rule I. The facts also point out, however, that Benny reasonably believed Cindy was about to steal from him. It was reasonable for Benny, then, to stop Cindy before she could make off with his property.

28. **(C)** As odd as it sounds, Cindy was falsely imprisoned. Applying Rule I to the facts of the case, we can see that Benny's actions restricted Cindy's freedom to move. But remember, the seeming artificiality of the result in question is a function of the special instructions with which we are forced to work.

29. **(D)** Rule II does not require that the property be valuable to warrant protection. Surely Benny is not required to allow Cindy to escape with clothing just because it is inexpensive. Since nothing turns on the value of the clothing, this must be a (D).

30. **(C)** As we previously argued, it was reasonable for Benny to detain Cindy until the police arrived. Notice that although Cindy had ditched the merchandise before Benny nailed her, Benny had every reason to believe she would have stolen it and that she still had it on her.

31. **(A)** Here we find presented the issue described in the set overview which requires a choice between the rules.

Set 7

OVERVIEW: The conflict here is the remedy to which Herman is entitled. It surely is the case that Deekins' disco constitutes a nuisance. The definitions of nuisance in both rules agree on that. The decision to be made is what remedy Herman is entitled to. According to Rule I, Herman is entitled to money compensation. According to Rule II, Herman can force Deekins to eliminate the nuisance.

32. **(C)** The two rules both agree on this. Deekins' disco diminished the value of Herman's cottage—as Deekins himself admitted. And the disco interfered with Herman's enjoyment of his cottage.

33. **(A)** This is the conflict of remedies presented by the rules which we described in the set overview.

34. **(A)** This is the same question as #33. It presents the choice of remedies.

35. **(C)** Even if the problem of the litter is solved, there is still the nuisance created by the late-night music.

SECTION VII

Explanation of Pressure Points and Exemplary Essay for Writing Sample

TOPIC: The Congress should adopt a national beverage for the United States.

PRESSURE POINTS: The following considerations might go through your mind as you examine the topic and seek to create an outline for your essay.

—What is a national beverage? What purpose? What effects? Why national?
—What would affect the selection of the beverage?
—What would affect the achievement of the purpose?
—How would the factors of selection interact with the achievement of purpose?
—How would the selection of a national beverage be viewed by different groups in the United States?

The following essay is only one of many that could have been written on this topic.

The suggestion that the Congress adopt a national beverage poses the following dilemma: Either the action will pass virtually unnoticed, in which case we have an empty and harmless formality; or the action will be significant, in which case we are faced with an impossible choice for the national beverage. It is important to keep in mind that the symbols of our nation fall into two general classes. There are those which are important because they represent for us some aspect of our heritage or national character. The bald eagle, the American flag, and the National Anthem are examples of this group. Then there is another group of relatively unimportant symbols, adopted to please some special interest group; and so we have a National Horse Day, or the pennant which flies on the limousine of some minor State Department dignitary. It must be admitted that this classification is somewhat over-simplified, but it raises a question—into which group shall we put the national beverage?

If the national beverage goes unremarked by the greater portion of our citizenry, it seems that there can be little or no objection to the Congress's adopting one. Since symbols derive their importance from the value with which they are endowed by people who use them as symbols, a symbol which no one uses is a dead symbol. It is difficult to build up any passion about a dead symbol.

If the national beverage, however, is embraced by most people, the choice of beverage becomes of paramount importance. Yet, a fair choice—fair because it captures in symbolic form some part of our heritage or character—is impossible. There is no single beverage which can fill the role. Many will argue for beer as the logical choice. Others, opposed to alcohol, will insist on milk. Still others will advocate a soft drink. In the final analysis, the choice of beverage must unfairly favor some groups of persons over others, some region over its neighbors, and some industry over its competitors. The idea of a national beverage is either doomed to obscurity or hopelessly unworkable.

ANSWER SHEET—PRACTICE EXAMINATION 2

SECTION I

1 Ⓐ Ⓑ Ⓒ Ⓓ Ⓔ	8 Ⓐ Ⓑ Ⓒ Ⓓ Ⓔ	15 Ⓐ Ⓑ Ⓒ Ⓓ Ⓔ	22 Ⓐ Ⓑ Ⓒ Ⓓ Ⓔ	29 Ⓐ Ⓑ Ⓒ Ⓓ Ⓔ
2 Ⓐ Ⓑ Ⓒ Ⓓ Ⓔ	9 Ⓐ Ⓑ Ⓒ Ⓓ Ⓔ	16 Ⓐ Ⓑ Ⓒ Ⓓ Ⓔ	23 Ⓐ Ⓑ Ⓒ Ⓓ Ⓔ	30 Ⓐ Ⓑ Ⓒ Ⓓ Ⓔ
3 Ⓐ Ⓑ Ⓒ Ⓓ Ⓔ	10 Ⓐ Ⓑ Ⓒ Ⓓ Ⓔ	17 Ⓐ Ⓑ Ⓒ Ⓓ Ⓔ	24 Ⓐ Ⓑ Ⓒ Ⓓ Ⓔ	31 Ⓐ Ⓑ Ⓒ Ⓓ Ⓔ
4 Ⓐ Ⓑ Ⓒ Ⓓ Ⓔ	11 Ⓐ Ⓑ Ⓒ Ⓓ Ⓔ	18 Ⓐ Ⓑ Ⓒ Ⓓ Ⓔ	25 Ⓐ Ⓑ Ⓒ Ⓓ Ⓔ	32 Ⓐ Ⓑ Ⓒ Ⓓ Ⓔ
5 Ⓐ Ⓑ Ⓒ Ⓓ Ⓔ	12 Ⓐ Ⓑ Ⓒ Ⓓ Ⓔ	19 Ⓐ Ⓑ Ⓒ Ⓓ Ⓔ	26 Ⓐ Ⓑ Ⓒ Ⓓ Ⓔ	33 Ⓐ Ⓑ Ⓒ Ⓓ Ⓔ
6 Ⓐ Ⓑ Ⓒ Ⓓ Ⓔ	13 Ⓐ Ⓑ Ⓒ Ⓓ Ⓔ	20 Ⓐ Ⓑ Ⓒ Ⓓ Ⓔ	27 Ⓐ Ⓑ Ⓒ Ⓓ Ⓔ	34 Ⓐ Ⓑ Ⓒ Ⓓ Ⓔ
7 Ⓐ Ⓑ Ⓒ Ⓓ Ⓔ	14 Ⓐ Ⓑ Ⓒ Ⓓ Ⓔ	21 Ⓐ Ⓑ Ⓒ Ⓓ Ⓔ	28 Ⓐ Ⓑ Ⓒ Ⓓ Ⓔ	35 Ⓐ Ⓑ Ⓒ Ⓓ Ⓔ

SECTION II

1 Ⓐ Ⓑ Ⓒ Ⓓ Ⓔ	6 Ⓐ Ⓑ Ⓒ Ⓓ Ⓔ	11 Ⓐ Ⓑ Ⓒ Ⓓ Ⓔ	16 Ⓐ Ⓑ Ⓒ Ⓓ Ⓔ	21 Ⓐ Ⓑ Ⓒ Ⓓ Ⓔ
2 Ⓐ Ⓑ Ⓒ Ⓓ Ⓔ	7 Ⓐ Ⓑ Ⓒ Ⓓ Ⓔ	12 Ⓐ Ⓑ Ⓒ Ⓓ Ⓔ	17 Ⓐ Ⓑ Ⓒ Ⓓ Ⓔ	22 Ⓐ Ⓑ Ⓒ Ⓓ Ⓔ
3 Ⓐ Ⓑ Ⓒ Ⓓ Ⓔ	8 Ⓐ Ⓑ Ⓒ Ⓓ Ⓔ	13 Ⓐ Ⓑ Ⓒ Ⓓ Ⓔ	18 Ⓐ Ⓑ Ⓒ Ⓓ Ⓔ	23 Ⓐ Ⓑ Ⓒ Ⓓ Ⓔ
4 Ⓐ Ⓑ Ⓒ Ⓓ Ⓔ	9 Ⓐ Ⓑ Ⓒ Ⓓ Ⓔ	14 Ⓐ Ⓑ Ⓒ Ⓓ Ⓔ	19 Ⓐ Ⓑ Ⓒ Ⓓ Ⓔ	24 Ⓐ Ⓑ Ⓒ Ⓓ Ⓔ
5 Ⓐ Ⓑ Ⓒ Ⓓ Ⓔ	10 Ⓐ Ⓑ Ⓒ Ⓓ Ⓔ	15 Ⓐ Ⓑ Ⓒ Ⓓ Ⓔ	20 Ⓐ Ⓑ Ⓒ Ⓓ Ⓔ	25 Ⓐ Ⓑ Ⓒ Ⓓ Ⓔ

SECTION III

1 Ⓐ Ⓑ Ⓒ Ⓓ Ⓔ	6 Ⓐ Ⓑ Ⓒ Ⓓ Ⓔ	11 Ⓐ Ⓑ Ⓒ Ⓓ Ⓔ	16 Ⓐ Ⓑ Ⓒ Ⓓ Ⓔ	21 Ⓐ Ⓑ Ⓒ Ⓓ Ⓔ	26 Ⓐ Ⓑ Ⓒ Ⓓ Ⓔ
2 Ⓐ Ⓑ Ⓒ Ⓓ Ⓔ	7 Ⓐ Ⓑ Ⓒ Ⓓ Ⓔ	12 Ⓐ Ⓑ Ⓒ Ⓓ Ⓔ	17 Ⓐ Ⓑ Ⓒ Ⓓ Ⓔ	22 Ⓐ Ⓑ Ⓒ Ⓓ Ⓔ	27 Ⓐ Ⓑ Ⓒ Ⓓ Ⓔ
3 Ⓐ Ⓑ Ⓒ Ⓓ Ⓔ	8 Ⓐ Ⓑ Ⓒ Ⓓ Ⓔ	13 Ⓐ Ⓑ Ⓒ Ⓓ Ⓔ	18 Ⓐ Ⓑ Ⓒ Ⓓ Ⓔ	23 Ⓐ Ⓑ Ⓒ Ⓓ Ⓔ	28 Ⓐ Ⓑ Ⓒ Ⓓ Ⓔ
4 Ⓐ Ⓑ Ⓒ Ⓓ Ⓔ	9 Ⓐ Ⓑ Ⓒ Ⓓ Ⓔ	14 Ⓐ Ⓑ Ⓒ Ⓓ Ⓔ	19 Ⓐ Ⓑ Ⓒ Ⓓ Ⓔ	24 Ⓐ Ⓑ Ⓒ Ⓓ Ⓔ	
5 Ⓐ Ⓑ Ⓒ Ⓓ Ⓔ	10 Ⓐ Ⓑ Ⓒ Ⓓ Ⓔ	15 Ⓐ Ⓑ Ⓒ Ⓓ Ⓔ	20 Ⓐ Ⓑ Ⓒ Ⓓ Ⓔ	25 Ⓐ Ⓑ Ⓒ Ⓓ Ⓔ	

SECTION IV

1 Ⓐ Ⓑ Ⓒ Ⓓ Ⓔ	6 Ⓐ Ⓑ Ⓒ Ⓓ Ⓔ	11 Ⓐ Ⓑ Ⓒ Ⓓ Ⓔ	16 Ⓐ Ⓑ Ⓒ Ⓓ Ⓔ	21 Ⓐ Ⓑ Ⓒ Ⓓ Ⓔ
2 Ⓐ Ⓑ Ⓒ Ⓓ Ⓔ	7 Ⓐ Ⓑ Ⓒ Ⓓ Ⓔ	12 Ⓐ Ⓑ Ⓒ Ⓓ Ⓔ	17 Ⓐ Ⓑ Ⓒ Ⓓ Ⓔ	22 Ⓐ Ⓑ Ⓒ Ⓓ Ⓔ
3 Ⓐ Ⓑ Ⓒ Ⓓ Ⓔ	8 Ⓐ Ⓑ Ⓒ Ⓓ Ⓔ	13 Ⓐ Ⓑ Ⓒ Ⓓ Ⓔ	18 Ⓐ Ⓑ Ⓒ Ⓓ Ⓔ	23 Ⓐ Ⓑ Ⓒ Ⓓ Ⓔ
4 Ⓐ Ⓑ Ⓒ Ⓓ Ⓔ	9 Ⓐ Ⓑ Ⓒ Ⓓ Ⓔ	14 Ⓐ Ⓑ Ⓒ Ⓓ Ⓔ	19 Ⓐ Ⓑ Ⓒ Ⓓ Ⓔ	24 Ⓐ Ⓑ Ⓒ Ⓓ Ⓔ
5 Ⓐ Ⓑ Ⓒ Ⓓ Ⓔ	10 Ⓐ Ⓑ Ⓒ Ⓓ Ⓔ	15 Ⓐ Ⓑ Ⓒ Ⓓ Ⓔ	20 Ⓐ Ⓑ Ⓒ Ⓓ Ⓔ	25 Ⓐ Ⓑ Ⓒ Ⓓ Ⓔ
				26 Ⓐ Ⓑ Ⓒ Ⓓ Ⓔ

SECTION V

1 Ⓐ Ⓑ Ⓒ Ⓓ Ⓔ	8 Ⓐ Ⓑ Ⓒ Ⓓ Ⓔ	15 Ⓐ Ⓑ Ⓒ Ⓓ Ⓔ	22 Ⓐ Ⓑ Ⓒ Ⓓ Ⓔ	29 Ⓐ Ⓑ Ⓒ Ⓓ Ⓔ
2 Ⓐ Ⓑ Ⓒ Ⓓ Ⓔ	9 Ⓐ Ⓑ Ⓒ Ⓓ Ⓔ	16 Ⓐ Ⓑ Ⓒ Ⓓ Ⓔ	23 Ⓐ Ⓑ Ⓒ Ⓓ Ⓔ	30 Ⓐ Ⓑ Ⓒ Ⓓ Ⓔ
3 Ⓐ Ⓑ Ⓒ Ⓓ Ⓔ	10 Ⓐ Ⓑ Ⓒ Ⓓ Ⓔ	17 Ⓐ Ⓑ Ⓒ Ⓓ Ⓔ	24 Ⓐ Ⓑ Ⓒ Ⓓ Ⓔ	31 Ⓐ Ⓑ Ⓒ Ⓓ Ⓔ
4 Ⓐ Ⓑ Ⓒ Ⓓ Ⓔ	11 Ⓐ Ⓑ Ⓒ Ⓓ Ⓔ	18 Ⓐ Ⓑ Ⓒ Ⓓ Ⓔ	25 Ⓐ Ⓑ Ⓒ Ⓓ Ⓔ	32 Ⓐ Ⓑ Ⓒ Ⓓ Ⓔ
5 Ⓐ Ⓑ Ⓒ Ⓓ Ⓔ	12 Ⓐ Ⓑ Ⓒ Ⓓ Ⓔ	19 Ⓐ Ⓑ Ⓒ Ⓓ Ⓔ	26 Ⓐ Ⓑ Ⓒ Ⓓ Ⓔ	33 Ⓐ Ⓑ Ⓒ Ⓓ Ⓔ
6 Ⓐ Ⓑ Ⓒ Ⓓ Ⓔ	13 Ⓐ Ⓑ Ⓒ Ⓓ Ⓔ	20 Ⓐ Ⓑ Ⓒ Ⓓ Ⓔ	27 Ⓐ Ⓑ Ⓒ Ⓓ Ⓔ	34 Ⓐ Ⓑ Ⓒ Ⓓ Ⓔ
7 Ⓐ Ⓑ Ⓒ Ⓓ Ⓔ	14 Ⓐ Ⓑ Ⓒ Ⓓ Ⓔ	21 Ⓐ Ⓑ Ⓒ Ⓓ Ⓔ	28 Ⓐ Ⓑ Ⓒ Ⓓ Ⓔ	35 Ⓐ Ⓑ Ⓒ Ⓓ Ⓔ

SECTION VI

1 Ⓐ Ⓑ Ⓒ Ⓓ Ⓔ	6 Ⓐ Ⓑ Ⓒ Ⓓ Ⓔ	11 Ⓐ Ⓑ Ⓒ Ⓓ Ⓔ	16 Ⓐ Ⓑ Ⓒ Ⓓ Ⓔ	21 Ⓐ Ⓑ Ⓒ Ⓓ Ⓔ
2 Ⓐ Ⓑ Ⓒ Ⓓ Ⓔ	7 Ⓐ Ⓑ Ⓒ Ⓓ Ⓔ	12 Ⓐ Ⓑ Ⓒ Ⓓ Ⓔ	17 Ⓐ Ⓑ Ⓒ Ⓓ Ⓔ	22 Ⓐ Ⓑ Ⓒ Ⓓ Ⓔ
3 Ⓐ Ⓑ Ⓒ Ⓓ Ⓔ	8 Ⓐ Ⓑ Ⓒ Ⓓ Ⓔ	13 Ⓐ Ⓑ Ⓒ Ⓓ Ⓔ	18 Ⓐ Ⓑ Ⓒ Ⓓ Ⓔ	23 Ⓐ Ⓑ Ⓒ Ⓓ Ⓔ
4 Ⓐ Ⓑ Ⓒ Ⓓ Ⓔ	9 Ⓐ Ⓑ Ⓒ Ⓓ Ⓔ	14 Ⓐ Ⓑ Ⓒ Ⓓ Ⓔ	19 Ⓐ Ⓑ Ⓒ Ⓓ Ⓔ	24 Ⓐ Ⓑ Ⓒ Ⓓ Ⓔ
5 Ⓐ Ⓑ Ⓒ Ⓓ Ⓔ	10 Ⓐ Ⓑ Ⓒ Ⓓ Ⓔ	15 Ⓐ Ⓑ Ⓒ Ⓓ Ⓔ	20 Ⓐ Ⓑ Ⓒ Ⓓ Ⓔ	25 Ⓐ Ⓑ Ⓒ Ⓓ Ⓔ

EXAMINATION FORECAST

Section Number	Type	Minutes	Questions
Section I	Issues & Facts	35	35
Section II	Analytical Reasoning	35	25
Section III	Reading Comprehension	35	28
Section IV	Logical Reasoning	35	26
Section V	Issue & Facts	35	35
Section VI	Analytical Reasoning	35	25
	Writing Sample	30	—
Total Time		4 hours	

A 15-minute break should be taken after Section IV.

The Writing Sample will usually be given before the rest of the LSAT and in this book is found at the end of the Practice Test.

PRACTICE EXAMINATION 2

SECTION I

Time—35 Minutes
35 Questions

Directions: Each of the following sets consists of a fact situation, a dispute and two rules. The rules may conflict, but you are to apply each rule independently. Do not treat a rule as subsidiary or as an exception to the other rule. The rules are followed by questions. You are to select from the following lettered choices (A) through (D) the one that best describes each question in the way it relates to the application of one or both of the rules to the dispute. Blacken the corresponding space on the answer sheet.

(A) a relevant question the answer to which requires a choice between the two rules
(B) a relevant question the answer to which does not require a choice between the two rules, but does require further facts or rules
(C) a relevant question that can be readily answered from the facts or rules or both
(D) an irrelevant question, the answer to which does not affect, or only tangentially affects, the outcome of the dispute

Set 1

FACTS: Barney was eating lunch in a drive-in restaurant when he noticed someone driving away in his car. Barney ran from the restaurant shouting for the driver to stop, but the driver did not stop. Barney looked around for a police officer, and seeing none gave pursuit on foot. Barney caught up with the car a block later when the driver was forced to stop at a traffic signal. Barney ran immediately to the driver's side of the car and without any warning to the driver jerked open the door and pulled the driver from the car. The driver was completely surprised by Barney and so offered no resistance, but he did stumble and fall to the street, incurring a broken arm. By this time a police car had arrived. The driver was identified as David, a student at a nearby high school, and David explained he had taken the car as part of a fraternity initiation and would have returned it to the restaurant parking lot an hour later. The police took David into custody, but the prosecutor declined to bring criminal charges against David, since David had never before been in trouble with the law.

DISPUTE: Later, David and his parents sued Barney for medical costs of having David's arm treated. Barney contested.

RULES: I. A person who touches the body of another person without that person's consent has committed a battery and is liable for any injuries which result from the contact.

II. The owner of personal property has the right to take action to recover that property from a person who has wrongfully taken it from him.

1. What was David's age at the time he took Barney's car?

2. What particular crime did David commit in taking Barney's car?

3. Is Barney liable to David and his parents for the costs of treating David's broken arm?

4. Had David consented to Barney's actions?

5. Did David wrongfully take Barney's car?

Set 2

FACTS: Annemarie had been a police officer on the Chicago police force for eleven years when her partner was arrested on charges of accepting bribes. Although Annemarie had not participated in her partner's wrongdoing and did not even know that he had taken bribes, she was suspended from active duty for an indefinite period until an investigation could be completed. Two weeks after her suspension, with the investigation still pending, Annemarie was returning to her home when she saw two men trying to wrestle a third man into the back seat of a car. Annemarie's police service revolver had been taken from her at the time of her suspension, but she carried a licensed pistol of her own, which she pulled out. She pointed her pistol at the two men, identified herself as a police officer and ordered the two to move away from their victim. One of the men, Hank, pulled a gun and fired at Annemarie. Annemarie returned the fire, striking the man with the gun and killing him instantly. The other man surrendered. Annemarie then learned that all three men were brothers, Hank, Randy, and Jerry, who worked together as plumbers, and the two men had been trying to get their brother, who was drunk, into a car to take him home. Annemarie telephoned for an ambulance, and in the confusion she slipped away. Afraid of the consequences of her mistake, she went home, packed a bag and went to the airport and caught a plane for Los Angeles. The Chicago police searched for Annemarie and could not find her. Randy and Jerry hired a private detective who traced Annemarie to a hotel in Los Angeles. Randy and Jerry flew to Los Angeles and forced Annemarie at gunpoint to return with them to Chicago in a rented car. They turned her over to the Chicago police.

DISPUTE: Annemarie was charged with manslaughter. Her lawyer pled her not guilty.

RULES: I. A person who willfully uses a deadly weapon on another person, with the result that the person attacked is killed, is guilty of manslaughter, unless the attack was justified as self-defense, the defense of a third party, the defense of personal property, or as a police officer acting in the line of duty.

II. Law enforcement officials of one state may not return a fugitive from justice to the officials of another state without proper extradition proceedings, and the remedy for such failure is dismissal of all charges.

6. Can Annemarie be convicted of manslaughter?

7. Was Annemarie acting in the line of duty when she confronted Hank and his brothers?

8. Was Annemarie acting in self-defense when she returned Hank's fire?

9. Is the judge required to dismiss the manslaughter charges against Annemarie for want of proper extradition proceedings?

10. Is Annemarie entitled to backpay and reinstatement on the police force?

11. At the time she intervened, did Annemarie believe she was acting on behalf of some third party?

Set 3

FACTS: Owens was an avid collector of Ulysses S. Grant memorabilia. She owned a sword worn by the general, a pair of reading glasses worn by his wife, and several of the general's letters. Nolan knew that Owens was usually in the market for such items, and he decided to fabricate some article which he could then sell to Owens. While doing research in the library on the Grant administration, Nolan discovered a seventy-five-year-old book containing some sample U.S. Army report forms from the 1890's. Nolan secretly cut one of these out. Later he carefully copied Grant's signature from an encyclopedia onto the form. Then Nolan set the paper in the sun for several days so that the signature would fade and appear older than it actually was. When the preparations were completed, Nolan took the document to Owens, and he offered to sell it to her for $500. Owens was taken in by Nolan's deception and paid him $500. Some time later, Owens was showing her collection to another collector who noticed that the form Nolan had used was one which was not used at a time when Grant could have signed it. Owens contacted Nolan and demanded her money back, but Nolan refused. Owens then contacted the police.

DISPUTE: Nolan was charged with forgery, but contested the indictment.

RULES: I. Forgery is the false making or material-altering, with intent to defraud, of any writing which, if genuine, might be the foundation for some legal liability of the signer of the document.

II. The crime of forgery is limited to documents such as deeds, checks, promissory notes, and receipts.

12. Is Nolan guilty of forgery?

13. What would have been the value of a true Grant signature on a document of the sort which Nolan sold to Owens?

14. Did Nolan materially alter or falsely make the document which he sold to Owens?

15. Is Nolan guilty of theft from the library?

Set 4

FACTS: In 1960, Tyrone executed a will which provided that his property was to be divided four ways. $10,000 was to go to his sister, Emily; $10,000 was to go to his nephew, Ivan; his house was to go to his daughter, Peggy; and the remainder of his estate was to go to an adopted son, Art. In 1965, Peggy married a man of whom Tyrone did not approve, and Tyrone ordered his attorney to draw up a new will leaving his, Tyrone's, house to the nephew, Ivan. Tyrone kept the new will in his desk drawer for several weeks but never executed it. Finally, he got over his anger at Peggy's marriage and tore it up without ever having executed it. In 1970, Tyrone's sister Emily died, and Tyrone had his attorney draft a new will deleting the provision for Emily, giving $20,000 to his nephew Ivan and the remainder of his estate to his daughter Peggy, with no provision for his adopted son, Art. The attorney drew up the will but the secretary made a typing error in the provision for Ivan, entering no amount at all. The mistake went unnoticed, and Tyrone executed his new will. He kept his new will and his old will in a desk drawer until his death in 1975.

DISPUTE: Ivan, Peggy, and Art each filed claims for a portion of Tyrone's estate.

RULES: I. A will may be completely revoked by a testator at any time before his death by physically destroying the will or by executing a new will.

II. The execution of a new will does not necessarily completely invalidate a previous will, and a judge will enforce all provisions of an earlier will which are not inconsistent with a later will.

16. Is Peggy entitled under Tyrone's will to receive the house?

17. Did Tryone's actions in 1965 constitute a complete revocation of his 1960 will?

18. Is Ivan to receive $20,000 or $2,000?

19. Which of the provisions of Tryone's 1960 will is inconsistent with those of his 1970 will?

20. How old was Tyrone at the time of his death?

Set 5

FACTS: Sandra was driving her car to a flea market. On the back seat was a box of plaster figurines which she hoped to sell for $5 apiece. Sandra was stopped at a red light when Herman, who was talking to his wife and not watching the road, ran into the back of Sandra's car. Sandra was not injured, but the car sustained damage and all but three of the figurines were shattered by the impact. The police officer who investigated the accident cited Herman for his recklessness. After the reports had been completed at the scene, Sandra discovered her car would not start. The investigating officer advised her to have the car towed to a garage, as there was a serious problem with car thieves and vandals in that area. Sandra asked Herman to call for a tow truck and pay the towing charges, but Herman refused. At that point, although Sandra had more than enough money for the towing fee, she told Herman she would leave the car there and would hold him responsible if anything happened to it. Sandra took a taxi home. The next day she came back with a mechanic to start the car, but during the night thieves had stripped the car and stolen the three unbroken figurines which Sandra had left in the back seat.

DISPUTE: Sandra sued Herman for all of the damage her car sustained, and for the value of the figurines. Herman contested Sandra's suit.

RULES: I. A person whose negligence causes damage to the property of another is legally responsible for all the damage caused directly or indirectly by his negligence.

II. The owner of property damaged by another's negligence must take reasonable steps to keep the amount of damage from being increased and the negligent party is not liable for any damage which is the result of the failure of the owner to take such steps.

21. Can Sandra recover for the damage done to her car by the car thieves?

22. How is the value of the lost figurines to be measured?

23. Is Herman liable to Sandra for the damage Sandra's car sustained in the accident?

24. Did Sandra take reasonable steps to keep the damage done to her car at a minimum?

Set 6

FACTS: Richard's old uncle, Zebadiah, was very ill and unable to care for himself. Richard was Zebadiah's only relation and was to inherit Zebadiah's estate, valued at least at $500,000, upon Zebadiah's death. Knowing that his uncle needed constant care, Richard hired Samuel to live with Zebadiah as his nurse and attendant. Richard explained to Samuel that he, Richard, did not have much money but that he expected to inherit a great deal of money upon Zebadiah's death. Richard and Samuel made a verbal agreement that Richard would pay Samuel $100 a week for his services for as long as Zebadiah lived, and then when he, Richard, collected the estate, Samuel would receive an additional $50,000. Samuel began to care for Zebadiah in March of 1965. He faithfully discharged his responsibilities until Zebadiah died in August of 1967. Zebadiah's estate was much less than Richard had expected, and he decided he could not afford to pay Samuel the $50,000.

DISPUTE: Samuel sued Richard for compensation for his services. Richard contested.

RULES: I. An oral agreement between two competent parties is a binding contract which is enforceable in a court of law.

II. An agreement that is not in writing will not be enforced if it is (1) for the sale of goods the value of which exceeds $500, or (2) by its own terms it cannot possibly be completed within one year of its making.

25. Is the verbal agreement between Samuel and Richard a binding and enforceable contract?

26. Aside from any contract, is Samuel entitled to the $50,000 as the reasonable value of his services to Zebadiah?

27. Was the contract between Samuel and Richard for goods the value of which exceeded $500?

28. Is Samuel entitled to the $50,000 as agreed to by Richard in the verbal agreement?

29. What was the actual size of the estate which Richard received upon Zebadiah's death?

30. Is it conceivable that Samuel's part of the contract could have been performed within one year?

Set 7

FACTS: In August, 1972, Revere signed a lease by which he agreed to rent an apartment from Grover for a period of four years, at a monthly rental of $250. At the time they signed the agreement, Revere pointed out to Grover that several items in the apartment needed attention. Specifically, he mentioned that the bathroom needed painting, there was a hole in the wall behind the refrigerator, and there was a torn screen on the bedroom window. Grover promised verbally to fix all three items, but he never replaced the torn screen. That winter the boiler in the building broke down and Revere and the other tenants were without heat for two days. The following winter, in December 1974, the boiler again broke down and remained out of service for four days. Then, in January, it broke down a third time during a severe cold spell. Attempted repairs were unsuccessful, and after fourteen days of living in temperatures around the freezing mark, Revere moved out of the apartment. He wrote Grover a letter saying that he considered their agreement was ended. Grover wrote back saying he was going to hold Revere liable for the rent due on the rest of the lease.

DISPUTE: Six months later, Grover sued Revere for thirty months' rent. Revere contested.

RULES:

I. A tenant who has signed a written lease is liable for all rents during the entire term of the lease whether or not he continues to reside at the premises, and the landlord may bring suit to collect those rents as they come due so long as he does not rent the premises to another tenant.

II. A tenant is relieved from liability for rent if he abandons the premises because the premises have become unfit for habitation because the landlord fails to supply essential services.

31. Is Grover entitled to recover the rent which has accumulated from the time Revere moved out of the apartment until the time he brought the suit against Revere?

32. Did Grover fail to provide essential services to Revere's apartment?

33. How much did Revere have to pay for the apartment into which he moved after leaving Grover's building?

34. If Grover finds a new tenant and rents the apartment to him in September, will Revere have any further liability for rent?

35. Was Grover eventually able to effect repairs to the boiler?

STOP

IF YOU FINISH BEFORE TIME IS CALLED, CHECK YOUR WORK ON THIS SECTION ONLY. DO NOT WORK ON ANY OTHER SECTION IN THE TEST.

SECTION II

Time—35 Minutes
25 Questions

Directions: Each group of questions is based on a set of propositions or conditions. Drawing a rough picture or diagram may help in answering some of the questions. Choose the best answer for each question and blacken the corresponding space on your answer sheet.

Questions 1–5

Jack Caribe, the ocean explorer, is directing a study of the parrot fish, an important part of coral reef ecology. Each day he must schedule the diving teams. His crew consists of four professional scuba divers—Ken, Leon, Mabel, and Nina—and four marine biologists—Peter, Quentin, Rosemary, and Sue.

No one can dive more than twice a day and a professional diver must always be on the boat as the dive-master. Jack is not assigned, but can do any task he wishes, including dive-master.

Each dive team must have at least one professional diver and one biologist.

Mabel and Peter have fought, and Jack won't put them together for now. Mabel, a strong swimmer, works very badly with slow-paced Quentin.

Sue and Ken are recently married and always dive together.

1. If Nina is dive-master supervising three diving teams, which of the following is NOT a possible dive team?
   (A) Ken, Sue, and Peter
   (B) Ken, Sue, and Quentin
   (C) Leon, Peter, and Quentin
   (D) Leon, Peter, and Rosemary
   (E) Mabel and Rosemary

2. If Jack is the dive-master with four teams diving, how many different possible two-diver teams are there?
   (A) 6
   (B) 7
   (C) 8
   (D) 9
   (E) 10

3. If Mabel is the dive-master, which of the following is NOT a possible dive team?
   I. Peter, Quentin, and Rosemary
   II. Leon and Nina
   III. Ken, Sue, and Quentin
   IV. Ken, Peter, and Rosemary

   (A) I and II only
   (B) I, II, and III only
   (C) I, II, and IV only
   (D) III only
   (E) I, II, III, and IV

4. If biologist Olga joins the expedition and Leon is away getting supplies, which of the following is a possible schedule for the morning dive teams?
   (A) Ken, Sue, and Peter; Mabel, Olga, and Rosemary; Nina, Jack, and Quentin
   (B) Ken, Mabel, and Sue; Nina, Rosemary, Peter, and Olga
   (C) Ken, Olga, and Quentin; Rosemary, Sue, and Mabel
   (D) Olga, Rosemary, and Peter; Ken and Sue; Nina and Peter
   (E) Mabel, Olga, and Peter; Ken, Sue, and Quentin; Nina, Jack, and Rosemary

5. If Peter and Mabel become friends again and Leon is the dive-master, which of the following is a possible diving team?
   (A) Peter, Mabel, and Ken
   (B) Peter, Mabel, and Sue
   (C) Peter, Quentin, and Rosemary
   (D) Peter, Mabel, Ken, and Sue
   (E) Mabel, Sue, and Rosemary

Questions 6–10

Farmer Brown has a large square field divided into nine smaller squares, all equal, arranged in three rows of three fields each. One side of the field runs exactly east-west.

The middle square must be planted with rice because it is wet.

The wheat and barley should be contiguous so that they can be harvested all at once by the mechanical harvester.

Two of the fields should be planted with soybeans.

The northwesternmost field should be planted with peanuts, and the southern third of the field is suitable only for vegetables.

Questions 6–8 refer to the following squares:

(A) the square immediately north of the rice
(B) the square immediately east of the rice
(C) the square immediately west of the rice
(D) the square immediately east of the peanuts
(E) the square immediately northeast of the rice

6. Which square cannot be planted with soybeans?

7. Which square cannot be planted with wheat?

8. If Farmer Brown decides to plant the wheat next to the peanuts, in which square will the barley be?

9. If the three southern squares are planted, from west to east, with squash, tomatoes, and potatoes, which vegetables could be planted next to soybeans?

I. Squash
II. Tomatoes
III. Potatoes

(A) I only
(B) II only
(C) III only
(D) I and III only
(E) I, II, and III

10. If Farmer Brown decides not to plant any peanuts or wheat, what is the maximum number of fields of vegetables that he could plant?
(A) 3
(B) 5
(C) 6
(D) 7
(E) 8

Questions 11–15

I. A cube has six sides, each of which is a different one of the following colors: Black, blue, brown, green, red, and white.
II. The red side is opposite the black.
III. The green side is between the red and the black.
IV. The blue side is adjacent to the white.
V. The brown side is adjacent to the blue.
VI. The red side is the bottom face.

11. Which statement adds no information which is not already given by the statements above it?
(A) II
(B) III
(C) IV
(D) V
(E) VI

12. The side opposite brown is
(A) white
(B) red
(C) green
(D) blue
(E) black

13. The four colors adjacent to green are
(A) black, blue, brown, red
(B) black, blue, brown, white
(C) black, blue, red, white
(D) black, brown, red, white
(E) blue, brown, red, white

14. Which of the following can be deduced from statements I, II, and VI?
(A) Black is on the top.
(B) Blue is on the top.
(C) Brown is on the top.
(D) Brown is opposite black.
(E) None of the above can be deduced.

15. If the red side is exchanged for the green side, and blue is swapped for black, which of the following is false?
(A) Red is opposite black.
(B) White is adjacent to brown.
(C) Green is opposite blue.

(D) White is adjacent to green.
(E) White is adjacent to blue.

Questions 16–20

A collie, poodle, retriever, setter, and sheepdog live in separate houses on a five-house block with the Joneses, Kings, Lanes, Murrays, and Neffs—not necessarily in that order.

The sheepdog lives next door to the Lanes, as does the collie.

The Joneses have the heaviest dog and live next to the sheepdog.

The retriever weighs more than the setter or the poodle.

The Lanes live two houses away from the Joneses and from the Kings.

The Kings do not own the setter.

The sheepdog lives with the Murrays.

16. Which of the following is definitely false?
(A) The poodle lives next to the collie.
(B) The poodle does not live next to the sheepdog.
(C) The sheepdog lives next to the collie.
(D) The setter lives next to the sheepdog.
(E) The retriever lives two houses from the setter.

17. Which of the following is definitely true?
(A) The Joneses live next to the Neffs.
(B) The Joneses live next to the collie.
(C) The Joneses live at the opposite end of the block from the Lanes.
(D) The Kings live next to the sheepdog.
(E) The Kings live next to the collie.

18. If a cat named Kitzen goes to live with the second heaviest dog, which of the following must be true?
(A) Kitzen lives with the Kings.
(B) Kitzen lives with the Lanes.
(C) Kitzen lives with the Murrays.
(D) Kitzen lives with the Neffs.
(E) The answer cannot be determined from the information given.

19. If the Neffs and the Joneses trade houses, but the dogs living in the houses stay with the houses, which of the following now becomes true?
(A) The poodle lives next to the Joneses.
(B) The sheepdog lives next to the Joneses.
(C) The setter lives next to the Neffs.
(D) The collie lives with the Lanes.
(E) The retriever lives with the Murrays.

20. If the Murrays move away and give their dog to the Lanes, which of the following would be true?
(A) The sheepdog now lives with the collie.
(B) The sheepdog does not now live with the poodle.
(C) The sheepdog lives next to the Joneses.
(D) The sheepdog lives next to the Kings.
(E) The sheepdog lives next to the setter.

Questions 21–25

Asters are not as pretty as lilacs and don't smell as nice as either lilacs or daffodils.

Daffodils are prettier than lilacs, but don't smell as nice.

Irises are not as pretty as lilacs and don't smell as nice as daffodils or roses.

Lilacs are prettier than roses, but don't smell as nice.

21. Which of the following statements is neither definitely true nor definitely false?
(A) Asters are not as pretty as lilacs.
(B) Daffodils are prettier than asters.
(C) Irises smell better than asters.
(D) Lilacs do not smell as nice as daffodils.
(E) Roses smell the best of all.

22. Which of the following is definitely true?
(A) Roses are as pretty as daffodils.
(B) Lilacs are as pretty as daffodils.
(C) Irises are prettier than asters.
(D) Daffodils do not smell as nice as irises.
(E) Asters don't smell as nice as roses.

23. If irises are prettier than roses, then they are definitely prettier than which of the following?
(A) asters only
(B) daffodils only
(C) lilacs only
(D) asters and roses only
(E) cannot be determined

24. Which of the following are both prettier and better smelling than asters?

    I. daffodils
    II. irises
    III. roses

    (A) I only
    (B) II only
    (C) III only
    (D) I and II only
    (E) I and III only

25. If dahlias are prettier than asters but do not smell as nice, then
    (A) dahlias might smell better than irises
    (B) dahlias might smell better than daffodils
    (C) dahlias might smell better than roses
    (D) dahlias cannot be prettier than lilacs
    (E) dahlias cannot be prettier than roses

STOP

IF YOU FINISH BEFORE TIME IS CALLED, CHECK YOUR WORK ON THIS SECTION ONLY. DO NOT WORK ON ANY OTHER SECTION IN THE TEST.

SECTION III

Time—35 Minutes
28 Questions

Directions: Below each of the following passages, you will find questions or incomplete statements about the passage. Each statement or question is followed by lettered words or expressions. Select the word or expression that most satisfactorily completes each statement, or answers each question in accordance with the meaning of the passage. After you have chosen the best answer, blacken the corresponding space on the answer sheet.

However important we may regard school life to be, there is no gainsaying the fact that children spend more time at home than in the classroom. Therefore, the great influence of parents cannot be ignored or discounted by the teacher. They can become strong allies of the school personnel or they can consciously or unconsciously hinder and thwart curricular objectives.

Administrators have been aware of the need to keep parents apprised of the newer methods used in schools. Many principals have conducted workshops explaining such matters as the reading readiness program, manuscript writing, and developmental mathematics.

Moreover, the classroom teacher, with the permission of the supervisors, can also play an important role in enlightening parents. The many interviews carried on during the year, as well as new ways of reporting pupils' progress, can significantly aid in achieving a harmonious interplay between school and home.

To illustrate, suppose that a father has been drilling Junior in arithmetic processes night after night. In a friendly interview, the teacher can help the parent sublimate his natural paternal interest into productive channels. He might be persuaded to let Junior participate in discussing the family budget, buying the food, using a yardstick or measuring cup at home, setting the clock, calculating mileage on a trip, and engaging in scores of other activities that have a mathematical basis.

If the father follows the advice, it is reasonable to assume that he will soon realize his son is making satisfactory progress in mathematics, and at the same time, enjoying the work.

Too often, however, teachers' conferences with parents are devoted to petty accounts of children's misdemeanors, complaints about laziness and poor work habits, and suggestions for penalties and rewards at home.

What is needed is a more creative approach in which the teacher, as a professional adviser, plants ideas in parents' minds for the best utilization of the many hours that the child spends out of the classroom.

In this way, the school and the home join forces in fostering the fullest development of youngsters' capacities.

1. The central idea conveyed in the above passage is:
   (A) Home training is more important than school training because a child spends so many hours with his parents.
   (B) Teachers can and should help parents to understand and further the objectives of the school.
   (C) Parents unwittingly have hindered and thwarted curricular objectives.
   (D) There are many ways in which the mathematics program can be implemented at home.
   (E) Parents have a responsibility to help students in doing homework.

2. The author directly discusses the fact that
   (A) parents drill their children too much in arithmetic.
   (B) principals have explained the new art programs to parents.
   (C) a father can have his son help him construct articles at home.
   (D) a parent's misguided efforts can be redirected to proper channels.
   (E) there is not sufficient individual instruction in the classroom.

3. It can reasonably be inferred that the author
   (A) is satisfied with present relationships between home and school

(B) feels that the traditional program in mathematics is slightly superior to the developmental program
(C) believes that schools are lacking in guidance personnel
(D) feels that parent-teacher interviews can be made much more constructive than they are at present
(E) is of the opinion that teachers of this generation are inferior to those of the last generation

4. A method of parent-teacher communication NOT mentioned or referred to by the author is
(A) classes for parents
(B) new progress report forms
(C) parent-teacher interview
(D) informal tea
(E) demonstration lesson

5. The author implies that
(A) participation in interesting activities relating to a subject improves one's achievement in that area
(B) too many children are lazy and have poor work habits
(C) school principals do more than their share in interpreting the curriculum to the parents
(D) only a small part of the school day should be set apart for drilling in arithmetic
(E) teachers should occasionally make home visits to parents

6. The author's purpose in writing this passage is to
(A) tell parents to pay more attention to the guidance of teachers in the matter of educational activities in the home
(B) help ensure that every child's capacities are actually fully developed when he leaves school
(C) urge teachers and school administrators to make use of a much underused resource—the parent
(D) improve the teaching of mathematics
(E) brainwash parents into doing the best thing for their child's education

7. It is most reasonable to infer that the author is a(n)
(A) elementary school teacher
(B) parent
(C) student
(D) college teacher
(E) professor of education

Hong Kong's size and association with Britain, and its position in relation to its neighbors in the Pacific, particularly China, determine the course of conduct it has to pursue. Hong Kong is no more than a molecule in the great substance of China. Its area is a mere 398 square miles. Fortunately, however, we cannot dispose of Hong Kong as simply as this. There are components in its complex and unique existence which affect its character and, out of all physical proportion, increase its significance.

Among these, the most potent are its people, their impressive achievements in partnership with British administration and enterprise, and the rule of law which protects personal freedom in the British tradition.

What is Hong Kong, and what is it trying to do? In 1841 Britain acquired outright, by treaty, the Island of Hong Kong, to use as a base for trade with China, and in 1860, the Kowloon Peninsula, to complete the perimeter of the superb harbor, which has determined Hong Kong's history and character. Hong Kong prospered as a center of trade with China, expanding steadily until it fell to the Japanese in 1941. Although the rigors of a severe occupation set everything back, the Liberation in 1945 was the herald of an immediate and spectacular recovery in trade. People poured into the Colony, and this flow became a flood during 1949–50, when the Chinese National Government was defeated by the Communists. Three-quarters of a million people entered the Colony at that stage.

Very soon two things affected commercial expansion. First, the Chinese Government restricted Hong Kong's exports to China, because it feared unsettled internal conditions, mounting inflation and a weakness in its exchange position. Secondly, during the Korean War, the United Nations imposed an embargo on imports into China, the main source of Hong Kong's livelihood. This was a crisis for Hong Kong; its China trade went overnight, and by this time it had over one million refugees on its hands. But something dramatic happened. Simply stated, it was this: Hong Kong switched from trading to manufacturing. It did it so so quickly that few people, even in Hong Kong, were aware at the time of exactly what was happening, and the rest of the world was not quickly convinced of Hong Kong's transformation into a center of manufacturers. Its limited industry began to expand rapidly and, although more slowly, to diversify, and it owed much to the immigrants from Shanghai, who brought their capital, experience, and expertise with them. Today Hong Kong must be unique among so-called developing countries in the dependence of its economy on industrialization. No less than 40 percent of the labor force is engaged in the manufacturing industries; and of the products from these, Hong Kong exports 90 percent, and it does this despite the fact that its industry is exposed to the full competition of the industrially mature nations. The variety of its goods now ranges widely from the products of shipbuilding, through textiles and plastics, to airconditioners, transistor radios, and cameras.

More than 70 percent of its exports are either wholly or partly manufactured in Hong Kong. In recent years these domestic exports have been increasing at about 15 percent a year. America is the largest market, taking 25 percent of the value of Hong Kong's exports; then follow the United Kingdom, Malaysia, West Germany, Japan, Canada, and Australia; but all countries come within the scope of its marketing.

8. The article gives the impression that
   (A) English rule constituted an important factor in Hong Kong's economic development
   (B) refugees from China were a liability to the financial status of Hong Kong
   (C) Hong Kong has taken a developmental course comparable to that of the new African nations
   (D) British forces used their military might imperialistically to acquire Hong Kong
   (E) there is a serious dearth of skilled workers in Hong Kong

9. The economic stability of Hong Kong since World War II is primarily attributable to
   (A) its shipbuilding activity
   (B) businessmen and workers from Shanghai who settled in Hong Kong
   (C) its political separation from China
   (D) its exports to China
   (E) a change in the type of business done in Hong Kong

10. Hong Kong's commerce was most adversely affected by the
    (A) liberation
    (B) Japanese occupation
    (C) British administration
    (D) retreat of the Chinese National Government
    (E) conversion from manufacturing to trading

11. From the passage it would appear that
    (A) the British succeeded in holding fast to Hong Kong through all events
    (B) the population of Hong Kong has grown steadily
    (C) the British were successful in their original plans for Hong Kong
    (D) a very small perçentage of the labor force accounts for almost all the exports
    (E) Hong Kong is still the trading capital of the Orient

12. In the decade following World War II, all of the following were stated or implied to be important factors in Hong Kong's economic development EXCEPT
    (A) capital from Shanghai
    (B) experts from Shanghai
    (C) manufacturing machinery from Shanghai
    (D) the Korean War
    (E) the United Nations

13. The author of this passage is most probably a(n)
    (A) Hong Kong politician
    (B) American journalist
    (C) Chinese econometrician
    (D) student of Far Eastern economic history
    (E) Oriental manufacturer

14. If the trends cited in the passage continue, which of the following is the most likely?
    (A) By the year 2000 the large majority of the Hong Kong work force will be engaged in manufacture for export.

(B) By the year 1995 the majority of Hong Kong's exports will have become manufactured items.
(C) By the year 1990 Hong Kong's population pressures will be absolutely unmanageable.
(D) By the year 1989 most Hong Kong businessmen will be very well-off.
(E) By the year 1988 Hong Kong will be one of the two major trading partners of the United States.

If present trends continue, nearly one out of every three of today's farms may not be around by the turn of the century.

The prime culprit won't be urban sprawl. Most of the decline in the number of farms will come as larger units absorb smaller ones, resulting in an increasing concentration of farmland and farm production among the biggest operations.

Of course, these projections are by no means inevitable. Farm policies, the economy, energy costs, technology, foreign market developments, and other perhaps unanticipated factors will all influence the future of U.S. agriculture.

While much of the move to larger operations will reflect farmers' expansion decisions, price inflation will also play a role in pushing farms into larger sales classes. These projections assume an average annual increase in farm prices of 7.5 percent—about equal to the average rate of the 1970's.

Under these conditions, about a third of the buildup in larger farms will reflect nothing more than changes in farm prices. A higher price inflation rate would shift more farms into the largest sales classes, while a lower rate would slow the trend.

In either case, U.S. agricultural production will become increasingly concentrated among fewer and larger farms. Recent figures show that the largest 1 percent of the farms produce about a fourth of the nation's food. In 20 years, they'll account for half of total U.S. output, while the smallest 50 percent of our farms will produce less than 1 percent of America's crops and livestock.

By then, farms with annual sales of $100,000 or more will produce virtually all the food going into commercial marketing channels.

The diminished role of small farms will partly reflect their size. Small farms of the year 2000 will be very small according to projections that the largest million farms will operate almost all of the nation's farmland. Three-fourths of the farmland will be in the hands of the top 200,000 operators.

Total farm wealth will show a similar pattern of concentration. Equity capital (farmers' ownership share of their total assets) was distributed evenly among farm sales classes in 1978—the small, medium, and large classes each accounted for about a third of total U.S. farm equity. In 20 years, however, two-thirds of the total wealth of the farm sector will be in farms with sales of $100,000 or more.

Partly for these reasons, it will become even more difficult for new farmers to get started. They may need about $2 million in assets for a farm to generate sales of more than $100,000, double the estimated requirement of 1978.

Of course, capital requirements for small farms will be much lower, and a large percentage of operators are now at the age where they'll be retiring sometime in the next few decades.

However, even when smaller, less expensive tracts of farmland are available for sale or rental, many aspiring young farmers will face intense competition from established farmers expanding their operations. There may also be sales competition from nonfarm investors seeking to develop the land or rent it to a "proven" operator. Those who do manage to enter farming on a small scale will be heavily dependent on off-farm income. Very few will succeed in making the transition to full-time farming. Most small farms won't generate enough income to support a family, let alone enough for expansion.

Also, as many of these units are bought up to expand existing farms, there will be fewer farms around for the future, particularly at the sizes a young person may be able to afford.

In fact, for every three operators who leave farms with sales of less than $100,000, only one will begin. The total number of new farmers under age 35 may shrink from about 377,000 just a few years ago to 233,000 by the end of the century.

Of course, the number of large farms will be expanding, but that won't open many doors for new entrants because the capital requirements will usually be far beyond their reach. Opportunities will be confined mostly to those who inherit a farm, and—more often than in the past—they'll be inheriting not an entire farm, but partnerships or shares in a family farm corporation that's highly specialized.

15. The tone of the passage is best described as
    (A) alarmed
    (B) cautious
    (C) factual
    (D) rustic
    (E) breezy

16. According to the passage a large farm is one which
    (A) produces two-thirds of the nation's crops and livestock
    (B) has sales of over $100,000 per year
    (C) covers more than 2 square miles
    (D) can support a family of six
    (E) currently involves $2 million in equity

17. The passage would be most likely to have appeared as an article in which of the following?
    (A) a publication of the United States Department of Defense
    (B) a publication of the University School of Forests and Mines
    (C) a publication of the United States Department of Agriculture
    (D) a publication of the United States Chamber of Commerce
    (E) a publication of Ford Foundation

18. The passage predicts all of the following EXCEPT
    (A) fewer younger farmers
    (B) fewer smaller farms
    (C) fewer farms producing relatively more
    (D) more families will be living on farms
    (E) concentration of farm assets in fewer hands

19. According to the passage, a lower rate of inflation would slow the trend to larger farms because
    (A) reduced inflation will slow the economy and make farming a less attractive investment
    (B) inflation is necessary for economic growth
    (C) population pressures will lower food prices
    (D) it is harder to manage large enterprises in low inflation periods
    (E) prices received for farm produce would increase less, and sales are the measure of farm size

20. It can be inferred from the passage that
    (A) predicting agricultural trends is a complex process
    (B) reducing the number of farms will surely increase productivity
    (C) increasing the size of farms will necessarily increase productivity
    (D) increasing farm size will increase the total wealth held by farmers
    (E) farming corporations are very common

21. Good advice for the aspiring farmer would be
    (A) "Go west, young man, go west"
    (B) "Make hay while the sun shines"
    (C) "Many are called, but few are chosen"
    (D) "Millions for defense, but not one cent for tribute"
    (E) "When the elephant moves, even the lion is wary"

In my early childhood I received no formal religious education. I did, of course, receive the ethical and moral training that moral and conscientious parents give their children. When I was about ten years old, my parents decided that it would be good for me to receive some formal religious instruction and to study the Bible, if for no other reason than that a knowledge of both is essential to the understanding of literature and culture.

As lapsed Catholics, they sought a group which had as little doctrine and dogma as possible, but what they considered good moral and ethical values. After some searching, they joined the local Meeting of the Religious Society of Friends. Although my parents did not attend Meetings for Worship very often, I went to First Day School there regularly, eventually completing the course and receiving an inscribed Bible.

At the Quaker school, I learned about the concept of the "inner light" and it has stayed with me. I was, however, unable to accept the idea of Jesus Christ being any more divine than, say, Buddha. As a result, I became estranged from the Quakers who, though believing in substantially the same moral and ethical values as I do, and even the same religious concept of the inner light, had arrived at these conclusions from a premise which I could not accept. I admit that my religion is the poorer for having no revealed word and no supreme prophet, but my inherited aversion to dogmatism limits my faith to a Supreme Being and the goodness of man.

Later, at another Meeting for Worship, I found that some Quakers had similar though not so strong reservations about the Christian aspects of their belief. I made some attempt to rejoin a Meeting for Worship, but found that though they remained far closer to me than any other organized religious group, I did not wish to become one again. I do attend Meetings for Worship on occasion, but it is for the help in deep contemplation which it brings rather than any lingering desire to rejoin the fold.

I do believe in a "Supreme Being" (or ground of our Being, as Tillich would call it). This Being is ineffable and not to be fully understood by humans. He is not cut off from the world and we can know him somewhat through the knowledge which we are limited to—the world. He is interested and concerned for humankind but on man himself falls the burden of his own life. To me the message of the great prophets, especially Jesus, is that good is its own reward, and indeed the *only* possible rewards are intrinsic in the actions themselves. The relationship between each human and the Supreme Being is an entirely personal one.

It is my faith that each person has this unique relationship with the Supreme Being. To me that is the meaning of the inner light. The purpose of life, insofar as a human can grasp it, is to understand and increase this lifeline to the Supreme Being, this piece of divinity that *every* human has. Thus, the taking of any life by choice is the closing of some connection to God, and unconscionable. Killing anyone not only denies them their purpose, but corrupts the purpose of all men.

22. The author of the preceding passage is most probably writing in order to
    (A) persuade a friend to convert to Quakerism
    (B) reassure a Friend that he has not become immoral
    (C) explain the roots of his pacifism
    (D) analyze the meaning of the "inner light"
    (E) recall his parents' religious teachings

23. If offered a reward for doing a good deed, the author would
    (A) spurn the reward indignantly
    (B) accept it only as a token of the other person's feelings of gratitude
    (C) neither take nor refuse the reward
    (D) explain to the offerer that rewards are blasphemous
    (E) make any excuse at all to avoid taking the reward

24. According to the passage, the Quakers
    (A) are the group he wishes to become a member of again
    (B) have historically been pacifists
    (C) are Christians, but only in a weak sense
    (D) share basic religious thought with the author
    (E) are relatively dogmatic and doctrinaire

25. Which of the following would the author likely see as most divine?
    (A) Jesus Christ
    (B) Buddha
    (C) Mohammed
    (D) Moses
    (E) They would be seen as equally divine.

26. It can be inferred that
    (A) the author views the inner light as uniquely an attribute of Quakers
    (B) Quakers treat all men the same, whether they have inner light or not
    (C) the Catholics are not concerned with killing
    (D) the author's parents found Catholic religious views unsuitable or inadequate
    (E) Buddhist belief is as congenial to the author as Quaker belief

27. The author argues that
    (A) we must seek greater comprehension of our own inner lights
    (B) humans must always seek to increase the number of inner lights; hence, population increase is desirable
    (C) the unique relationship between each person and his inner light makes him more divine than those without an inner light

(D) only a person without an inner light could kill
(E) faith is essential to life, especially faith based on those most divine persons who are often called prophets

28. If the author were faced with a situation where the killing of another human would occur both by his action and his inaction, then
(A) he could not act because it would kill someone
(B) he could not fail to act because it would kill someone
(C) he would have to kill himself to avoid the situation
(D) he would have to abandon his beliefs
(E) he would have to choose to act or not act on some basis other than whether a human would die

STOP

IF YOU FINISH BEFORE TIME IS CALLED, CHECK YOUR WORK ON THIS SECTION ONLY. DO NOT WORK ON ANY OTHER SECTION IN THE TEST.

SECTION IV

Time—35 Minutes
26 Questions

Directions: In this section, the questions ask you to analyze and evaluate the reasoning in short paragraphs or passages. For some questions, all of the answer choices may conceivably be answers to the question asked. You should select the *best* answer to the question, that is, an answer which does not require you to make assumptions which violate commonsense standards by being implausible, redundant, irrelevant or inconsistent. After choosing the best answer, blacken the corresponding space on the answer sheet.

Questions 1 and 2

On his first trip to the People's Republic of China, a young U.S. diplomat of very subordinate rank embarrassed himself by asking a Chinese official how it was that Orientals managed to be so inscrutable. The Chinese official smiled and then gently responded that he preferred to think of the inscrutability of his race in terms of a want of perspicacity in Occidentals.

1. Which of the following best describes the point of the comment made by the Chinese official?
   (A) It is not merely the Chinese, but all Oriental people who are inscrutable.
   (B) Most Americans fail to understand Chinese culture.
   (C) What one fails to perceive may be attributable to carelessness in observation rather than obscurity inherent in the object.
   (D) Since the resumption of diplomatic relations between the United States and Communist China, many older Chinese civil servants have grown to distrust the Americans.
   (E) If the West and the East are ever to truly understand one another, there will have to be considerable cultural exchange between the two.

2. Which of the following best characterizes the attitude and response of the Chinese official?
   (A) anger
   (B) fear
   (C) caution
   (D) indifference
   (E) compassion

3. People waste a surprising amount of money on gadgets and doodads that they hardly ever use. For example, my brother spent $25 on an electric ice-cream maker two years ago, but he has used it on only three occasions. Yet, he insists that regardless of the number of times he actually uses the ice-cream maker, the investment was a good one because __________.

   Which of the following best completes the thought of the paragraph?
   (A) the price of ice cream will go up in the future.
   (B) he has purchased the ice-cream maker for the convenience of having it available if and when he needs it.
   (C) in a society that is oriented toward consumer goods one should take every opportunity to acquire things.
   (D) today $25 is not worth what it was two years ago on account of the inflation rate.
   (E) by using it so infrequently he has conserved a considerable amount of electrical energy.

4. A poet was once asked to interpret a particularly obscure passage in one of his poems. He responded, "When I wrote that verse, only God and I knew the meaning of that passage. Now, only God knows."

   What is the point of the poet's response?
   (A) God is infinitely wiser than man.
   (B) Most men are unable to understand poetry.
   (C) Poets rarely know the source of their own creative inspiration.

(D) A great poem is inspired by the muse.
(E) He has forgotten what he had originally meant by the verse.

5. A recent survey by the economics department of an Ivy League university revealed that increases in the salaries of preachers are accompanied by increases in the nationwide average of rum consumption. From 1965 to 1970 preachers' salaries increased on the average of 15% and rum sales grew by 14.5%. From 1970 to 1975 average preachers' salaries rose by 17% and rum sales by 17.5%. From 1975 to 1980 rum sales expanded by only 8% and average preachers' salaries also grew by only 8%.

Which of the following is the most likely explanation for the findings cited in the paragraph?
(A) When preachers have more disposable income, they tend to allocate that extra money to alcohol.
(B) When preachers are paid more, they preach longer; and longer sermons tend to drive people to drink.
(C) Since there were more preachers in the country, there were also more people; and a larger population will consume greater quantities of liquor.
(D) The general standard of living increased from 1965 to 1980 which accounts for both the increase in rum consumption and preachers' average salaries.
(E) A consortium of rum importers carefully limited the increases in imports of rum during the test period cited.

6. Since all four-door automobiles I have repaired have eight-cylinder engines, all four-door automobiles must have eight-cylinder engines.

The author argues on the basis of
(A) special training
(B) generalization
(C) syllogism
(D) ambiguity
(E) deduction

7. Two women, one living in Los Angeles, the other living in New York City, carried on a lengthy correspondence by mail. The subject of the exchange was a dispute over certain personality traits of Winston Churchill. After some two dozen letters, the Los Angeles resident received the following note from her New York City correspondent, "It seems you were right all along. Yesterday I met someone who actually knew Sir Winston, and he confirmed your opinion."

The two women could have been arguing on the basis of all of the following EXCEPT
(A) published biographical information
(B) old news film footage
(C) direct personal acquaintance
(D) assumption
(E) third party reports

8. Judging by the architecture, I would say that the chapel dates from the early eighteenth century. Furthermore, the marble threshold to the refectory is worn to a depth of one and three-eighths inches at the middle. Since the facilities were designed to accommodate approximately forty monks, I estimate that the monastery was occupied for approximately seventy-five years before it was abandoned, and that date would coincide with the violent civil and religious wars of the first decade of the 1800's.

Which of the following is NOT an assumption made by the author in describing the dates of the buildings?
(A) The marble threshold he studied is the same one originally included in the building.
(B) Architectual features can be associated with certain historical periods.
(C) The monastery he is investigating was nearly fully occupied during the time span in question.
(D) There is a correlation between usage and wear of marble flooring.
(E) Religious organizations have often abandoned outlying monasteries during times of political strife.

9. *Daily Post* newspaper reporter Roger Nightengale let it be known that Andrea Johnson, the key figure in his award-winning series of articles on prostitution and drug abuse, was a composite of many persons and

not a single, real person, and so he was the subject of much criticism by fellow journalists for having failed to disclose that information when the articles were first published. But these were the same critics who voted Nightengale a prize for his magazine serial *General,* which was a much dramatized and fictionalized account of a Korean War military leader whose character was obviously patterned closely after that of Douglas MacArthur.

In which of the following ways might the critics mentioned in the paragraph argue that they were NOT inconsistent in their treatment of Nightengale's works?

I. Fictionalization is an accepted journalistic technique for reporting on sensitive subject matter such as prostitution.
II. Critic disapproval is one of the most important ways members of the writing community have for ensuring that reporting is accurate and to the point.
III. There is a critical difference between dramatizing events in a piece of fiction and presenting distortions of the truth as actual fact.

(A) I only
(B) I and II only
(C) II and III only
(D) III only
(E) I, II, and III

10. Why pay outrageously high prices for imported sparkling water when there is now an inexpensive water carbonated and bottled here in the United States at its source—Cold Springs, Vermont. Neither you nor your guests will taste the difference, but if you would be embarrassed if it were learned that you were serving a domestic sparkling water, then serve Cold Springs Water—but serve it in a leaded crystal decanter.

The advertisement rests on which of the following assumptions?

I. It is difficult if not impossible to distinguish Cold Springs Water from imported competitors on the basis of taste.
II. Most sparkling waters are not bottled at the source.
III. Some people may purchase an imported sparkling water over a domestic one as a status symbol.

(A) I only
(B) II only
(C) III only
(D) I and II only
(E) I and III only

11. Choose the best completion of the following paragraph.

Parochial education serves the dual functions of education and religious instruction, and church leaders are justifiably concerned to impart important religious values regarding relationships between the sexes. Thus, when the administrators of a parochial school system segregate boys and girls in separate institutions, they believe they are helping to keep the children pure by removing them from a source of temptation. If the administrators realized, however, that children would be more likely to develop the very attitudes they seek to engender in the company of the opposite sex, they would __________.

(A) put an end to all parochial education
(B) no longer insist upon separate schools for boys and girls
(C) abolish all racial discrimination in the religious schools
(D) stop teaching foolish religious tripe, and concentrate instead on secular educational programs
(E) reinforce their policies of isolating the sexes in separate programs

12. Professor Branch, who is chairman of the sociology department, claims she saw a flying saucer the other night. But since she is a sociologist instead of a physicist, she cannot possibly be acquainted with the most recent writings of our finest scientists that tend to discount such sightings, so we can conclude her report is unreliable.

Which of the following would be the most appropriate criticism of the author's analysis?

(A) He makes an irrelevant attack on Professor Branch's credentials.

(B) He himself may not be a physicist, and therefore may not be familiar with the writings he cites.
(C) Even the U.S. Air Force cannot explain all of the sightings of UFO's which are reported to them each year.
(D) A sociologist is sufficiently well-educated that he can probably read and understand scientific literature in a field other than his own.
(E) It is impossible to get complete agreement on matters such as the possibility of life on other planets.

13. INQUISITOR: Are you in league with the devil?
VICTIM: Yes.
INQUISITOR: Then you must be lying, for those in league with the "Evil One" never tell the truth. So you are not in league with the devil.

The inquisitor's behavior can be described as paradoxical because he
(A) charged the victim with being in league with the devil but later recanted
(B) relies on the victim's answer to reject the victim's response
(C) acts in accordance with religious law but accuses the victim of violating that law
(D) questions the victim about his ties with the devil but does not himself believe there is a devil
(E) asked the question in the first place, but then refused to accept the answer that the victim gave

14. "Whom did you pass on the road?" the King went on, holding his hand out to the messenger for some hay.
"Nobody," said the messenger.
"Quite right," said the King. "This young lady saw him, too. So, of course, Nobody walks slower than you."

The King's response shows that he believes
(A) the messenger is a very good messenger
(B) "Nobody" is a person who might be seen
(C) the young lady's eyesight is better than the messenger's
(D) the messenger is not telling him the truth
(E) there was no person actually seen by the messenger on the road

15. MARY: All of the graduates from Midland High School go to State College.
ANN: I don't know. Some of the students at State College come from North Hills High School.

Ann's response shows that she has interpreted Mary's remark to mean that
(A) most of the students from North Hills High School attend State College
(B) none of the students at State College are from Midland High School
(C) only students from Midland High School attend State College
(D) Midland High School is a better school than North Hill High School
(E) some Midland High School graduates do not attend college

16. Total contributions by individuals to political parties were up twenty-five percent in this most recent presidential election over those of four years earlier. Hence, it is obvious that people are no longer as apathetic as they were but are taking a greater interest in politics.

Which of the following, if true, would considerably weaken the preceding argument?
(A) The average contribution per individual actually declined during the same four-year period.
(B) Per capita income of the population increased by fifteen percent during the four years in question.
(C) Public leaders continue to warn citizens against the dangers of political apathy.
(D) Contributions made by large corporations to political parties declined during the four-year period.
(E) Fewer people voted in the most recent presidential election than in the one four years earlier.

17. The harmful effects of marijuana and other drugs have been considerably overstated. Although parents and teachers have expressed much concern over the dangers which widespread usage of marijuana and other drugs pose for high school and junior high school students, a national survey of 5,000 students of ages 13 to 17 showed that fewer than 15% of those students thought such drug use was likely to be harmful.

    Which of the following is the strongest criticism of the author's reasoning?
    (A) The opinions of students in the age group surveyed are likely to vary with age.
    (B) Alcohol use among students of ages 13 to 17 is on the rise, and is now considered by many to present greater dangers than marijuana usage.
    (C) Marijuana and other drugs may be harmful to users even though the users are not themselves aware of the danger.
    (D) A distinction must be drawn between victimless crimes and crimes in which an innocent person is likely to be involved.
    (E) The fact that a student does not think a drug is harmful does not necessarily mean he will use it.

18. AL: If an alien species ever visited Earth, it would surely be because they were looking for other intelligent species with whom they could communicate. Since we have not been contacted by aliens, we may conclude that none have ever visited this planet.

    AMY: Or, perhaps, they did not think human beings intelligent.

    How is Amy's response related to Al's argument?
    (A) She misses Al's point entirely.
    (B) She attacks Al personally rather than his reasoning.
    (C) She points out that Al made an unwarranted assumption.
    (D) She ignores the detailed internal development of Al's logic.
    (E) She introduces a false analogy.

19. I maintain that the best way to solve our company's present financial crisis is to bring out a new line of goods. I challenge anyone who disagrees with this proposed course of action to show that it will not work.

    A flaw in the preceding argument is that it
    (A) employs group classifications without regard to individuals
    (B) introduces an analogy which is weak
    (C) attempts to shift the burden of proof to those who would object to the plan
    (D) fails to provide statistical evidence to show that the plan will actually succeed
    (E) relies upon a discredited economic theory

20. If quarks are the smallest sub-atomic particles in the universe, then gluons are needed to hold quarks together. Since gluons are needed to hold quarks together, it follows that quarks are the smallest sub-atomic particles in the universe.

    The logic of the above argument is most nearly paralleled by which of the following?
    (A) If this library has a good French literature collection, it will contain a copy of *Les Conquerants* by Malraux. The collection does contain a copy of *Les Conquerants;* therefore, the library has a good French literature collection.
    (B) If there is a man-in-the-moon, the moon must be made of green cheese for him to eat. There is a man-in-the-moon, so the moon is made of green cheese.
    (C) Either helium or hydrogen is the lightest element of the periodic table. Helium is not the lightest element of the periodic table, so hydrogen must be the lightest element of the periodic table.
    (D) If Susan is taller than Bob, and if Bob is taller than Elaine, then if Susan is taller than Bob, Susan is also taller than Elaine.
    (E) Whenever it rains, the streets get wet. The streets are not wet. Therefore, it has not rained.

21. The following statements are a scrambled paragraph.

I. To increase court revenues, judges invented new forms of action which brought more cases before them.
II. In the earliest stages of the common law, a party could have his case heard by a judge only upon the payment of a fee to the court and then only if his case fit within one of the forms for which there existed a writ.
III. Consequently, the motivating force for the expansion in judicial power was at first economic, not political.
IV. The number of such formalized causes of action was very small.

Which of the following arrangments of these sentences is most logical?

(A) I, II, IV, III
(B) II, III, IV, I
(C) I, IV, III, II
(D) II, IV, I, III
(E) III, II, IV, I

22. If Martin introduces an amendment to Evans' bill, then Johnson and Lloyd will both vote the same way. If Evans speaks against Lloyd's position, Johnson will defend anyone voting with him. Martin will introduce an amendment to Evans' bill only if Evans speaks against Johnson's position.

If the above statements are true, each of the following can be true EXCEPT:

(A) If Evans speaks against Johnson's position, Lloyd will not vote with Johnson.
(B) If Martin introduces an amendment to Evans' bill, then Evans has spoken against Johnson's position.
(C) If Evans speaks against Johnson's position, Martin will not introduce an amendment to Evans' bill.
(D) If Martin introduces an amendment to Evans' bill, then either Johnson will not vote with Lloyd or Evans did not speak against Johnson's position.
(E) If either Evans did not speak against Lloyd's position or Martin did not introduce an amendment to Evans' bill, then either Johnson did not defend Lloyd or Martin spoke against Johnson's position.

23. Judging from the content of the following statements and the apparent authoritativeness of the speakers, which is the most reasonable and trustworthy?
(A) ECONOMIST: We can expect a long and hard winter because the ants are digging deeper and deeper colonies.
(B) LIBRARIAN: No one would dare try to steal a book from this library. All of our students are much too honest for that.
(C) DAIRY FARMER: During the past three months, milk producion of my herd has dropped off 14%.
(D) BUSINESS EXECUTIVE: The best way to combat inflation in this country is to make sure that every person on welfare who is not disabled is given a job working at the minimum wage.
(E) ELEMENTARY-SCHOOL TEACHER: Administrators should require more core curriculum courses for freshmen college students. As it is, students are allowed too much freedom in course selection.

Questions 24–26

The blanks in the following passage indicate deletions from the text. Select the completion that is most appropriate to the context.

Contemporary legal positivism depends upon the methodological assumption that a theory of law may be conceptual without, at the same time, being normative. In point of fact this assumption is a composite principle. It makes the fairly obvious claim that a conceptual theory, which strives to be ___(24)___ rather than normative, says what the law is—not what it ought to be. A conceptual theory must be supplemented by a normative theory, and the arguments in favor of a particular content for law are couched in terms of the results which are expected to flow from proposed legal acts. It is never a part of an argument for what the law ought to be, in the positivist's view, that to be a law it must have a certain content. While the normative argument refers ultimately to agreed-upon ends, it does not assert that these ends ___(25)___. Rather, that they are accepted and acted upon is a merely contingent matter. The second part of the methodological premise is more subtle: A conceptual theory such as legal positivism does not claim that the particular description it offers is uniquely correct. Proponents of legal positivism regard their study of law as analogous to the physicists' study of the universe: They have one theory of legal institutions,____(26)____.

24. (A) concise
    (B) descriptive
    (C) comprehensive
    (D) independent
    (E) simple

25. (A) must be pursued as a matter of logical necessity
    (B) are not the best ends for any modern legal system
    (C) would not be adopted by courts in a democratic society
    (D) could be undermined by dissident elements in the community
    (E) are shared by everyone

26. (A) and that is the only possible correct theory of law
    (B) and someday, with sufficient work, that theory will be able to generate societal goals for us to pursue
    (C) but that theory may, someday, be displaced by a better one
    (D) although no theory of the physical universe is as reliable as the positivistic theory of law
    (E) which is, however, strongly supported by the findings of modern science

STOP

IF YOU FINISH BEFORE TIME IS CALLED, CHECK YOUR WORK ON THIS SECTION ONLY. DO NOT WORK ON ANY OTHER SECTION IN THE TEST.

SECTION V

Time—35 Minutes
35 Questions

Directions: Each of the following sets consists of a fact situation, a dispute and two rules. The rules may conflict, but you are to apply each rule independently. Do not treat a rule as subsidiary or as an exception to the other rule. The rules are followed by questions. You are to select from the following lettered choices (A) through (D) the one that best describes each question in the way it relates to the application of one or both of the rules to the dispute. Blacken the corresponding space on the answer sheet.

(A) a relevant question the answer to which requires a choice between the two rules
(B) a relevant question the answer to which does not require a choice between the two rules, but does require further facts or rules
(C) a relevant question that can be readily answered from the facts or rules or both
(D) an irrelevant question, the answer to which does not affect, or only tangentially affects, the outcome of the dispute

Set 1

FACTS: Walter was a famous jazz musician and the acknowledged master of the trumpet style which he had invented. Deidra, who was very wealthy, had been studying the trumpet for several years and wanted to learn to play as Walter played. She spoke with Walter by telephone, and he agreed to give Deidra a series of twenty-five two-hour lessons, to be spaced out over a twelve-month period. The fee for each lesson was to have been $250. Deidra rented a practice room at a music studio and met Walter there. Walter began by having Deidra play some musical scales. Shortly after Deidra began to play, Walter realized that Deidra had no musical talent and that he could not hope to teach her to play even acceptably well. Further, Deidra's playing was so bad that it offended Walter's sensibilities. Walter explained nicely to Deidra that he thought she would benefit more from studying fundamental techniques with some other teacher before taking lessons from him. Deidra, however, was quite insistent about the lessons and was outraged when Walter flatly refused to continue.

DISPUTE: Deidra then sued Walter to force Walter to give her the twenty-five lessons. Walter contested.

RULES: I: If the subject matter of a contract is unique, the remedy for breach of contract is to compel the breaching party to render to the injured party the promised performance.

II. A court will not order the specific performance of a contract where the promised performance is of such a nature that it would be impracticable to try to force the breaching party to carry out his bargain.

1. Was the performance which Walter promised unique?

2. If the court decides it will not force Walter to give the lessons, is Deidra entitled to receive money compensation from Walter for his failure to continue the lessons?

3. Is it practicable to force Walter to continue giving trumpet lessons to Deidra?

4. Is Deidra entitled to have the court order Walter to continue giving her trumpet lessons?

Set 2

FACTS: Brett's six-year-old child Martin had a severe emotional problem. At the suggestion of her family physician, she had him admitted to a state psychiatric hospital for special counseling. With the exception of some volunteer nurses, everyone who worked at the hospital was an employee of the state government. The doctor who treated Martin prescribed some medicine for him and wrote out specific instructions for the duty nurse regarding the dosage and frequency the medicine was to be given. One evening, after the doctor had gone home, the nurse who was to give Martin his medicine was in a hurry to go home. She made an error in the dosage and gave Martin ten times what the doctor had prescribed. Martin had an adverse reaction to the medicine and nearly died. He was in intensive care for three weeks.

DISPUTE: Brett sued the state hospital for damages as compensation for the injury Martin suffered as the result of the nurse's negligence. The hospital contested.

RULES: I. An employer is liable for all injuries caused by the negligence of his employees provided that the negligent action was within the ordinary scope of his employment.

II. A state government and all its agencies enjoy sovereign immunity, and no suit for negligence may be maintained against the state unless specifically authorized by statute.

5. Was the nurse who gave Martin the incorrect dosage of medicine an employee of the state or one of its agencies?

6. Is Brett entitled to maintain her suit for the injuries which Martin suffered?

7. Was the nurse acting within the scope of her employment when she administered the medicine to Martin?

8. If no statute has specifically authorized lawsuits of the sort brought by Brett, is Brett entitled to maintain her suit?

9. If Brett is unable to recover on Martin's behalf from the state hospital, does she have any legal rights against the nurse who administered the wrong dosage to Martin?

Set 3

FACTS: In June, 1972, Lionel, who was then only twelve years of age, was riding with his mother in their family car when another car, driven by Quincy, ran a stop sign and collided with the passenger side of the car in which Lionel was riding. Lionel's mother was not hurt, but Lionel himself sustained a broken arm and a broken leg. The doctor who treated Lionel advised Lionel and his parents that while the injuries would eventually heal and allow Lionel to lead a fairly normal life, Lionel had sustained some injury to the kneecap and would never be able to participate in certain sports such as skiing. This was a big disappointment for Lionel, who had been an avid skier. Lionel's parents thought of suing Quincy for the injuries sustained by Lionel, but their family attorney advised against it since it appeared that Quincy was uninsured and did not have any assets of his own. So Lionel's parents did not press the matter. In March of 1977, Quincy won $1.2 million in the state lottery.

DISPUTE: The next month Lionel filed suit against Quincy for damages for the injuries which he had sustained in the 1972 accident. Quincy's attorney claimed that Lionel had delayed too long and that the suit was barred by the statute of limitations.

RULES: I. An action for personal injuries must be brought within two years after the injuries are sustained, otherwise the action is barred by the statute of limitations.

II. The statute of limitations is tolled (its running is supended) if the injured party has not yet reached the age of eighteen.

10. Is Lionel entitled to recover compensation from Quincy for his inability to ski?

11. Was the statute of limitations tolled for Lionel?

12. Is Lionel's action barred by the statute of limitations?

13. What was Quincy's age at the time the accident occurred?

14. If Lionel's parents had sued on Lionel's behalf in 1973 and lost, would Lionel be able to maintain his suit against Quincy in 1977?

15. If Lionel had waited to bring his suit until 1980, would the suit have been barred by the statute of limitations?

Set 4

FACTS: On December 15, 1978, Raymond and Frank entered into a written contract whereby Raymond agreed to deliver to Frank's warehouse in New York on August 3, 1979, 3,000 "Haruka-made dolls attired in traditional Korean garments." The price for the dolls was $15,000. Raymond placed an order with Haruka on January 10, 1979 and expected to have the dolls in his own warehouse by mid-June. Unfortunately, Seoul, where Haruka was located, experienced considerable political activity during that period, and on April 12, 1979 the government closed down Haruka's plant. As a result, Raymond did not receive the dolls he had been promised until September 30, 1979. Raymond telephoned Frank on July 9, 1979, and advised him of the situation, but Frank told Raymond he expected Raymond to meet the contract. When Raymond tried to deliver the dolls in October, Frank refused them.

DISPUTE: Frank then brought a lawsuit against Raymond for breach of contract, alleging that because Raymond had failed to deliver the dolls on schedule, he, Frank, had lost a profit of $30,000. Raymond contested.

RULES: I. A party who breaches a contract is obligated to pay compensation to the injured party in the amount of the net value the injured party would have received if the transaction had been carried out.

II. An unanticipated event which occurs subsequent to the formation of a contract and renders performance of the contract impossible relieves both parties from liability to perform.

16. Was the action by the Korean government an event subsequent to the formation of the contract between Raymond and Frank?

17. Why did the Korean government close the Haruka plant?

18. Is Frank entitled to damages from Raymond for Raymond's failure to deliver the Haruka dolls on August 3, 1979?

19. How much would Frank have been able to sell the dolls for if they had been delivered on schedule?

20. How much was Raymond supposed to have paid Haruka for the dolls?

21. If Raymond's failure to deliver the dolls had been caused not by the Korean government's action, but by loss of the shipment of dolls in a storm at sea, would Raymond be liable to Frank for breach of contract?

Set 5

FACTS: Alfred lived in San Francisco. While playing golf on vacation in Dallas, he dropped a gold ring out of his pocket. Alfred did not realize he had dropped the ring until he returned home to San Francisco. Alfred figured he must have lost the ring somewhere near the seventeenth green, and he thought he could have found it had he known that he dropped it. The ring was worth only $200, so Alfred decided its loss did not justify a trip to Texas to look for it. Six weeks later, however, Alfred returned to Dallas on business. While there, he thought he would look for his ring. He went to the golf course and explained to the club pro that he had returned to look for his ring. The pro told Alfred that a woman named Sylvia had found a ring three days earlier near the seventeenth green and had taken it home with her. Alfred described the ring and the club pro confirmed that that was the ring which Sylvia had found. Alfred contacted Sylvia to get his ring back. Sylvia refused to return it.

DISPUTE: Alfred sued Sylvia to recover the ring. Sylvia contested.

RULES: I. The finder of lost property is entitled to possess that property against anyone except the true owner of the property.

II. A person who recovers abandoned property and takes it into his possession thereby becomes the true owner of that property.

22. Is Alfred entitled to recover the ring from Sylvia?

23. If Alfred abandoned the ring, is Sylvia entitled to keep it as against Alfred?

24. Is Alfred the true owner of the ring?

25. Did Sylvia take the ring into her possession?

26. How much would it have cost Alfred to return to Dallas to search for the ring immediately after he discovered it was missing?

Set 6

FACTS: The Bloomington Glass Company kept a substantial quantity of hydrofluoric acid in its plant. The acid was used in etching glass. Bloomington was very careful to store the acid in proper containers and in a special part of the plant, because when hydrofluoric acid is exposed to air it vaporizes, creating a highly toxic gas. In the twenty years which Bloomington had kept hydrofluoric acid on its premises, only one incident had occurred involving the acid. A worker inadvertently failed to seal one of the containers, and he was slightly injured when he inhaled a whiff of the gas. His co-workers quickly contained the gas. What Bloomington did not realize, however, was that a freak occurrence had caused some of the oldest containers to start to leak. The acid in those containers had reacted with some trace elements in the containers over a long time period, and the result was that the acid was changed into another chemical compound. When it leaked out, it did not vaporize as hydrofluoric acid would have done; instead it soaked into the ground. Eventually, the chemical found its way into the Victory City water supply. Several of the city's residents became ill from drinking the contaminated water.

DISPUTE: The persons who had been taken ill sued Bloomington. The company contested the suits.

RULES: I. A company is liable only for those injuries caused by its conduct that were resonably foreseeable and that would result at the time it did the act.

II. A company which maintains dangerous substances on its premises, that is, substances which if they escaped could cause serious injury or death, is liable for all injuries which result from their keeping of the dangerous substances.

27. Could Bloomington have foreseen the injuries which the leaking containers caused?

28. Is Bloomington liable for the injuries which the chemicals caused to the residents of Victory City?

29. Was the chemical kept by Bloomington a dangerous substance?

30. Can Victory City sue Bloomington to force it to dispose of all the hydrofluoric acid stored at the Bloomington plant?

31. Was Bloomington careless in storing the hydrofluoric acid as it did?

Set 7

FACTS: Al rented from Franny an apartment in a building with twelve other apartments. Both Al and Franny signed copies of the lease which stipulated that Al was to pay $250 a month for the apartment, and that the lease was to last two years. The lease provided that Franny was to provide essential services, and that Al was to use the apartment only as a residence. At the time he signed the lease, Al gave Franny $500, $250 for the first month's rent, and another $250 for security, which he was to receive at the end of the lease—provided that all rents were paid and no damage was done to the apartment. After six months, Al's neighbors began to complain to Franny about Al's behavior. He played his stereo very loudly and had large parties. On two occasions the police had come and ordered Al to quiet down. Franny spoke with Al, who promised to be more quiet, but two weeks later Al had another loud party. The following day Franny read Al's lease and found that no provision in the lease said anything about making noise.

DISPUTE: The other tenants continued to complain about Al, so Franny brought a suit to have him evicted. Al contested.

RULES: I. A tenant who is in possession of premises under the terms of the lease is entitled to hold those premises during the term of that lease so long as he abides by the terms of the lease.

II. Regardless of the terms of a lease, a tenant who uses leased premises for illegal purposes or who maintains a nuisance on the premises likely to interfere with the rights of other tenants on the premises may be evicted by the landlord.

32. Is Franny entitled to have Al evicted?

33. Did Al's conduct constitute a nuisance?

34. Did Al's conduct violate any of the terms of the lease?

35. Is Al entitled to receive his $250 security deposit?

STOP

IF YOU FINISH BEFORE TIME IS CALLED, CHECK YOUR WORK ON THIS SECTION ONLY. DO NOT WORK ON ANY OTHER SECTION IN THE TEST.

SECTION VI

Time—35 Minutes
25 Questions

Directions: Each group of questions is based on a set of propositions or conditions. Drawing a rough picture or diagram may help in answering some of the questions. Choose the best answer for each question and blacken the corresponding space on your answer sheet.

Questions 1–6

The National Zoo has a very active panda bear colony. One day six of the pandas broke out of their compound and visited the seals. After they were returned to their compound, they were examined by the Panda-keeper. The following facts were recorded.

Bin-bin is fatter than Ging-ging and drier than Eena.
Col-col is slimmer than Fan-fan and wetter than Ging-ging.
Dan-dan is fatter than Bin-bin and wetter than Ging-ging.
Eena is slimmer than Ging-ging and drier than Col-col.
Fan-fan is slimmer than Eena and drier than Bin-bin.
Ging-ging is fatter than Fan-fan and wetter than Bin-bin.

1. Which of the pandas is (are) fatter than Eena and drier than Ging-ging?
   (A) Dan-dan only
   (B) Fan-fan only
   (C) Bin-bin only
   (D) both Fan-fan and Col-col
   (E) both Dan-dan and Bin-bin

2. Which of the pandas is both slimmer and wetter than Eena?
   (A) Ging-ging
   (B) Fan-fan
   (C) Dan-dan
   (D) Col-col
   (E) Bin-bin

3. Which of the following is (are) both fatter and wetter than Ging-ging?
   (A) Fan-fan
   (B) Dan-dan
   (C) Col-col
   (D) Fan-fan and Col-col
   (E) Eena and Dan-dan

4. Which of the following is the driest?
   (A) Col-col
   (B) Dan-dan
   (C) Eena
   (D) Fan-fan
   (E) Ging-ging

5. Which of the following statements must be false?
   I. Dan-dan is drier than Col-col.
   II. Fan-fan is wetter than Dan-dan.
   III. Dan-dan is three inches fatter than Ging-ging.

   (A) I only
   (B) II only
   (C) III only
   (C) I and II only
   (E) II and III only

6. A new panda, Yin-yin, is purchased from the Peking Zoo. If dominance in panda bears is determined by fatness, then what will Yin-yin's rank be if he is fatter than Fan-fan and slimmer than Bin-bin?
   (A) second from the top
   (B) third from the top
   (C) fourth from the top
   (D) next to the bottom
   (E) cannot be determined from the information given

Questions 7–13

Captain Mulhouse is choosing the last part of his crew for the sailboat *Fearsome,* with which he hopes to earn the right to defend the America's Cup. He needs four more crew members, of whom at least two must be grinders for the winches, with the others being sail trimmers.

The candidates for grinder are David, Erica, and Francis.
The candidates for trimmer are Larry, Mary, Nancy, and Paul.
Nancy will not crew with Paul.
Erica will not crew with Larry.
David will not crew with Nancy.

7. If Nancy is chosen, which of the following must be the other members of the crew?
(A) David, Erica, and Mary
(B) Erica, Francis, and Larry
(C) Erica, Francis, and Mary
(D) Erica, Francis, and Paul
(E) Francis, Larry, and Mary

8. If Paul is chosen, which of the following combinations of candidates CANNOT be chosen to be on the crew?
(A) David, Erica, and Francis
(B) David, Erica, and Mary
(C) David, Francis, and Larry
(D) David, Francis, and Mary
(E) Erica, Francis, and Larry

9. Given the above statements about the relationships among the potential crew members, which of the following must be true?

I. If David is rejected, then Mary must be chosen.
II. If David is rejected, then Francis must be chosen.
III. If David is chosen, then Paul must also be chosen.

(A) II only
(B) III only
(C) I and II only
(D) I and III only
(E) II and III only

10. If Larry is chosen as a trimmer, which of the following could be the other members of crew?

I. David, Francis, and Mary
II. David, Francis, and Nancy
III. David, Francis, and Paul

(A) I only
(B) II only
(C) III only
(D) I and II only
(E) I and III only

11. Which of the following statements must be true?

I. If Captain Mulhouse chooses Larry now, then Francis must also be chosen now.
II. If Captain Mulhouse chooses Mary now, then Nancy must also be chosen now.
III. Larry and Nancy never crew together.

(A) I only
(B) I and II only
(C) I and III only
(D) II and III only
(E) I, II, and III

12. If Paul is chosen to be part of the *Fearsome*'s crew and David is not, who must be the other members of the crew?
(A) Erica, Francis, and Larry
(B) Erica, Francis, and Mary
(C) Erica, Francis, and Nancy
(D) Erica, Mary, and Nancy
(E) Francis, Larry, and Mary

13. If Erica makes the crew and Francis does not, which of the following statements must be true?

I. Paul will be a member of the crew.
II. Mary will be a member of the crew.

(A) both I and II
(B) neither I nor II
(C) I only
(D) II only
(E) either I or II, but not both

Questions 14–17

The first three names in each set are names usually used for males.

The last two names in each set are names usually used for females.

Each name in a set begins with a different letter.

Each name in a set contains the same number of letters.

I.	Jack	Paul	Dave	June	Edna
II.	Pete	Mike	Henry	Emma	Mary
III.	Frank	James	Chuck	Nancy	Betty
IV.	Louis	Tommy	Greta	Linda	Annie
V.	Phil	Dick	Mona	Alma	Inga

14. Which name would correctly complete the following set?

Allen Wally _____ Eliza Julia

(A) Ethel
(B) Mabel
(C) Waldo
(D) Harry
(E) Angus

15. All of the conditions established above are met by which of the sets?
(A) I only
(B) III only
(C) I and V only
(D) II and IV only
(E) III and V only

16. Which set satisfies all of the conditions except the third?
(A) I
(B) II
(C) III
(D) IV
(E) V

17. Which of the following substitutions would make its set meet the stated conditions?
(A) "Mark" for "June" in set I
(B) "Lila" for "Henry" in set II
(C) "Boris" for "Frank" in set III
(D) "Simon" for "Louis" in set IV
(E) "Fred" for "Mona" in set V

Questions 18–21

I. L, M, Z, and P are all possible.
II. All M are L.
III. All L are Z.
IV. No M are Z.
V. Some Z are L.
VI. No P are both M and L, but not Z.

18. Which of the above statements contradicts previous ones?
(A) III
(B) IV
(C) V
(D) VI
(E) none of the statements contradict previous statements.

19. If statements II and III are true, which of the other statements must also be true?
(A) IV only
(B) V only
(C) VI only
(D) IV and V only
(E) V and VI only

20. If X is an L it must also be a(n)
(A) M only
(B) P only
(C) Z only
(D) L and Z only
(E) L, P, and Z

21. Given the above statements, which of the following must be false?
(A) There are some L's.
(B) Some Z are not L.
(C) There are some P's which are Z's but not M or L.
(D) There cannot be any Z's that are not L or M.
(E) None of the above are necessarily false.

Questions 22–25

Four companies have just merged and their computer programmers are trying to coordinate their different communications computers. They have six computers: F, G, H, J, K, and L, which can input and output only the computer languages specified below:

F can fully use Optico, but can only input Newton.
G can fully use Optico, but can only input Mantra and Newton.
H can fully use Newton, but can only input Mantra.
J can fully use Optico and Praxis.
K can fully use Mantra, but can only input Optico.
L can fully use Praxis.

22. Which of the following computers has (have) the capacity to output data directly to at least three of the other computers?

    I. J
    II. G
    III. F

    (A) I only
    (B) II only
    (C) I and III only
    (D) II and III only
    (E) I, II and III

23. Between which of the following pairs of computers can J serve as a link so that data can be transmitted in both directions?
    (A) K and F
    (B) K and G
    (C) K and H
    (D) L and G
    (E) L and K

24. If H and J are to linked together, which of the following is (are) true?

    I. H can input data from J, but cannot send data to J.
    II. If F is linked to J and H, data can be transmitted in both directions between J and H through F.
    III. If G is linked to J and H, J can input data from H through G, but H cannot input data from J through G.

    (A) I only
    (B) II only
    (C) III only
    (D) I and III only
    (E) II and III only

25. In which of the following linkages could data be transmitted from the first computer to the third computer through the second computer, but NOT in the reverse direction?
    (A) K—H—F
    (B) J—L—H
    (C) H—G—L
    (D) G—J—L
    (E) F—G—J

STOP

IF YOU FINISH BEFORE TIME IS CALLED, CHECK YOUR WORK ON THIS SECTION ONLY. DO NOT WORK ON ANY OTHER SECTION IN THE TEST.

WRITING SAMPLE

Time—30 Minutes

Directions: Write an essay about the question listed below. You may support or attack the question or discuss it in any way that you wish. Be sure to make your points clearly and cogently and to write as neatly as possible. Write your essay within the margins of the pages. Additional paper may be used as scratch paper, but only these pages can be used for the actual essay.

TOPIC: Some parents have urged that elementary school children should be taught computer programming as early as second grade. They point out that children will be growing up in a world in which there will be computers and that understanding computers will be critical to a successful life. Other parents oppose too great an emphasis on computer programming at that age, arguing that very few children will ever become programmers themselves and that, at that age, there are too many other things that children should be learning. They should not be spending the time needed to become proficient programmers that early in their schooling.

You are a member of the board of directors of the Parents Association. Prepare a brief position paper on this topic to be presented to the board.

ANSWER KEY
PRACTICE EXAMINATION 2

SECTION I

1. D	8. C	15. D	22. B	29. D
2. D	9. C	16. C	23. C	30. C
3. A	10. D	17. C	24. C	31. A
4. C	11. C	18. A	25. C	32. C
5. C	12. C	19. C	26. B	33. D
6. C	13. D	20. D	27. C	34. C
7. B	14. C	21. A	28. C	35. D

SECTION II

1. D	8. E	15. B	22. E
2. A	9. D	16. C	23. E
3. C	10. B	17. E	24. A
4. B	11. B	18. E	25. A
5. D	12. A	19. A	
6. E	13. D	20. B	
7. C	14. A	21. C	

SECTION III

1. B	8. A	15. C	22. C
2. D	9. E	16. B	23. B
3. D	10. B	17. C	24. D
4. E	11. C	18. D	25. E
5. A	12. C	19. E	26. D
6. C	13. D	20. A	27. A
7. E	14. A	21. B	28. E

SECTION IV

1. C	8. E	15. C	22. D
2. E	9. D	16. E	23. C
3. B	10. E	17. C	24. B
4. E	11. B	18. C	25. A
5. D	12. A	19. C	26. C
6. B	13. B	20. A	
7. C	14. B	21. D	

SECTION V

1. C	8. A	15. B	22. A	29. C
2. B	9. B	16. C	23. C	30. B
3. C	10. B	17. D	24. A	31. D
4. A	11. C	18. A	25. C	32. A
5. B	12. A	19. B	26. D	33. C
6. B	13. D	20. D	27. C	34. C
7. C	14. B	21. B	28. A	35. B

SECTION VI

1. C	6. E	11. A	16. A	21. D
2. D	7. C	12. B	17. E	22. E
3. B	8. E	13. A	18. B	23. D
4. D	9. C	14. D	19. C	24. C
5. B	10. E	15. B	20. C	25. A

EXPLANATORY ANSWERS

SECTION I

Set 1

OVERVIEW: Glancing at the two rules, we can already begin to imagine situations in which they would conflict. Specifically, it will be a case in which a person touches another person without that person's consent *while* trying to recover property which belongs to him. This situation arises in our facts. Barney does touch David without David's consent. We know this since the facts make it clear that Barney surprises David, and acts suddenly before David can consent or object. The issue here is whether Barney is liable for the medical costs.

1. **(D)** Although David's age might be relevant in determining for some other rule whether David had committed a crime (for example, perhaps David is a juvenile), this information would be irrelevant to the question of whether Barney is liable to David or David's parents for the injuries sustained by David. Notice that although the information is not supplied by the passage, this is not a (B) since the *answer* to this question would not help us apply either rule.

2. **(D)** Again the *answer* to the question asked would not give us any information useful in determining whether Barney is liable in this case. (Remember our first question in the attack strategy was to ask, "Would the *answer* to this question provide useful information?") Although Rule II does require that David wrongfully take the car, this can be deduced from the facts we are given. After all, Barney did not consent to David's taking his car, and Barney obviously objected to David's taking his car (he pursued David). So we really do not need to know what crime David has committed to conclude that David wrongfully took Barney's car.

3. **(A)** This is the question which highlights the conflict mentioned in the set overview. According to Rule I, Barney is liable because he touched David without David's consent. But according to Rule II, Barney was justified in doing so, so given that Barney had a right to take action in this case, he could not be liable. Incidentally, we note in passing that had Barney not been justified by some rule such as II, he would have committed a battery. There are two kinds of battery in the law—a civil battery and a criminal battery. The criminal battery is the one we read about in newspapers. It is violent. But a civil battery need not be violent. In any event, this is just a further reminder not to presume anything about the law.

4. **(C)** The set overview answers this question. We pointed out there that Barney completely surprised David, so we can deduce that there was no consent since there was no time for David to give consent.

5. **(C)** Again, the set overview makes it clear that David wrongfully took Barney's car. Barney surely did not consent to the taking, and even David realized that it was wrong (he said he planned to return it).

Set 2

OVERVIEW: The kind of facts in which these two rules would conflict might involve police officers returning someone who had committed a crime to their jurisdiction. In this case, we would be looking for the crime of manslaughter which involves the taking of another's life which is not excused by any of the exceptions. A preview of the rules would alert you to look for the exceptions. Now, interestingly enough, in this case there is no conflict of rules, because Rule II never comes into play. Rule II applies only to the actions of *officials,* not to the actions of *individuals* acting in their private capacity. So regardless of how Rule I fits the facts, there can be no answer (A) in this sequence of questions because there can be no conflict between Rules I and II.

6. **(C)** This is not an (A) for reasons noted above. The question does raise a (C)-type issue. Annemarie did kill someone, but then we must ask further whether her actions come within any of the exceptions articulated in Rule I. It may be a close call whether she was acting as a police officer (see #7), but it is quite clear that she did fire in self-defense. She does not have to fall within all of the exceptions, only one, and that is sufficient to tell us she cannot be convicted.

7. **(B)** This is an open question. If you picked (C), it should only have been after much debate: "Well, she was still a police officer, but then she was suspended, etc." When you have such misgivings about your conclusion, that should tip you off to the fact that your conclusion is in doubt. Therefore, an answer (B), that we need more information, is in order—not an answer (C).

8. **(C)** Unlike #7, this question can be answered by deduction. Since Annemarie was fired upon first, we can conclude that her returning of the fire was to protect herself.

9. **(C)** Referring again to the set overview, we know that this cannot be an (A). The actions of the brothers in hiring a detective are not the actions of officials. Since Rule II is not applicable we can deduce that the answer to this question is "no." This cannot be an irrelevant issue in this case since the presence of Rule II makes it at least an arguable objection to the charges against Annemarie.

10. **(D)** This question is clearly a (D). Obviously, whether she ever is compensated for the time of her suspension is not relevant to the question of manslaughter. And, even if you argue that her reinstatement (as opposed to back pay) is relevant because it would show she was not involved in her partner's wrongdoing, this cannot affect whether she was acting in the line of duty when she fired the gun in the first place. Either she was acting in the line of duty at that time or she was not. Later events cannot alter that.

11. **(C)** You must read the questions carefully, as this item illustrates. This question asks "Did Annemarie believe. . . . ?" We know from the facts that she did believe she was acting to save someone else. We do not have to raise the issue "Was she acting in the defense of a third party?" That might be a (B) or (C)—it is too close to say—and since we do not have to, we reserve judgment on that point.

Set 3

OVERVIEW: In this set a potential conflict arises if there is an alteration of some writing which is not one of those enumerated in Rule II. For example, if someone altered a contract, we might have a conflict. The alteration of a writing might fit the conditions of Rule I (alteration of a liability-creating document), and yet a contract would not fit within the list of Rule II. As the facts are actually presented, we do not have a conflict at all. The document which Nolan altered was not one which would create some legal liability for the signer (Grant was long since dead). This shows the importance of reading all of the words in the rule. A student who overlooked this important qualification might have thought Nolan had committed a forgery (except for Rule II).

12. **(C)** If you noted in Rule I that a forgery can be committed only by altering a liability-creating document, you had no trouble with this question. Since the document altered by Nolan could not have created any liability for Grant, there was no forgery. A person who answered (A) probably did so because he overlooked that element of the rule.

13. **(D)** This is irrelevant to the question of whether there was a forgery in the first place. Nothing in the rule states that there must be some minimum amount to constitute a forgery. So far as the rule mentions, any amount, even 1¢, could be enough for forgery.

14. **(C)** This can be answered on the basis of the facts. We know Nolan did alter the document—the facts say so. There is no forgery, however, for the reasons given in #12.

15. **(D)** This is irrelevant. We are concerned only in determining whether Nolan is guilty of forgery. Whether he is guilty of some other crime is completely beside the point.

Set 4

OVERVIEW: In this case there is a possibility of conflict if there is a new will, some of the provisions of which do *not* conflict with the earlier will. According to Rule I, the earlier will is completely revoked by a new will, which says that any earlier provision does not survive. According to Rule II, however, a provision in an earlier will may survive, provided that it is not inconsistent with a later will. Notice that the provision does not have to be incorporated into the later will; it is necessary only that the earlier provision not contradict the later one. This is what happened in the provision for Ivan. Both wills leave him something, but the later will fails to specify the amount.

16. **(C)** Since Peggy was to receive the house under both wills, there is no conflict. Notice that the 1965 document was never signed and so never became a will. Notice further that this does not require any knowledge about the law; the problem is drafted in such a way that clue words let you know that the 1965 document was not a will ("never executed it").

17. **(C)** This is deducible for the reasons explained in #16. The will never became effective at all because Tyrone never executed it.

18. **(A)** According to Rule I, the second will must govern since it completely revokes the earlier will. But according to Rule II, the earlier will remains in effect as long as there is no inconsistency between their provisions. Here there is no inconsistency, since the one speaks on a subject while the other is silent. So the court must decide whether to enforce the earlier (but consistent) provisions or the later.

19. **(C)** Since the provisions of the two wills are completely known, the only question is whether you can tell if they are inconsistent. There is no reason to look for another rule to interpret this commonsense word. Each provision in the 1960 will can be directly compared to the 1970 will, and vice versa, and the consistency determined.

20. **(D)** Since the rules do not make the age at which the testator died important, this question is irrelevant.

Set 5

OVERVIEW: The conflict between the rules will arise in the following manner: Someone causes an accident, but the full extent of the damages is not manifested immediately. There is an opportunity for the injured party to take action to mitigate the extent of his loss. Now, if he fails to do so, Rule I yields the result that he may recover those damages despite his failure to mitigate them. But according to Rule II, he cannot recover for those damages.

21. **(A)** This is the conflict just outlined in the set overview. Sandra would be entitled to all damages under Rule I, but under Rule II she cannot recover for those damages which she might have prevented by some reasonable precaution. Since she could have prevented the damage done by the car thieves by having the car towed (and the officer did warn her), she cannot recover according to Rule II. So we have a conflict.

22. **(B)** Notice that Sandra has sued for the value of the figurines. But what is their value? Is it the cost she paid for them? Is it the cost of replacing them now? Or might it

be the profit she would have made at the flea market? And given that some of the figurines were smashed in the accident while others survived but were stolen, should we assume that value is the same for both groups? No, the answer to this question is (B). We need some more information.

23. **(C)** Notice that this question stipulates "at the time of the accident." This means that Rule II is not called into play. It applies to later damages, which Sandra might have avoided. Rule I tells us that Sandra is entitled to recover those damages which occurred at the time of collision.

24. **(C)** This involves only one of the rules, the second. Can we conclude, given the facts, Sandra did not take reasonable steps? Yes, we can conclude that. The passage says that Sandra knew the danger, that she had it within her power to have the car removed, yet she obstinately refused to do anything. Such behavior is not reasonable. So we are able to deduce the answer to this question: (C).

Set 6

OVERVIEW: The possible conflict between these two rules is easily envisioned. If we find an oral agreement, Rule I says that it is enforceable. But Rule II says that it is enforceable only if it is for goods valued at less than $500 or it is possible to perform it within one year. Now, if a contract is verbal and for more than $500, we will have a conflict. As it turns out, the facts do not present us with a conflict. The contract for personal services *could* have been performed within one year—if Zebadiah had died. Note, it is irrelevant whether Zebadiah did or did not die within a year. Rule II says only that if the contract cannot *possibly* be completed within a year, it is unenforceable.

25. **(C)** Since the contract could possibly have been performed within a year (if Zebadiah had died), Rule II does not apply to these facts. Only Rule I applies, and it says the contract is enforceable.

26. **(B)** Notice that the wording of the problem says that Samuel sued for compensation for his services. To be sure, he would probably want to collect the entire $50,000; but if he cannot get that under his contract, there may be some other way for him to collect. After all, he did render the services, and that suggests he is entitled to something. Is he or is he not? We just do not have enough information to decide. We need an additional rule to tell us whether his contract is the only way he can recover, or whether he might be able to get some money, such as the reasonable value of his services, because he did do the work.

27. **(C)** We can deduce the answer to the question, and our answer (if we were required to answer rather than just say how it affects the case) would be "no!" This was no contract for the *sale of goods*. So you do not have to wonder what the true value of the contract was.

28. **(C)** Again, we recall that there is no conflict between the rules in this case since the contract could have been performed within one year.

29. **(D)** This is irrelevant to the question of whether Samuel is entitled to some compensation. Once we have established that Samuel is entitled to recover on his contract, it is not important why Richard decided not to fulfill his half of the bargain.

30. **(C)** The answer to this question is "yes." It is conceivable, as we have stressed, that Zebadiah might have died within the year. Since he *might* have died within the year, it is also unimportant that he did not.

Set 7

OVERVIEW: A conflict between the two rules would occur in a case where a tenant, who had signed a lease, abandoned the premises because the landlord failed to provide needed services. According to Rule I, the tenant would be liable for the entire term of the lease, and the landlord would be entitled to the rents *as they came due*.

But according to Rule II, the tenant has no obligation after he has moved out.

31. **(A)** This is the conflict just described. Notice that the question specifies "rent which has accumulated." Even without regard to a possible conflict, the landlord cannot recover those rents which have not yet become due; Rule I allows him to recover only for those which have already fallen due.

32. **(C)** It will not do to strain at gnats and question whether heat is an essential service. After all, if heat is not, it is difficult to imagine anything which a landlord is supposed to provide which *is* essential (the roof?).

33. **(D)** How much rent Revere had to pay at his new location is irrelevant to how much he owes Grover. Had the question stipulated that Grover rented Revere's old apartment, that information would have been relevant to how much Revere owned to Grover. See #34.

34. **(C)** As we noted in #33, if Grover rerents the apartment Revere lived in, then Revere does not owe any rent for months after that time.

35. **(D)** This information is given in the facts and is irrelevant since Grover did fail at one time to provide the services.

SECTION II

Questions 1–5

Arranging the Information

Previewing these problems and the information makes it clear that all we have is a partial description of what might be the diving arrangements. We can classify this either algebraically by writing equations such as: "M not P or Q," "K with S," or we can make a diagram showing the connections which are stated:

DIVERS — BIOLOGISTS

AT LEAST ONE PER TEAM OF EACH CATEGORY

ALWAYS WITH

KEN ←——→ SUE

NEVER WITH

MABEL ←——→ {PETER, QUENTIN}

LEON — ROSEMARY

NINA

DIVE-MASTER FROM THIS GROUP

Answering the Questions

1. **(D)** You must note the condition that there are three dive teams. Since there are seven people, not counting Jack or Nina, to be divided into 3 teams (one could stay aboard ship, but it doesn't matter) the teams must be 2, 2, and 2 or 3 persons. Ken and Sue are on one team. Mabel can't be with either Peter or Quentin so she must be with Rosemary, hence (D) is not possible, yielding (D) as the correct answer.

   That leaves Leon to be with either Peter or Quentin and the other of that pair to go with either Ken or Leon's team or stay on ship.

   If you wished to choose (A) or (B) you may have thought the newlyweds wouldn't dive with anyone, but all that was said was that they dive together. (C) and (E) are valid possibilities as previously explained, which leaves (D).

2. **(A)** Ken and Sue are one team. Since Mabel won't dive with the two male biologists, she must dive with Rosemary as a two-diver team. Nina and Ken on the one hand, and Peter and Quentin on the other, can trade freely and they can team up four ways (M & P, M & Q, N & P, and N & Q) for a grand total of six.

3. **(C)** Mabel's being the dive-master opens things up a little, but the basic restrictions still hold. I is not possible because they are all biologists. II is not possible because they are both professional divers with no biologist. III is possible in a way similar to that

discussed in problem 1. IV is not possible because it involves splitting Ken and Sue. Hence, (C).

4. **(B)** (C) is out because it parts Ken and Sue. (D) has a team composed only of biologists or only of professional divers, and thus fails. (A) and (E) both fail to keep anyone on board as a dive-master. (B) is, thus, the answer. There is no limit to the size of the teams.

5. **(D)** (A), (B), and (E) all split Ken and Sue and thus are not possible. (C) fails for having only biologists. (D) is possible and the answer.

Questions 6–10

Arranging the Information

This problem set describes a layout or map situation. One clue is its being a set of regular shapes and the other is the use of compass directions. You have to distinguish between conditions which lead to definite squares being definite crops and ones which simply describe relationships between crops.

If two sides of the field runs east-west, the other sides run north-south, and the field is aligned with the compass.

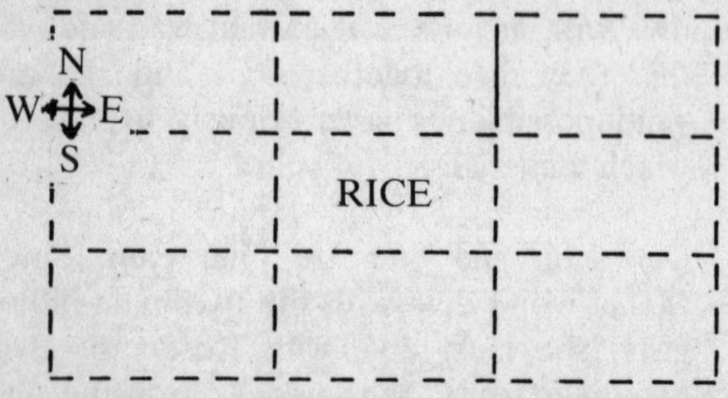

The information about wheat and barley cannot be coded into the diagram now, nor can the information about the soybeans, but peanuts can.

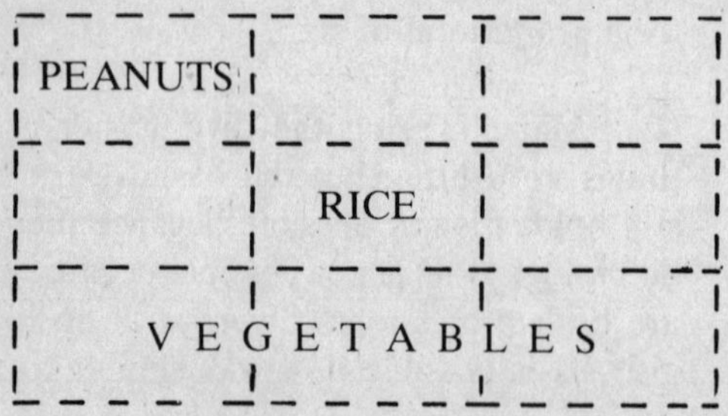

Answering the Questions

Questions 6, 7, and 8 refer to five squares. Let us locate them on the map:

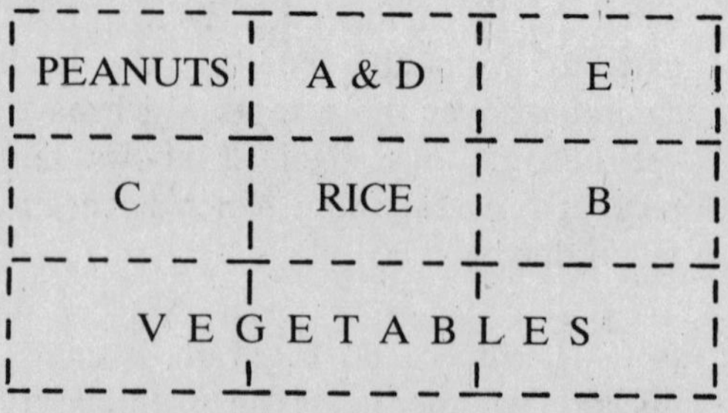

If the four unallocated fields are to be planted with one field of wheat, one of barley, and two of soybeans, the wheat and barley have to be two of the upper-right-hand fields in order to be next to each other.

6. **(E)** If field (E) is planted with soybeans, then the wheat and barley cannot be next to each other.

7. **(C)** If (C) is planted with wheat, the barley cannot be next to it.

8. **(E)** Although there are two fields next to the peanuts, we have already eliminated (C) from consideration as a wheat field. Thus, the wheat must be in the field just north of the rice (A)/(D) and the barley must be in field (E) to be next to the wheat.

9. **(D)** The rice is in the middle, so the tomatoes cannot be next to the soybeans, eliminating II—and answer choices (B) and (E). Either of the fields to the east or west of the rice field could be planted with the soybeans as previously discussed, thus, I and III are possible, and (D) is correct.

   Note that the squash actually must be next to the soybeans, but that also means it is possible.

10. **(B)** It is a fair assumption that the other crops mentioned are to be planted and only the ones specifically omitted are not planted (to do otherwise would be mere nitpicking). This means that there will be one field of rice and barley, and two of soybeans—leaving five for vegetables.

Questions 11–15

Arranging the Information

Some people can easily either visualize or draw a cube and label the sides accordingly. However, such powers are not necessary to the solution of the problem. Simply note that a cube, like a room, has a top, a bottom, and four sides, and draw the diagram as follows:

TOP	
SIDES	
BOTTOM	

At first it is not clear how this information is to be arranged since the top and bottom are not clear until the end of the information. If you noticed that the last statement gave the bottom side's color, you could have done that first. If not, just assign one side to the top or bottom and then shift if it turns out to be wrong.

Since question 11 asks about redundancy from the top down, it is best to do the statements in that order, at least until #11 is solved.

Problem 11 is solved by noting that if red and black are opposite sides, ALL of the other sides are between them, so that statement III must be true given II and, thus, (B) is the answer to #11.

Code in I:

TOP	BLACK
SIDES	
BOTTOM	RED

As previously noted, III adds nothing new.

Code in IV. Note that these other sides are all in the middle of the diagram, so even though they are not specifically related to red/black, we still do know where in the diagram they go.

TOP	BLACK
SIDES	BLUE WHITE
BOTTOM	RED

Code in V:

TOP	BLACK
SIDES	BROWN BLUE WHITE
BOTTOM	RED

From the preceding diagram we can put the last color, green, next to white and between white and brown—since that is the only place left.

TOP	BLACK
SIDES	BROWN BLUE WHITE GREEN
BOTTOM	RED

The colors of the sides could be rotated in any way so long as their relative order is preserved. VI places red on the bottom, so this is the final diagram.

Answering the Questions

11. **(B)** This is analyzed in "Arranging the Information."

12. **(A)** Sides that are separated by one other side are opposite, just as the wall in front of you is one wall away from the wall in back of you (if you are in a box-like room, anyway). Thus, white is opposite brown.

13. **(D)** Since green is one of the side colors, the top and bottom—red and black—are adjacent to it, eliminating (B) and (E). From the diagram, we can see that white and brown are adjacent sides, thus, (D).

14. **(A)** Since the statements in the question mention specific positions only of red and black, answers (B), (C), and (D) cannot be supported. If red is the bottom (VI) and black is opposite it (II), then black must be the top—(A).

15. **(B)** This problem calls for a readjustment of the diagram, which now becomes:

TOP	GREEN
SIDES	BROWN BLACK WHITE RED
BOTTOM	BLUE

This was a tricky but easy question since the statement which is false, (B), was false in the original configuration. The diagram shows that (A), (C), (D), and (E) are all true. (A) is also a little tricky since this very important original relationship is preserved.

Questions 16–20

Arranging the Information

There are three kinds of information—house order on the block, family name, and type of dog—and there are five items of each sort. Thus, we will have a grid that is 5 by 3.

HOUSE ORDER	1	2	3	4	5
DOG*					
FAMILY					

*Note that two of the dogs begin with the letter "s" so more than initials must be used.

Since the preview of the questions reveals no questions about subsets of the information set nor any questions about contradictions or redundancies, we can safely start with any statement and pick the third-from-last which gives order of house information.

Setting up the preceding diagram is the most efficient way to approach the problem. Note that much of the other information does concern house order even though it does not directly number houses.

If the Lanes live two houses from both the other families, then the Lanes must live in the middle and the others at the ends. We will put the others in as 1 and 5, but remember that they might flip-flop.

HOUSE ORDER	1	2	3	4	5
DOG					
FAMILY	KINGS		LANES		JONESES

Now we can link in the next-to-last statement and the second statement's items.

HOUSE ORDER	1	2	3	4	5
DOG	NOT SETTER NOT SHEEP NOT COLLIE	SHEEP? COLLIE?	NOT SHEEP NOT COLLIE	SHEEP? COLLIE?	NOT SHEEP NOT COLLIE
FAMILY	KINGS		LANES		JONESES

Entering the third item, we find that the Kings can't have the sheepdog (since it is next to the Joneses) or any dog other than the poodle, and thus must have the poodle. Since the sheepdog lives next to the Joneses, it must be in position 4 (always remembering that the order could be left-to-right or right-to-left). This in turn means that the only slot available for the collie is at house 2.

HOUSE ORDER	1	2	3	4	5
DOG	POODLE	COLLIE	NOT SHEEP NOT COLLIE NOT POODLE	SHEEP	NOT SHEEP NOT COLLIE NOT POODLE HEAVIEST DOG
FAMILY	KINGS		LANES		JONESES

The next statement, that the retriever weighs more than the setter or poodle, means that the Joneses don't have either of the lighter dogs, which makes four dogs eliminated for them and they must have the retriever. If the Joneses have the retriever, then the only dog left for the Lanes is the setter.

HOUSE	1	2	3	4	5
DOG	POODLE	COLLIE	SETTER	SHEEPDOG	RETRIEVER
FAMILY	KINGS		LANES		JONESES

The last statement now fills in the last two families as being:

HOUSE	1	2	3	4	5
DOG	POODLE	COLLIE	SETTER	SHEEPDOG	RETRIEVER HEAVIEST DOG
FAMILY	KINGS	NEFFS	LANES	MURRAYS	JONESES

Answering the Questions

Almost all of these questions are largely a matter of reading from the diagram.

16. **(C)** The second statement also shows the falseness of (C) by itself.

17. **(E)** This can only be gotten quickly from the diagram.

18. **(E)** Although the heaviest dog is known (retriever), the rank- order of the other dogs by weight is not known, thus the answer to this question is not determinable.

19. **(A)** The Neffs now live with the collie and the Joneses with the retriever, in houses 2 and 5 respectively. When swapped, the Joneses in house 2 are next to the Kings and the poodle. Note that since we are looking for something which now BECOMES true, it must be something to do with the Joneses or the Neffs. Thus, (D) and (E) are improbable.

20. **(B)** The sheepdog will now be in house 3 with the Lanes and the setter, thus, (B) is correct and (A) false. (B) is the most general statement available, and thus deserving of a thorough review early in your work on the problem.

Questions 21–25

Arranging the Information

This problem set concerns items arranged along two different and non-connected parameters: Smell and prettiness. Since there is no connection between the two parameters (such as prettier flowers smell better, or whatever) the two can be analyzed separately.

←PRETTIER—— less PRETTY→

A less pretty than L	L A
D prettier than L	D L A
I less pretty than L	D L A ←I→
L prettier than R	D L A ←I→ ←R→

Now for the smell	←BETTER—SMELL—WORSE→
A not as nice as L or D	L A ←D→
D not as nice as L	L D A
I not as nice as D or R	L D A ←R × I→
L not as nice as R	R L D A ←I→

Answering the Questions

21. **(C)** We are looking for indeterminacies, and as the diagram shows the smell relationship between irises and asters is unknown. (A), (B), and (E) are all definitely true, while (D) is false.

22. **(E)** (A), (B), and (D) are false, with (C) being possible, but unknown. (E) is definitely true since roses smell the best of all.

23. **(E)** The bottom of the prettiness scale has irises, roses, and asters all being in one group, whose interrelationships are not known. Even knowing how irises and roses relate does not solve the problem of how asters fit into the scheme of things. Thus, it is not determinable just what, if anything, irises are prettier than.

24. **(A)** The diagrams make it clear that only daffodils qualify. As discussed in problem 23, the relationship between the prettiness of roses, irises, and asters is not known.

25. **(A)** Be careful when you enter this new item not to conclude too much. Even though the diagram happens to list irises and asters next to each other in the smell scale, putting dahlias below the asters does not make it below the irises. The new diagram is:

	←BETTER—SMELL—WORSE→
L not as nice as R	R L D A←Dahlia→ ←I→

Thus, dahlias overlap irises and (A) is correct. The other choices are false.

SECTION III

1. **(B)** The number of hours at home is seen by the author as an opportunity to extend the work of the school, but not as being more important. The author says it is a great influence, but not that it is the greatest, thus, (A) fails. (C) and (D) are both stated in the passage, but they are used as examples of (B)'s more general idea. (E) is, if anything, opposed since the example of the parent helping with the homework was largely negative. If the more general mathematics usage ideas are considered helping with homework, then this is like (C) and (D): Only an example of (B).

2. **(D)** (A) is incorrect since no generalization is made, only an example used. (B) and (E) are absent from the passage altogether. (C) is attractive, but not actually in the passage. It sounds like one of the things which might be done to help math, perhaps using the yardstick that is mentioned, but this is not, in fact, mentioned. (D) is the subject of the entire passage and the last several paragraphs in particular.

3. **(D)** (B), (C), and (E) are without foundation, and (A) is false. (D) is precisely what is urged by the author.

4. **(E)** This is a detail question. (E), a demonstration lesson, is not necessarily included in classes for parents since the classes for the parents would focus on what the parents should do at home, rather than reviewing, as such, what the children do at school. New progress report methods are mentioned, (B), as are (D) and (C).

5. **(A)** The passage made its point by giving an example in which interesting related activities led to improvement. Although the example was abstract to some extent, the author's use of it as a piece of evidence implies that he believes it to be true, thus, (A) is implied.

   (D) picks up on the passage's negative evaluation of drill in the home and the types of non-drill reinforcements recommended by the author; however, since the focus of the passage is exclusively on home activities, only the weakest of inferences can be made about the author's views on activities at school. (D) is probably the second-best answer.

   None of the other choices is much connected with the passage. (B) alleges laziness, but only inadequate support is seen as the student's problem in the passage. The only mention of a principal, (C), is in reference to his approval being sought for innovative or unusual teacher initiatives. (E) refers to visits by teachers to the parents at home, but the only parent-teacher communication urged in the passage is the reference to informal interviews, which need not be conducted at the parent's home.

6. **(C)** All of the answers touch upon the substance of the passage and it is the differences among them which give the answer choice. The passage is aimed at teachers and specifies actions to be taken by teachers in order to influence the parents' future actions. Thus, (A) errs in claiming the passage speaks directly to the parent, as does (E). (E) also suffers from the pejorative word *brainwash,* since the author believes that many parents are willing and eager to help their children and lack only proper guidance.

   (D) takes the example of mathematics as the point, when all subjects are at issue.

   (B) and (C) have the most merit. There can be no doubt that the author hopes to serve the purpose outlined in (B), to some small extent, by writing his passage. BUT, the goal of having the child's capacities totally developed is most general and abstract, while the passage has a closer, clearer purpose as expressed by (C). (C) fits the passage much more closely than does (B), which could describe the ultimate purpose of hundreds of articles.

7. **(E)** Since the tone is one of instructing the teacher, (E) is very attractive, but the others must be eliminated. (B) and (C) fail because

of the passage's instructions-to-the-teacher tone. (D) is not supported in the passage, since no reference to college is needed or present. (A) has the merit of focusing on the right sort of person since the passage refers to elementary school subjects such as arithmetic. However, while an elementary school teacher could be instructing his fellow teachers, it is precisely the job of the professor of education to do so, hence (E) is preferable.

8. **(A)** The most impressive thing about Hong Kong is the achievements of its people in partnership with the British administration, thus, (A). (B) is refuted by the example of the refugees from Shanghai; (C) by the unique developmental course of Hong Kong; and (E) by the ease with which the transition to manufacturing was accomplished as well as the generally complimentary attitude towards the people. (D) is slightly supported by the reference to the acquisition of Hong Kong by treaty as opposed to purchase or lease, but this is much weaker than (A).

9. **(E)** (C) and (D), if relevant at all, refer to the China trade which ended shortly after the war, and thus are either irrelevant or refer to unstabilizing factors. (A) and (B) are part of the basis of economic stability, but we are seeking a primary basis, thus, (E) is best because it includes (A) and (B), and much more.

10. **(B)** This is a detail question. (A) and (C) were definitely positive factors so they are not what we seek here. (E) is backwards, since it was actually a conversion from trading to manufacturing that occurred, with beneficial results. This question seeks something that actually happened and had bad results. If a potentially poor move for the future was sought, (E) might be a strong contender, but it is weak here.

    The defeat of the Chinese National Government did lead to the reduction of trade with China which was—at least temporarily—a setback for Hong Kong commerce. BUT the answer choice refers to the "retreat" of the government which is not in the passage and which is not the same as the defeat. Thus, (B) remains the only clearly adverse influence.

11. **(C)** The British acquired Hong Kong as a base for trade with China. This was largely successful until recently. (B) is seductive since we know from reading the newspapers that population virtually everywhere has grown a great deal. The passage, however, must be our guide and inspiration here and the only population changes it mentions were not steady, but the sudden immigration of hundreds of thousands of refugees.

    (A) and (D) are contrary to the statements of the passage since the Japanese occupied Hong Kong and the 40% of the labor force which works in manufacturing cannot be called a very small percentage. (E) is unknown since the passage only says that Hong Kong was the capital of the trade with China, not of trade in the entire Orient.

12. **(C)** No manufacturing machinery is stated to have come with the refugees from Shanghai. (A), capital, and (B), experts (or expertise), did. Note that the question stem merely asks what was important, not what was good or bad. (D) and (E) together led to the embargo of trade with China, which is certainly important.

13. **(D)** (D) covers the waterfront very well. All we know about the author in this passage is that he is the sort of person who would write this sort of passage. Since the passage is about an element of Far Eastern economic history, this is a good answer.

    (A) is poor because there is little of specifically political character in the passage. (B) is not as good as (D) since the passage is more of a treatise than an article in a newspaper or magazine of general circulation. In addition there is nothing to label the author as being American. (C) suffers from the same lack of national identifiers, though the econometrician part is fine. (D) is preferable to (C) since (C) has the burden of the unproven assertion of nationality. (E) has only superficial merit since a merely Oriental manufacturer is not specifically concerned with the history of

Hong Kong—(D) is concerned with history generally. (E)'s virtue is primarily that it reminds us of what would have been a wonderful answer—a writer for the Hong Kong chamber of commerce, but that is not what (E) is.

14. **(A)** This seemingly difficult question can be approached by considering which ideas are most important in the passage. The development of Hong Kong into a manufacturing center is key. Therefore, (A), which shows the central trend continuing, is the best answer.

(B) fails because the majority of Hong Kong's exports already are manufactured items, so this is not a continuation of a trend. (C) again echoes common knowledge about population growth, but it is information not in the passage. The word *absolutely* is very strong and would require a strong statement in the passage to justify the answer choice; such a statement is lacking.

(D) is tempting since we are given the impression that things are good in Hong Kong, but that is not really stated since there is only a discussion of the overall picture. Further, it may be that only the manufacturers are doing well and not all of the other businessmen.

(E) is getting things backwards. As we learn from Logical Reasoning, just because we are Hong Kong's main trading partner doesn't mean they are ours.

15. **(C)** The passage is a dry report of the facts, hence, (C). While the facts may give cause for alarm in some quarters, it is not the major tone of the passage. "Cautious," (B), has some appeal, but the caution expressed is largely caution to remain factual. "Rustic," (D), is a play on the farming topic, and (E) is unsupported.

16. **(B)** This requires a little spadework. It is not enough that $100,000 is constantly referred to in the passage. In the paragraph on farm wealth it is stated that at present the wealth is distributed in even thirds for small, medium, and large farms. By contrast, the future will see two-thirds in the over-$100,000 category. If we assume that $100,000 is one of the breakpoints (which the extent of the discusson DOES support) then it cannot be the line between small and medium since two-thirds of the wealth is already above that point according to the passage. Thus, it is a strong inference that $100,000 is the dividing point between medium and large.

(A) is eliminated by the article *a* in the question. *A* farm which produced two-thirds of the nation's crops is certainly large, but that is not in the passage.

(C) and (D) refer to measures that, though reasonable, are not used for this purpose in the passage. (E) refers to an amount the passage says will be the future equity of a $100,000 farm. Even if it were the present equity—which would not be seen on a real question—you could not choose the equity choice in preference to the sales figure since equity is referred to in terms of size of sales in the passage.

17. **(C)** The topic of the passage is agriculture, hence, (C) has great merit. All the other answer choices are possible, but there is no special reason to support them, except (D) perhaps which is still poorer than (C).

18. **(D)** The reference in the passage to families and farms is that there will be more family corporations, which has nothing to do with residence. Actually, (D) is probably opposed by the passage since fewer farms will be available for residency. All the others are explicitly stated in the passage.

19. **(E)** The fifth paragraph states that a third of the shift of farms to higher sales categories will be the result of inflation of the sales figures causing farms still selling the same produce to move up in sales dollars.

(A) has some merit, but it is based more on common knowledge than the passage, which makes it inferior to (E) which is straight from the passage. (B), (C), and (D) are unrelated to the passage as stated.

20. **(A)** The disclaimer in the beginning of the passage lists five major influences and hints at even more; this is certainly complex. The other choices fail because they are too

strong. (B) and (C) allege a definite link between greater size and greater productivity, which is much stronger than any inference of that sort which the passage could support. (E) harks back to the last paragraph which merely stated that family corporations will be more common, not VERY common. (D) echoes the statement in the passage that the wealth of each farmer will increase, but since there will be fewer farmers, the total wealth will not necessarily increase. Note that the choice refers only to the linkage between the increase in farm size and the increase in wealth. The increased wealth resulting from inflation is, thus, excluded.

21. **(B)** The aspiring farmer is not now a farmer. Since it will become increasingly difficult to enter farming, he should act as soon as possible. While (B) does have the additional implication that now is a particularly good time, it is fair to say that now is as good a time as there is likely to be. (A), (D), and (E) have no relevance. (C) has some small virtue in that it indicates that mere desire is not enough, but this would be a better answer to a question seeking consoling words for the disappointed aspirant than this one which asks for advice.

22. **(C)** The form of this essay is to recount a number of formative historical aspects of the author's personal religious and moral development. The last paragraph states the author's current faith which has resulted from these influences. Thus, (C) is a good description of the passage's workings and purpose.

(A) catches the tone of the passage as being explanatory and directed, but the author does not consider himself a Quaker and thus it is improbable that (A) is correct. (B) has the word *Friend* with a capital letter, thus indicating that a Quaker is addressed. However, while the passage might serve the purpose stated in (B), it would only do so through the idea of (C), and indeed the significant differences which the author does find between himself and Quakers might upset (B)'s purpose.

(D) is only relevant to a very small portion of the passage and the analysis of the inner light that does occur primarily sets the stage for the pacifism of the last paragraph, which still leaves (C) preferable to (D). (E) is not really in the passage, since it is only the parents' attitudes toward religious dogmatism which are discussed, rather than any explicit teachings.

23. **(B)** Two types of reward are played with between this question and the passage. In the passage the idea of a good deed being its own reward refers to inner feelings generated by the knowledge of having done a good deed. In the question, the connotation is one of a financial or material reward. While these are different, there is no reason to believe that the author would refuse a financial reward—he has sworn no vow of poverty—but at the same time he would not want it to seem that the financial reward was the reason for the good deed.

(C) is impossible or unnecessarily complicated. You may have thought that this answer choice was a way of referring to the possibility of having the financial reward given to a charity or some such, but it does not say that and if you choose it you are reading too much into the answer choice.

(D) fails since there is no basis in the passage for having any idea as to what, if anything, the author might consider blasphemous. The financial reward does not necessarily obviate the spiritual one.

(A) and (E) both suppose that the author is totally opposed to receiving a financial reward, which is more than we know from the passage. We would only entertain an answer of this sort if all others were totally impossible—and even then you should be unhappy with so weak an answer.

In contrast to the other answer choices, (B) has the virtue of being considerate of the other person's feelings, which seems to be implied in the author's respect for the divinity of all other persons.

24. **(D)** The author states that the idea of "inner light" is basic to his views and he uses it in that way. He got this idea from the Quakers and restates that it is a shared thought.

(B) is something that some people may know to be true of many—though not all—Quakers in the real world. In this passage, however, the author makes absolutely no reference to the pacifism of the Quakers, and indeed only discusses his own pacifism after he has dissociated himself from the Quakers. If one were forced to choose between the Quakers being pacifists and preachers of holy crusades, the passage would support the former over the latter, but nothing is said about the HISTORICAL nature of Quakerism in the passage.

(A) and (E) are specifically rejected in the passage and (C) is known to be true only of some Quakers at one Meeting for Worship.

25. **(E)** The author sees no reason for Jesus being more divine "than, say, Buddha." Thus, he likely sees all major religious leaders as being equally divine.

26. **(D)** The position taken by the author's parents can be inferred from the first sentence of the second paragraph where the parents' dislike of doctrine and dogmas is traced to their lapsed Catholicism, and thus a probable reason for the lapse.

(A) is false both because the author has an inner light and sees himself as a non-Quaker and because the last paragraph refers to "this piece of divinity that EVERY human has."

(B) is false because the inner light views of the author and the Quakers are stated to be the same, so the Quakers view all men as having an inner light.

(C) has no basis in the passage since the author's parents' dissatisfaction with Catholic views is not said to be in the matter of killing.

(E) is incorrect since the author states that he is closer to the Quakers than to any other organized religious group. While the organization of Buddhism is not the same as many Christian religions, it could not be called unorganized.

27. **(A)** (A) is stated in the last paragraph. (B) plays on the statement that we must "increase this lifeline" ("the inner light"). The increase is linked with understanding and better refers to increased strength rather than numbers. (C) and (D) fail for the same reasons as #26 (A) and (B). (E) is either unsupported or, better, rejected in the passage since the author has a faith without help of prophets which appears to be adequate for him, even though he says that it is "poorer" for lacking a prophet, etc. The extra divinity of prophets is also a questionable inference to base on this passage.

28. **(E)** This is a logical reasoning question. If both action and inaction will cause death, then death is no longer a difference between the options available and cannot be used to make the decision as to which option should be taken. (C) does not avoid the situation because it would simply be a method of choosing inaction. (D) fails because beliefs should not be abandoned because of the existence of situations to which they do not apply. Note that when the author argues against "the taking of any life by choice" this does not mean only by action. Inaction is a choice, too.

SECTION IV

1. **(C)** The point of the Chinese official's comment is that the Chinese appear to Westerners to be inscrutable because Westerners simply do not pay very careful attention to what is directly before them. (C) is correct because it points this out. (A) is misleading. The Chinese official refers to Occidentals in general, but he never mentions Orientals in general. Even so (A) misses the main point of the anecdote. (B) is better than (A), since it is at least generally related to the point of the Chinese official, but the precise point is not that Americans (rather Occidentals) fail to understand Chinese culture, rather that they suffer from a more specific myopia. They find they are not able to penetrate the motivations of the Chinese. In any event, the point of the passage is not just that there is such a failure, but further that such failure is attributable to the lack of insight of Westerners—not any real inscrutability of the

Chinese. (E) mentions the problem of understanding, but the difficulty described in the passage is one way only. Nowhere is it suggested that the Chinese have difficulty in understanding Westerners. Finally, (D) would be correct only if the passage had contained some key word to qualify the official's response, such as *hesitatingly* or *cautiously*.

2. **(E)** Once it is seen that the passage is humorous, this question is fairly easy. The official "smiles" and he "gently" responds. Further, the scenario is set by the first sentence: a *junior* official *embarrassed* himself. This shows the situation is uncomfortable for the American, but it is not a serious international incident. And the Chinese official's response is kind—not angry (A), not fearful (B), not indifferent (D). (C) is the second-best response, but by comparison "compassion" better fits the description of the official's action—smiling and gentle.

3. **(B)** Here the problem is to make sense out of the brother's claim that a device he rarely used and may never use again is still a good investment. It is not land, a work of art, or some similar thing, so it does not appear as though it will appreciate in value. The advantage, then, of owning must come from merely being able to possess it. Thus, answer (B), which cites the convenience of having the item to use if and when he should decide to do so, is best. (A) can be disregarded because the brother regards the investment as a good one *even if* he never again uses the device. To save money on ice cream, he would have to use it. (C) is highly suggestive—is the brother saying that it is a good idea to have things around in case one needs them? If so, then (C) sounds a bit like (B). But (C) is not nearly so direct as (B), and it requires some work to make it into (B). (D) is wrong because saving money by having purchased earlier would be worthwhile only if the item is actually needed. After all, a great deal you made by buying a ton of hay is not a great deal just because the price of hay is going up—you need an elephant (or a horse, or a plan to resell, or something) to make it worthwhile. Just buying hay because its a "bargain" is no bargain at all. (E) is fairly silly. It is like saying: "The bad news is you are to be executed tomorrow morning; the good news is you would have had liver for lunch." Or perhaps closer to this example would be: "The bad news is that someone stole your car; the good news is that the price of gasoline went up by 25¢ a gallon this morning." The point is that you will avoid some trivial injury or cost at the expense of something more serious.

4. **(E)** Again, the passage is somewhat lighthearted. The poet is saying that the poem is obscure: When he wrote it only he and the Almighty could understand it, and now (it is so difficult) even he has forgotten the point of the verse. (A) is somewhat attractive because the passage does state that God knows what man does not. Of course, once one understands the point of the passage, (A) can be discarded. Even so, there is something about (A) that lets you know it is wrong—"infinitely." One might infer from the poet's comments that man is not so wise as God, but it is not possible to conclude, on the basis of the one example, that God is infinitely wiser than man. (B) is also attractive, for the poet is saying that it is difficult to understand this particular poem. But (B) is wrong because he is not saying that men cannot understand poetry in general. (C) and (D) are distractions. They play on the term "God" in the paragraph. The poet cites God as the one who understands the verse—not the one who inspired it.

5. **(D)** Here we have one final humorous passage. Now this should not lead you to conclude that *many* LSAT paragraphs are amusing—to generalize to that conclusion on the basis of three examples would be a fallacy in and of itself—but taken individually each is reflective of the LSAT. And even if the LSAT does not string together three or four in a row, we hope that you have found them diverting. After all, study for this test is not itself the most enjoyable pastime available to human beings. But back to the task at hand. . . . You must always be careful of naked correlations. Sufficient

research would probably turn up some sort of correlation between the length of skirts and the number of potatoes produced by Idaho, but such a correlation is obviously worthless. Here too, the two numbers are completely unrelated to one another at any concrete cause-and-effect level. What joins them is the very general movement of the economy. The standard of living increases; so, too, does the average salary of a preacher, the number of vacations taken by factory workers, the consumption of beef, the number of color televisions, and the consumption of rum. (D) correctly points out that these two are probably connected only in this way. (A) is incorrect for it is inconceivable that preachers, a small portion of the population, could account for so large an increase in rum consumption. (B) is wildly implausible. (C), however, is more likely. It strives for that level of generality of correlation achieved by (D). The difficulty with (C) is that it focuses upon *total* preachers, not the *average* preacher; and the passage correlates not *total* income for preachers with rum consumption, but *average* income for preachers with consumption of rum. (E) might be arguable if only one period had been used, but the paragraph cites three different times during which this correlation took place.

6. **(B)** This is a relatively easy question. The argument is similar to "All observed instances of S are P, therefore, all S must be P." (All swans I have seen are white; therefore, all swans must be white.) There is little to suggests the author is a mechanic or a factory worker in an automobile plant; therefore, (A) is incorrect—and would be so even if the author were an expert because he does not argue using that expertise. A syllogism is a formal logical structure such as: "All S are M, All M are P; therefore, All S are P," and the argument about automobiles does not fit this structure—so (C) is wrong. By the same token, (E) is wrong since the author generalizes—he does not deduce, as by logic, anything. Finally, (D) is incorrect because the argument is not ambiguous, and one could hardly argue on the basis of ambiguity anyway, especially on the LSAT.

7. **(C)** The key phrase here—and the problem is really just a question of careful reading—is "who actually knew." This reveals that neither of the two knew the person whom they were discussing. There are many ways, however, of debating about the character of people with whom one is not directly acquainted. We often argue about the character of Napoleon or even fictional characters such as David Copperfield. When we do, we are arguing on the basis of indirect information. Perhaps we have read a biography of Napoleon (A), or maybe we have seen a news film of Churchill (B). We may have heard from a friend, or a friend of a friend, that so and so does such and such (E). Finally, sometimes we just make more or less educated guesses, (D). At any event, the two people described in the paragraph could have done all of these things. What they could not have done—since they finally resolved the problem by finding someone who actually knew Churchill—was to have argued on the basis of their own personal knowledge.

8. **(E)** Here we are looking for the unstated or hidden assumptions of the author. (A) is one because the author dates the building by measuring the wear and tear on the threshold, but if that were a replacement threshold installed, say 50 years after the building was first built, the author's calculations would be thrown off completely. So to reach the conclusion he does, he must have assumed that he was dealing with the original threshold. (C) is very similar. The calculations work—based as they are on the estimated capacity of the monastery—only if the author is right about the number of people walking across the door sill. So it also follows that (D) is something he assumes. After all, if marble tended to wear out spontaneously instead of under use—if sometimes it just evaporates—then the whole process of calculating time as a function of wear would be ill-founded. (E) is correct. The author uses the wars he cites to help him date *this particular group* of buildings. He never suggests that this has occurred "often."

9. **(D)** The insight required to solve this problem is that the apparent contradiction can be resolved by observing that the two cases are essentially different. The one is supposed to be a factual story; the other is a fictional account. Only III properly expresses this distinction, and II is simply irrelevant. While it may be true that disapproval is one way of trying to keep members of the profession honest, that has nothing to do with the seeming contradiction in the behavior of the critics. Finally, I contradicts the explicit wording of the passage, which stated that the critics rejected the fictionalization.

10. **(E)** The main point of the advertisement is that you should not hesitate to buy Cold Springs Water even though it is not imported. According to the ad, you will not be able to taste the difference. Thus, I is an assumption of the ad: "Neither you nor your guests will taste the difference" and it is explicitly mentioned. We know it is an assumption for if there were a taste difference the appeal of the ad would be seriously undermined. III is an assumption, too—but it is hidden or suppressed. Implicit in the ad is a rebuttal to the objection: "Yes, but it is not imported?" Whether it is imported or not can have only to do with status since the ad also states (assumes) that the tastes of Cold Springs and imported waters are indistinguishable. II is not an assumption. Although it is mentioned that Cold Springs is bottled at the source, the ad does not depend on where other imported or domestic waters are bottled. They could be bottled fifty miles away from the source, and that would not affect the appeal of the ad.

11. **(B)** Careful reading of the paragraph shows that the author's attitude toward parochial education is that he believes the insistence on instruction in religious values is *justifiable;* he disagrees, however, on the question of how best to inculcate those values. He believes that the proper attitude toward relations between the sexes could best be learned by children in the company of the other sex. Thus, (E) is diametrically opposite to the policy the author would recommend. (A) and (D) must be wrong because the passage clearly indicates the author supports parochial schools and the religious instruction they provide. (C) is a distraction. It plays on the association of segregation and racial discrimination. Racial segregation is not the only form of segregation. The word *segregation* means generally to separate or to keep separate.

12. **(A)** In this story, the identity of the person who reports the incident is irrelevant. So long as it is not someone with a special infirmity (very poor eyesight, for example) or poor credibility (an inveterate liar), then the person is quite capable of reporting what he saw—or what he thought he saw. The most serious weakness of the analysis presented is that it attacks Professor Branch's credentials. To be sure, one might want to question the accuracy of the report: At what time did it occur? What were the lighting conditions? Had the observer been drinking or smoking? But these can be asked independently of attacking the qualifications of the source. Thus, (D) must be wrong, for special credentials are just not needed in this case, so the wrong way to defend Professor Branch is to defend those. By the same token, it makes no sense to defend Branch by launching a counter-*ad hominem* attack on her attacker, so (B) is incorrect. (C) and (E) may or may not be true, but they are surely irrelevant to the question of whether this particular sighting is to be trusted.

13. **(B)** The inquisitor's behavior is paradoxical—that is, internally inconsistent or contradictory. The victim tells him that he is in league with the devil, so the inquisitor refuses to believe him because those in league with the devil never tell the truth. In other words, the inquisitor refuses to believe the victim because he accepts the testimony of the victim. Thus, (B) is correct. (A) is incorrect because the inquisitor does not *withdraw* anything he has said; in fact, he lets everything he has said stand, and that is how he manages to contradict himself. (E) is a bit more plausible, but it is incomplete. In a certain sense, the inquisitor does not accept the answer, but the real point of the

passage is that his basis for *not* accepting the answer is that he *does* accept the answer: He believes the victim when he says he is in league with the devil. (C) and (D) find no support in the paragraph. Nothing suggests that the inquisitor is violating any religious law, and nothing indicates that the inquisitor does not himself believe in the devil.

14. **(B)** The key here is that the word *nobody* is used in a cleverly ambiguous way—and, as many of you probably know, the "young lady" in the story is Lewis Carroll's Alice. This is fairly representative of his wordplay. (E) must be incorrect since it misses completely the little play on words: "I saw Nobody," encouraging a response such as "Oh, is he a handsome man?" (D) is beside the point, for the King is not interested in the messenger's veracity. He may be interested in his reliability (A); but if anything, we should conclude the King finds the messenger unreliable since "nobody walks slower" than the messenger. (C) is wrong because the question is not a matter of eyesight. The King does not say "If you had better eyes, you might have seen Nobody."

15. **(C)** Ann's response would be appropriate only if Mary had said, "All of the students at State College come from Midland High." That is why (C) is correct. (D) is wrong, because they are talking about the background of the students, not the reputations of the schools. (E) is wrong, for the question is from where the students at State College come. (B) is superficially relevant to the exchange, but it, too, is incorrect. Ann would not reply to this statement, had Mary made it, in the way she did reply. Rather, she would have said, "No, there are some Midland students at State College." Finally, Ann would have correctly said (A) only if Mary had said, "None of the students from North Hills attend State College." Or "Most of the students from North Hills do not attend State College." But Ann makes neither of these responses, so we know that (A) cannot have been what she thought she heard Mary say.

16. **(E)** If you wanted to determine how politically active people are, what kind of test would you devise? You might do a survey to test political awareness; you might do a survey to find out how many hours people devote to political campaigning each week or how many hours they spend writing letters, etc.; or you might get a rough estimate by studying the voting statistics. The paragraph takes contributions as a measure of political activity. (E) is correct for two reasons. One, the paragraph says nothing about individual activity. It says total contributions were up, not average or per person contributions. Second, (E) cites voting patterns which seem as good as or better an indicator of political activity than giving money. This second reason explains why (A) is wrong. (A) may weaken the argument, but a stronger attack would use voting patterns. (D) confuses individual and corporate contributions, so even if campaign giving were a strong indicator of activity, (D) would still be irrelevant. (B) does not even explain why contributions *in toto* rose during the four years, nor does it tell us anything about the pattern of giving by individual persons. Finally, (C) seems the worst of all the answers, for it hardly constitutes an attack on the author's reasoning. It seems likely that even in the face of increased political activity, public leaders would continue to warn against the dangers of political apathy.

17. **(C)** If you want to determine whether or not drug use is harmful to high school students, you surely would not conduct a survey of the students themselves. This is why (C) is correct. That a student does not *think* a drug is harmful does not mean that it *is not* actually harmful. (E) misses the point of the argument. The author is not attempting to prove that drug use is not widespread; he is trying to show it is not dangerous. (D) is part of an argument often used in debates over legalization of drugs by proponents of legalization. Here, however, it is out of place. The question is whether the drugs are harmless, that is, whether they are, in fact, victimless. (D) belongs to some other part of the debate. (A) sounds like the start of an argument. One might suggest that students

change their minds as they get older, and eventually many acknowledge the danger of such drugs. But (A) does not get that far; and, even if it did, (C) would be stronger for it gives us the final statement up to which that argument would only be leading. Finally, (B) is irrelevant. The question here is the harm of drugs, and that issue can be resolved independent of whether other things are harmful, e.g., alcohol or drag-racing.

18. **(C)** Amy points out that Al assumes that any extraterrestrial visitors to Earth, seeking intelligent life, would regard human beings here on Earth as intelligent, and therefore contact us. Amy hints that we might not be intelligent enough to interest them in contacting us. This is why (C) is the best answer. (A) is wrong. Amy does not miss Al's point: She understands it very well and criticizes it. (B) is wrong since Amy is not suggesting that Al is any less intelligent than any other human being, just that the aliens might regard us all as below the level of intelligence which they are seeking. (D) is more nearly correct than any other choice save (C). The difficulties with it are three-fold: One, there really is not all that much internal development of Al's argument, so (D) does not seem on target; two, in a way she does examine what internal structure there is—she notes there is a suppressed assumption which is unsound; finally, even assuming what (D) says is correct, it really does not describe the point of Amy's remark nearly so well as (C) does. Finally, (E) is incorrect because Amy does not offer an analogy of any sort.

19. **(C)** The problem with this argument is that it contains no argument at all. Nothing is more frustrating than trying to discuss an issue with someone who will not even make an attempt to prove his case, whose only constructive argument is: "Well, that is my position, if I am wrong, you prove I am wrong." This is an illegitimate attempt to shift the burden of proof. The person who advances the argument naturally has the burden of giving some argument for it. (C) points out this problem. (A) is incorrect because the author uses no group classifications. (B) is incorrect because the author does not introduce any analogy. (D) is a weak version of (C). It is true the author does not provide statistical evidence to prove his claim, but then again he provides no kind of argument at all to prove his claim. So if (D) is a legitimate objection to the paragraph (and it is), then (C) must be an even stronger objection. So any argument for answer (D)'s being the correct choice ultimately supports (C) even more strongly. The statement contained in (E) may or may not be correct, but the information in the passage is not sufficient to allow us to isolate the theory upon which the speaker is operating. Therefore, we cannot conclude that it is or is not discredited.

20. **(A)** Let us assign letters to represent the complete clauses of the sentence from which the argument is built. "If quarks . . . universe" will be represented by the letter P, the rest of the sentence by Q. The structure of the argument is, therefore: "If P then Q. Q. Therefore, P." The argument is obviously not logically valid. If it were, it would work for any substitutions of clauses for the letters, but we can easily think up a case in which the argument will not work: "If this truck is a fire engine, it will be painted red. This truck is painted red; therefore, it is a fire engine." Obviously, many trucks which are not fire engines could also be painted red. The argument's invalidity is not the critical point. Your task was to find the answer choice that paralleled it—and since the argument first presented was incorrect, you should have looked for the argument in the answer choices which makes the same mistake: (A). It has the form: "If P then Q. Q. Therefore, P." (B) has the form: "If P, then Q. P. Therefore, Q," which is both different from our original form and valid to boot. (C) has the form: "P or Q. Not P. Therefore, Q." (D) has the form: "If P, then Q. If Q, then R. Therefore, if P, then R." Finally, (E) has the form: "If P then Q. Not Q. Therefore, not P."

21. **(D)** The easiest starting point here is to recognize that I and III are a pair. The word *consequently* shows that the author is deduc-

ing a conclusion from something directly preceding. So III needs to be preceded by a sentence referring to something economic, and I contains the proper reference. On this basis alone, the remaining answers could have been rejected. Beyond that, you might have noticed that only II is an appropriate opening sentence. III is definitely not a good choice, because it begins with *consequently.* IV is no better because the word *such* refers to something earlier in the paragraph. I is possible, but then there would be no place to put II. If you began with I, you would follow it by III; but then neither II not IV would have represented a logical continuation.

22. **(D)** As we did in #20, let us use letters to represent the form of the argument. The first sentence is our old friend: "If P, then Q." Now, we must be careful not to use the same letter to stand for a different statement. No part of the second sentence is also a part of the first one, so we must use a new set of letters: "If R, then S." Do not be confused by the internal structure of the sentences. Though the second clause of the first sentence speaks about Johnson and Lloyd voting the same way, the second clause of the second sentence speaks about Johnson's defending someone. So the two statements are different ideas and require different letters. The first clause of the third sentence is the same idea as the first clause of the first sentence, so we use letter P again, but the second clause is different, T. The third sentence uses the phrase *only if,* "P only if T," which can also be written: "If P, then T." Our three sentences are translated as:
    1. If P, then Q.
    2. If R, then S.
    3. If P, then T.

    Now we can find which of the answers cannot be true.
    (A) "If R, then not Q." That is a possibility. While it cannot be deduced from our three assumptions, nothing in the three assumptions precludes it. So (A) could be true.
    (B) "If P, then T." This is true, a restatement of the final assumption.
    (C) "If T, then not-P." This is possibly true. #3 tells us "If P then T," which is the same thing as "if not-T, then not-P"; but it does not dictate consequences when the antecedent clause (the if-clause) is T.
    (D) "If P, then either not-Q or not-T." This must be false, since #1 and #3 together tell us that from P must follow both Q and T.
    (E) "If not-T or not-P, then either not-S or U." We have to add a new letter: U. In any event, this is possible for the reasons mentioned in (C).

23. **(C)** Again remember we are looking for the best answer, even though it may be open to some objection. As for (A), we can reject it on two grounds: (1) implausible content, and (2) the speaker is an economist, not a meteorologist. (B) is not the most reliable because the content of the claim seems terribly naive. (D) can be rejected for two reasons: (1) there is a hint here of self-interest, and (2) the notion seems pretty outlandish. (E) can be rejected on the grounds that the speaker is out of his particular area of experience. Finally, (C) is the most reliable. It is a purely factual claim which, unlike (A), (B), and (D), seems to be fairly modest in its scope; and it is made by a dairy farmer within the scope of his expertise, unlike (A) and (E).

24. **(B)** The author is trying to draw a contrast between two elements of a pair of concepts. They must be opposites because the structure of the sentence is "______ rather than normative." A normative theory would be one which makes recommendations about behavior; its opposite would be a theory which merely states facts or describes how things are—"what the law is"—not how it ought to be. Perhaps theories should be concise (A) and comprehensive (C); but those notions are not in order here, for neither contrasts with normative. Similarly, a theory perhaps ought to be simple (E), but simplicity does not contrast with normative. (D) confuses the idea of supplementing a descriptive theory with a normative one which is introduced in the next sentence. It is true that the conceptual theory must be independent of the normative one, but that fails to complete the contrast we need for #24.

25. **(A)** The ends of law, according to legal positivism, are to be agreed upon—"accepted as a contingent matter." They are values which the community adopts; they are not handed down by God, nor are they dictated by logic. (B) actually reverses the point. The legal positivist probably would say he does not claim these ends are the best for all modern legal systems. He does not want to commit himself to anything beyond a mere factual description of things as they are. The normative theory ultimately reduces to a question of practical politics—whatever succeeds. (C) can be rejected because the question raised by the normative theory is what values the law ought to generally embody, not just what values the courts ought to promote. (D) is incorrect because while it is perhaps true, it does not address itself to the *status* of the normative values: Are they universally held and dictated by logic? Are they given by God? etc. (E) is similar to (D) in that it may be true simply as a matter of fact, but again (E) does not address itself to the status of the values. It is true that the values are those the community chooses, but that that status is *selected* rather than dictated is not undermined because there is not complete agreement on the values. Whatever values are selected will be chosen by more or less unanimous agreement.

26. **(C)** The analogy to physical theory is highly suggestive. The physicist advances a theory which represents an improvement on existing theories, but he is aware that tomorrow another theory may be proposed which is more correct than his. So the legal postivist advances a descriptive theory, that is, a description of existing legal institutions, but new information or advances in theory may displace that theory. (A) is directly contrary to the legal positivist's position that no one theory is uniquely correct. (B) ignores the radical and complete divorce of description and normative recommendation upon which the legal positivist insists. (D) just confuses the point of the analogy to physics. The author introduces the analogy to explain how the legal positivist views his theory—in the same way the physicist views his—not to compare the reliability of physics with jurisprudence. (E) makes a mistake similar to that committed by (D).

SECTION V

Set 1

OVERVIEW: We will find that the two rules conflict if the case involves a performance which is unique but cannot be ordered because it is just not practicable to force that sort of performance. In our facts, the promised performance is unique, because Walter is the originator and master of the style. No one else could quite take Walter's place. On the other hand, it is not practicable to force Walter to give those lessons. Teaching, particularly in this situation, requires that the person doing the work really wants to do it. Otherwise, there would be no way of ensuring the work was properly done. So in this set, we find a conflict between the two rules.

1. **(C)** This is deducible given the facts. As we noted in the set overview, Walter is unique in that he is the only person in the world who is the master of the musical (his own) style. The facts make it clear that there is no one else who could do the job in quite the way Walter could.

2. **(B)** The rules present a conflict as to whether Walter can be compelled to perform his contract by giving the lessons. Neither rule says anything about money compensation. So our answer cannot be (C) or (A). The question itself makes this relevant by stipulating that Deidra is not entitled to the lessons. Is she then entitled to some other compensation? That is an important question we are not in a position to answer without further rules.

3. **(C)** As we discussed in the set overview, it would not be practicable to force Walter to work. How could one ever hope to judge whether he had done the job properly?

4. **(A)** This is the conflict between the two rules which we isolated in the set overview.

Set 2

OVERVIEW: The general rule here, I, is that employers are liable for the injuries caused by the careless actions of their employees. But Rule II carves out a very important exception to that. The state government is not liable under the doctrine of sovereign immunity. So any case involving injury by a state employee, which injury is not covered by some statute, will present us with a conflict between the two rules. In the facts of this case, we have such a situation. We know the state is the employer at the hospital, but we do not know whether there is a statute covering Martin's case. So Martin would be entitled to bring his suit under Rule I, but Rule II says he is not allowed to bring his suit.

5. **(B)** This is surely a very important issue. An employer has liability only if the person who acted is his employee. The employer is surely not liable for a stranger. We do not know first of all whether the attending nurse was a volunteer or an official employee of the state hospital. Further, even if the nurse was one of the volunteers, it might be argued that such persons are acting as employees and should therefore be treated as such. Any way you look at it, we need more information, facts, and rules to solve this issue.

6. **(B)** We cannot apply Rule II until we determine whether there is a statute authorizing the action or not, so this is a very important question which requires additional information.

7. **(C)** This is deducible. Although the nurse performed the duty very poorly, she was still acting within the scope of her employment. Now it will not do to argue that a badly performed duty is automatically the performance of a "non-duty." For in that case, Rule I would cover no cases. If an employee's carelessness removed him from the scope of his duties, then there could be no employer liability at all. Yet, Rule I assesses employer liability in some cases.

8. **(A)** This is the conflict we uncovered in the set overview. If there is no statute, Rule II precludes Brett's maintaining an action, while Rule I allows it without regard to the existence of a statute.

9. **(B)** The question stem asks us to make relevant the question of the nurse's liability, but we have no basis for deciding under what conditions the nurse would be liable. Our rules speak only of employers, not employees. So we would need more information to make this decision.

Set 3

OVERVIEW: In this set of rules, Rule I sets down a general limitation on the bringing of cases. If you wait more than two years to bring your suit, it is barred. Rule II creates an exception to this: Even though you waited more than two years, you may bring your suit if you were not eighteen at the time the injury occurred. In our facts, we learn that Lionel was only twelve when the accident occurred. So Lionel has until two years after he reaches his eighteenth birthday to bring his suit, or until 1980 (18−12=6) plus the two years for the running of the statute of limitations.

10. **(B)** The two rules we have deal with whether Lionel has brought his suit in time to avoid the statute of limitations. Nothing in either of them helps us out with the underlying substantive issue, so to answer this question, which is relevant to the dispute between Lionel and Quincy, we must have further guidance.

11. **(C)** Rule II defines "toll." The statute of limitations is suspended for the time until Lionel reaches his eighteenth birthday.

12. **(A)** This requires a choice between the two rules. Remember they are both to be regarded as of equal importance. By the terms of Rule I, Lionel's action is barred. The incident occured in 1972, and Lionel did not bring his suit before 1975. But by Rule II, Lionel has until 1980 to bring his suit, so it is not barred. To decide this issue we would have to choose between the two rules.

13. **(D)** While Lionel's age at the time of the accident is very important for applying Rule

II, nothing in either rule requires us to know Quincy's age.

14. **(B)** This raises another possible ground for barring Lionel's suit. If they sued and lost, can Lionel try it on his own? That raises an obviously important question, but one which must be settled by some appropriate rule. Since we do not have that rule, we must classify this as a (B).

15. **(B)** Since we do not know *precisely* when Lionel reached his eighteenth birthday, nor *precisely* when in 1980 he brings the suit, we cannot compute whether two years have passed since Lionel reached his eighteenth birthday.

Set 4

OVERVIEW: Here we find another set of rules which may trouble those people who have preconceived ideas about what the law really is. As surprising as it may seem, these are really rules of law. Even though you have a contract, you may be relieved of performing that contract if something unanticipated (and outside of your control) happens to prevent you from completing your end of the bargain. In our facts, we have such a situation. Raymond finds he cannot deliver the dolls on time because an event, which he neither anticipated nor created, prevents him from doing so. Thus, the two rules present a choice for us. By Rule I, Raymond has made a deal and did not complete it, so he is liable for damages; but by Rule II, Raymond is excused from performance because of the Korean government's action.

16. **(C)** The word *subsequent* in Rule II is very important in determining whether Rule II fits the situation. Had the event occurred *prior* to the entering of the contract, Rule II would just not have applied to the situation. As things turned out, we know the government's closure of Haruka's plant took place after the contract was made. So this is an important issue which can be deduced from the facts of the case.

17. **(D)** This, however, is irrelevant. Why the government closed Haruka's plant is not something we must know in order to decide whether Rule II applies to Raymond.

18. **(A)** This question presents the conflict we discussed in the set overview. By Rule I Frank is entitled to damages, but by Rule II Raymond is not liable, owing to the government's action against Haruka—which made it impossible for Raymond to deliver.

19. **(B)** The first rule requires that we know how much Frank would have made (net value) on the transaction so that we can assess damages. Since we do not have that information, this item represents a factual element which must be supplied before we can apply the rule.

20. **(D)** Contrast this question with #19. While Frank's anticipated gain is an important aspect of Rule I, Raymond's financial picture is not relevant. We are concerned with deciding whether (and if so, how much) Raymond owes damages to Frank.

21. **(B)** At first glance this looks like a (C), like #16. But a closer look suggests that the event may not have been unanticipated. It is one thing to fail to foresee the action of some government—political fortunes are notoriously unpredictable. While any particular storm at sea might be unanticipated, the general idea of the danger of loss at sea is not. To decide whether a storm is an unanticipated event, we would need further clarification of this concept.

Set 5

OVERVIEW: The conflict here arises over the definition of "lost" versus "abandoned" property. If the ring was lost property, then Alfred is entitled, under Rule I, to recover it from Sylvia. But if the ring was abandoned by Alfred, then Sylvia gets to keep it on the basis of Rule II. So to decide whether Alfred is entitled to his ring, we must choose between these two rules.

22. **(A)** This is the conflict we just outlined. Rule I will return the ring to Alfred because he is the true owner while Sylvia is just the

finder. Rule II awards the ring to Sylvia, because one who recovers property which has been abandoned has a claim superior to all others.

23. **(C)** The answer to this issue is deducible. If we operate on the assumption that the property is abandoned, then Sylvia has a better claim than Alfred because, according to Rule II, she has become the true owner.

24. **(A)** This is the same question as that posed by #22. In order to determine whether Alfred is the true owner we must choose whether Alfred lost the property or abandoned it. If he lost only it, then he remains the true owner, but if he abandoned it (see #23), Sylvia has become the true owner.

25. **(C)** This is deducible from the facts. Sylvia found the ring and took it home with her, thereby keeping it in her possession.

26. **(D)** Alfred's reasons for not returning to Dallas are not relevant to the question of whether he lost or abandoned the property. To be sure, it might be argued that because he did not return to look for the ring, he thereby abandoned it, but that argument does not depend on Alfred's *reasons* for not returning. The argument could be made, and just as effectively, that Alfred had not returned because he could not afford to take off time from his job.

Set 6

OVERVIEW: In this case, the rules set up a conflict regarding the extent of a company's liability. According to Rule I, the company is liable only for damages which it should have been aware might occur. So under Rule I, a company is not liable for freak accidents. But under Rule II, if the company is keeping dangerous substances on its premises, it is liable for anything which happens in connection with those substances—whether or not it could have anticipated the event. In the facts of the case, it appears that Bloomington could not have foreseen that the containers would begin to leak, allowing liquid to seep into the ground. Bloomington was well aware of the danger that would follow if the acid turned into a gas, but the accident which actually occurred was a "freak" one. So by the terms of Rule I, Bloomington should not be liable, but by the terms of Rule II, it is liable because it maintained dangerous substances on its premises.

27. **(C)** This is an essential element of applying Rule I, and the answer to the question raised is contained within the facts. It was a freak accident.

28. **(A)** Even though Rule I would not impose liability on Bloomington, Rule II would, and this is the conflict which we sketched in the set overview.

29. **(C)** As with #27, this is an essential part of one of the rules, here Rule II, and the answer to the issue raised is contained in the facts. The dangers of hydrofluoric acid are described in sufficient detail to warrant our drawing the conclusion that this is a substance which fits the definition of dangerous given in Rule II.

30. **(B)** This question raises an important issue, but it is one which neither of the two rules we have can handle. Both rules which we are given are applicable only after the fact of the damage. To decide whether the city is entitled to protect itself before the incident demands that we have further rules.

31. **(D)** Nothing in either rule makes the company's carelessness important in determining liability. As far as the rules are concerned, a company might be careful and still be liable for any injury which results.

Set 7

OVERVIEW: The conflict in this case arises between the lease and Al's conduct. By the terms of Rule I, Al, who is a tenant under a lease, is entitled to remain in possession for the term of the lease so long as he pays the rent and complies with the other provisions of the lease. Since nothing is said in the lease about noise (or so far as we are told, anything related to disturbances), Rule I will allow Al to remain in the apartment.

Rule II, however, says that regardless of the provisions in the lease, a landlord has the right to evict a tenant who constitutes a nuisance, as Al certainly did. So by Rule II, Franny ought to win.

32. **(A)** This is the conflict which we just outlined in the set overview. By Rule II Franny is entitled to have Al evicted, but by Rule I, since the lease is silent (so to speak) about the noise, Al is entitled to remain.

33. **(C)** This is a term which is critical to Rule II and is defined there by reference to interference with the rights of other tenants. Since Al repeatedly made enough noise to bother them (sufficient to warrant a visit or two from the local authorities) we do have enough information to deduce a conclusion to the question.

34. **(C)** We are told in the facts that Al apparently violated no specific provision of the lease. If he had, there would be no conflict between the rules in this case. On either, Al could be evicted.

35. **(B)** This raises another aspect of the dispute between Al and Franny. Since we do not know whether Al was current with the rent, or whether Al damaged the apartment, we do not have enough information to determine whether he should get his $250 back.

SECTION VI

Questions 1–6

Arranging the Information

Previewing the question stems for this set of questions shows that there is only one conditional question and it is based on a new individual. This leads you to suppose that you should be able to completely describe this situation. In addition, a preview of the general information at the start of the problem set indicates that there are only two ways in which the pandas are to be related to each other and that the two ways—wet/dry and fat/slim—are both separate.

Let us first arrange the information into a usable format starting with the fat/slim idea. Each piece of information must fit in with some previously arranged piece of information in order to create a complete and valid arrangement. Since each panda's name begins with a different letter, we can use single letters to indicate each panda.

	←FATTER———SLIMMER→
B fatter than G	B G
C slimmer than F—can't do now	
D fatter than B	D B G
E slimmer than G	D B G E
F slimmer than E	D B G E F
C slimmer than F—can do now	D B G E F C
G fatter than F—redundant	

Now we can do the dry/wet idea.

	←DRIER———WETTER→
B drier than E	B E
C wetter than G—can't do now	
D wetter than G—can't do now	
E drier than C	B E C
C wetter than G—can do now	B E C ←G
D wetter than G—can do now	B E C ←—— G D →
F drier than B	F B E C ←—— G D →
G wetter than B	F B E C ←—— G D →

Answering the Questions

1. **(C)** Only B is on the fatter (left) side of E and also on the drier (left) side of G.

2. **(D)** Only C is both slimmer (right) and wetter (right) than E.

3. **(B)** Only D is both fatter (left) and wetter (right) than G. Even though the exact wetness position of D is not known, it is wetter than G.

4. **(D)** F is the driest (leftmost) in the final diagram.

5. **(B)** I is not false for sure because the exact wetness relationship between D and C is not known. D might be wetter or drier than C. II is definitely false since F is drier than D. III is not knowable from the given information since the exact amounts by which the various pandas are fatter or slimmer is not stated. D is fatter than G, but not necessarily by three inches. However, the statement is not false because it might be true. Thus, only II is definitely false.

6. **(E)** The exact rank cannot be determined because the new panda Y's being slimmer than B and fatter than F leaves unclear the relationship between Y and pandas G and F.

Questions 7–13

Arranging the Information

Previewing the questions shows that most of them are conditional questions, and the set-up of the situation is of that nature, too. This means that most of the work will be in answering the questions rather than in determining the arrangement of the information.

At least 2 of D E F

Either 1 or 2 from L M N P

Total of 4

N not=P

E not=L

D not=N, thus, if N, neither P or D

Answering the Questions

7. **(C)** If Nancy is chosen, then both David and Paul are out. Since at least two out of the trio of David, Erica, and Francis must be chosen, the elimination of David results in the forced selection of Erica and Francis, which eliminates answer choices (A) and (E). Since Nancy will not work with Paul, he cannot be a member of the crew and answer choice (D) is eliminated. Since Erica is selected as previously noted, and Erica will not work with Larry, answer choice (B) is eliminated, and we find that the crew will be David, Erica, Mary, and Nancy.

8. **(E)** If Paul is chosen, the only direct restriction is that Nancy is eliminated from the crew. This leaves only the restriction of the grinders versus the sail trimmers. If you wanted to select answer choice (A) because you thought there could only be two grinders, you missed the fact that the only restriction on the numbers of grinders versus sail trimmers was that AT LEAST two of the crew additions had to be grinders, which leaves open the possibility of all three of the grinder candidates being accepted. Thus, answer choice (A) is possible.
   Answer choice (E), however, is not possible because Erica will not work with Larry as the answer choice requires. The other answer choices (B), (C), and (D) do not violate any of the restrictions laid down by the problem.

9. **(C)** I must be true because if David is rejected, then the only two remaining grinder candidates—Erica and Francis—must be chosen. The selection of Erica means the elimination of Larry, leaving Mary, Nancy, and Paul. However, since Nancy will not work with Paul, only one of those two may be chosen, which gives Mary a definite berth on the boat.

II follows from the first sentence of the discussion of I.

III does not have to be true. The selection of David permits the selection of a crew such as David, Francis, Mary, and Paul or the selection of a crew without Paul—such as David, Francis, Mary, and Larry.

Thus, the answer is that I and II must be true and III is a maybe.

10. **(E)** As hinted at by the structure of the three roman numeral propositions, the acceptance of Larry as a crew member eliminates Erica from consideration, and thus requires the selection of David and Francis. The selection of David means that Nancy cannot be chosen, which leaves either Mary or Paul as acceptable candidates to fill the last sail trimmer slot with Larry. I and III are, thus, possible and II is not.

11. **(A)** I must be true since the choice of Larry eliminates Erica and requires the choice of David and Francis as noted in #10.

    II is not necessarily true since the choice of Mary imposes no further restrictions on the choice of crew, so Mary and Nancy may or may not crew together.

    III need not be true because it refers to all future time and it is possible that Nancy and Paul will be able to make peace in the future. The difference between the form of this statement and that of statements I and II is a good clue that the ground has been shifted.

    Thus, only I must be true, and II and III might or might not be true.

12. **(B)** The choice of Paul eliminates Nancy, and thus answer choices (C) and (D). The omission of David forces the choice of Erica and Francis, which in turn eliminates Larry, and thus answer choices (A) and (E), leaving only Mary to fill out the crew, as stated in answer choice (B).

13. **(A)** If Erica makes the crew and Francis does not, this leaves David to fill in the second grinder slot. Erica's presence eliminates Larry, and David's eliminates Nancy, leaving a crew of David, Erica, Mary, and Paul. Thus, both I and II must be true.

Questions 14–17

Arranging the Information

This problem is one which presents a set of conditions and a group of situations to which the conditions are to be applied. The five sets do not necessarily meet all of the conditions. A preview of the question stems indicates that it is worthwhile to identify errors in the sets. It is probably more efficient to check all of them at once, condition by condition, since they are laid out so nicely.

In checking the first stated condition, that the first three names in each set should be typically male names, you can just read down the columns of names. All of the names in columns one and two for all five sets are male names. In column three, however, you find that the last two, Greta and Mona from sets IV and V respectively, are female names and, thus, errors. You could circle or underline them to indicate the fact that they are errors.

Checking the second condition, that the names in the last two columns should be female names, produces no errors.

The requirement that each name in a set begin with a different letter does produce some errors. Remember that the duplication of first letters indicates that either of the two or more failing to meet the condition could be wrong. This sort of condition is somewhat different than the previous ones. With the first two conditions you could check each item individually and know for sure whether it was wrong. This condition is one of limitation where you cannot say whether it is Jack or June which is the problem in set I, Mike or Mary in II, or Louis or Linda in IV. Technically it is not the names which are in error but the sets.

A check of the last condition, that each of the names in a set be the same number of letters, shows Henry in II as the only problem. Again technically it may not be Henry which is wrong, but the lack of agreement within the set. It could be that all four of the other names are wrong.

Answering the Questions

14. **(D)** The missing name must be a male name in accordance with the first require-

ment, thus eliminating (A) and (B). The correct answer choice must also have a different first letter from any of the other names already in the set. Waldo (C) duplicates Wally, and Angus (E) duplicates Allen, which leaves only (D).

15. **(B)** Our general review of the conditions gives the answer to this problem. I is out because of the *J*'s. II is out because of the *M*'s and Henry. III is OK. IV and V are out for the female names in position three and the *L*'s in IV. Answer choice (B).

16. **(A)** The third condition is having different first letters for all of the names. Set III satisfies all of the conditions without exception so it cannot be the answer to this problem, which eliminates choice (C). Set I has only the error of the *J*'s as described in the general discussion and in the discussion of problem 15, thus, choice (A) is correct. The other sets cited in answer choices (B), (D), and (E) have other forms of error, as previously described in the discussion of arranging the information.

17. **(E)** You have to be careful with a question like this which seeks to correct some sort of error in the given information. Some of the suggested answers may correct one error only to make a new one. Answer choice (A), for example, corrects the problem of the *J*'s in set I, but puts a male name in the fourth position which is a new error.

   (B) makes a similar error because in the act of correcting the number of letters problem with Henry, a female name is placed where a male name should go.

   (C) makes a change in an already correct set, which means that it is not going to "make" set III correct. In addition, the Boris would duplicate a first letter with Betty, and thus create an error.

   (D) does accurately correct an error in set IV—the *L*'s—without making a new error, but this is not enough to make the set correct since it still has a female name in the third position.

   (E) is the correct answer because the substitution of Fred for Mona in set V solves the only problem that set had without creating any new errors.

Questions 18–21

Arranging the Information

This is a problem where the main issue is the overlapping of different sets or groups, which means that Venn diagrams are a good method of arranging the information. This type of problem usually requires that the majority of your time be spent in the arranging of the information and somewhat less in the answering of the questions. However, a previewing of the questions indicates that some of the statements might contradict some of the other statements. Question 19 indicates that statements I, II, and III are to be taken as true and question 18, which asks about contradiction, only asks about possible contradiction after I, II, and III. Thus, it would seem that I, II, and III could be arranged without any problems.

The most efficient arrangement of I and II's information is in a three-circle (Venn) diagram with circles standing for L, M, and Z. Remember that a Venn diagram is only good for up to three categories.

We will now draw a three-circle diagram for L, M, and Z.

Statement I only indicates that there is some possibility of there being each of the four categories. It does not mean, for instance, that there will be an L by itself that is not any of the others, etc. This does not affect the diagram.

Statement II is coded into the diagram by marking out the parts of the diagram where M is not L.

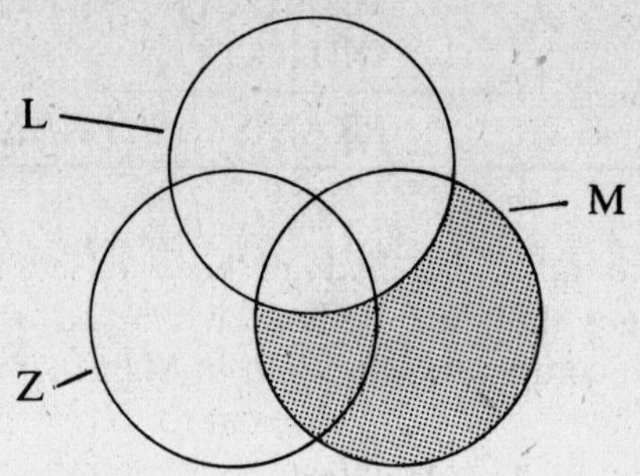

Statement III is coded into the diagram by eliminating the parts of the diagram where L is not Z, leaving us with this:

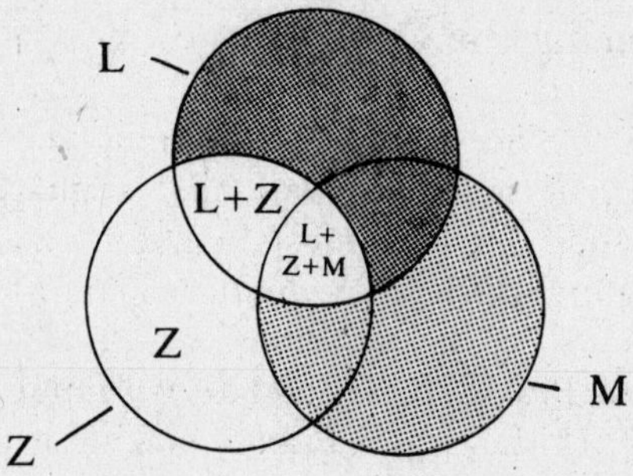

Thus, what remains possible is L with Z, L with M and Z, and Z by itself.

Answering the Questions

18. (**B**) Statement III was successfully integrated with the previous statements without encountering any problem, so answer choice (A) is eliminated. Statement IV, however, does present a problem. If no M are Z, this means that there can be no M found inside the Z circle. However, the only place where M can be found, after coding the first three statements, is inside the Z circle. The elimination of the possibility of having L, M, and Z together will eliminate the possibility of having M altogether, which is forbidden by statement I. Thus, answer choice (B) is correct. Note that one must proceed in order in this particular problem because the question asks about contradictions with all previous statements, which means that the first one with a contradiction must be the answer sought. Both statements V and VI are fully compatible with the following diagrams:

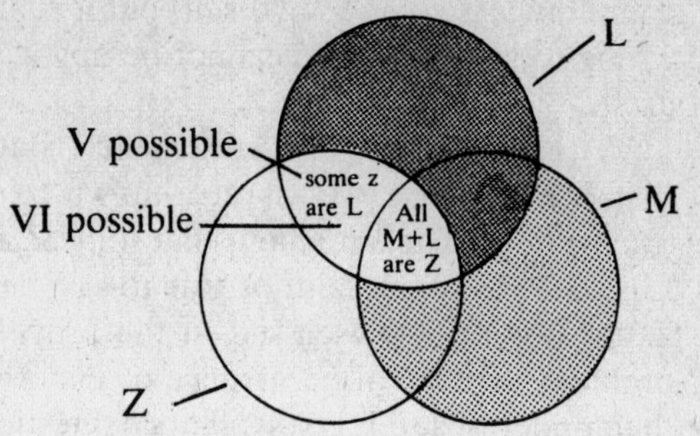

19. (**C**) In the previous question we saw that statement IV was contradictory to the previous statements which excludes it from being deducible from statements II and III, eliminating answer choices (A) and (D). Statement V is not deducible from the others because it states that there are actually some Z. The existence of any Z is definitely not known since the two statements II and III only discuss the relationships that pertain to the groups if there happen to be any members of the groups. This eliminates answer choices (B) and (D) (again), and (E).

Answer choice (C) is deducible because the only place that L and M overlap is the location where L and M and also Z apply. Thus, anything, such as P, which is going to be both L and M must also be Z.

20. (**C**) From the diagram we can see that there are two possible locations within the L area. One location is the L + M + Z area and the other is the L + Z area. Thus, all L are Z as statement III has said. The only reason that you would use the diagram instead of just relying on the original statement is to make sure that there was no further limitation that had snuck in as happened with M, all of which are also Z (ignoring the contradiction problem). You cannot make any statement about the overlap between P and X because statement VI only says where P will not be found and makes no promises that there are P's that actually are M and L, etc.

21. (**D**) The diagram shows that there is a definite possible area of Z which does not overlap any part of the L or M areas; therefore, it is still possible for Z to be by

itself. It would be wrong to say that there definitely was some Z by itself, but it is also wrong to say that there cannot be any Z by itself.

(A) is not false since statement I states that L is possible. (B) is not known to be true or false. The statement that some Z are L does not make it false or true to say some Z are not L. As discussed in the previous problem, the actual occurrence of P's other than under M and L is still an open question, and (C) is, thus, not false. (E) is eliminated with the discovery that (D) is false.

Questions 22–25

Arranging the Information

This can be regarded as either a linkage or a table question. The idea of linkages comes from the question stems which show you that the major idea is that the various computers can output data in certain languages and that the other computers will only be able to receive the data if they can input the same language. This could be expressed by labelled arrows, but the number of different computers and the number of languages indicates that a table will probably be easier to keep track of.

The phrase "can fully use" means that both input and output can be done in the language mentioned. This is both logically reasonable and inferable from the question stems which first introduce the specific term "output." Thus, the table will show the input and output capacities of the various computers, since that is what the questions ask about.

COMPUTER	INPUT	OUTPUT
F	OPTICO NEWTON	OPTICO
G	OPTICO NEWTON MANTRA	OPTICO
H	NEWTON MANTRA	NEWTON
J	OPTICO PRAXIS	OPTICO PRAXIS
K	MANTRA OPTICO	MANTRA
L	PRAXIS	PRAXIS

If the questions had all been based on the languages that each computer handled, such as, "Which computers can input in Mantra?" then it might have been more efficient to have organized the table with the languages as the margin and the computers as the entries instead of the other way around, as here. In principle, either manner of organization will give you the right answers, and the difference in this question set is rather small.

Answering the Questions

22. **(E)** Since only one of the computers, J, can output in more than one language, that stands out. We must look for other computers which have *input* capacities the same as J's *output* capacities, which are Optico and Praxis. F, G, and K can input Optico and L can input Praxis, making a total of four for J. F and G can both output in Optico which is received by three other computers, F/G, J, and K. Thus all three propositions are correct.

23. **(D)** A two way link through J is desired and J can input and output Optico and Praxis. Since there are fewer possibilities for the other computers in outputting, this should be checked first. H outputs only Newton and K only Mantra, neither of which can be input by J. Thus choices (A), (B), (C), and (E) are eliminated. (D) is correct since L can communicate in both directions with J in Praxis and G can do the same in Optico.

24. **(C)** Proposition I is easily disposed of. Since H and J have no common languages at all, I is false. II asks about the linkage J—F—H. H can output to F in Newton and F can output that data to J in Optico, so that direction is OK. However, while J can output to F in Optico, H cannot input anything that F can output; thus, II is false. Proposition III is true. III is the same

situation as II for all practical purposes, since the only difference in capacities between F and G is that G can output Mantra, which neither of the other two can input. However, the statement is different. This time it correctly describes the problem that data can flow in only one direction and thus III is true and (C) is the answer.

25. **(A)** In (A), K can output to H in Mantra with H outputting to F in Newton, but H cannot output to K in the reverse direction. This meets the specifications of the question. (B) fails since L can only output in Praxis, which H cannot input. (C) fails similarly because G cannot output to L. (D) and (E) fail for a different reason. They are too good. Both of those trios can communicate in both directions, while the question stem asks for one-way communication only.

Explanation of Pressure Points and Exemplary Essay for Writing Sample

TOPIC: Some parents have urged that elementary school children should be taught computer programming as early as second grade. They point out that the children will be growing up in a world in which there will be computers and that understanding computers will be critical to a successful life. Other parents oppose too great an emphasis on computer programming at the age, arguing that very few children will ever become programmers themselves and that at that age, there are too many other things that the children should be learning. They should not be spending the time needed to become proficient programmers that early in their schooling.

You are a member of the board of directors of the Parents Association. Prepare a brief position paper on this topic to be presented to the board.

PRESSURE POINTS: The following considerations might go through your mind as you examine the topic and seek to create an outline for your essay.

—What is the purpose of elementary education?

—Is computer programming appropriate for elementary school children? Is it too abstract?

—What other school programs might be helped or hindered by the introduction of computer programming at this age? Academically, financially, teacher resources, student time?

—Is familiarity with computers the same as being able to program them? Will computers in the future work with people so that the people do not have to be programmers, like arcade games do now?

The following essay is only one of many that could have been written on this topic.

The proposal to have second grade children learn computer programming is both too much and too little. It proposes too much in making an unrealistic demand on the children for abstract thought that is largely beyond their capacities at that age, and it is too little in that programming by itself is not enough to ask in terms of developing the ability to cope with the world as it will be when they are grown.

Young children, of the age mentioned in this proposal, can benefit from rigorous work, but it is important that the work be of a type that they can succeed at so that they do not grow discouraged in their pursuit of education and knowledge. The students need to be introduced to computers so that they are not afraid of them. This requires a simple introduction and a gradual one, probably spread over many years, or even done at different paces for different children.

Like any other form of problem-solving, programming must involve good habits of thought. Care and discipline are important in any intellectual discipline, and these must be mastered before full programming can be done. If the programming instruction can be used to develop these mental skills, that is much more important than the specific matter of learning programming, and such instruction is very desirable. If the instruction in programming is not being used as a method of improving problem-solving and mental discipline in a way that works with the rest of the curriculum, then it will take too much valuable class time from other, more important topics.

Thus, the simple proposal to teach computer programming in the second grade is not specific enough to be evaluated. When the specific curriculum is developed, a better evaluation can be made.

ANSWER SHEET—PRACTICE EXAMINATION 3

SECTION I

1 Ⓐ Ⓑ Ⓒ Ⓓ Ⓔ	6 Ⓐ Ⓑ Ⓒ Ⓓ Ⓔ	11 Ⓐ Ⓑ Ⓒ Ⓓ Ⓔ	16 Ⓐ Ⓑ Ⓒ Ⓓ Ⓔ	21 Ⓐ Ⓑ Ⓒ Ⓓ Ⓔ
2 Ⓐ Ⓑ Ⓒ Ⓓ Ⓔ	7 Ⓐ Ⓑ Ⓒ Ⓓ Ⓔ	12 Ⓐ Ⓑ Ⓒ Ⓓ Ⓔ	17 Ⓐ Ⓑ Ⓒ Ⓓ Ⓔ	22 Ⓐ Ⓑ Ⓒ Ⓓ Ⓔ
3 Ⓐ Ⓑ Ⓒ Ⓓ Ⓔ	8 Ⓐ Ⓑ Ⓒ Ⓓ Ⓔ	13 Ⓐ Ⓑ Ⓒ Ⓓ Ⓔ	18 Ⓐ Ⓑ Ⓒ Ⓓ Ⓔ	23 Ⓐ Ⓑ Ⓒ Ⓓ Ⓔ
4 Ⓐ Ⓑ Ⓒ Ⓓ Ⓔ	9 Ⓐ Ⓑ Ⓒ Ⓓ Ⓔ	14 Ⓐ Ⓑ Ⓒ Ⓓ Ⓔ	19 Ⓐ Ⓑ Ⓒ Ⓓ Ⓔ	24 Ⓐ Ⓑ Ⓒ Ⓓ Ⓔ
5 Ⓐ Ⓑ Ⓒ Ⓓ Ⓔ	10 Ⓐ Ⓑ Ⓒ Ⓓ Ⓔ	15 Ⓐ Ⓑ Ⓒ Ⓓ Ⓔ	20 Ⓐ Ⓑ Ⓒ Ⓓ Ⓔ	25 Ⓐ Ⓑ Ⓒ Ⓓ Ⓔ

SECTION II

1 Ⓐ Ⓑ Ⓒ Ⓓ Ⓔ	6 Ⓐ Ⓑ Ⓒ Ⓓ Ⓔ	11 Ⓐ Ⓑ Ⓒ Ⓓ Ⓔ	16 Ⓐ Ⓑ Ⓒ Ⓓ Ⓔ	21 Ⓐ Ⓑ Ⓒ Ⓓ Ⓔ	26 Ⓐ Ⓑ Ⓒ Ⓓ Ⓔ
2 Ⓐ Ⓑ Ⓒ Ⓓ Ⓔ	7 Ⓐ Ⓑ Ⓒ Ⓓ Ⓔ	12 Ⓐ Ⓑ Ⓒ Ⓓ Ⓔ	17 Ⓐ Ⓑ Ⓒ Ⓓ Ⓔ	22 Ⓐ Ⓑ Ⓒ Ⓓ Ⓔ	27 Ⓐ Ⓑ Ⓒ Ⓓ Ⓔ
3 Ⓐ Ⓑ Ⓒ Ⓓ Ⓔ	8 Ⓐ Ⓑ Ⓒ Ⓓ Ⓔ	13 Ⓐ Ⓑ Ⓒ Ⓓ Ⓔ	18 Ⓐ Ⓑ Ⓒ Ⓓ Ⓔ	23 Ⓐ Ⓑ Ⓒ Ⓓ Ⓔ	28 Ⓐ Ⓑ Ⓒ Ⓓ Ⓔ
4 Ⓐ Ⓑ Ⓒ Ⓓ Ⓔ	9 Ⓐ Ⓑ Ⓒ Ⓓ Ⓔ	14 Ⓐ Ⓑ Ⓒ Ⓓ Ⓔ	19 Ⓐ Ⓑ Ⓒ Ⓓ Ⓔ	24 Ⓐ Ⓑ Ⓒ Ⓓ Ⓔ	
5 Ⓐ Ⓑ Ⓒ Ⓓ Ⓔ	10 Ⓐ Ⓑ Ⓒ Ⓓ Ⓔ	15 Ⓐ Ⓑ Ⓒ Ⓓ Ⓔ	20 Ⓐ Ⓑ Ⓒ Ⓓ Ⓔ	25 Ⓐ Ⓑ Ⓒ Ⓓ Ⓔ	

SECTION III

1 Ⓐ Ⓑ Ⓒ Ⓓ Ⓔ	6 Ⓐ Ⓑ Ⓒ Ⓓ Ⓔ	11 Ⓐ Ⓑ Ⓒ Ⓓ Ⓔ	16 Ⓐ Ⓑ Ⓒ Ⓓ Ⓔ	21 Ⓐ Ⓑ Ⓒ Ⓓ Ⓔ
2 Ⓐ Ⓑ Ⓒ Ⓓ Ⓔ	7 Ⓐ Ⓑ Ⓒ Ⓓ Ⓔ	12 Ⓐ Ⓑ Ⓒ Ⓓ Ⓔ	17 Ⓐ Ⓑ Ⓒ Ⓓ Ⓔ	22 Ⓐ Ⓑ Ⓒ Ⓓ Ⓔ
3 Ⓐ Ⓑ Ⓒ Ⓓ Ⓔ	8 Ⓐ Ⓑ Ⓒ Ⓓ Ⓔ	13 Ⓐ Ⓑ Ⓒ Ⓓ Ⓔ	18 Ⓐ Ⓑ Ⓒ Ⓓ Ⓔ	23 Ⓐ Ⓑ Ⓒ Ⓓ Ⓔ
4 Ⓐ Ⓑ Ⓒ Ⓓ Ⓔ	9 Ⓐ Ⓑ Ⓒ Ⓓ Ⓔ	14 Ⓐ Ⓑ Ⓒ Ⓓ Ⓔ	19 Ⓐ Ⓑ Ⓒ Ⓓ Ⓔ	24 Ⓐ Ⓑ Ⓒ Ⓓ Ⓔ
5 Ⓐ Ⓑ Ⓒ Ⓓ Ⓔ	10 Ⓐ Ⓑ Ⓒ Ⓓ Ⓔ	15 Ⓐ Ⓑ Ⓒ Ⓓ Ⓔ	20 Ⓐ Ⓑ Ⓒ Ⓓ Ⓔ	25 Ⓐ Ⓑ Ⓒ Ⓓ Ⓔ
				26 Ⓐ Ⓑ Ⓒ Ⓓ Ⓔ

SECTION IV

1 Ⓐ Ⓑ Ⓒ Ⓓ Ⓔ	8 Ⓐ Ⓑ Ⓒ Ⓓ Ⓔ	15 Ⓐ Ⓑ Ⓒ Ⓓ Ⓔ	22 Ⓐ Ⓑ Ⓒ Ⓓ Ⓔ	29 Ⓐ Ⓑ Ⓒ Ⓓ Ⓔ
2 Ⓐ Ⓑ Ⓒ Ⓓ Ⓔ	9 Ⓐ Ⓑ Ⓒ Ⓓ Ⓔ	16 Ⓐ Ⓑ Ⓒ Ⓓ Ⓔ	23 Ⓐ Ⓑ Ⓒ Ⓓ Ⓔ	30 Ⓐ Ⓑ Ⓒ Ⓓ Ⓔ
3 Ⓐ Ⓑ Ⓒ Ⓓ Ⓔ	10 Ⓐ Ⓑ Ⓒ Ⓓ Ⓔ	17 Ⓐ Ⓑ Ⓒ Ⓓ Ⓔ	24 Ⓐ Ⓑ Ⓒ Ⓓ Ⓔ	31 Ⓐ Ⓑ Ⓒ Ⓓ Ⓔ
4 Ⓐ Ⓑ Ⓒ Ⓓ Ⓔ	11 Ⓐ Ⓑ Ⓒ Ⓓ Ⓔ	18 Ⓐ Ⓑ Ⓒ Ⓓ Ⓔ	25 Ⓐ Ⓑ Ⓒ Ⓓ Ⓔ	32 Ⓐ Ⓑ Ⓒ Ⓓ Ⓔ
5 Ⓐ Ⓑ Ⓒ Ⓓ Ⓔ	12 Ⓐ Ⓑ Ⓒ Ⓓ Ⓔ	19 Ⓐ Ⓑ Ⓒ Ⓓ Ⓔ	26 Ⓐ Ⓑ Ⓒ Ⓓ Ⓔ	33 Ⓐ Ⓑ Ⓒ Ⓓ Ⓔ
6 Ⓐ Ⓑ Ⓒ Ⓓ Ⓔ	13 Ⓐ Ⓑ Ⓒ Ⓓ Ⓔ	20 Ⓐ Ⓑ Ⓒ Ⓓ Ⓔ	27 Ⓐ Ⓑ Ⓒ Ⓓ Ⓔ	34 Ⓐ Ⓑ Ⓒ Ⓓ Ⓔ
7 Ⓐ Ⓑ Ⓒ Ⓓ Ⓔ	14 Ⓐ Ⓑ Ⓒ Ⓓ Ⓔ	21 Ⓐ Ⓑ Ⓒ Ⓓ Ⓔ	28 Ⓐ Ⓑ Ⓒ Ⓓ Ⓔ	35 Ⓐ Ⓑ Ⓒ Ⓓ Ⓔ

SECTION V

1 Ⓐ Ⓑ Ⓒ Ⓓ Ⓔ	6 Ⓐ Ⓑ Ⓒ Ⓓ Ⓔ	11 Ⓐ Ⓑ Ⓒ Ⓓ Ⓔ	16 Ⓐ Ⓑ Ⓒ Ⓓ Ⓔ	21 Ⓐ Ⓑ Ⓒ Ⓓ Ⓔ
2 Ⓐ Ⓑ Ⓒ Ⓓ Ⓔ	7 Ⓐ Ⓑ Ⓒ Ⓓ Ⓔ	12 Ⓐ Ⓑ Ⓒ Ⓓ Ⓔ	17 Ⓐ Ⓑ Ⓒ Ⓓ Ⓔ	22 Ⓐ Ⓑ Ⓒ Ⓓ Ⓔ
3 Ⓐ Ⓑ Ⓒ Ⓓ Ⓔ	8 Ⓐ Ⓑ Ⓒ Ⓓ Ⓔ	13 Ⓐ Ⓑ Ⓒ Ⓓ Ⓔ	18 Ⓐ Ⓑ Ⓒ Ⓓ Ⓔ	23 Ⓐ Ⓑ Ⓒ Ⓓ Ⓔ
4 Ⓐ Ⓑ Ⓒ Ⓓ Ⓔ	9 Ⓐ Ⓑ Ⓒ Ⓓ Ⓔ	14 Ⓐ Ⓑ Ⓒ Ⓓ Ⓔ	19 Ⓐ Ⓑ Ⓒ Ⓓ Ⓔ	24 Ⓐ Ⓑ Ⓒ Ⓓ Ⓔ
5 Ⓐ Ⓑ Ⓒ Ⓓ Ⓔ	10 Ⓐ Ⓑ Ⓒ Ⓓ Ⓔ	15 Ⓐ Ⓑ Ⓒ Ⓓ Ⓔ	20 Ⓐ Ⓑ Ⓒ Ⓓ Ⓔ	25 Ⓐ Ⓑ Ⓒ Ⓓ Ⓔ

SECTION VI

1 Ⓐ Ⓑ Ⓒ Ⓓ Ⓔ	6 Ⓐ Ⓑ Ⓒ Ⓓ Ⓔ	11 Ⓐ Ⓑ Ⓒ Ⓓ Ⓔ	16 Ⓐ Ⓑ Ⓒ Ⓓ Ⓔ	21 Ⓐ Ⓑ Ⓒ Ⓓ Ⓔ	26 Ⓐ Ⓑ Ⓒ Ⓓ Ⓔ
2 Ⓐ Ⓑ Ⓒ Ⓓ Ⓔ	7 Ⓐ Ⓑ Ⓒ Ⓓ Ⓔ	12 Ⓐ Ⓑ Ⓒ Ⓓ Ⓔ	17 Ⓐ Ⓑ Ⓒ Ⓓ Ⓔ	22 Ⓐ Ⓑ Ⓒ Ⓓ Ⓔ	27 Ⓐ Ⓑ Ⓒ Ⓓ Ⓔ
3 Ⓐ Ⓑ Ⓒ Ⓓ Ⓔ	8 Ⓐ Ⓑ Ⓒ Ⓓ Ⓔ	13 Ⓐ Ⓑ Ⓒ Ⓓ Ⓔ	18 Ⓐ Ⓑ Ⓒ Ⓓ Ⓔ	23 Ⓐ Ⓑ Ⓒ Ⓓ Ⓔ	28 Ⓐ Ⓑ Ⓒ Ⓓ Ⓔ
4 Ⓐ Ⓑ Ⓒ Ⓓ Ⓔ	9 Ⓐ Ⓑ Ⓒ Ⓓ Ⓔ	14 Ⓐ Ⓑ Ⓒ Ⓓ Ⓔ	19 Ⓐ Ⓑ Ⓒ Ⓓ Ⓔ	24 Ⓐ Ⓑ Ⓒ Ⓓ Ⓔ	
5 Ⓐ Ⓑ Ⓒ Ⓓ Ⓔ	10 Ⓐ Ⓑ Ⓒ Ⓓ Ⓔ	15 Ⓐ Ⓑ Ⓒ Ⓓ Ⓔ	20 Ⓐ Ⓑ Ⓒ Ⓓ Ⓔ	25 Ⓐ Ⓑ Ⓒ Ⓓ Ⓔ	

EXAMINATION FORECAST

Section Number	Type	Minutes	Questions
Section I	Analytical Reasoning	35	25
Section II	Reading Comprehension	35	28
Section III	Logical Reasoning	35	26
Section IV	Issues & Facts	35	35
Section V	Analytical Reasoning	35	25
Section VI	Reading Comprehension	35	28
	Writing Sample	30	—
Total Time		4 hours	

A 15-minute break should be taken after Section IV.

The Writing Sample will usually be given before the rest of the LSAT and is found at the end of the Practice Test in this book.

PRACTICE EXAMINATION 3

SECTION I

Time—35 Minutes
25 Questions

Directions: Each group of questions is based on a set of propositions or conditions. Drawing a rough picture or diagram may help in answering some of the questions. Choose the best answer for each question and blacken the corresponding space on your answer sheet.

Questions 1–5

City College is selecting a four-person debate team. There are seven candidates of equal ability: X, Y, and Z, who attend the West campus, and L, M, N, and P, who attend the East campus. The team must have two members from each campus. Also, the members must be able to work well with all the other members of the team.

Debaters Y and L, Z and N, and L and M are incompatible pairs.

1. If debater Y is rejected and M is selected, the team will consist of
   (A) L, M, X, and Z
   (B) M, N, X, and Z
   (C) M, N, P, and X
   (D) M, N, P, and Z
   (E) M, P, X, and Z

2. If debater L is on the team, what other debaters must be on the team as well?
   (A) M, X, and Z
   (B) N, X, and Z
   (C) P, N, and Z
   (D) P, X, and Y
   (E) P, X, and Z

3. If both Y and Z are selected, which of the other debaters are thereby assured of a place on the team?
   (A) both L and M
   (B) both M and P
   (C) only N
   (D) both N and P
   (E) only P

4. Which of the following must be false?
   I. Debaters M and Z cannot be selected together.
   II. Debaters N and Y cannot be selected together.
   III. Debaters P and Z cannot be selected together.

   (A) I only
   (B) II only
   (C) III only
   (D) I and III only
   (E) I, II, and III

5. Which of the following statements is true of debater X?
   I. Debater X must be selected as one of the West campus members of the team.
   II. Debater X must be selected if debater N is selected.
   III. Debater X cannot be selected if both L and N are rejected.

   (A) I only
   (B) II only
   (C) III only
   (D) I and II only
   (E) I, II, and III

Questions 6–10

Paul, Quincy, Roger, and Sam are married to Tess, Ursula, Valerie, and Wilma, not necessarily in that order. Roger's wife is older than Ursula. Sam's wife is older than Wilma, who is Paul's sister. Tess is the youngest of the wives. Roger was the best man at Wilma's wedding.

6. If Quincy and his wife have a boy named Patrick, then
   (A) Tess will be Patrick's aunt
   (B) Valerie will be Patrick's aunt
   (C) Paul will be Patrick's cousin
   (D) Ursula will be Patrick's mother
   (E) None of the above.

7. Which of the following is true?
   (A) Roger's wife is younger than Valerie.
   (B) Roger's wife is younger than Wilma.
   (C) Paul's wife is younger than Ursula.
   (D) Sam's wife is older than Valerie.
   (E) Quincy's wife is older than Ursula.

8. If each husband is exactly two years older than his wife, which of the following must be false?
   (A) Roger is older than Ursula.
   (B) Tess is younger than anyone.
   (C) Paul is younger than Sam.
   (D) Quincy is younger than Paul.
   (E) Valerie is younger than Paul.

9. If the wives were—from youngest to oldest—28, 30, 32, and 34 years old; and Paul, Quincy, Roger, and Sam were respectively 27, 29, 31, and 33 years old, which of the following must be false?
   (A) Tess is older than her husband.
   (B) Valerie is older than her husband.
   (C) Ursula is younger than Valerie's husband.
   (D) Wilma is younger than Ursula's husband.
   (E) Tess is younger than Wilma's husband.

10. If Tess and Valerie get divorced from their current husbands and marry each other's former husband then
   (A) Sam's wife will be younger than Paul's wife
   (B) Sam's wife will be younger than Roger's wife
   (C) Roger's wife will be older than Quincy's wife
   (D) Roger's wife will be older than Paul's wife
   (E) Paul's wife will be younger than Quincy's wife

Questions 11–15

Williams is the director of investments for a major pension fund. He believes that blue chip common stocks and government securities will generally not do as well as corporate bonds in the coming year, but government regulations require that at least one-third of the fund's capital be in blue chip common stocks and another third in government securities.

11. Under current regulations, what seems to be the best way for Williams to invest the pension fund?
   (A) two-thirds government securities, one-third blue chip stock
   (B) two-thirds government securities, one-third corporate bonds
   (C) one-third government securities, two-thirds corporate bonds
   (D) one-third each government securities, blue chip stocks, and corporate bonds
   (E) half government securities and half blue chip stocks

12. If the pension fund has $6 billion in assets, what is the maximum that Williams could invest in blue chip stocks?
   (A) $2 billion
   (B) $3 billion
   (C) $4 billion
   (D) $5 billion
   (E) $6 billion

13. If the government regulations are changed to require only one-quarter where one-third was previously required, Williams will probably
   (A) increase the fund's holdings of government securities
   (B) increase the fund's holdings of corporate bonds
   (C) increase the fund's holdings of blue chip stock
   (D) hold less cash
   (E) hold more cash

14. If the return on government securities suddenly goes up five percentage points, Williams will probably
    (A) sell blue chip stock to buy government securities
    (B) sell corporate bonds to buy government securities
    (C) sell both corporate bonds and blue chip stocks to buy government securities
    (D) keep the fund the way it was
    (E) act, but his action cannot be predicted

15. In the middle of the year, the fund is invested equally in corporate bonds, blue chip stock, and government securities. The sudden merger of one of the main employers serviced by the fund results in the early retirement of thousands of workers, creating in turn a cash shortage for the fund. To generate the needed cash, Williams might do any one of the following EXCEPT
    (A) sell two times more corporate bonds than blue chip stocks
    (B) sell two times more corporate bonds than government securities
    (C) sell only corporate bonds and blue chip stocks
    (D) sell only government securities and blue chip stock
    (E) sell only government securities and corporate bonds

Questions 16–20

Max is planning his sales calls for the next day. He is judged and paid by his company both on the basis of the number of calls he makes and the amount of sales he generates.

Acme Co. will take only one hour and will probably result in an order of 5 boxes.

Bell Corp. will take three hours and will either result in an order of 20 boxes or nothing.

Camera Shops, Inc. will take one hour and yield an order of 10 boxes.

Deland Bros. will take from one to three hours and probably result in an order of 10–30 boxes.

16. Under these conditions, what is the greatest number of boxes Max can reasonably hope to sell in a seven-hour working day?
    (A) 65
    (B) 60
    (C) 45
    (D) 40
    (E) 35

17. Under these conditions, what is the minimum number of boxes that Max can reasonably expect to sell in eight working hours?
    (A) none
    (B) 15
    (C) 20
    (D) 25
    (E) 35

18. If Max has sold 20 boxes to Deland Bros. and then his car breaks down and is not fixed until 2:00 P.M., what is the maximum sales figure for the day he can reasonably hope to achieve by 5:00 P.M.?
    (A) 20 boxes
    (B) 35 boxes
    (C) 40 boxes
    (D) 45 boxes
    (E) 55 boxes

19. If Max has an unbreakable thirty-minute luncheon appointment at 1:30 P.M., what is his best schedule for a 9:00 A.M. to 5:00 P.M. day?
    (A) Acme and Camera, then Bell and Deland
    (B) Bell and Acme, then Camera, and if time permits, Deland
    (C) Bell and Camera, then Deland, and if time permits, Acme
    (D) Camera and Bell, then Acme and Deland
    (E) Deland and Acme, then Camera and Bell

20. If Max is sick and has to carry all his calls over to the next day when he must be at Edwards & Co. from 10:30 A.M. to 1:30 P.M., what would be his best schedule for the day from 9:00 A.M. to 5:00 P.M.?
    (A) Deland, Edwards, Camera, and Bell
    (B) Camera, Edwards, Deland, and if time permits, Acme
    (C) Camera, Edwards, Acme, and if time permits, Deland
    (D) Acme, Edwards, Deland, and if time permits, Camera
    (E) Bell, Edwards, Deland, and if time permits, Camera

Questions 21–25

I. Some L are P.

II. All Y are P.

III. Only P can be an L.

IV. More Y are P and L, than are P and not L.

21. Statements I and II together imply that
 (A) All L are P.
 (B) All P are L.
 (C) All Y are L.
 (D) Some P are L.
 (E) Some L are Y.

22. Which of the following must be true?
 (A) Some Y are L.
 (B) Some Y that are P are not L.
 (C) Some L are not P.
 (D) Some Y that are L are not P.
 (E) All of the above must be true.

23. Which of the following must be false?
 (A) Some Y are P.
 (B) Not all P are L or Y.
 (C) Not all Y are L.
 (D) Not all L are P or Y or both.
 (E) No P are not Y.

24. Which of the following is neither definitely true nor definitely false?
 (A) All Y must be either L or P.
 (B) All L must be either P or Y.
 (C) All P must be either L or Y.
 (D) No Y can be L.
 (E) None of the above.

25. If there are exactly ten P that are both Y and L, which of the following could be true?

 I. There are exactly ten P that are Y and/or L.
 II. There are exactly ten P that are neither Y nor L.
 III. There are exactly ten P that are L and not Y.

 (A) I only
 (B) II only
 (C) III only
 (D) II and III only
 (E) I, II, and III

STOP

IF YOU FINISH BEFORE TIME IS CALLED, CHECK YOUR WORK ON THIS SECTION ONLY. DO NOT WORK ON ANY OTHER SECTION IN THE TEST.

SECTION II

Time—35 Minutes
28 Questions

Directions: Below each of the following passages, you will find questions or incomplete statements about the passage. Each statement or question is followed by lettered words or expressions. Select the word or expression that most satisfactorily completes each statement or answers each question in accordance with the meaning of the passage. After you choose the best answer blacken the corresponding space on the answer sheet.

There is a confused notion in the minds of many persons, that the gathering of the property of the poor into the hands of the rich does no ultimate harm, since in whosesoever hands it may be, it must be spent at last, and thus, they think, return to the poor again. This fallacy has been again and again exposed; but granting the plea true, the same apology may, of course, be made for blackmail, or any other form of robbery. It might be (though practically it never is) as advantageous for the nation that the robber should have the spending of the money he extorts, as that the person robbed should have spent it. But this is no excuse for the theft. If I were to put a turnpike on the road where it passes my own gate, and endeavor to exact a shilling from every passenger, the public would soon do away with my gate, without listening to any pleas on my part that it was as advantageous to them, in the end, that I should spend their shillings, as that they themselves should. But if, instead of outfacing them with a turnpike, I can only persuade them to come in and buy stones, or old iron, or any other useless thing, out of my ground, I may rob them to the same extent, and be, moreover, thanked as a public benefactor and promoter of commercial prosperity. And this main question for the poor of England—for the poor of all countries—is wholly omitted in every treatise on the subject of wealth. Even by the laborers themselves, the operation of capital is regarded only in its effect on their immediate interests, never in the far more terrific power of its appointment of the kind and the object of labor. It matters little, ultimately, how much a laborer is paid for making anything; but it matters fearfully what the thing is, which he is compelled to make. If his labor is so ordered as to produce food, fresh air, and fresh water, no matter that his wages are low—the food and the fresh air and water will be at last there, and he will at last get them. But if he is paid to destroy food and fresh air, or to produce iron bars instead of them,—the food and air will finally *not* be there, and he will *not* get them, to his great and final inconvenience. So that, conclusively, in political as in household economy, the great question is, not so much what money you have in your pocket, as what you will buy with it and do with it.

1. We may infer that the author probably lived in the
   (A) 1960's in the United States
   (B) early days of British industrialization
   (C) 18th-century France
   (D) Golden Age of Greece
   (E) England of King Arthur

2. It can be inferred that the author probably favors
   (A) capitalism
   (B) totalitarianism
   (C) socialism
   (D) anarchism
   (E) theocracy

3. According to the passage, the individual should be particularly concerned with
   (A) how much wealth he can accumulate
   (B) the acquisition of land property rather than money
   (C) charging the customer a fair price
   (D) the quality of goods which he purchases with his funds
   (E) working as hard as possible

4. The passage implies that
   (A) "A stitch in time saves nine."
   (B) "It is better late than never."
   (C) "He who steals my purse steals trash."

(D) "None but the brave deserve the fair,"
(E) "All's well that ends well."

5. It can be inferred that in regard to the accumulation of wealth the author
   (A) equates the rich with the thief
   (B) thinks that there are few honest businessmen
   (C) condones some dishonesty in business dealings
   (D) believes destruction of property is good because it creates consumer demand
   (E) says that the robber is a benefactor

6. What is the "main question for the poor" referred to by the author in the passages?
   (A) the use to which the laborer can put his money
   (B) the methods by which capital may be accumulated
   (C) the results of their work and their lack of authority to determine to what ends their work shall be put
   (D) whether full measure of recompense shall be accorded to the laboring person for the investment of his time in worthy work
   (E) the extent to which a man can call his life his own

7. According to the views expressed in the passage, people should be happiest doing which of the following?
   (A) mining ore for the manufacture of weapons
   (B) cleaning sewage ponds at a treatment plant
   (C) waiting tables for a rich man
   (D) helping a poor man do his job
   (E) studying economic theory

The Planning Commission asserts that the needed reduction in acute care hospital beds can best be accomplished by closing the smaller hospitals, mainly voluntary and proprietary. This strategy follows from the argument that closing entire institutions saves more money than closing the equivalent number of beds scattered throughout the health system.

The issue is not that simple. Larger hospitals generally are designed to provide more complex care. Routine care at large hospitals costs more than the same care given at smaller hospitals. Therefore, closure of all the small hospitals would commit the city to paying considerably more for inpatient care delivered at acute care hospitals than would be the case with a mixture of large and small institutions. Since reimbursement rates at the large hospitals are now based on total costs, paying the large institutions a lower rate for routine care would simply raise the rates for complex care by a comparable amount. Such a reimbursement rate adjustment might make the charges for each individual case more accurately reflect the actual costs, but there would be no reduction in total costs.

There is some evidence that giant hospitals are not the most efficient. Service organizations—and medical care remains largely a service industry—frequently find that savings of scale have an upper limit. Similarly, the quality of routine care in the very largest hospitals appears to be less than optimum. Also, the concentration of all hospital beds in a few locations may affect the access to care.

Thus, simply closing the smaller hospitals will not necessarily save money or improve the quality of care.

Since the fact remains that there are too many acute care hospital beds in the city, the problem is to devise a proper strategy for selecting and urging the closure of the excess beds, however many it may turn out to be.

The closing of whole buildings within large medical centers has many of the cost advantages of closing the whole of smaller institutions, because the fixed costs can also be reduced in such cases. Unfortunately, many of the separate buildings at medical centers are special use facilities, the relocation of which is extremely costly. Still, a search should be made for such opportunities.

The current lack of adequate ambulatory care facilities raises another possibility. Some floors or other large compact areas of hospitals could be transferred from inpatient to ambulatory uses. Reimbursement of ambulatory services is chaotic, but the problem is being addressed. The overhead associated with the entire hospital should not be charged even *pro rata* to the ambulatory facilities. Even if it were, the total cost would probably be less than that of building a new facility. Many other issues would also need study, especially the potential overcentralization of ambulatory services.

The Planning Commission language seems to imply that one reason for closing smaller hospitals is that they are "mainly voluntary and proprietary," thus preserving the public hospital system by making the rest of the hospital system absorb the needed cuts. It is important to preserve the public hospital system for many reasons, but the issue should be faced directly and not hidden behind arguments about hospital size, if indeed that was the Commission's meaning.

8. The best title for the passage would be
   (A) Maintaining Adequate Hospital Facilities
   (B) Defending the Public Hospitals
   (C) Methods of Selecting Hospital Beds to be Closed
   (D) Protecting the Proprietary and Voluntary Hospitals
   (E) Economic Efficiency in Hospital Bed Closings

9. The Planning Commission is accused by the author of being
   (A) unfair
   (B) racist
   (C) foolish
   (D) shortsighted
   (E) ignorant

10. On the subject of the number of hospital beds, the author
    (A) is in complete agreement with the Planning Commission
    (B) wishes to see large numbers of beds closed
    (C) wishes to forestall the closing of any more hospital beds
    (D) is unsure of the number of excess beds there really are
    (E) wishes to avoid exchanging quantity for quality

11. All of the following are reasons the author opposes the Planning Commission's recommendation EXCEPT
    (A) service industries have an upper limit for savings of scale
    (B) single buildings of large centers may be closable instead of smaller hospitals
    (C) public hospitals have a unique contribution to make and should not be closed
    (D) the smaller hospitals recommended for closure provide services more cheaply than larger hospitals
    (E) hospitals are service organizations

12. With which of the following would the author probably NOT agree?
    (A) Large medical centers provide better and more complex care than smaller hospitals.
    (B) Reimbursement rates do not necessarily reflect the actual costs of providing medical care to a given patient.
    (C) Patients needing only routine medical care can often be distinguished from those requiring complex care prior to hospitalization.
    (D) Too much centralization of ambulatory care is possible.
    (E) Access to medical care is an important issue.

13. The author's purpose in discussing ambulatory care is to
    (A) discuss alternatives to closing hospital beds
    (B) present a method of reducing the fiscal disadvantages of closing only parts of larger hospitals.
    (C) show another opportunity for saving money
    (D) help preserve the public hospital system
    (E) attack the inefficient use of space in larger hospitals

14. With which of the following is the author LEAST likely to agree?
    (A) a proposal to save costs in a prison system by building only very large prison complexes
    (B) a plan to stop the closing of any hospital beds whatsoever in the city, until the costs of various alternatives can be fully considered
    (C) an order by the Planning Commission mandating that no public hospitals be closed
    (D) a proposal by an architecture firm that new hospital buildings have centralized record systems
    (E) a mayoral commission being formed to study the plight of the elderly

It is almost a definition of a gentleman to say he is one who never inflicts pain. This description is both refined and, as far as it goes, accurate. He is mainly occupied in merely removing the obstacles which hinder the free and unembarrassed action of those about him; and he concurs with their movements rather than takes the initiative himself. His benefits may be considered as parallel to what are called comforts or conveniences in arrangements of a personal nature: such as an easy chair or a good fire, which do their part in dispelling cold and fatigue, though nature provides both means of rest and animal heat without them. The true gentleman, in like manner, carefully avoids whatever may cause a jar or a jolt in the minds of those with whom he is cast—all clashing of opinion, or collision of feeling, all restraint, or suspicion, or gloom, or resentment; his great concern being to make everyone at their ease and at home. He has his eyes on all his company; he is tender towards the bashful, gentle towards the distant, and merciful towards the absurd; he can recollect to whom he is speaking; he guards against unseasonable allusions, or topics which may irritate; he is seldom prominent in conversation, and never wearisome. He makes light of favors while he does them, and seems to be receiving when he is conferring. He never speaks of himself except when compelled, never defends himself by a mere retort, he has no ears for slander or gossip, is scrupulous in imputing motives to those who interfere with him, and interprets everything for the best. He is never mean or little in his disputes, never takes unfair advantage, never mistakes personalities or sharp sayings for arguments, or insinuates evil which he dare not say out. From a longsighted prudence, he observes the maxim of the ancient sage, that we should ever conduct ourselves towards our enemy as if he were one day to be our friend. He has too much good sense to be affronted at insults, he is too well employed to remember injuries, and too indolent to bear malice. He is patient, forbearing, and resigned on philosophical principles; he submits to pain, because it is inevitable, to bereavement, because it is irreparable, and to death, because it is his destiny. If he engages in controversy of any kind, his disciplined intellect preserves him from the blundering discourtesy of better, perhaps, but less educated minds, who, like blunt weapons, tear and hack instead of cutting clean; who mistake the point in argument, waste their strength on trifles, misconceive their adversary, to leave the question more involved than they find it. He may be right or wrong in his opinion, but he is too clear-headed to be unjust; he is as simple as he is forcible, and as brief as he is decisive. Nowhere shall we find greater candor, consideration, indulgence: he throws himself into the minds of his opponents, he accounts for their mistakes. He knows the weakness of human reason as well as its strength, its province, and its limits. If he be an unbeliever, he will be too profound and large-minded to ridicule religion or to act against it; he is too wise to be a dogmatist or fanatic in his infidelity. He respects piety and devotion; he even supports institutions as venerable, beautiful, or useful, to which he does not assent; he honors the ministers of religion, and it contents him to decline its mysteries without assailing or denouncing them. He is a friend of religious toleration, and that, not only because his philosophy has taught him to look on all forms of faith with an impartial eye, but also from the gentleness and effeminacy of feeling, which is the attendant on civilization.

Not that he may not hold a religion too, even when he belongs to no formal congregation. In that case his religion is one of imagination and sentiment; it is the embodiment of those ideas of the sublime, majestic, and beautiful, without which there can be no large philosophy. Sometimes he acknowledges the being of God, sometimes he invests an unknown principle or quality with the attributes of perfection. And this deduction of his reason, or creation of his fancy, he makes the occasion of such excellent thoughts, and the starting-point of so varied and systematic a teaching, that he even seems like a disciple of Christianity itself. From the very accuracy and steadiness of his logical powers, he is able to see what sentiments are consistent in those who hold any religious doctrine at all, and he appears to others to feel and to hold a whole circle of theological truths, which exist in his mind not otherwise than as a number of deductions.

15. According to the passage, the gentleman when engaged in debate is
    (A) soothing and conciliatory
    (B) brilliant and insightful
    (C) opinionated and clever
    (D) concise and forceful
    (E) quiet and charming

16. A gentleman, here, is analogized to
    (A) a jar or jolt
    (B) an easy chair or a good fire
    (C) a blunt weapon
    (D) a sharp saying
    (E) collisions and restraints

17. A person who is "scrupulous in imputing motives" is
    (A) careful about accusing others of base motives
    (B) eager to prove another guilty of improper intentions
    (C) willing to falsify another's moods
    (D) unable to make decisions about people's motives
    (E) suspicious concerning the actions of others and the reasons for them

18. This passage does not take into account the commonly held concept that a gentleman is known for his
    (A) consideration for others
    (B) refusal to slander
    (C) leniency toward the stupid
    (D) neatness in attire
    (E) willingness to forgive

19. The most appropriate title for this passage would be
    (A) A Gentleman Now and Before
    (B) Definition of a Gentleman
    (C) Intellectualism and the Gentleman
    (D) Can a Gentleman Be Religious?
    (E) The Gentleman's Thought

20. The word "effeminacy" as used in the end of the first paragraph in this selection really means
    (A) womanliness
    (B) childishness
    (C) cowardice
    (D) indecision
    (E) delicacy

21. According to the passage
    (A) gentlemen will never disagree with each other
    (B) gentlemen can have the same religious beliefs as common men and in the same way
    (C) the power of a gentleman's thought on religious matters can give him the appearance of a true Christian
    (D) the gentleness of a gentleman disarms all who would oppose him
    (E) the kindness of a gentleman moves all who know him to love him

Consumers rely on several methods to acquire information about product quality. The most straightforward, of course, is to "experience" the product—eat it or use it. Low-priced, frequently purchased products require the experience approach, but some goods have "search" characteristics. Information on search goods can be obtained by inspection, asking one's friends, or even reading technical reports.

Nelson has suggested advertising intensity as yet another index of product quality. Based largely on the experience and search characteristics and rational behavior by consumers, his theory is noteworthy in light of the widespread controversy over the information content of advertising.

Television advertising has often been criticized on the grounds that it lacks concrete product information. But Nelson finds fault with the criticisms. If advertising provides no information, then why do consumers respond to it? If there was truly no information provided, consumers would most likely learn to ignore or to be quite skeptical of the many commercials they see each day. Finally, only a relatively small proportion of products are heavily advertised. Apparently, there are many products for which advertising does not elicit strong consumer response.

Search product advertising is relatively noncontroversial, since it provides "hard" information (such as price, location, brand, objective quality ratings, etc.) to consumers probably more cheaply than they can get it elsewhere. It can also be checked for accuracy before buying. It is advertising of experience goods that is often criticized for its lack of informational value and its effect on market performance.

Because such information may be misleading and consumers have no way of separating the truthful from the misleading, consumers have good reason not to respond to "informational" advertising about experience characteristics. Thus, there is less incentive for advertisers of experience goods to provide hard information beyond the product's function. Do heavy expenditures on experience goods advertising provide any benefit to consumers if little accurate product information is conveyed? Nelson contends that they do. He says that heavy advertising is itself indirect information. Advertising is costly, and this cost may be incurred long before appreciable sales are made. Makers of heavily advertised, inferior products cannot expect repeated sales. Consumers will learn through experience that the brand is inferior. On the other hand, consumers who purchase a heavily advertised, superior product are likely to make further purchases as their experience reveals the product's superiority. For that reason, Nelson argues that the makers of superior products can expect a greater return from advertising (more sales per unit of advertising) than can the makers of inferior products.

Producers of inferior products gain only initial purchases in response to advertising, while makers of superior products net initial plus repeat purchases. Since producers of superior products expect a higher return from their advertising, they have a greater incentive to advertise. If producers respond to this incentive, then superior products should be more heavily advertised than inferior, and consumers can with good reason use advertising as an indicator of product quality.

Nelson's contention, that more heavily advertised products provide more quality for the price, is still quite controversial. It depends crucially on the ability of consumers to accurately assess product characteristics after purchase. His hypothesis is not concerned with characteristics whose quality cannot be determined even after use (for example, the efficacy of a drug). Nor is it concerned with the issue of whether advertising alters consumers' perceptions. The validity of Nelson's hypothesis is difficult to test.

Recently, some preliminary tests of the hypothesis have been undertaken. Advertised brands in 11 different food product classes were selected for the test. Quality ratings of each brand were obtained from *Consumer Reports*. Sales and brands within each class were ranked according to their advertising expenditure per unit of sales. The research question was whether there was any tendency for brands ranked high in quality to also be ranked high in advertising per unit of sales. The results indicate a tendency for advertising intensity and quality to be positively associated in those samples. The coefficient was negative only for one product class.

The samples in this preliminary study are small, ranging from 5 to 12 brands in each product class; for that reason an inference that our estimates would hold for all brands in a product class is not justified. In addition, we are not testing Nelson's strong contention that heavily advertised products provide more quality per dollar, but a weaker contention (held by most adherents to Nelson's position) that heavily advertised products are of higher quality (without consideration of price).

Given the small sample size, we cannot say that the hypothesis is conclusively supported, nor can we make precise assertions about the strength of associations between advertising-sales ratios and product quality. However, Nelson's hypothesis cannot be rejected on the basis of our data—he may be right and his theory deserves to be taken seriously. A key factor may be the extent to which consumers actually learn through experience.

22. The author's purpose in writing this article is to
    (A) support Nelson's theory
    (B) oppose Nelson's theory
    (C) present and discuss some tests of Nelson's theory
    (D) present an alternative to Nelson's theory
    (E) show the development of Nelson's theory

23. The author's tone is
    (A) skeptical
    (B) intensive
    (C) supportive
    (D) thorough
    (E) scientific

24. The preliminary study reported
    (A) confirms Nelson
    (B) disputes Nelson
    (C) gives some support to Nelson
    (D) supports further funding of Nelson's research
    (E) shows consumers respond to advertising

25. According to the passage, Nelson's theory can be characterized by all of the following EXCEPT that it is
    (A) hard to test in its strongest form
    (B) based on rational decision-making by consumers

(C) opposed to the idea that television advertising has no informational content
(D) dependent on others for testing
(E) limited to product characteristics determinable by consumers

26. Which of the following future research findings would, if true, tend to weaken Nelson's hypothesis?

I. New brands tend to be both heavily advertised and perceived as high quality.
II. Most non-search product advertising succeeds in blunting the consumer's ability to evaluate the true quality of a product.
III. The reason many products are not advertised is that the response which is sure to be generated is hard to convert to profits for the advertiser when the product is not branded.

(A) I only
(B) II only
(C) III only
(D) I and III
(E) II and III

27. Nelson's hypothesis would apply to all of the following EXCEPT
(A) tomato soup
(B) caviar
(C) fish fillets
(D) milk
(E) cheese

28. The passage seems to
(A) treat television advertising as the major part of advertising
(B) give too much weight to Nelson's hypothesis
(C) be overly cautious in its interpretations
(D) confuse "experience" products with "search" products
(E) give too much credit to consumers and advertisers

STOP

IF YOU FINISH BEFORE TIME IS CALLED, CHECK YOUR WORK ON THIS SECTION ONLY. DO NOT WORK ON ANY OTHER SECTION IN THE TEST.

SECTION III

Time—35 Minutes
26 Questions

Directions: In this section, the questions ask you to analyze and evaluate the reasoning in short paragraphs or passages. For some questions, all of the answer choices may conceivably be answers to the question asked. You should select the *best* answer to the question, that is, an answer which does not require you to make assumptions which violate commonsense standards by being implausible, redundant, irrelevant or inconsistent. After choosing the best answer, blacken the corresponding space on the answer sheet.

1. Which of the following activities would depend upon an assumption which is inconsistent with the judgment that you cannot argue with taste?
(A) a special exhibition at a museum
(B) a beauty contest
(C) a system of garbage collection and disposal
(D) a cookbook filled with old New England recipes
(E) a movie festival

2. If George graduated from the University after 1974, he was required to take Introductory World History.

The statement above can be logically deduced from which of the following?
(A) Before 1974, Introductory World History was not a required course at the University.
(B) Every student who took Introductory World History at the University graduated after 1974.
(C) No student who graduated from the University before 1974 took Introductory World History.
(D) All students graduating from the University after 1974 were required to take Introductory World History.
(E) Before 1974, no student was not permitted to graduate from the University without having taken Introductory World History.

3. Largemouth bass are usually found living in shallow waters near the lake banks wherever minnows are found. There are no largemouth bass living on this side of the lake.

Which of the following would logically complete an argument with the preceding premises given?

I. Therefore, there are no minnows on this side of the lake.
II. Therefore, there are probably no minnows on this side of the lake.
III. Therefore, there will never be any minnows on this side of the lake.

(A) I only
(B) II only
(C) III only
(D) I and III only
(E) II and III only

4. TOMMY: That telephone always rings when I am in the shower and can't hear it.
JUANITA: But you must be able to hear it, otherwise you couldn't know that it was ringing.

Juanita's response shows that she presupposes that
(A) the telephone does not ring when Tommy is in the shower
(B) Tommy's callers never telephone except when he is in the shower
(C) Tommy's callers sometimes hang up thinking he is not at home
(D) Tommy cannot tell that the telephone has rung unless he actually heard it
(E) the telephone does not always function properly

5. ADVERTISEMENT: You cannot buy a more potent pain-reliever than RELIEF without a prescription.

Which of the following statements is inconsistent with the claim made by the advertisement?

I. RELIEF is not the least expensive non-prescription pain-reliever one can buy.
II. Another non-prescription pain-reliever, TOBINE, is just as powerful as RELIEF.
III. Some prescription pain-relievers are not as powerful as RELIEF.

(A) I only
(B) II only
(C) I and II only
(D) I, II, and III
(E) none of the statements is inconsistent with the advertisement

Questions 6 and 7

A behavioral psychologist interested in animal behavior noticed that dogs who are never physically disciplined (e.g., with a blow from a rolled-up newspaper) never bark at strangers. He concluded that the best way to keep a dog from barking at strange visitors is to not punish the dog physically.

6. The psychologist's conclusion is based on which of the following assumptions?

I. The dogs he studied never barked.
II. Dogs should not be physically punished.
III. There were no instances of an unpunished dog barking at a stranger which he had failed to observe.

(A) I only
(B) II only
(C) III only
(D) II and III only
(E) I, II, and III

7. Suppose the psychologist decides to pursue his project further, and he studies twenty-five dogs which are known to bark at strangers. Which of the following possible findings would undermine his original conclusion?

I. Some of the owners of the dogs studied did not physically punish the dog when it barked at a stranger.
II. Some of the dogs studied were never physically punished.
III. The owners of some of the dogs studied believe that a dog which barks at strangers is a good watchdog.

(A) I only
(B) II only
(C) I and II only
(D) II and III only
(E) I, II, and III

8. Everything a child does is the consequence of some experience he has had before. Therefore, a child psychologist must study the personal history of his patient.

The author's conclusion logically depends upon the premise that
(A) everything that a child is doing he has already done before
(B) every effect is causally generated by some previous effect
(C) the study of a child's personal history is the best way of learning about that child's parents
(D) a child will learn progressively more about the world because experience is cumulative
(E) it is possible to ensure that a child will grow up to be a mature, responsible adult

9. It is sometimes argued that we are reaching the limits of the earth's capacity to supply our energy needs with fossil fuels. In the past ten years, however, as a result of technological progress making it possible to extract resources from even marginal wells and mines, yields from oil and coal fields have increased tremendously. There is no reason to believe that there is a limit to the earth's capacity to supply our energy needs.

Which of the following statements most directly contradicts the conclusion drawn above?
(A) Even if we exhaust our supplies of fossil fuel, the earth can still be mined for uranium for nuclear fuel.
(B) The technology needed to extract fos-

sil fuels from marginal sources is very expensive.

(C) Even given the improvements in technology, oil and coal are not renewable resources; so we will sometime exhaust our supplies of them.

(D) Most of the land under which marginal oil and coal supplies lie is more suitable to cultivation or pasturing than to production of fossil fuels.

(E) The fuels which are yielded by marginal sources tend to be high in sulphur and other undesirable elements which aggravate the air pollution problem.

Questions 10–12 refer to the following arguments.

(A) The Bible must be accepted as the revealed word of God, for it is stated several times in the Bible that it is the one, true word of God. And since the Bible is the true word of God, we must accept what it says as true.

(B) It must be possible to do something about the deteriorating condition of the nation's interstate highway system. But the repairs will cost money. Therefore, it is foolish to reduce federal appropriations for highway repair.

(C) The Learner Commission's Report on Pornography concluded that there is a definite link between pornography and sex crimes. But no one should accept that conclusion because the Learner Commission was funded by the Citizens' Committee Against Obscenity, which obviously wanted the report to condemn pornography.

(D) People should give up drinking coffee. Of ten people who died last year at City Hospital from cancer of the pancreas, eight of them drank three or more cups of coffee a day.

(E) Guns are not themselves the cause of crime. Even without firearms crimes would be committed. Criminals would use knives or other weapons.

10. Which of the above arguments contains circular reasoning?

11. Which of the above arguments contains a generalization which is based on a sample?

12. Which of the above arguments addresses itself to the source of the claim rather than to the merits of the claim itself?

13. Some sociologists believe that religious sects such as the California-based Waiters, who believe the end of the world is imminent and seek to purify their souls by, among other things, abstaining completely from sexual relations, are a product of growing disaffection with modern, industrialized and urbanized living. As evidence, they cite the fact that there are no other active organizations of the same type which are more than fifty or sixty years old. The evidence, however, fails to support the conclusion for ______.

Which of the following is the most logical completion of the passage?

(A) The restrictions on sexual relations are such that the only source of new members is outside recruitment, so such sects tend to die out after a generation or two.

(B) It is simply not possible to gauge the intensity of religious fervor by the length of time the religious sect remains viable.

(C) The Waiters group may actually survive beyond the second generation of its existence.

(D) There are other religious sects which emphasize group sexual activity which currently have several hundred members.

(E) The Waiters are a California-based organization and have no members in the northeast which is even more heavily urban and industrialized than California.

14. Any truthful auto mechanic will tell you that your standard 5,000-mile checkup can detect only one-fifth of the problems which are likely to go wrong with your car. Therefore, such a checkup is virtually worthless and a waste of time and money.

Which of the following statements, if true, would weaken the above conclusion?

I. Those problems which the 5,000-mile checkup will turn up are the ten leading causes of major engine failure.

II. For a new car, a 5,000-mile checkup is required to protect the owner's warranty.
III. During a 5,000-mile checkup the mechanic also performs routine maintenance which is necessary to the proper functioning of the car.

(A) I only
(B) II only
(C) I and II only
(D) II and III only
(E) I, II, and III

Questions 15 and 16

In recent years, unions have begun to include in their demands at the collective bargaining table requests for contract provisions which give labor an active voice in determining the goals of a corporation. Although it cannot be denied that labor leaders are highly skilled administrators, it must be recognized that their primary loyalty is and must remain to their membership, not to the corporation. Thus, labor participation in corporate management decisions makes about as much sense as ___________.

15. Which of the following represents the best continuation of the passage?
(A) allowing inmates to make decisions about prison security
(B) a senior field officer asking the advice of a junior officer on a question of tactics
(C) a university's asking the opinion of the student body on the scheduling of courses
(D) Chicago's mayor inviting the state legislators for a ride on the city's subway system
(E) the members of a church congregation discussing theology with the minister

16. The author's reasoning leads to the further conclusion that
(A) the authority of corporate managers would be symbolically undermined if labor leaders were allowed to participate in corporate planning
(B) workers have virtually no idea of how to run a large corporation
(C) workers would not derive any benefit in hearing the goals of corporate management explained to them at semiannual meetings
(D) the efficiency of workers would be lowered if they were to divide their time between production line duties and management responsibilities
(E) allowing labor a voice in corporate decisions would involve labor representatives in a conflict of interest

17. Wilfred commented, "Of all the musical instruments I have studied, the trombone has the least pleasing sound because I have the most difficulty in playing the notes precisely."

Which of the following statements, if true, would most seriously weaken Wilfred's conclusion?
(A) The trombone is relatively easy for trumpet players to learn.
(B) Wilfred has not studied the trombone as seriously as he has other instruments.
(C) Wilfred also has some difficulty in playing the viola and the cello.
(D) The trombone is easier to learn as a second instrument than as a first.
(E) There are several other instruments Wilfred has not studied and which are more difficult to play than the trombone.

18. I. No student who commutes from home to a university dates a student who resides at a university.
II. Every student who lives at home commutes to his university, and no commuter student ever dates a resident student.

Which of the following best describes the relationship between the two sentences above?
(A) If II is true, I must also be true.
(B) If II is true, I must be false.
(C) If II is true, I may be either true or false.
(D) If I is true, II is unlikely to be false.
(E) If II is false, I must also be false.

19. All books from the Buckner collection are kept in the Reserve Room.

All books kept in the Reserve Room are priceless.
No book by Hemingway is kept in the Reserve Room.
Every book kept in the Reserve Room is listed in the card catalogue.

If all of the statements above are true, which of the following must also be true?
(A) All priceless books are kept in the Reserve Room.
(B) Every book from the Buckner collection which is listed in the card catalogue is not valuable.
(C) No book by Hemingway is priceless.
(D) The Buckner collection contains no books by Hemingway.
(E) Every book listed in the card catalogue is kept in the Reserve Room.

20. The new car to buy this year is the Goblin. We had one hundred randomly selected motorists drive the Goblin and the other two leading sub-compact cars. Seventy-five drivers ranked the Goblin first in handling. Sixty-nine rated the Goblin first in styling. From the responses of these one hundred drivers, we can show you that they ranked Goblin first overall in our composite category of style, performance, comfort, and drivability.

The persuasive appeal of the advertisement's claim is most weakened by its use of the undefined word
(A) randomly
(B) handling
(C) first
(D) responses
(E) composite

21. Recently the newspaper published the obituary notice of a novelist and poet which had been written by the deceased in anticipation of the event. The last line of the verse advised the reader that the author had expired a day earlier and gave as the cause of death "a deprivation of time."

The explanation of the cause of the author's death is
(A) circular
(B) speculative
(C) self-serving
(D) medically sound
(E) self-authenticating

22. Since Ronnie's range is so narrow, he will never be an outstanding vocalist.

The statement above is based on which of the following assumptions?

I. A person's range is an important indicator of his probable success or failure as a professional musician.
II. Vocalizing requires a range of at least two and one-half octaves.
III. Physical characteristics can affect how well one sings.

(A) I only
(B) II only
(C) I and II
(D) III only
(E) I, II, and III

Questions 23 and 24

During the 1970's the number of clandestine CIA agents posted to foreign countries increased 25 percent and the number of CIA employees not assigned to field work increased by 21 percent. In the same period, the number of FBI agents assigned to case investigation rose by 18 percent, but the number of non-case working agents rose by only 3 percent.

23. The statistics best support which of the following claims?
(A) More agents are needed to administer the CIA than are needed for the FBI.
(B) The CIA needs more people to accomplish its mission than does the FBI.
(C) The proportion of field agents tends to increase more rapidly than the number of non-field agents in both the CIA and the FBI.
(D) The rate of change in the number of supervisory agents in an intelligence gathering agency or a law-enforcement agency is proportional to the percentage change in the results produced by the agency.
(E) At the end of the 1960's, the CIA was more efficiently administered than the FBI.

24. In response to the allegation that it was more overstaffed with support and supervisory personnel than the FBI, the CIA could best argue:
    (A) The FBI is less useful than the CIA in gathering intelligence against foreign powers.
    (B) The rate of pay for a CIA non-field agent is less than the rate of pay for a non-investigating FBI agent.
    (C) The number of FBI agents should not rise so rapidly as the number of CIA agents given the longer tenure of an FBI agent.
    (D) A CIA field agent working in a foreign country requires more back-up support than does an FBI investigator working domestically.
    (E) The number of CIA agents is determined by the Congress each year when they appropriate funds for the agency, and the Congress is very sensitive to changes in the international political climate.

Questions 25 and 26

When we reflect on the structure of moral decisions we come across cases in which we seem to be subject to mutually exclusive moral demands. But the conflict is just that, a seeming one. We must be careful to distinguish two levels of moral thinking: The *prima facie* and the critical. A *prima facie* moral principle is analogous to a work-a-day tool, say a (n)____(25)____. It is versatile, that is, useful in many situations, and at your fingertips, to wit, no special skill is needed to use it. Unfortunately, the value of a *prima facie* principle derives from its non-specific language, which means in some situations it will turn out to be an oversimplification. For example, two fairly straightforward moral rules of the sort "keep all promises" and "assist others in dire need," which work well enough in most cases, seem to clash in the following scenario: "I have promised a friend I will run a very important errand on his behalf (and he is relying on me); but while *en route* I happen across a person in need of emergency medical assistance, which I can provide, but only at the cost of leaving my original purpose unaccomplished." The appearance of conflict arises from the choice of tools used in analyzing the situation—the two *prima facie* rules do not cut finely enough. What is wanted, therefore, is a more refined analysis which will be applicable to the specific situation. At this the second level of moral thinking, critical moral thinking employs a finer system of categories so that the end result is____(26)____.

25. (A) surgical scalpel
    (B) kitchen knife
    (C) electrical generator
    (D) tuning fork
    (E) library book

26. (A) not two conflicting moral judgments, but a single consistent moral judgment
    (B) an advance for the human species over the savagery of our forebears
    (C) the improvement of medical care for the population in general
    (D) moral principles of higher levels of abstraction which are applicable to larger numbers of cases
    (E) that value judgments will no longer depend on the particulars of any given situation

STOP

IF YOU FINISH BEFORE TIME IS CALLED, CHECK YOUR WORK ON THIS SECTION ONLY. DO NOT WORK ON ANY OTHER SECTION IN THE TEST.

SECTION IV

Time—35 Minutes
35 Questions

Directions: Each of the following sets consists of a fact situation, a dispute and two rules. The rules may conflict, but you are to apply each rule independently. Do not treat a rule as subsidiary or as an exception to the other rule. The rules are followed by questions. You are to select from the following lettered choices (A) through (D) the one that best describes each question in the way it relates to the application of one or both of the rules to the dispute. Blacken the corresponding space on the answer sheet.

(A) a relevant question the answer to which requires a choice between the two rules
(B) a relevant question the answer to which does not require a choice between the two rules, but does require further facts or rules
(C) a relevant question that can be readily answered from the facts or rules or both
(D) an irrelevant question, the answer to which does not affect, or only tangentially affects, the outcome of the dispute

Set 1

FACTS: Hart and his friend Jackson were engaged in robbing a liquor store, a felony. Hart stayed outside the store as the lookout while Jackson entered the store, pointed a pistol at the clerk, Merrick, and demanded the receipts from the cash register. Merrick pretended to reach for the money but produced a shotgun which he kept under the counter for protection. Merrick fired the weapon, hitting Jackson. When Hart heard the shot, he pulled out his own pistol and ran into the store. When he saw that Jackson, his friend, had been wounded, Hart flew into a rage. He cursed Merrick for having shot Jackson, and then shot Merrick, intending only to wound him. Then Hart ran to the cash register and took the money, after which he helped Jackson to their car which they had parked just outside of the store. Hart was not aware that Merrick had been fatally wounded, and having recovered from his fit of rage and feeling remorse, he drove to the nearest pay telephone and called an ambulance for Merrick.

DISPUTE: Later, when Hart sought medical treatment for Jackson, the police arrested the pair and charged them with robbery and murder, but they maintained their innocence.

RULES: I. A person who kills another person accidentally or in an uncontrollable rage is guilty only of voluntary manslaughter.

II. A person who participates in the commission of a felony during which any person is killed is guilty of first degree murder.

1. Is Hart guilty of manslaughter?

2. How severe were Jackson's wounds?

3. Did Merrick commit any crime in shooting Jackson?

4. Is Jackson guilty of first degree murder?

Set 2

FACTS: Farnsworth bought a farm known as White Oaks in 1942. In 1944, Binkley, who owned the neighboring farm, Corn Acres, was killed in a fire which destroyed all of the buildings on Corn Acres. According to the terms of Binkley's will, the farm passed to his nephew, Ditmore. Ditmore lived in a large city several hundred miles away. He visited the farm shortly after he became owner and decided not to rebuild the buildings. Instead, he calculated that rising land prices would eventually make Corn Acres a valuable piece of property, so he determined to leave the land idle until he would sell it. In 1948, Farnsworth began to use part of Corn Acres for his crops. Each year he used a little more of Corn

Acres for his crops. Then, in 1953, Farnsworth died and his son-in-law Gardner became owner of White Oaks. Gardner, assuming that he had also inherited Corn Acres, immediately built a new house right on the spot where the fire had destroyed the old buildings. Gardner lived there until 1976, when Ditmore finally decided to sell Corn Acres. The prospective buyer, however, inspected the land and refused to go through with the sale when he found Gardner was living on the land.

DISPUTE: Ditmore then brought an action to have Gardner thrown off the land as a trespasser. Gardner contested, claiming a right to stay.

RULES: I. A person who enters upon or remains on land which he does not own without the permission of the owner is a trespasser and the owner may bring a legal action at any time to have him removed.

II. A person who lives on land or otherwise uses it in a manner inconsistent with another's ownership, claiming it as his own, without interruption for twenty years acquires ownership of that land by adverse possession.

5. Was Farnsworth a trespasser on Corn Acres at the time he first began to farm the land?

6. Is Ditmore entitled to have Gardner removed as a trespasser?

7. Could Ditmore have had Gardner removed as a trespasser if he had brought his suit when he first inherited Corn Acres from Farnsworth?

8. Has Gardner lived on Corn Acres long enough to acquire the property by adverse possession?

9. For what price did Ditmore agree to sell Corn Acres?

10. If Ditmore had sued to have Gardner removed as a trespasser in 1969, would Gardner be entitled to adverse possession of Corn Acres by virtue of the time his father-in-law had lived on the land?

Set 3

FACTS: Blackwell was driving his pickup truck north on Main Street. Blackwell was in a hurry because he was late for work and was driving 40 miles per hour in a 30-mile-per-hour speed zone. Williams was driving east on Elm Street, well within the speed limit. Williams' car, however, did not have a current inspection sticker; but Williams himself was an amateur mechanic and maintained his car in perfect condition. As Williams approached the intersection of Elm and Main, he failed to notice that the light had changed to yellow until it was too late to stop. For that reason he accelerated into the intersection in an effort to beat the light. Unfortunately, he was right in the middle of the intersection when the light turned red and Blackwell struck the rear quarter-panel of Williams' car. Although Blackwell had a legal right to be in the intersection when the accident occurred, the accident would not have happened if Blackwell had not been exceeding the speed limit.

DISPUTE: Blackwell sued Williams for the damage his truck sustained in the collision. Williams contested.

RULES: I. A person is liable for all personal injuries or property damage he causes by the careless operation of a motor vehicle.

II. A person may not recover compensation for personal injury or property damage sustained in an accident caused by the careless conduct of another if he was guilty of contributory negligence, that is, if his own careless or criminal conduct directly contributed to the occurrence of the accident.

11. What criminal penalty is Williams liable to for having failed to obtain a proper inspection sticker?

12. Was Blackwell contributorily negligent in

the occurrence of the collision between his truck and Williams' car?

13. Is Blackwell entitled to receive compensation from Williams for the damage to his pickup truck?

14. Did Williams' failure to secure a valid inspection sticker constitute careless operation of his car?

15. Supposing that Blackwell had been travelling at 35 miles per hour when Williams' car struck his pickup truck, and supposing further that Blackwell could not have avoided the accident even if he had been travelling at 30 miles per hour, would Blackwell have been contributorily negligent in the accident?

Set 4

FACTS: Taylor and her husband Stone were involved in a criminal scheme to defraud elderly people of money. Taylor would introduce herself to likely targets in the park. Then, after she had gained their confidence, she would introduce them to Stone, who she would claim was an investment banker. Stone had, in fact, once been a stock market analyst, so he was able to impress the potential victim with his knowledge of financial matters. He would then tell the potential victim that he had some inside information regarding a stock and suggest that if the victim were willing to invest some money in it through him, he could guarantee a substantial return. Once Taylor and Stone had gotten the money, they simply disappeared and kept the money. After several similar successful operations, Taylor divorced Stone on the grounds that he was impotent. Later, it developed that Taylor had acquired a new accomplice and was again operating a criminal scheme to defraud victims, this time widows. The police arrested Taylor and charged her with criminal fraud. Stone was called to testify against his former wife, and the prosecution granted Stone immunity from prosecution for his own criminal acts.

DISPUTE: When Stone was asked about his marriage to Taylor, their divorce and their scheme, he refused to answer any questions for he feared that the grounds for their divorce would become public. The prosecution asked the judge to hold Stone in contempt of court for refusing to answer the questions.

RULES: I. A person is not required to answer any question asked at a trial if the answer to the question would tend to show that he had been involved in a criminal activity, and he may refuse to answer such questions without any penalty.

II. A person who has been granted immunity from prosecution for a crime he has committed may not refuse to answer questions on the grounds that his answers might show he had been involved in that criminal activity, and failure to answer places him in contempt of court, the penalty for which is fine or imprisonment.

16. Would Stone's answers to the questions posed by the prosecution tend to show that he had been involved in criminal activity?

17. Is Stone's refusal to answer the questions contempt of court?

18. Is Taylor guilty of criminal fraud?

19. If Stone had not been granted immunity from prosecution, would his answers to questions about the grounds for his divorce tend to show that he had been involved in criminal activity?

20. Can Stone be subjected to any penalty for his refusal to answer the prosecution's questions?

Set 5

FACTS: Ekhard owned three antique automobiles of the same model which he had decided to sell. So he took out an ad in a collector's newsletter, *The Antique Auto Collector,* published quarterly, which stated: "For sale, three

MG-TD Roadsters, perfect condition, $12,000 each or $30,000 for all three. Respond by mail, Box 39, New City, Vt." Garner was looking through the newsletter one day while in the waiting room of his dentist Perkins, and Garner knew that Perkins was a collector of antique autos. Perkins contacted Ekhard and eventually paid Ekhard $12,000 for one of the cars. Perkins also mentioned the ad to a friend, Martin, who was also an antique auto collector. Martin wanted to buy a car of the kind Perkins had bought, but he did not have the money. Two months later, however, Martin inherited a substantial sum of money from a distant relative. He wrote to Ekhard telling him that he, Martin, wished to purchase one of the cars. Ekhard wrote back saying that he had sold all but one, and that he had decided to keep that one. Martin wrote back to Ekhard offering $25,000. Ekhard then contacted Perkins to try to get one of the cars back so he could resell it to Martin. Perkins refused.

DISPUTE: Martin sued Ekhard for failing to fulfill a contract to sell him one of the cars, and Ekhard in turn sued Perkins, claiming there never was a contract between him and Perkins.

RULES: I. A binding contract is made when the terms of an offer are accepted by the person or persons to whom the offer of an agreement is directed.

II. When an offer fails to specify a time limit, it remains open only for a reasonable period of time, at which time it is deemed to expire and the party making the offer may refuse to honor an acceptance of its terms.

21. Was there a contract between Ekhard and Perkins for the sale of one of the cars?

22. Was there a contract between Martin and Ekhard for the sale of one of the cars?

23. Was the offer to sell the three cars directed at Martin?

24. Had the offer to sell the cars expired before Martin contacted Ekhard?

25. Is Martin entitled to receive one of the cars from Ekhard?

Set 6

FACTS: Gordon, a police officer, was on routine patrol in a squad car when he observed another car run through a red light. Gordon pulled the car over. It was late at night with little traffic on the road, so he planned to give the driver a warning and not a summons. As he approached the car, he observed by the light of a nearby street lamp actions by the driver and the one passenger as though they were secreting some object beneath the front seat. Gordon asked Baker, the driver, for his license. Baker appeared to be very nervous, and at first he claimed to have lost his license but then produced a license issued to him which had expired two months earlier. Gordon asked Baker if he could look into the trunk of the car, but Baker said "No." At that moment, the passenger, Cooke, stated that he was the owner of the car and that Gordon could, if he wished, look into the trunk. As Cooke exited from the car, he kicked something on the floor board. From his viewpoint outside of the car, Gordon was able to see the barrel of a gun. He immediately ordered both Baker and Cooke to stand against the side of the car. Gordon entered the car and found a gun partially concealed under the front seat.

DISPUTE: Baker and Cooke were charged with possession of an illegal weapon. They pled not guilty on the grounds the evidence was not admissible.

RULES: I. Police may not enter or search a vehicle which has been stopped for a traffic infraction unless the driver specifically consents to a search, and any evidence obtained in violation of this requirement is not admissible in a criminal trial.

II. Police may legally seize any evidence of a crime which is lying in a place in plain view from where they are standing while discharging their duties.

26. Did the driver of the car specifically consent to Gordon's search under the car's seat?

27. Is the gun Gordon found under the front seat admissible evidence against Baker and Cooke?

28. Was the gun Gordon seized lying in plain view?

29. Are Baker and Gordon guilty of possessing an illegal weapon?

30. If Gordon had searched the trunk of the car with Cooke's permission and found illegal drugs, would those drugs have been admissible at a trial as evidence against Baker?

Set 7

FACTS: Oliver was employed by Rapid Delivery Service as a messenger. Oliver's job was to drive a panel van and to make pick-ups and deliveries of small packages. Occasionally, during the summer months, Oliver would have his teenaged son ride with him on his routes. When accompanied by his son, Oliver was able to complete his assignments more quickly. Morton, the owner of Rapid Delivery Service, knew that Oliver sometimes took his son with him, and though he did not really approve of the practice, he did nothing to stop it. One day, Oliver was accompanied by his son and assigned to make a delivery in a large office building to Garments, Inc. Another firm, Time Pieces Corporation, also had offices in the same building. The employees of Time Pieces were on strike and had surrounded the building with pickets. When the pickets saw Oliver pull up in front of the building, they incorrectly assumed that he had some business with Time Pieces and refused to let him pass. Oliver was anxious to make the delivery, so he told his son to take the package and run past the pickets while he, Oliver, distracted them. One of the pickets, Brook, saw the son trying to sneak past and grabbed him. Seeing this, Oliver ran over and seized Brook by the arm, spun him around, and hit him in the face as hard as he could, breaking Brook's jaw. As Brook fell, Oliver's son, angered at having been manhandled by Brook, kicked Brook in his side, breaking three ribs. By this time, the police arrived and restored order. Oliver made his delivery to Garment.

DISPUTE: Later, Brook sued Rapid Delivery Service for the injuries inflicted by Oliver and his son. Rapid Delivery Service contested.

RULES:

I. An employer is liable for all injuries caused by the actions of his employees while they are in the course of discharging their assigned duties.

II. An employer is not responsible for any injuries which are intentionally inflicted by an employee whether or not the employee is performing a task assigned by the employer.

31. Is Rapid Delivery Service liable to Brook for the injuries he sustained when Oliver struck him in the face?

32. Was Oliver's son an employee of Rapid Delivery Service?

33. Is Rapid Delivery Service liable to Brook for the broken ribs he sustained when Oliver's son kicked him?

34. Was Oliver discharging his assigned duties when he struck Brook in the face?

35. What was the value of the package which Oliver's son was trying to deliver at the time of the altercation?

STOP

IF YOU FINISH BEFORE TIME IS CALLED, CHECK YOUR WORK ON THIS SECTION ONLY. DO NOT WORK ON ANY OTHER SECTION IN THE TEST.

SECTION V

Time—35 Minutes
25 Questions

Directions: Each group of questions is based on a set of propositions or conditions. Drawing a rough picture or diagram may help in answering some of the questions. Choose the best answer for each question and blacken the corresponding space on your answer sheet.

Questions 1–5

The letters S, T, U, V, W, X, Y, and Z represent eight consecutive whole numbers, not necessarily in that order.

W is four more than Z and three less than X.
S is more than T and less than X.
U is the average of V and X.

1. If the lowest number of the series is 8, what is the value of W?
(A) 10
(B) 11
(C) 12
(D) 13
(E) 14

2. Which of the following is (are) true?

I. W is not the greatest number in the series.
II. Z is not the greatest number in the series.
III. X is not the greatest number in the series.

(A) I only
(B) II only
(C) I and II only
(D) I and III only
(E) I, II, and III

3. If V is less than W, which one of the following is a possible order of the numbers, starting with the highest number on the left?
(A) X, S, U, W, V, T, Y, Z
(B) X, S, T, W, V, U, Y, Z
(C) Z, S, T, W, U, V, Y, X
(D) X, T, S, V, W, U, Z, Y
(E) X, U, S, T, W, V, Y, Z

4. If U did not have to be greater than V, which of the following is a new possibility?
(A) X is one greater than U.
(B) U is one greater than Z.
(C) U is four less than W.
(D) Z is two greater than U.
(E) U is equal to W.

5. If Y is three greater than Z, which of the following is (are) true?

I. W is greater than U.
II. S is greater than W.
III. Y is greater than V.
IV. V is two less than Y.

(A) I and II only
(B) I and III only
(C) I, II, and IV only
(D) II, III, and IV only
(E) none of the above

Questions 6–9

John is trying to figure out the best arrangement of spices in the spice rack of his small efficiency kitchen. The rack has two shelves with three spaces on each shelf. He decides that the six spices he uses most often, and thus wishes to put in the rack, are: Basil, cumin, fennel, pepper, salt, and thyme. Since the thyme and the basil look similar and come in similar containers, the chances of confusion will be reduced if they are not placed next to each other either horizontally or vertically. Since the pepper and salt are usually both used at the same time they should be next to each other on the same shelf.

6. Given the above information, which of the following arrangements is (are) unacceptable?

I. Thyme and basil can be on the same shelf.
II. Thyme and cumin can be on the same shelf.

III. Thyme and salt can be on the same shelf.

(A) Any of the above are acceptable.
(B) I only
(C) II only
(D) II and III only
(E) All cannot be true.

7. If the two left-hand spices on the upper shelf are thyme and cumin, respectively, which of the following is an acceptable arrangement of the lower shelf, reading from left to right?
(A) fennel, salt, basil
(B) fennel, pepper, basil
(C) basil, salt, pepper
(D) salt, pepper, basil
(E) salt, fennel, pepper

8. If the lower shelf has salt, pepper, and basil from left to right, then how many possible arrangements are there for the upper shelf?
(A) 2
(B) 3
(C) 4
(D) 5
(E) 6

9. John buys a new brand of thyme and basil because it has more flavor. If the new containers are very similar to one another, and also are too tall to fit on the lower shelf, which of the following describes an acceptable arrangement?
(A) Either salt or pepper will be next to or below fennel.
(B) Salt will be below thyme.
(C) Pepper will be next to either fennel or cumin.
(D) Thyme will be above either salt or pepper.
(E) Basil will be above either salt or pepper.

Questions 10–13

To apply for a Dark Days Fellowship a student must see the Dean of Students, fill out a financial statement, and obtain a thesis approval from either Professor Fansler or Professor Cross.

A student must see the Dean of Students before filling out the financial statement in order to make sure that it is filled out correctly.

The Dean of Students has office hours for students only on Thursday and Friday mornings, and Monday and Tuesday afternoons.

The Financial Aid Office, where the financial statement has to be filed in person, is open only Monday and Tuesday mornings, Wednesday afternoons, and Friday mornings.

Professor Fansler is in her office only on Monday and Tuesday mornings.

Professor Cross is in his office only on Tuesday and Friday mornings.

10. A student has already seen the Dean of Students and wishes to complete the rest of the application process in one day. If he must obtain his approval from Professor Fansler, when should he come to the campus?
(A) Monday morning only
(B) Tuesday morning only
(C) Friday morning only
(D) either Monday or Tuesday morning
(E) either Monday, Tuesday, or Friday morning

11. If a student completed her application process in one visit, which of the following must be false?

I. She got her thesis approved by Professor Cross.
II. She got her thesis approved by Professor Fansler.
III. She completed everything in the afternoon.

(A) I only
(B) II only
(C) III only
(D) I and III only
(E) II and III only

12. If a student wanting to apply for a Dark Days Fellowship has classes only on Tuesdays and Thursdays and doesn't want to make an extra trip to the campus, which of the following is true?

I. The thesis approval must be obtained from Professor Fansler.

II. The thesis approval must be obtained from Professor Cross.
III. The entire application process can be completed in one day.
IV. The entire application process can be completed within the same school week.

(A) I and II only
(B) II and III only
(C) I, II, and III only
(D) None of the statements are true.
(E) All of the statements are true.

13. A student has already obtained thesis approval from Professor Fansler. She wishes to complete the application process in only one more visit. When can she do this?
(A) Monday or Tuesday only
(B) Monday, Tuesday, or Friday only
(C) Friday morning only
(D) any morning except Wednesday
(E) any morning except Wednesday or Thursday

Questions 14–18

There are four grades of milk cows in the Bellman herd: AA, AAA, AAAA, and AAAAA. These are sometimes called 2A, 3A, 4A and 5A. These classifications are based on the amount and quality of the milk produced by a cow, or in the case of a bull, the qualities of the bull's mother. AA cows produce less milk of lesser quality and AAAAA cows produce the greatest quantity and the highest quality. The Bellmans have an extensive breeding program. The primary goal of the breeding program is to produce better grades of cattle, but sometimes other factors such as resistance to disease, fertility, and even temperament are considered in making the breeding decisions.

The milk producing abilities of a cow are inherited primarily from its mother; but if the father is two or more grades different from the mother, then the offspring's grade will be one grade different from the mother's grade in the direction of the father's grade.

14. If a calf is grade 3A, which of the following pairs could have been its parents?
(A) A father who was grade AAAAA and a mother who was grade AA.
(B) A father who was grade AA and a mother who was grade AAAAA.
(C) A father who was grade AAA and a mother who was grade AA.
(D) A father who was grade AAAA and a mother who was grade AAAAA.
(E) A father who was grade AAAAA and a mother who was grade AAAA.

15. If it is found that resistance to hoof and mouth disease is associated with having had grade 2A or 3A fathers, which of the following grades of cows will probably be least resistant?
(A) AA
(B) AAA
(C) AAAA
(D) AAAAA
(E) All grades will have the same resistance.

16. If the Bellmans notice that the offspring of grade 4A cattle are the gentlest and easiest to handle, which of the following is the best method of quickly introducing the trait of gentleness into the largest part of the herd while getting the best milk results?
(A) Breeding AAAA bulls to all the cows.
(B) Breeding AAAA bulls to the AAAAA cows and AAAA cows to all the other bulls.
(C) Breeding AAAA cows to all the bulls.
(D) Breeding AAAAA cows to all the bulls.
(E) Instituting a random breeding program.

17. Which of the following must be true?

I. AA and AAAAA cannot be interbred.
II. A 2A bull and a 4A cow produce a higher grade calf than a 4A bull and a 3A cow.
III. The father of a 4A bull must have been grade 3A, 4A, or 5A.

(A) None of the statements must be true.
(B) I only
(C) II only

(D) I and III only
(E) II and III only

18. A certain hide color is found to breed true, that is, if either parent has the hide color, the calf will have the hide color. If the hide color is first noticed in grade AA cattle, at least how many generations, not including the first 2A cow or bull with the hide color, will it take to have a grade AAAAA cow with the hide color?
(A) two
(B) three
(C) four
(D) five
(E) six

Questions 19–25

A Scout Troop is planning the menu for the lunches and dinners of their five-day camping trip. The menus must conform to the following conditions:

Lunches can be one of three foods: cheese, tuna, or hot dogs.
Dinners can be one of three foods: hot dogs, stew, or ham.
The same food cannot be served twice on the same day, nor can the same food be served two days in a row.
The dinner on day 1 will be stew.
The menu on day 4 will be cheese for lunch and hot dogs for dinner.

19. Which of the following statements about the menus must be true?
(A) Hot dogs will be served on only one day.
(B) Tuna will be served on only one day.
(C) Stew will be served on only one day.
(D) Tuna will be served on at least two days.
(E) Hot dogs will be served on at least two days.

20. If ham is served for dinner on day 3, all of the following are possible EXCEPT
(A) Tuna is served for lunch on day 1.
(B) Hot dogs are served for lunch on day 2.
(C) Cheese is served for lunch on day 2.
(D) Ham is served for dinner on day 5.
(E) Stew is served for dinner on day 5.

21. Which of the following must be true?
(A) Tuna is served for lunch on day 1.
(B) Stew is served for dinner on day 2.
(C) Stew is served for dinner on day 3.
(D) Hot dogs are served for dinner on day 5.
(E) Tuna is served for lunch on day 5.

22. If hot dogs are served for lunch only once, which of the following must be true?
(A) Ham can be served no more than twice.
(B) Tuna can be served no more than twice.
(C) Cheese can be served no less than twice.
(D) Stew can be served no more than once.
(E) Hot dogs can be served no less than three times.

23. Which of the following is a possible menu for day 2?

I. Tuna and Hot Dogs
II. Cheese and Hot Dogs
III. Hot Dogs and Ham

(A) I only
(B) III only
(C) I and III only
(D) II and III only
(E) I, II, and III

24. If hot dogs are served for lunch on day 1, which of the following must be true?
(A) Tuna is served for lunch on day 2.
(B) Hot dogs are served for lunch on day 2.
(C) Ham is served for dinner on day 2.
(D) Stew is served for dinner on day 2.
(E) Ham is served for dinner on day 3.

25. If the trip is extended to six days and hot dogs are served for dinner on the sixth day, which of the following must be true?
(A) Cheese is served for lunch on day 6.
(B) Tuna is served for lunch on day 6.
(C) Hot dogs are served for dinner on day 5.
(D) Stew is served for dinner on day 5.
(E) Cheese is served for lunch on day 5.

STOP

IF YOU FINISH BEFORE TIME IS CALLED, CHECK YOUR WORK ON THIS SECTION ONLY. DO NOT WORK ON ANY OTHER SECTION IN THE TEST.

SECTION VI

Time—35 Minutes
28 Question

Directions: Below each of the following passages, you will find questions or incomplete statements about the passage. Each statement or question is followed by five lettered words or expressions. Select the word or expression that most satisfactorily completes each statement or answers each question in accordance with the meaning of the passage. After you have chosen the best answer, blacken the corresponding space on the answer sheet.

The job of attracting the right young people into business will be facilitated if businessmen and the world at large understand the real benefits of an education designed to prepare young people for business and the fact that such an education does breed the broad-gauge man who can stand with feet planted in both Column A and Column B. The continued success of our business democracy requires no less.

Education for business must avoid the purely intellectual for something with a more pragmatic focus. And what is wrong with an education that has a pragmatic focus? Plato—in his *Republic*—was far more pragmatic than we ever think of being.

But even if education for business should be unashamedly pragmatic, it cannot be an end in itself. Any young person entering management, from school, regardless of what degree he has earned, is going to have to continue his education throughout his life. Things are happening too fast today for anyone to feel fully educated after four years, or six years, or ten years! What he will have to do is to be retrained or retooled as the years go by. The kind of education needed is that which opens the young person's eyes to the need for a lifetime of study and gives him the foundations on which his continued study can be based.

Rather than being narrowly vocational, modern business education in many ways leads in the liberality of its approach. Beginning with courses in human relations, and ending up permeating all its activities, is the concept of participative management. Why? Because as business becomes more scientific, more intellectual, more complex, no one man can have the total knowledge required to make sound decisions arbitrarily. When things become so highly complex, group management is the logical answer.

It is in modern business education that this type of leadership is taught and researched. This is of crucial importance to the well-being of our nation, because if the leaders of our business democracy cannot meet the challenge of the collective economy which boasts it will bury us, we may indeed be buried—and not just economically. Modern business education teaches how to lead without a sacrifice of freedom; how to exercise control and direction, while at the same time respecting opinions of others more qualified in highly specialized areas as well as respecting their essential dignity as humans; and how to learn to lead by freeing the latent potentialities of gifted advisers–not by stifling them.

Perhaps it will be the business schools of this nation which will remind American education not only that democracy and strong leadership are *not* contradictory terms, but that leadership can and *must* be taught. No other part of our university system seemingly is paying much, if any, attention to *doing* something about, rather than talking about, education for democratic leadership. To some faculties, leadership itself is a jingoistic word echoing back to Teddy Roosevelt. Not so to the faculties of our modern business schools—and not so to the masses of American students who are revolting against the lofty disengagement of many academics from the complex—and often unclean—realities of our world.

Thus, business will be serving the nation's interest as well as its own—*if* it recognizes that the *right* kind of young people it needs for tomorrow's managers are the brighter students who are not purely intellectual, or purely pragmatic; *if* it offers them a career that will satisfy their values; and *if* it does what it can to encourage their development.

1. The most appropriate title for this passage is
   (A) Businessmen and Business Schools
   (B) Youth and Business
   (C) Business Schools
   (D) Bright Students and Business
   (E) The Relationship Between Business Education and Business

2. The passage implies that
   (A) a business education is more easily obtained than a Liberal Arts education
   (B) business schools are in the forefront in the matter of liberalizing curricula
   (C) a Liberal Arts education is superior to a technical education
   (D) education is of little importance to success in the business world
   (E) business is not challenging to most students

3. According to the passage, the future economic well-being of the country depends primarily on
   (A) businessmen who are hard-headed
   (B) businessmen who can get along with government
   (C) business school faculties
   (D) business leaders from a wide range of backgrounds
   (E) business leaders skilled in group management

4. The author uses the term "both Column A and Column B" to indicate
   (A) the need for students to be able to do well on standardized tests
   (B) the desirability of businessmen being educated both in business and in general learning skills
   (C) the appropriateness of having as broad an education as possible
   (D) the value of the physical element in education
   (E) the requirement for dual modality in business thinking

5. The author feels that the modern student is
   (A) committed to business education
   (B) aware of the value of a modern business education
   (C) eager to have a career combining reality with intellectual vigor
   (D) opposed to studying theory
   (E) revolted by the unclean aspects of academic life

6. If the passage's predictions for the future are true, a young person entering business can count on
   (A) being a great success
   (B) going back to school several times during his career
   (C) becoming a leader of his country
   (D) doing what most students want to do
   (E) having to learn many new things during his career

7. The author indicates that
   (A) business methods have drastically changed in the last decade
   (B) there has been too much government interference in business
   (C) the larger universities are far too impersonal in their dealings with students
   (D) the importance of vocational education is much over-rated
   (E) business success, in the final analysis, spells success for the entire nation

Whenever two or more unusual traits or situations are found in the same place, it is tempting to look for more than a coincidental relationship between them. The high Himalayas and the Tibetan plateau certainly have extraordinary physical characteristics and the cultures which are found there are also unusual, though not unique. However, there is no intention of adopting Montesquieu's view of climate and soil as cultural determinants. The ecology of a region merely poses some of the problems faced by the inhabitants of the region, and while the problems facing a culture are important to its development, they do not determine it.

The appearance of the Himalayas during the late Tertiary Period and the accompanying further raising of the previously established ranges had a marked effect on the climate of the region. Primarily, of course, it blocked the Indian monsoon from reaching Central Asia at all. Secondarily, air and moisture from other directions was also reduced.

Prior to the raising of the Himalayas, the land now forming the Tibetan uplands had a dry continental climate with vegetation and animal life similar to that of much of the rest of the region on the same parallel, but somewhat different than that of the areas further north, which were already drier. With the coming of the Himalayas and the relatively sudden drying out of the region, there was a severe thinning out of the animal and plant populations. The ensuing incomplete Pleistocene glaciation had a further thinning effect, but significantly did not wipe out life in the area. Thus, after the end of the glaciation there were only a few varieties of life extant from the original continental species. Isolated by the Kunlun range from the Tarim basin and Turfan depression species which had already adapted to the dry steppe climate, and would otherwise have been expected to flourish in Tibet, the remaining native fauna and flora multiplied. Armand describes the Tibetan fauna as not having great variety, but being "striking" in the abundance of the particular species that are present. The plant life is similarly limited in variety, with some observers finding no more than seventy varieties of plants in even the relatively fertile Eastern Tibetan Valleys, with fewer than ten food crops. Tibetan "tea" is a major staple, perhaps replacing the unavailable vegetables.

The difficulties of living in an environment at once dry and cold, and populated with species more usually found in more hospitable climes, are great. These difficulties may well have influenced the unusual polyandrous societies typical of the region. Lattimore sees the maintenance of multiple husband households as being preserved from earlier forms by the harsh conditions of the Tibetan uplands, which permitted no experimentation and "froze" the cultures which came there. Kawakita, on the other hand, sees the polyandry as a way of easily permitting the best householder to become the head husband regardless of age. His detailed studies of the Bhotea village of Tsumje do seem to support this idea of polyandry as a method of talent mobility in a situation where even the best talent is barely enough for survival.

In sum, though arguments can be made that a pre-existing polyandrous system was strengthened and preserved (insofar as it has been) by the rigors of the land, it would certainly be an overstatement to lay causative factors of any stronger nature to the ecological influences in this case.

8. What are the "unusual situations and traits" referred to in the first sentence?

I. Patterns of animal and plant growth
II. The limited variety of food available to the upland Tibetans
III. Social and familial organization of typical Tibetan society

(A) I only
(B) II only
(C) III only
(D) I and III only
(E) I, II, and III

9. What was the significance of the fact that the Pleistocene glaciation did not wipe out life entirely in the area?
(A) Without life, man could not flourish either.
(B) The drying out was too sudden for most plants to adapt to the climate.
(C) If the region had been devoid of life, some of the other species from nearby arid areas might possibly have taken over the area.
(D) The variety of Tibetan life was decreased.
(E) None of the above.

10. Which of the following most likely best describes Tibetan "tea"?
(A) a pale brown, clear broth-like drink
(B) a dark brown tea drink, carefully strained
(C) a nutritious mixture of tea leaves and rancid yak butter
(D) a high caffeine drink
(E) a green tinted drink similar to Chinese basket-fried green tea

11. The purpose of the passage is to
(A) describe Tibetan fauna and flora
(B) describe the social organization of typical Tibetan villages
(C) analyze the causes of Tibet's unusual animal and plant populations
(D) analyze the possible causal links between Tibetan ecology and society
(E) probe the mysteries of the sudden appearance of the Himalayas

12. The author's knowledge of Tibet is probably
(A) based on first-hand experience
(B) the result of life-long study

(C) derived only from books
(D) derived from Chinese sources
(E) limited to geological history

13. In which ways are the ideas of Lattimore and Kawakita totally opposed?
(A) Lattimore forbids change and Kawakita requires it.
(B) Kawakita opposes change and Lattimore favors it.
(C) Lattimore sees polyandry as primitive and Kawakita views it as modern.
(D) Lattimore criticizes polyandry as inefficient, but Kawakita finds it highly efficient.
(E) Their ideas are not totally opposed on any point.

14. According to the passage, which of the following would probably be the most agreeable to Montesquieu?
(A) All regions have different soils, and thus different cultures.
(B) Some regions with similar climates will have similar cultures.
(C) Cultures in the same area, sharing soil and climate, will be essentially identical.
(D) European cultures are liberated to some degree from determinism.
(E) The plants of a country, by being the food of its people, cause the people to have similar views to one another.

Every profession or trade, every art, and every science has its technical vocabulary, the function of which is partly to designate things or processes which have no names in ordinary English, and partly to secure greater exactness in nomenclature. Such special dialects, or jargons, are necessary in technical discussion of any kind. Being universally understood by the devotees of the particular science or art, they have the precision of a mathematical formula. Besides, they save time, for it is much more economical to name a process than to describe it. Thousands of these technical terms are very properly included in every large dictionary, yet, as a whole, they are rather on the outskirts of the English language than actually within its borders.

Different occupations, however, differ widely in the character of their special vocabularies. In trades and handicrafts and other vocations, such as farming and fishing, that have occupied great numbers of men from remote times, the technical vocabulary is very old. It consists largely of native words, or of borrowed words that have worked themselves into the very fibre of our language. Hence, though highly technical in many particulars, these vocabularies are more familiar in sound, and more generally understood, than most other technicalities. The special dialects of law, medicine, divinity, and philosophy have also, in their older strata, become pretty familiar to cultivated persons, and have contributed much to the popular vocabulary. Yet, every vocation still possesses a large body of technical terms that remain essentially foreign, even to educated speech. And the proportion has been much increased in the last fifty years, particularly in the various departments of natural and political science and in the mechanic arts. Here new terms are coined with the greatest freedom, and abandoned with indifference when they have served their turn. Most of the new coinages are confined to special discussions, and seldom get into general literature or conversation. Yet, no profession is nowadays, as all professions once were, a closed guild. The lawyer, the physician, the man of science, the cleric, all associate freely with his fellow creatures, and do not meet them in a merely professional way. Furthermore, what is called "popular science" makes everybody acquainted with modern views and recent discoveries. Any important experiment, though made in a remote or provincial laboratory, is at once reported in the newspapers, and everybody is soon talking about it—as in the case of the Roentgen rays and wireless telegraphy. Thus, our common speech is always taking up new technical terms and making them commonplace.

15. Which of the following words is least likely to have started its life as jargon?
(A) sun
(B) calf
(C) plow
(D) loom
(E) hammer

16. The author's main purpose in the passage is to
(A) describe a phenomenon
(B) argue a belief
(C) propose a solution

(D) stimulate action
(E) be entertaining

17. When the author refers to professions as no longer being "closed guilds" he means that
    (A) it is much easier to become a professional than in the past
    (B) there is more social intercourse between professionals and others
    (C) popular science has told its secrets to the world
    (D) anyone can now understand anything in a profession
    (E) apprenticeships are no longer required

18. If the author of the passage wished to study a new field, he would probably
    (A) call in a dictionary expert
    (B) become easily discouraged
    (C) look to the histories of the words in the new field
    (D) pay careful attention to the new field's technical vocabulary
    (E) learn how to coin new jargon in the field

19. The writer of this article was probably a(n)
    (A) linguist
    (B) attorney
    (C) scientist
    (D) politician
    (E) physician

20. The author of the passage probably lived in
    (A) 1904 in India
    (B) 1914 in the United States
    (C) 1944 in Russia
    (D) 1964 in England
    (E) 1974 in France

21. It seems that the passage implies that
    (A) English is always becoming larger and larger
    (B) the words of the English language are always changing
    (C) one can never be sure of what a word means without consulting an expert
    (D) technical terms in most non-scientific fields have little chance of becoming part of the main body of the language in these scientific days
    (E) such old-time farming words as *harrow* and *farrow* are not really technical terms at all

Just as the non-manager is dependent on his boss for motivational opportunities, so is the manager dependent on his boss for conditions of motivation which have meaning at his level. Since the motivation of an employee at any level is strongly related to the supervisory style of his immediate boss, sound motivation patterns must begin at the top. Being closer to the policy-making level, the manager has more opportunity to understand and relate his work to company goals. However, high position alone does not guarantee motivation or self-actualization.

Motivation for the manager, as well as the non-manager, is usually both a consequence and a symptom of effective job performance. Job success is dependent on cyclical conditions created by interpersonal competence, meaningful goals, and helpful systems. After sustained conditioning in the developmental cycle, an individual has amazing capacity and incentive to remain in it. Moreover, if forced into the reductive cycle, unless he has pathological needs to remain there, organizational conditions must be remarkably and consistently bad to suppress his return to the developmental cycle.

Sustained confinement of a large percentage of the work force in the reductive cycle is symptomatic of organizational illness. It is usually a culmination of a chain of events beginning with top management, and is reversible only by changes at the top. Consequences of reductive conditions such as militant unionism and other forms of reactive behavior usually provoke management into defensive and manipulative behavior which only reinforces the reductive cycle. The vicarious pleasure sought by the rank and file through seeing the management giant felled by their union is a poor substitute for the self-actualization of being a whole person doing a meaningful job, but in the absence of motivational opportunities, it is an understandable compromise.

The seeds of concerted reactive behavior are often brought to the job from broadly shared frustrations arising from social injustice, economic deprivation, and moral decadence either to sprout in a reductive climate or become infertile in a developmental climate. Hence, the unionization of a work group is usually precipitated by management failure to provide opportunities for employees to achieve personal goals through the achievement of organization goals. Organizations survive these failures only because most other companies are equally handicapped by the same failures.

Management failures in supervision do not, of course, stem from intentional malice. They may result, in part, from a lingering tradition of "scientific management" which fractionated tasks and "protected" employees from the need to think, and perpetrated management systems based on automaton conformity. But more often such failures stem from the manager's insensitivity to the needs and perceptions of others, particularly from his inability to see himself as others see him.

Insensitivity or the inability to empathize is manifested not only as interpersonal incompetence, but also as the failure to provide meaningful goals, the misuse of management systems, or a combination of both. Style of supervision, then, is largely an expression of the personality characteristics and mental health of the manager, and his potential for inducing developmental or reductive cyclical reactions.

22. A reductive cycle is one in which
    (A) an employer attempts to reduce costs
    (B) the work-force is gradually reduced in number
    (C) costs decrease as a firm gains experience
    (D) a union, step-by-step, takes over control of a business
    (E) there is less productive effort on the part of employees

23. Upon whom do managers and other employees ultimately depend for their motivation?
    (A) their spouses
    (B) their chief executive officers
    (C) their union
    (D) their fellow workers
    (E) themselves

24. The passage indicates that the unionization of a work group is most commonly brought about by management's failure to provide
    (A) opportunities for the workers to realize individual objectives by way of group objectives
    (B) opportunities for the workers to achieve a feeling of self-identification
    (C) more pleasant working surroundings, including modern conveniences available both at their work and during rest-periods and lunch-periods
    (D) greater fringe benefits, including more holidays and health insurance
    (E) opportunities for socialization during working hours as well as after work

25. If a substantial number of the employees remain in the reductive cycle, one may assume that
    (A) the organization is enjoying increased business
    (B) the personnel department has been functioning effectively
    (C) the boss is not giving sufficient attention to the business
    (D) the organization is failing to provide adequate motivation for its employees
    (E) they belong to unions

26. Which of the following is likely to result initially from reductive conditions in an organization?

    I. militant unionism
    II. pension plans
    III. higher wages

    (A) I only
    (B) II only
    (C) I and II only
    (D) I and III only
    (E) I, II, and III

27. Employees will get together to seek an improvement of conditions because of dissatisfactions stemming from

    I. social injustice
    II. economic deprivation
    III. moral decadence

    (A) I only
    (B) II only
    (C) I and II only
    (D) I and III only
    (E) I, II, and III

28. According to the author, management failures in supervision are mainly attributable to the supervisor or manager's
    (A) currying favor with the boss
    (B) being soft-hearted
    (C) ignorance
    (D) lack of feeling
    (E) inability to gain respect

STOP

IF YOU FINISH BEFORE TIME IS CALLED, CHECK YOUR WORK ON THIS SECTION ONLY. DO NOT WORK ON ANY OTHER SECTION IN THE TEST.

WRITING SAMPLE

Time—30 Minutes

Directions: Write an essay about the question listed below. You may support or attack the question or discuss it in any way that you wish. Be sure to make your points clearly and cogently and to write as neatly as possible. Write your essay within the margins of the pages. Additional paper may be used as scratch paper, but only these pages can be used for the actual essay.

TOPIC: When you meet someone, it is better not to make the first impression your best impression, because thereafter you will not be able to live up to your new acquaintance's expectations. It is better to make a bad first impression, so that later you will seem to be more impressive.

ANSWER KEY
PRACTICE EXAMINATION 3

SECTION I

1. E	6. A	11. D	16. A	21. D
2. E	7. C	12. C	17. D	22. B
3. B	8. D	13. B	18. C	23. D
4. E	9. C	14. E	19. C	24. E
5. B	10. A	15. D	20. B	25. D

SECTION II

1. B	8. E	15. D	22. C
2. C	9. D	16. B	23. E
3. D	10. D	17. A	24. C
4. E	11. C	18. D	25. D
5. A	12. A	19. B	26. B
6. C	13. B	20. E	27. B
7. B	14. A	21. C	28. A

SECTION III

1. B	8. B	15. A	22. D
2. D	9. C	16. E	23. C
3. B	10. A	17. B	24. D
4. D	11. D	18. A	25. B
5. E	12. C	19. D	26. A
6. C	13. A	20. E	
7. B	14. E	21. A	

SECTION IV

1. A	8. C	15. B	22. A	29. B
2. D	9. D	16. C	23. C	30. C
3. D	10. B	17. C	24. B	31. A
4. C	11. D	18. D	25. B	32. C
5. D	12. C	19. C	26. C	33. B
6. A	13. A	20. A	27. A	34. B
7. C	14. D	21. C	28. C	35. D

SECTION V

1. C	6. A	11. E	16. B	21. A
2. C	7. D	12. D	17. A	22. A
3. A	8. C	13. C	18. A	23. D
4. B	9. A	14. A	19. D	24. C
5. E	10. D	15. D	20. B	25. A

SECTION VI

1. E	8. E	15. A	22. E
2. B	9. C	16. A	23. B
3. E	10. C	17. B	24. A
4. B	11. D	18. D	25. D
5. C	12. C	19. A	26. A
6. E	13. E	20. B	27. E
7. E	14. C	21. B	28. D

EXPLANATORY ANSWERS

SECTION I

Questions 1–5

Arranging the Information

The major issue is who can and can't be on the team with particular other candidates.

WEST CAMPUS EAST CAMPUS

TWO FROM EACH CAMPUS

X P

Y←NOT WITH→L←NOT WITH→M

Z←NOT WITH→N

Answering the Questions

1. **(E)** The rejection of Y requires the selection of X and Z. The selection of Z forbids N. The selection of M bars L, leaving only M, N, X, and Z, choice (E).
   (C) and (D) fail for lack of two West campus members. (A) puts L and M together, which is wrong, and (B) puts Z and N together, which is forbidden.

2. **(E)** L's inclusion bars Y and M. Y's omission requires the inclusion of X and Z to have two West campus members, leaving only (E).
   (A) and (D) wrongly put L with M and Y respectively. (B) has Z and N, which is not permitted, while (C) has only one West campus member.

3. **(B)** The selection of Y and Z excludes L and N respectively, thus assuring the selection of P and M, choice (B).
   (A), (C), and (D) wrongly claim the selection of excluded members and (E) omits the necessity of having M.

4. **(E)** The answer to problem 3 gives an example of M, P, and Z being on the same team, thus falsifying statements I and III. N, P, Y, and X is a possible team which shows the error of II, hence, (E).

5. **(B)** I is not true since we can select team Y, Z, P, and M. II is true since N's selection eliminates Z, requiring the selection of both X and Y to ensure that there are two West campus members. III is false since the rejection of L and N, while not requiring the selection of X, still permits it: M, P, X, and Z.

Questions 6–10

Arranging the Information

This is a situation with so few items in it that it looks likely to be completely determined once everything is fitted in. It is probably going to be helpful to keep track of the cross-references in a separate chart.

Entering the first item: Roger's wife is older than Ursula, and hence not Ursula.

PAUL	QUINCY	ROGER	SAM
		not U older than U	

TESS	URSULA	VAL	WILMA
	not R		

	P	Q	R	S
T				
U			N	
V				
W				

"N" MEANS NOT SPOUSE OF

"Y" MEANS IS SPOUSE OF

Sam's wife is older than Wilma (and hence not Wilma), who is Paul's sister (and hence not Paul's wife).

Sam's wife is older than Wilma, hence, Wilma is not Roger's wife.
Wilma is Paul's sister, hence, not his wife.
Wilma is not P's, R's, or S's wife, so must be Q's wife, and Q's wife is not V, U, or T.

	P	Q	R	S
T		N		
U		N	N	
V		N		
W	N	Y	N	N

"N" MEANS NOT SPOUSE OF
"Y" MEANS IS SPOUSE OF

Tess is the youngest, and hence not Sam's or Roger's wife, is P's wife.

	P	Q	R	S
T	Y	N	N	N
U	N	N	N	
V	N	N		
W	N	Y	N	N

"N" MEANS NOT SPOUSE OF
"Y" MEANS IS SPOUSE OF

This leads to the further deduction that U can only go with S, leaving R and V to go with each other.

	P	Q	R	S
T	Y	N	N	N
U	N	N	N	Y
V	N	N	Y	N
W	N	Y	N	N

"N" MEANS NOT SPOUSE OF
"Y" MEANS IS SPOUSE OF

We have the miscellaneous information that the ages of the wives are also in order. V, as R's wife, is older than U who is older than W, with T the youngest, yielding, in age, V > U > W > T.

Paul is Wilma's brother.

Answering the Questions

6. **(A)** Quincy's wife's (Wilma) brother's (Paul) wife, Tess, will be Patrick's aunt, (A). You must look to Paul since that is the only brother/sister relationship, which is the only thing that could yield an aunt relationship.

7. **(C)** This is just a matter of checking on who is married to whom and using the age relationships previously developed. Paul's wife is Tess, who is youngest of all.

8. **(D)** The main idea here is to use the age relationships of the wives to help sort out the husbands. Since Wilma is older than Tess, their husbands Quincy and Paul must have the same relationship, thus, (D) is false.
   (A) is true since Roger, older than the oldest wife, must be the oldest of the group, and (B) is true since Tess must be the youngest of all. The husbands are older than the wives and she is the youngest wife. (C) is true since the wives of these two have just that relationship.
   (E) might or might not be true, but it is certainly not definitely false. The wives might be one day older than each other, or decades.

9. **(C)** Since the answer choices are all in terms of the marriages, let us arrange the information that way:

PAUL	27	QUINCY	29
TESS	28	WILMA	30
ROGER	31	SAM	33
VAL.	34	URS.	32

Note that since the husband are generally younger, it is not surprising that in three of the couples the wife is older.
Reading from this chart we see that (C) is false.

10. **(A)** This goes back to the original information and does not use the information from the previous problem. We simply have to sort out who is married to whom, and use the age relationships developed previously. The couples are P/V, Q/W, R/T, S/U and the ages are V > U > W > T. Sam's wife is still Ursula, and she is younger than only Valerie who is now Paul's wife, choice (A), eliminating (B). (C) and (D) would be correct before the switch in spouses, when Valerie, the oldest wife, was married to

Roger. Now, however, Tess, the youngest wife, is married to Roger so they are false. (E) similarly would have been true before the divorces and remarriages, but not now.

Questions 11–15

Arranging the Information

This is a problem where most of the action occurs in the questions rather than in the arranging of the given information. It is important, however, to get a grasp of what conditions there are.

There are three types of investments: corporate bonds, blue chip common stocks, and government securities. That is all there is unless something new is introduced in one of the questions. There is one regulation: One-third each in blue chips and government securities, which means that only the last third is discretionary for Williams. His other idea is that for the next year he would like bonds.

Answering the Questions

11. **(D)** Since Williams thinks that bonds are the best investment, but he can only put one-third of the fund's assets into them because of the regulations, one-third to each type of investment is the best he can do, choice (D).

    (B) and (C) violate the regulation. (A) and (E) violate Williams' sense of what is the best investment at this time.

12. **(C)** Although we noted in the previous problem that the best investment strategy, according to Williams' view of things, is one-third to each type of investment, he COULD invest two-thirds in blue chip stocks. The regulation only says that there is to be a minimum of the two categories, not a maximum. Two-thirds of $6 billion is $4 billion.

13. **(B)** This is a matter of what his preferences are. He likes bonds, so if the opportunity presents itself, he will buy them. (D) and (E) are entirely outside the scope of the problem set.

14. **(E)** Although the increase in the return of government securities sounds very large, this is not a question that depends on how closely you follow the investment markets. Within the scope of the problem, we cannot tell what this increase will mean. (A), (B), and (C) would only be good ideas if the new rate for government securities were higher than the rates for the other investments, which we simply do not know. If the rates were higher, he might well wish to change his investments, hence, (D) is not adequate. (E) is the only possible answer.

15. **(D)** The key here is that he has invested one-third each in the three types of investments. This means that he has the minimum possible amount of government securities and blue chip stocks. If he sells off, he must take care to maintain at least one-third of each of the required investments. Selling only government securities and blue chip stocks will definitely lead him to an illegal situation, so (D) is not possible.

    The others are all acceptable since he can have more than one-third of the fund invested in a required security if he wants. Let us work (A) in detail as an example: Suppose he starts with 30 units of each type of investment:

    BONDS 30 STOCKS 30 GOV'T. SEC. 30

    If he sells twice as many bonds as stocks, say 20 and 10, he will still be legal since the stocks will still be one-third.

    BONDS 10 STOCKS 20 GOV'T. SEC. 30

    Similar arguments apply to (B), and in a more general way to (C) and (E).

Questions 16–20

Arranging the Information

In a problem set of this sort, the major purpose of arranging the information in the beginning is to make it clear and easy to use. Unlike the first two problem sets in this section, there will not be many deductions to make prior to starting work on the problems.

The points to note are that BOTH calls and sales are used to judge Max's performance, so we cannot concentrate on just one of those factors. The statements that are phrased as "probably" should be construed as basically definite, especially in comparision to the even less certain other statements.

CUSTOMER	HOURS NEEDED	SALES IN BOXES
A	1	5
B	3	0 OR 20
C	1	10
D	1 TO 3	10 TO 30

Note that for Bell, the sale will be either 0 or 20—not anything in between. Also, for Deland there is no connection between the number of hours he is there and the size of the order he lands. It will take as long as it takes, and he will make the sale that he makes.

Answering the Questions

16. **(A)** The reasonable maximum will be what happens if everything goes as well as it possibly can. If Deland takes two hours or less, Max can see all four customers. If he gets the maximum order from each he will sell 5 + 20 + 10 + 30 = 65 boxes.

17. **(D)** Again the word *reasonably* implies that nothing really unexpected will happen. (A), none, is not at all expected. There is no real question about what the minimum for each customer is from the preceding chart. The real question is whether he sees them all or not. The problem answers this by noting that he will work eight hours, which is long enough for him to see all four customers. The minimum is, thus, 5 + 0 + 10 + 10 = 25 boxes.

18. **(C)** Max has 20 boxes sold, so the question is how many additional boxes can he sell from 2:00 P.M. to 5:00 P.M. If he sees Acme and Camera he will probably sell 15 boxes, but if he spends those three hours at Bell he might sell 20 boxes. Thus, the maximum is 20 boxes to Deland and possibly 20 more to Camera for a total of 40.

    If you wanted to say (A), you probably were just saying how many he could sell in the afternoon, while the problem requested the "daily" sales figure.

19. **(C)** If Max schedules Deland after 2:00 P.M., that is improper. He could not know that he will have enough time since he must allow three hours for Deland if it happens to take that long. In addition, he would not want to omit Deland since they might give him his biggest order of the day and have the largest minimum probable order (tie with Camera).

    For these reasons, (A), (B), and (D) are poor schedules.

    (E) is defective because it schedules four hours of work starting at 2:00 P.M., which runs past the 5:00 P.M. deadline set by the problem.

    Under schedule (C), Max will certainly see his best possibilities and still has a chance of seeing the fourth customer if things move quickly at Deland.

20. **(E)** In this situation, there is a 1½-hour slot before Edwards and 3½ hours afterwards. (A) and (E) try to fit a three-hour customer into the 1½-hour slot, which is wrong. (C) claims to provide for seeing Deland if time permits, but the only flexibility is the Deland appointment itself, which cannot be forecast, thus, (C) fails.

    The difference between (D) and (B) is whether to be sure of Acme or Camera. Since Camera is a larger sale, it should get the guaranteed spot in the morning, eliminating (D).

    A consideration not used much here, but of theoretical interest, is the choice between seeing Bell or Deland. He cannot see both of the three-hour customers. Deland is preferable to Bell for three reasons: (1) the minimum expected sale is higher, (2) the maximum expected sale is higher, and (3) there is the possibility of finishing early enough to also get to another customer.

Questions 21–25

Arranging the Information

This sort of information set is best approached with Venn, or three-circle, diagrams. This might even be true if there was a fourth category, but since there are only L, P, and Y, three circles will cover all the possibilities. First, the three circles without limitations:

DIAGRAM 1

Using statement I:

DIAGRAM 2

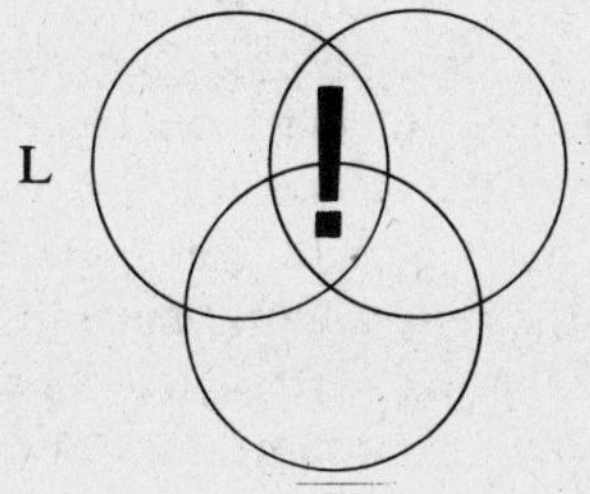

"!" = SOME

Using statement II: (See this for question 21.)

DIAGRAM 3

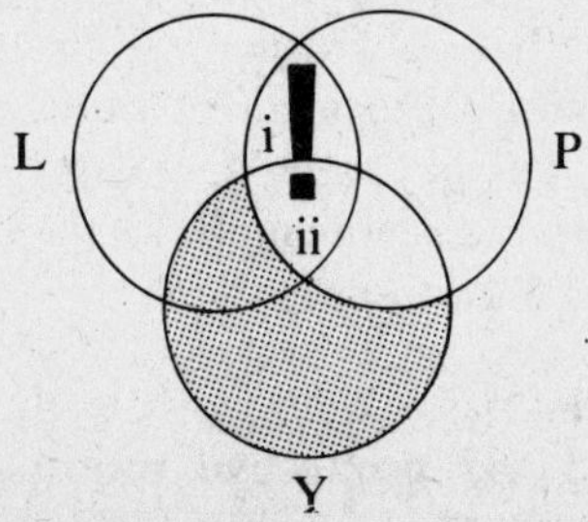

Using statement III:

DIAGRAM 4

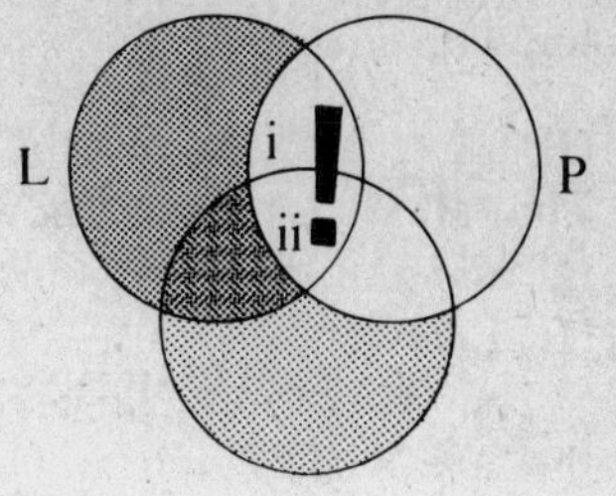

Statement IV is not, strictly speaking, the sort of information which is usually entered into a Venn diagram, but we must improvise. You could simply make a note on the side, but it is usually best to mark as much information in the diagram as possible. One way that this could be done here is to put a greater than sign (>) on the border between the two areas. This works well here since there are only two possible locations being addressed.

DIAGRAM 5

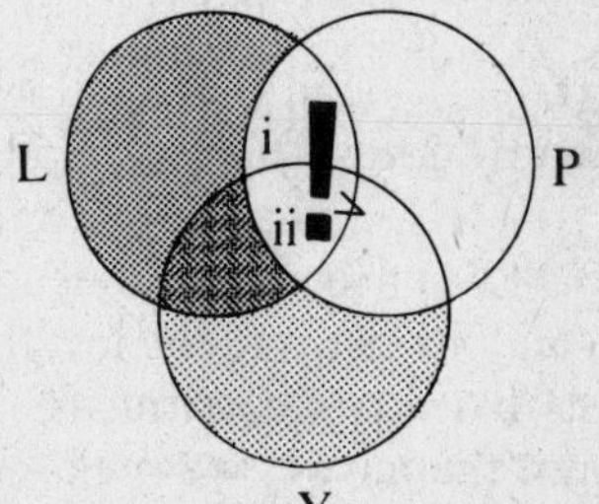

Answering the Questions

21. **(D)** First, let us approach this even without a diagram. If there are some L that are P, as statement I tells us, then those same L that are P are examples of P that are L. If some land animals are mammals, then some mammals are land animals. This justifies choice (D).

    Looking at the diagrams, we can see the same thing. The difficulty here is that the coding of the "some" idea seems inexact. The exclamation point deliberately covers two areas (marked i and ii in diagram 3) because it might be that either one of them is empty. We merely know that between the two of them there are some members. This is why (E) is not necessarily true. (B) and (C) are simply not justified from the diagram at all.

(B) does turn out to be true—LATER. With only I and II to go on, it cannot be known.

22. **(B)** Let us clear out the underbrush first. That all the L are P is known from statement III and the diagram, thus, (C) is false and (E) falls with it.

The other three choices concern the areas that are Y and P only and Y, P, and L, which are the two areas divided by the greater than sign. As previously noted, the exclamation sign written out does not mean that there must be anything in the latter category, so (A) might be true but need not be true.

(D) cannot be true since all Y are P, leaving (B).

(B) must be true since even if in that case the category L + P + Y is empty, the category of Y and P but not L is larger than L + P + Y and, thus, must contain at least one member.

23. **(D)** (A) and (E) are saying the same thing and address the same ideas discussed for #22 (B), and are true for the same reasons.

(C) concerns the same idea as (A) and (E) (and #22B), and the fact that there are some L that are P confirms (C) as true, and thus not the answer we seek.

(B) may not be true, since the area where P is by itself is only a possibility, but it certainly need not be false, so it is out.

(D) must be false since we have seen that all L are P (statement III) and if they are P they must be P or Y. If all giraffes are mammals, then it follows that all giraffes are either mammals or baseballs.

24. **(E)** What we are looking for is a statement that is uncertain. If a statement is certain, it is not the answer.

(A) is definitely true, from the diagram and statement II.

(B) is true for the same reasons as discussed above for #23 (D).

(C) is definitely false because of the word *must.* It is wrong to say that they "must," even though it might be true that they are that way.

(D) is false for the reasons discussed in #22.

Thus, (E) is correct.

25. **(D)** This problem revolves around the greater than sign in the diagram, which derives from statement IV of the original information.

I is false, because there are more P that are Y and not L than the ten who are all three at once, so the total sharing P and Y is 21 or more.

II could be true since there is no information about the number of members of the P-only portion of the diagram.

III is also possible since that area (i of diagram three) is not limited as to its numbers. Hence, (D) is correct.

SECTION II

1. **(B)** The passage makes only one geographic reference and that is to England, with the use of "this is the question" for England. Thus, (A), (C), and (D) are out. Since the author is doing a fairly modern analysis of the problems of distributing wealth, it is not likely that he lived in King Arthur's time. Hence, (B) rather than (E).

2. **(C)** (B), (D), and (E) are eliminated on the simple grounds that there is nothing in the passage on which to base them. The preference for (C) over (A) is not great, but can be arrived at by considering that what the author is advocating is paying less attention to the wages and the money part of the economy and more towards its ultimate ends. The denial of the virtue of money and the implication that the rich are robbers (by analogy) also tend away from capitalism at least, if not toward socialism.

3. **(D)** (D) is included in the concluding sentence of the passage. (A) and (E) are specifically disputed in the passage, since it is the entire process that matters and not merely the pay rate or effort. (C) is not disputed, but is not emphasized either, while (B) is simply absent.

4. **(E)** The passage emphasizes that it is the ends of the productive process that are critical, thus, giving some support to (E). (C) has some appeal since money as such is

not too important to the author, but its uses are important. (A), (B), and (D) derive any attractiveness they may have solely from the relative obscurity of (E).

5. **(A)** While the author stops short of outright accusation of the rich as robbers, they are treated in much the same manner in the passage, which creates the analogy desired.
   (E) is untrue. The author says that one might as well say the robber is a benefactor, or at least does no harm, but this is a way of disputing a statement, not agreeing with it.
   (D) fails since destruction is generally opposed to waste, while (B) and (C) are incorrect because only dishonesty is mentioned in relation to business.

6. **(C)** The choice is between (A) and (C). (B) is of no interest to the author, while (D) is only acceptable for the last three words. (E) is relevant but far too general.
   (A) refers to the last sentence and (C) refers to the sentence immediately after the posing of the great question. The distinction here is that (A) describes the great question for ALL members of society, while (C) describes the plight of the poor specifically.

7. **(B)** (B) is preferable because it is something that helps to provide the necessities of life—clean air and water, etc. (D) fails since it does not specify the job. (A) is not strong since weapons are generally destructive, though this is not impossible. (C) is less attractive than (B) since it has no stated positive value. The dislike of the rich would also enter into it. (E) is attractive since it is clear that this is something of which the author has done a great deal. It is clearly the second-best choice, but is not as good as (B), since there is no clear message in the passage as to the value of studying theory. If (E) specifically were the arousal of the laborer to his best interests, that might be even better than (B) since it would mean all would do good work and not just the one.

8. **(E)** (D) is of no interest to the author. (A), (B), and (C) are topics mentioned in the passage, but only as serving the general analysis of the Planning Commission's proposal. Thus, (E) is more descriptive of the actual passage.

9. **(D)** The author's argument essentially states that the commission may be right as far as it goes, but it "is not that simple." This implies that the commission has been shortsighted. It is true that because of the shortsightedness, the author views the plan as foolish, and perhaps somewhat ignorant, but these derive from the shortsightedness, and the tone is respectful rather than condemnatory. (A) and (B) have no basis.

10. **(D)** (A) is attractive, but the word "complete" kills it. The author is clearly unsure of the number of beds that should be closed and sees that as a future issue. (B) and (C) fail for the same reason. (E) sounds good, but is not really mentioned.

11. **(C)** All of the statements are agreeable to the author, but (C) is specifically stated by the passage not to be properly addressed in the context of the commission's proposal. Because of (A) and (E), large hospitals may not be more efficient. (B) and (D) are both reasons why small hospitals should not be closed.

12. **(A)** (A) is only half agreeable. The author states the larger centers provide more complex care, and if the larger hospitals do not provide the most efficient care—as the author claims they don't—then it is certainly probable that they do not definitely provide better care than smaller hospitals of the sort that can be received at both kinds of facilities.
    (B) is inferable from the statement that only overall costs are used to set rates. (C) is inferable from the author's support of the existence of institutions that can only provide that sort of care, while also supporting quality. (D) is stated to be a possible problem. (E) is inferable from the concern shown for greater or lesser access in the third and fifth paragraphs.

13. **(B)** The author knows that he cannot simply say to the commission that they shouldn't close the smaller hospitals. He

must present evidence that it is not the best approach to the agreed goal of saving money and closing unneeded beds, hence, (B). (A) is false since closing beds is agreed with by the author. (C) is true, but not as precise as (B); also the word *another* is troublesome since it is actually an alternative which is proposed. (D) is not currently at issue. (E) is appealing, but the inefficiencies of larger hospitals are not stated to be in the use of space.

14. **(A)** Prisons are, in a manner of speaking, service organizations (like hospitals), and thus very large ones may not be more efficient, according to the author. Thus, (A). (B) is probably just what the author wants, since he is unsure of the number of beds that should be closed anyway. (C) is stated to be agreeable to the author in the last paragraph. (D) and (E) are indeterminable. There is no basis for agreement or disagreement given in the passage.

15. **(D)** (D) is directly from the passage. (A) is attractive, but is the reason that the gentleman rarely engages in debate. Once he is engaged, he is as (D) would have it; similarly for (E).

16. **(B)** The fourth sentence of the first paragraph provides the source of answer (B). All the others are unpleasant, and the gentleman is pleasant.

17. **(A)** "Scrupulous" means careful, and since the gentleman is always generous in his interpretations of the actions of others, he will be slow to believe ill of their motives, as (A) states. (B), (C), and (E) all are unpleasant failings that a gentleman does not have. (D) only follows if you see the gentleman as a wimp, which the author does not.

18. **(D)** Clothes may make the man, but not the gentleman according to this author, or at least he is silent on that subject. Clothes are a physical attribute, while all of the others are spiritual, which is what the passage is about.

19. **(B)** (B) is hard to fault and is nearly perfect. (E) has some small merit since the passage does concern mental and spiritual qualities, but much of the passage concerns the actions of a gentleman as well.

20. **(E)** The intention is to be positive in the assessment of the gentleman's feeling at this point, so (B), (C), and (D) are out. (A) has merit only in the root meaning of the word, but this is a special use and delicacy is intended, thus, (E) not (A).

21. **(C)** He seems like a "disciple," but not from faith but only from reason. (A) fails since a gentleman is not even always right in his disputes, and thus they could oppose each other—in a gentlemanly way. (B) is specifically opposed by the preceding discussion of (C). (D) and (E) are too extreme. While admirable, the gentleman is not without opposition and dislike from others less meritorious than he.

22. **(C)** The author makes it clear in the latter part of the passage that he neither endorses nor opposes Nelson's theory, nor does he present an alternative, thus, (A), (B), and (D) are out. (E) is the second-best choice and is one part of the passage, but it is included in (C), while (C) covers the passage well without error.

23. **(E)** Skeptical is not merely questioning, but bordering on definite disinclination to believe, which makes (A) too strong for the passage, which is rather scientific, (E). Though thorough to a degree, there are many points at which further details could be stated and are not included—which brands and expenses, etc.

24. **(C)** (A), (B), and (E) are without merit, but both (D) and (C) have some support in the author's statements that Nelson's theory is somewhat supported by the findings. (D) fails because the needed research does not have to be done by Nelson.

25. **(D)** There is no reason stated in the passage that Nelson could not have tested his

own theory, nor indication that he isn't doing so. (A), (B), (C), and (E) are stated in the passage and logically related to the theory.

26. **(B)** This is almost a Logical Reasoning question. I would more confirm than oppose Nelson's theory, though only for the special case of new products.

II violates Nelson's requirement that the advertising not affect the consumer's ability to make evaluations of the product. If most advertising did this, then at the very least Nelson's hypothesis would apply to relatively little advertising and would be less powerful, if not actually wrong.

III is merely a statement of why some products are not advertised. Nelson's hypothesis is that those that ARE advertised heavily are good and he does not imply that the non-advertised products are bad or that there cannot be reasons other than quality that they are not advertised heavily. Thus, II only, (B).

27. **(B)** Nelson's hypothesis applies to "experience" products that are relatively cheap products that are bought frequently. Of the available options, caviar, (B), is clearly the least cheap and the least likely to be bought frequently.

28. **(A)** The second paragraph ends with a statement of the controversy about the informational content of advertising generally, but the third paragraph picks up with television advertising in particular, which supports the inference that television advertising is the major part of advertising—at least as far as the article is concerned. (B) is untenable since the hypothesis is never accepted, but only stated to be weakly supported. (C) has more justification, but there seem to be reasons enough for the caution of the author. (D) and (E) simply don't happen.

SECTION III

1. **(B)** The proposition that you cannot argue with taste says that taste is relative. Since we are looking for an answer choice inconsistent with that proposition, we seek an answer choice that argues that taste, or aesthetic value, is absolute, or at least not relative; that there are standards of taste. (B) is precisely that.

(C) and (D) are just distractions, playing on the notion of taste in the physical sense and the further idea of the distasteful; but these superficial connections are not strong enough.

(A), (B), and (E) are all activities in which there is some element of aesthetic judgment or appreciation. In (A), the holding of an exhibition, while implying some selection principle and thus some idea of a standard of taste, does not truly purport to judge aesthetics in the way that (B), precisely a beauty *contest,* does. The exhibition may be of historical or biographical interest, for example. (E) also stresses more of the exhibition aspect than the judging aspect. You should not infer that all movie festivals are contests, since the word "festival" does not require this interpretation and, in fact, there are festivals at which the judging aspect is minimal or non-existent. The Cannes Film Festival, while perhaps the best-known, is not the only type of movie festival there is. The questions are not tests of your knowledge of the movie industry.

2. **(D)** Note the question stem very carefully: We are to find the answer choice *from which* we can deduce the sample argument. You must pay very careful attention to the question stem in every problem. (D) works very nicely as it gives us the argument structure: All post-1974 students are required. . . . George is a post-1974 student. Therefore, George is required. . . . Actually, the middle premise is phrased in the conditional (with an "if"), but our explanation is close enough, even if it is a bit oversimplified. (A) will not suffice, for while it describes the situation before 1974, it just does not address itself to the post-1974 situation. And George is a post-1974 student. (B) also fails. From the fact that all of those who took the course graduated after 1974, we cannot conclude that George was

one of them (any more than we can conclude from the proposition that all airline flight attendants lived after 1900 and that Richard Nixon, who lived after 1900, was one of them). (C) fails for the same reason that (A) fails. (E) is a bit tricky because of the double negative. It makes the sentence awkward. The easiest way to handle such a sentence is to treat the double negative as an affirmative. The negative cancels the negative, just as in arithmetic a negative number times a negative number yields a positive number. So (E) actually says that before 1974 the course was not required. That is equivalent to (A) and must be wrong for the same reason.

3. **(B)** II is the only one of the three which is completely supported by the argument. III is easily dismissed. That there are no minnows on this side of the lake now surely does not mean that there will never be any, any more than the fact that there are no children in the park now means that there never will be any children in the park. I is very close to II and differs only in the qualification introduced by the word *probably,* but that is an important qualification. The author states specifically that bass are *usually* found wherever there are minnows. So where there are no bass, he *expects* to find no minnows. But, of course, he cannot be certain. Perhaps there are other reasons for the absence of bass: The water is too cold or too shallow or too muddy for bass though not for minnows. So I overstates the case. The author apparently allows that you may find minnows without bass—but not usually.

4. **(D)** Juanita wonders how Tommy knows the phone has rung if he couldn't hear it because of the shower. She overlooks the possibility that he learned the phone had rung without actually hearing it himself. Perhaps someone else lives with him who heard it; perhaps Tommy has an answering machine and later learned that the phone rang while he was in the shower; maybe the caller calls back and tells Tommy he called earlier and Tommy says "Oh, I must have been in the shower and didn't hear it." Juanita overlooks these possibilities. (A) is incorrect because Juanita apparently assumes the phone does ring and that Tommy can hear it ringing. (C) and (E) may or may not be true, but they do not address themselves to Juanita's statement. (B) could only underlie Juanita's objection to Tommy's remarks if hearing calls were the only possible way in which Tommy could learn of the call. But as we show, there are other possibilities.

5. **(E)** I is not inconsistent with the advertisement since the ad is touting the strength of the pain reliever, not its price. III, too, can easily be seen not to be inconsistent. The ad speaks of non-prescription pain-relievers, but III brings up the irrelevant matter of prescription pain-relievers. II is not inconsistent because RELIEF does not claim to be the one strong*est* pain-reliever, only that no other non-prescription pain-reliever is stronger. So none of the statements contradicts the ad.

6. **(C)** III is an assumption of the psychologist. He observed the dogs for a certain period of time, and found that each time a stranger approached they kept silent. From those observed instances he concluded that the dogs never barked at strangers. Obviously his theory would be disproved (or at least it would have to be seriously qualified) if, when he was not watching, the dogs barked their heads off at strangers. I is not assumed, however. The psychologist was concerned only with the dogs' reactions to strangers. As far as we know, he may have seen the dogs barking during a frolic in the park, or while they were being bathed, or at full moon. II is not an assumption the author makes. The author makes a factual claim: Dogs treated in this way do not bark at strangers. We have no basis for concluding that the author does or does not think that dogs ought or ought not to bark at strangers. In fact, it seems as likely that the author thinks a great way to train watchdogs is to hit them with rolled-up newspapers.

7. **(B)** II would undermine the psychologist's thesis that "only a beaten dog barks." It cites instances in which the dog was not

beaten and still barked at strangers. This would force the psychologist to reconsider his conclusion about the connection between beating and barking. I is not like II. It does not state the dogs were never beaten; it states only that the dogs were not beaten when they barked at strangers. It is conceivable that they were beaten at other times. If they were, then even though they might bark at strangers (and not be beaten at that moment), they would not be counter-examples to the psychologist's theory. III is not an assumption of the psychologist, as we saw in the preceding question, so denying it does not affect the strength of his argument. The psychologist is concerned with the factual connection between beating a dog and its barking; information about the owners' feelings can hardly be relevant to that factual issue.

8. **(B)** Here the author must assume that every effect which is part of the child's experience has been generated by a cause which was also a part of the child's experience, but that is possible only on the assumption that that cause, which is an effect itself, is the result of some previous cause. In other words, every effect flows from some earlier effect. Now, admittedly that seems to lead to a pretty absurd conclusion: Therefore, there could be no beginning of experience for the child—it must stretch back infinitely. But the question stem does not ask us to critique the argument, only to analyze it and uncover its premises. (A) is wrong because the author does not say all experiences are alike, only that the one today has its roots in the one yesterday. For example, sometimes the presence of moisture in the atmosphere causes rain, sometimes snow. (C) oversimplifies matters in two respects. One, while the author may agree that a child's experiences may tell us *something* about the parents (assuming the child is in intimate contact with them), we surely would not want to conclude that is the *best* way to learn about the parents. Two, the parents are not the only source of experience the child has, so the later effects would be the result of non-parental causes as well. (D) is incorrect because the author need not assume that experience is cumulative. In some cases, the cause and effect sequence may only reiterate itself so that experience is circular rather than cumulative. Finally, (E) is another example of going too far—of extending a simple factual statement beyond the scope the author originally gave it. Here the author says that experience causes experience, but he never suggests that we are in a position to use this principle practically, to manipulate the input to mold the child.

9. **(C)** The author's claim is that we have unbounded resources, and he tries to prove this by showing that we are getting better and better at extracting those resources from the ground. But that is like saying "I have found a way of get the last little bit of toothpaste out of the tube, therefore, the tube will never run out." (C) calls our attention to this oversight. (A) does not contradict the author's claim. In fact, it seems to support it. He might suggest, "Even if we run out of fossil fuels, we still have uranium for nuclear power." Now, this is not to suggest that he would. The point is only to show that (A) supports rather than undermines the author's contention. (B) is an attack on the author's general stance, but it does not really *contradict* the particular conclusion he draws. The author says, "We have enough." (B) says, "It is expensive." Both could very well be true, so they cannot contradict one another. (D) is similar to (B). Yes, you may be correct, the technology is expensive, or in this case wasteful, but it will still get us the fuel we need. Finally, (E) is incorrect for pretty much these same reasons. Yes, the energy will have unwanted side effects, but the author claimed only that we could get the energy. The difficulty with (B), (D), and (E) is that though they attack the author's general *position,* though they undermine his general suggestion, they do not *contradict* his *conclusion*.

Questions 10–12

10. **(A)** 11. **(D)** 12. **(C)** Argument (A) is circular. It is like saying, "I never tell a lie; and you must believe that because, as I have

just told you, I never tell a lie." So (A) is the answer to question 10. (E) might seem circular: Guns do not cause crimes, people do. But it is not. The author's point is that these crimes would be committed anyway, and he explains how they would be committed. (C) is an *ad hominem* attack. It rejects the conclusion of the argument not because the argument is illogical but because it comes from a particular source. Remember, as we learned in the statement credibility questions, not all *ad hominem* are illegitimate. It is perfectly all right to inquire into possible biases of the source, and that is just what occurs here. So (C) is the answer to question 12. (D) is a fairly weak argument. It takes a handful of observed instances and generalizes to a strong conclusion. But even though it may be weak, it does fit the description "generalization," so (D) is the answer to question 11. (B) is just left over and fits none of the descriptions.

13. **(A)** The author places himself in opposition to the sociologists whom he cites. He claims an alternative interpretation of the evidence. In other words, the most logical continuation of the passage will be the one which explains why such sects are not a recent phenomenon even though there are no old ones around. (A) does this neatly. Since the members abstain from sexual relations, they will not reproduce members and the sect will tend to die out. This explains why there are none more than fifty or sixty years old. (C), if anything, supports the position of the sociologists for it implicitly gives up trying to explain the evidence differently and also undercuts the explanation the author might have given. (B) is irrelevant because intensity of religious fervor is irrelevant to the length of the sect's existence; it cannot possibly help the author explain away the evidence of the sociologists. (D) is irrelevant for another reason. The author needs to explain why the sects are all relatively young without having recourse to the thesis of the sociologists that they are a recent phenomenon. That there are other organizations which encourage sexual relationships of whatever kind cannot help the author explain a phenomenon such as the Waiters. Finally, (E) is a distraction, picking up as it does on a minor detail. The author needs to explain the short-livedness of groups of which the Waiters is only an example.

14. **(E)** The conclusion of the speaker is that the checkup has *no* value, so anything which suggests the checkup does have value will undermine the conclusion. I shows a possible advantage of having the checkup. It says, in effect, while the checkup is not foolproof, and will not catch everything, it does catch some fairly important things. II also gives us a possible reason for visiting our mechanic for a 5,000-mile checkup. Even if it won't keep our car in running order, it is necessary if we want to take advantage of our warranty. Finally, III also gives us a good reason to have a checkup: the mechanic will make some routine adjustments. All three of these propositions, then, mention possible advantages of having a checkup. So all three weaken the author's conclusion that the checkup is *worthless* and a waste of money and time.

15. **(A)** Here we are looking for the most perfect analogy. Keep in mind, first, that the author opposes the move, and second, all of the features of the union-management situation, in particular that they are adversaries. (A) captures both elements. The relationship between prison administrators and inmates is adversarial, and the suggestion that inmates make decisions on security is outrageous enough that it captures also the first element. (B) fails on both counts. First, the two are not on opposites of the fence; second, the senior officer is *asking* for advice—not deferring to the opinion of his junior officer. (C) is very similar. First, the administration of the university and the student body are not necessarily adversaries; at least, although they may disagree on the best means for advancing the goals of the university, there is often agreement about those goals. Second, the administration is, as with (B), *asking* advice, not abdicating responsibility for the decision. In (D) we lack both elements; the mayor need not be an adversary of the state legislators (he may be seeking their assis-

tance); nor is he giving them his authority to make decisions. Finally, (E) lacks both elements as well; the minister is a leader, not an adversary, who is discussing questions, not delegating authority.

16. **(E)** The author's reason for rejecting the notion of labor participation in management decisions is that the labor leaders first have a responsibility to the people they represent and that the responsibility would color their thinking about the needs of the corporation. His thinking is reflected in the adage, and this could easily have been worked into an LSAT-type question: No man can serve two masters. (B) is incorrect for the author is referring to the labor *leaders,* not the rank-and-file; and he specifically mentions that the leaders are skilled administrators. (D) is incorrect because it, too, fails to respect the distinction between union leader and union member. (A) is a distraction. The notion that the authority would be "symbolically undermined" is edifying but finds no support in the paragraph. In any event, it entirely misses the main point of the paragraph as we have explained it. (C) also fails to observe the distinction between leader and worker, not to mention also that it is only remotely connected with the discussion.

17. **(B)** The difficulty with Wilfred's position is that he tries to blame the trombone rather than himself for the poor sound. Only (B) points up this deficiency in Wilfred's argument: Since he has not studied it as thoroughly as he has other instruments, he should not expect to meet with the same success he has with others. Whether some persons find the trombone easy or difficult relative to other instruments has no bearing on the fact that Wilfred has not *studied* the trombone sufficiently, so (A) and (D) are incorrect. Also, instruments which Wilfred has not studied have no relevance to his claim about those he has studied, so (E) is wrong. Finally, (C) is somewhat like (B), but it just does not zero in on the weakness in Wilfred's argument in the way (B) does. It may be true that Wilfred has studied some other instruments which he does not find easy, but what we are looking for is an answer choice which attacks the argument in some way. (C) does not uncover and attack a hidden assumption as (B) does, for whether other instruments have been difficult for Wilfred is irrelevant. Nor does (C) attack the linkage between the premise (I have trouble playing this instrument) and the conclusion (It does not have a nice sound) in the way (B) does.

18. **(A)** If II is true, then both independent clauses of II must be true. This is because a sentence which has the form "P and Q" (Eddie is tall and John is short) can be true only if both sub-parts are true. If either is false (Eddie is not tall or John is not short) or if both are false, then the entire sentence makes a false claim. If the second clause of II is true, then I must also be true, for I is actually equivalent to the second clause in II. That is, if "P and Q" is true, then Q must itself be true. On this basis, (B) and (C) can be seen to be incorrect. (D) is wrong, for we can actually define the interrelationship of I and II as a matter of logic: we do not have to have recourse to a probabilistic statement; i.e., it is *unlikely*. (E) is incorrect since a statement of the form "P and Q" might be false and Q could still be true—if P is false "P and Q" is false even though Q is true.

19. **(D)** Again, let us resort to the use of capital letters to make it easier to talk about the propositions. Incidentally, you may or may not find this technique useful under test conditions. Some people do, but others do not. We use it here because it makes explanation easier. Let us render the four premises as:

(1)	All B are R.	(All Buckner are Reserve)
(2)	All R are P.	(All Reserve are Priceless)
(3)	No H is R.	(No Hemingway is Reserve)
(4)	All R are C.	(All Reserve are Catalogue)

From this we can deduce:	(5) All B are P.	(using 1 and 2)
and:	(6) No H is B.	(using 1 and 3)

Since "No B is H" is equivalent to "no H is B" (there is no overlap between the two categories), (D) must be our correct answer. From (2), we would not want to conclude "all P are R," any more than we would go from "all station wagons are cars" to "all cars are station wagons"; so (A) is not a proper inference and cannot be our answer. As for (B), we can show that "all B are C" (using 1 and 4) and also "all B are P" (5), so we would be wrong in concluding that "no B are not P." As for (C), while we know that "no H is R," we would not want to conclude that "no H is P." After all, books by Hemingway may be priceless, but the Buckner collection and the Reserve Room may just not contain any. Finally, (E) is not deducible from our four propositions. We cannot deduce "all C is R" from "all R is C."

20. **(E)** Now, it must be admitted that a liar can abuse just about any word in the English language, and so it is true that each of the five answer choices is *conceivably* correct. But it is important to keep in mind that you are looking for the BEST answer, which will be the one word which, more than all the others, is likely to abuse. As for (A), while there may be different ways of doing a random selection, we should be able to decide whether a sample was, in fact, selected fairly. Although the ad may be lying about the selection of participants in the study, we should be able to determine whether they are lying. In other words, though they may not have selected the sample randomly, they cannot escape by saying, "Oh, by *random* we meant anyone who liked the Goblin." The same is true of (C), *first.* That is a fairly clear term. You add up the answers you got, and one will be at the top of the list. The same is true of (D), a "response" is an answer. Now (B) is open to manipulation. By asking our question correctly, that is, by finagling a bit with what we mean by *handling,* we can influence the answers we get. For example, compare: "Did you find the Goblin handled well?" "Did you find the Goblin had a nice steering wheel?" "Did you find the wheel was easy to turn?" We could keep it up until we found a question that worked out to give a set of "responses" from "randomly" selected drivers who would rank the Goblin "first." Now, if the one category itself is susceptible to manipulation, imagine how much easier it will be to manipulate a "composite" category. We have only to take those individual categories in which the Goblin scored well, construct from them a "composite" category, and announce the Goblin "first" in the overall category. There is also the question of how the composite was constructed, weighted, added, averaged, etc.

21. **(A)** The explanation given is no explanation at all. It is like a mechanic saying to a motorist, "Your car did not get over this steep hill because it did not have enough grade climbing power." While the author may have speculated about when and how his death would occur, it cannot be said that his explanation is speculative. So (A) is correct, not (B). Of course, since the explanation is merely circular, it cannot be considered medically sound, any more than our hypothetical mechanic's answer is sound as a matter of automotive engineering, so (D) must be wrong. As for (C), while the author's *announcement* may be self-serving, designed to aggrandize his reputation, the *explanation* he gives in the announcement is not. Finally, the explanation is not self-authenticating, that is, it does not provide that standard by which its own validity is to be measured. So (E) can be overruled.

22. **(D)** It is important not to attribute more to an author than he actually says or implies. Here the author states only that Ronnie's range is narrow so he will not be an *outstanding vocalist. Vocalizing* is only one kind of music career, so I, which speaks of professional *musicians,* takes us far beyond the claim the author actually makes. II also goes beyond what the author says. He never specifies what range an outstanding vocalist needs, much less what range is required to vocalize without being outstanding. Finally, III is an assumption since the author moves from a physical characteristic to a conclusion regarding ability.

23. **(C)** You should remember that there is a very important distinction to be drawn between "numbers" and "percentages." For example, an increase from one murder per year to two murders per year can be

described as a "whopping big 100% increase." The argument speaks only of percentages, so we would not want to conclude anything about the numbers underlying those percentages. Therefore, both (A) and (B) are incorrect. They speak of "more agents," and "more people," and those are numbers rather than percentages. Furthermore, if we would not want to draw a conclusion about numbers from data given in percentage terms, we surely would not want to base on percentages a conclusion about efficiency or work accomplished. Thus, (D) and (E) are incorrect. What makes (C) the best answer of the five is the possibility of making percentage comparisons *within* each agency. Within both agencies, the number of field agents increased by a greater *percentage or proportion* than the non-field agents.

24. **(D)** Keeping in mind our comments about (D) and (E) in the preceding question, (A) must be wrong. We do not want to conclude from sheer number of employees anything about the actual work accomplished. (B) and (E) are incorrect for pretty much the same reason. The question stem asks us to give an argument *defending* the CIA against the *claim* that it is *overstaffed*. Neither rate of pay nor appropriations has anything to do with whether or not there are too many people on the payroll. (C) is the second-best answer, but it fails because it does not keep in mind the ratio of non-field to field agents. Our concern is not with the number of agents generally, but the number of *support* and *supervisory* workers (reread the question stem). (D) focuses on this nicely by explaining why the CIA should experience a faster increase (which is to say, a greater percentage increase) in the number of its supervisory personnel than the FBI.

25. **(B)** This is essentially an analogy question. Argument from analogy is an important form of argument, and the LSAT has many different ways of determining whether or not a student can use that argumentative technique. In this question, we are looking for the tool which is most analogous to a rule-of-thumb moral principle. Our task is made easier by the string of adjectives which follows the blank. We need a tool which is useful in many situations, which rules out a tuning fork (D) and an electrical generator (C), both of which have highly specialized functions. Moreover, we need a tool which requires no special training, so we can eliminate answer (A). Finally, although a library book requires no special training, it has only one use—to be read. Though the knowledge it contains may be generally useful, the book itself, *qua* book, has only one use.

26. **(A)** The point of the passage is that a moral decision sometimes seems difficult because we are using moral principles which are too general. They work most of the time, but sometimes they are too abstract, and as a result, two or more of them give contradictory results. (D) and (E) are wrong, then, for they confuse the value of abstract and particular principles. When a conflict arises, we need principles which are more specific, not more abstract, (D) and particularly (E). (C) is a distraction; the medical character of the example was purely fortuitous and irrelevant to the author's point about moral reasoning. (B) is edifying but hardly a logical completion of the paragraph. The author is not trying to explain advances in moral reasoning; he is explaining two different levels of moral reasoning available to us now.

SECTION IV

Set 1

OVERVIEW: In this set, the two rules conflict because they define two different crimes. Either someone is guilty of manslaughter under Rule I, or he is guilty of felony murder under Rule II. Here is where we perhaps caught some students who have some prior familiarity with the law. Some students probably thought the two rules were consistent. They reasoned even if you cannot get him for murder, you can get him for manslaughter since the one is a lesser-included offense of the other. While this is true in the real world—that is, if the prosecutor cannot get a conviction for the more serious crime, he may settle for a conviction on the less serious count—

we must remember that the LSAT instructs to treat these rules as being of equal importance. Either someone fits under Rule I or he fits under Rule II. There is no middle ground of the sort that this fits well under Rule I and Rule II.

1. **(A)** This is the conflict we just mentioned. Hart's actions do fit within Rule I, because he shot the gun in a rage. But Hart's actions also fit with Rule II since he was involved in the commission of a felony at the time the shooting occurred. Since the rules are mutually exclusive, defining as they do two separate crimes, we must choose between the two.

2. **(D)** This question would not help us resolve the dispute. We certainly do not need it for the application of Rule II, and for the application of Rule I we need only know that Hart was in a rage. Hart was in a rage because Jackson was shot, but Hart may not have known the extent of Jackson's wounds (that is left open), and we do not need that information to read the plain statement that Hart flew into a rage.

3. **(D)** This is irrelevant to the dispute at the end of the facts. We are trying to decide whether Hart and Jackson are guilty of some crime. Whether Merrick, too, is guilty of some crime in keeping a gun is irrelevant to assessing the guilt of the other two.

4. **(C)** Since Jackson did not fire the gun in the first place, his actions do not fall within the scope of the first rule, so there cannot be a conflict here. Only Rule II applies to Jackson's actions, and they fit nicely within the rule. He was committing a felony and someone was killed in the process. Rule II says anyone participating is guilty of first degree murder, so Jackson need not have been the one to pull the trigger.

Set 2

OVERVIEW: The general rule is that an owner can have a trespasser removed (Rule I), but Rule II states that there are circumstances under which the owner cannot have the trespasser removed, i.e., if the trespasser has been there long enough he becomes the owner, displacing the original owner. In our case we have just such a situation. Gardner built a house on Corn Acres in 1953 and lived there, claiming Corn Acres as his own (he believed he owned it, according to the facts). So when Ditmore tries to have Gardner removed in 1976, twenty years have passed making Rule II applicable to the situation. This would force a choice between Rule I, by which Ditmore wins, and Rule II, by which Gardner wins.

5. **(D)** When Farnsworth first began to farm the land, he was a trespasser, but that information, while deducible through an application of Rule I, does not bear on the issue of current ownership. Gardner lived on Corn Acres long enough to establish his ownership without regard to Farnsworth's actions. But compare #10 which follows.

6. **(A)** This is the conflict we spotted in the set overview. According to Rule I, Gardner is a trespasser on Ditmore's land, and Ditmore may have him removed. But by the terms of Rule II, the land now belongs to Gardner, who has acquired it by adverse possession. The rules give different results, so a choice would be required.

7. **(C)** This question asks us to make an additional assumption. Suppose that Ditmore had brought his action in 1953. What would Gardner's status have been then? Rule II does not apply since Gardner had not yet been there for the required twenty years; but Rule I would have applied, so we can deduce that Ditmore could have had Gardner removed at that time.

8. **(C)** This question asks us to make an application of the second rule to the facts. To acquire by adverse possession one must have resided on the land for twenty years. Did Gardner live there for twenty years? The answer is "yes," from 1953 until 1976. Notice that this is not an answer (A) because we are not asked about the ultimate outcome of the case, only one of the preliminary issues leading up to the ultimate outcome.

9. **(D)** This is irrelevant to the application of the rules. Neither mentions the value of the

property, so even if we had this information, it would not further our understanding of how to apply the rules.

10. **(B)** This is an interesting question. In 1969, Gardner would not have accumulated enough time to give him adverse possession (1953 through 1969 is only sixteen years, not twenty). On the other hand, Farnsworth had used the land for sometime before that, enough time so that if Gardner could add that to his own time, Gardner could claim adverse possession in 1969. But is that legitimate? Well, it certainly seems plausible, but we would admittedly need some additional rule. So, (B).

Set 3

OVERVIEW: The kind of case in which these rules conflict will be one in which one person is injured through the careless actions of another, but in circumstances in which his own careless conduct contributed something to the accident. In such circumstances, Rule I allows the injured person to recover, while Rule II denies him recovery. In our case Blackwell was injured by Williams' carelessness. Williams ran the red light. On the other hand, although Blackwell had the right-of-way, the accident would not have occurred but for his own speeding. So Blackwell's own carelessness added something to the collision. Whether Blackwell is entitled to recover against Williams would require us to make a choice between the two rules.

11. **(D)** This is irrelevant to the application of either rule. Now, it is true that the facts state that driving without a valid inspection sticker is a crime, but the lack of a sticker in no way contributed to the accident. The facts clearly state the car was in *perfect* condition.

12. **(C)** This does not require a choice between the two rules; it requires only an application of a key concept in the second rule to the facts. Using the concept of contributory negligence given us in Rule II, we can deduce that Blackwell was indeed negligent in a way which contributed to the occurrence of the accident.

13. **(A)** This question raises the ultimate issue: Will Blackwell win or lose? This issue, as we observed in the set overview, will require a choice between the two rules. On Rule I, Blackwell will win since the accident was caused (at least partially) by Williams' running the light. On the other hand, Rule II states Blackwell cannot win since he contributed to the accident.

14. **(D)** This is irrelevant since Williams is the defendant. The question of contributory negligence, and the conflict we highlight in #13, is important only with regard to the suing party. The rule never mentions anything about contributory negligence by a defendant.

15. **(B)** This seems to present us with an open question. On the one hand, Blackwell was speeding and would not even have been in the intersection at the time of the collision if he had been driving within the speed limit. (He would have arrived later, after Williams had gone through.) But then again, it seems that driving slower would not have prevented the accident if he had been there at the time. This suggests that we need some further rule to assess the importance of Blackwell's violating the speed laws.

Set 4

OVERVIEW: According to Rule I, a person does not have to answer questions which might incriminate him, and his refusal to do so does not expose him to any penalty. According to Rule II, however, if he has been granted immunity from prosecution for those crimes, his refusal to answer questions about them constitutes contempt of court and that carries a penalty. So the two rules conflict in those cases where a person has been granted immunity and still refuses to respond regarding some criminal activity. Remember, we must treat the two rules as being of equal importance; neither can override or subsume the other.

16. **(C)** The answer to this question is affirmative. Stone's answers would show that he had been involved in such activity, and that

information is critical in determining whether, by the terms of Rule I, Stone is liable to penalties for his refusal to answer.

17. **(C)** Again, the answer to this question is yes, and it is preliminary to determining whether Stone is liable to any penalty. According to Rule II, he would be because he is in contempt. But compare #20, which follows.

18. **(D)** Whether or not Taylor will ultimately be convicted of fraud has no bearing on the question whether Stone must answer the questions put to him by the prosecution.

19. **(C)** The answer to this question is in the negative. That Stone was impotent was not a crime. Notice this question asks about the grounds of divorce, not about his prior criminal activity.

20. **(A)** This is the conflict we outlined in the set overview.

Set 5

OVERVIEW: Again, it is of surpassing importance to keep in mind that the rules are equal in status. Rule I states that an acceptance of an offer creates a contract, and since it does not mention anything about the time limit, we must conclude that insofar as Rule I is concerned, acceptance at any time—no matter how late—would result in a contract. Taking Rule I, then, in isolation, it looks like Martin has a contract with Ekhard. But Rule II states that the offer expires after a reasonable time. What is a reasonable time? Well, here that is difficult to say. The magazine was a quarterly and Martin did respond two months after he saw the ad. But, then again, how old was the magazine when Martin first saw the ad? Whether the offer had expired seems an open question. In any event, both rules cannot simultaneously govern the case, since Rule II, if it is applicable, might give a different result.

21. **(C)** There was no question here of the expiration of the offer. Both parties agreed; there was an offer and an acceptance, so by the terms of Rule I, there was a contract.

22. **(A)** This requires the choice of rules we outlined previously. If Rule I alone is applicable, there is definitely a contract. If Rule II governs the cases, there may or may not be a contract, depending on how the issue of "reasonable" period is resolved.

23. **(C)** Since the offer was made in an advertisement, the person making the offer intended that anyone who read the magazine could accept the terms of the offer. Admittedly, it was not personally directed at Martin, but then again it was not personally directed at anyone in particular.

24. **(B)** This is the open question we discussed previously. There are arguments on both sides of the issue, and we need additional facts before we can decide whether the acceptance from Martin came too late.

25. **(B)** This question requires some additional information. Even if we establish by choice of rules that there was a contract, we have not yet laid down a rule for the appropriate remedy. We have no basis for concluding that Martin's remedy will be receiving one of the cars, as opposed to some money compensation.

Set 6

OVERVIEW: The possible conflict between the two rules arises over the limits of a search. According to Rule I, no search may be conducted without the consent of the driver of the car. But according to Rule II, the police officer may enter the car if he sees something lying in plain view. In our case, Gordon did not have Baker's consent to conduct a search, but he did see a gun lying in plain view. According to Rule I, Gordon was not permitted to enter the car, but by the terms of Rule II he was allowed to do so. Notice further that Cooke gave permission for the search of the trunk, and that Cooke was not the driver.

26. **(C)** We know from the facts that Baker, who is the driver, did not consent to the search. Gordon undertook to enter the car when he saw the gun's barrel protruding from under the seat.

27. **(A)** This requires us to choose between the rules. By the terms of the first, Gordon has violated the rule against entering the car without permission; but according to the second, he was allowed to do so to retrieve the object which was already in his sight.

28. **(C)** This is deducible from the facts. Gordon could see the barrel of the gun from where he was standing outside the car.

29. **(B)** This question will require some additional information. First, we need the rule defining possession of an illegal weapon. What is such a weapon? What is possession—is the driver or the owner of the car, or perhaps both, guilty of possession of an illegal weapon in the car? Then, we will probably need some more facts: Who knew about it? In any event, since we require something more, the correct answer is (B).

30. **(C)** Since Cooke was not the driver of the car, Rule I establishes that the search would have been impermissible.

Set 7

OVERVIEW: The conflict between the rules in the case is relatively straightforward. Rule I holds the employer liable for actions, intentionally or otherwise, of his employees, so long as they were acting to discharge their duties. Rule II, however, specfically exempts intentional wrongdoing from liability. Since Oliver intentionally hit Brook, we are faced with a conflict of rules. Rule I will put liability for that action on Rapid Delivery, but Rule II will exempt Rapid Delivery from liability.

31. **(A)** This is the conflict we just outlined in the set overview.

32. **(C)** This is a relatively easy question. Whether the son was an employee or not is an important question, since the employer is not liable under either rule except for employees. By the facts we can deduce that the son was not employed by the company.

33. **(B)** Although the son is not an employee, and although Rapid Delivery cannot be liable to Brook for the broken ribs under either rule (since both speak of employees), there may be other rules which hold Rapid liable for the son's actions. After all, he was helping his father, who was engaged in making deliveries for Rapid. We cannot be sure what the scope of Rapid's liabilities is without further rules.

34. **(B)** Although Oliver was generally doing what he was told to do by his employer—delivery of packages—we can wonder whether or not his unorthodox method for making delivery takes him outside of the scope of his *assigned* duties. On the one hand, he was making deliveries; but on the other hand, his employer surely did not assign that method of delivery. So in order to determine whether this unusual conduct comes within the scope of assigned duties, we will need another rule.

35. **(D)** Admittedly, the value of the package could be relevant on further assumptions: suppose it were extremely valuable and Rapid had told Oliver to guard it with his life. But again, we remind the student that such speculation is out of place.

SECTION V

Questions 1–5

Arranging the Information

The eight numbers are arranged, like all numbers, along a single line. The original information tells us that they are consecutive, so the diagram will be of eight slots, each right next to the other. Enter the information one item at a time.

This is the diagram:

←GREATER——SMALLER→

__ __ __ __ __ __ __ __

W is four more than Z and three less than X—this defines the endpoints and W.

←GREATER____SMALLER→

X __ __ W __ __ __ Z

S greater than T—can not do now.

S less than X—redundant since X is largest, but these establish the relationship: X > S > T.

U is the average of V and X—this means that U is greater than V because the average is between two numbers and X is the largest number in the group. Furthermore, for every step that U is below X, V is the same number of steps below U. This establishes some possibilities:

←GREATER____SMALLER→

possibility #1 X U? V? W __ __ __ Z

possibility #2 X __ U? W V? __ __ Z

These are the only possibilities because U cannot take W's place and if U is below W, then V will be below Z which is not possible within the context of eight consecutive numbers. The final diagram shows the two possibilities and the notation that S is greater than T. Nothing is known about Y at all.

Answering the Questions

1. **(C)** Z is the lowest number in the series and W is four greater, and thus equal to 8 + 4 = 12.

2. **(C)** I. As previously discussed, W cannot be the greatest number because it is less than X. As for II, Z cannot be the greatest number because it is less than W. Thus, I and II are true.

   III is false because X, being 7 greater than Z in a series of eight consecutive numbers, must be the greatest number.

3. **(A)** The question asks for a possible arrangement, so elimination of impossibilities is the proper approach. X is the greatest number, not Z, which eliminates answer choice (C). Z is the lowest number, which eliminates answer choices (C) (again) and (D). W is three less than X, and thus must be the fourth number from the left, which again eliminates answer choice (D) as well as (E). U, being the average of X and V, must lie exactly between them, which it does not in answers (B), (C), (D), and (E). All of these considerations lead to the conclusion that only (A) is possible.

4. **(B)** Under the original conditions, U could not have been immediately above Z since there had to be room for V below U. With the removal of that requirement (B) is now possible. (A) was a possibility anyway, so it is not the newly created possibility for which the problem asks. (C) is not possible because the eight numbers are consecutive numbers, and thus not equal to each other. (E) is wrong for the same reason. (D) violates the limitation that the numbers be a string of eight consecutive numbers. By placing U below Z the difference between the highest and lowest numbers in the string becomes too great.

5. **(E)** If Y is three greater than Z, it goes just below W. This eliminates possibility #2 shown previously and gives the following diagram. Once U and V and Y are tied down, so are S and T.

   ←GREATER____SMALLER→

   X U V W Y S T Z

   Inspection of the diagram indicates that none of the four statements is true, hence, answer choice (E) is correct.

Questions 6–9

Arranging the Information

Since three of the four questions are conditional questions introducing different variations or new information, you know that you will not get a definite result from the original set of information. This means that you should quickly sketch out the limitations and requirements in the original information, and spend most of your time in the answering of the questions.

In addition to the basic setup of there being two shelves with three spaces on each, there are only three relationships which are specified.

Thyme and basil are not next to each other.

Thyme and basil are not above or below each other.

Salt and pepper must be next to each other on the same shelf.

Answering the Questions

In answering the sort of question where there are many possibilities, it is often most efficient to focus on the limiting factors since there are fewer of them.

6. **(A)** All that the question asks is whether the three arrangements are unacceptable, thus, all you have to do for each arrangement is find one possibility of its being acceptable in order to eliminate the arrangement from consideration.

I. Thyme and basil on same shelf but not next to each other.

T	___	B
___	___	___

Salt and pepper must be on the other shelf to be together.

Others fit in without problem.

T	C	B
S	P	F

(This is only one possible arrangement.)

Thus, I is possible.

II is shown to be possibly acceptable by the same arrangement as given above for I. If you happened to have made a different arrangement for I, you would need to start with T and C on the same shelf, and see if you could fill it all in without violating any of the restrictions of the problem.

III: for T and S to be on the same shelf requires that one shelf be T, S, P (or any arrangement of the three which has S and P together). For example:

T	S	P
C	F	B

B can be added without being under T.

So III is acceptable also.

Since all of the arrangements are acceptable, the correct answer is (A).

7. **(D)** The wording of the problem means that your job is to find the four answer choices which are not acceptable. The correct answer choice is not necessarily the only way to meet the conditions, but merely a possibility.

One general rule is that salt and pepper have to be next to each other, therefore, any shelf arrangement which does not have them next to each other is wrong. This eliminates (A), (B), and (E).

The difference between the remaining answer choices—(C) and (D)—is whether the basil is on the left or on the right. If the basil is on the left, it will be immediately below the thyme, which is forbidden, hence, (D) is the only acceptable arrangement.

8. **(C)** The problem sets up this starting point:

___	___	___
S	P	B

This means that thyme cannot be in the upper right-hand slot, but there are no restrictions on cumin or fennel. The possibilities are these:

T	C	F
S	P	B

T	F	C
S	P	B

C	T	F
S	P	B

F	T	C
S	P	B

Since thyme is the limiting item, you should start your work with it. First place thyme in the left-hand slot and flip-flop the other two, then put thyme in the middle slot and flip-flop the other two again = 4 ways.

9. **(A)** This is a problem where a condition is added. Even though new containers are bought, they are similar, and thus still must not be placed next to each other. The new condition is that they must both be in the top shelf. This means that the top shelf must have basil at one end and thyme at the other. Since salt and pepper still must be next to each other and there is only one empty space on the upper shelf, salt and pepper must be on the bottom shelf, though

they can slide from side to side and could be placed with pepper on the left or on the right of the salt.

There are two ways of approaching this problem. Either you can focus on elimination of answer choices that are not acceptable by constructing counter examples, or you can focus on trying to find an acceptable arrangement that meets the new conditions. Since it is a fairly loosely constrained situation, the former is more efficient, especially since it will at least provide the elimination of some answer choices.

If you try the elimination route, it is best to start with the simplest and most definite arrangements since their unacceptability will likely be easier to demonstrate.

(B) is not necessarily true because the salt could be on the left of the pepper, and the pair could be all the way to the other side from the thyme.

B	___	T
S	P	___

The same diagram shows that (D) is not necessarily acceptable. (D) can be eliminated with this diagram, among others:

B	___	T
___	S	P

We chose to work with these three answers first because they used the smallest number of items, and thus would be the quickest and easiest to work with. (A) and (C) require the filling in of the whole spice rack, or nearly so.

A counter example to (C) can be found by seeing the problem as one of looking for an arrangement that walls pepper off from the other spices. If pepper is in the lower left- or right-hand corner, only salt will be next to it, thus eliminating (C).

As a practical matter you would end your work here, since only one answer choice remains, and go on to the next problem, only returning to the task if you had extra time. The elimination of four answer choices IF CORRECTLY DONE will require the fifth to be the right answer. Since (A) is the most permissive of all the answer choices, this is an intuitively reasonable result.

(A)'s merit can be seen by considering the first diagram we made for this problem. Four of the slots are taken. The ends of the upper shelf are taken by thyme and basil in whatever order, and salt and pepper form a pair on the bottom shelf in whatever order. Since (A) refers to "either salt or pepper" it is really addressing the pair on the bottom shelf. Fennel will either be on the upper shelf in the middle position, in which case it will be above one of the salt/pepper pair, or fennel will be in the one empty space on the bottom shelf, in which case it will be next to one of the salt/pepper pair. Hence, (A) is correct.

Questions 10–13

Arranging the Information

This problem has two aspects, the order in which items have to be done and the times during the week when the various offices and individuals are available. Note that although the first statement in the information set does seem to give some feeling that thesis approval by the professors must come after the filling out of the application, this would be reading too much into the problem. In fact, the further statements about the required order of events indicate, by silence about the timing of thesis approval, that the approval can come after the visit to the dean. Question 17 supports this by putting the approval process ahead of the other items. The filing at the Financial Aid Office must be last.

Since the information is given to us in terms of mornings and afternoons, that is the way to arrange it. There are no immediate interactions between the items of information (such as might have been the case if Professor Fansler's office hours were always three days after Professor Cross's, or if the dean's hours were described in terms of those of the Financial Aid Office), therefore, a straight listing of the information on hours is all that is required.

	MON.	TUES.	WED.	THUR.	FRI.
AM	Fin. Aid Fansler	Fin. Aid Fansler Cross		Dean	Dean Fin. Aid Cross
PM	Dean	Dean	Fin. Aid		

DEAN MUST PRECEDE FIN. AID, FIN. AID LAST, PROF'S PRE/POST DEAN

Answering the Questions

10. **(D)** Since the thesis must be approved by Fansler only and not by Cross, only Monday and Tuesday mornings are possibilities, which eliminates (C) and (E). The student also has to go to the Financial Aid Office after seeing the professor. Since the Financial Aid Office is open on both Monday and Tuesday mornings, both of those times are good, hence (D), rather than (A) or (B).

11. **(E)** This problem is, of course, separate from the preceding one, so we must consider that the student is starting out fresh and needs to see the dean, a professor, and the Financial Aid Office. They are asking for what must be false, so we seek elimination by seeing possibilities.

    I is not necessarily false because it is possible to have thesis approval from Professor Cross and complete the job in one day. On Friday morning all three of the required parties are open for business, and ignoring waiting time (which you do because if they didn't bring it up, you shouldn't), there would be no problem. This eliminates answer choices (A) and (D).

    II is false because Professor Fansler's approval can only be obtained on Monday or Tuesday morning. While it is true that both the Financial Aid Office and the dean are open on Mondays and Tuesdays, the order is wrong. By the time the dean is open for business the Financial Aid Office is closed so the application cannot be filed that day. This eliminates answer (C).

    III is also false because neither of the professors is available in the afternoon. Hence, (B) is out and (E) is correct.

12. **(D)** This problem does not require that the process be completed in any particular time, but only that all the action take place on Tuesdays and Thursdays. Since both professors have office hours on Tuesdays, statements I and II are not necessarily true. As it happens, this is enough to give you the answer since all of the answer choices except (D) allege that either I or II or both are true.

    III is false because on Thursdays only the dean is open, and because on Tuesdays the Financial Aid Office closes before the dean opens, as was previously discussed.

    IV requires you to interpret what a school week might be. If a mere six-day period was intended (start on Thursday and complete on the following Tuesday) that would not be called a "school" week. A school week is Monday through Friday, and the application cannot be done on a consecutive Tuesday and Thursday. Thus, all four of the statements are false.

13. **(C)** On Wednesday and Thursday only one of the proper offices is open, so they are not possible one-visit days, but this only eliminates (D). Friday morning is a possibile one-visit time, which eliminates answer choice (A). Monday and Tuesday mornings, while blessed with open offices for the professors and the Financial Aid Office, do not have the dean, so (E) is eliminated (as is (D) for the second time).

    Monday and Tuesday have the problem of order of office openings previously referred to, and thus are not one-visit days—which eliminates (B), leaving (C) as the answer.

Questions 14–18

Arranging the Information

The whole first paragraph is mostly background. The real meat of the setup is in the second paragraph, where the method of determining the grade of a calf from the grades of its parents is laid out.

If father = mother or +/− 1 grade, child = mother.

If father +2 or 3 from mother, child = mother +1.
If father −2 or 3 from mother, child = mother −1.
Permissible grades 2A, 3A, 4A, and 5A.

Since the questions stems are largely conditional, this small amount of information in the arranging end of the job is to be expected. Most of the work will be in the questions.

Answering the Questions

14. **(A)** A 2A mother's calf will be raised one grade if the father is either 4A or 5A, hence answer choice (A) yields a 3A child.

    Since the calf's grade must always be within one grade of its mother's grade, a 3A calf could not have had a 5A mother. This eliminates answer choices (B) and (D). Count the A's carefully.

    (C) fails because although the father is higher than the 2A mother, he is only one grade higher, and thus cannot lift the calf to 3A. (E)'s breeding will produce a 4A calf, which while preferable from the Bellman's perspective perhaps, is not a preferable answer choice when you are trying to explain a 3A result.

15. **(D)** The least resistant grades will be those which could not possibly have had 2A or 3A fathers, if any. 5A offspring can only be the result of 5A mothers and 5A or 4A fathers. Any other father would be sufficiently below the 5A mother to lower the offspring to 4A. By the same sort of reasoning the 2A offspring would be the most resistant since they must have had a 2A or 3A father. The others would be in-between since it is likely that some of them did have 2A or 3A fathers. As the discussion shows, it is not true that all of the grades will have the same resistance, thus, (E) fails.

16. **(B)** Answer choices (A), (B), and (C) all have some merit since they each will result in all of the next generation of cattle having at least one 4A parent, and thus presumably being more gentle. Though (D) does improve the milk-producing qualities of the herd, it will do nothing to enhance gentleness. Thus, (D) is eliminated. (E) could not be correct since a random breeding program would leave some non-gentle offspring, which (B) avoids.

    Since (A), (B), and (C) all have good results on gentleness, you must tell them apart and choose the best answer on the basis of their effect on milk quality and quantity. (A) will upgrade the 2A cows' offspring, but the other cows will have the same grade calves as they are themselves. (C), on the other hand, will eliminate 5A grades from the herd altogether.

    (B) is preferable to either (A) or (C) because it will preserve 5A grades, unlike (C), and it will improve the herd more than (C)—since it is using higher grade cows rather than higher grade bulls, and the cows will pull up the grades more than the bulls according to the given information.

17. **(A)** Statement I has no basis whatever in the problem set, so it cannot be known to be true. II is not true because a 2A bull and 4A cow produce a 3A offspring, and so does the breeding of a 4A bull to a 3A cow. III is also false since a 2A bull and a 5A cow will produce a 4A calf. Thus, all three statements are false.

18. **(A)** The key to this problem is the phrase "at least," which permits you to assume the most favorable permissible conditions without worrying about what might actually happen down on the dairy farm. Since we want to raise the grade rapidly and a high-grade mother will raise grade more rapidly than a high-grade father, we will assume that we start with a hide color 2A bull which is bred to a 5A cow, producing a 4A bull offspring. That is the first generation. This 4A hide color bull is then bred to another 5A cow to produce a 5A hide color offspring in the second generation after the first hide color animal.

Questions 19–25

Arranging the Information

The natural structure in which to arrange this information is to make a table or grid which shows both the days and lunch and dinner for each day. The general conditions are simply that there is no repetition from day to day. It is important to remember that even though this is stated in the form of not having day 4 duplicate day 3, this also means that if day 4 is known, then day 3 cannot be the same.

Entering the three known meals:

	1	2	3	4	5
LUNCH				CHEESE	
DINNER	STEW			HOT DOG	

Since the same item cannot be served two days in a row:

	1	2	3	4	5
LUNCH			NOT CHEESE NOT HOT DOG	CHEESE	NOT CHEESE NOT HOT DOG
DINNER	STEW	NOT STEW	NOT HOT DOG	HOT DOG	NOT HOT DOG

By elimination we find that the only possibility for lunch on days 3 and 5 is tuna, which can then not be served on day 2.

	1	2	3	4	5
LUNCH		NOT TUNA	TUNA	CHEESE	TUNA
DINNER	STEW	NOT STEW	NOT HOT DOG	HOT DOG	NOT HOT DOG

Answering the Questions

19. **(D)** The diagram above justifies (D). (A) fails since hot dogs could be served a second time on day 2 lunch or dinner, or day 1 lunch. Question 22 can give a hint of this. (B) is clearly wrong when (D) is right. (C) is not true since stew could be served for dinner on day 3 or 5. (E) is not true since it is only possible to serve hot dogs twice, not required. Day 1 could be tuna and day 2 cheese for lunch and the dinners could be stew, ham, stew, hot dogs, and stew or ham, for instance.

20. **(B)** If ham is served for dinner on day 3, then ham cannot be served for dinner on day 2 and the table looks like this:

	1	2	3	4	5
LUNCH		NOT TUNA	TUNA	CHEESE	TUNA
DINNER	STEW	NOT STEW NOT HAM	HAM	HOT DOG	NOT HOT DOG

This in turn leaves only the option of hot dogs for dinner on day 2, which eliminates hot dogs from consideration for lunch or dinner on days 1 and 3 or lunch on day 2:

	1	2	3	4	5
LUNCH	NOT HOT DOG	NOT TUNA NOT HOT DOG	TUNA	CHESE	TUNA
DINNER	STEW	HOT DOG	HAM	HOT DOG	NOT HOT DOG

Thus cheese is the only possibility for lunch on day 2, meaning lunch on day 1 cannot be either hot dog or cheese, and thus must be tuna, giving:

	1	2	3	4	5
LUNCH	TUNA	CHEESE	TUNA	CHEESE	TUNA
DINNER	STEW	HOT DOG	HAM	HOT DOG	NOT HOT DOG

Checking the answer choices against this chart reveals (B) as the answer. (A), (C), and (D) are wrong and (E) is not definitely true, but only possible.

21. **(E)** Referring to the chart at the end of the Arranging the Information section, (E) is seen to be true. (A), (B), and (C) are just possibilities, and (D) is not possible since hot dogs are served for dinner on day 4.

22. **(A)** This question stem practices some misdirection. The issue is not so much that they can only be served once for lunch as what the implications are if they are served the one time it IS possible to serve them. As shown in the original arrangement, hot dogs could be served for lunch on either day 1 or day 2. In either case, the only effect is on the possibilities for dinner on day 2 since hot dogs are already forbidden for day 3. Since stew is also forbidden for dinner on day 2, ham must be served for dinner on day 2. Thus ham cannot be served for dinner on day 3:

	1	2	3	4	5
LUNCH	HOT DOG		TUNA	CHEESE	TUNA
DINNER	STEW	HAM	NOT HOT DOG NOT HAM	HOT DOG	NOT HOT DOG

This in turn requires that stew be served for dinner on day 3 as the only remaining possibility:

	1	2	3	4	5
LUNCH	HOT DOG	NOT TUNA	TUNA	CHEESE	TUNA
DINNER	STEW	HAM	STEW	HOT DOG	NOT HOT DOG

From this table, the truth of (A) is clear since only day 5's dinner is open. (B) is not true since tuna could be served on Day 1 if hot dogs are served on day 2. Cheese could likewise be served on either day 1 or 2 but it does not have to be served, thus (C) is not true. (D) is definitely false as shown above. (E) is false since hot dogs cannot be served for dinner on day 5.

23. **(D)** Referring to the original arrangement of the information shows that tuna and stew are not permitted on day 2. This eliminates proposition I, but the other two are possible, hence (D), II and III only, is correct.

24. **(C)** The explanation and diagrams are similar to those for question 22, except hot dogs are in day 1 lunch and thus day 2's lunch can be neither hot dogs nor tuna, and must therefore be cheese:

	1	2	3	4	5
LUNCH	HOT DOG	CHEESE	TUNA	CHEESE	TUNA
DINNER	STEW	HAM	STEW	HOT DOG	NOT HOT DOG

Thus (C) is true and the other answer choices are false.

25. **(A)** Adding the sixth day information to the original table gives:

	1	2	3	4	5	6
LUNCH		NOT TUNA	TUNA	CHEESE	TUNA	
DINNER	STEW	NOT STEW	NOT HOT DOG	HOT DOG	NOT HOT DOG	HOT DOG

Lunch on Day 6 cannot be hot dogs because of dinner on day 6, nor can it be tuna, because of lunch on day 5; thus it must be cheese:

	1	2	3	4	5	6
LUNCH		NOT TUNA	TUNA	CHEESE	TUNA	CHEESE
DINNER	STEW	NOT STEW	NOT HOT DOG	HOT DOG	NOT HOT DOG	HOT DOG

This shows (A) to be true. (B) was false because lunch on day 5 was tuna. (B) is false because dinner on day 4 is hot dogs, and the same for dinner on day 6. (D) is possible, but need not be true since ham is also a possibility. (E) is false from the original information that cheese is served for lunch on day 4.

SECTION VI

1. **(E)** Only (E) covers the main ideas of the passage as stated in the first sentence. (A) omits the idea of youth, (B) that of schooling, (C) youth and business, and (D) introduces the untrue idea that ONLY bright students are the topic of the passage, when it is the education to be pursued by the future managers which is of primary interest.

2. **(B)** In both (B) and the passage the term "liberalizing" means the opening up of the curriculum and including leadership training in it. This is an area which the passage finds that business schools excel at, hence, (B). (A) fails since little is said of difficulty. If any implication is drawn it would be that business education is harder since it includes much of Liberal Arts, and adds technical and practical ideas. (C) is not stated and the passage requires both for its definition of a complete business education. (D) is stated to be false, and (E) fails for the same reasons as (A).

3. **(E)** All the answer choices refer to business in some way, so further distinctions among the answer choices must be found. (C) refers to only the business schools, which seems too limited for the question stem's "primarily." The other four refer to the qualities of the businessmen or leaders.

While (A) and (B) are certainly nice, they are not the focus of the passage. The passage emphasized leaders with a wide range of competencies rather than backgrounds, eliminating (D). (E) is stated at the end of the fourth paragraph to be essential to competent business management, which is in turn stated in the last paragraph to be essential to the economic well-being of the country. This last linkage could have been worked backwards to find the answer.

4. **(B)** The reference in the passage is, to be frank, obscure, but it is equated with a "broad-gauged man" who is clearly one with both specific business knowledge for the present and learning skills for the future, thus, (B). (C) has some merit, but the passage does not advocate all forms of education, only the ones previously mentioned, as such. (D) is not mentioned, and like (E) it is not clear to what it might really refer. (A) is flack.

5. **(C)** The end of the last paragraph gives the author's view that careers combining reality with intellectual rigor will be serving the students' desires as well as the nation's needs. In the previous paragraph, the author stated that modern students, in general, are desirous of more reality, which permits the widening of the view of the last paragraph to all students.

   (D) is false since opposition to avoiding reality is not opposition to studying theory. (E) is false since the unclean aspects were of reality, which the students wished to study. (A) and (B) fail for lack of support in the passage since only some students will end up in business, and the purpose of the passage has to do with informing the world at large about the values of a proper business education.

6. **(E)** The third paragraph makes the point supporting (E). (B) also bases itself on the need for reschooling that the future businessman is certain to face, but no mention is made of returning to school. In fact, the emphasis on the school's equipping the student to do his own future learning implies that further schooling is probably not contemplated. (A), (C), and (D) all fail because the person referred to in the question stem is not stated to be prepared according to the ideals set out by the author.

7. **(E)** (E) is the idea put forward in the fifth paragraph. (A) and (D) have some basis in the paragraph. (D) is supported by the author's insistence on a broad education, which is not what is usually meant by vocational education. Yet, in the strict sense of vocational education being a training for a vocation, this is what the author is lauding, so (D) is not clearly indicated, and is thus much less desirable than (E).

   (A) plays on the author's idea that business is changing, which he does say. However, there is nothing in the passage to indicate that drastic changes have been made in the last decade, as opposed to some other period. (B) and (C) are not stated in the passage, whatever their possible truth in the real world.

8. **(E)** I and III are clearly indicated by the phrase "physical characteristics and cultures." II is a combination of the two. Food is a physical characteristic in terms of what is available and the preparation is a cultural aspect. Hence, all three are referred to in the passage, (E).

9. **(C)** (B) is the result primarily of the Himalaya's sudden appearance, rather than the glaciation, and (D) is of both. What we need is the idea of what would have been different if the existing plants had been entirely wiped out. (A) and (C) both speak to that, and (A) has some merit, though it is weakened by the word *flourish,* which seems extreme. Though the use of *life* without any adjective seems odd, this is done in both (A) and (C). In (A), however, there is no sense of development or implication. (C) tells us what would have been different to the concern of the passage at that point—the diversity and type of fauna and flora. Note that the word *possibly* in (C) protects it from the criticism that the Kunlun range cut off other life from coming in, as does the non-specific reference to nearby arid areas. (E) would only be chosen if all of the others were definitely bad.

10. **(C)** We know only two things about the Tibetan "tea." First, it is in quotes, which means it is not just regular tea. Second, it is a possible replacement for vegetables. These both fit (C) better than any of the other answer choices. If you were reluctant to choose (C) because it sounded unlikely, you are wrong for two reasons. First, and most important, it is almost exclusively the relationship to the passage that matters. Second, that is what Tibetan tea really is.

11. **(D)** (A), (B), and (C) are all in the passage, but they serve the purpose stated in (D). (E) is not mentioned as mysterious.

12. **(C)** The passage is full of references to the findings of others, which supports (B) and (C). (A) is unsupported by the few statements made in the passage without references. None of the statements refers to any first-hand experience by the author, eliminating (A). There is no special emphasis on China to support (D), and there is much in the passage other than geology, (E). Between (B) and (C), one must choose between the strong items in each choice—"life-long" and "only." While the passage displays some erudition, it is not clear that a life-long study is indicated, but all of the information can come from books and almost all of it certainly does, hence, (C).

13. **(E)** Although Lattimore and Kawakita have different emphases as to the source of the polyandry, it is not stated nor required that polyandry must be either preserved from earlier forms or an efficient way of selecting the householder. The other answers reflect differences which are not required.

14. **(C)** Montesquieu is stated to believe that climate and soil are cultural determinants, that is, they determine what the culture of the inhabitants of an area will be. (D) is unrelated to this idea, and (E) focuses on the food, not the soil and climate as such. (A) and (B) mention only one of the two factors said to be important to Montesquieu. (C) clearly states the idea of soil and climate being determinative of culture.

15. **(A)** "Jargon" is stated to be a technical term, though the passage notes that in farming and other old and widespread occupations, the words will often be generally familiar. (A), "sun," is not a technical term in any field, while the other four are technical terms for, respectively, husbandry, farming, weaving, and carpentry.

16. **(A)** None of the answer choices has any statement of the topic of the passage, but only general form. The passage is descriptive only, hence, (A). (C) and (D) are not done, and (E) seems unlikely in this rather dry passage. (B) has the slight merit of the fact that the description given is a sort of argument that the phenomenon described does exist, but that is not so well described as a belief, hence, (A) not (B).

17. **(B)** It is important not to let outside knowledge interfere with understanding how THIS author is using a term. Although guilds in the Middle Ages were hard to get into (A), and often required apprenticeships (E), this is not in the passage since it is modern times that are under discussion.

(D) is too strong and (C)'s references to secrets is a little strange since it is only the reports, not the secrets, that are broadcast; but the strength of (B) is that it is one of the two specific statements following the phrase at issue. (C), the second-best answer, is not precisely what is stated about popular science in the passage.

18. **(D)** Since the author thinks of vocabulary to write an article about it, he likely would study it since it reflects the best way to discuss things in the field, as the passage states. (A), (B), and (E) have little to do with the passage. (D) is preferable to (C) because (D) includes (C) and also refers to actually learning knowledge in the new field.

19. **(A)** Since the passage primarily concerns words and their uses, meanings, and history, (A) is the best answer. There is no specific support for any of the other answers.

20. **(B)** The last two sentences give us our best evidence for time and place. "Roentgen

rays" and "wireless telegraphy" are key terms. They are obsolete terms for X-rays and radio, respectively, and certainly have an old-fashioned feel about them. The sentence with *provincial* in it tells us that the country of the author probably has both advanced science and many newspapers. The omission of radio and television from the list of media is also significant. (D) and (E) fail because of date, since television and radio would surely be mentioned in those years. (A) fails since India was not a science center (nor a media center) in 1904. (B) is preferable to (C) since 1944 had radio and 1914 didn't.

21. **(B)** Since technical words come and go, (B) is very strong. (A) would only be true if words never left the language, which the passage does not say and common sense forbids. (C) fails since it refers to all words. (D) is shown to be false by the last sentence, if not the whole passage. (E) overlooks the author's position that such words as these ARE still technical words, even though common.

22. **(E)** A reductive cycle is a negative aspect of the psychology of the individual worker, hence, (E). (A), (B), and (C) play on the everyday meaning of *reduce.* (D) may result from a long-term reductive cycle, but is not the cycle itself, which can be changed before (D) occurs.

23. **(B)** The passage says "sound motivation patterns begin at the top." The top is (B).

24. **(A)** This passage traces unionization to failures in the psychological setting of the job. (B), (C), and (D) are more commonly the sorts of things thought of as leading to unionization, but not here. (B) refers to nothing in the passage, but appears to refer to "self-actualization," the lack of which is associated in the passage with unionization. (A) describes the elements of "self-actualization" which must be missing for unionization to occur.

25. **(D)** The passage indicates that motivation is the key. (D) is the cause of a continued reductive cycle. (A) and (B) pretend that a reductive cycle is good, and are thus eliminated. (E) is something that may result from the continued situation, but is here stated in the present rather than future tense, so it fails. (C) is true, but (D) is the specification of just which way the boss is failing.

26. **(A)** Note that the question stem speaks of initial results only. There is some temptation to seek an answer which says that none of the listed propositions is an initial result of reductive conditions since the unionism results from continued reductive conditions and the other two, presumably, result from unionism, though that latter is weak in this passage. However, since that is not an available choice, we choose I only, (A), since that clearly precedes the others.

27. **(E)** All three of these conditions are mentioned in the fourth paragraph. The fact that these are not the only roots of collective action is irrelevant to answering the question.

28. **(D)** The root of the manager's failure is stated to be lack of sensitivity to the needs, etc., of the employees under him. (D) best describes this lack of empathy. (C) may be a cause of the lack of empathy and (E) a possible result, but they are not mentioned specifically in the passage, and thus have a conditional connection to the question at best. (A) and (B) are not the cause of failures or anything else in the passage.

SECTION VII

Explanation of Pressure Points and Exemplary Essay for Writing Sample

TOPIC: When you meet someone, it is better not to make the first impression your best impression, because thereafter you will not be able to live up to your new acquaintance's expectations. It is better to make a bad first impression, so that later you will seem to be more impressive.

PRESSURE POINTS: The following considerations might go through your mind as you examine the topic and seek to create an outline for your essay.

—What are overall benefits and costs of this recommendation?
—Why be concerned about impressions, first or later?
—Do "best" and "bad" have to be all there is?
—Are impressions that controllable? Should they be?
—Who is the "someone"? Friend, business acquaintance, superior, subordinate? Someone important, unimportant? Can the same rule apply for all situations?

The following essay is only one of many that could have been written on this topic.

The position outlined in the topic statement is an oversimplification for two reasons. First, the topic statement fails to allow that there is a middle position between a good and a bad first impression. Second, the statement fails to distinguish different kinds of first encounters.

First, the topic statement presupposes that one has a choice of only two first impressions, a good one or a bad one. There is a middle ground, however. One need not try to overwhelm a new acquaintance, trying to impress him with knowledge and wit. Nor is it necessary to present a character which is too self-effacing. A better choice for a first meeting would be a cautious presentation of one's character, that is, rather than putting on a mask, it would be better to wear what comes naturally, tempering enthusiasm with caution until such time as a fuller disclosure appears in order.

Second, the topic statement fails to distinguish between first encounters with some specific goal and those which have no defined purpose. As for the first, there are some first meetings which have pre-established objectives so that the first impression must be a good one or the meeting is a failure. A job interview illustrates this point. Unless a good first impression is made, there will be no opportunity for a second one. In such cases, the advice of the topic statement is just plain wrong. Even for other meetings, however, the advice seems weak. After all, no form of deception is a good foundation for a lasting friendship.

ANSWER SHEET—PRACTICE EXAMINATION 4

SECTION I

1 Ⓐ Ⓑ Ⓒ Ⓓ Ⓔ	6 Ⓐ Ⓑ Ⓒ Ⓓ Ⓔ	11 Ⓐ Ⓑ Ⓒ Ⓓ Ⓔ	16 Ⓐ Ⓑ Ⓒ Ⓓ Ⓔ	21 Ⓐ Ⓑ Ⓒ Ⓓ Ⓔ	26 Ⓐ Ⓑ Ⓒ Ⓓ Ⓔ
2 Ⓐ Ⓑ Ⓒ Ⓓ Ⓔ	7 Ⓐ Ⓑ Ⓒ Ⓓ Ⓔ	12 Ⓐ Ⓑ Ⓒ Ⓓ Ⓔ	17 Ⓐ Ⓑ Ⓒ Ⓓ Ⓔ	22 Ⓐ Ⓑ Ⓒ Ⓓ Ⓔ	27 Ⓐ Ⓑ Ⓒ Ⓓ Ⓔ
3 Ⓐ Ⓑ Ⓒ Ⓓ Ⓔ	8 Ⓐ Ⓑ Ⓒ Ⓓ Ⓔ	13 Ⓐ Ⓑ Ⓒ Ⓓ Ⓔ	18 Ⓐ Ⓑ Ⓒ Ⓓ Ⓔ	23 Ⓐ Ⓑ Ⓒ Ⓓ Ⓔ	28 Ⓐ Ⓑ Ⓒ Ⓓ Ⓔ
4 Ⓐ Ⓑ Ⓒ Ⓓ Ⓔ	9 Ⓐ Ⓑ Ⓒ Ⓓ Ⓔ	14 Ⓐ Ⓑ Ⓒ Ⓓ Ⓔ	19 Ⓐ Ⓑ Ⓒ Ⓓ Ⓔ	24 Ⓐ Ⓑ Ⓒ Ⓓ Ⓔ	
5 Ⓐ Ⓑ Ⓒ Ⓓ Ⓔ	10 Ⓐ Ⓑ Ⓒ Ⓓ Ⓔ	15 Ⓐ Ⓑ Ⓒ Ⓓ Ⓔ	20 Ⓐ Ⓑ Ⓒ Ⓓ Ⓔ	25 Ⓐ Ⓑ Ⓒ Ⓓ Ⓔ	

SECTION II

1 Ⓐ Ⓑ Ⓒ Ⓓ Ⓔ	6 Ⓐ Ⓑ Ⓒ Ⓓ Ⓔ	11 Ⓐ Ⓑ Ⓒ Ⓓ Ⓔ	16 Ⓐ Ⓑ Ⓒ Ⓓ Ⓔ	21 Ⓐ Ⓑ Ⓒ Ⓓ Ⓔ
2 Ⓐ Ⓑ Ⓒ Ⓓ Ⓔ	7 Ⓐ Ⓑ Ⓒ Ⓓ Ⓔ	12 Ⓐ Ⓑ Ⓒ Ⓓ Ⓔ	17 Ⓐ Ⓑ Ⓒ Ⓓ Ⓔ	22 Ⓐ Ⓑ Ⓒ Ⓓ Ⓔ
3 Ⓐ Ⓑ Ⓒ Ⓓ Ⓔ	8 Ⓐ Ⓑ Ⓒ Ⓓ Ⓔ	13 Ⓐ Ⓑ Ⓒ Ⓓ Ⓔ	18 Ⓐ Ⓑ Ⓒ Ⓓ Ⓔ	23 Ⓐ Ⓑ Ⓒ Ⓓ Ⓔ
4 Ⓐ Ⓑ Ⓒ Ⓓ Ⓔ	9 Ⓐ Ⓑ Ⓒ Ⓓ Ⓔ	14 Ⓐ Ⓑ Ⓒ Ⓓ Ⓔ	19 Ⓐ Ⓑ Ⓒ Ⓓ Ⓔ	24 Ⓐ Ⓑ Ⓒ Ⓓ Ⓔ
5 Ⓐ Ⓑ Ⓒ Ⓓ Ⓔ	10 Ⓐ Ⓑ Ⓒ Ⓓ Ⓔ	15 Ⓐ Ⓑ Ⓒ Ⓓ Ⓔ	20 Ⓐ Ⓑ Ⓒ Ⓓ Ⓔ	25 Ⓐ Ⓑ Ⓒ Ⓓ Ⓔ
				26 Ⓐ Ⓑ Ⓒ Ⓓ Ⓔ

SECTION III

1 Ⓐ Ⓑ Ⓒ Ⓓ Ⓔ	8 Ⓐ Ⓑ Ⓒ Ⓓ Ⓔ	15 Ⓐ Ⓑ Ⓒ Ⓓ Ⓔ	22 Ⓐ Ⓑ Ⓒ Ⓓ Ⓔ	29 Ⓐ Ⓑ Ⓒ Ⓓ Ⓔ
2 Ⓐ Ⓑ Ⓒ Ⓓ Ⓔ	9 Ⓐ Ⓑ Ⓒ Ⓓ Ⓔ	16 Ⓐ Ⓑ Ⓒ Ⓓ Ⓔ	23 Ⓐ Ⓑ Ⓒ Ⓓ Ⓔ	30 Ⓐ Ⓑ Ⓒ Ⓓ Ⓔ
3 Ⓐ Ⓑ Ⓒ Ⓓ Ⓔ	10 Ⓐ Ⓑ Ⓒ Ⓓ Ⓔ	17 Ⓐ Ⓑ Ⓒ Ⓓ Ⓔ	24 Ⓐ Ⓑ Ⓒ Ⓓ Ⓔ	31 Ⓐ Ⓑ Ⓒ Ⓓ Ⓔ
4 Ⓐ Ⓑ Ⓒ Ⓓ Ⓔ	11 Ⓐ Ⓑ Ⓒ Ⓓ Ⓔ	18 Ⓐ Ⓑ Ⓒ Ⓓ Ⓔ	25 Ⓐ Ⓑ Ⓒ Ⓓ Ⓔ	32 Ⓐ Ⓑ Ⓒ Ⓓ Ⓔ
5 Ⓐ Ⓑ Ⓒ Ⓓ Ⓔ	12 Ⓐ Ⓑ Ⓒ Ⓓ Ⓔ	19 Ⓐ Ⓑ Ⓒ Ⓓ Ⓔ	26 Ⓐ Ⓑ Ⓒ Ⓓ Ⓔ	33 Ⓐ Ⓑ Ⓒ Ⓓ Ⓔ
6 Ⓐ Ⓑ Ⓒ Ⓓ Ⓔ	13 Ⓐ Ⓑ Ⓒ Ⓓ Ⓔ	20 Ⓐ Ⓑ Ⓒ Ⓓ Ⓔ	27 Ⓐ Ⓑ Ⓒ Ⓓ Ⓔ	34 Ⓐ Ⓑ Ⓒ Ⓓ Ⓔ
7 Ⓐ Ⓑ Ⓒ Ⓓ Ⓔ	14 Ⓐ Ⓑ Ⓒ Ⓓ Ⓔ	21 Ⓐ Ⓑ Ⓒ Ⓓ Ⓔ	28 Ⓐ Ⓑ Ⓒ Ⓓ Ⓔ	35 Ⓐ Ⓑ Ⓒ Ⓓ Ⓔ

SECTION IV

1 Ⓐ Ⓑ Ⓒ Ⓓ Ⓔ 6 Ⓐ Ⓑ Ⓒ Ⓓ Ⓔ 11 Ⓐ Ⓑ Ⓒ Ⓓ Ⓔ 16 Ⓐ Ⓑ Ⓒ Ⓓ Ⓔ 21 Ⓐ Ⓑ Ⓒ Ⓓ Ⓔ
2 Ⓐ Ⓑ Ⓒ Ⓓ Ⓔ 7 Ⓐ Ⓑ Ⓒ Ⓓ Ⓔ 12 Ⓐ Ⓑ Ⓒ Ⓓ Ⓔ 17 Ⓐ Ⓑ Ⓒ Ⓓ Ⓔ 22 Ⓐ Ⓑ Ⓒ Ⓓ Ⓔ
3 Ⓐ Ⓑ Ⓒ Ⓓ Ⓔ 8 Ⓐ Ⓑ Ⓒ Ⓓ Ⓔ 13 Ⓐ Ⓑ Ⓒ Ⓓ Ⓔ 18 Ⓐ Ⓑ Ⓒ Ⓓ Ⓔ 23 Ⓐ Ⓑ Ⓒ Ⓓ Ⓔ
4 Ⓐ Ⓑ Ⓒ Ⓓ Ⓔ 9 Ⓐ Ⓑ Ⓒ Ⓓ Ⓔ 14 Ⓐ Ⓑ Ⓒ Ⓓ Ⓔ 19 Ⓐ Ⓑ Ⓒ Ⓓ Ⓔ 24 Ⓐ Ⓑ Ⓒ Ⓓ Ⓔ
5 Ⓐ Ⓑ Ⓒ Ⓓ Ⓔ 10 Ⓐ Ⓑ Ⓒ Ⓓ Ⓔ 15 Ⓐ Ⓑ Ⓒ Ⓓ Ⓔ 20 Ⓐ Ⓑ Ⓒ Ⓓ Ⓔ 25 Ⓐ Ⓑ Ⓒ Ⓓ Ⓔ

SECTION V

1 Ⓐ Ⓑ Ⓒ Ⓓ Ⓔ 6 Ⓐ Ⓑ Ⓒ Ⓓ Ⓔ 11 Ⓐ Ⓑ Ⓒ Ⓓ Ⓔ 16 Ⓐ Ⓑ Ⓒ Ⓓ Ⓔ 21 Ⓐ Ⓑ Ⓒ Ⓓ Ⓔ 26 Ⓐ Ⓑ Ⓒ Ⓓ Ⓔ
2 Ⓐ Ⓑ Ⓒ Ⓓ Ⓔ 7 Ⓐ Ⓑ Ⓒ Ⓓ Ⓔ 12 Ⓐ Ⓑ Ⓒ Ⓓ Ⓔ 17 Ⓐ Ⓑ Ⓒ Ⓓ Ⓔ 22 Ⓐ Ⓑ Ⓒ Ⓓ Ⓔ 27 Ⓐ Ⓑ Ⓒ Ⓓ Ⓔ
3 Ⓐ Ⓑ Ⓒ Ⓓ Ⓔ 8 Ⓐ Ⓑ Ⓒ Ⓓ Ⓔ 13 Ⓐ Ⓑ Ⓒ Ⓓ Ⓔ 18 Ⓐ Ⓑ Ⓒ Ⓓ Ⓔ 23 Ⓐ Ⓑ Ⓒ Ⓓ Ⓔ 28 Ⓐ Ⓑ Ⓒ Ⓓ Ⓔ
4 Ⓐ Ⓑ Ⓒ Ⓓ Ⓔ 9 Ⓐ Ⓑ Ⓒ Ⓓ Ⓔ 14 Ⓐ Ⓑ Ⓒ Ⓓ Ⓔ 19 Ⓐ Ⓑ Ⓒ Ⓓ Ⓔ 24 Ⓐ Ⓑ Ⓒ Ⓓ Ⓔ
5 Ⓐ Ⓑ Ⓒ Ⓓ Ⓔ 10 Ⓐ Ⓑ Ⓒ Ⓓ Ⓔ 15 Ⓐ Ⓑ Ⓒ Ⓓ Ⓔ 20 Ⓐ Ⓑ Ⓒ Ⓓ Ⓔ 25 Ⓐ Ⓑ Ⓒ Ⓓ Ⓔ

SECTION VI

1 Ⓐ Ⓑ Ⓒ Ⓓ Ⓔ 6 Ⓐ Ⓑ Ⓒ Ⓓ Ⓔ 11 Ⓐ Ⓑ Ⓒ Ⓓ Ⓔ 16 Ⓐ Ⓑ Ⓒ Ⓓ Ⓔ 21 Ⓐ Ⓑ Ⓒ Ⓓ Ⓔ
2 Ⓐ Ⓑ Ⓒ Ⓓ Ⓔ 7 Ⓐ Ⓑ Ⓒ Ⓓ Ⓔ 12 Ⓐ Ⓑ Ⓒ Ⓓ Ⓔ 17 Ⓐ Ⓑ Ⓒ Ⓓ Ⓔ 22 Ⓐ Ⓑ Ⓒ Ⓓ Ⓔ
3 Ⓐ Ⓑ Ⓒ Ⓓ Ⓔ 8 Ⓐ Ⓑ Ⓒ Ⓓ Ⓔ 13 Ⓐ Ⓑ Ⓒ Ⓓ Ⓔ 18 Ⓐ Ⓑ Ⓒ Ⓓ Ⓔ 23 Ⓐ Ⓑ Ⓒ Ⓓ Ⓔ
4 Ⓐ Ⓑ Ⓒ Ⓓ Ⓔ 9 Ⓐ Ⓑ Ⓒ Ⓓ Ⓔ 14 Ⓐ Ⓑ Ⓒ Ⓓ Ⓔ 19 Ⓐ Ⓑ Ⓒ Ⓓ Ⓔ 24 Ⓐ Ⓑ Ⓒ Ⓓ Ⓔ
5 Ⓐ Ⓑ Ⓒ Ⓓ Ⓔ 10 Ⓐ Ⓑ Ⓒ Ⓓ Ⓔ 15 Ⓐ Ⓑ Ⓒ Ⓓ Ⓔ 20 Ⓐ Ⓑ Ⓒ Ⓓ Ⓔ 25 Ⓐ Ⓑ Ⓒ Ⓓ Ⓔ
26 Ⓐ Ⓑ Ⓒ Ⓓ Ⓔ

EXAMINATION FORECAST

Section Number	Type	Minutes	Questions
Section I	Reading Comprehension	35	28
Section II	Logical Reasoning	35	26
Section III	Issues & Facts	35	35
Section IV	Analytical Reasoning	35	25
Section V	Reading Comprehension	35	28
Section VI	Logical Reasoning	35	26
	Writing Sample	30	—
Total Time		4 hours	

A 15-minute break should be taken after section IV.

The Writing Sample will usually be given before the rest of the LSAT and is found at the end of the Practice Test in this book.

PRACTICE EXAMINATION 4

Section I

Time—35 Minutes
28 Questions

Directions: Below each of the following passages, you will find questions or incomplete statements about the passage. Each statement or question is followed by five lettered words or expressions. Select the word or expression that most satisfactorily completes each statement or answers each question in accordance with the meaning of the passage. After you choose the best answer, blacken the corresponding space on the answer sheet.

Shams and delusions are esteemed for soundest truths, while reality is fabulous. If men would steadily observe realities only, and not allow themselves to be deluded, life, to compare it with such things as we know, would be like a fairy tale and the Arabian Nights' entertainments. If we respect only what is inevitable and has a right to be, music and poetry would resound along the streets. When we are unhurried and wise, we perceive that only great and worthy things have any permanent and absolute existence—that petty fears and petty pleasures are but the shadow of the reality. This is always exhilarating and sublime. By closing the eyes and slumbering, and consenting to be deceived by shows, men everywhere establish and confirm their daily life of routine and habit, which still is built on purely illusory foundations. Children, who play life, discern its true law and relations more clearly than men, who fail to live it worthily, but who think that they are wiser by experience; that is, by failure.

I have read in a Hindu book that there was a king's son who, being expelled in infancy from his native city, was brought up by a forester, and, growing up to maturity in that state, imagined himself to belong to the barbarous race with which he lived. One of his father's ministers, having discovered him, revealed to him what he was, and the misconception of his character was removed, and he knew himself to be a prince. "So soul," continues the Hindu philosopher, "from the circumstances in which it is placed, mistakes its own character, until the truth is revealed to it by some holy teacher, and then it knows itself to be *Brahme.*"

We think that that *is* which *appears* to be. If a man should give us an account of the realities he beheld, we should not recognize the place in his description. Look at a meeting-house, or a court-house, or a jail, or a shop, or a dwelling-house, and say what that thing really is before a true gaze, and they would all go to pieces in your account of them. Men esteem truth remote, in the outskirts of the system, behind the farthest star, before Adam and after the last man. In eternity there is indeed something true and sublime. But all these times and places and occasions are now and here. God himself culminates in the present moment, and will never be more divine in the lapse of all ages. And we are enabled to apprehend at all what is sublime and noble only by the perpetual instilling and drenching of the reality that surrounds us. The universe constantly and obediently answers to our conceptions; whether we travel fast or slow, the track is laid for us. Let us spend our lives in conceiving then. The poet or the artist never yet had so fair and noble a design but some of his posterity at least could accomplish it.

1. The writer's attitude toward the arts is one of
   (A) indifference
   (B) suspicion
   (C) admiration
   (D) repulsion
   (E) reluctant respect

2. The author believes that children are often more acute than adults in their appreciation of life's relations because
   (A) children know more than adults
   (B) children can use their experience better
   (C) children's eyes are unclouded by failure
   (D) experience is the best teacher
   (E) the child is father to the man

3. The passage implies that human beings
   (A) cannot distinguish the true from the untrue
   (B) are immoral if they are lazy
   (C) should be bold and fearless
   (D) believe in fairy tales
   (E) have progressed culturally throughout history

4. The word *fabulous* in the second line means
   (A) wonderful
   (B) delicious
   (C) birdlike
   (D) incomprehensible
   (E) illusory

5. The author is primarily concerned with urging the reader to
   (A) meditate on the meaninglessness of the present
   (B) look to the future for enlightenment
   (C) appraise the present for its true value
   (D) honor the wisdom of past ages
   (E) spend more time in leisure activities

6. The passage is primarily concerned with problems of
   (A) history and economics
   (B) society and population
   (C) biology and physics
   (D) theology and philosophy
   (E) music and art

7. Which of the following best describes the author's idea of the relationship between man and the universe?
   (A) Each person's mind can control the galaxies.
   (B) What you see is what you get.
   (C) Our lives are predetermined.
   (D) We may choose to live quickly or slowly.
   (E) Poets cannot conceive of their posterity.

Suppose you go into a fruiterer's shop, wanting an apple—you take up one, and on biting it you find it is sour; you look at it, and see that it is hard and green. You take up another one, and that, too, is hard, green, and sour. The shopman offers you a third; but, before biting it, you examine it, and find that it is hard and green, and you immediately say that you will not have it, as it must be sour, like those that you have already tried.

Nothing can be more simple than that, you think; but if you will take the trouble to analyze and trace out into its logical elements what has been done by the mind, you will be greatly surprised. In the first place you have performed the operation of induction. You found that, in two experiences, hardness and greenness in apples went together with sourness. It was so in the first case, and it was confirmed by the second. True, it is a very small basis, but still it is enough from which to make an induction; you generalize the facts, and you expect to find sourness in apples where you get hardness and greenness. You found upon that a general law, that all hard and green apples are sour; and that, so far as it goes, is a perfect induction. Well, having got your natural law in this way, when you are offered another apple which you find is hard and green, you say, "All hard and green apples are sour; this apple is hard and green, therefore, this apple is sour." That train of reasoning is what logicians call a syllogism, and has all its various parts and terms—its major premise, its minor premise, and its conclusion. And, by the help of further reasoning, which, if drawn out, would have to be exhibited in two or three other syllogisms, you arrive at your final determination, "I will not have that apple." So that, you see, you have, in the first place, established a law by induction, and upon that you have founded a deduction, and reasoned out the special particular case.

Well now, suppose, having got your conclusion of the law, that at some times afterwards, you are discussing the qualities of apple with a friend; you will say to him, "It is a very curious thing, but I find that all hard and green apples are sour!" Your friend says to you, "But how do you know that?" You at once reply, "Oh, because I have tried them over and over again, and have always found them to be so." Well, if we were talking science instead of common sense, we should call that an experimental verification. And, if still opposed, you go further, and say, "I have heard from the people in Somersetshire and Devonshire, where a large number of apples are grown, and in London, where many apples are sold and eaten, that they have observed the same thing. It is also found to be the case in Normandy, and in North America. In short, I find it to be the universal experience of mankind wherever attention has been directed to the subject." Whereupon, your friend, unless he is a very unreasonable man, agrees with you, and is convinced that you are quite right in the conclusion you have drawn. He believes, although perhaps he does not know he believes it, that the more extensive verifications have been made, and results of the same kind arrived at—that the more varied the conditions under which the same results are attained, the more certain is the ultimate conclusion, and he disputes the question no further. He sees that the experiment has been tried under all sorts of conditions, as to time, place, and people, with the same result; and he says with you, therefore, that the law you have laid down must be a good one, and he must believe it.

8. The writer is probably
   (A) French
   (B) English
   (C) American
   (D) Italian
   (E) none of the above

9. "All giraffes are beautiful and graceful.
   Twiga is a giraffe.
   Twiga is beautiful and graceful."

   According to the passage, the above reasoning is a(n)
   (A) empirical verification
   (B) induction from cases
   (C) syllogism
   (D) experimental conclusion
   (E) developmental sequence

10. Apples are used
    (A) in order to convince the reader that fruit has no intellect
    (B) to illustrate the subject of the passage
    (C) to give color to the story
    (D) to show how foolish logic is
    (E) to compare various types of persons

11. The author has the approach of a(n)
    (A) scientist
    (B) artist
    (C) novelist
    (D) economist
    (E) businessman

12. The term "natural law" as it appears in the text refers to
    (A) common sense
    (B) the "honor system"
    (C) the result of an induction
    (D) the order of nature
    (E) a scientific discovery

13. Which of the following would be the best title for the passage?
    (A) Discovering the Natural Laws of Apples
    (B) The Uses of Induction
    (C) Syllogistic Reasoning in Common Circumstances
    (D) Experimental Verification As an Adjunct to Reasoning
    (E) The Logic of Everyday Reasoning

14. If you find a hard and green apple that is not sour, you should
    (A) try further apples to see if the natural law has changed
    (B) eat the rest of the apple at once
    (C) reject the law stating hard and green apples are usually sour
    (D) conduct further investigations and make adjustments to the law of apples as necessary
    (E) all of the above

The origin of continental nuclei has long been a puzzle. Theories advanced so far have generally failed to explain the first step in continent growth, or have been subject to serious objections. It is the purpose of this article to examine the possible role of the impact of large meteorites or asteroids in the production of continental nuclei.

Unfortunately, the geological evolution of the Earth's surface has had an obliterating effect on the original composition and structure of the continents to such an extent that further terrestrial investigations have small chance of arriving at an unambiguous answer to the question of continental origin. Paradoxically, clues to the origin and early history of the surface features of Earth may be found on the moon and planets, rather than on Earth, because some of these bodies appear to have had a much less active geological history. As a result, relatively primitive surface features are preserved for study and analysis.

In the case of both the moon and Mars, it is generally concluded from the appearance of their heavily cratered surfaces that they have been subjected to bombardment by large meteoroids during their geological history. Likewise, it would appear a reasonable hypothesis that Earth has also been subjected to meteoroid bombardment in the past, and that very large bodies struck Earth early in its geological history.

The largest crater on the moon listed by Baldwin has a diameter of 285 km. However, if we accept the hypothesis of formation of some of the mare basins by impact, the maximum lunar impact crater diameter is probably as large as 650 km. Based on a lunar analogy, one might expect several impact craters of at least 500-km diameter to have been formed on Earth. By applying Baldwin's equation, the depth of such a crater should be about 20 km. Baldwin admits that his equation gives excessive depths for large craters so that the actual depth should be somewhat smaller. Based on the measured depth of smaller lunar craters, a depth of 10 km is probably a conservative estimate for the depth of a 500-km impact crater. Baldwin's equation gives the depth of the zone of brecciation for such a crater as about 75 km. The plasticity of Earth's mantle at the depth makes it impossible to speak of "brecciation" in the usual sense. However, local stresses may be temporarily sustained at that depth, as shown by the existence of deep-focus earthquakes. Thus, short-term effects might be expected to a depth of more than 50 km in the mantle.

Even without knowing the precise effects, there is little doubt that the formation of a 500-km crater would be a major geological event. Numerous authors have considered the geological implications of such an event. Donn et al. have, for example, called on the impact of continent-size bodies of sialic composition to form the original continents. Two major difficulties inherent in this concept are the lack of any known sialic meteorites, and the high probability that the energy of impact would result in a wide dissemination of sialic material, rather than its concentration at the point of impact.

Gilvarry, on the other hand, called on meteoroid impact to explain the production of ocean basins. The major difficulties with this model are that the morphology of most of the ocean basins is not consistent with impact, and that the origin and growth of continents are not adequately explained.

We agree with Donn et al. that the impact of large meteorites or asteroids may have caused continent formation, but would rather think in terms of the localized addition of energy to the system, rather than in terms of the addition of actual sialic material.

15. The author's purpose in writing the passage was to
    (A) examine the relationship between meteors and other problems
    (B) discuss the possible causes of continent formation
    (C) review lunar continent formation
    (D) discuss the theories of continental nuclei formation
    (E) analyze ways in which asteroids and meteorites could have influenced the development of continents on Earth

16. A mare basin is most probably
    (A) an area where animal life flourished at one time
    (B) a formula for determining the relationship between the depth and width of craters
    (C) a valley that is filled in when a spatial body has impact with the moon or Earth
    (D) a planetoid (small planet) created when a meteorite, upon striking the moon, breaks off a part of the moon
    (E) an area of the moon that is the result of collision between the moon and some other body

17. As used in the passage, the term "brecciation" seems to mean
    (A) volcanism
    (B) breaking and bending

(C) utter destruction
(D) mountain building
(E) sea bed raising

18. According to the passage, the largest crater that is found on the moon today is approximately
    (A) 1.6 km across
    (B) 20 km across
    (C) 50 km across
    (D) 500 km across
    (E) 650 km across

19. The writer does NOT believe that
    (A) an asteroid is larger than a meteorite
    (B) material from space, upon hitting the Earth, was eventually distributed
    (C) oceans were formerly craters
    (D) Earth, at one time, had craters
    (E) tremendous meteorites, in early times, fell upon our planet

20. The passage is primarily concerned with
    (A) the origin of continents on Earth
    (B) the origin of craters on the moon
    (C) differences of opinion among schools of geological thought
    (D) the relationship between asteroids and meteorites and other space bodies
    (E) planetary surface features of all kinds

21. It may be inferred from the passage that the author believes geologists researching continental origins and development would do well to devote much, if not most, of their study to
    (A) asteroids and large meteorites
    (B) Earth
    (C) the sun
    (D) planetoids
    (E) other planets and the moon

When the television is good, nothing—not the theatre, not the magazines, or newspapers—nothing is better. But when television is bad, nothing is worse. I invite you to sit down in front of your television set when your station goes on the air and stay there without a book, magazine, newspaper, or anything else to distract you and keep your eyes glued to that set until the station signs off. I can assure you that you will observe a vast wasteland. You will see a procession of game shows, violence, audience-participation shows, formula comedies about totally unbelievable families, blood and thunder, mayhem, more violence, sadism, murder, Western badmen, Western goodmen, private eyes, gangsters, still more violence, and cartoons. And, endlessly, commercials that scream and cajole and offend. And most of all, boredom. True, you will see a few things you will enjoy. But they will be very, very few. And if you think I exaggerate, try it.

Is there no room on television to teach, to inform, to uplift, to stretch, to enlarge the capacities of our children? Is there no room for programs to deepen the children's understanding of children in other lands? Is there no room for a children's news show explaining something about the world for them at their level of understanding? Is there no room for reading the great literature of the past, teaching them the great traditions of freedom? There are some fine children's shows, but they are drowned out in the massive doses of cartoons, violence, and more violence. Must these be your trademarks? Search your conscience and see whether you cannot offer more to your young beneficiaries whose future you guard so many hours each and every day.

There are many people in this great country, and you must serve all of us. You will get no argument from me if you say that, given a choice between a Western and a symphony, more people will watch the Western. I like Westerns and private eyes, too—but a steady diet for the whole country is obviously not in the public interest. We all know that people would more often prefer to be entertained than stimulated or informed. But your obligations are not satisfied if you look only to popularity as a test of what to broadcast. You are not only in show business; you are free to communicate ideas as well as to give relaxation. You must provide a wider range of choices, more diversity, more alternatives. It is not enough to cater to the nation's whims—you must also serve the nation's needs. The people own the air. They own it as much in prime evening time as they do at six o'clock in the morning. For every hour that the people give you—you owe them something. I intend to see that your debt is paid with service.

—excerpt from speech by Newton H. Minow, chairman of the Federal Communications Commission, before the National Association of Broadcasters.

22. The wasteland referred to by the author describes
    (A) western badlands
    (B) average television programs
    (C) morning television shows
    (D) television shows with desert locales
    (E) children's programs generally

23. The author's attitude toward television can best be described as
    (A) sullenness at defeat
    (B) reconciliation with the broadcasters
    (C) righteous indignation
    (D) determination to prevail
    (E) hopelessness over the size of the problem

24. The author is primarily concerned to tell broadcasters that
    (A) the listener, not the broadcaster, should make the decisions about which programs are aired
    (B) all children's shows are worthless
    (C) mystery programs should be banned
    (D) they had better mend their ways
    (E) televised instruction should become a substitute for classroom lessons

25. Concerning programs for children, it may be inferred that Minow believes that such programs should
    (A) include no cartoons at all
    (B) include ones which provide culture
    (C) be presented only during the morning hours
    (D) be presented without commercial interruption
    (E) not deal with the Old West

26. The statement that "the people own the air" implies that
    (A) citizens have the right to insist on worthwhile television programs
    (B) television should be socialized
    (C) the government may build above present structures
    (D) since air is worthless, the people own nothing
    (E) the broadcasters have no right to commercialize on television

27. It can be inferred from the passage in regard to television programming that the author believes
    (A) the broadcasters are trying to do the right thing but are failing
    (B) foreign countries are going to pattern their programs after ours
    (C) there is a great deal that is worthwhile in present programs
    (D) the listeners do not necessarily know what is good for them
    (E) six o'clock in the morning is too early for a television show

28. Which of the following would NOT be inferable from the passage?
    (A) The needs of minorities must be met by television.
    (B) Minow would probably favor more television stations being established, if they were responsible stations.
    (C) Violence is not a good ingredient for children's television shows.
    (D) Children's television is uniformly terrible.
    (E) Minow believes that better shows are possible.

STOP

IF YOU FINISH BEFORE TIME IS CALLED, CHECK YOUR WORK ON THIS SECTION ONLY. DO NOT WORK ON ANY OTHER SECTION IN THE TEST.

SECTION II

Time–35 Minutes
26 Questions

Directions: In this section, the questions ask you to analyze and evaluate the reasoning in short paragraphs or passages. For some questions, all of the answer choices may conceivably be answers to the question asked. You should select the *best* answer to the question, that is, an answer which does not require you to make assumptions which violate commonsense standards by being implausible, redundant, irrelevant or inconsistent. After choosing the best answer, blacken the corresponding space on the answer sheet.

1. Two ardent cinema buffs argued over dinner one night about the merits of a very old and rarely exhibited silent movie. At length, they finished their meal and as they were leaving the restaurant one of them said to his companion, "Someday we must actually see this film."

   The two persons were arguing on the basis of
   (A) revelation
   (B) induction
   (C) deduction
   (D) assumption
   (E) semantics

2. When this proposal to reduce welfare benefits is brought up for debate, we are sure to hear claims by the liberal Congressmen that the bill will be detrimental to poor people. These politicians fail to understand, however, that budget reductions are accompanied by tax cuts—so everyone will have more money to spend, not less.

   Which of the following, if true, would undermine the author's position?

   I. Poor people tend to vote for liberal Congressmen who promise to raise welfare benefits.
   II. Poor people pay little or no taxes so that a tax cut would be of little advantage to them.
   III. Any tax advantage which the poor will receive will be more than offset by cuts in the government services they now receive.

   (A) I only
   (B) II only
   (C) II and III only
   (D) III only
   (E) I, II, and III

3. Many people ask, "How effective is Painaway?" So to find out we have been checking the medicine cabinets of the apartments in this typical building. As it turns out, eight out of ten contain a bottle of Painaway. Doesn't it stand to reason that you, too, should have the most effective pain-reliever on the market?

   The appeal of this advertisement would be most weakened by which of the following pieces of evidence?
   (A) Painaway distributed complimentary bottles of medicine to most apartments in the building two days before the advertisement was made.
   (B) The actor who made the advertisement takes a pain-reliever manufactured by a competitor of Painaway.
   (C) Most people want a fast, effective pain-reliever.
   (D) Many people take the advice of their neighborhood druggists about pain-relievers.
   (E) A government survey shows that many people take a pain-reliever before it is really needed.

Questions 4 and 5

An artist must suffer for his art say these successful entrepreneurs who attempt to pass themselves off as artists. They auction off to the highest bidder, usually a fool in his own right, the most mediocre of drawings; and then, from their well-laid tables, they have the unmitigated gall to imply that they themselves____(4)____.

4. Choose the answer which best completes the paragraph.
   (A) are connoisseurs of art
   (B) suffer deprivation for the sake of their work
   (C) are artists
   (D) know art better than the art critics do
   (E) do not enjoy a good meal

5. Which of the following must underlie the author's position?

   I. One must actually suffer to do great art.
   II. Financial deprivation is the only suffering an artist undergoes.
   III. Art critics have little real expertise and are consequently easily deceived.

   (A) I only
   (B) II only
   (C) I and II only
   (D) II and III only
   (E) I, II, and III

Questions 6 and 7

Stock market analysts always attribute a sudden drop in the market to some domestic or international political crisis. I maintain, however, that these declines are attributable to the phases of the moon which also cause periodic political upheavals and increases in tension in world affairs.

6. Which of the following best describes the author's method of questioning the claim of market analysts?
   (A) He presents a counter-example.
   (B) He presents statistical evidence.
   (C) He suggests an alternative causal linkage.
   (D) He appeals to generally accepted beliefs.
   (E) He demonstrates that market analysts' reports are unreliable.

7. It can be inferred that the author is critical of the stock analysts because he
   (A) believes that they have oversimplified the connection between political crisis and fluctuations of the market
   (B) knows that the stock market generally shows more gains than losses
   (C) suspects that stock analysts have a vested interest in the stock market, and are therefore likely to distort their explanations
   (D) anticipates making large profits in the market himself
   (E) is worried that if the connection between political events and stock market prices becomes well-known, unscrupulous investors will take advantage of the information

8. This piece of pottery must surely date from the late Minoan period. The dress of the female figures, particularly the bare and emphasized breasts, and the activities of the people depicted, note especially the importance of the bull, are both highly suggestive of this period. These factors, when coupled with the black, semi-gloss glaze which results from firing the pot in a sealed kiln at a low temperature, makes the conclusion a virtual certainty.

   Which of the following is a basic assumption made by the author of this explanation?
   (A) Black semi-gloss glazed pottery was made only during the late Minoan period.
   (B) The bull is an animal which was important to most ancient cultures.
   (C) Throughout the long history of the Minoan people, their artisans decorated pottery with semi-nude women and bulls.
   (D) By analyzing the style and materials of any work of art, an expert can pinpoint the date of its creation.
   (E) There are key characteristics of works of art which can be shown to be typical of a particular period.

9. Most radicals who argue for violent revolution and complete overthrow of our existing society have no clear idea what will emerge from the destruction. They just assert that things are so bad now that any change would have to be a change for the better. But surely this is mistaken, for things might actually turn out to be worse.

The most effective point which can be raised against this argument is that the author says nothing about

(A) the manner in which the radicals might foment their revolution
(B) the specific results of the revolution which would be changes for the worse
(C) the economic arguments the radicals use to persuade people to join in their cause
(D) the fact that most people are really satisfied with the present system so that the chance of total revolution is very small
(E) the loss of life and property which is likely to accompany total destruction of a society

Questions 10 and 11

Having just completed Introductory Logic 9, I feel competent to instruct others in the intricacies of this wonderful discipline. Logic is concerned with correct reasoning in the form of syllogisms. A syllogism consists of three statements, two of which are premises, the third of which is the conclusion. Here is an example:

MAJOR PREMISE: The American buffalo is disappearing.
MINOR PREMISE: This animal is an American buffalo.
CONCLUSION: Therefore, this animal is disappearing.

Once one has been indoctrinated into the mysteries of this arcane science, there is no statement he may not assert with complete confidence.

10. The reasoning of the author's example is most similar to that contained in which of the following arguments?
    (A) Any endangered species must be protected; this species is endangered; therefore, it should be protected.
    (B) All whales are mammals; this animal is a whale; therefore, this animal is a mammal.
    (C) Engaging in sexual intercourse with a person to whom one is not married is a sin; and since pre-marital intercourse is, by definition, without the institution of marriage, it is, therefore, a sin.
    (D) There are sixty seconds in a minute; there are sixty minutes in an hour; therefore, there are 3600 seconds in an hour.
    (E) Wealthy people pay most of the taxes; this man is wealthy; therefore, this man pays most of the taxes.

11. The main purpose of the author's argument is to
    (A) provide instruction in logic
    (B) supply a definition
    (C) cast doubt on the value of formal logic
    (D) present an argument for the protection of the American buffalo
    (E) show the precise relationship between the premises and the conclusion of his example

Questions 12 and 13

On a recent trip to the Mediterranean, I made the acquaintance of a young man who warned me against trusting Cretans. "Everything they say is a lie," he told me, "and I should know because I come from Crete myself." I thanked the fellow for his advice but told him in light of what he had said I had no intention of believing it.

12. Which of the following best describes the author's behavior?
    (A) It was unwarranted because the young man was merely trying to be helpful to a stranger.
    (B) It was paradoxical for in discounting the advice he implicitly relied on it.
    (C) It was understandable inasmuch as the young man, by his own admission, could not possibly be telling the truth.
    (D) It was high-handed and just the sort of thing that gives American tourists a bad name.
    (E) It was overly cautious for not everyone in a foreign country will try to take advantage of a tourist.

13. Which of the following is most nearly analogous to the warning issued by the young man?
    (A) An admission by a witness under cross-examination that he has lied.

(B) A sign put up by the Chamber of Commerce of a large city alerting visitors to the danger of pickpockets.
(C) The command of a military leader to his marching troops to do an about-face.
(D) A sentence written in chalk on a blackboard which says, "This sentence is false."
(E) The advice of a veteran worker to a newly hired person: "You don't actually have to work hard so long as you look like you're working hard."

14. Doctors, in seeking a cure for *aphroditis melancholias* are guided by their research into the causes of *metaeritocas polymanias* because the symptoms of the two diseases occur in populations of similar ages, manifesting symptoms in both cases of high fever, swollen glands, and lack of appetite. Moreover, the incubation period for both diseases is virtually identical. So these medical researchers are convinced that the virus responsible for *aphroditis melancholias* is very similar to that responsible for *metaeritocas polymanias.*

The conclusion of the author rests on the presupposition that
(A) *metaeritocas polymanias* is a more serious public health hazard than *aphroditis melancholias*
(B) for every disease, modern medical science will eventually find a cure
(C) saving human life is the single most important goal of modern technology
(D) *aphroditis melancholias* is a disease which occurs only in human beings.
(E) diseases with similar symptoms will have similar causes

15. Judging from the content and source of the following statements, which is the most reasonable and trustworthy?
(A) MEMBER OF THE FOOTBALL BOOSTER CLUB: This year our team is sure to win the state championship because we have Gardner at quarterback.
(B) SALES REPRESENTATIVE FOR A COSMETIC COMPANY: This new lip gloss is sure to attract a lot of attention. We even tested it in popular singles spots around the city, and the results were fantastic.
(C) JET FIGHTER PILOT AND HIS CO-PILOT: At on-nine-hundred hours we spotted a silver object on the eastern horizon moving at twice the speed of sound.
(D) RUNNER-UP IN A CONTEST: I deserved to win. My entry was far and away the most original.
(E) UNION REPRESENTATIVE: All that we ask for is a fair settlement, one which will compensate our members for the wage increases they have already foregone in an effort to help the company expand.

Questions 16 and 17

The federal bankruptcy laws illustrate the folly of do-good protectionism at its most extreme. At the debtor's own request, the judge will list all of his debts, take what money the debtor has, which will be very little, and divide that small amount among his creditors. Then the judge declares that those debts are thereby satisfied, and the debtor is free from those creditors. Why, a person could take his credit card and buy a car, a stereo, and a new wardrobe and then declare himself bankrupt! In effect, he will have conned his creditors into giving him all those things for nothing.

16. Which of the following adages best describes the author's attitude about a bankrupt debtor?
(A) "A penny saved is a penny earned."
(B) "You've made your bed, now lie in it."
(C) "Absolute power corrupts absolutely."
(D) "He that governs least governs best."
(E) "Millions for defense, but not one cent for tribute."

17. Which of the following does the author imply?
(A) A judge will not use all of a debtor's assets, including personal possessions, to pay his creditors.
(B) Most persons who own credit cards are financially irresponsible.
(C) A bankrupt debtor ought to be imprisoned until he is able to raise the money to pay all of his debts.

(D) Most personal bankruptcy proceedings are initiated at the request of the creditors.
(E) Borrowing money is immoral.

18. Either you punish a child severely when he is bad or he will grow up to be a criminal.
Your child has just been bad.
Therefore, you should punish him severely.

All EXCEPT which of the following would be appropriate objection to the argument?
(A) What do you consider to be a severe punishment?
(B) What do you mean by the term "bad"?
(C) Isn't your "either-or" premise an oversimplification?
(D) Don't your first and second premises contradict one another?
(E) In what way has this child been bad?

19. The Supreme Court's recent decision is unfair. It treats non-resident aliens as a special group when it denies them some rights ordinary citizens have. This treatment is discriminatory, and we all know that discrimination is unfair.

Which of the following arguments is most nearly similar in its reasoning to the above argument?
(A) Doing good would be our highest duty under the moral law, and that duty would be irrational unless we had the ability to discharge it; but since a finite, sensuous creature could never discharge that duty in his lifetime, we must conclude that if there is a moral law, the soul is immortal.
(B) Required core courses are a good idea because students just entering college do not have as good an idea about what constitutes a good education as do the professional educators; therefore, students should not be left complete freedom to select coursework.
(C) This country is the most free nation on Earth largely as a result of the fact that the founding fathers had the foresight to include a Bill of Rights in the Constitution.
(D) Whiskey and beer do not mix well; every evening that I have drunk both whiskey and beer together, the following morning I have had a hangover.
(E) I know that this is a beautiful painting because Picasso created only beautiful works of art, and this painting was done by Picasso.

20. Creativity must be cultivated. Artists, musicians, and writers all practice, consciously or unconsciously, interpreting the world from new and interesting viewpoints. A teacher can encourage his pupils to be creative by showing them different perspectives for viewing the significance of events in their daily lives.

Which of the following, if true, would most undermine the author's claim?
(A) In a well-ordered society, it is important to have some people who are not artists, musicians, or writers.
(B) A teacher's efforts to show a pupil different perspectives may actually inhibit development of the student's own creative process.
(C) Public education should stress practical skills, which will help a person get a good job, instead of creative thinking.
(D) Not all pupils have the same capacity for creative thought.
(E) Some artists, musicians, and writers "burn themselves out" at a very early age, producing a flurry of great works and then nothing after that.

21. Opponents to the mayor's plan for express bus lanes on the city's major commuter arteries objected that people could not be lured out of their automobiles in that way. The opponents were proved wrong; following implementation of the plan, bus ridership rose dramatically, and there was a corresponding drop in automobile traffic. Nonetheless, the plan failed to achieve its stated objective of reducing average commuting time.

Which of the following sentences would be the most logical continuation of this argument?
(A) The plan's opponents failed to realize that many people would take advantage of improved bus transportation.

(B) Unfortunately, politically attractive solutions do not always get results.
(C) The number of people a vehicle can transport varies directly with the size of the passenger compartment of the vehicle.
(D) Opponents cited an independent survey of city commuters showing that before the plan's adoption only one out of every seven used commuter bus lines.
(E) With the express lanes closed to private automobile traffic, the remaining cars were forced to use too few lanes and this created gigantic traffic tie-ups.

22. Last year, Gambia received $2.5 billion in loans from the International Third World Banking Fund, and its Gross National Product grew by 5%. This year Gambia has requested twice as much money from the ITWBF, and its leaders expect that Gambia's GNP will rise by a full 10%.

Which of the following, if true, would undermine the expectations of Gambia's leaders?

I. The large 5% increase of last year is attributable to extraordinary harvests due to unusually good weather conditions.
II. Gambia's economy is not strong enough to absorb more than $3 billion in outside capital each year.
III. Gambia does not have sufficient heavy industry to fuel an increase in its GNP of more than 6% per year.

(A) I only
(B) II only
(C) I and II only
(D) II and III only
(E) I, II, and III

23. Efficiency experts will attempt to improve the productivity of an office by analyzing production procedures into discrete work tasks. They then study the organization of those tasks and advise managers on techniques to speed production, such as rescheduling of employee breaks or relocating various equipment such as the copying machines. I have found a way to accomplish increases in efficiency with much less to do. Office workers grow increasingly productive as the temperature drops, so long as it does not fall below 68°F.

The passage leads most naturally to which of the following conclusions?

(A) Some efficiency gains will be short-term only.
(B) To maintain peak efficiency an office manager must occasionally restructure office tasks.
(C) Employees are most efficient when the temperature is 68°F.
(D) The temperature-efficiency formula is applicable to all kinds of work.
(E) Office workers will be equally efficient at 67°F and 69°F.

Questions 24–26

PRO-ABORTION SPEAKER: Those who oppose abortion upon demand make the foundation of their arguments the sanctity of human life, but this seeming bedrock assumption is actually as weak as shifting sand. And it is not necessary to invoke the red herring that many anti-abortion speakers would allow that human life must sometimes be sacrificed for a greater good, as in the fighting of a just war. There are counter-examples to the principle of sanctity of life which are even more embarrassing to pro-life advocates. It would be possible to reduce the annual number of traffic fatalities to virtually zero by passing federal legislation mandating a nationwide fifteen-mile-per-hour speed limit on *all* roads. You see, implicitly we have always been willing to trade off quantity of human life for quality.

ANTI-ABORTION SPEAKER: The analogy my opponent draws between abortion and traffic fatalities is weak. No one would propose such a speed limit. Imagine people trying to get to and from work under such a law, or imagine them trying to visit a friend or relatives outside their own neighborhoods, or taking in a sports event or a movie. Obviously such a law would be a disaster.

24. Which of the following best characterizes the anti-abortion speaker's response to the pro-abortion speaker?
(A) His analysis of the traffic fatalities case

actually supports the argument of the pro-abortion speaker.
(B) His analysis of the traffic fatalities case is an effective rebuttal of the pro-abortion argument.
(C) His response provides a strong affirmative statement of the anti-abortionist position.
(D) His response is totally irrelevant to the issue raised by the pro-abortion speaker.
(E) His counter-argument attacks the character of the pro-abortion speaker instead of the merits of his argument.

25. Which of the following represents the most logical continuation of the reasoning contained in the pro-abortion speaker's argument?
(A) Therefore, we should not have any laws on the books to protect human life.
(B) We can only conclude that the anti-abortionist is also in favor of strengthening enforcement of existing traffic regulations as a means to reducing the number of traffic fatalities each year.
(C) So the strongest attack on the anti-abortionist position is that he contradicts himself when he agrees that we should fight a just war even at the risk of considerable loss of human life.
(D) Even the laws against contraception are good examples of this tendency.
(E) The abortion question just makes explicit that which for so long has remained hidden from view.

26. In his argument, the pro-abortionist makes which of the following assumptions?

I. It is not a proper goal of a society to protect human life.
II. The human fetus is not a human life.
III. The trade-off between the number of human lives and the quality of those lives is appropriately decided by society.

(A) I only
(B) II only
(C) I and II only
(D) III only
(E) I, II, and III

STOP

IF YOU FINISH BEFORE TIME IS CALLED, CHECK YOUR WORK ON THIS SECTION ONLY. DO NOT WORK ON ANY OTHER SECTION IN THE TEST.

SECTION III

Time—35 Minutes
35 Questions

Directions: Each of the following sets consists of a fact situation, a dispute and two rules. The rules may conflict, but you are to apply each rule independently. Do not treat a rule as subsidiary or as an exception to the other rule. The rules are followed by questions. You are to select from the following lettered choices (A) through (D) the one that best describes each question in the way it relates to the application of one or both of the rules to the dispute. Blacken the corresponding space on the answer sheet.

(A) a relevant question the answer to which requires a choice between the two rules
(B) a relevant question the answer to which does not require a choice between the two rules, but does require further facts or rules
(C) a relevant question that can be readily answered from the facts or rules or both.
(D) an irrelevant question, the answer to which does not affect, or only tangentially affects, the outcome of the dispute

Set 1

FACTS: Greg was a sales representative for a large pharmaceutical manufacturer. The company provided Greg with a car which he used in making his sales calls. By the terms of Greg's employment agreement with the company, Greg was also allowed to use the car for his personal needs. Greg was to arrange for all repairs and maintenance on the car, paying the bills out of his own pocket and submitting vouchers to the company for reimbursement. One morning as Greg was driving to an appointment with an important customer, the car's engine began to malfunction. Greg pulled into the nearest garage, Third Street Service Station, and asked the mechanic and owner, Pardee, to take a look at the engine. Pardee checked the engine and explained to Greg that the fuel pump was "about to go" and that the car might or might not get him to his destination. Pardee told Greg that he could fix the problem in an hour. Since Greg's appointment was an important one, he had allowed himself some extra time. Greg told Pardee to fix the car, but he explained carefully to Pardee about his appointment and told him that he, Greg, stood to lose $175 if he missed it. Pardee replied he understood and that the car would be ready in an hour. After Pardee had begun work on the car, he learned that he did not have the proper replacement for the fuel pump. He had to send an assistant to find one, and the repairs took four hours. As a result, Greg missed his appointment and lost a medium-sized order on which he would have earned a commission of $175. Not only that, but Greg later learned that his regular customer had invited a business associate to meet Greg and that Greg would have received a very large order from him on which he would have earned a commission of $1,000.

DISPUTE: Greg sued Pardee for his lost commissions and the cost of the repairs. Pardee contested.

RULES: I. A party who fails to perform his contractual obligation must pay compensation for any loss suffered by the non-breaching party to the contract, and the amount of that compensation is the profit or other value the injured person would have realized had the contract been fulfilled.

II. A party who breaches a contract is liable for only those damages he was in a position to see would likely result from his failure to fulfill the contract.

1. What was the amount of the written estimate given to Greg by Pardee?

2. Can Greg recover damages from Pardee for the $175 commission he lost as the result of Pardee's failure to finish the repairs on time?

3. If Greg's company also sues Pardee, can it recover compensation from Pardee for the sale Greg would have made to his regular customer?

4. Can Greg recover damages from Pardee for the $1,000 commission he would have realized from the new prospect?

5. Did Pardee sign his name to the written estimate he gave to Greg?

6. Can Greg recover the cost of the repairs from Pardee?

Set 2

FACTS: Grant and Nebel were both members of the Midtown Health and Racquet Club. Though each had seen the other in the club, they had never actually met until they were introduced. Grant and Nebel learned that they had a common interest in squash and made arrangements to play a match on one of the club's squash courts. All members of the Midtown Health and Racquet Club were required upon registering and paying the Club's annual fee to sign a release form absolving the Club from liability in the case of injury while using any of the Club's facilities. Grant and Nebel had played one complete game, which Nebel had won, and were midway through a second with the score tied, when Grant, playing hard, carelessly swung his racket for a high shot, not realizing that Nebel was standing closely behind him. The racket struck Nebel above the right eye, opening a cut which eventually required several stiches and left a noticeable scar. Grant apologized and made attempts to assist Nebel. Nebel, however, incorrectly believed that Grant had intentionally inflicted the wound because he, Nebel, had beaten him, Grant, in the first game. Consequently, Nebel swung his own racket at Grant, striking Grant in the mouth and knocking out a tooth.

DISPUTE: Nebel sued Grant for his injuries and Grant brought a counter-suit against Nebel for his own injuries.

RULES: I. A person who is injured by the careless action of another person is entitled to money compensation to the extent that those injuries were the natural and foreseeable consequence of the action.

II. A person who is injured by the careless actions of another may not recover compensation for those injuries if he assumed the risk of those injuries by placing himself in a position where he was knowingly exposed to them.

7. Can Nebel recover compensation from Grant for the injury he suffered when Grant struck him?

8. Is the Club liable for Grant's injuries?

9. Who introduced Grant and Nebel to one another?

10. Is Nebel liable to Grant for the injury he caused Grant when he hit him with his racket?

11. Did Nebel assume the risk of the injuries he suffered when Grant hit him with his racket?

Set 3

FACTS: Patrick grew up in a home where the parents were strictly opposed to the consumption of alcohol, and at age thirty-one Patrick had never drunk any alcohol—not even a glass of beer. Patrick worked as a mechanic in a factory, and was promoted to the position of foreman. His fellow workers were very happy for Patrick and insisted upon taking him out for a drink. Patrick too was excited and so did not object when his co-workers drove him to a bar. Since Patrick was not familiar with alcoholic beverages, when his friends asked him what he wanted to drink Patrick responded, "I don't know." When pressed on the issue, Patrick said, "Well you order for me, but I am really ready to have a good time." Patrick drank several drinks and became quite intoxicated. Late in the evening, Patrick became hostile. The bartender asked Patrick to leave, but Patrick responded that he did not wish to leave. Patrick then picked up his glass and threw it against the mirror behind the bar. Next Patrick took a broken piece of glass and lunged at several of the patrons in the bar, but no one was actually injured.

DISPUTE: The bartender called the police, who arrested Patrick and charged him with criminal assault. Patrick claimed he was innocent of criminal assault.

RULES: I. A criminal assault is any attempt with force or violence to intentionally inflict bodily injury on another person.

II. A person is not guilty of a crime if at the time he acted he was involuntarily intoxicated.

12. Was Patrick involuntarily intoxicated?

13. How many people were in the bar when Patrick attacked the other bar patrons?

14. Is Patrick civilly liable for the damage he caused in the bar?

15. Is Patrick guilty of criminal assault?

Set 4

FACTS: Roberta owned a cow which she believed to be barren, since several attempts to impregnate the cow had all failed. She verbally agreed to sell the cow to Oscar for $100, about one-tenth of the value of a similar animal able to bear calves. Oscar paid Roberta the $100 at that time. Oscar picked up the cow two weeks later in a truck and transported it to his farm about thirty miles away. Oscar planned to fatten the cow up and slaughter it for beef which he planned to feed to his own family. A month later Oscar began to suspect that the cow was with calf, and he called the veterinarian who confirmed that she was indeed carrying a calf.

DISPUTE: When Roberta heard that the cow was not barren she demanded that Oscar undo their deal. Oscar refused, so Roberta sued Oscar to regain possession of the cow. Oscar contested.

RULES: I. A contract which has been completely carried out is completely enforceable regardless of whether the underlying agreement was ever reduced to writing.

II. Where two parties enter into a contract for the sale of something, and it turns out that there was a mutual mistake regarding the value of the item of sale which greatly affects the bargain, either party may have the contract rescinded, and both parties will be restored to their original positions.

16. If the court decides to rescind the contract, is Oscar entitled to the return of his $100?

17. What was the age of the cow?

18. Was the cow carrying the calf when Oscar took delivery of the cow?

19. Is Roberta entitled to possession of the cow?

20. If the court orders that Roberta is entitled to possession of the cow, is Oscar required to bear the cost of transporting the animal back to Roberta's farm?

21. Were all the provisions of the contract between Oscar and Roberta completely carried out?

Set 5

FACTS: Elizabeth Bergson was born in 1910. In 1935 she married Garrett Hargrove, and the couple had three children, Michael, Harriet, and Victor. Michael died as an infant, and Victor was killed during the Second World War. In 1955, Elizabeth and Garrett were divorced. Garrett was remarried in 1959 to Victoria Dickenson. Elizabeth remained unmarried until 1971, at which time she took a new husband, Paul Parker. Parker, a widower, had two children—Paulette, age seventeen, and Damion, age thirteen. Shortly after her marriage to Paul, Elizabeth asked her attorney to rewrite her will. Before the change, Harriet, her child by her first marriage, was to have received all of her property. Elizabeth owned a summer home in New England valued at about $150,000 as well as $150,000 in stocks and bonds, plus personal items such as jewelry. Under the terms of the new will, Harriet was to receive one-half of Elizabeth's estate while the rest was to go to the Carson Foundation, a charity. Elizabeth properly executed the will in the presence of two witnesses at her attorney's office in 1972. Elizabeth died in 1979.

DISPUTE: Paul Parker sued on his own behalf and on behalf of his children for a portion of Elizabeth's estate. The Carson Foundation contested.

RULES: I. A will which is signed in the presence of two witnesses is valid, and a court must honor its provisions in the distribution of the property of the deceased.

II. If a will does not make a specific provision for the spouse of the deceased, the surviving spouse is entitled to one-third of the value of the estate of the deceased.

22. What was the cause of Elizabeth's death?

23. Is Paul Parker entitled to a portion of Elizabeth's estate?

24. Are Paul's children entitled to a portion of Elizabeth's estate?

25. Is Paul entitled to receive the summer home which Elizabeth owned at the time of her death?

26. If the summer house in New England were destroyed by fire after Elizabeth's death, but before the final decision on how to distribute Elizabeth's property, which of the persons concerned would bear the loss?

Set 6

FACTS: Gary brought his three-year-old child, Carl, to the play area in the apartment complex where they lived. Another parent warned Gary that the fence which surrounded the swimming pool, then empty for cleaning, had a large hole. The owner of the apartment complex had promised to fix the hole ten days earlier but had not yet sent workmen to fix it, despite repeated protests by parents living in the complex that the hole was dangerous to small children. While Carl was playing in the sand box, Gary decided to walk to a grocery store a block away and buy a pack of cigarettes. The line in the grocery was very long, and Gary did not return for twenty minutes. While Gary was gone, Carl wandered through the hole in the fence and fell into the empty swimming pool, breaking his leg.

DISPUTE: Gary sued the owner of the apartment complex for the injuries Carl suffered in his fall.

RULES: I. A landlord is liable for any injuries which result from his failure to maintain the premises in safe condition.

II. A landlord is not liable for injuries suffered on his premises when it can be shown that the injured party, or in the case of a child, the adult responsible for the child, exercised less than reasonable care.

27. Is the owner of the apartment complex liable for Carl's injuries?

28. At what time of day did Carl sustain his injuries?

29. Had the owner of the apartment complex maintained the premises in safe condition?

30. Did Gary exercise reasonable care in supervising Carl?

Set 7

FACTS: Timothy borrowed $500 from Eugene in 1978, promising to pay him back in four equal installments on January 1, April 1, July 1, and October 1 of 1979. Timothy did make the first three installments, but he failed to make the October 1 payment of $125. In November,

Timothy entered into a contract with Glenn to paint Glenn's house for $125. At the time Timothy and Glenn were discussing the matter, Timothy said to Glenn, "I owe Eugene $125, so instead of your paying the money to me, pay it directly to Eugene." Glenn agreed to do so. Timothy finished the job in accordance with the provisions of his agreement with Glenn; but Glenn did not pay Eugene the money, thinking he would wait until Eugene demanded it. In December, Eugene contacted Timothy and insisted that Timothy pay him the $125. Timothy told Eugene about his, Timothy's, arrangement with Glenn. Eugene then demanded the money from Glenn who claimed he no longer had it.

DISPUTE: Eugene then sued Glenn for the $125. Glenn contested.

RULES: I. Only a party to a contract can maintain a legal action to enforce the terms of the contract.

II. A third-party beneficiary to a contract, that is anyone for whose specifically mentioned benefit the contract is undertaken, can bring an action to enforce a contract as though he were an actual party to the contract.

31. Is Eugene entitled to maintain his action against Glenn?

32. Could Timothy maintain an action to force Glenn to pay Eugene the $125?

33. Could Eugene sue Timothy to recover his $125?

34. Did Timothy and Glenn sign a written contract?

35. Is Eugene a third-party beneficiary of the contract between Timothy and Glenn?

STOP

IF YOU FINISH BEFORE TIME IS CALLED, CHECK YOUR WORK ON THIS SECTION ONLY. DO NOT WORK ON ANY OTHER SECTION IN THE TEST.

SECTION IV

Time—35 Minutes
25 Questions

Directions: Each group of questions is based on a set of propositions or conditions. Drawing a rough picture or diagram may help in answering some of the questions. Choose the best answer for each question and blacken the corresponding space on your answer sheet.

Questions 1–5

The tribe of Ater is divided into three clans—first, second, and third.

Only men and women of the same clan may marry.

On maturity, sons of couples in the first and second clans move down one rank, while sons of the third clan join the first.

On maturity, daughters of the second and third clans move up a rank and daughters of the first clan join the third.

Only mature Ater may marry.

1. Is it ever possible for an Ater woman born of the first clan to marry her nephew?
   (A) Yes, but only the son of her brother.
   (B) Yes, but only the son of her sister.
   (C) Yes, but only the daughter of her brother.
   (D) Yes, but only the daughter of her sister.
   (E) No.

2. Into what clans were the parents of an adult second clan male born?
   (A) father first clan, mother first clan
   (B) father first clan, mother third clan
   (C) father second clan, mother third clan
   (D) father second clan, mother first clan
   (E) father third clan, mother second clan

3. If a baby is born into the third clan, its mother's mother's mother could have been born to adult parents of what clan(s)?
   (A) first, second, or third
   (B) first and second only
   (C) first and third only
   (D) second only
   (E) third only

4. An Ater man has a granddaughter who is married to a man in the second clan. In what clan(s) could he be?
   (A) first only
   (B) second only
   (C) third only
   (D) first or second
   (E) second or third

5. Which of the statements about the Ater may be inferred from the information given?

   I. A sister and brother may not marry.
   II. A man may not marry his mother.
   III. A woman may not marry her grandson.

   (A) I only
   (B) II only
   (C) I and II only
   (D) I and III only
   (E) I, II, and III

Questions 6–10

J, K, L, M, N, P, and Q get on an empty express bus at 10th Street. The bus only stops every ten blocks. No one else gets on the bus, and no one leaves and gets back on. Nobody gets off at 30th Street or at 60th Street. When the bus pulls away from 80th Street, there are three people left on the bus.

Both P and Q get off before 80th Street, with P getting off at an earlier stop than Q.

6. If J gets off the bus on the second stop after M does, at which street(s) could J have gotten off?
   (A) 20th and 40th
   (B) 20th, 40th, and 70th
   (C) 40th and 70th
   (D) 50th, 70th, and 80th
   (E) 70th and 80th

7. If L, M, and N are on the bus after 80th Street, which of the following is true?

I. Each of the other passengers could have gotten off at separate stops.
II. There was at least one stop at which no one got off.
III. No one got off at 80th Street.

(A) I only
(B) I and II only
(C) I and III only
(C) II and III only
(E) I, II, and III

8. If K and L get off at separate stops before 80th Street, which of the following must be false?
(A) J did not get off the bus.
(B) M did not get off the bus.
(C) N did not get off the bus.
(D) Q did not get off the bus.
(E) None of the above.

9. If P left the bus after M did, and no one got off at 70th Street, then
(A) everyone who left the bus left at a different stop
(B) Q left at either 50th or 80th Streets
(C) P left at either 50th or 80th Streets
(D) M left after J
(E) Q left after J

10. If X, Y, and Z got on the bus at 20th, 30th, and 40th Streets, respectively, and stayed on the bus for 3, 4, and 5 stops, respectively, how many persons were on the bus when it arrived at 90th Street?
(A) 1
(B) 2
(C) 3
(D) 4
(E) cannot be determined from the information given

Questions 11–15

Jon is decorating his apartment and is trying to arrange his six pop art paintings on the east and west walls of his living room. The paintings are each multicolor representations of one of the letters of the alphabet: E, H, M, O, R, T.

Jon does not want the three letters on each wall to make any common English words. Also, the colors of the O and E do not look good next to each other, nor do the T and O go together well.

11. If Jon puts the M, O, and T on the west wall, which of the following is true?

I. O will be on one end of the west wall.
II. H and R will not be, respectively, the left and right paintings on the east wall.
III. E cannot be in the middle of the east wall.

(A) I only
(B) II only
(C) I and II only
(D) I and III only
(E) I, II, and III

12. If Jon puts the E, H, and M on the east wall, which of the following must be true?
(A) The E cannot be in the center of the east wall.
(B) The O cannot be in the center of the west wall.
(C) The R and M cannot face each other.
(D) The T and M cannot face each other.
(E) The H and R cannot face each other.

13. If Jon's mother is coming to visit and Jon decides to celebrate the visit by having his paintings spell "mother" starting with the leftmost painting on the east wall and going on around the room, which of the following must be false?
(A) T is next to O.
(B) H is next to E.
(C) O is opposite E.
(D) T is opposite R.
(E) None of the above.

14. Which of the following is not possible?
(A) H, M, and R to be on the same wall
(B) T, H, and E to be on the same wall
(C) T and O to be opposite each other
(D) M and O to be opposite each other
(E) E and O to be opposite each other

15. If Jon trades his M painting for another O painting just like the one he has now, which of the following must be false?
(A) Either R or H will be next to either T or E.
(B) Either R or H will be next to an O.
(C) The O's can be on opposite walls in the middle.

(D) The T will be opposite either O or E.
(E) All of the above are possible.

Questions 16–20

Coach Nelson is putting together a four-member handball team from right-handed players R, S, and T and left-handed players L, M, N, and O. He must have at least two right-handed players on the team, and all players must be able to practice with each other.

S cannot practice with L.
T cannot practice with N.
M cannot practice with L or N.

16. If L is on the team, what other individuals must also be on the team?
(A) R and T only
(B) R, T, and N
(C) R, T, and O
(D) R only
(E) M and O only

17. If O is not on the team, which of the other players must be on the team?
(A) No other particular player must be on the team if O is not chosen.
(B) M only
(C) R and S only
(D) R, S, T, and M
(E) S only

18. If both S and T are chosen for the team, what other individuals must be on the team with them?
(A) L only
(B) M only
(C) M and O only
(D) O only
(E) None of the above.

19. How many different teams can be formed without R?
(A) 0
(B) 1
(C) 2
(D) 3
(E) more than 3

20. If T were to become a left-handed player, then how many different teams could be formed?
(A) 0
(B) 1
(C) 2
(D) 3
(E) more than 3

Questions 21–25

I. Some Z are not Y.
II. Some Y are not X.
III. Some X are not Z.
IV. All X are not Y.

21. Which of the following can be deduced from conditions I, II, and III?
(A) There are no X that are both Y and Z.
(B) Some X are not Y.
(C) Some Z are not X.
(D) Some Y are not Z.
(E) None of the above.

22. Which of the following must be false given conditions I, II, III, and IV?
(A) There are no X that are neither Y nor Z.
(B) There are no Z that are not X.
(C) There are no X that are Z.
(D) There are no Y that are Z.
(E) None of the above.

23. Given the above conditions, which of the following conditions adds no new information?

I. No Z are both X and Y.
II. Some X are neither Z nor Y.
III. Some Y are neither X nor Z.

(A) I only
(B) II only
(C) III only
(D) I and II only
(E) I and III only

24. Which of the following are inconsistent with the given information?
(A) Some Z are not X.
(B) Some Y are not Z.
(C) No X are not Z.
(D) No Y are not X.
(E) All of the above are inconsistent with the given information.

25. If no Z are Y and no X are Z, which of the following must be false?
(A) Some Z are neither X nor Y.
(B) Some Y are neither X nor Z.
(C) Some X are neither Y nor Z.
(D) No Z are never X.
(E) No Z are never non-Y.

STOP

IF YOU FINISH BEFORE TIME IS CALLED, CHECK YOUR WORK ON THIS SECTION ONLY. DO NOT WORK ON ANY OTHER SECTION IN THE TEST.

SECTION V

Time—35 Minutes
28 Questions

Directions: Below each of the following passages, you will find questions or incomplete statements about the passage. Each statement or question is followed by lettered words or expressions. Select the word or expression that most satisfactorily completes each statement or answers each question in accordance with the meaning of the passage. After you choose the best answer, blacken the corresponding space on the answer sheet.

It is a measure of how far the Keynesian revolution has proceeded that the central thesis of "The General Theory" now sounds rather commonplace. Until it appeared, economists, in the classical (or non-socialist) tradition, had assumed that the economy, if left to itself, would find its equilibrium at full employment. Increases or decreases in wages and in interest rates would occur as necessary to bring about this pleasant result. If men were unemployed, their wages would fall in relation to prices. With lower wages and wider margins, it would be profitable to employ those from whose toil an adequate return could not previously have been made. It followed that steps to keep wages at artificially high levels, such as might result from the ill-considered efforts by unions, would cause unemployment. Such efforts were deemed to be the principal cause of unemployment.

Movements in interest rates played a complementary role by insuring that all income would ultimately be spent. Thus, were people to decide for some reason to increase their savings, the interest rates on the now more abundant supply of loanable funds would fall. This, in turn, would lead to increased investment. The added outlays for investment goods would offset the diminished outlays by the more frugal consumers. In this fashion, changes in consumer spending or in investment decisions were kept from causing any change in total spending that would lead to unemployment.

Keynes argued that neither wage movements nor changes in the rate of interest had, necessarily, any such agreeable effect. He focused attention on the total of purchasing power in the economy—what freshmen are now taught to call aggregate demand. Wage reductions might not increase employment; in conjunction with other changes, they might merely reduce this aggregate demand. And he held that interest was not the price that was paid to people to save but the price they got for exchanging holdings of cash, or its equivalent, their normal preference in assets, for less liquid forms of investment. And it was difficult to reduce interest beyond a certain level. Accordingly, if people sought to save more, this wouldn't necessarily mean lower interest rates and a resulting increase in investment. Instead, the total demand for goods might fall, along with employment and also investment, until savings were brought back into line with investment by the pressure of hardship which had reduced saving in favor of consumption. The economy would find its equilibrium not at full employment but with an unspecified amount of unemployment.

Out of this diagnosis came the remedy. It was to bring aggregate demand back up to the level where all willing workers were employed, and this could be accomplished by supplementing private expenditure with public expenditure. This should be the policy wherever intentions to save exceeded intentions to invest. Since public spending would not perform this offsetting role if there were compensating taxation (which is a form of saving), the public spending should be financed by borrowing—by incurring a deficit. So far as Keynes can be condensed into a few paragraphs, this is it. "The General Theory" is more difficult. There are nearly 400 pages, some of them of fascinating obscurity.

1. According to the passage, "The General Theory" advances which of the following ideas?

   I. Government intervention is necessary to curtail excessive unemployment.

   II. Sometimes public spending must be financed by borrowing.

III. Steps to increase wages create unemployment.

(A) I only
(B) II only
(C) I and II only
(D) II and III only
(E) I, II, and III

2. Keynes emphasized that
(A) unemployment was largely caused by high wages
(B) interest rate fluctuations were desirable
(C) lowering salaries would eventually create more jobs
(D) the government should go into debt, if necessary, to provide jobs
(E) an internal laissez faire policy is advantageous

3. The writer's attitude toward the Keynesian economic philosophy seems to be generally
(A) antagonistic
(B) questioning
(C) favorable
(D) mocking
(E) bombastic

4. It may be inferred from the passage that Keynes would
(A) favor the full employment of only those who wished to be employed
(B) favor full employment at the cost of forcing unwilling workers to work
(C) oppose government spending in conjunction with private spending
(D) oppose a government deficit
(E) force people to work

5. The "central thesis" referred to in the first sentence of the passage is the theory that
(A) unemployment can only be reduced by government spending
(B) unemployment is a function of the willingness of workers to work
(C) interest in employment will decline with lowered wages
(D) the equilibrium point of an economy will include some amount of unemployment
(E) savings by consumers will increase government spending

6. It can be inferred from the passage that Keynes
(A) was widely admired in his day
(B) was not a socialist
(C) had no idea of what his theories would mean
(D) could not agree on the role of interest rates in developing economies
(E) thought widely and deeply on many topics besides economics

7. According to Keynes, people prefer which of the following?
(A) blue chip stocks
(B) government securities
(C) savings accounts
(D) corporate bonds
(E) cash

A Polish proverb claims that fish, to taste right, should swim three times—in water, in butter, and in wine. The early efforts of the basic scientists in the food industry were directed at improving the preparation, preservation, and distribution of safe and nutritious food. Our memories of certain foodstuffs eaten during the Second World War suggest that, although these might have been safe and nutritious, they certainly did not taste right nor were they particularly appetizing in appearance or smell. This neglect of the sensory appeal of foods is happily becoming a thing of the past. Indeed, in 1957 the University of California considered the subject of sufficient importance to warrant the setting-up of a course in the analysis of foods by sensory methods. The book, *Principles of Sensory Evaluation of Food,* grew out of this course. The authors hope that it will be useful to food technologists in industry and also to others engaged in research into the problem of sensory evaluation of foods.

The scope of the book is well illustrated by the chapter headings: "The Sense of Taste"; "Olfaction"; "Visual, Auditory, Tactile, and Other Senses"; and "Factors Influencing Sensory Measurements." There are further chapters on panel testing, difference and directional difference tests, quantity-quality evaluation, consumer studies, statistical procedures (including design of experiments), and physical and chemical tests. An attempt has clearly been made to collect every possible piece of information which might be useful, more than one thousand five hundred references being quoted. As a result, the book seems at first sight to be an exhaustive and critically useful review of the literature. This it certainly is, but this is by no means its only achievement, for there are many suggestions for further lines of research, and the discursive passages are crisply provocative of new ideas and new ways of looking at established findings.

Of particular interest is the weight given to the psychological aspects of perception, both objectively and subjectively. The relation between stimuli and perception is well covered, and includes a valuable discussion of the uses and disadvantages of the Weber Law of Sensory Perception in the evaluation of differences. It is interesting to find that in spite of many attempts to separate and define the modalities of taste, nothing better has been achieved than the familiar classification into sweet, sour, salty, and bitter. Nor is there as yet any clear-cut evidence of the physiological nature of the taste stimulus. With regard to smell, systems of classification are of little value because of the extraordinary sensitivity of the nose and because the response to the stimulus is so subjective. The authors suggest that a classification based on the size, shape and electronic status of the molecule involved merits further investigation, as does the theoretical proposition that weak physical binding of the stimulant molecule to the receptor site is a necessary part of the mechanism of stimulation.

Apart from taste and smell, there are many other components of perception of the sensations from food in the mouth. The basic modalities of pain, cold, warmth, and touch, together with vibration sense, discrimination, and localization may all play a part, as, of course, does auditory reception of bone-conducted vibratory stimuli from the teeth when eating crisp or crunchy foods. In this connection the authors rightly point out that this type of stimulus requires much more investigation, suggesting that a start might be made by using subjects afflicted with various forms of deafness. It is, of course, well-known that extraneous noise may alter discrimination, and the attention of the authors is directed to the work of Prof. H. J. Eysenck on the "stimulus hunger" of extroverts and the "stimulus avoidance" of introverts. (It is perhaps unfair to speculate, not that the authors do, that certain breakfast cereals rely on sound volume to drown any deficiencies in flavor, or that the noisier types are mainly eaten by extroverts.)

8. The author uses a Polish proverb at the begining of the article in order to
   (A) introduce, in an interesting manner, the discussion of food
   (B) show the connection between food and nationality
   (C) indicate that there are various ways to prepare food
   (D) bring out the difference between American and Polish cooking
   (E) impress upon the reader the food value of fish

9. The author's appraisal of *Principles of Sensory Evaluation of Food* is one of
   (A) mixed feelings
   (B) indifference
   (C) derogation
   (D) high praise
   (E) faint praise

10. The writer of the article does not express the view, either directly or by implication, that
   (A) more sharply defined classifications of taste are needed than those which are used at present
   (B) more research should be done regarding the molecular constituency of food
   (C) food values are objectively determined by an expert "smeller"
   (D) psychological consideration would play an important part in food evaluation
   (E) temperature is an important factor in the appraisal of food

11. The authors of the book suggest the use of deaf subjects because
   (A) deaf people are generally introverted
   (B) all types of subjects should be used to insure the validity of an experiment
   (C) they are more objective in their attitude than normal subjects would be when it comes to food experimentation
   (D) the auditory sense is an important factor in food evaluation
   (E) they are more fastidious in their choice of foods

12. Which of the following can be inferred from

the chapter headings of *Principles of Sensory Evaluation of Food* as cited by the passage?
(A) The sense of smell is less important than the sense of taste.
(B) The sense of taste is less important than the sense of smell.
(C) The sense of taste is less important than the sense of sound.
(D) The sense of smell is less important than the sense of touch.
(E) The sense of touch is less important than the sense of smell.

13. Which of the following Webers is most likely to have originated the Weber's Law referred to in the passage?
(A) Max Weber (1881–1961), an American painter
(B) Ernest Heinrich Weber (1795–1878), German physiologist
(C) Baron Karl Maria Friedrich Ernest von Weber (1786–1826), German composer
(D) Max Weber (1864–1920), German political economist and sociologist
(E) George Weber (1808–1888), a German historian

14. The famous *Guide Michelin* includes ambience in rating the quality of restaurants. The author of the passage would likely
(A) prefer that only food be considered in rating restaurants
(B) object that French cooking should not be the standard for the world
(C) be uninterested in the opinions of restaurant foods
(D) endorse the ratings of the *Guide Michelin*
(E) agree to the inclusion of ambience in the rating system

As befits a nation made up of immigrants from all over the Christian world, Americans have no distinctive Christmas symbols; but we have taken the symbols of all the nations and made them our own. The Christmas tree, the holly, and the ivy, the mistletoe, the exchange of gifts, the myth of Santa Claus, the carols of all nations, the plum pudding and the wassail bowl are all elements in the American Christmas of the mid-twentieth century. Though we have no Christmas symbols of our own, the American Christmas still has a distinctive aura by virtue of two characteristic elements.

The first of these is that, as might be expected in a nation as dedicated to the carrying on of business as the American nation, the dominant role of the Christmas festivities has become to serve as a stimulus to retail business. The themes of Christmas advertising begin to appear as early as September, and the open season on Christmas shopping begins in November. Fifty years ago, Thanksgiving Day was regarded as the opening day of the season for Christmas shopping; today, the season opens immediately after Halloween. Thus, virtually a whole month has been added to the Christmas season—for shopping purposes.

Second, the Christmas season of festivities has insensibly combined with the New Year's celebration into one lengthened period of Saturnalia. This starts with the "office parties" a few days before Christmas. It continues on Christmas Eve, now the occasion in America of one of two large-scale revels that mark the season—save that the Christmas Eve revels are often punctuated by a visit to one of the larger churches for midnight Mass, which has increasingly tended to become blended into a part of the entertainment aspect of the season—and continues in spirited euphoria until New Year's Eve, the second of the large-scale revels. New Year's Day is spent resting, possibly regretting one's excesses, watching a football "bowl" game, and indulging in the lenitive of one's choice. January 2 marks, for most, the return to temperance and decorum and business as usual.

15. The author's attitude toward the manner in which Christmas is celebrated in the United States in one of
(A) great disapproval
(B) humorous confusion
(C) laudatory acclaim
(D) objective analysis
(E) great optimism

16. Which of the following would be most in accord with the main ideas of the passage?
(A) In Puritan Massachusetts Bay Colony, it was a crime, punishable by the stocks, to fail to observe Christmas.
(B) Christmas customs in Europe and

America that are associated with the Feast of the Nativity were not originally Christian.
(C) Rudolph the Red-Nosed Reindeer has become a traditional aspect of Christmas, yet was created only a few years ago by commercial interests.
(D) The custom of wassailing continued well into the nineteenth century.
(E) In widely separated areas of the world, religious observances tend to cluster around striking natural phenomena.

17. According to the passage, the American celebration of the Christmas season has
(A) demonstrated great symbolic originality
(B) little justification for existing
(C) departed completely from the example of early settlers
(D) made little attempt to promote a variety of entertainment
(E) borrowed extensively from the traditions of other countries

18. Which of the following does the author find to be distinctive to the American Christmas season?
(A) the purchase and exchange of Christmas gifts
(B) eating and drinking in celebration
(C) going to midnight mass on Christmas Eve
(D) the timing of Christmas
(E) the dedication to commerce

19. What would the author of the passage likely say by way of analysis of the use of Christmas cards by Americans to celebrate Christmas?
(A) The sending of large numbers of expensive cards is largely an extension of the business aspect of the American Christmas celebration.
(B) The reaching out to many friends, both close and far, through the cards, is an extension of the festive spirit of the American Christmas celebration.
(C) The multiplicity of cards and forms is a reflection of the very heterogenous views of Americans on the celebration of Christmas.
(D) The cards, once religious in meaning, have, like the Christmas Eve masses at churches, become part of the general Saturnalia with which the months-long Christmas season is crowned.
(E) The extension of the Christmas season has permitted more cards to be sent and handled by the overworked postal system.

20. Which of the following would be the best counter to the author's argument that spurring retail trade is the major purpose of Christmas giving?
(A) Many other countries have similar, if smaller, traditions of gift giving during the Christmas season.
(B) It is the natural joy of the citizens of a wealthy nation and their generous desire to share their wealth which leads to so many gifts being given.
(C) Many retail businesses do large volumes of business all year long.
(D) Many other celebrations are accompanied by business purposes.
(E) The author's argument cannot be countered in any way.

21. Which of the following can best be inferred from the passage?
(A) The great waves of immigrants from many countries in the late 1800's and early 1900's had a significant effect on the American celebration of Christmas.
(B) Only the earliest settlers brought traditions on which the American Christmas celebration is based.
(C) Every year sees the start of a new Christmas "tradition."
(D) The Saturnalia of Christmas week is a release from the hard work of the Christmas shopping season.
(E) New Year's is indistinguishable from Christmas Eve at this point.

Davis, California, like many other American cities, has been threatened by unchecked growth, swarming automobiles, and steeply rising energy costs. But unlike towns and cities which leave energy policy to the federal government or energy corporations, the citizens of Davis have acted on their own.

After lengthy debate, Davis' City Council moved to curb growth. It turned against the automobile and embraced the bicycle as a means of transport. It sponsored an inquiry into energy uses and endorsed a series of measures aimed at reducing energy consumption by as much as one half. It cut back the use of petroleum-derived pesticides on the thousands of trees and shrubs that shade the city's streets, adopting instead a policy of biological control for insects. The city's own cars and trucks have been transformed into a fleet of compact vehicles. When a Davis employee has to get around town, he borrows a bike from the city rack. Davis even passed a law formally and solemnly sanctioning the clothesline.

The citizens of Davis have been involved in progressive city planning and energy conservation since 1968, when they persuaded the City Council to facilitate bicycle transportation by developing a system of bikeways. The city's general plan for development, drawn up in 1972, was based on questionnaires distributed to residents. When a survey of residents showed that automobiles represented 50% of energy consumption and space heating and cooling accounted for 25%, transportation and building construction became important focal points in the Davis plan.

Armed with survey information revealing that a building's east-west orientation on a lot, as well as its insulation, window area, roof and wall colors, overhang shading, and other factors greatly influenced space heating and cooling needs, the City Council drew up a building construction code which greatly reduces the cost of winter heating and eliminates the need for air conditioning even on Davis' hottest (114°+) days. To demonstrate to local builders and developers methods for complying with the new code, Davis built two model solar homes, a single-family dwelling which takes advantage of natural southern exposure sunlight and a duplex adaptable to difficult siting situations where direct sunlight is blocked. Many of Davis' measures simply facilitate natural solar heating or sun-shading. Where most communities require that fences be built close to houses, Davis realized that that practice meant blocking winter sunlight. New fences in Davis must be placed closer to the street, giving residents the benefit of natural solar heat in winter. Reducing required street widths provided more shade and saved asphalt to boot.

Davis' other energy-conserving moves run the gamut—from a city ordinance encouraging cottage industry (to cut down on commuting and the need for new office building construction) to planting evergreens on city streets to reduce leaf pickup in the fall, from a ban on non-solar swimming pool heaters to a recycling center that supports itself selling $3,000 worth of recyclables a month.

22. It can be inferred from the passage that Davis' City Council felt that
    (A) bicycles are healthful because they promote physical fitness
    (B) control of automobile traffic is an essential part of energy management
    (C) Davis citizens are always ready to do the most modern, up-to-date thing
    (D) clotheslines are an important part of energy management for everyone
    (E) survey results should always determine legislative actions

23. Why did Davis build two model solar homes instead of just one?
    (A) To show what they could do when they put their minds to it.
    (B) To show that even the hottest days could be mastered without air conditioning.
    (C) To demonstrate that even multiple dwellings in difficult locations could be solar powered.
    (D) To indicate that other cities were inadequate to the job.
    (E) To prove that winter sunlight could be used for heating.

24. The purpose of this article is probably to
    (A) congratulate Davis on their fine work
    (B) help Davis to spread their message
    (C) chide the federal government for not doing enough to help cities like Davis
    (D) poke fun at Davis' "clothesline law"
    (E) hold up Davis as an example to other cities

25. We may infer from the article all of the following EXCEPT
    (A) air conditioning need not be as important in new houses as many people make it
    (B) the City Council had grave doubts

about the accuracy of the energy survey.
(C) the City Council realized that they were making major decisions when they enacted their energy and growth laws
(D) more people will generally use more energy
(E) lighting and sun direction influence house energy efficiency

26. It appears that Davis is
(A) a "good old American town"
(B) committed to social justice
(C) a medium- to small-sized city
(D) governed by a Council-Manager form of municipal government
(E) blessed by a strong radical element in the population

27. The passage supports the conclusion that
(A) Davis does not have much industry
(B) Davis cannot go any further than it already has toward being energy efficient
(C) Davis' example will work for any city
(D) the days of the automobile are numbered
(E) planning can solve all our problems

28. If, after continuing its programs, Davis did another energy survey in 1992 and found that its total energy use had gone up from 1972, all of the following could help to explain this finding, EXCEPT
(A) population growth might have been substantial because Davis became such a nice place to live
(B) builders were unable to comply with the stringent and complex building code
(C) new facilities were constructed that used considerable energy even with advanced design
(D) as the population got older they could no longer use bicycles as much and had to use cars more
(E) the 1972 energy survey seriously underestimated the energy used at that time

STOP

IF YOU FINISH BEFORE TIME IS CALLED, CHECK YOUR WORK ON THIS SECTION ONLY. DO NOT WORK ON ANY OTHER SECTION IN THE TEST.

SECTION VI

Time—35 Minutes
26 Questions

Directions: In this section, the questions ask you to analyze and evaluate the reasoning in short paragraphs or passages. For some questions, all of the answer choices may conceivably be answers to the question asked. You should select the *best* answer to the question, that is, an answer which does not require you to make assumptions which violate commonsense standards by being implausible, redundant, irrelevant or inconsistent. After choosing the best answer, blacken the corresponding space on the answer sheet.

1. All effective administrators are concerned about the welfare of their employees, and all administrators who are concerned about the welfare of their employees are liberal in granting time off for personal needs; therefore, all administrators who are not liberal in granting time off for their employees' personal needs are not effective administrators.

   If the argument above is valid, then it must be true that
   (A) no ineffective administrators are liberal in granting time off for their employees' personal needs
   (B) no ineffective administrators are concerned about the welfare of their employees
   (C) some effective administrators are not liberal in granting time off for their employees' personal needs
   (D) all effective administrators are liberal in granting time off for their employees' personal needs
   (E) all time off for personal needs is granted by effective administrators

2. CLYDE: You shouldn't drink so much wine. Alcohol really isn't good for you.

   GERRY: You're wrong about that. I have been drinking the same amount of white wine for fifteen years, and I never get drunk.

   Which of the following responses would best strengthen and explain Clyde's argument?
   (A) Many people who drink as much white wine as Gerry does get very drunk.
   (B) Alcohol does not always make a person drunk.
   (C) Getting drunk is not the only reason alcohol is not good for a person.
   (D) If you keep drinking white wine, you may find in the future that you are drinking more and more.
   (E) White wine is not the only drink that contains alcohol.

3. In considering the transportation needs of our sales personnel, the question of the relative cost of each of our options is very important. The initial purchase outlay required for a fleet of diesel autos is fairly high though the operating costs for them will be low. This is the mirror image of the cost picture for a fleet of gasoline powered cars. The only way, then, of making a valid cost comparison is on the basis of ________.

   Which of the following best completes the above paragraph?
   (A) projected operating costs for both diesel and gasoline powered autos
   (B) the average costs of both fleets over the life of each fleet
   (C) the purchase cost for both diesel powered and gasoline powered autos.
   (D) the present difference in the operating costs of the two fleets
   (E) the relative amount of air pollution which would be created by the one type of car compared with the other

4. The Dormitory Canteen Committee decided that the prices of snacks in the Canteen vending machines were already high enough, so they told Vendo Inc., the company holding the vending machine concession for the Canteen, either to maintain prices at the then current levels or to forfeit the concession. Vendo, however, managed

to thwart the intent of the Committee's instructions without actually violating the letter of those instructions.

Which of the following is probably the action taken by Vendo referred to in the above paragraph?

(A) The president of Vendo met with the University's administration, and they ordered the Committee to rescind its instructions.
(B) Vendo continued prices at the prescribed levels but reduced the size of the snacks vended in the machines.
(C) Vendo ignored the Committee's instructions and continued to raise prices.
(D) Vendo decided it could not make a fair return on its investment if it held the line on prices, so it removed its machines from the Dormitory Canteen.
(E) Representatives of Vendo met with members of the Dormitory Canteen Committee and offered them free snacks to influence other members to change the Committee's decision.

5. The president of the University tells us that a tuition increase is needed to offset rising costs. That is simply not true. Weston University is an institution approximately the same size as our own University, but the president of Weston University has announced that they will not impose a tuition increase on their students.

The author makes his point primarily by

(A) citing new evidence
(B) proposing an alternative solution
(C) pointing out a logical contradiction
(D) drawing an analogy
(E) clarifying an ambiguity

6. Only White Bear gives you all-day deodorant protection and the unique White Bear scent.

If this advertising claim is true, which of the following cannot also be true?

I. Red Flag deodorant gives you all-day deodorant protection.
II. Open Sea deodorant is a more popular deodorant than White Bear.
III. White Bear after-shave lotion uses the White Bear scent.

(A) I only
(B) II only
(C) III only
(D) I and III only
(E) all of the propositions could be true

7. Clara prefers English Literature to Introductory Physics. She likes English Literature, however, less than she likes Basic Economics. She actually finds Basic Economics preferable to any other college course, and she dislikes Physical Education more than she dislikes Introductory Physics.

All of the following statements can be inferred from the information given above EXCEPT

(A) Clara prefers Basic Economics to English Literature
(B) Clara likes English Literature better than she likes Physical Education
(C) Clara prefers Basic Economics to Advanced Calculus
(D) Clara likes World History better than she likes Introductory Physics
(E) Clara likes Physical Education less than she likes English Literature

8. In *The Adventure of the Bruce-Partington Plans,* Sherlock Holmes explained to Dr. Watson that the body had been placed on top of the train while the train paused at a signal.

"It seems most improbable," remarked Watson.

"We must fall back upon the old axiom," continued Holmes, "that when all other contingencies fail, whatever remains, however improbable, must be the truth."

Which of the following is the most effective criticism of the logic contained in Holmes' response to Watson?

(A) You will never be able to obtain a conviction in a court of law.
(B) You can never be sure you have accounted for all other contingencies.
(C) You will need further evidence to satisfy the police.

(D) The very idea of putting a dead body on top of a train seems preposterous.
(E) You still have to find the person responsible for putting the body on top of the train.

9. PROFESSOR: Under the rule of primogeniture, the first male child born to a man's first wife is always first in line to inherit the family estate.

STUDENT: That can't be true; the Duchess of Warburton was her father's only surviving child by his only wife and she inherited his entire estate.

The student has misinterpreted the professor's remark to mean which of the following?
(A) Only men can father male children.
(B) A daughter cannot be a first-born child.
(C) Only sons can inherit the family estate.
(D) Illegitimate children cannot inherit their fathers' property.
(E) A woman cannot inherit her mother's property.

10. The following sentences are a scrambled paragraph.

I. Then they were absorbed into the bloodstreams of infants drinking the water.
II. In an effort to check the spread of plant-eating insects, farmers in the valley launched a massive program of pesticide spraying.
III. The chemicals then migrated to the liver, causing enlargement in eight out of ten infants born in the valley after the beginning of the sprayings.
IV. Some of the chemicals in the pesticides dissolved into rain water and washed into the valley water supply.

Which of the following arrangements of these sentences is most logical?

(A) IV, III, II, I
(B) I, II, IV, III
(C) III, I, II, IV
(D) II, I, IV, III
(E) II, IV, I, III

11. Mr. Mayor, when is the city government going to stop discriminating against its Hispanic residents in the delivery of critical municipal services?

The form of the question above is most nearly parallelled by which of the following?
(A) Mr. Congressman, when is the Congress finally going to realize that defense spending is out of hand?
(B) Madam Chairperson, do you anticipate the committee will take luncheon recess?
(C) Dr. Greentree, what do you expect to be the impact of the Governor's proposals on the economically disadvantaged counties of our state?
(D) Gladys, since you're going to the grocery store anyway, would you mind picking up a quart of milk for me?
(E) Counselor, does the company you represent find that its affirmative action program is successful in recruiting qualified minority employees?

12. The main ingredient in this bottle of Dr. John's Milk of Magnesia is used by nine out of ten hospitals across the country as an antacid and laxative.

If this advertising claim is true, which of the following statements must also be true?

I. Nine out of ten hospitals across the country use Dr. John's Milk of Magnesia for some ailments.
II. Only one out of ten hospitals in the country do not treat acid indigestion and constipation.
III. Only one out of ten hospitals across the country do not recommend Dr. John's Milk of Magnesia for patients who need a milk of magnesia.

(A) I only
(B) II only
(C) I and III only
(D) I, II, and III
(E) none of the statements is necessarily true

Questions 13 and 14

I. All wheeled conveyances which travel on the highway are polluters.
II. Bicycles are not polluters.
III. Whenever I drive my car on the highway, it rains.
IV. It is raining.

13. If the above statements are all true, which of the following statements must also be true?
(A) Bicycles do not travel on the highway.
(B) Bicycles travel on the highway only if it is raining.
(C) If my car is not polluting, then it is not raining.
(D) I am now driving my car on the highway.
(E) My car is not a polluter.

14. The conclusion "my car is not polluting" could be logically deduced from statements I–IV if statement
(A) II were changed to: "Bicycles are polluters."
(B) II were changed to: "My car is a polluter."
(C) III were changed to: "If bicycles were polluters, I would be driving my car on the highway."
(D) IV were changed to: "Rainwater is polluted."
(E) IV were changed to: "It is not raining."

15. Statistics published by the State Department of Traffic and Highway Safety show that nearly 80% of all traffic fatalities occur at speeds under 35 miles per hour and within twenty-five miles of home.

Which of the following would be the most reasonable conclusion to draw from these statistics?
(A) A person is less likely to have a fatal accident if he always drives over 35 miles per hour and always at distances greater than twenty-five miles from his home.
(B) There is a direct correlation between distance driven and the likelihood of a fatal accident.
(C) The greater the likelihood that one is about to be involved in a fatal accident, the more likely it is that he is driving close to home at a speed less than 35 miles per hour.
(D) If it were not the case that a person were about to be involved in a fatal traffic accident, then he would not have been driving at the speed or in the location he was, in fact, driving.
(E) Most driving is done at less than 35 miles per hour and within twenty-five miles of home.

16. Usually when we have had an inch or more of rain in a single day, my backyard immediately has mushrooms and other forms of fungus growing in it. There are no mushrooms or fungus growing in my backyard.

Which of the following would logically complete an argument with the premises given above?

I. Therefore, there has been no rain here in the past day.
II. Therefore, there probably has been no rain here in the past day.
III. Therefore, we have not had more than an inch of rain here in the past day.
IV. Therefore, we probably have not had more than an inch of rain here in the past day.

(A) I only
(B) II only
(C) III only
(D) IV only
(E) II and IV only

17. Judging from the nature of the following statements and the apparent authoritativeness of their sources, which is the most reasonable and trustworthy?
(A) WITNESS UNDER OATH: Yes, that's the person I saw with the car. He drove under a streetlight about three blocks from where I was standing.
(B) BUSINESS EXECUTIVE TO REPORTER: The toxic waste spill is not the fault of our corporation. We have always been very careful to dispose of such chemicals properly—even before the news media publicized the dangers of toxic waste.

(C) TWO TRAINED PARAMEDICS: When we arrived, the patient was all but dead. We administered cardio-pulmonary resuscitation, and after twenty minutes the patient regained consciousness.
(D) PH.D. CANDIDATE IN BIOLOGY: Religious leaders are clearly wrong when the claim that Providence is responsible for the presence of life on earth.
(E) PRESIDENT OF A SMALL BUSINESS: All of my employees love me. We're really like one big, happy family here.

18. I recently read a book by an author who insists that everything man does is economically motivated. Leaders launch wars of conquest in order to capture the wealth of other nations. Scientists do research in order to receive grants or find marketable processes. Students go to college to get better jobs. He even maintains that people go to museums to become better informed on the off-chance that some day they will be able to turn that knowledge to their advantage. So persuaded was I by the author's evidence that, applying his theory on my own, I was able to conclude that he had written the book ___________.

Which of the following provides the most logical completion of the above paragraph?
(A) as a labor of love
(B) in order to make money
(C) as a means of reforming the world by calling man's attention to his greed
(D) as an exercise in scientific research
(E) in response to a creative urge to be a novelist

19. Judging from the tenor of the following statements and the apparent authoritativeness of their sources, which is the most reasonable and trustworthy?
(A) PROFESSIONAL MARRIAGE COUNSELOR: My wife and I had a perfect marriage, and she even told her friends so several times before she ran off with another man.
(B) GRADUATE OF WILSON COLLEGE: Wilson College has probably the best pre-business major in the country because the department is headed by Professor Johnson, who actually has an MBA.
(C) PRINCIPAL DANCER OF A BALLET COMPANY: Our performance last night was not as good as usual: The orchestra was ragged, the company was sloppy, and I danced very poorly.
(D) HEART SURGEON: *David Copperfield* was perhaps Charles Dickens' most balanced work and ranks far above *A Tale of Two Cities* in literary method.
(E) MOTORCYCLE OWNER: Many people say motorcycles are unsafe, but that's not true. Riding on a motorcycle is just as safe as riding in a car.

20. In our investigation of this murder, we are guided by our previous experience with the Eastend Killer. You will recall that in that case, the victims were also carrying a great deal of money when they were killed but the money was not taken. As in this case, the murder weapon was a pistol. Finally, in that case also the murders were committed between six in the evening and twelve midnight. So we are probably after someone who looks very much like the Eastend Killer, who was finally tried, convicted, and executed: 5′11″ tall, a mustache, short, brown hair, walks with a slight limp.

The author makes which of the following assumptions?

I. Crimes similar in detail are likely to be committed by perpetrators who are similar in physical appearance.
II. The Eastend Killer has apparently escaped from prison and has resumed his criminal activities.
III. The man first convicted as the Eastend Killer was actually innocent, and the real Eastend Killer is still loose.

(A) I only
(B) II only
(C) III only
(D) I and II only
(E) I and III only

21.

I. Everyone who has not read the report either has no opinion in the matter or holds a wrong opinion about it.

II. Everyone who holds no opinion in the matter has not read the report.

Which of the following best describes the relationship between the two above propositions?

(A) If II is true, I may be either false or true.
(B) If II is true, I must also be true.
(C) If II is true, I is likely to be true.
(D) If I is true, II must also be true.
(E) If I is false, II must also be false.

22. The idea that women should be police officers is absurd. After all, women are on the average three to five inches shorter than men and weigh twenty to fifty pounds less. It is clear that a woman would be less effective than a man in a situation requiring force.

Which of the following, if true, would most weaken the above argument?

(A) Some of the female applicants for the police force are larger than some of the male officers presently on the force.
(B) Police officers are required to go through an intensive eighteen month training program.
(C) Police officers are required to carry pistols and are trained in the use of their weapons.
(D) There are a significant number of desk jobs in the police force which women could fill.
(E) Many criminals are women.

23. No sophomores were selected for Rho Rho Phi. Some sophomores are members of the Debating Society. Therefore, some members of the Debating Society were not selected for Rho Rho Phi.

Which of the following is logically most similar to the argument given above?

(A) Everyone who exercises in the heat will get ill. I never exercise in the heat, so I will probably never be ill.
(B) Drivers who wish to avoid expensive automobile repairs will have their cars tuned up regularly. My uncle refuses to have his car tuned up regularly. Therefore, he enjoys paying for major repairs.
(C) Some books which are beautiful were written in French, and French literature is well-respected. Therefore, any book which is beautiful is well-respected.
(D) All pets are excluded from this apartment complex. But many pets are valuable. Therefore, some valuable animals are excluded from this apartment complex.
(E) St. Paul is a long way from London. Minneapolis is a long way from London. Therefore, St. Paul is a long, long way from Minneapolis.

24. All Burrahobbits are Trollbeaters, and some Burrahobbits are Greeblegrabbers.

If these statements are true, which of the following must also be true?

I. If something is neither a Trollbeater nor a Greeblegrabber, it cannot be a Burrahobbit.
II. It is not possible not to be a Trollbeater without being a Greeblegrabber.
III. Any given thing either is a Trollbeater or it is not a Burrahobbit.

(A) I only
(B) II only
(C) III only
(D) I and II only
(E) I, II, and III

25. If the batteries in my electric razor are dead, the razor will not function. My razor is not functioning. Therefore, the batteries must be dead.

Which of the following arguments is most similar to that presented above?

(A) If Elroy attends the meeting, Ms. Barker will be elected club president. Ms. Barker was not elected club president; therefore, Elroy did not attend the meeting.
(B) All evidence is admissible unless it is tainted. This evidence is inadmissible. Therefore, it is tainted.
(C) If John committed the crime, fingerprints will be found at the scene. John's fingerprints were found at the

scene; therefore, John committed the crime.

(D) Grant is my uncle. Sophie is Grant's niece. Therefore, Sophie is my sister.

(E) Jonathan will wear his dark glasses if the coast is clear. The coast is clear. Therefore, Jonathan will wear his dark glasses.

26. All general statements are based solely on observed instances of a phenomenon. That the statement has held true up to a certain point in time is no guarantee that it will remain unexceptionless. Therefore, no generalization can be considered free from possible exception.

The logic of the above argument can best be described as

(A) self-defeating
(B) circular
(C) ill-defined
(D) valid
(E) inductive

STOP

IF YOU FINISH BEFORE TIME IS CALLED, CHECK YOUR WORK ON THIS SECTION ONLY. DO NOT WORK ON ANY OTHER SECTION IN THE TEST.

WRITING SAMPLE

Time—30 Minutes

Directions: Write an essay about the question listed below. You may support or attack the question or discuss it in any way that you wish. Be sure to make your points clearly and cogently and to write as neatly as possible. Write your essay within the margins of the pages. Additional paper may be used as scratch paper, but only these pages can be used for the actual essay.

TOPIC: The Traffic Safety Council has proposed that a new law be enacted which requires that all prospective drivers take a much more stringent driving test than is required at present. The new test will require the demonstration of total control of the vehicle as well as extensive knowledge of traffic laws relevant to the type of vehicle for which the license is being sought. The Council proposes that this new requirement only apply to persons seeking their first driver's license, and predicts a savings of hundreds of lives per year when the program is implemented. Opponents argue that accidents are caused by such things as speeding and drinking rather than not knowing how to handle a car and that the costs of preparing for the more extensive test will impose a significant economic burden on the society as a whole and on poorer citizens in particular.

You are a state legislator on the Transportation Committee and you are to prepare a brief position paper to be presented to the Committee in your absence.

ANSWER KEY
PRACTICE EXAMINATION 4

SECTION I

1. C	8. B	15. E	22. B
2. C	9. C	16. E	23. D
3. A	10. B	17. B	24. D
4. E	11. A	18. E	25. B
5. C	12. C	19. C	26. A
6. D	13. E	20. A	27. D
7. B	14. D	21. E	28. D

SECTION II

1. D	8. E	15. C	22. E
2. C	9. B	16. B	23. C
3. A	10. E	17. A	24. A
4. B	11. C	18. D	25. E
5. B	12. B	19. E	26. D
6. C	13. D	20. B	
7. A	14. E	21. E	

SECTION III

1. D	8. D	15. A	22. D	29. C
2. C	9. D	16. C	23. A	30. C
3. B	10. B	17. D	24. C	31. A
4. A	11. C	18. D	25. B	32. C
5. D	12. B	19. A	26. B	33. C
6. B	13. D	20. B	27. A	34. D
7. A	14. B	21. C	28. D	35. C

SECTION IV

1. A	6. C	11. C	16. C	21. E
2. E	7. B	12. B	17. D	22. A
3. E	8. D	13. D	18. E	23. D
4. D	9. B	14. A	19. B	24. C
5. C	10. D	15. C	20. E	25. D

SECTION V

1. C	8. A	15. D	22. B
2. D	9. D	16. C	23. C
3. C	10. C	17. E	24. E
4. A	11. D	18. E	25. B
5. D	12. E	19. A	26. C
6. B	13. B	20. B	27. A
7. E	14. E	21. A	28. B

SECTION VI

1. D	8. B	15. E	22. A
2. C	9. C	16. D	23. D
3. B	10. E	17. C	24. A
4. B	11. A	18. B	25. C
5. D	12. E	19. C	26. A
6. E	13. A	20. A	
7. D	14. E	21. A	

EXPLANATORY ANSWERS

SECTION I

1. **(C)** The author first uses a comparison to the Arabian Nights as a positive example, and then uses music and poetry in the streets as an example of true bliss. At the end he refers to artists having "fair and noble" designs. The focus on reality should not be seen as antithetical to arts, which can be seen as mirrors of reality rather than "mere" fictions.

   (E), perhaps the second-best, fails because there is no reluctance to be found in the admiration. The indifference, suspicion and repulsion in the passage are all for lies and fictions, not art, thus (A), (B), and (D) fail.

2. **(C)** The end of the first paragraph equates experience with failure, an unusual thought that should stand out to your eye. This directly eliminates (B) and (D), and argues for (C). (A) is wrong because it is in discernment that children excel, not in amount of knowledge, which the author feels may even interfere with discernment. (E) means that childhood sets many patterns for the adult that is to come, but here the author is saying that the adult is less able than the child.

3. **(A)** The first sentence says just what (A) says. (D) is incorrect because the reference to Arabian Nights is to show the wonder of reality. (B), (C), and (E) have no basis in the passage.

4. **(E)** The first sentence describes the situation that the author sees as actually going on in the world—delusions are seen as real and reality as delusion—everything is backwards. Thus, (E) makes the best sense. Note that he is speaking of the perceptions of the actual reality. (A) is a common meaning of the word *fabulous* but not the one used in this sentence. The whole passage is about how to comprehend reality, hence, (D) fails while (C) and (B) are unrelated entirely.

5. **(C)** In the last paragraph all the true and sublime are stated to be true now and the emphasis is on the value of properly and truly perceiving the present, hence (C), rather than (A), (B), or (D). (E) is an attempt to lure the unwary into thinking that children and Arabian Nights refer to leisure.

6. **(D)** The issues dealt with in the passage are the good, the true, and the soul—hence, (D). (C) and (A) have little connection to the passage. (B)'s word *society* connects, but *population* does not. (E)'s reference to the arts confuses the celebration with the cause for celebration.

7. **(B)** (B) is admittedly a little glib and has a light-hearted tone not entirely in keeping with the passage, but is the only choice which conveys the meaning of the passage, albeit by using this expression somewhat differently than common usage does. The passage indicates that we can achieve what we see, but will be limited by our false perceptions of the world if we let ourselves be blinded. The universe's answering to our perceptions is just that—the limits are set by us, not the universe.

   (A) plays on the universe answering idea; however, physical control is not the issue, but rather spiritual matters. (C) is opposite to the theme of the passage and a trap for those who think of any reference to Eastern religion as meaning all is fated. (D) plays with the fast and slow tracks, which we may choose, but it is not physical speed, but mental life to which is referred. Perceiving fully makes us experience more and more quickly. (E) is simply false since the last sentence has the posterity, in fact, doing what the poet conceived.

8. **(B)** The references to the shires and London are detailed and imply a closeness to hand, and are first mentioned. (A), France, is only mentioned with one reference, and thus is less good than (B). America, (C), is only supported by a reference to North America which is insufficiently detailed to override the English references. (D) is nowhere mentioned.

9. **(C)** The only trick here is to remember that the third line of a syllogism does not always have the word *thus* or its equivalent. The other methods are all in the passage, but not for this sort of reasoning. See also the instructional materials for the Logical Reasoning questions.

10. **(B)** While it is true that the use of apples gives the story a pedestrian flavor, this is merely to exemplify the author's view that there is real reasoning even in very ordinary events. The apples are the subject of an analogy between the situation and all everyday reasoning, which is likened and explained through that example. (C) has a little merit, but (B) is far better since it goes with the basic ideas of the passage. (D) is attractive, but false since the author shows how common logic is—not how foolish. (A) and (E) are merely flack.

11. **(A)** While the answer choice of "philosopher" would be better yet, the scientist's reference to experimental method and logic make (A) the best available choice. All the others may use logic and experiment, of course, but the topic here is science—in the sense of its root meaning "knowing"—not art, fiction, economics, or business, nor the distinguishing methods of those fields.

12. **(C)** The passage notes that you establish a natural law as the result of the induction in just those words, hence (C). (D) and (E) are other meanings of the term "natural law" but not the ones used in this particular passage. (A) and (B) have little connection to the passage.

13. **(E)** All the answer choices reflect part of the passage, but (E) covers the largest portion of the passage, and thus is best. Each of the others can be subsumed under it since (A) is the example used, and (B), (C), and (D) are the methods of everyday reasoning brought out through the use of the example of apples.

14. **(D)** The law of apples is a construct based, as noted in the passage, on experimental verification of an induction. If further verification should show that the law is not perfect, then it must be modified as (D) suggests. (C) is particularly attractive, but the word *usually* makes it fail, since it is still the case that hard and green apples are usually sour. If (C) had said "always" it would be hard to refuse.

    (A) is subsumed under (D) and is incorrect in supposing that the nature of apples has changed, when it is only that our original understanding of them proved to be inadequate. (B), while attractive in the real world where tasty apples are all too rare, has little to do with standardized tests. Since (A), (B), and (C) are faulty, (E) does not apply.

15. **(E)** While much of the discussion in the passage is of the moon, the purpose of the discussion is to shed light on the history of Earth. The moon happens to be convenient for that purpose, but only as a guide, hence, (C) is incorrect.

    (B) and (C) are much more general than (E) in that they refer to many other causes of continent formation or of continental nuclei formation, while the passage only discusses the possibilities of having the continental nuclei formed by meteorites or asteroids (treated here as essentially a single class of objects). (A) is also more general than (E), but in a different way. (A) considers meteors in relationship to all other problems, while (E) correctly limits the discussion to meteors and continental nuclei formation.

16. **(E)** This is something of a detail question, but the fourth paragraph states that mare basins are on the moon and does so in the context of how big a crater is formed upon

impact, hence (E). (A) fails for lack of any connection with the passage at all. (B) refers to the right paragraph, but the wrong part of it. (C) would be good, but it mentions Earth as well, while the paragraph in question refers only to the moon. (D) is not mentioned in the passage.

17. **(B)** The term "brecciation" is obviously jargon and is not well defined in the passage. You are not expected to know its dictionary definition. Since we are talking about a sum effect of the impact of a large meteor leaving a crater, (D) and (E) are not immediately meritorious and should be eliminated. The latter part of the paragraph discussing the major craters speaks of minor stresses at the depth at which brecciation is referred to as occurring. This eliminates (C). While we have all heard of theories that volcanism could be caused by major meteor impacts, there is none of that really being discussed here, so (A) is without support. (B) is intuitively reasonable as well as logical, and is correct.

18. **(E)** The answer choices are helpful here. The two large crater sizes mentioned for the moon are 285 km and 650 km. Since 285 is not available, we choose 650 km, answer choice (E).

19. **(C)** That the author believes (A) is inferable from the first paragraph which refers to large meteorites and asteroids as the same. (B) is merely one theory, but it is endorsed by the author in the last paragraph where he rejects the concentration of material, thus agreeing that it was distributed. (C) fails because in the next to last paragraph the author rejects the notion that ocean basins are created by craters. (D) is stated, as is (E).

20. **(A)** See also the discussion of #15. The first paragraph makes clear the intentions of the author. The moon is introduced only as a surrogate for Earth.

21. **(E)** The sad fact is that Earth's geology is active and the surface of the planet has been scoured by wind, rain, etc., thus, its history is hidden. On airless, but otherwise similar bodies, the history may be more readily available. (A) is fruitless since it is the effect of these bodies on Earth that is at issue, though they are of some interest as to their composition. (B) is exactly the problem. (C) is foolish since the sun is a star and totally different. (D) is just like (A). Hence, (E).

22. **(B)** The author states that there are some good shows, but from the start to the end of the television day the average is bad.

23. **(D)** He is telling the industry what it must do, "I intend . . . ", hence (D). He is not defeated, (A), nor hopeless, (E). While he is righteous, (C), the intention to prevail is dominant. There is no reconciliation, (B), at all.

24. **(D)** The whole thing is an extended shape-up-or-else statement, with justifications. (A) is not intended, and while there is an obligation to the listener or viewer, it is in seeking only to please the viewer that the author sees error, thus (A) is incorrect. (B) and (C) fail since good children's shows are said to exist and it is only the steady diet of mystery, etc., which is objectionable. (E) fails because the teaching referred to is not classroom instruction.

25. **(B)** Literature and great traditions of freedom are urged as subjects for children's shows and these are certainly culture. None of the others are objected to, except cartoons, and there it is the massive doses only. The entire speech is a plea for moderation.

26. **(A)** (C) and (D) wrongly refer to air as the thing we breathe, while the author is referring to the broadcasting of television programs. (E) fails since the author nowhere opposes commercial television, but only insists that it should provide real service in return for using the common property that the airwaves represent, thus, (E) fails. (B) has some merit since clearly the idea that the airwaves are owned by the people could be part—though only part—of an argument to say that the people should actually run everything to do with the airwaves through

their government, but this is not part of the author's speech and only if government oversight is to be equated with socialism can (B) ultimately be supported. We are, thus, left with (A), which is correct. While other rights may accrue to the people from their "ownership" of the airwaves, the right to have worthwhile use made of their property is certainly a permissible inference.

27. **(D)** The author states explicitly that the popularity of shows should not be the only criterion for selecting them. Since he has separated merit from popularity, he must believe that not all listeners or viewers know what is good for them. (A) and (C) have some appeal, but the author accuses the networks of catering to the nation's whims, which is hardly consonant with trying to do the right thing. He certainly does agree that they are failing, but that is not enough to justify choosing (A). The author's statements that there are some worthwhile shows is not enough to justify (C). (B) and (E) are flack.

28. **(D)** The citation of some good children's shows, even though they are overwhelmed by trash, is sufficient to choose (D). While (A) is not currently fashionable, the author is talking about meeting the needs of all of the population. (C) and (E) are directly stated, while (B) can be derived from the author's emphasis on opportunity of choice.

SECTION II

1. **(D)** The concluding remark of the one party shows that the two people never actually saw the movie they were discussing. Therefore, they must have been arguing on the basis of what they assumed to be true of the film. (E) is the second-best answer. It is conceivable that an argument could proceed on the basis of semantics where the parties had no direct knowledge of the subject at issue, but (E) is not as good an answer as (D) because there is no support for this further conjecture in the passage. It is, however, evident on the face of the paragraph that the parties must be arguing on the basis of what they assume to be true about the film. (A) requires a good deal of imagination to accept: that the two persons have access to some supernatural knowledge. (B) and (C) are incorrect because they are just not appropriate terms to describe the progress of the argument. "Induction" is generalization on the basis of observed instances; "deduction" is reasoning as a matter of the meanings of terms (strict logical connection).

2. **(C)** The author is arguing that the budget cuts will not ultimately be detrimental to the poor since the adverse effects will be more than offset by beneficial ones. II and III attack both elements of this reasoning. II points out that there will be no beneficial effects to offset the harmful ones, and III notes that the harmful effects will be so harmful that they will outweigh any beneficial ones that might result. I, however, is not relevant to the author's point. The author is arguing a point of economics. How the Congressmen get themselves elected has no bearing on that point.

3. **(A)** The author reasons from the premise "there are bottles of this product in the apartments" to the conclusion "therefore, these people believe the product is effective." The ad obviously wants the hearer to infer that the residents of the apartments decided themselves to purchase the product because they believed it to be effective. (A) directly attacks this linkage. If it were true that the company gave away bottles of the product, this would sever that link. (B) does weaken the ad, but only marginally. To be sure, we might say to ourselves, "Well, a person who touts a product and does not use it himself is not fully to be trusted." But (B) does not aim at the very structure of the argument as (A) does. (C) can hardly weaken the argument, since it appears to be a premise on which the argument itself is built. (C), therefore, actually strengthens the appeal of the advertisement. It also does not link to Painaway's effectiveness. (D) seems to be irrelevant to the *appeal* of the ad. The ad is designed to *change* the hearer's

mind, so the fact that he does not now accept the conclusion of the ad is not an argument against the ability of the ad to accomplish its stated objective. Finally, (E) is irrelevant to the purpose of the ad for reasons very similar to those cited for (D).

4. **(B)** The author is accusing the artists of being inconsistent. He claims they give lip service to the idea that an artist must suffer, but that they then live in material comfort—so they do not themselves suffer. Only (B) completes the paragraph in a way so that this inconsistency comes out. (A) and (D) can be dismissed because the author is concerned with those whom he attacks as *artists,* not as connoisseurs or purchasers of art, nor as critics of art. (D) is inadequate for it does not reveal the inconsistency. The author apparently allows that these people are, after a fashion, artists; what he objects to is their claiming that it is necessary to suffer while they do not themselves suffer. (E) is the second-best answer, but it too fails. The difficulty with (E) is that the author's point is that there is a contradiction between the actions and the words of those he accuses: They claim to suffer but they do not. But the claimed suffering goes beyond matters of eating and has to do with deprivation generally.

5. **(B)** II is an assumption of the author because the inconsistency of which he accuses others would disappear if, though they were not poor, they nonetheless endured great suffering, e.g., emotional pain or poor health. I is not an assumption of the author. He is trying to prove that he has uncovered a contradiction in another's words and actions: It is the others who insist suffering is necessary. The author himself never says one way or the other whether he considers that suffering is necessary to produce art—only that these others claim it is, and then eat well. Finally, III incorrectly construes the author's reference to purchasers of art. He never mentions the role of the critic.

6. **(C)** Take careful note of the exact position the author ascribes to the analysts: They *always* attribute a sudden drop to a crisis. The author then attacks this simple causal explanation by explaining that, though a crisis is followed by a market drop, the reason is not that the crisis causes the drop but that both are the effects of some common cause, the changing of the moon. Of course, the argument seems implausible, but our task is not to grade the argument, only to describe its structure. (A) is not a proper characterization of that structure since the author never provides a specific example. (B), too, is inapplicable since no statistics are produced. (D) can be rejected since the author is attacking generally accepted beliefs rather than appealing to them to support his position. Finally, though the author concedes the reliability of the reports in question, he wants to draw a different conclusion from the data, (E).

7. **(A)** Given the implausibility of the author's alternative explanation, he is probably speaking tongue-in-check, that is, he is ridiculing the analysts for *always* attributing a drop in the market to a political crisis. But whether you took the argument in this way or as a serious attempt to explain the fluctuations of the stock market, (A) will be the correct answer. (E) surely goes beyond the mere factual description at which the author is aiming, as does (D) as well. The author is concerned with the *causes* of fluctuations; nothing suggests that he or anyone else is in a position to exploit those fluctuations. (C) finds no support in the paragraph for nothing suggests that he wishes to attack the credibility of the source rather than the argument itself. Finally, (B) is inappropriate to the main point of the passage. Whether the market ultimately evens itself out has nothing to do with the causes of the fluctuations.

8. **(E)** The assumption necessary to the author's reasoning is the fairly abstract or minimal one that there is a connection between the characteristics of a work of art and the period during which it was produced. If there were no such connection, that is, if there were not styles of art which lasted for some time but only randomly produced works unrelated to one another by

medium, content, or detail, the argument would fail. Every other answer, however, attributes too much to the author. (D) for example states that the expert can *pinpoint* the date of the work, but this goes far beyond the author's attempt to date generally the piece of pottery he is examining. (C) says more than the author does. He mentions that the details of semi-nude women and bulls are characteristic of the *late* Minoan period, not that they generally characterize the entire history of that people. (B) also goes far beyond the details offered. The author connects the bull with a period of *Minoan* civilization—not ancient civilizations in general. Finally, (A) fails because, while the author apparently believes that Minoan pottery of this period was made in a certain way, he does not claim that all such pottery came from this period. He uses a group of characteristics in combination to date the pottery: It is the combination which is unique to the period, not each individual characteristic taken in isolation.

9. **(B)** The weakness in the argument is that it makes an assertion without any supporting argumentation. The author states that things might turn out to be worse, but he never mentions any specific way in which the result might be considered less desirable than what presently exists. As for (A), the author might have chosen to attack the radicals in this way, but that he did not adopt a particular line of attack which was available to him is not nearly so severe a criticism as that expressed by (B)—that the line of attack he did adopt is defective, or at least incomplete. The same reasoning applies to both (C) and (E). It is true the author might have taken the attack proposed by (C), but that he chose not to is not nearly so serious a weakness as that pointed out by (B). (E) comes perhaps the closest to expressing what (B) says more explicitly. (E) hints at the specific consequences which might occur, but it is restricted to the *transition* period. It is not really detailing the bad results which might finally come out of a revolution, only the disadvantages of undertaking the change. Finally, (D) describes existing conditions, but it does not treat the question whether there *should* be a revolution; and, in any event, to defend against the question whether there *should* be a revolution by arguing there *will not be* one would itself be weak, had the author used the argument.

10. **(E)** The sample syllogism uses its terms in an ambiguous way. In the first premise the category "American buffalo" is used to refer to the group as a whole, but in the second premise it is used to denote a particular member of that group. In the first premise, *disappearing* refers to extinction of a group, but in the second premise *disappearing* apparently means fading from view. (E) is fraught with similar ambiguities. The argument there moves from wealthy people as a group to a particular wealthy person, an illegitimate shifting of terminology; and it uses the word frequently in two difference senses, first to mean the occurrence of unrelated incidents but in the second to mean the occurrence of a series of events. (A) is a distraction. It mentions subject matter similar to that of the question stem, but our task is to parallel the *form* of the argument, not to find an argument on a similar topic. (A), incidentally, is an unambiguous and valid argument. So, too, is (B), and a moment's reflection will reveal that it is very similar to (A). (C) is not similar to (A) and (B), but then again it is not parallel to the question stem. (C) contains circular reasoning—the very thing to be proved had to be assumed in the first place—but while circular reasoning is incorrect reasoning, it does not parallel the error committed by the question stem: ambiguity. (D) is clearly a correct argument so it cannot be parallel to the question stem which contains a fallacious argument.

11. **(C)** The tone of the paragraph is tongue-in-cheek. The author uses phrases such as "mysteries of this arcane science" and "wonderful discipline," but then gives a silly example of the utility of logic. Obviously, he means to be ironic. The real point he wants to make is that formal logic has little utility and that it may even lead one to make foolish errors. (A) cannot be correct be-

cause the example is clearly not an illustration of correct reasoning. (B) can be rejected since the author does not attempt to define the term "logic," he only gives an example of its use. (D) is a distraction. The author's particular illustration does mention the American buffalo, but he could as easily have taken another species of animal or any other group term which would lend itself to the ambiguous treatment of his syllogism. (E) is incorrect since the author never examines the relationship between the premises and the conclusion. He gives the example and lets it speak for itself.

12. **(B)** The author's behavior is paradoxical because he is going along with the young man's paradoxical statement. He concludes the young man is lying because the young man told him so, but that depends on believing what the young man told him is true. So he accepts the content of the young man's statement in order to reject the statement. Once it is seen that there is a logical twist to this problem, the other answer choices can easily be rejected. (A), of course, overlooks the paradoxical nature of the tourist's behavior. The stranger may have been trying to be helpful, but what is curious about the tourist's behavior is not that he rejected the stranger's offer of advice, *but* that he relied on that very advice at the moment he rejected it! (C) also overlooks the paradox. It is true the tourist rejects the advice, but his rejection is not *understandable;* if anything it is self-contradictory, and therefore completely incomprehensible. (D) is the poorest possible choice since it makes a value judgment totally unrelated to the point of the passage. Finally, (E) would have been correct only if the tourist were possibly being victimized.

13. **(D)** As we explained in the previous question, the tourist's behavior is self-contradictory. So, too, the sentence mentioned in (D) is self-contradictory. For if the sentence is taken to be true, what it asserts must be the case, so the sentence turns out to be false. On the other hand, if the sentence is taken to be false, then what it says is correct, so the sentence must be true. In other words, the sentence is true only if it is false, and false only if it is true: a paradox. (A) is not paradoxical. The witness *later* admits that he lied in the first instance, thus, though his later testimony contradicts his earlier testimony, the statements taken as a group are not internally inconsistent, since he is not claiming that the first and the second are true *at the same time.* (B) and (C) do not have even the flavor of paradox. They are just straightforward statements. Do not be deceived by the fact that (C) refers to an about-face. To change directions, or even one's testimony, is not self-contradictory—see (A). Finally, (E) is a straightforward, self-consistent statement. Although the worker is advised to dissemble, he does not claim that he is both telling the truth and presenting a false image at the same time.

14. **(E)** The author cites a series of similarities between the two diseases, and then in his last sentence he writes, "So . . . ," indicating that his conclusion that the causes of the two diseases are similar rests upon the other similarities he has listed. Answer (E) correctly describes the basis of the argument. (A) is incorrect, for nothing in the passage indicates that either disease is a public health hazard, much less that one disease is a greater hazard than the other. (B) is unwarranted for the author states only that the scientists are looking for a cure for *aphroditis melancholias.* He does not state that they will be successful; and even if there is a hint of that in the argument, we surely would not want to conclude on that basis that scientists will eventually find a cure for *every* disease. (C), like (A), is unrelated to the conclusion the author seeks to establish. All he wants to maintain is that similarities in the symptoms suggest that scientists should look for similarities in the causes of these diseases. He offers no opinion of the ultimate goal of modern technology, nor does he need to do so. His argument is complete without any such addition. (D) is probably the second-best answer, but it is still completely wrong. The author's argument based on the assumption that similarity of effect depends upon similarity of cause would neither gain nor lose persuasive force

if (D) were true. After all, many diseases occur in both man and other animals, but at least (D) has the merit—which (A), (B), and (C) all lack—of trying to say something about the connection between the causes and effects of disease.

15. **(C)** (A) can be seriously questioned on two points. First, there is the very obvious bias of the speaker in making the statement; and second, even were he a reliable, unbiased source, the statement is still a prediction in a difficult and uncertain field. (B) also smacks of bias: The sales representative is expected to defend his products, so we tend to discount his claims, deflate them a bit, since we rightly worry that he may be puffing up his wares. (D) is a variation on the bias element found in (A) and (B): Although the runner-up *may* be correct, it is still a good idea to be suspicious that his judgment has been clouded by his own interest in the matter. (E) also is a statement made by a person who is likely to have an ulterior motive for making his claim. In this case, the union representative would obviously speak in the interests of the workers he represents. (C), on the other hand, suffers from neither a defect of source nor a defect of content. As to the source, we have not one, but two, highly trained professionals making the observation, and there is no reason to suspect that such a statement would carry any personal advantage for them. Second, as to the content, there is nothing outlandish about it; it could have been another aircraft or a missile—do not conclude that they must have spotted a UFO; there is no reason to attribute that to the speakers.

16. **(B)** The author's attitude toward the bankruptcy law is expressed by his choice of terms, "folly," "protectionism," "conned." He apparently believes that the debtor who has incurred these debts ought to bear the responsibility for them and that the government should not help him get off the hook. (B) properly expresses this attitude: You have created for yourself a situation by your own actions, now you must accept it. The author may share (A) as well, but (A) is not a judgment he would make about the bankrupt, that is, a person who does not have a penny to save. (C) is completely unrelated to the question at hand; the bankrupt has no power to wield. The author may believe (D)—in fact, he opposes at least this one instance of government interference and hints that he is, in general, opposed to government interference for the protection of people from themselves—but the question stem asks for the author's attitude about the bankrupt debtor, not the government. (D) would be appropriate to the latter, but it has no bearing on the question at hand. Finally, (E) would be applicable if the government were giving money to pay a ransom to terrorists or some similar situation. The assistance it provides to the bankrupt debtor is not such a program. It does not pay tribute to the debtor.

17. **(A)** For the author's conclusion to follow from his premises—the debtor will make out like a bandit with the goods he procured with credit—it must be the case that after the proceedings are completed the debtor will be left with those goods. At least the author leads us to believe this is the way the law works. As a matter of fact, that implication is incorrect (in part) and is a serious defect in the author's position; but for present purposes we do not need to worry what the "real" law is nor whether the suggestion is *mis*leading or not—only that the author does lead in that direction. (B) is incorrect because it attributes more to the author than he actually claims. He is making an argument about people who abuse credit; he never even hints that most persons who can obtain credit through use of a card abuse their credit. (C), too, takes us far beyond what the author has specifically claimed. The author only argues that the bankruptcy laws are too favorable to the debtor; he never extends his argument to say what sort of substitute he would advocate. And we certainly do not, without evidence, want to attribute to the author anything so drastic as imprisonment of the debtor as an appropriate remedy. (D) fails for it is highly speculative. Such a conclusion finds no support in the passage because the author is silent

about how many debtors take advantage of the law; and, in any event, if there is such an implication in the paragraph, it must surely be that the debtors and not the creditors are the ones to initiate the proceedings. (E) fails for the same reasons that (B) and (C) fail. The author never even hints at such a position.

18. **(D)** The argument commits several errors. One obvious point is that the first premise is very much an oversimplification. Complicated questions about punishment and child-rearing are hardly ever easily reduced to "either-or" propositions. Thus, (C) is a good objection. Beyond that, the terms "severely punish" and "bad" are highly ambiguous. It would be legitimate to ask the speaker just what he considered to be bad behavior, (B), and severe punishment, (A). Also, since the speaker has alleged the child has been "bad," and since that term is ambiguous, we can also demand clarification on that score, (E). The one objection it makes no sense to raise is (D). The premises have the very simple logical structure: If child is bad and not punished, then he becomes a criminal. Child X is bad. There is absolutely no inconsistency between those two statements.

19. **(E)** The argument given in the question stem is circular, that is, it begs the question. It tries to prove that the decision is unfair by claiming that it singles out a group, which is the same thing as discriminating, and then concludes that *since* all discrimination is unfair so, too, the court's decision is unfair. Of course, the real issue is whether singling out this particular group is unfair. After all, we do make distinctions, e.g., adults are treated differently than children, businesses differently than persons, soldiers differently than executives. The question of fairness cannot be solved by simply noting that the decision singles out some persons. (E) also is circular: It tries to prove this is a beautiful painting because all paintings of this sort are beautiful. (A) is perhaps the second-best answer, but notice that it is purely hypothetical in its form: *If* this were true, *then* that would be true. As a consequence, it is not as similar to the question stem as (E), which is phrased in categorical assertions rather than hypothetical statements. (B) moves from the premise that students are not good judges of their needs to a conclusion about the responsibility for planning course work. The conclusion and the premise are not the same so the argument is not circular. (C) is not, technically speaking, even an argument. Remember from our instructional material at the beginning of the book, an argument has premises and a conclusion. These are separate statements. (C) is one long statement, not two short ones. It reads: "A because B, not A, therefore B." For example, the statement "I am late because the car broke down" is not an inference, but a causal statement. In (D), since the premise (everything after the semicolon) is not the same as the conclusion (the statement before the semicolon), the argument is not a circular argument and so does not parallel the stem argument.

20. **(B)** The author's claim depends in a very important way on the assumption that the assistance he advocates will be successful. After all, any proposed course of action which just won't work clearly ought to be rejected. (B) is just this kind of argument: Whatever else you say, your proposed plan will not work, therefore, we must reject it. (A) opens an entirely new line of argument. The author has said only that there is a certain connection between guidance and creativity; he never claims that everyone can or should be a professional artist. Thus, (A) is wrong, as is (E) for the same reason. (C) is wrong for a similar reason. The author never suggests that all students should be professional artists; and, in fact, he may want to encourage students to be creative no matter which practical careers they may choose. (E) is probably the second-best answer; it does, to a certain extent, try to attack the workability of the proposal. Unfortunately, it does not address the general connection the author says exists between training and creativity. In other words, (E) does not say the proposal will not work at all; it merely says it may work too well. Further, (E) is wrong because it does not attribute the

"burn out" to the training of the sort proposed by the author.

21. (E) What we are looking for here is an intervening causal link which caused the plan to be unsuccessful. The projected train of events was: (1) Adopt express lanes, (2) fewer cars, and (3) faster traffic flow. Between the first and the third steps, however, something went wrong. (E) alone supplies that unforeseen side effect. Since the cars backed up on too few lanes, total flow of traffic was actually slowed, not speeded up. (A) is irrelevant since it does not explain what went wrong *after* the plan was adopted. (B) does not even attempt to address the sequence of events which we have just outlined. Although (C) is probably true and was something the planners likely considered in their projections it does not explain the plan's failure. Finally, (D) might have been relevant in deciding whether or not to adopt the plan, but given that the plan was adopted, (D) cannot explain why it then failed.

22. (E) We have all seen arguments of this sort in our daily lives, and perhaps if we have not been very careful, we have even made the same mistakes made by the leaders of Gambia. For example, last semester, which was fall, I made a lot of money selling peanuts at football games, therefore, this spring semester I will make even more money. All three propositions point out weaknesses in the projections made by Gambia's leaders. I: Of course, if the tremendous increase in GNP is due to some unique event (my personal income increased last semester when I inherited $2,000 from my aunt), it would be foolish to project a similar increase for a time period during which that event cannot repeat itself. II: This is a bit less obvious, but the projection is based on the assumption that Gambia will receive additional aid, *and* will be able to put that aid to use. If they are not in a position to use that aid (I cannot work twice as many hours in the spring), they cannot expect the aid to generate increases in GNP. Finally, III also is a weakness in the leaders' projections. If there are physical limitations on the possible increases, then the leaders have made an error. Their projections are premised on the existence of physical resources which are greater than those they actually have.

23. (C) The conclusion of the paragraph is so obvious that it is almost difficult to find. The author says office workers work better the cooler the temperature—provided the temperature does not drop below 68°. Therefore, we can conclude, the temperature at which workers will be most efficient will be precisely 68°. Notice that the author does not say what happens once the temperature drops below 68° except that workers are no longer as efficient. For all we know, efficiency may drop off slowly or quickly compared with improvements in efficiency as the temperature drops to 68°. So (E) goes beyond the information supplied in the passage. (D) also goes far beyond the scope of the author's claim. His formula is specifically applicable to *office* workers. We have no reason to believe the author would extend his formula to non-office workers. (B) is probably not a conclusion the author would endorse since he claims to have found a way of achieving improvements in efficiency in a different and seemingly permanent way. Finally, (A) is not a conclusion the author seems likely to reach since nothing indicates that his formula yields only short-term gains which last as long as the temperature is kept constant. To be sure, the gains will not be repeatable, but then they will not be short-run either.

24. (A) The anti-abortion speaker unwittingly plays right into the hands of the pro-abortion speaker. The "pro" speaker tries to show that there are many decisions regarding human life in which we allow that an increase in the quality of life justifies an increase in the danger to human life. All that the "anti" speaker does is to help prove this point. He says the quality of life would suffer if we lowered the speed limits to protect human life. Given this analysis, (B) must be incorrect, for the "anti" speaker's position is completely ineffective as a rebuttal. Moreover, (C) must be incorrect for his

response is not a strong statement of an anti-abortion position. (D) is incorrect, for while his response is of no value to the position he seeks to defend, it cannot be said that it is irrelevant. In fact, as we have just shown, his position is very relevant to that of the "pro" speaker's because it supports that position. Finally, (E) is not an appropriate characterization of the "anti" speaker's position, for he tries, however ineptly, to attack the merits of the "pro" speaker's position, not the character of that speaker.

25. **(E)** The "pro" speaker uses the example of traffic fatalities to show that society has always traded the quality of life for the quantity of life. Of course, he says, we do not always acknowledge that that is what we are doing; but, if we were honest we would have to admit that we were making a trade-off. Thus, (E) is the best conclusion of the passage. The author's defense of abortion amounts to the claim that abortion is just another case in which we trade off one life (the fetus) to make the lives of others (the survivors) better. The only difference is that the life being sacrificed is specifiable and highly visible in the case of abortion, whereas in the case of highway fatalities, no one knows in advance on whom the ax will fall. (A) certainly goes far beyond what the author is advocating. If anything, he probably recognizes that sometimes the trade-off will be drawn in favor of protecting lives, and thus we need some such laws. (B) must be wrong, first, because the "anti" speaker claims this is not his position, and second, because the "pro" speaker would prefer to show that the logical consequence of the "anti" speaker's response is an argument in favor of abortion. (C) is not an appropriate continuation because the author has already said this is a weak counter-example and that he has even stronger points to make. Finally, the author might be willing to accept contraception (D) as yet another example of the trade-off, but his conclusion can be much stronger than that. The author wants to defend abortion, so the conclusion of his speech ought to be that abortion is an acceptable practice—not that contraception is an acceptable practice.

26. **(D)** This is a very difficult question. That III is an assumption the author makes requires careful reading. The author's attitude about the just war tips us off. He implies that this is an appropriate function of government, and further that there are even clearer cases. Implicit in his defense of abortion is that a trade-off must be made and that it is appropriately a collective decision. I is not an assumption of the argument. Indeed, the author seems to assume, as we have just maintained, that the trade-off is an appropriate goal of society. Finally, the author does not assume II; if anything, he almost states that he accepts that the fetus is a life but it may be traded off in exchange for an increase in the quality in the lives of others.

SECTION III

Set 1

OVERVIEW: The kind of conflict which might arise between these two rules is over the appropriate measure of damages for breach of contract. Rule I specifies that the breaching party is liable for all the profit the injured party would have made. Rule II softens this quite a bit by limiting the liability of the breaching party to those losses he could have foreseen would result from his breach. In our facts, there are two different losses which Greg suffers. One, Greg was aware in advance of the loss, and he told Pardee about it. The other would have been a windfall; Greg did not know he would have received the other commission. So, too, Pardee did not know about the possibility of a second commission. It appears, then, that Pardee is liable for the first commission, the one about which Greg knew and told Pardee. Both rules are in accord here. But the second commission, the one neither person knew about and Pardee had no reason to suspect would occur, requires us to choose between the two rules. If Rule I is used, Greg wins; if Rule II is used, Pardee wins.

1. **(D)** This information, even if we had it, would not help us apply either rule. The written estimate for the work on the car will

not aid us in determining what Pardee knew, or should have known, would be the result of his breaching the contract.

2. **(C)** As we have already discussed, the two rules agree in their treatment of the commission about which Pardee was aware. Greg expected to make the $175, so Rule I would award that to him. Pardee knew Greg expected to make $175, so Rule II would also award Greg that money.

3. **(B)** This question sets up additional problems. Supposing that Greg's company sues. What will be the result? We cannot call this a (D), since we are asked to alter the problem structure so that Greg's company sues. So whether the company can win the suit is made an issue for us. But neither of the rules applies to Greg's company. The first does not apply to the company because it is specifically applicable only to the "party to the contract." Since II is really an exception to I, or a restriction on I, II cannot apply either. On the other hand, the company is out some money, and maybe it does have some rights against Pardee. But we lack any rule to tell us that, so the correct answer here is (B).

4. **(A)** This is the conflict we outlined in the overview. Applying Rule I, Greg is entitled to the second commission, but applying Rule II, Greg is not entitled to the second commission.

5. **(D)** Since nothing in the rules mentions any requirement that a contract be in writing, the question of whether the agreement was signed is completely irrelevant to the problem of damages.

6. **(B)** Greg sues for the repairs, but the rules apply only to the expected gain. It may be that Greg is entitled to receive a refund even though he is not entitled to recover from Pardee for the loss of the unexpected commission.

Set 2

OVERVIEW: The conflict in this case centers around the question of whether Nebel assumed the risk that he would be injured. According to Rule I, an injured party may recover without restriction for any injury which another carelessly inflicts on him. Rule II considerably curtails the scope of I. It provides that a person who is injured by another's carelessness may not recover if he assumed the risk of that injury by placing himself in a position where he might be injured in that way. Nebel did place himself in just such a position. The facts indicate that the game was proceeding normally. Grant got a bit overexuberant and Nebel was standing too close. Although Grant was admittedly careless, Nebel implicitly assumed that risk since he agreed to play with Grant. Seeing that we can reason to the conclusion that Nebel assumed the risk of such an injury, we can also see that the two rules conflict in this case.

7. **(A)** This is the conflict we just described in the set overview. On Rule I Nebel does recover from Grant; on Rule II Nebel does not.

8. **(D)** This is a red herring. Although there is mention made of a release being signed, this release was for the Club. It has nothing to do with the dispute between Nebel and Grant.

9. **(D)** Clearly this is unimportant. Even if we knew who made the introduction, this would not help us apply the two rules to the facts.

10. **(B)** Grant carelessly hurt Nebel, but Nebel *intentionally* hit Grant. Neither of the two rules is applicable to this part of the facts. So to decide this aspect, we will need further guidance.

11. **(C)** This is deducible from the facts. The injury seems to be one of those which might occur in the ordinary course of events—one player becoming just a bit too aggressive. So we can conclude that Nebel assumed the risk, because he got out there to play the game in the first place.

Set 3

OVERVIEW: The possible conflict between these two rules is easily imagined. Rule I defines a criminal assault as the attempt to intentionally injure another, and Rule II creates a general exception to criminal liability. A person who is involuntarily intoxicated is not criminally liable for his actions. Notice that the word *involuntarily* is an extremely important restriction on the scope of Rule II. A person is not relieved of criminal liability merely because he is intoxicated; he escapes liability only if the intoxication was involuntary, e.g., someone forced him to drink to excess. Although no question in this particular series turns on your having picked up on this word (#12 specifically mentions the word, so you could hardly have missed it), we might easily have written a set of facts such that the person willingly intoxicated himself. In that case, Rule II would not have applied and there would have been no conflict between the two rules.

12. **(B)** As we have just pointed out in the set overview, the word *involuntarily* introduces a very important qualification on Rule II. To apply that rule, we must decide whether Patrick was voluntarily or involuntarily intoxicated. We could argue that the intoxication was voluntary because he did go with his friends and he did say he wanted to have a good time. On the other hand, given that Patrick had no prior experience with the effects of alcohol (at least not inside his own body) and probably had no way of knowing how much alcohol he could consume without becoming intoxicated, we can argue that he did not mean to become intoxicated. In any event, the decision as to the voluntariness of the intoxication cannot be made by logically deducing the conclusion from the facts and the rules, and the issue is relevant in applying Rule II, so the correct answer is (B).

13. **(D)** Would the information provided by an answer to this question help us apply either rule? No. Rule I requires only that Patrick have attacked at least one person. Further, it will not do to argue, "Yes, but each time Patrick attacked someone he committed another crime." While that may be true (the rule does not definitely support that conclusion), the question does not ask, "How many people did Patrick attack?" It asks, "How many people were in the bar?"

14. **(B)** Rule I defines Patrick's criminal liability for his actions in the bar. If we want to know also whether Patrick is civilly liable, we will need the rule which defines civil liability. Notice that this cannot be an (A), because we do not have a rule governing civil liability. In fact, for all we know, while voluntary intoxication is a defense against a criminal prosecution, it may not be a defense against a civil suit.

15. **(A)** Here, however, we find our conflict between the two rules. As we explained in the overview to this set, Rule II is a general exception to criminal liability. If we take Rule I in isolation, Patrick is guilty of criminal assault. If we take Rule II, Patrick cannot be criminally liable for anything (depending on the issue of intoxication).

Set 4

OVERVIEW: This set of rules is likely to cause some head-shaking among those students who have preconceived notions about the law. Those students are likely to believe that Rule I is a real rule of law, while Rule II is something we made up just for purposes of writing this section. The reaction is based on the mistaken notion that the law says "a deal is a deal." In reality, Rule II is a very old and well-entrenched rule of law. Although the general principle is articulated by Rule I, Rule II creates an exception to that principle. If the two parties were mistaken about the value of the goods sold at the time of the contract, then either party may ask that the court rescind the contract. In this case, both parties were mistaken about the value of the cow. Rule I would insist upon the enforcement of the contract, but Rule II would allow the judge to rescind the contract and put both parties back in their original positions.

16. **(C)** This we can deduce from Rule II. If the court orders recision, it must restore *both* parties to their original positions.

17. **(D)** Although it might be possible to make this remotely relevant, e.g., the older the cow the less likely she is to bear calves, this would be straining at gnats. To avoid classi-

fying this as a (D), you would have to mark it a (B), but you surely would not want to insist that this is a *major* issue in the case. To be sure, the question whether the cow is barren is a major issue, but the age of the cow would be minor at best, so better to call this (D).

18. **(D)** In this question, unlike #17, there is some justification for answering (B), but (B) is still wrong. Some students will reason, "It is important to know whether the cow was pregnant at the time so I can tell whether both parties were mistaken." But this line of reasoning depends on distorting Rule II. Rule II requires there be a mutual mistake. The mistake in this case was over whether the cow was barren. Even if she had gotten pregnant after leaving Roberta's farm and moving to Oscar's place, this would have shown she was not barren. So when she got with calf is irrelevant. That she did so is important.

19. **(A)** This highlights the conflict we discussed in the set overview. According to Rule I, Roberta made a deal and she is stuck with it. According to Rule II, since both parties made a mistake and did not quite realize the real implications of their deal, the deal can be called off.

20. **(B)** In this question we assume that the judge picks Rule II to govern the case and that he decides the cow belongs to Roberta. We noted in 16 that on this assumption Oscar will have his $100 returned. But who has to move the cow? It takes some time and money to move a big animal 30 miles. The rule does not say how this part of the recision will be carried out. To determine which of the two parties has to bear the cost we would need another rule.

21. **(C)** Here we apply a concept of Rule I to our facts. Was the contract carried out? The answer to this question will be important in determining whether Rule I applies to the facts, and the answer is affirmative. Roberta got her $100, and Oscar got the cow.

Set 5

OVERVIEW: Rule II creates a possible exception to Rule I. Rule I establishes that a will must be enforced, that is, the court will follow its directions in distributing the property of the deceased. Rule II says, however, that if the deceased failed to make some provision for the spouse, the provisions of the will are not to be enforced—at least not enforced to the extent that one-third of the property is to go to the spouse regardless of what the will says. In our case, Elizabeth's will leaves her estate to Harriet and to the Foundation, with no provision for her spouse. Paul is not entitled to anything under Rule I, but he is entitled to one-third of the estate under Rule II. Notice that Rule II does not specify which third Paul will receive. It does not tell us that Paul gets to pick what he will receive from his third. That is an open issue which would require another rule.

22. **(D)** The cause of death will not help us apply either rule. Again, do not strain at gnats (i.e., but what if Paul killed her?). If Paul had killed her, it would have been made explicit, and then that would have been a major issue in the case. As it is, to make this relevant you would only be speculating. You might as well speculate that she is not really dead, only in a deep trance. Such straining will get you nowhere on the test.

23. **(A)** This is the conflict we outlined in the set overview. According to Rule I, Paul gets nothing, but by Rule II he gets one-third of the estate.

24. **(C)** At first glance you might think this a (B). But by applying the rules, even without choosing between them, we know the children are entitled to nothing. By the terms of Rule I, only Harriet and the Foundation receive portions of the estate. Even taking Rule II into account, only Paul, Harriet, and the Foundation receive portions. So the two rules taken together show us the children will receive nothing.

25. **(B)** As we noted in the set overview, Rule

II is silent on how the assets are to be selected for distribution. Paul is entitled to one-third of the estate, but how that third is to be selected is an open question. Notice that although the value of the house, $150,000, is one-half of the value we are told about (stocks, etc., total $150,000), we cannot deduce that Paul is not entitled to the house because the value exceeds one-third of the entire estate. There is the value of the jewelry to take into account, and that is unknown. You should not conclude that it is, or is not, a large amount.

26. **(B)** This would obviously affect the value of the estate. No matter whether we are working with Rule I or Rule II, we would still have to readjust the distribution. The pie would be smaller and so the shares would also be smaller. But whose share would shrink the most and by how much can be determined only on the basis of some further guidance by rules.

Set 6

OVERVIEW: In this set, a conflict will arise if there is an injury that the landlord would ordinarily be responsible for which occurs while an adult should be supervising a child. Carl's injury does fit within the terms of Rule I. There was the hole in the fence; the landlord was warned it was dangerous; the condition was dangerous; Carl was injured. But Rule II lets the landlord off the hook in that Carl would not have been injured if he had been properly supervised by an adult. You can use the facts to deduce that there was not proper supervision. Carl is a three-year-old. Gary left him and walked a block away and stayed away for twenty minutes. So we have a conflict in the case.

27. **(A)** This is the conflict we just outlined. According to Rule I the landlord is liable, but Rule II yields a different result since Carl would not have been injured had Gary not left him unattended.

28. **(D)** Although this might be remotely relevant to the issue of Gary's failure to supervise, we do not need it since the facts say the play yard was deserted except for Carl. If the facts had been silent on this issue, this question would have bordered on a (B) choice. Had Gary walked away while there were ten other parents present, it would be harder to decide whether he had or had not been irresponsible.

29. **(C)** This is something we can deduce using the facts. The landlord knew about the hole. The hole was dangerous since children played near the pool. And of course, this conclusion is critical in determining whether Rule I is applicable to the facts of the case.

30. **(C)** As we have previously argued, Gary was not reasonable in his supervision. He left a three-year-old child unattended in a deserted play yard when he knew, according to the facts, that there was a hole in the fence. You do not really need any more information to conclude that Gary did not behave in a responsible manner.

Set 7

OVERVIEW: A conflict will arise between these two rules if a person not a party to a contract sues claiming that he is a third-party beneficiary. The term "third-party beneficiary" is a legal term, but you were not expected to know its meaning. The term is defined for you in Rule II. In this case, Eugene is apparently a third-party beneficiary. At the time Timothy and Glenn made their contract, it was agreed that the contract would be for the benefit of Eugene.

31. **(A)** This is the conflict we described in the set overview. According to Rule I, since Eugene is not a party to the contract, he cannot maintain his action, but according to the wording of Rule II, he can since he is a third-party beneficiary.

32. **(C)** Since Timothy is a party to the contract in the first place, an application of Rule I tells us that he is entitled to maintain a suit to enforce it.

33. **(C)** This is similar to #32. Since Eugene was a party to his agreement with Timothy, Rule I tells us that Eugene has the proper status to allow him to sue Timothy.

34. **(D)** This is a red herring. Nothing in the rules requires anything to be in writing. Although the facts are silent on whether the agreement was reduced to writing, this is not a (B). The answer to this question—was it in writing?—would not help you apply either rule. Since neither rule mentions any requirement of writing, the additional information would be superfluous.

35. **(C)** Eugene fits the description of a "third-party beneficiary" as that term is defined by Rule II.

SECTION IV

Questions 1—5

Arranging the Information

Since the transfer from clan to clan takes place upon reaching adulthood, a person can be referred to either by the clan into which they were born or by the one in which they are adults. The requirement that only mature Ater may marry simply keeps order. The basic information can be organized in this way

MEN		WOMEN	
BORN	ADULT	BORN	ADULT
1	2	1	3
2	3	2	1
3	1	3	2

Answering the Questions

1. **(A)** Answers (C) and (D) are flack and can be dismissed.

   The nephew we are seeking is the son of a sister OR of a brother. Since marriage is permitted only within a clan, the question is whether the nephew can ever be the same clan.

   The woman and her brother or sister would have been born into the same clan—the first. Sisters born into the first clan would both become third clan adults and the son of a third clan person becomes a first clan adult and is not able to marry the third clan adult woman who is the subject of the question. This eliminates (B).

   A brother and sister born into the first clan would be in separate clans as adults, the woman moving to the third and the man to the second. The brother's son would be born second clan and be a third clan adult, who is eligible to marry his aunt. Hence, (A). (E) is eliminated by this reasoning also.

2. **(E)** An adult second clan male was born into the first clan, thus, both parents must be first clan adults. The father, as an adult first clan male must have been born third clan, which gives the answer (E). The mother, as an adult first clan, must have been born into the second clan.

3. **(E)** Tracing the lineage:

   BABY 3 → MOTHER 3 ADULT → 1 BORN → GRANDMOTHER 1 ADULT → 2 BORN → GREATGRANDMOTHER 2 ADULT → 3 BORN.

4. **(D)** Tracing the lineage possibilities:

   GRANDDAUGHTER 2 ADULT → 3 BORN → (branch here)

   because the subject of the question could be related through either the father or the mother of the granddaughter.

   → FATHER/SON ADULT 3 → BORN 2, AND THUS GRANDFATHER IS A 2 OR
   → MOTHER/DAUGHTER ADULT 3 → BORN 1, THUS GRANDFATHER IS A 1

   Note that we are concerned only with the adult status of the subject of the question since he is clearly an adult now.

5. **(C)** I is inferable since a sister and brother are born into the same clan and move in

different directions, they cannot marry each other.

II is inferable since a son will move out of his birth clan and his mother will stay in it, thus, they cannot marry.

III is not inferable, since it is possible for the grandson to be the same clan as she, and clan membership is the only restriction on who may marry whom. For example:

woman adult 3 → daughter born 3 → adult 2 → grandson born 2 → adult 3, same as grandmother.

Questions 6–10

Arranging the Information

This is similar to an elevator problem or any other sequence or arrival and departure problem. You can refer to the express stops as 1 through 8, with 3 and 6 not used. P gets off earlier than Q, with three on after 8.

10	20	30	40	50	60	70	80	
		xx			xx			3 left
		P < Q						

Answering the Questions

6. **(C)** J is M + 2. At first it seems as though M can get off anywhere except 30th and 60th (10th is not possible). But since there is the two stop differential, J cannot get off at 10th, 20th, 30th, 50th (because M can't leave at 30th), 60th, or 80th (because M can't get off at 60th). This leaves only 40th and 70th.

7. **(B)** The seeming addition of information actually does nothing except to specify which were the three who were still on the bus after 80th. There are four passengers and five available exit stops (20th, 40th, 50th, 70th, and 80th), so I and II are both possible. III however is not known for sure since the unused stop could have been any other available stop. Hence, (B).

8. **(D)** Learning that K and L got off before 80th, coupled with the information that P and Q also got off before 80th, means that J, M, and N are still on the bus. Thus, (A), (B), and (C) are true. The original information tells us that (D) must be false.

9. **(B)** If M precedes P, and therefore Q, this couples with the original information that P preceded Q to produce M < P < Q. Since Q had to wait through at least two available stops, he could not have exited at either 20th or 40th, but used 50th, 70th, or 80th, but the question stem rules out 70th, leaving (B).

   (A) is not necessarily true since the fourth departing passenger may have left at the same time as M, P, or Q.

   (C) is not necessarily true since P could have left as early as 40th. (D) and (E) fail since we do not even know that J left at all.

10. **(D)** We know from the original information that three of the original persons were still on the bus after 80th Street, so the answer cannot be (A) or (B).

    X enters on 20th and leaves at 50th, Y enters at 30th and leaves at 70th, but Z enters at 40th and leaves at 90th, thus, adding one to the three otherwise known to be on the bus after 80th. Hence, (D).

Questions 11–15

Arranging the Information

O will not go next to T or E. The condition of not forming a common three-letter word cannot be usefully listed out. A simple alertness to the words formed is sufficient. English words are formed only left to right, however.

Answering the Questions

11. **(C)** I is true because if O is in the middle, it will be next to T, which is forbidden. II is a little more complicated. If M, O, and T are on one wall, then H, E, and R are the paintings on the other wall. These will form the word *her* if H and R are the left and right paintings on the east wall.

    III is, however, not required since the east

wall could be REH, which is not a common English word.

12. **(B)** O cannot be the center painting since it would then be between R and T, placing it next to T, which is forbidden. Also, both ROT and TOR are words, though TOR is not so common.

(A) is not correct since MEH is possible. (C) is possible with:

T R O

E M H

(D) is possible with:

M H E

T R O

(E) is possible with:

M H E

T R O

13. **(D)** The diagram is this:

M O T

R E H

Since the word runs from left to right as you turn around in the middle of the room. (A), (B), and (C) are true, while (D) is false. (E) fails when (D) succeeds.

14. **(A)** If H, M, and R are on one wall, this leaves only E, O, and T for the other wall, which is incorrect since O would have to be next to at least one forbidden partner.

(B) is possible if the wall is arranged E H T, so no word is formed. (C) is possible:

H T E

M O R

(D) is also possible:

T M E

R O H

(E) is possible too:

E R T

O M H

15. **(C)** After the trade Jon has O, O, T, H, E, and R. Note that the new O painting is the same color as the original, and thus also cannot go next to T or E.

(C) is impossible, since to have the O's in the middle of both walls would guarantee that they would be next to the T and the E, which is not permitted. The diagram looks like this:

O O

R/H

T E

However, the order on each side could be different.

The O's cannot be on the same side as the T or E. Answers (A) and (B) both turn on the same idea that either the R or the H will be on one side or the other.

(D) can be false, but is not necessarily false, and thus is not the answer sought.

Questions 16–20

Arranging the Information

LEFT-HANDED RIGHT-HANDED

M← NOT WITH→ { L← NOT WITH→ S ; N← NOT WITH→ T } 4 TOTAL

O R

MUST BE 2

Answering the Questions

16. **(C)** If L is on, that eliminates M and S, and thus choice (E) is out. The elimination of S means that T and R must be on the team since two right-handers are needed, which eliminates (D). The inclusion of T means the exclusion of N, and thus choice (B). Thus, L, O, R, and T are the team, answer choice (C).

17. (**D**) This is a little tricky since you have to remember that the only handedness limitation is that at least two right-handers must be on the team. It is OK if only one left-hander is on the team.

If O is omitted, then the only way to have two left-handers is to have L and N, since neither of those can go with M. But, if L and N are used, then S and T can't be, which leaves only one right-hander, R, and a team of only three players. This means that "L and N" cannot be right, so the left-hander component must be M only, since M cannot go with L or N. (Note that using only L or N will still leave only three players even though two right-handers will be achieved.)

If only M is taken from the left-handers, then all three right-handers must be used, hence (D).

The key was to start with the information you had—about left-handers—and build on that.

18. (**E**) If S and T are chosen, then L and N are excluded. At first glance this seems to require M and O also to be chosen, but remember that, as discussed in 7, there can be three right-handers, so any two of M, O, and R could be chosen, which means (E) is correct since none of the answer choices has sufficient flexibility.

19. (**B**) If R is omitted, S and T are chosen. If S and T are chosen, then L and N are out and only M and O are left, which is only one possibility, M, O, S, and T—answer choice (B).

20. (**E**) Changing T to a left-handed player does not eliminate the restriction that T cannot go with N, or any other restriction or condition. If T is left-handed, then S and R must be on the team as the two needed right-handers. S eliminates L and we are left with R, S, and two of the others. Let us count the ways:

If N is chosen, T and M are out, giving R, S, N and O—1.

If T is chosen, N is out, but it could be combined with either M or O giving R, S, T, and M/O for two more—3 so far.

If M is chosen, N is out leaving T and O. R, S, M, and T/O. The combination with T has already been counted, but R, S, M, and O is a fourth possibility, thus answer choice (E).

Questions 21–25

Arranging the Information

If we indicate the idea of there being "some" by putting the number of the proposition with a question mark over the two areas of a Venn diagram, we will get the following for propositions I, II, and III:

We use Venns or circles because it is the interaction between the groups which is primarily of interest here.

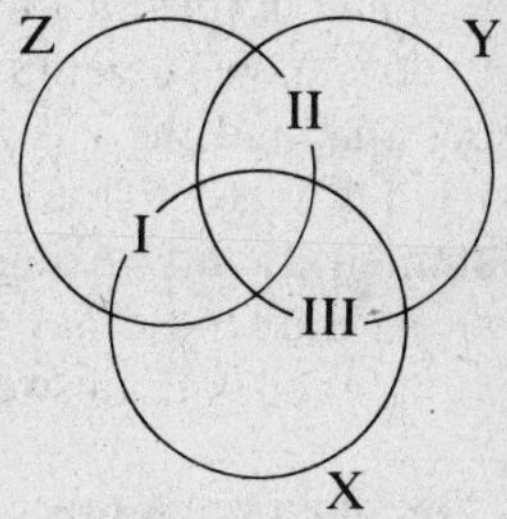

Diagram 1:

Adding the information from proposition IV, we get:

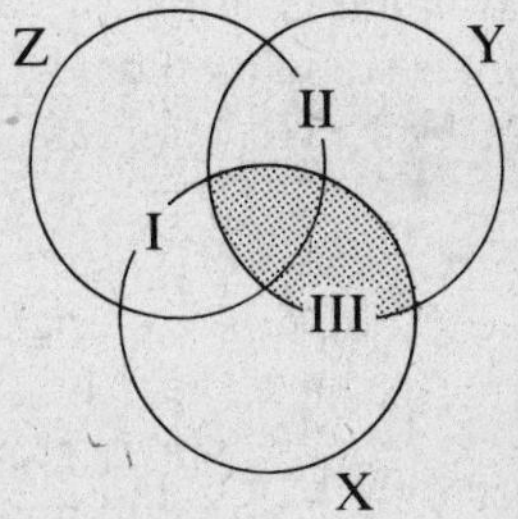

Diagram 2:

Answering the Questions

21. (**E**) Refer to diagram 1. The three statements we are dealing with here are simply indications as to where some things are and say nothing about where things aren't, thus, (A) cannot be known to be true from I, II, and III, and is eliminated.

The same general argument eliminates answer choices (B), (C), and (D). Since the "some" statements covered areas divided into two parts in the diagram, we cannot know which of the two areas is the actual inhabited location, or perhaps both are. The areas pointed to in the three answer choices are indicated here:

Diagram 3:

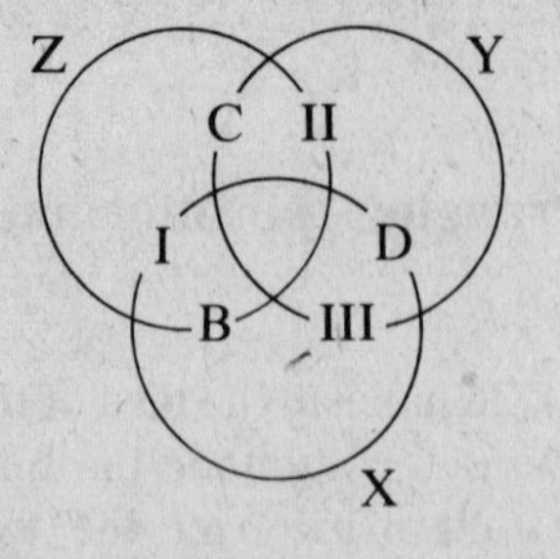

22. **(A)** Referring to diagram 2, we see that one of the areas at first thought to be possibly inhabited in accordance with statement III is rendered impossible by statement IV's obliteration of the overlap between X and Y. This, in turn, means that the area of X only does have something in it, hence (A) is impossible and the answer sought.

(B) and (C) refer to the two areas governed by statement I, and we do not know whether one or both of these has members. Similar reasoning applies to answer choice (D).

23. **(D)** I is already known since statement IV of the original information forbids X to be also Y. II is known for the same reasons that (A) in #22 is false. III is uncertain since II of the original information says only that there is either some member of Y only or of Y + Z, or both. Hence, (D).

24. **(C)** The answer choice (C) is false since the combination of original statements III and IV require there to be some X that are only X, as shown in diagram 2. (A), (B), and (D) are all indeterminate for the same reasons as (C), (D), and (E) in #22.

25. **(D)** Coding in the additional information gives us this diagram:

Diagram 4:

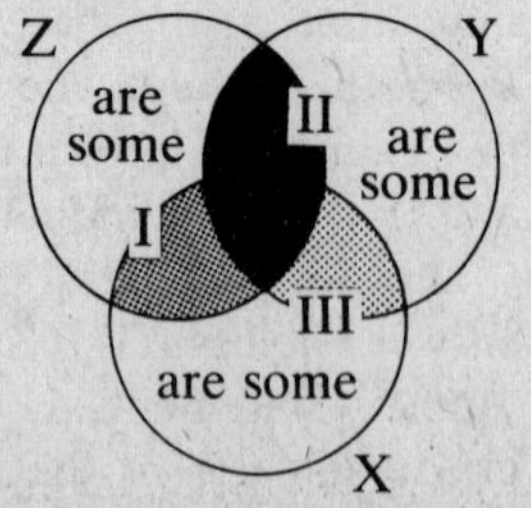

From this diagram we see that there are some individual items which are only X, others only Y, and others only Z. No overlap of any sort is permitted. (D) falsely states that Z must be X, which is wrong. (E) states that you cannot find a Z except for those Z that are not Y, which is correct.

SECTION V

1. **(C)** I is stated in the passage. The only possible objection is that it may sometimes be the case that unemployment can be reduced through the operation of forces other than government intervention. The word *excessive* copes with that.

II is the result of I and the idea that taxation to produce the revenue needed for public spending would defeat the purposes of the spending.

III, however, is not advanced by Keynes as the author explains him. This refers to the author's discussion of the ideas which preceded Keynes.

2. **(D)** (D) is essentially the same idea as #1, I and II, while (A) is similar to III in the same problem. (B), (C), and (E), like (A), refer to the ideas that preceded Keynes.

3. **(C)** There is not much in the passage which yields tone or attitude. This lack of strong attitude is itself the best reason for eliminating (A), (D), and (E), which are all strong attitudes that would need some strong evidence. (B), questioning, is not supported since there is no statement of doubt, nor is there any questioning. The reference to Keynes' work having some "fascinating obscurity" could mean many things depending on the tone of voice with which it is delivered. Unfortunately, as written there is no tone, so we must take it straight as an indication of the difficulty of the work, and of its fascination. Thus, this becomes more a support of (C) than (B).

4. **(A)** (A), (B), and (E) make a good contrast. Their difference, the question of whether Keynes would favor forcing people to work or not, is resolvable from the passage, which refers to willing workers. (C)

fails because nowhere is it even hinted that Keynes is opposed to private spending. Actually, the passage indicates that insufficient private spending can be one of the causes of unemployment. (D) is simply false.

5. **(D)** (B), (C), and (E) are relatively easy to dispose of as being, respectively, unfounded, irrelevant, and too distant from the passage as well as too strong. (A) and (D) are more difficult. (A) is somewhat too strong since it is only in certain circumstances that unemployment is far enough advanced to require government intervention, but such remedy is the final remedy proposed by Keynes. The real key is to remember that this question has a certain focus in the passage—the very beginning—where the term at issue was used. In the first paragraph, the sentence immediately after the one including the term "central thesis" discusses the previous theory's assumption that the equilibrium point of an economy was full employment. Since the two theories are being contrasted—"until it appeared"—this is the point of difference.

6. **(B)** Only (B) has any basis in the passage. Keynes' theory is stated to be the successor to certain prior classical or non-socialist theories, hence, he is a non-socialist theoretician.

7. **(E)** The passage states that it is necessary to give interest in order to get people to let go of their cash, hence (E).

8. **(A)** The slight disconnectedness of the first sentence's proverb from the rest of the passage supports (A). So does elimination of the other answer choices. The passage does not deal with the differences between foods of different nations, (B) and (D); nor does it principally discuss various ways of preparing food, (C), or the food value of fish, (E).

9. **(D)** The author praises the book's intelligence, scope, and writing style. There is no criticism of the book.

10. **(C)** The passage states that the objective classification of the sense of smell is of little use because the response to stimulus is so subjective, just the opposite of (C).

Since the author is so approving of the book, the book's points can be taken to be agreeable to the author. (B) and (D) are stated explicitly in the third paragraph, as is (E) in the fourth. (A) may be implied because of the locution that "nothing better" has been devised than the current one. While this is a relatively weak inference, (C)'s definite disagreement with the passage makes the answer to the question clear.

11. **(D)** The book states that sound stimulus may alter the discrimination between tastes and bases the proposal to use deaf research subjects on that fact. (A) appeals to the last statement in the passage that noisy cereals might be thought to be eaten by extroverts, but remember our Logical Reasoning overview. The allegation that extroverts eat the cereal does not mean that people who do not eat the cereal are not extroverts. (E) has only superficial merit since there is nothing in the passage which indicates that it might be correct. (B) and (C) sound a little scientific, and (B) is a nice general rule, but the correct answer is most likely some specific idea in the passage such as (D). (C)'s merit is that deaf subjects will be better for SOME experiments, but there is no reason to suppose that they are better for ALL food experiments as the answer choice alleges. General and specific are always an issue.

12. **(E)** Our attention is directed only to the chapter headings listed at the top of the second paragraph. This is similar to a partial information question for Analytical Reasoning, where only part of the given information is to be used in answering the question. The book is stated to be well-organized and the chapter headings are specifically stated to be a good representation of the scope of the book. Therefore, we can use the differences in the way the different senses are listed in the chapter headings to indicate their relative importance. Taste and smell (olfaction) are given separate chapters, and thus are likely more important than the other senses which are lumped together into

one chapter. Since we cannot tell whether taste is more important than smell, (A) and (B) cannot be inferred. (C) and (D) can be inferred to be false since each alleges that a "separate-chapter" sense is less important than one with only part of a chapter devoted to it. (E) has it the other way around and can be inferred.

13. **(B)** This interesting question is best approached by examining the differences among the answer choices. The names do not matter since they are all Weber. The dates and the fields are the differences. The passage brings up Weber's law in relation to the relation between stimuli and response for taste and smell and refers to this as a psychological aspect of perception. Our first choice, then, would be a psychologist, but there is not one available. We have two artists, one a painter, and one a composer, two social scientists, one an historian and one an economist-sociologist; and a physiologist. The last is the best answer since it is the senses of smell and taste which are being referred to and these are—at least in part—physiological matters, hence (B). (D) is probably the second-best choice.

14. **(E)** You do not need prior familiarity with the *Guide Michelin*. The question stem tells you that it is a restaurant rating guide. "Ambience" means the surroundings. Ambience includes sound, and extraneous sound is agreed by the author to affect taste discrimination, and thus he would most likely agree that this should be a standard of rating restaurants, (E), rather than be excluded, as (A) would have it. (B), while possible, is not supported by the passage. The reference to the Polish proverb does not endorse Polish cooking. (C) has some merit since the author does seem to be primarily interested in the scientific aspects of the matter, but his comments about the World War II food indicate that he is not entirely uninterested in good food. (D) is too strong since there is much difference between agreeing to the inclusion of one of several criteria and agreeing with the outcome of the entire rating process.

15. **(D)** The author maintains a tone devoid of judgmental words, thus (A) and (C) fail. There may be some humor in the passage, but the author does not feel confused about anything, eliminating (B). There is no projection of the future, and thus no basis for either optimism or pessimism, which causes (E) to fail and leaves (D).

16. **(C)** Commercialization of Christmas in America in the past half-century is the theme of the passage. (C) is an example of that and also of the eclecticism of American traditions. None of the other answer choices strikes either of these chords.

17. **(E)** (E) is stated in the first paragraph, which eliminates (A). (B) is a judgment that could perhaps be made, but is not present in the passage. (D) seems false given the revelling and Saturnalia aspect of the season, though the clinging to the Christmas Eve Mass as entertainment may give a shred of support to this choice. (C) has some merit since the passage does cite the changes in the past fifty years and we certainly know of our own knowledge that the early settlers did not have large department stores in which to shop. However, (C) is not supported in the passage nearly as well as (E).

18. **(E)** (A) is very attractive for two reasons. First, the gift-giving is a part of the commercialism noted by the author as the first distinctive part of the American Christmas celebration. Second, only the exchange of gifts is cited as being borrowed from other lands in the first paragraph. However, (E) much more clearly conveys the passage's idea than (A), since it is the stimulus to retail business (commerce) which is cited by the author. (B) and (C) are clearly not exclusively American and it is the length of the eating and drinking celebration, not the fact of it, that is the second distinction found by the author. (D) is flack.

19. **(A)** In a question asking you to extend the author's analysis to another situation or time, you must always give preference to anything which carries forward the precise ideas of the passage. (A) focuses on com-

mercialism, and thus precisely continues the ideas of the passage. (B) and (D) try to reach the Saturnalia distinction, but (A) cites "large numbers of expensive cards" and money is the more important issue. (C) and (E) are nice, but unconnected to the passage.

20. **(B)** This is similar to a "weakening the argument" question in Logical Reasoning. The author's argument is essentially based on the size of the gift-giving enterprise and concludes that so much buying and selling must be its own purpose. (B) proposes a somewhat plausible alternative. (C) also has some merit, but still leaves the Christmas gifting as a commercial enterprise. (A) and (D) actually support, or at least are consistent with, the author's argument. (E) fails when (B) succeeds.

21. **(A)** (C) and (D) have no basis in the passage. (E) is inconsistent with the passage since Christmas Eve has the Mass. We are, thus, left with the choice of (A) or (B). It is true that we cannot know exactly where the traditions noted in the passage came from, nor when, but the passage does call attention to the role of immigrants in enriching the American Christmas symbology, and thus (A) is better than (B).

22. **(B)** The council acted on the basis of a study that showed that automobiles were the major users of energy in the city. Further, the encouragement of bicycles and other automobile-use-reducing measures indicated that (B) is correct. (A), while perhaps true and an ancillary benefit of the bikeways, is not mentioned in the passage. (D) is false since the strong terms "important" and "everyone" are unsupported by the passage's almost humorous reference to this action of the council. (E) is similarly too strong because of "always." (C) has some superficial merit, but the passage does not really say that the measures undertaken by Davis are all modern or up-to-date. Some might well be viewed as old-fashioned, though excellent for saving energy. The standard applied to the actions was whether they save energy, not whether they are fashionable.

23. **(C)** The purpose of the demonstration homes was to show the local contractors that the new regulations could be met with ease. (B) and (E), thus, have some appeal, but the question asks why two instead of just one, which (C) addresses. (A) has a little merit in that it is certainly true that a demonstration project shows what you can do, but that was not why two houses instead of one were built. (D) has no basis.

24. **(E)** Here we must look to the reasons for writing an article about Davis. The first paragraph provides the best support for (E), though both (A) and (B) have some appeal. (C) is not an implication of the passage and (D) is trivial. (B) fails since the passage does not state that Davis wishes or needs to "spread" its message since its actions were intended to be suited to its own particular circumstances. (A) is part of (E) and if (E) stands up, as it does, then it is preferable to (A) since it covers more of the passage.

25. **(B)** (A) and (E) are implied by the fact that codes take these positions. (D) is implied by the statement that the codes are to curb growth in order to limit energy use. (C) is implied by the lengthy debate held by the council. (B) is probably false since the council acted on the basis of the survey and would likely have delayed action, or refused it if the survey was of doubtful accuracy. Thus, (B) is a better answer than (C).

26. **(C)** The fact that Davis has thousands of trees and a fleet of cars indicates that it is not a tiny town, yet the utility of bikeways for general transportation even by city employees indicates that Davis is not too large either. The limitation of the model homes to single and two family dwellings also indicates less than major urban concentration, as does the recycling center's sales volume.

(A) is a meaningless term not defined in the passage. (B) has to do with social issues not dealt with in the passage at all. The citizens of Davis could be all kinds of horrible things, and still be concerned enough to save energy. (D) has the tempting half-truth that it is known that the city has a council, but nothing is said of a manager, mayor, or whatever else there might be. The lack of reference to a mayor is some small argument against it, but not for a manager. (E) is unsupported by the passage in any way.

27. **(A)** The analysis of energy-use patterns in Davis does not even mention industry, and thus supports (A). (B) has some merit, but is stated in terms—"any further"—too strong to be supported. If (C) means that the same actions will work in any city, this is clearly false, since Davis' actions are based on a close analysis of its own situation. The passage does support the idea that other cities should do something about their energy use, but it is perhaps too strong to say "any" city. (E) is good and bad in the same ways as (C). Yes, planning helps, but not necessarily to solve all problems. Also, the passage only speaks to energy management, not to crime, etc. (D) has no support. Even in Davis, the automobile was only restricted, not eliminated, and nothing in the passage would support that conclusion.

28. **(B)** (B) is known to be false since the feasibility of meeting the new code was demonstrated by the two model houses. The answer choice does not address the question of whether the builders will meet the code, only that they can.

(A) will mean more energy even if each person uses less. (C) clearly means more energy and (E) explains the discrepancy very easily. (D) shows that more cars were used, but has the weakness that we are unsure of the breakdown between cars and bicycles before the energy survey. However, the passage noted that the town had been involved in building bikeways in 1968, four years before the 1972 survey. This means that reduced bicycle use will reflect on the 1972 results.

SECTION VI

1. **(D)** Let us use letters to represent the categories. "All effective administrators" will be A. "Concerned about welfare" will be C. "Are liberal" will be L. The three propositions can now be represented as:

1. All A are W.
2. All W are L.
3. All non-L are not A.

Proposition #3 is equivalent to "all A are not non-L," and that is in turn equivalent to "all A are L." Thus, (D) follows fairly directly as a matter of logic. (A) is incorrect, for while we know that "all A are L," we would not want to conclude that "No L are A"—there might be some ineffective administrators who grant time off. They could be ineffective for other reasons. (B) is incorrect for the same reason. Even though all effective administrators are concerned about their employees' welfare, this does not mean that an ineffective administrator could not be concerned. He might be concerned but ineffective for another reason. (C) is clearly false given our propositions; we know that all effective administrators are liberal. Finally, (E) is not inferable. Just because all effective administrators grant time off does not mean that all the time granted off is granted by effective administrators.

2. **(C)** The weakness in Gerry's argument is that he assumes, incorrectly, that getting drunk is the only harm Clyde has in mind. Clyde could respond very effectively by pointing to some other harms of alcohol. (A) would not be a good response for Clyde since he is concerned with Gerry's welfare. The fact that other people get drunk when Gerry does not is hardly a reason for Gerry to stop drinking. (B) is also incorrect. That other people do or do not get drunk is not going to strengthen Clyde's argument against Gerry. He needs an argument which will impress Clyde, who apparently does not get drunk. (D) is perhaps the second-best answer, but the explicit wording of the paragraph make it unacceptable. Gerry has been drinking the same quantity for fifteen years. Now, admittedly it is possible he will begin to drink more heavily, but that *possibility* would not be nearly so strong a point in Clyde's favor as the *present* existence of harm (other than inebriation). Finally, (E) is irrelevant, since it is white wine which Gerry does drink.

3. **(B)** The point of the passage is that a meaningful comparison between the two systems is going to be difficult since the one is cheap in the short run, but expensive in the long run, while the other is expensive in the short run and cheap in the long run. The only appropriate way of doing the cost comparison is by taking account of both costs—which is what (B) does. To take just the long run costs would be to ignore the short run costs involved, so (A) is wrong; and taking the short run costs while ignoring the long run costs is no better, so (C) is wrong. If (A) is wrong, then (D) also has to be wrong, and the more so because it is not even projecting operating costs. Finally, (E) is a distraction—the connection between diesel fuel and air pollution is irrelevant in a paragraph which is concerned with a cost comparison.

4. **(B)** One way of "making more money" other than raising the price of a product is to lower the size or quality of the product. This is what Vendo must have done. By doing so, they accomplished the equivalent of a price increase without actually raising the price. (C) contradicts the paragraph which states that Vendo did not violate the letter of the instructions—that is the literal meaning—though they did violate the intention. (D) also contradicts the paragraph. Had Vendo forfeited the franchise, that would have been within the letter of the "either-or" wording of the instructions. (A) and (E) require much speculation beyond the information given, and you should not indulge yourself in imaginative thinking when there is an obvious answer such as (B) available.

5. **(D)** The author's argument seems fairly weak. He introduces the example of the second university without explaining why we should consider that case similar to the one we are arguing about (except for size). This shows that the author is introducing an analogy—though not a very strong one. (A) is perhaps the second-best answer. But it would be correct only if there were a *contention* which the author had introduced new evidence in support of the argument. He does not articulate a contention and then adduce evidence for it. (B) is wrong because the author really has no solution to the problem—he wants to argue the problem does not exist. Finally, (C) and (E) must be wrong because the author never mentions a logical contradiction nor does he point to any ambiguity in his opponent's argument.

6. **(E)** Careful reading of the ad shows that all three propositions could be true even if the ad is correct. First, another deodorant might also give all-day protection. The ad claims that White Bear is the only deodorant which gives you *both* protection and scent—a vacuous enough claim since White Bear is probably the only deodorant with the White Bear scent. Of course, III is not effected by this point, since the White Bear Company may put its unique scent into many of its products. Finally, II is also not inconsistent with the ad—that another product is more popular does not say that it has the features the ad claims for the White Bear deodorant.

7. **(D)** The easiest way to set this problem up is to draw a relational line:

PE IP EL BE
Dislikes ————→ Likes

We note that Clara likes Basic Economics better than anything else, which means she must like it better than Advanced Calculus. So even though Advanced Calculus does not appear on our line, since we know that Basic Economics is the maximum, Clara must like Advanced Calculus less than Basic Economics. So (C) can be inferred. But we do not know where World History ranks on the preference line, and since Introductory Physics is not a maximal or a minimal value, we can make no judgment regarding it and an unplaced course. Quick reference to the line will show that (A), (B), and (E) are inferable.

8. **(B)** We have seen before examples of the form of argument Holmes has in mind: "P or Q; not-P; therefore, Q." Here, however, the first premise of Holmes' argument is more complex: "P or Q or R . . . S," with as

many possibilities as he can conceive. He eliminates them one-by-one until no single possibility is left. The logic of the argument is perfect, but the weakness in the form is that it is impossible to guarantee that all contingencies have been taken into account. Maybe one was overlooked. Thus, (B) is the correct answer. (A), (C), and (E) are wrong for the same reason. Holmes' method is designed to answer a particular question—in this case, "Where did the body come from?" Perhaps the next step is to apply the method to the question of the identity of the murderer, as (E) suggests, but at this juncture he is concerned with the preliminary matter of how the murder was committed. In any event, it would be wrong to assail the logic of Holmes' deduction by complaining that it does not prove enough. Since (A) and (C) are even more removed from the particular question raised, they, too, must be wrong. Finally, (D) is nothing more than a reiteration of Watson's original comment, and Holmes has already responded to it.

9. (C) Notice that the student responds to the professor's comment by saying, "That can't be true," and then uses the Duchess of Warburton as a counter-example. The Duchess would only be a counter-example to the professor's statement had the professor said that women cannot inherit the estates of their families. Thus, (C) must capture the student's misinterpretation of the professor's statement. What has misled the student is that he has attributed too much to the professor. The professor has cited the general rule of primogeniture—the eldest male child inherits—but he has not discussed the special problems which arise when no male child is born. In those cases, presumably a non-male child will have to inherit. (E) incorrectly refers to inheriting from a mother, but the student is discussing a case in which the woman inherited her father's estate. (D) is wrong for the student specifically mentions the conditions which make a child legitimate: born to the wife of her father. (A) was inserted as a bit of levity: Of course, only men can *father* children of either sex. Finally, first-born or not, a daughter cannot inherit as long as there is any male child to inherit, so (B) must be incorrect.

10. (E) (A) can be rejected because sentence IV—first in this choice—begins with the phrase *some of the chemicals,* which apparently refers to information provided earlier; thus, IV cannot be a first sentence. (B) is wrong for a similar reason. The word *then* (I) is not a good choice for beginning the paragraph. By the same token, (C) is a poor choice because it, too, contains a transitional phrase, *then,* and should not open the paragraph. (D) has the proper first sentence (II), but (D) has the chemicals getting into the bloodstream (I) before they entered the water supply (IV).

11. (A) The question stem contains a hidden assumption: It is a loaded question. It presupposes that the person questioned agrees that the city is discriminating against its Hispanic residents. (A) is a pretty nice parallel. The questioner assumes that the Congressman agrees that defense spending is out of hand, which may or may not be true. (B) makes no such assumption. It can be answered with a simple "yes" if the chairperson plans to take a luncheon recess, otherwise a "no" will do the job. (C) requires more than a "yes" or "no" answer, but it still contains no presuppositions. Since the question asks "what," the speaker may respond by saying much, little, or none at all. (D) may be said to make a presupposition—Gladys is going to the store—but here the presupposition is not concealed. It is made an explicit condition of the answer. Finally, (E) is a little like (B) in that a simple "yes" or "no" can communicate the counselor's opinion. It might be objected that (E) presupposes that the company has an affirmative action program, and that this makes it similar to the question stem. Two responses can be made. First, (E) is in this way like (D): The assumption—if there is one—is fairly explicit. Second, (E) does not have the same loaded tone as (A) does, so by comparison (A) is a better choice.

12. (E) The ad is a little deceptive. It tries to create the impression that if hospitals are using Dr. John's Milk of Magnesia, people

will believe it is a good product. But what the ad actually says is that Dr. John uses the same *ingredient* which hospitals use (milk of magnesia is a simple suspension of magnesium hydroxide in water). The ad is something like an ad for John's Vinegar which claims it has "acetic acid," which is vinegar. I falls into the trap of the ad and is therefore wrong. II is not inferable since there may be treatments other than milk of magnesia for these disorders. Finally, since I is incorrect, III must certainly also be incorrect. Even it I had been true, III might still be questionable since use and recommendation are not identical.

13. **(A)** Statements I and II combine to give us (A). If all wheeled conveyances which travel on the highway are polluters, and a bicycle does not travel on the highway, then a bicycle cannot be a polluter. If then (A) is correct, (B) must be incorrect because bicycles do not travel on the highways at all. (C) and (D) make the same mistake. III must be read to say "if I am driving, it is raining," not "if it is raining, I am driving." (E) is clearly false since my car is driven on the highway. Don't make the problem harder than it is.

14. **(E)** Picking up on our discussion of (C) and (D) in the previous question, III must read "if I am driving, then it is raining." Let that be: "If P, then Q." If we then had not-Q, we could deduce not-P. (E) gives us not-Q by changing IV to "it is not raining." Changing I or II or even both is not going to do the trick, for they don't touch the relationship between my driving my car and rain—they deal only with pollution and we need the car to be connected. Similarly, if we change III to make it deal with pollution, we have not adjusted the connection between my driving and rain, so (C) must be wrong. (D) is the worst of all the answers. Whether rainwater is polluted or not has nothing to do with the connection between my driving and rain. Granted, there is the unstated assumption that my car only pollutes when I drive it, but this is OK.

15. **(E)** Common sense dictates that where one is driving in relationship to his home (within or without a twenty-five mile radius) has little or nothing to do with the safety factor. Moreover, common sense also says that a person driving under 35 miles per hour is (usually) safer than one driving at 60 miles per hour. The explanation, then, for the fact that most traffic fatalities occur under conditions contrary to those which would be suggested by common sense is that more driving is done under those conditions. Just as common sense indicates, the driving is safer per mile, but there are so many more miles driven under those conditions that there are many fatalities. (A) is obviously inconsistent with common sense. And the directions for the Logical Reasoning section explicitly say that the BEST answer will be one which does not require you to make such assumptions. (B) is incorrect since the statistics mention the location of the accident—how far away from home—not how far the driver had driven at the time of the accident. Even though the accident occurred, say, twenty-six miles from home, you would not want to conclude the driver had driven twenty-six miles. (C) compounds the error made by (A). Not only does it take the general conclusion regarding fatalities and attempt to apply it to a specific case without regard to the individual variety of those cases, but it commits the further error of conditioning the speed of driving on the occurrence of an accident. (D) does exactly the same thing and is also wrong.

16. **(D)** The author states that a certain amount of rain in a given time *usually* results in mushrooms growing in his backyard. I and II are wrong for the same reason. From the fact that there has not been the requisite minimum rainfall required for mushrooms, we would not want to conclude that there has been *no* rain at all. III overstates the author's case and is for that reason wrong. The author specifically qualifies his claim by saying it "usually" happens this way. Thus, he would not want to say that the absence of mushrooms and fungus definitely means that the requisite amount of rain has not fallen—only that it seems likely or probable that there has not been enough rain.

17. **(C)** (C) is the most reliable here. We have two trained paramedics talking about their work. Notice the paramedics have given first aid—they are not discussing open heart surgery, which would exceed the scope of their training. Notice further that they report in almost clinical terms the fact that the patient recovered. (A) is unreliable because the witness is not likely to be able to make such an identification given the conditions of observation. (B) is not as reliable as (C) because there is an almost palpable element of self-interest in the statement. Even if we were charitable and allowed that this particular spill was not the fault of the company represented by the executive, the second element might give us pause. Now, this is not to say that the executive is not to be believed; we are simply comparing his statement with (C). And by comparison there seems to be more reason to believe (C) than (B). (D) is wrong not because the biology student is not qualified to speak about life on Earth but because he is making a claim about something that is not susceptible to verification. How would it ever be proved or disproved by scientific inquiry that God did or did not create life on Earth—not to mention all of the collateral questions about what we mean by God, etc. Finally, (E) is wrong because it is a self-serving statement.

18. **(B)** The author's claim is self-referential—it refers to itself or includes itself in its own description. The author says that *every* action is economically motivated; therefore, we may conclude that his own motivation in making such a claim and in writing a book about it is also economically motivated. The speaker in our passage says he is going to apply the author's theory to his (the author's) own actions. This is why (B) is correct. Neither (A) nor (E) can be correct inasmuch as the author of the book claims that there are no such motivations. Ultimately, he says, all motivations can be reduced to one, economics. (C) has to be wrong since the author of the book claims that everything done is economically motivated. His examples make it clear that even a reformer with some seemingly non-economic motive would be "pure" only on the surface, with a deeper, economic motivation for reforming. Finally, (D) can be rejected since it conflicts with one of the examples given by the author of the book.

19. **(C)** (C) is an excellent choice for two reasons. First, we have a highly trained professional speaking within the scope of that training. Second, not only is there no hint that the statement is self-serving; if anything the statement is self-critical. Compare this with (B), where there is an element of self-interest making it less reliable than (C). Compare (C) also with (D) in which the speaker is outside of field. (A) is unreliable not because the speaker is not an authority on the subject about which he is speaking. (A) is unreliable on the basis of its content: my wife and I had a perfect marriage which didn't work out. Finally, in (E) there is an element akin to the element of self-interest in (B). Here we suspect wishful thinking. The speaker rides a motorcycle, so we would hardly expect him to say that he is exposing himself to great danger in doing so. And if under other circumstances he did *boast* about the dangers of riding a motorcycle, that, too, would make his statement unreliable.

20. **(A)** The argument makes the rather outlandish assumption that the physical characteristics of the criminal dictate the kind of crime he will commit. But as unreasonable as that may seem in light of common sense, it *is* an assumption made by the speaker. (We did not make the assumption, he did.) II is not an assumption of the argument, since the paragraph specifically states that the killer was executed—he can not have escaped. III does not commit the blatant error committed by II, but it is still wrong. Although III might be a better explanation for the crimes now being committed than that proposed by our speaker, our speaker advances the explanation supported by I, not III. In fact, the speaker uses phrases such as "looks very much like" which tell us that he assumes there are two killers.

21. **(A)** The form of the argument can be represented using letters as:
I. All R are either O or W. (All non-

Readers are non-Opinion holders or Wrong.)
II. All O are R.

If II is true, I might be either false or true, since it is possible that there are some who have not read the report who hold right opinions. That is, even if II is true and all O are R, that does not tell us anything about all the R's, only about all the O's. The rest of the R's might be W's (wrong opinion holders) or something else altogether (right opinion holders). By this reasoning we see that we cannot conclude that I is definitely true, so (B) must be wrong. Moreover, we have no ground for believing I to be more or less likely true, so (C) can be rejected. As for (D), even if we assume that all the R's are *either* O or W, we are not entitled to conclude that all O's are R's. There may be someone without an opinion who has not read the report. Finally (E), if it is false that all the O's (non-opinion holders) are not R's, tells us nothing about all R's and their distribution among O and W.

22. **(A)** The fallacy in the author's argument is that he takes a group term ("the average size of women") and applies it to the individual. (A) calls attention to this fallacy. The average size of women is irrelevant in the case of those women who are of sufficient size. (D) concedes too much to the author. We do not have to settle for the conclusion that some women may be suitable for desk jobs. We can win the larger claim that some women may be suitable to be police officers—or at least as suitable as their male counterparts. (B), (C), and (E) are possible arguments to be used against the author's general position. We might want to claim, for example, that training or weapons will compensate for want of size, but again there is no reason even to grant the author that much. We do not even have to concede that the *average* size is relevant. Finally, (E) also gives away too much. Although the use of pistols is sometimes called "deadly force," the author's linkage of size to force specifies force as being a strength or size idea.

23. **(D)** We can use our capital letters to see why (D) is the correct answer. The structure of the stem argument is:

No S are R.
Some S are D.
Therefore, Some D are not R.

(D) shares this form:

All pets are excluded:	No P are A.	(A = allowed)
Many = Some:	Some P are V.	
Therefore, Some V are not A.		

(A) has a very different form since it is presented as a probabilistic, not a deductive or logical, argument. (B)'s conclusion goes beyond the information given in the premises. We cannot conclude that uncle *enjoys* paying the bills, even though he may incur them. (C) has the form:

Some BB are F.
All F is WR.
Therefore, All BB are WR.

This does not parallel our question stem for two reasons. First, our stem argument is valid, while the argument in (C) is not. Second, (D) is more nearly parallel to the stem argument than (C); for even if we rearrange the assumptions in (C) to put the "all" proposition first and the "some" proposition second, the "all's" and the "some's" of (C) do not parallel those of the question stem. (E) does not share the stem form. First, it is not the same argument form (all, some, etc.). Second, (E) is clearly not a proper logical argument.

24. **(A)** Perhaps a little diagram is the easiest way to show this problem.

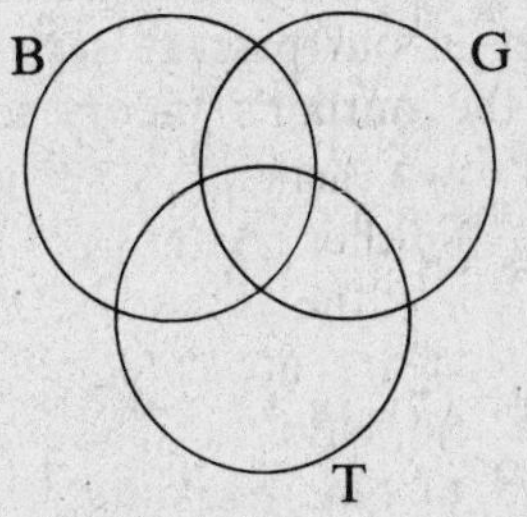

We will show all B are T by eliminating that portion of the diagram where some area of B is not also inside T:

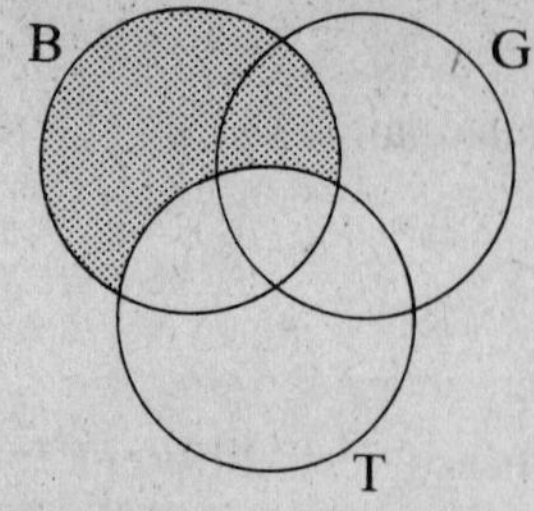

Now, let us put an *x* to show the existence of those B's which are G's:

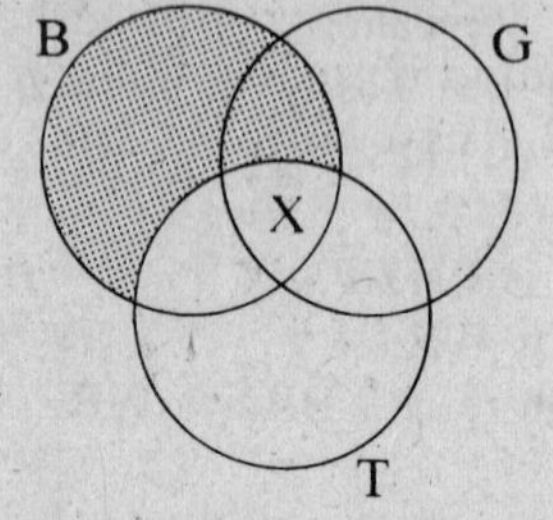

The diagram shows us that I is true. Since the only areas left for B's are within the T circle, the G condition is unimportant. II is not inferable. Although there is some overlap of the G and T circles, there is also some non-overlap. This shows that it may be possible to be a T without also being a G. III is not inferable since our diagrams are restricted to the three categories B, G, and T and say nothing about things outside of those categories.

25. **(C)** The stem argument has the form: "If P, then Q. Q, therefore, P." The argument is invalid. There may be other reasons that the razor is not functioning, e.g., the switch is not on, it is broken, etc. (C) has this form also. John's fingerprints might have been found at the scene, yet he may not have committed the crime. (A) has the form: "If P, then Q. Not Q, therefore, not P," which not only is not parallel to the question stem, but is valid and thus a poor parallel to the invalid original argument as well. (B) has the form: "P or Q. Not P, therefore, Q." This, too, does not parallel the stem argument, and, like (B), is valid. (D) is invalid, but the fallacy is not the same as what we find in the stem argument. The stem argument is set up using "if, then" statements. (D) does not parallel this form. (E) does use "if, then" statements, but its form is: "If P, then Q. P, therefore P." This argument is clearly valid.

26. **(A)** The author's statement is self-contradictory or paradoxical. It says in effect "no statement is always correct," but then that statement itself must be false—since it attempts to make a claim about "always." The author's statement is inductive, that is, a generalization; but (E) is not as good an answer as (A) because it fails to pick up on the fact that the statement is internally contradictory. The statement cannot be valid, (D), since the author tries to pass it off as a generalization. Generalizations can be strong or weak, well-founded or ill-founded, but they cannot be valid or invalid. (C) is incorrect for there is nothing ambiguous or poorly defined in the argument. Finally, the argument is not circular, (B), because the author does not seek to establish his conclusion by assuming it. As we have noted, the statement is self-contradictory, so it could not possibly be circular.

Explanation of Pressure Points and Exemplary Essay for Writing Sample

TOPIC: The Traffic Safety Council has proposed that a new law be enacted which requires that all prospective drivers take a much more stringent driving test than is required at present. The new test will require the demonstration of total control of the vehicle as well as extensive knowledge of traffic laws relevant to the type of vehicle for which the license is being sought. The Council proposes that this new requirement only apply to persons seeking their first driver's license, and predicts a savings of hundreds of lives per year when the program is fully implemented. Opponents argue that accidents are caused by such things as speeding and drinking rather than not knowing how to handle a car and that the costs of preparing for the more extensive test will impose a significant economic burden on the society as a whole and on poorer citizens in particular.

You are a state legislator on the Transportation Committee and you are to prepare a brief position paper to be presented to the Committee in your absence.

PRESSURE POINTS: the following considerations might go through your mind as you examine the topic and seek an outline for your essay.

—Is there a problem from traffic fatalities?

—What are the causes of a traffic problem? Poor training, ignorance of the law, ignorance of car-handling, carelessness, irresponsibility, drinking, etc?

—Will the proposal address these causes?

—What is the cost of NOT reducing traffic deaths?

—Is discrimination a relevant objection when life and death are involved? What are statistics on economic status and traffic safety?

The following essay is only one of many that could have been written on this topic.

The proposed law attempts to cure a serious problem, but while its effect would be beneficial, the roots of the problem would not be addressed. Therefore, the law should not be passed as currently drafted.

The deaths and injuries caused by traffic accidents are a tragedy. The causes of the tragedy are primarily the foolish driving habits of irresponsible drivers. While greater knowledge of the handling characteristics of cars and of the traffic safety laws might cause a few drunks and fools to avoid accidents, it is not sufficient. On the other hand, the economic costs of giving such difficult and extensive tests might spread already overburdened traffic safety and police resources even thinner and thus cause other deaths and injuries, possibly even more than the new licensing procedures would save.

While it can be argued that it cannot be a waste to learn better car handling or more about the traffic laws, the cost of preparing the entire population to learn these things will be very high. Not only will thousands of classroom and teacher hours be needed, but also large numbers of specially equipped training cars will also probably be required. These costs would be in addition to the greater testing costs already mentioned. If these costs are borne by the individuals seeking licenses, the effective discrimination against poor people could cause considerable bitterness and perhaps a very great social cost in increased racial and class strife. It is even possible that the money spent on driver training might reduce the money available for car purchases and operation. The economic consequences of any disruption of the country's major industry would be a strong argument against adopting the proposal.

In summary, the proposal seems to address some of the wrong causes of traffic accidents and have too many potentially serious costs to merit adoption now.